THE PROCESS OF PARENTING

SEVENTH EDITION

Jane B. Brooks

Boston   Burr Ridge, IL   Dubuque, IA   New York   San Francisco   St. Louis
Bangkok   Bogotá   Caracas   Kuala Lumpur   Lisbon   London   Madrid   Mexico City
Milan   Montreal   New Delhi   Santiago   Seoul   Singapore   Sydney   Taipei   Toronto

Higher Education

To my grandparents and parents, and my children and their children

THE PROCESS OF PARENTING, SEVENTH EDITION
Published by McGraw-Hill, a business unit of The McGraw-Hill Companies, Inc., 1221 Avenue of the
Americas, New York, NY 10020. Copyright © 2008 by The McGraw-Hill Companies, Inc. All rights
reserved. Previous editions © 1999, 1996, 1991, 1987, 1981 by Mayfield Publishing Company. No part of
this publication may be reproduced or distributed in any form or by any means, or stored in a database or
retrieval system, without the prior written consent of The McGraw-Hill Companies, Inc., including, but
not limited to, any network or other electronic storage or transmission, or broadcast for distance learning.

Some ancillaries, including electronic and print components, may not be available to customers
outside the United States.

3 4 5 6 7 8 9 0 DOC/DOC 0 9 8

ISBN: 978-0-07-313145-0
MHID: 0-07-313145-8

Editor-in-chief: *Emily G. Barrosse*
Sponsoring editor: *David S. Patterson*
Development editor: *Emily Pecora*
Marketing manager: *Sarah Martin*
Production editor: *David Blatty*
Cover designer: *Marianna Kinigakis*
Interior designer: *Violeta Diaz*
Art manager: *Robin Mouat*
Photo researcher: *Nora Agbayani*
Production supervisor: *Rich Devitto*

The text was set in 10.5/12 Berkeley by Laserwords Private Limited, Chennai, India and printed on
acid-free, 45# New Era Matte by RR Donnelley, Crawfordsville.

The credits for this book begin on page C-1, a continuation of the copyright page.

Library of Congress Cataloging-in Publication Data
Brooks, Jane B.
    The process of parenting / Jane B. Brooks.—7th ed.
       p. cm.
    Includes bibliographical references and index.
    ISBN-13: 978-0-07-313145-0 (pbk. : alk. paper)
    ISBN-10: 0-07-313145-8 (pbk. : alk. paper)
       1. Parenting—United States. I. Title.

HQ755.8.B75 2008
649'.1—dc22   2006046926

The Internet addresses listed in the text were accurate at the time of publication. The inclusion of a
website does not indicate an endorsement by the authors or McGraw-Hill Higher Education, and
McGraw-Hill does not guarantee the accuracy of the information presented at these sites.

www.mhhe.com

BRIEF CONTENTS

C O N T E N T S

CHAPTER **2**

Seeking Guidance 38

CHAPTER 4

Nurturing Close Emotional Relationships 126

CHAPTER **5**

Supporting Children's Growth and Development 158

PART II
Parenting at Developmental Stages 205

CHAPTER 6
Becoming Parents 206

CHAPTER **7**

Parenting Infants: The Years from Birth to Two 244

C H A P T E R **8**

Parenting in Early Childhood: The Years from Two to Five 278

CHAPTER **9**

Parenting Elementary School Children 310

CHAPTER **10**

Parenting Early Adolescents 345

CHAPTER **11**

Parenting Late Adolescents 376

CHAPTER **12**
Parenting Adults 407

PART III
Parenting in Varying Life Circumstances 433

CHAPTER 13
Parenting and Working 434

CHAPTER **14**

Parenting in Diverse Family Structures 461

CHAPTER **15**

Parenting at Times of Loss, Trauma, Disaster, or Violence 498

PREFACE

"For most adult humans, parenthood is still the ultimate source of the sense of meaning. For most adults, the question 'What does life mean?' is automatically answered once they have children; better yet it is no longer asked," writes the psychologist David Gutmann, after testing and interviewing men and women about the impact of parenthood on their lives.[1]

Do people receive training to succeed in this important activity? No! Anyone who drives a car or cuts hair for pay must have a license and must demonstrate a certain level of skill before being permitted to engage in these activities independently. But nowhere does society require systematic parenting education, which may matter most of all.

This book attempts to fill this educational gap. As did the earlier editions, the seventh edition of *The Process of Parenting* shows how parents and caregivers can translate their love and concern for children into effective parenting skills. The book strives to bring to life the child's world and concerns, so that parents can better understand their children. The book also describes the myriad thoughts and feelings—positive and negative—of parents, so that they can better understand themselves. Finally, the book highlights the influence of the social context on both parents and children.

THE APPROACH OF *THE PROCESS OF PARENTING*

I have selected topics and written this book from the points of view of a parent, a clinician, a researcher, and a teacher of parenting skills. I have the firm conviction that anyone who wants to invest attention and effort in becoming a competent, caring parent can do so in his or her own way. The single prerequisite is the desire to succeed, along with the willingness to invest time and energy, and the results are well worth the effort. My experience as a clinician has shown me that children face many difficult situations; with a loving, supportive caregiver, children can live life fully and happily even if temporarily engulfed by trauma.

Children are not the only ones enriched by adults' efforts to be effective parents. Helping children grow is an intense and exciting experience that brings special rewards to us as parents. Our physical stamina, agility, and speed increase as we care for infants and toddlers. Our emotional stamina grows as we deal with our own intense feelings toward our children and help children learn to express and modulate their feelings. Our intellectual skills grow as we answer young children's questions and, later, help them learn school subjects. In helping children grow, we gain for ourselves an inner vitality and richness that affects all our relationships.

ORGANIZATION

Organizing and writing the seventh edition has proven a challenging endeavor that demanded careful thought and clear writing. The aim has been to retain the overall organization of the book and its emphasis on children's development in the many different contexts that influence the process of parenting. At the same time I have made a strong effort to connect academic research more directly and more meaningfully to parents' experiences in everyday life. Chapters include additional boxes describing parents' actual experiences in situations or programs designed to deal with special problems. To engage the student more quickly in the reading, each chapter begins with five provocative, true/false questions dealing with practical issues that the chapter material will answer.

With the addition of several topics reviewers suggested, the book is longer, but it provides the instructor with greater flexibility to focus on topics that may be particularly pertinent to class members. For example, when the class includes foster parents, that section can become a focus. If many students are in the health professions and work with children with illnesses, then that section can become a focus.

To make the detailed and factual material more meaningful to students in the class, the Instructor's Manual includes suggestions for role-playing assignments that can help students translate facts and figures into actual life experiences. For example, drawing on material presented in Chapter 1, students are asked to role-play two parents telling a therapist all their frustrations in being parents, and the recommendations the therapist has to make. Or a couple can role-play deciding whether or not to have children, worrying about their responsibilities and their ability to be parents.

Let me now describe the organization of the book and other new features as they appear.

Like the sixth edition, the seventh edition has three parts. Part I, "General Concepts, Goals, and Strategies of Parenting," includes Chapters 1–5. As before, Chapter 1 describes the roles and interactions of the three participants in the process of parenting—the child, the parent, and the social system—and the ways social forces shape parenting. Chapter 2 includes a new section on the history of parent-child relationships and then describes theories of development. The chapter shows how each theory contributes to parents' effectiveness by describing the insights each brings to our understanding of a common parenting problem: dealing with a child's difficulty in school. A new section illustrates how popular parenting experts have drawn on theories and research to help parents.

Chapter 3 continues to focus on the cultural influences on parenting, including cultural models of parenting strategies and the values and distinctive influences of six major ethnic groups: Native Americans, European Americans, African Americans, Latinas/os, Asian Americans, and Middle Eastern Americans. The experiences of specific ethnic groups continue to appear throughout the text as they relate to the topic of discussion. For example, ethnic identity formation and prejudice are discussed in the chapters dealing with identity formation. Chapter 3 has an expanded section on the influence of social status and interventions to counter the effects of economic hardship on parenting.

As in previous editions, Chapter 4 discusses creating close emotional relationships and presents information on the power of physical closeness and positive words to increase closeness. Chapter 5 has a new emphasis on all the activities parents undertake to support and stimulate children's growth—ensuring safety and health, guarding against destructive media influences, and providing a collaborative family atmosphere that stimulates children's developing the many competencies needed for independence and adult life. This chapter still includes strategies available when positive support has not been sufficient to prevent difficulties.

Part II, "Parenting at Developmental Stages," begins with Chapter 6, on how parents make the transition to parenthood. This chapter focuses on how the methods and timing of becoming parents influence the process of parenting. Beginning with Chapter 7, Part II describes the ways general concepts and basic strategies are applied to children at six different stages of development: infancy (the years from birth to two), early childhood (the years from two to five), the elementary school years, early adolescence, late adolescence, and adulthood.

Chapters 7–11 deal with children from birth through the high school years. Each chapter presents information on children's physical, intellectual, and personal-social development during the five age periods, emphasizing ways parents can promote positive behaviors. This edition continues to pay particular attention to understanding and promoting children's emotional regulation, especially the regulation of anger and sadness.

Chapter 12 describes the tasks of parenting children from age eighteen onward. The main sections deal with parenting children in the transition to adulthood, parenting independent adult children, parenting dependent adult children, parenting children who move back and forth between independence and dependence, parenting dependent adults, and, finally, parenting one's own parent. Strategies used with children of younger ages are applied when appropriate.

Part III, "Parenting in Varying Life Circumstances," describes how parents adapt parenting strategies to meet the challenges of everyday life: parenting and working (Chapter 13), parenting in diverse family structures (Chapter 14), and parenting in times of loss or trauma (Chapter 15). Chapters 13 and 14 emphasize understanding the nature of the circumstances and challenges involved in each situation, and discuss how to promote effective functioning in parents and children—in combining working and parenting and in less traditional family structures, respectively. Chapter 14 includes a new section on foster families. In Chapter 15, we look at different forms of loss and trauma for children and also for their parents, including physical illness, death, child maltreatment, community violence, natural disasters, and the current threat of terrorism. We discuss ways to minimize the threat of trauma, ways to cope with it when it occurs, and how parents help children feel safe in a world that is sometimes unsafe.

PROBLEM SOLVING

A portion of each chapter in Part II deals with common problems children experience and parents must handle. Because each child is a unique individual, parents require a variety of strategies and techniques for handling problems, depending on the child and the circumstances. Parents are encouraged to define the problem specifically, get the child's point of view, make certain the problem is the child's and not the parent's, maintain positive interactions and good times with children, consider possible actions, take action, evaluate the results, and start again if necessary.

THE JOYS OF PARENTING

In addition to describing what parents do, the book describes how parents feel as they raise children. Stages of parenthood are identified, and interviews with parents provide information about what parents wish they had known about parenting before they started. The book also emphasizes the joys that parents experience. In 1948, Arthur Jersild[2] and his colleagues at Columbia University observed that most research on parenting was focused on the problems parents experience, and little attention was given to "the cheerful side of the ledger." Because this is still true today, I try in this text to redress the imbalance.

INTEGRATED COVERAGE OF PARENTING CHILDREN WITH SPECIAL NEEDS AND SUPPORTS FOR PARENTS

The seventh edition continues to present a more complete picture of parenting children at specific ages by including material on children with special needs throughout the book. For example, the discussion of adoption is in the chapter on the transition to parenthood, and the discussion of depression has been moved to the chapter on late adolescence. Similarly, material on supports for parents is included in appropriate chapters, such as supports for parents of infants in the chapter on infancy.

SPECIAL FEATURES

The book includes, at the start of each chapter, a short outline of important topics and a brief newspaper summary highlighting a topic of contemporary interest relating to the chapter. A new feature is a brief test of the student's current knowledge of some of the important topics. Many chapters contain practical questions of interest and significance to parents, such as, What do parents do if they think their child is not developing according to the usual timetables of growth? When in conflict, should parents stay together for the sake of the children? Is child care more important than parenting in predicting children's competence?

SUPPLEMENTAL MATERIALS

Instructor's Manual and Test Bank: Accompanying the book is an instructor's manual and test bank. Please contact McGraw-Hill for more information.

ACKNOWLEDGMENTS

Writing acknowledgments is one of the pleasures of completing a book. As I read manuscript and page proofs, I am constantly reminded of all the people who have helped make this book a reality.

I wish to thank all the clinicians and researchers who gave generously of their time, not only for the interviews themselves but also to review the excerpts and clarify points: Jay Belsky, Judy Dunn, Susan Harter, Sylvia Hewlett, Barbara Keogh, Anneliese Korner, Jacqueline Lerner, Richard Lerner, James Levine, Susan McHale, Emily Visher, John Visher, Emmy Werner, and Steven Wolin.

I thank the following people for a review of the sixth edition of this book, as their comments enabled me to make more insightful revisions:

Shera Atkinson, Texas Tech University

Kathryn Bojczyk, Florida State University

Lane Brigham, Nicholls State University

Mary Jo Graham, Marshall University

Mary Hanrahan, Northern Virginia Community College

Kere Hughes, Iowa State University

Erin Kraan, Miami University of Ohio

Nancy Lee, East Carolina University

Linda Maier, Marshall University

Judith Myers-Walls, Purdue University

Carol West, Humboldt State University

Special appreciation goes to Robert Kremers, former Chief of the Department of Pediatrics of Kaiser Medical Center, for his willingness to place questionnaires about the joys of parenting in the waiting rooms. I thank the many anonymous parents who completed them there and in parenting classes. Most particularly, I express my gratitude to all those parents I interviewed about the joys of parenting and the ways they changed and grew through the experience. I gained valuable insights about the process of parenting, and their comments enliven the book immeasurably. These parents are Michelle Brown, Steve Brown, Kevin Carmack, Laura Carmack, Mark Clinton, Wendy Clinton, Judy Davis, Douglas Dobson, Linda Dobson, Jill Fernald, Otie Gould, Warren Gould, Caryn Gregg, Robert Gregg, Michael Hoyt, Henrietta Krueger, Richard Krueger, Patricia Landman, Jennifer Lillard, Kathy Malone, Chris McArtor, Robert McArtor, Charles Nathan, Jean Oakley, Paul Opsvig, Susan Opsvig, Sherry Proctor, Stewart Proctor, Robert Rosenbaum, David Schmidt, Nancy Schmidt, Moshe Talmon, Raymond Terwilleger, Anthony Toney, Patricia Toney, Steven Tulkin, Elizabeth Whitney, Julie Whitney, Kenneth Whitney, Leon Whitney, Richard Whitney, Barbara Woolmington-Smith, Craig Woolmington-Smith, and Iris Yotvat-Talmon.

My coworkers at the Kaiser Medical Center at Hayward were supportive and helpful throughout. Beckey Hoxsey, our medical librarian, obtained all the books and articles I requested; pediatricians and pediatric advice nurses have given helpful information about parents' concerns. I greatly appreciate the leadership at Kaiser, especially that of Annabel Anderson Imbert, former Physician-in-Chief, and Jerome Rauch, former Chief of Psychiatry, who promote an atmosphere in which creativity flourishes.

I am extremely grateful to the staff and freelancers at McGraw-Hill for helping me to develop the new features of this edition and for transforming the manuscript into a book. The reviewers made valuable suggestions regarding new topics, and everyone at McGraw-Hill gave additional time and attention to make the new features a reality. Sponsoring editor David Patterson had a parent's interest and enthusiasm in reading the book, and so his comments reflected the voice of experience. I am especially indebted to editorial coordinator Emily Pecora, who read early drafts of chapters. She read with the new student in mind, and her insights improved the content and organization of the material. She was always available for practical questions and answered them immediately. She is a pleasure to work with.

The Production staff has been outstanding in making the book a reality. David Blatty, production editor, has moved the whole process along so everything fell into place seamlessly. Copy editor April Wells-Hayes has been a kind and tireless worker in including my suggestions and new inserts without complaint. Her ability to clarify points and sharpen the focus of the writing with a few editorial changes commands admiration. I deeply appreciate her help and her willingness to do extra work. Photo researcher Nora Agbayani selected pictures with the eye of a new parent and added to quality of the book.

I am grateful to the late Paul Mussen, who, fifteen years ago, suggested that I use comments from researchers to make material more vivid for students. His concern with the social forces impinging on parenting has continued to influence my thinking.

Finally, I thank my family and friends for their thoughtfulness and company. I thank my patients for sharing their lives and experiences with me. I hope they have learned as much about life from me as I have learned from them. Most particularly, I thank my children, who are now grown and live away from home. They are very much in my mind as I write, and I relive our experiences together as I explore the different developmental periods. I find that I have learned the most important truths of parenting from our interactions. I believe that, when I have paid attention, they have been my best teachers.

FOREWORD*

The author of this book, Jane Brooks, has had a wide variety of professional and personal experiences that qualify her as an expert in child development. She is a scholar, researcher, and writer in the discipline of child psychology; a practicing clinician working with parents and children; and a mother. Drawing on the knowledge and insights derived from this rich background of experience, she has produced a wise and balanced book that parents will find valuable in fostering the optimal development of their children—helping them to become secure, happy, competent, self-confident, moral individuals. Dr. Brooks offers guidelines that are explicitly linked to major theorists (for example, Freud, Piaget, Erikson) and findings of scientific research in child development, so that the reader is also presented with a wealth of information on physical, cognitive, social, and emotional development. Students of human development and all who work with children professionally, as well as parents, will profit greatly from reading this book.

Brooks's approach to parenting incorporates many noteworthy features. Her coverage of the fundamental tasks and issues in child rearing is comprehensive. Included are tasks shared by all parents (for example, preparing for the birth of the infant, feeding, toilet training, adjusting to nursery school or kindergarten, the adolescent's growing interest in sex) as well as special, although common, problems (such as temper tantrums, delinquency, use of drugs, and physical or mental handicaps). Critical contemporary experiences such as divorce, single parenting, and stepparenting are also treated with insight and sympathy. Brooks's suggestions for ways of dealing with these problems are reasonable, balanced, and practical; her writing is straightforward, clear, and jargon-free.

Authorities in child development generally agree that the principal theories and accumulated findings of scientific investigations are not in themselves adequate to provide a comprehensive basis for directing parents in child rearing. Given the limitations of the present state of knowledge, guidance must be based on established principles of human development *plus* the cumulative wisdom and insights of specialists who have worked systematically and successfully in child-guidance settings. Yet many, perhaps most, academically trained child psychologists pay little attention to the writing of such clinicians as Briggs, Dreikurs, Ginott, Gordon, and Spock, regarding them as unscientific "popular" psychologists. This is not true of Dr. Brooks. After careful and critical reading of their work, she concluded that, as a consequence of their vast clinical experience, these specialists have achieved some profound insights about children and have thus developed invaluable techniques for analyzing and dealing effectively with many problems that parents face. Furthermore,

*This foreword was written by the late Paul Mussen for the third, fourth, and fifth editions. As the book continues to have the features he discusses, the foreword is included in this edition.

Brooks believes that parents themselves can successfully apply some of these techniques to resolve specific problems. Some of the experts' suggestions are therefore incorporated, with appropriate acknowledgment, where they are relevant.

The book is not doctrinaire or prescriptive, however; the author does not advise parents simply to unquestioningly adopt some "system," plan, or set of rules. On the contrary, Brooks stresses the uniqueness of each individual and family, the complex nature of parent-child relations, and the multiple determinants of problem behavior. In Brooks's view, each problem must be placed in its developmental context and evaluated in terms of the child's level of physical, cognitive, and emotional maturity. The processes of parenting are invariably bidirectional: Parents influence children *and* children influence parents. Furthermore, families do not function in isolation; each family unit is embedded in a wider network of social systems that affect its functioning. Successful child rearing depends on parents' accepting these complexities, yet also attempting to understand themselves and their children and maintaining a problem-solving orientation.

It is a pleasure to note the pervasive optimistic, yet realistic, tone of the book. The author has recognized that promotion of children's welfare and happiness is one of the highest parental goals, and she communicates her confidence that most parents *can* achieve this. Underlying this achievement is parents' deep-seated willingness to work hard and to devote thought, time, energy, and attention to their children's development and their problems. Reading this book will increase parental understanding and thus make the difficult tasks of parenting easier.

Paul Mussen
Former Professor Emeritus of Psychology,
Former Director, Institute of Human Development
University of California, Berkeley

I

General Concepts, Goals, and Strategies of Parenting

1

Parenting Is a Process

IN THE NEWS

New York Times, June 15: "That Wild Streak? Maybe It Runs in the Family."[1] For a discussion of the role of genes, parenting, and personal choice in behavior, see pages 21–25 and pages 31–32.

Test Your Knowledge: Fact or Fiction?

1. As the wealthiest industrialized country in the world, the United States has the lowest rate of infant mortality.
2. Because the many changes in the forms of family life over the past thirty-five years have resulted in parents' spending less time with children, adolescents and young adults now do not feel as close to their parents as their parents did to their own parents in 1970.
3. In a large survey, parents reported more than twice as many joys and satisfactions as problems in raising children.
4. Parents' behavior toward their children determines the kind of parents their children will be when they grow up.
5. Most parents who were abused as children will abuse their children.

Parenthood transforms people. After a baby comes, parents are no longer the same people they once were. A whole new role begins, and they start a new way of life. Why do people undertake this new and demanding role? What is parenting really all about?

How does society help or hinder parents? In this chapter, we explore parenting as a co-operative venture among parents, their children, and society. We define parenting, describe the roles of parents and society in rearing children, and focus on how society both helps and hinders parents and children. The chapter describes parents' important influence on children's lives and the ways children change their parents. Finally, we explore the influence of parents' childhood experiences on their parenting.

WHAT IS PARENTING?

Would you apply for this position?

> Wanted: Caregiver to rear one or two children from birth to maturity. A seven-day-a-week, twenty-four-hour-a-day position. No salary or benefits such as sick leave or holiday pay, no retirement plan. Caregiver must supply all living expenses for self and children; in the event of any absence, even for a few minutes with younger children, must supply substitute care. No opportunity to meet child or children to determine compatibility before taking the position. Motivation and job satisfaction must come from within applicant, as neither children nor society regularly express gratitude or appreciation.

Although such a newspaper advertisement might attract few applicants, in everyday life the parents of 4 million babies accept such a position each year![2] In fact, many exert extraordinary effort and pay thousands of dollars for help getting pregnant or locating children to adopt so they can take on this job.

The advertisement describes the time commitment and selfless nature of the job, but it does not tell us what parenting is. Here, we define a parent as an individual who fosters all facets of a child's growth—who nourishes, protects, and guides new life through the course of its development.[3] Box 1-1 lists parents' responsibilities in caring for children. This general list encompasses thousands of specific actions carried out over many years. Parenting draws on all the skills and abilities parents possess. It takes over the lives of adults, who at the same time must carry on lives at home with spouses and at work. Most parents would say parenting never ends; they feel that, as long as they live, they will be trying to help their children grow and be happy.

WHY DO PEOPLE TAKE ON THE JOB?

People are drawn to parenting for several reasons. First, we appear to be preprogrammed to respond positively to babies.[4] The young of all species have a quality of babyishness—heads are proportionately larger; foreheads and eyes are more prominent; cheeks are fatter; limbs are shorter in relation to the torso; and there is a clumsiness to their movements. Women's pupils grow bigger (a sign of attraction) when they look at pictures of babies. When people are shown drawings of human and animal faces, their pupils grow larger as the faces become more and more babylike.

Box 1-1
SOCIETY'S EXPECTATIONS OF PARENTS AND OF ITSELF

Of parents:
- Feed, clothe, and shelter the child.
- See that the child has access to medical and dental care.
- Provide responsible discipline; avoid injurious and cruel criticism and physical punishment.
- Ensure the child's intellectual and moral education.
- Prepare the child to become an independent adult.
- Take responsibility for the child's actions in the larger society.

Of itself:
- Provide free public education from ages five to eighteen.
- Give other assistance only if the child is economically disadvantaged or physically or psychologically disabled.

Adapted from: Diana Baumrind and Ross A. Thompson, "The Ethics of Parenting," in *Handbook of Parenting*, 2nd ed., ed. Marc H. Bornstein, vol. 5: *Practical Issues in Parenting* (Mahwah, NJ: Erlbaum, 2002), 3–34.

Not everyone is equally attracted to babies, and the fact that there may be a biological contribution to the attraction does not mean that people are required to have children. It suggests only that there may be a biological contribution in addition to the social prescriptions for parenthood.

Second, society's strong encouragement is a major influence in having children. Society needs children if it is to flourish and continue, and so it emphasizes the positive value of having children. More than work or marriage, society describes parenthood as a sign of maturity and adulthood.[5] Being a parent means that you are grown up, ready to take on responsibilities, and that you are unselfish and generous. A married couple feels pressure to have children not only from the larger society but also from their own parents, who want to be grandparents. Social pressure for parenthood was stronger after World War II, when parents were encouraged to have three or four children. It decreased somewhat because of growing concerns about overpopulation. But in some European countries and Japan, pressure is increasing because the population is diminishing.[6] Currently, in our society most couples expect to have children, and most do.

Although no one should feel pressured to have children against his or her will, a little push to have children may be beneficial. The reason is this: Most parents describe profound joys and satisfactions with their children. One mother said, "You never imagined you could love someone this much."[7] Another father said, "It is the first time in my life I know what the term *unconditional love* means. The wonder of this little girl and nature! I have never experienced anything like that. It is 'Yes'

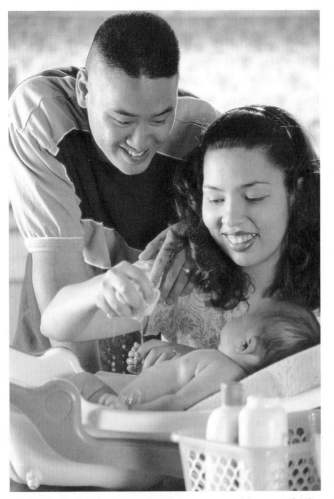

The main reason men and women, parents and nonparents alike, give for having children is to love and feel close to the child. One father said, 'It's the first time in my life I know what the term *unconditional love* means.'

without any 'Buts.' "[8] Yet, it is difficult, if not impossible, to experience such pleasures with other people's children or to know them in advance of having children. As one father said, he would really have regretted not having children. Society tries to make sure that few have that regret.

When asked to list their reasons for having children, men and women, parents and nonparents alike, give similar reasons. In general, people give these reasons (listed in Table 1-1) in similar order of importance in all ethnic groups, with the exception that African Americans and rural residents are more likely than other groups to view children as providing economic help and security in old age, and people with more education are less likely to see that as a reason for having children.[9]

The list indicates that people want children to love and be close to. They want to see children grow, develop new skills, take on new challenges. In helping children grow, parents feel a sense of creativity and accomplishment. People want to meet

■ **T A B L E 1-1**
PARENTS' REASONS FOR WANTING CHILDREN

1. Love and satisfying relationship with others.

2. Stimulation and excitement at watching the child grow.

3. A means of self-development—becoming more responsible, more sensitive, more skilled in relationships.

4. A way of achieving adult status—parenthood is "proof" of maturity.

5. A sense of creativity and achievement in helping the child grow.

6. An expression of moral and religious belief.

7. Utility—the belief that children will care for parents when parents are older or ill.

Adapted from: Lois Wladis Hoffman and Jean Denby Manis, "The Value of Children in the United States: A New Approach to the Study of Fertility," *Journal of Marriage and the Family* 41 (1979): 583–596.

society's—and in some instances, their religion's—expectations of them. Parents find satisfaction in being more adult, responsible, and caring. And for some groups, children offer a feeling of greater security in the case of sickness or old age.

The largest study of joys and problems in child rearing found that, by and large, parents get what they hope for in parenthood.[10] Arthur Jersild and his colleagues interviewed 544 parents. Although the study is fifty years old, it is the only extensive study of parenting's joys as well as its problems. Parents reported more than twice as many joys (18,121) as problems (7,654) in rearing children. The most common joys described are children's special qualities as a person, companionship and affection, pleasure in watching the child grow in intellectual and social skills, feelings of satisfaction in helping the child grow and in the general role of parent, and satisfactions in sibling relationships. You can see that parents' joys relate not to children's outstanding or spectacular achievements but to everyday life experiences and interactions that are readily available to all parents. And, fortunately, the joys are what parents hope to experience when they decided to become parents.

Reasons given by couples for not having children center on three broad factors: restrictions (loss of freedom, loss of time for other activities, increase in workload), negative feelings in relation to children (worries concerning their health and well-being, difficulties in discipline, fear of disappointments in children or in self as a parent), and concerns about the child being poorly cared for.[11]

These couples anticipated the kinds of problems parents actually report. The problems parents described in Jersild's study centered on the child's difficult personality traits, difficulties in getting cooperation in routines, concerns about sibling conflicts, disappointments in self as a parent.[12] Interestingly, few parents (only 15 percent) reported lack of closeness with the child as a problem, so the difficulties did not prevent the closeness that is the main reason parents want children. Many parents reported health issues as a problem (18 percent), but few parents (only 2 percent) reported good health as a satisfaction.

As we talk about parents' many activities in helping children grow, and the work and the effort involved, it is wise to recall that there are many more satisfactions than problems in parenting. We just don't talk about them as much.

PARENTING IS A PROCESS

We have described parents' responsibilities to protect and nurture children, but parenting is not a one-way street in which the parent directs the child to adulthood. It is a process of action and interaction between parent and child, a process in which both parties change each other as children grow to adulthood.

Jay Belsky identifies three major influences on the process of parenting: (1) the child's characteristics and individuality; (2) the parents' personal history, psychological characteristics, and resources; and (3) the social context of stresses and supports.[13] The child, the parent, and the social context all influence the process of parenting and in turn are changed by it. Let us look at the contributions of each.

THE ROLE OF THE CHILD

Evolutionary psychologists point out that the organized, cooperative, social behavior of human tribal society depends on a large brain capacity.[14] The large brain and head require that human babies are born in a very immature state, so that the mother's body can accommodate the child's head and body size in the birth process. Children's immaturity at birth and for several years thereafter requires that parents and society care for them and meet their physical and social needs for a long period if the children are to survive.

Babies' physical needs are straightforward, but they can be met in many different ways, depending on the environment and the society in which they are born. They require shelter, food, clothing, and warmth. Their psychological and social needs are more complex.

Urie Bronfenbrenner and Pamela Morris describe a child's basic psychological need for "one or more other persons with whom the child develops a strong, mutual, irrational attachment, and who are committed to the child's development, preferably for life." The child need not be biologically related to the caregiver or live in a two-parent family, but the caregiver must have a long-term, "irrational" attachment to and love for the child. They use the term *irrational* to refer to the total love and commitment felt for the child, the one you would save first in a fire. The caregiver-child relationship requires the attachment and support of a second adult "who assists, encourages, spells off, gives status to, and expresses admiration and affection for the person caring for and engaging in joint activity with the child."[15]

Children grow through interactions with caregivers and with objects and symbols in the environment. Interactions must occur regularly and for long periods of time for the interactions to become more complex and stimulate further development.

In addition to their basic human needs, children's individual qualities—gender, temperament, physical health—affect parents' actions and the effects of these actions on children. For example, the mother of fraternal twins, a boy and a girl, commented that, if she had had either child alone, she would have thought that she was either the best or the worst mother in the world. Her daughter was a quiet, adaptable, easygoing baby, happy with whatever her mother did, and her mother felt herself to be an excellent mother. Her son was an intense, colicky baby, and nothing his mother did seemed to make him happy in the first few months, so she felt very inadequate as his mother. She was the same person with the same skills, but her behavior had a different impact on each child as a result of the child's temperament, and her impact on the babies affected how she felt about herself as a mother.

A child's health influences parenting. Genetic or birth complications can make child care more demanding for parents. If babies' basic abilities to nurse, to adapt to stimulation, and to sleep are affected, soothing and caring for them is more complex.

Another factor in the parenting process is the "goodness of fit" between the child's qualities and those of the parent and family.[16] For example, the behavior of a slow-moving, slow-to-adapt child may present a problem in an active, boisterous, on-the-go family but no problem in a family in which most members are quiet and slow moving.

Children's Importance to Parents and Society

As we noted earlier, children meet parents' basic needs for closeness, for a sense of accomplishment, and for a sense of creativity and maturity in life. They also meet parents' needs for personal growth. Parents undertake new activities, meet new people, and become more involved in communities as they go about meeting children's needs. Parents also experience more stress and daily anger than nonparents, and they become more skillful in managing their emotional reactions.[17] We discuss other changes parenting initiates in individuals later in this chapter.

We do not often think about how children meet society's critical needs, but they do. Children ensure that society will continue. They maintain traditions and rituals, and they transmit social values to the next generation. Very importantly, they grow into economic producers who support the aging members of society as well as their own children. In a society like ours, in which children represent an ever-smaller percentage of the population, every child is a valued participant. As Richard Lerner, Elizabeth Sparks, and Laurie McCubbin write, "Children constitute 100 percent of the future human and social capital on which our nation must depend."[18]

THE ROLE OF THE PARENT

Parents' role is to nurture and protect children, and Box 1-1 (page 4) listed parents' activities in carrying out the role. Society gives parents primary authority to meet children's needs because parents are assumed to have their dependent children's best interests at heart.[19] So parents choose where children live, what schools they go to, what religion they practice, what forms of discipline are used. Society intervenes only in cases of abandonment, neglect, physical harm, or potential harm to children, or in conflicts parents cannot resolve themselves.

Parents bring a complex set of needs and qualities to the process of parenting. As do children, they bring their gender and temperamental qualities.[20] They also bring their personalities and the relationships they have forged with the other parent and with their broader social network of extended family, friends, and coworkers. Unlike children, who come to the parenting process fresh and inexperienced, parents come with a history of relationships with their own parents and with other authority figures and friends.

Parents may well carry over past ways of relating into their relationships with their children. For example, studies have shown that mothers who had less authoritarian parenting in their preschool years, whose mothers experienced positive, supportive, and open relationships with their mothers in childhood and adolescence, grew into warm, sensitive, stimulating mothers with their own children.[21] Conversely, when parents had difficulties in previous relationships with their parents, when they feel irritable and angry they are more likely to misinterpret children's behavior as willful and behave harshly toward the children.[22]

Other dimensions of parents' lives influence parenting as well. The positive or negative qualities of marriages and work environments can support or stress parents' relationships with children, as we see in Chapters 13 and 14.

Paul Amato uses the term *human capital* to refer to all the skills, abilities, and knowledge that parents bring to the parenting role. In addition to human capital, he says, parents bring *financial capital*—the income that enables them to provide food, shelter, housing, access to lessons and educational opportunities. And parents also bring *social capital,* a term that refers to the quality of relationships within the home and the relationships between the parents and the larger community.[23]

The three terms suggest that these categories are independent of one another, but they often are not. A parent with confidence and self-esteem is more likely to pursue advanced education and to have an occupation with a higher salary that, in turn, enables the family to live in a neighborhood with recreational resources and less violence. Another example can be seen in families when parents lose jobs, experience more irritability and marital tension, and then become harsh in parenting their children. When parents can remain supportive of each other, parenting skills do not decrease.[24]

Parents' Importance to Children and Society

We explore parents' vital importance to children in a later, expanded section of the chapter (pages 21–26). Parents play a critical role in our society as they rear children who will maintain society. They provide round-the-clock care for eighteen years, and they pay all their children's expenses. When society is forced to intervene in family life, it is difficult if not impossible, as we shall see, for society to provide the level and continuity of personal care that parents happily give children.

THE ROLE OF SOCIETY

Children live in families, and families live in neighborhoods and communities in a larger society that, in turn, influences how parents carry out their tasks. Society provides values, standards of conduct, and shared views of the world. Because children are the future of society, society has a strong interest in their care and growth. Thus, it provides a set of beliefs about (1) the roles of the parents, (2) the role of the child, (3) the roles of the extended family members and the community, (4) the goals of parenting, and (5) approved methods of care and discipline.[25] Our diversified society has many views on these topics, as cultural groups as well as state laws differ one from another. However, we can talk about general principles.

Legal Definitions and Enforcement of Roles

Society's legal system defines the roles of parent and child:

> Generally, the law defines parenthood in terms of relationship—a woman's biological relationship to a child, a man's marital relationship to a child's natural mother, or a non-biological relationship established by adoption or marriage. Less commonly, the law may acknowledge an emotional or psychological relationship between people who are otherwise unrelated. Within these various definitions, both legal and social traditions stress the primacy of the nuclear family and the functions it fulfills in the lives of children.[26]

Laws regarding rights of parenting figures prior to birth—sperm donor, egg donor, surrogate parent, rearing parent—are still vague, but, in general, prebirth figures give up rights to the child. When a child is born to a married woman, her husband is presumed to be the father. Because *fatherhood* has been defined as being married to the biological mother, unwed fathers traditionally had no rights with regard to their children until 1972, when the Supreme Court decided that, if unwed fathers participated in children's care, they were entitled to claim parental rights. The law, however, is still vague in the scope of unwed fathers' parental rights or what they must do to ensure them.

In cases of conflict about parenthood, the biological tie is the first consideration, provided the parent is fit, but it is not the only consideration. For example, even though the biological mother was fit, children were awarded to their stepmother after their biological father died, because the children had been living with her, and she was in a sense the psychological parent.[27] See Box 1-2 for another example of a nonbiological "parent" obtaining custody of a child.

Society defines not only a parent but also the basic requirements of parenting. Because parents are expected to make most of the decisions, society imposes few but important requirements. Parents must see that children have immunizations before the age of five and ongoing medical care, and that children receive education between the ages of five and eighteen. Society also insists that parents use accepted forms of discipline and rear law-abiding children.

Society defines the role of the child as well as that of the parent.[28] Children are considered inexperienced and dependent and are expected to follow parents' rules and requests. Children are considered incapable of making informed decisions, and so, prior to a child's eighteenth birthday, parents must give consent for routine medical care, driver's license, entry into military service, and marriage. Most states make exceptions to this general rule and permit teens to seek treatments for substance abuse, pregnancy, contraception, reproductive health, and mental health counseling without parental consent. Further, parents cannot obtain information about their teens' medical care in these areas.[29]

Most often, society looks at family issues from the point of view of the parents but at the same time tries to keep in mind the best interests of the child. The child's interests are usually the main concern in custody issues.

The law imposes few rules on parents, but it does enforce these rules and takes action if it determines that parents are neglectful or abusive or are putting the child at risk. Child protective agencies can remove children from parents' custody and charge parents with crimes if they feel that parents have endangered their

---

Box 1-2
DO YOU AGREE WITH THE CALIFORNIA APPELLATE COURT OR THE CALIFORNIA SUPREME COURT?*

The California Supreme Court recently awarded legal custody of a child to mother's ex-boyfriend over mother's objections that he was not the biological parent. The state appellate court had declared that the ex-boyfriend could not be a legal father because he was not the biological father. The state supreme court reversed the ruling and established that the man was the legal father of the child because he had cared for the seven-year-old since birth, and no biological father had stepped forward. He was considered the constant in the child's life; without him, the child would be fatherless and homeless. The court wrote, "A man who receives a child into his home and openly holds the child out as his natural child is presumed to be the natural father of the child."

If the biological father had been located when the child was seven and was as fit a parent as the boyfriend, should the court have given custody to him rather than to the natural father? Why or why not?

*From: Michael Janofsky, "Custody Case in California Paves Way for 'Fathers,'" *New York Times*, 6 June, 2002, p. A13.

---

children. For example, a mother was sent to jail for nine years—not for what she did but for what her boyfriend did. (See Box 1-3.) In addition to holding parents responsible for their behavior, society sometimes holds them legally responsible for their children's actions—paying fines, making restitution when children have destroyed property.

The law also takes action to ensure that children and teens obey parents' rules.[30] Children and teens can go to juvenile detention for repeatedly violating reasonable parental rules or for running away. Further, society has also removed the legal protections given to children in the past. For example, children and teens are now considered responsible for violent crimes and are charged, sentenced, and jailed as adults would be. Recently, an eleven-year-old girl with no previous record of violence was charged with felony assault because she hit an eight-year-old boy with a rock and made a $1\frac{1}{2}$-inch cut on his forehead, requiring stitches.[31] The boy had hit her with water balloons and rocks, and she threw one of the rocks back. When she resisted arrest, she was handcuffed, taken to juvenile hall for five days, then released with an electronic ankle bracelet that was removed after a hearing a month later.

There was little protest in the girl's city, but national and international attention brought protests about the harsh treatment of a minority child in a poor neighborhood whose family had few legal resources. Authorities further investigated the incident. The two children and their families were given the opportunity to reach a negotiated settlement. A scheduled trial was postponed pending the outcome of the negotiations.

Box 1-3
WOULD YOU HAVE SENT THIS MOTHER TO JAIL?*

In 1995, Tabatha Pollock was convicted of first-degree murder and sentenced to thirty-six years in jail because her boyfriend, Mr. English, hit twice, choked, and killed her three-year-old daughter at three in the morning while Ms. Pollock was sleeping. When her boyfriend woke her and she found the child, she immediately called authorities and sought medical help.

No witnesses testified that the boyfriend was suspected of physical abuse. In his confession, he said that Ms. Pollock knew nothing of such behavior, although prosecutors said she should have noticed that her children had many scrapes and bruises. She was convicted on a negligence theory, that she should have known of potential harm even though she did not. In other cases, parents have been held responsible only when they witnessed or knew of the threat. An appeals court upheld Ms. Pollock's conviction, and her lawyer at that time said there were no legal grounds to appeal to the state supreme court.

After her conviction and incarceration, Ms. Pollock lost her parental rights regarding her other three children, the youngest of whom was the son of Mr. English. After years in jail, Ms. Pollock was able to secure legal help from the Northwestern University Law School clinic. Lawyers there were able to persuade the state supreme court to hear an appeal even though the deadline had expired. The supreme court overturned her conviction, stating that the negligence theory—that she should have known what she did not know—had no basis in law. After seven years in prison, she was released.

Mary Becker, professor of family and domestic violence law at DePaul University in Chicago, said, "We hold mothers responsible beyond all logic, beyond any possibility that they could stop it. We live in a culture where we want mothers to do everything, and where whenever something goes wrong, it's the mother's fault."

*Adam Liptak, "Judging a Mother for Someone Else's Crime," *New York Times,* 27 November 2002, p. A14.

Cultural Expectations of Parents' and Children's Roles

Cultural expectations influence parents and children as well. Although the law's requirements are few, focus on observable behaviors, and extend to all groups, cultural expectations can be numerous and sometimes contradictory, can refer to feelings as well as acts, and can vary from group to group. In general, it is middle-class notions of roles that are most widely presented in print and in the media, but we should be aware that middle-class views do not reflect the opinions of all Americans or all groups within the country.

We more fully explore past conceptions of parents' roles in the next chapter. Currently, society has demanding roles for men and women alike. Both parents are expected to share all parenting activities equally. Men are expected not only to provide financial resources for families but also to be sensitive caregivers of children.[32]

Women are expected to develop their abilities fully, to contribute to the economic well-being of families, to nurture children, and to provide them with the experiences necessary for achievement and success in life.[33] See Box 1-4 for two statements of role expectations and the frustrations that can come from meeting them without training or support.

Society also has expectations about children.[34] Because their labor frequently is not needed, children have an extended dependency on parents, and their roles become those of learners and consumers of material goods and entertainment.

Providing the Social Fabric of Life

Society not only defines the roles of parent and child, it also creates the social context in which parents and children play out their roles. Although our society is a diverse one, we describe here the middle-class culture that is presented to all Americans via the media. In Chapter 3, we review ways of seeing the world and the behaviors encouraged in different cultures within our society.

Social Climate   One looks for a common cultural theme that underlies the American experience for all groups and finds it in philosopher Jacob Needleham's book, *The American Soul*. Needleham describes the hope America has inspired in all its citizens and aspiring citizens:

> The hope of America lies and has consisted in the fact that its political ideals and forms of government, its iconic actions and archetypal heroes, reflect in two directions at once—toward the external good of a life of liberty and equality and the reasonable search for a normal life of community and creative aspiration; and at the same time inwardly toward the search for inner development, the life of conscience and reason that defines the true nature of humanity and gives life its ultimate meaning. The hope of America lies in large measure in the extent to which its ideals and forms of action, and its main symbols of identity, point in two directions at once: to the outer and inner simultaneously.[35]

At times, our culture reflects these ideals with stories of people's achievements against great odds, of individuals' giving their lives to bring civil rights to underserved groups in our society, of generosity in endowing scholarships so that poor students have opportunities for education. Often, however, the popular press and electronic media express, as psychologist Jim Taylor writes, a culture of materialism, violence, greed, and corruption in business and on the part of government leaders, superficial sexuality, and self-centeredness.[36] These messages come to families over hundreds of radio and television channels, in movies, in contemporary music, and in computer and video games. Not only numerous, such influences are pervasive throughout the waking hours of children and adolescents through videos, DVDs, iPods, and games playable anywhere youth are.

Supports and Stressors   Society presents not only messages but also tangible supports and stresses for parents as they go about rearing children. Although we think of ourselves as a culture that values children and provides excellent care for them, our infant mortality rate (the number of deaths of a child under one year of age per 1,000 live births) is twice as high as that of Japan (6.6 compared to 3.3) and higher than that of any European country.[37] Our rate is about the same as that of

Box 1-4
CHALLENGING ROLES FOR CONTEMPORARY PARENTS*

Society's roles for parents can be demanding. Here, a mother and father identify problems they see in their role expectations.

Judith Warner, author of *Perfect Madness: Motherhood in the Age of Anxiety*, describes the heavy burden society's role prescriptions place on mothers. The Mommy Mystique, as Warner terms society's demands, makes mothers totally responsible for their children's development and well-being. Mothers are expected to be physically available to children at all times, to meet all their needs for physical care, love, and stimulation, and then to see that children have access to the best physical, social, and educational programs. Mothers must excel in the role so their children can succeed in our competitive society. Mothers are failures if their children have difficulties or cannot achieve high levels of success. Such total responsibility for the child's well-being is especially hard for contemporary mothers who have been raised to have strong commitments to their work as well.

Although society demands much of mothers, it gives little help in meeting these expectations. Mothers are often required to work to help support their families, but good-quality, affordable day care is often not available, especially for mothers who work part-time; little after-school care is available for older children as well, so much of mothers' pay goes for substitute care while they work. Many mothers who are financially able have stopped working or have reduced their work hours, but they may still experience anxiety and guilt because they are not fulfilling their career aspirations.

These expectations and the lack of help in meeting them create tremendous stress for mothers as they run around frantically trying to accomplish all their tasks. The role demands also arouse intense anxiety in mothers about their children's future performance and guilt whenever children fail to keep up with other children or when they develop problems. The expectations also affect children, who sense their mothers' stress and tension.

Warner believes that this situation will not change until parents band together and insist on programs to reduce maternal stress, such as affordable, good-quality day care, tax credits and benefits for part-time workers, and more parent-friendly workplaces with flexible hours and work. A *Newsweek* article[†] Warner wrote that described mothers' dilemmas drew almost six hundred letters, some disagreeing with her, some offering solutions to the problems. For example, Rob Reiner, Hollywood director and advocate for children's programs, wrote about Parents' Action for Children, a parent group he has formed to exert political pressure for family support programs like child care and medical care programs. Jennifer Blaske wrote to describe a nongovernmental organization, the International MOMS Club, that provides support to stay-at-home mothers with baby-sitting, play groups, and discussion clubs.

Still other readers believe that stress can be managed when individuals make informed choices as to how to balance work and family commitments. Jennifer Regen Bisbee wrote, "I can relate to the challenges that Judith Warner illuminates, but I was surprised that she only hinted at the one solution available to every harried mom: the power to say no . . . No, I tell my children, you can't participate in more than one after-school activity, but that keeps our family schedule remotely sane. No,

Box 1-4

I tell myself, I will not take on another client right now, which would mean more money but also more nights away from my children. We are a generation of young women raised to believe we can do it all. We also need the self-discipline and wisdom to understand we can't do it all *right now*."

Joe Ehrmann[‡] identifies a misguided role expectation for men. A former NFL football player who became an inner-city minister in Baltimore following the death from cancer of a much-loved younger brother, he has observed that society values and teaches a "false masculinity" (p. 36), which gives boys and men approval for excelling at physical games, attracting and impressing women, and building up financial wealth. Boys are taught to compete and win and to hide their feelings, especially when they feel hurt. But masculinity that emphasizes power and dominance prevents men from developing close relationships and becoming loving husbands and fathers. Such masculinity brings no lasting sense of worth and happiness in life. Genuine masculinity, he believes, depends on creating close relationships and caring for others and for causes beyond oneself.

Ehrmann believes that, in the context of high school football, he and the co-coach, businessman Biff Poggi, and the eight assistant coaches can encourage adolescents' positive relationships with others by teaching these four basic traits of masculinity: (1) to take responsibility for their actions, (2) to "lead others courageously," (3) to "enact justice on behalf of others" (p. 140), and (4) to be responsible and accountable to a higher set of principles or greater authority such as God, representing a cause greater than myself. The boys learn responsibility by being on time, following team and school rules, and meeting academic standards. They also take responsibility for finding and developing their skills to the fullest. The boys learn to care about each other and look after each other. They are taught to include people—for example, always to ask the person eating alone at school to join the group. Ehrmann terms this program, which he carries out at a secular, private high school, "Building Men for Others."

Ehrmann and the coaches give the boys the experience of being nurtured and encouraged. Many of the team practices begin with Biff or Joe asking the boys, "What is our job as coaches?" The boys answer, "To love us." "And what is your job?" "To love each other" (pp. 3, 43). Ehrmann believes that, over time and with the coaches' examples, their ways of interacting with the boys, and the fun activities of the team, adolescents can learn to take responsibility for what they do and become. The following excerpt is from an interview with Ehrmann in Jeffrey Marx's book, *Season of Life*[§]:

> "Nobody grows up in a perfect family, simply does not exist, and we certainly do not live in a perfect society, so we find ourselves with an awful lot of nurturing wounds," Joe said. "And then what we get from that is a tendency to blame others or make an alibi for our own decisions and action."

Joe offered an example. "A father walks out on his wife and kids. The kids struggle without a male role model in the house. Then come the problems."

(continued)

Box 1-4
CONTINUED

"But as a kid," Joe said, "even though your dad walked away, you've still eventually got to assume responsibility for yourself. And you've got to assume responsibility not to do that to *your* kids the next go-round. . . .

"It's not so much what your father did, it's more that the responsibility is on what you do with that fact." Everything in our culture teaches men to either deny or suppress or ignore this kind of pain. But we have to work through our own woundedness and whatever happened to us. We simply have to be responsible for what we do with the stuff that happens to us. (p. 141)

As we shall see in a later section, many adults have done just this, worked through the hurt feelings of childhood so they do not repeat them with their own children.

*Judith Warner, *Perfect Madness: Motherhood in the Age of Anxiety* (New York: Penguin, 2005).
†Judith Warner, "Mommy Madness," *Newsweek*, 21 February 2005, pp. 42–49.
‡"Letters," *Newsweek*, 7 March 2005, p. 15.
§Jeffrey Marx, *Season of Life* (New York: Simon & Schuster, 2003).

Taiwan and South Korea. These trends continue in the mortality figures for children under the age of five.[38] Further, approximately one in nine children in our country lacks insurance for medical care.[39]

Unless a child has a specific disability or the family lives below the poverty line, the United States provides only a free education for children from ages five to eighteen, a specific tax exemption for each dependent child, and a tax credit for child care. Parents in our society have the option to take unpaid leave for up to three months at the time of a baby's birth, but ours is one of only six countries in the world that does not give paid maternal or paternal leave (the others are Australia, New Zealand, Lesotho, Swaziland, and Papua New Guinea).[40]

Although supports are few, parents' stressors exist at many levels. First, at the most general level, the international scene of unpredictable terrorist attacks, bombings, killings, and terrorist alerts creates fear and insecurity in children and parents alike. Parents worry about children's reactions and seek to reassure them, but global insecurity has become a fact of contemporary life and will continue to be so for the foreseeable future. So, parents must find ways to help children cope with that ongoing but unpredictable stress. We discuss ways to do that in Chapter 15.

Second, at the most immediate level is the day-to-day stress of caring for infants and young children and meeting their needs. Warner voices the many worries parents have as they do this.[41] Peter Stearns also describes the anxieties parents feel in a modern world in which threats of mortal illness and epidemics are few but the potential threats of psychological harm and damage to children abound.[42] Parents fear they may be the source of damage—damaging self-esteem, creating trauma for the child—but they also feel helpless in the face of possible harm from outside their sphere of influence—kidnapping, abuse, bullying at school or on the playing field, and so forth.

Our communities also create stress for parents. James Garbarino describes what he terms the "socially toxic environment" that children and parents inhabit in our country.[43] Garbarino points to high levels of childhood poverty, abuse, and community violence as sources of toxicity, and also to disruptions in families and an increased sense of despair among children. He specifically cites the increase in problem behaviors parents report about children. In 1976, 10 percent of children were described as having problems in need of treatment, and in 1989 the comparable figure was 18 percent.

Aware of such statistics, child psychiatrist and researcher Michael Rutter writes, "If we had a proper understanding of why society has been so spectacularly successful in making things psychologically worse for children and young people, we might have a better idea as to how we can make things better in the future."[44]

We are not doomed to endure the present culture. Culture is a changing, dynamic force that can be redirected. Looking at changes in the social system over the last one hundred and twenty years helps to put contemporary culture in perspective and to suggest changes that can be made.

The Changing Context of Social Supports and Stresses   Vern Bengtson points to four major forms of family life in the last century: the extended farm family, the nuclear family, the diverse family, and the multigenerational family.[45] *The extended farm family,* the primary form of family life in this country until the late nineteenth century, was a productive economic and social institution based on law and custom. Industrialization, urbanization, and growing secularism led to the formation of *the nuclear family,* consisting of parents and children. The function of the nuclear family, which was based on companionship and love, was to socialize children and meet the emotional needs of family members.

The traditional nuclear family was the primary form of family life for much of the twentieth century. In the 1970s, however, social and economic changes led to a decrease in the number of nuclear families in which fathers worked and mothers reared children. Such factors as (1) economic changes requiring more than one parent's income to support families, (2) women's entrance into the workforce, (3) a secularism that permitted greater acceptance of divorce and childbearing outside marriage led to *diverse families:* dual-career families, single-parent families, and stepfamilies.

Recently, young families have faced economic difficulties caused by unstable employment, increasing housing costs and child-care expenses, and reduced incomes in single-parent families. Fewer emotional resources are available because of parents' decreased availability due to work and divorce. Bengtson believes that the limited material and emotional resources available for children have led to *multigenerational families'* reliance on two or more generations to sustain the young. "For many Americans, multigenerational bonds are becoming more important than nuclear ties for well-being and support over the course of their lives."[46]

Multigenerational families rely on two or more generations to provide strong emotional ties and resources for children.

Demographic changes in the population have made this shift possible. In the last hundred years, the lengthening of the life span has led to an extended period for shared relationships between older adults and their children and grandchildren. In 1900, the average life expectancy was 49 years for women and 46.4 years for men; today, the average is 79.4 years for women and 73.6 for men.[47] Thus, there are thirty more years for adult children to relate to their parents, and for grandparents and great-grandparents to be involved with children. In this same period, the average number of children per family has dropped from 4.1 in 1900 to 1.9 in 1990.

These figures mean that the proportion of children in our society has decreased. Although the age structure of the population in 1900 resembled a pyramid, with many young people at the base and fewer older individuals at the top, it now resembles a bean pole, according to Bengtson, with equal proportions of people at all ages. Thus, adults of many ages are available to nourish the small number of children. Grandparents and great-grandparents step in and meet children's emotional needs for closeness. Referred to as "latent kin networks" or the "family national guard," they "muster up and march out when an emergency arises regarding younger generation members' well-being."[48]

Bengtson states that, despite all the changes in family structure, adolescents and youth feel as much solidarity with mothers and fathers in 1997 as their parents did with their own parents in 1971. He cites data from the Longitudinal Study of Generations collected from four generations of working and middle-class families from 1971 to 1997.[49]

Figure 1-1 compares the early life experiences of Generation 3 (termed *Baby Boomers*) with the life experiences of their children, Generation 4 (termed *Gen Xers*), including feelings of family solidarity with mothers and fathers. Baby Boomers grew up in families with more siblings, with fathers and mothers who had less education, with mothers who were more likely to be full-time homemakers, and with fewer divorces than their Gen X children. Yet the family solidarity scores of Baby Boomers in 1971 were very similar to the scores of their children in 1997.

Children not only feel close to their parents, they maintain similar values with regard to achievement as well. Maternal employment has not changed self-esteem or values, with the exception that Gen X young women have higher occupational aspirations than either their mothers or Gen X young men.

Data from a multinational study of young adults' subjective well-being support Bengtson's view that multigenerational help can compensate for the difficulties children experience when nuclear families are under stress.[50] In a large multicultural

■ **FIGURE 1-1**
HISTORICAL CHANGES IN FAMILY STRUCTURE AND PARENTAL ATTRIBUTES: GENERATION X COMPARED WITH THEIR BABY-BOOMER PARENTS AT THE SAME AGE

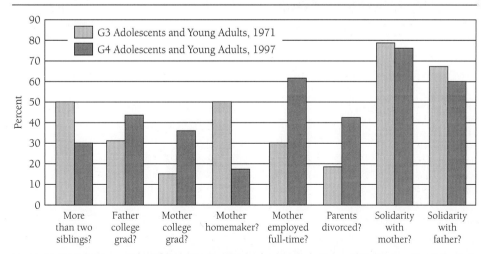

Vern L. Bengtson, "Beyond the Nuclear Family: The Increasing Importance of Multigenerational Bonds," *Journal of Marriage and Family* 63 (2001): 11. Reprinted with permission.

study on the relationship between divorce and young adults' feelings of life satisfaction and positive mood, researchers found that children of divorced parents in collectivist cultures (in which children receive more support from extended family members as well as the community) feel greater life satisfaction and more positive moods as adults than do the children of divorced parents living in individualistic cultures (in which families have less support from family and community).

INTERACTIONS AMONG CHILD, PARENT, AND SOCIETY

We have seen that children, parents, and society play their own vital roles in the process of parenting, that each participant is affected by the actions of the other two, and that all are affected by historical time.

Jay Belsky and his colleagues provide a model of how children, parents, and society interact, to predict the probability of child competence—a combination of abilities reflected in the child's feeling emotionally secure, having the capacity for independent behavior and good social skills with peers, and achieving at school.[51] (See Table 1-2.) When all factors are supportive, the probability of child competence is high. When two of the three factors are supportive, there is still a good probability of child competence. For example, if a child has a learning disability, but the parents' personal resources are strong and the school personnel provide practical help and emotional support, the probability of child competence is high.

■ **TABLE 1-2**
RELATIVE PROBABILITY OF A CHILD'S DEVELOPING COMPETENTLY

Probability of Child Competence	Conditions of the Parental Subsystems*		
	Parent's Personal Resources	**Subsystems of Support**	**Child's Characteristics**
High	+	+	+
↑	+	+	−
	+	−	+
	−	+	+
	+	−	−
	−	+	−
↓	−	−	+
Low	−	−	−

*(+) stands for supportive mode; (−) stands for stressful mode.

From J. Belsky, E. Robins, and W. Gamble, "Theoretical model of the probability of a child's developing competently in all possible conditions of the parenting system," in *Beyond the Dyad*, ed. Michael Lewis (New York: Plenum Press, 1984), p. 272. Reprinted by permission.

Conversely, even when the child has many skills and positive qualities, lack of social support and parental involvement lowers the probability of child competence. Belsky and his colleagues believe that, even when all goes wrong, if the parent brings his or her personal resources to bear on behalf of the child, there is a good chance that the child will develop average competence.

HOW IMPORTANT ARE PARENTS IN CHILDREN'S LIVES?

Parents invest time, emotional energy, and money in rearing children. They want to think that what they are doing really matters in the lives of children, that the sacrifices they make help children's growth. For most of human history, there has been little question that parents matter most; parents have been considered children's guardians, responsible for their health, well-being, and moral virtue, the figures that stood between children and death.

Beginning in the 1980s, two strands of research stimulated questions about parents' importance. On the one hand, research indicating the major role of genetic influences on children's development challenged the view of parents' behavior as the major influence on children. Popular writer Judith Rich Harris advised parents in 1998 that their role in children's development ". . . had been oversold. You have been led to believe that you have more influence over your child's personality than you really do."[52] She believed that parents nurtured children in the first five years but that parents' genes and children's peer experiences were the major determiners of children's adult personalities and life success. A number of social scientists agreed with her on the primary importance of genes.

At the same time that research on genes indicated a reduced role for parents' influence, research concerning the plasticity of the brain at birth led some observers to conclude that parents played a critical role in providing the early stimulation the brain requires for proper development. Parental anxieties increased because they feared they were not providing sufficient and appropriate stimulation.

So what does research suggest about the role of parents? Overall, it supports Belsky and his colleagues' contention that parents' behavior and efforts are the most important, though not the only, influences on children's growth and competence.[53]

Genes play an important role in providing a baby with a range of potential behaviors that are refined by interactions with people and the environment. It is not a question of either genetic or environmental influences; these are inseparable, and both play a significant role in all behavior. Even when a behavior or trait is very much under the control of the genes (as, for example, height), the environment can affect it. Around the world, average heights increased during the twentieth century because of better diets; in our own country, we have examples of Japanese Americans who are significantly taller than their Japanese grandparents because of enriched diets here.[54]

Genes exist only in an environment, and from the moment of conception, parents have the largest role in providing or monitoring the quality of that environment. Even before birth, the parental environment influences and can dramatically change the genetic potential. Although most parents' lifestyles protect intrauterine development, mothers who expose their fetuses and growing babies to alcohol or drugs can irreparably damage the genetic contributions to their children.[55] Recent research indicates that a prospective father's work environment, alcohol, smoking, and drug habits can affect the quality of the sperm and the coming baby as well.[56]

In this section, we look at four areas of parental influence after the child is born: (1) providing an environment of protection rather than one of risk, (2) providing experiences that lead to the development of maximum potential, (3) serving as an advocate in the larger community, and (4) being an irreplaceable force in a child's life.

Providing a Protective Social Environment

Parents' personal characteristics, their forms of interactions with children, and their interactions with social institutions create an environment of protection or risk for children that is more consistent than the child's own characteristics, as researchers discovered in the Rochester Longitudinal Study.[57] They followed children from birth through adolescence and looked at the number of protective and risk factors in each child's life and the relationships of these factors to children's social and emotional functioning. (See Table 1-3.) Only maternal qualities were included because few fathers participated in the study.

Protective factors were defined as those factors related to positive changes in intellectual and social-emotional functioning in children between four and thirteen years of age.[58] As can be seen, protective factors concern the general positive atmosphere of the family—the mother's good feeling about herself, her positive comments to children, children's self-esteem and sense of the world's predictability, and the amount of social support for the family.

Risk factors were those associated with poor outcomes for children. Risks centered on mothers' difficulties—anxiety, lack of emotional stability, lower education, and unskilled occupational status—and on negative family interactions and stressful events, especially when they occurred in larger families.[59] Researchers found no one special risk that led to a poor outcome for children. It was the accumulation of risks that mattered. Children in protective environments with no risks scored thirty points higher on intelligence tests than children with eight or more risks. Children with more risk factors had more emotional problems as well.

Children's environments greatly expanded or limited their range of competencies. The least resilient or resourceful child living in a low-risk environment scored higher on measures of competence than did the most resilient or resourceful child living in a high-risk environment. "The negative effects of a disadvantaged environment seem to be more powerful contributors to child achievement at every level than the personality characteristics of the child."[60]

Finally, researchers concluded that no single change could be made—increased income, change in marital status from single to married—that would eliminate the risks for children. Efforts to improve high-risk environments must focus on making changes in a broad constellation of factors—encouraging positive parent-child relationships, improving mothers' emotional stability, improving education and occupational status—because it is the combination of all the risks "that sap the lives of families."[61]

■ **T A B L E 1-3**
PROTECTIVE AND RISK FACTORS

Protective Factors[*]

Mothers' Characteristics

When children were preschoolers:

　encouraging children to think and reflect

When children were early adolescents:

　feeling positive about themselves and their children

　making positive rather than critical comments to children

　voicing fewer dissatisfactions, scoring lower on a scale of depression

　feeling support from confidantes and social networks

　encouraging self-direction in children rather than conformity

Children's Characteristics

When children were early adolescents:

　self-esteem

　a sense of social support

　a sense of predictability about the world

Environmental Characteristics

　fewer negative events

　social support for the family

Risk Factors[†]

Mothers' Characteristics

　serious mental instability

　high anxiety

　rigid beliefs about development

　few positive mother-child interactions

　minimal education

　unskilled occupation

　disadvantaged minority status

　single parenthood

　large family size

Environmental Characteristics

　stressful life events

---

[*]Ronald Seifer et al., "Child and Family Factors That Ameliorate Risk between 4 and 13 Years of Age," *Journal of the American Academy of Child and Adolescent Psychiatry* 31 (1992): 893–903.

[†]Arnold Sameroff et al., "Family and Social Influences on the Development of Child Competence," in *Families, Risk, and Competence*, ed. Michael Lewis and Candice Fearing (Mahwah, NJ: Erlbaum, 1998), 161–185.

Providing Experiences That Lead to Maximal Growth and Potential

Like the study of height and diet, many studies point to the nourishing effects of positive parenting in helping children achieve their maximal potential even when genetic influences make offspring susceptible to problems.

Let us look for a moment at animal studies because it is easier to manipulate the environmental experiences of animals with known genetic traits.[62] Rats and monkeys both differ in emotional reactivity at birth. Highly reactive animals in both species tend to be timid in exploring their environments and easily stressed. When nurturant foster mothers rear such reactive rats and monkeys, the animals grow up to be less anxious, more able to explore the environment, and more stress resistant. When highly nurturant foster mothers rear highly reactive monkeys, the monkeys not only decrease in anxiety but show many competencies and become leaders among peers.[63] They are skilled in avoiding stress and gaining support from other monkeys. If female, the foster monkeys of nurturant mothers become competent mothers, whereas emotionally reactive monkeys reared by control mothers in the average range of nurturance show deficits with their offspring. So, superlative mothering can compensate for reactive temperamental traits.

We have a similar finding with infants. Within the more usual range of temperamental qualities, parenting can modify in babies even those qualities that are thought to be genetically determined. Jerome Kagan's longitudinal research documented that highly reactive infants showing fretful crying and much motor activity at four months were less fearful as toddlers when mothers were firm and set reasonable limits with their babies.[64] The babies then seemed to find ways to settle down. Mothers who were responsive to the child's fretting and did not set limits had toddlers who continued to be fearful.

Skilled parenting can stimulate intellectual development.[65] The IQs of adoptive children correlate highly with those of their biological mothers; however, the children have significantly higher average IQs than their mothers. Average IQ increases as the socioeconomic status of the adoptive family increases. When adopted into homes with limited resources, the children gained an average of 8 IQ points, but when adopted into homes with ample resources, they gained 19 points on average.

A Swedish study shows how the environment provided by adoptive parents can influence social development and affect susceptibility to criminal behavior.[66] The study examined 862 men born out of wedlock but adopted by nonrelatives, on average, by age eight months. Researchers classified the risk of petty criminality (nonviolent, infrequent, minor crimes, usually property offenses) for both biological and adoptive parents and noted the rate of petty criminality of the adopted men as adults. The men's risk varied with the risk of adoptive as well as biological parents. When neither biological nor adoptive parents were at risk, the men's risk of petty criminality was 3 percent; when the adoptive parent was at risk but the biological parent was not, the men's risk was 7 percent; when a biological parent was at risk but an adoptive parent was not, the men's risk was 12 percent; when both the biological and adoptive parents were at risk, the men's risk was 40 percent. When a biological parent was at risk for petty criminality, the risk for the child was reduced by two-thirds if that child was reared by parents not at risk. Conversely, the risk for petty criminality increased more than three times when a child at biological risk was reared by an adoptive parent at risk.

Parents as Advocates

We think of parental influence as parents' directly influencing children's behavior by teaching, modeling, encouraging, supporting, and loving their children. But parents also influence children's behavior indirectly by assembling resources and helping children draw on them to promote growth.

For example, parents who have children with health or developmental problems and who have worked to help their children develop their full potentials have changed our culture's way of viewing disabilities and have greatly expanded the resources and opportunities available to children with disabilities and their parents.[67] These parents have lobbied for improvements in educational programs, living arrangements, and community respect for children so that their children can become more fully integrated into the mainstream. Parents' advocacy has resulted in fewer children living in institutions and more children living with biological or adoptive families. More community living arrangements for disabled adults have also been created. Parents have demanded and obtained more educational resources, greater community integration, and expanded occupational opportunities for children.

In addition to improving society's treatment of their children with special needs, parents' efforts at home make special contributions to their children's lives. Parents "frequently have expectations that help to elevate the functioning of their children with disabilities in a positive version of a self-fulfilling prophecy. They think their children can learn so they create favorable environments in which to teach them, and thus they do learn more than they would in less favorable environments."[68]

Children of outstanding achievements also benefit from parents' extra efforts and commitment. Benjamin Bloom and his coworkers studied 120 young men and women who achieved international recognition for high levels of performance in a variety of fields.[69] The researchers interviewed the individuals, their family members, teachers, and coaches to understand the process by which children achieved such excellence.

Few of the individuals, the researchers noted, were identified as special in the beginning. A combination of individual commitment, family support, and outstanding instruction led to accomplishment. Parents sought instruction for children, structured practices, and provided support and encouragement, emphasizing the ethic of hard work and doing one's best. As children's skills grew, parents found more advanced teachers and coaches and made financial and time commitments not only to provide instruction but also to attend recitals, games, and meets. In fact, the whole family's schedule sometimes changed to accommodate the child's training and performance schedule.

As children advance, parents continue their emotional and financial support. Studies of talented and world-class achievers emphasize that enormous effort on the part of many people goes into the gradual development of superior accomplishment.

Clearly, whether children have special difficulties or potential talents, parental support is essential along the way.

Indispensable Caring Figures in Children's Lives

We noted earlier that when families are unable to provide adequate care for children, society attempts to provide it. Numerous cases in many states illustrate the difficulties social institutions face in doing so. There really is no substitute for a caring adult figure in a child's life, be it a parent, a relative, or a friend.

A recent New Jersey case vividly demonstrated the difficulties state agencies face when they take on the role of parent. In January 2003, the physically abused body of a seven-year-old boy was found in a trunk in a locked cellar, and his twin and four-year-old brothers were found chained nearby.[70] Their mother had been reported to the Division of Youth and Family Services for abuse and neglect eleven times in a ten-year period, but the agency had closed the case on the family the year before. At the time, there was a report that the mother beat and burned her children, but it was not investigated because the agency could not locate the children.

The governor declared a state of emergency at the agency, and the workers were ordered to investigate immediately the 280 outstanding cases of children reported as victims of abuse. Workers could not locate 110 of the possible victims.[71] A review of cases reported to the Division of Youth and Family Services in the previous five years revealed that eighty-two children had died or had been critically injured, despite the reports of abuse to the agency.[72]

Although New Jersey and, at times, New York and Florida have drawn national attention because of difficulties in their management of child abuse cases, a federal survey revealed that they are not alone in having problems.[73] Not one of the fifty states fully met government standards in providing safe, permanent homes for children who were abused. "Some of these children are no better off in the care of the state than they were in the hands of abusive and negligent parents," said Carole Strayhorn, a Texas official reporting on the level of care in that state.[74]

Awareness of parents' great responsibilities in rearing children creates anxiety and frustration when parents lack social supports. But when social supports exist, stress decreases to manageable proportions. Given parents' importance in children's lives, should we consider licensing parents? (See Box 1-5.) How can we acknowledge our debt of gratitude to parents? (See Box 1-6.) Does Sylvia Hewlett provide answers in her interview on page 34?

HOW RAISING CHILDREN CHANGES ADULTS

Parents write about their intense love for their children and their appreciation of what children bring to their everyday lives. They also write about stress and worries. But they write less often about the positive changes parents allude to when they talk about how parenting has changed them (see Voices of Experience, page 29). They use such phrases as "a better person," "more patient," "more kind," "more responsible," "more oriented toward the future."

Katherine Ellison's *recent* book, *The Mommy Brain: How Motherhood Makes Us Smarter,* looks at a wide range of research supporting the view that mothers especially, but fathers and nonrelated caregivers as well, experience many positive changes in their personalities and behavior as a result of caring for children.[75]

🌳 **Box 1-5**
SHOULD A PARENTING LICENSE BE REQUIRED?

Given the importance of parents in children's lives, should we require parents to get a license to have children? Although some behavior geneticists minimize parents' role in children's behavior, David Lykken is not among them. Despite the fact that his work has demonstrated high heritability for certain traits, he nevertheless believes that parents have such a profound influence on children's lives that parents should be licensed to have children. Having studied criminal behavior and its antecedents, he is convinced that immature, impulsive parents doom a child to a life of difficulties.

> Most of the 1,400,000 men currently locked up in American prisons would have become tax-paying neighbors had they been switched in the hospital nursery and sent home with a mature, self-supporting, married couple. The parent with whom they did go home would in most instances not have been fit to adopt someone else's baby. . . . For evolutionary reasons, human beings are reluctant to interfere with the procreational rights of any person, no matter how immature, incompetent, or unsocialized he or she might be. In consequence human beings tend not to think about the rights of a child to a reasonable opportunity for life, liberty, and the pursuit of happiness.*

Lykken would require prospective parents to get a license, just as adults must to drive a car or operate a truck. Like the requirements for adoptive parents, a parenting license would require (1) proof of legal age, (2) proof of marriage, (3) proof of employment or economic independence, and (4) no history of violent criminal behavior. If parenting courses were available, a certificate of completion would be required as well. Proof of marriage would be required because Lykken believes the biggest risk factor for adult problems is absence of a biological father. If couples object to marriage, they can sign a legal contract indicating they plan to stay together for twelve years to provide stability in the child's life. Gay or lesbian parents can appeal to a family court for a license. If parents had a child without a license, the child would be removed and placed for permanent adoption. If a divorce occurred after the child was born, the child would remain with the parents.

To critics of licensure, Lykken replies that no system will eliminate all problems, but, he insists, "Parenthood is both a privilege and a responsibility. The privilege of parenthood would not be determined by test scores or family trees, but by behavior. . . . If you wish to have a child, all you have to do is to grow up, keep out of trouble, get a job, and get married."†

Few might agree with the specifics of Lykken's plan, but how would *you* go about balancing the needs of the child with the rights of the parent?

*David T. Lykken, "Parental Licensure," *American Psychologist* 56 (2001): 885–886.
†David T. Lykken, "The Causes and Costs of Crime and a Controversial Cure," *Journal of Personality* 68 (2000): 598.

Box 1-6
HOW CAN WE ACKNOWLEDGE PARENTS' CONTRIBUTIONS TO OUR SOCIETY?

Jay Belsky and John Kelly, summarizing observations from Belsky's study of new parents, wrote in 1994 words that still apply today:*

> As I watched our couples cope with financial concerns and with all the other challenges of the transition, I found myself deeply moved. The quiet dignity and courage of our fathers and mothers—especially our employed mothers—was inspiring to behold. But as I watched them, I also found myself deeply troubled by how little public acknowledgment, how little public support and gratitude they and other new parents receive for their selflessness and devotion.
>
> In its better moods our society now treats the family with benign neglect; in its darker moods as a source of parody. None of our participants complained about the lack of public support for their family building, but it affected them—in many cases by making the routine sacrifices of the transition that much harder. It is difficult to sacrifice oneself when the larger society says the overriding purpose in life is devotion to self, not devotion to others. And in a few cases it made those sacrifices too far to go. . . . Ills that plague the American family are complex and have many sources. But I think one major source is that our society no longer honors what I witnessed every day in the Project—the quiet heroism of everyday parenting. (p. 23)

Does the interview with Sylvia Hewlett (see page 34) provide ways for society to express its gratitude? Are there other ways?

* From Jay Belsky and John Kelly, *The Transition to Parenthood* (New York: Delacorte, 1994), 23.

Ellison became interested in the topic when she discovered, after the births of her two boys, that "I was complaining a lot more. But I was accomplishing a lot more" (two books in a four-year period while caring for her family and managing a freelance writing career). "Though I often felt frazzled, I was more motivated, excited by all I was learning at work and at home. My children not only had inspired my future-oriented interest in the environment but also had provided me with the 'excuse' to insist on a more flexible work life; this, in turn, allowed me more creativity. The children were also giving me constant lessons in human nature: theirs and my own."[76]

Ellison felt supported in her personal insights when she read a study finding that the learning and memory abilities of mother rats exceeded those of "bachelorette" rats. Mother rats caring for young pups were able to locate and recall the location of food more efficiently than the bachelorettes. They retained their improved perceptual

VOICES OF EXPERIENCE

How Parenting Has Changed Me as a Person

"It has changed my priorities, my perspective. I am much more protective. If I see someone driving like an idiot, I get much more upset. I feel more like a regular person, more grown up." FATHER OF A TODDLER

"Now I'm officially grown up. It's kind of funny because I am a forty-year-old person who is just feeling grown up. For me, it's being less caught up in myself, more unselfish; I don't do everything I want to do all the time, and that's changing, and it's okay. I used to resent that. I'm less self-centered, less concerned with myself and how I'm doing, how I'm feeling, what's up. Now I am thinking more about him. For both my husband and me, I don't know whether this is going to change, but we are more oriented toward the future." MOTHER OF A TODDLER

"My own personal sense of the meaningfulness of life in all its aspects has really gone through a dramatic change. It's just been so gratifying and meaningful and important to have this other little life, in a sense, in my hands, to be responsible for it." FATHER OF A TODDLER

"It has changed my sense of the past. I appreciate more of what my parents must have gone through for me. No matter what their problems or shortcomings, gee, they had to do all this for me." FATHER OF A TODDLER

"It's that overused word, *maturity*. It happened for both of us, my husband and me. We look back on our lives before our son and afterwards. Our whole lives were what we wanted, every hour of every day. Along came the baby and, by choice, there was a reverse, almost 100 percent. We don't go out like we used to. It seems like an agony sometimes, but we are growing up as a couple and a family. It's very enriching." MOTHER OF A TODDLER

"It has changed me for the better. It matured me, really at the core. I am much more responsible because I want to be a good example for them, provide stability for them. It has helped me to see into myself. I recall things I did as a child, and I understand better what was happening then. It has changed the kind of things I think of as fun." FATHER OF ELEMENTARY SCHOOL CHILD AND EARLY ADOLESCENT

"Having children makes you more patient, more humble, better able to roll with the punches because life is not so black and white. You can't just base your life on platitudes. You have the experience of having things go not the way you would have them go, having your children do things you would not have them do, and you have to roll with that. You learn it; it either kills you or you go on, and you have a different view of life. You become more patient and, I think, more kind." MOTHER OF EARLY AND LATE ADOLESCENTS

"I want to be a good father so it makes me evaluate what I do and say; I look at mistakes as you would in any important and intense relationship, so it certainly makes me more self-examining and more aware of myself and how I am being experienced by the other person. It is also a challenge to be tolerant when I don't feel very tolerant. So in developing certain interpersonal skills, I think being a parent has helped me to become a better person." FATHER OF ELEMENTARY SCHOOL CHILD

and memory abilities into old age. Spurred by the research, Ellison reviewed studies, interviewed scientists overseas, and documented the positive changes that occur for mothers and for all who have close contact with and provide care for children. She cautioned that, for children to get the advantages of caregiving, stress levels of caregivers have to be under control.

Ellison identified five areas in which abilities improve: (1) perception, (2) efficiency, (3) resiliency, (4) motivation, and (5) social skills. Mothers' visual and auditory perceptions increase. They are more sensitive to infants' cries, can differentiate their own infants' cries from those of other infants in the hospital, can identify their infants' clothes by smell. In one study, they are better able than nonmothers to read the body language and identify the emotional reactions of adults. Personality inventories given before and several years after having children reveal that mothers are more responsible and more understanding of themselves and others after having children.

She believes these changes are most dramatic for mothers because of the numerous hormonal changes during pregnancy, the birth process, and, later, nursing. For example, increases in levels of the hormones prolactin and oxytocin at the end of pregnancy and during nursing may trigger feelings of calm, relaxation, closeness to others, and fearlessness in protecting the young. These hormonal changes may produce lifelong changes in the brain that facilitate women's enjoyment of social relationships and social activism on behalf of children and others in need of help. Research is suggestive but not yet definitive in this area.

Clearly, hormonal changes are not required for maternal behaviors. When adoptive mothers are matched with first-time mothers with regard to maternal and paternal age and education as well as socioeconomic status, adoptive mothers' attachment to infants is as secure as that of biological mothers.[77] Further, fathers respond to infants' cries in ways similar to those of mothers.[78] They, too, increase in their ability to read body language and identify emotional reactions.[79] They do not experience the dramatic hormonal changes mothers do, but they do show some increase in prolactin and decrease in testosterone.[80]

A survey of mothers', fathers', and teachers' views on ways children have changed them identified four areas of change similar to those of Ellison.[81] First, children have heightened their awareness of environmental issues and motivated them to change bad habits like smoking or drinking. "One mother said, 'It wasn't so much that he (her son) would say anything, it was just how he would look at me, like he was really worried when I smoked. It would kill me. He cared so much. He really helped me to care for myself better. I haven't had a cigarette in over a year.'"[82]

Second, children have helped them to understand and integrate experiences from their own childhoods. They may hear themselves saying or doing things their parents did and understand their parents better. Or they may use such an experience as a wake-up call to change their behavior with their own children. Parents may recall important, long-forgotten childhood experiences and thus gain greater knowledge of themselves. Third, adults say they have become more knowledgeable and more creative in helping children learn and master tasks. Fourth, children's awe and wonder at life trigger parents' wonder. "Parents and teachers report that children wrestle with life's mysteries, stand awestruck before the most mundane of spectacles, and hunger for meaning and value by which to live their life. When adults interact with children, the familiar categories and concepts adults use to organize the world can be challenged and even cracked open by the child."[83]

So, we grow in many ways as a result of caring for children. As researchers studying the satisfactions and problems of parenting wrote, "Perhaps no other circumstance in life offers so many challenges to an individual's powers, so great an array of opportunities for appreciation, such a varied emotional and intellectual stimulation."[84]

A PRACTICAL QUESTION: IS MY PARENTING DETERMINED BY WHAT MY PARENTS DID?

Many parents and prospective parents worry when they read in newspapers and magazines that parents who physically abused their children were often abused themselves as children, or that alcoholic parents themselves grew up in families with an alcoholic parent. Or they worry when they read that warm, sensitive mothers grew up in families with support, understanding, and encouragement, and they themselves did not have such experiences. They worry even more when they read that genes control a lot of what we do—gain or lose weight, make friends easily or feel too shy to go to a party, become violent or retreat in fear—because they fear they are genetically destined to do what their parents did.

Is parenting limited by genes or what parents experienced as children? The answer, in brief, is "No." Genetic influences, in terms of temperamental qualities such as irritability or an easygoing nature, surely affect what we do as parents; they can make certain parenting behaviors involving emotional control harder or easier for parents to carry out. As we shall see, such parenting behaviors can be modified with effort. Childhood experiences with parents influence our development, often in very complex ways that we are just beginning to understand, but research indicates that parents can come to terms with childhood experiences and develop the behaviors they want to have as parents.

Although it is true, for example, that parents who were physically abused as children have a higher risk of being abusive than parents who did not experience abuse—between 25 and 35 percent grow up to maltreat their own children—still, the vast majority do not abuse their children.[85] And those parents who feel they are on the verge of hurting a child can learn new behaviors.

This is true in other areas as well. The majority of children who grow up with an alcoholic parent do not themselves become alcoholics. The risk is increased, but as adults parents can decrease the risk through certain actions.[86]

Steven Wolin found that some families with an alcoholic parent acted deliberately to prevent transmission of alcoholic behavior to the next generation by protecting family rituals and routines such as Christmas and birthdays from the alcohol abuse of the parent.[87] The family persisted with important holidays and rituals, even in times of trouble. Major holidays were the most important to safeguard, because everyone in the culture celebrates them, and participating in celebrations enables family members to still feel part of the larger society despite the alcoholic parent's behavior.

When couples, all of whom grew up with one alcoholic parent, came from families with protected rituals and made conscious decisions to protect their new families' rituals, then their children did not become alcoholics. Parents who did not transmit alcoholic behavior had healthy patterns of communication; parents talked together about their goals and planned satisfying holidays and routines, sometimes by doing the opposite of what had been done when they were children. Such planning prevented the development of alcoholic behavior in their children who were the grandchildren of alcoholics.[88]

Parents who worry about repeating other negative ways of relating learned in childhood can deal with their feelings about their parents' behavior and adopt new ways of relating. One study found that a group of parents who experienced early hardships and difficulties in their relationships with their parents were able to find new ways to solve problems and relate to other people. With the emotional support of a therapist, spouse or friend, these parents, as adults, were able to look at their childhood experiences, identify the negative emotional experiences, and accept that their parents could not give them what they needed or wanted. With insights and acceptance of what had been, they were then able to create the kinds of relationships they wanted to have with their sons and daughters. These parents' childhoods were difficult, and they had many sad and depressed feelings about them, but their painful feelings did not limit them. They acknowledged the pain and went on to develop the flexible, warm style of parenting they desired.[89]

Drawing on insights from neurobiology, attachment theory, and parent education classes, the book *Parenting from the Inside Out: How a Deeper Self-Understanding Can Help You Raise Children Who Thrive,* by child psychiatrist Daniel Siegel and teacher-educator Mary Hartzell, shows parents how, through awareness of their present feelings and reflections on the sources of these feelings, parents can gain the self-understanding that allows them to be the parents they want to be. "By freeing ourselves from the constraints of our past, we can offer our children the spontaneous and connecting relationships that enable them to thrive."[90]

Siegel and Hartzell encourage parents to live in the present moment with children, focusing on the feelings and perceptions as they occur. They show parents how to see beyond the child's external behaviors to understand the internal ways the child thinks and feels. With a full appreciation of what parent and child are experiencing, parents can choose actions that meet children's basic needs.

Sometimes, parents' feelings interfere with effective parenting. When parents find themselves reacting to children's behavior with intense feelings they do not understand or in ways they do not approve, parents are encouraged to look for the unresolved feelings, left over from other situations, that interfere with parenting. In such situations, the authors recommend journal writing about the situation because the reflection that occurs in the process of writing often gives parents insights and understanding. Sometimes, others' comments, including the child's, provide insight.

Mary Hartzell illustrates how her feelings from childhood took the joy out of her boys' shoe shopping. The trip would start with the boys excitedly choosing the shoes they wanted. She would encourage them to select what they wanted but then would begin to criticize the choices—the cost, the color, the fit, the practicality. Finally, the boys would give up in frustration and tell her to choose the shoes. She would find it very hard to choose, but after a great deal of indecision, she would choose. She and the boys, all worn out and frustrated, left the store with shoes that nobody really wanted. This scenario was repeated many times until one of the boys asked her, "Didn't you like to get new shoes as a kid?" She immediately answered a heartfelt, "No!"[91]

She then recalled her childhood shoe-buying trips. As one of nine children, she never had a choice of the shoes she really wanted. Her mother had to save money and buy the cheapest shoes on sale. Her older sister, however, had an odd-shaped foot that was hard to fit, and her shoes were never on sale, so she always got to choose the shoes she wanted. Mary's foot was easy to fit, so there were always some shoes for her on sale, but they were never the ones she wanted. Her mother was often irritated with the shopping trip—the number of shoes to buy and the cost—and ignored Mary's protests about the choice of shoes. So Mary and her mother always left the store angry and resentful. Her son's question made her realize that she was creating the same experience for her children. Insight helped her change.

They conclude,

> We don't need to have had great parents in order to parent our own children well. Being a parent gives us the opportunity to reparent ourselves by making sense of our own early experiences. Our children are not the only ones who will benefit from this making-sense process: We ourselves will come to live a more vital and enriched life because we have integrated our past experiences into a coherent ongoing life story.[92]

Student Advisory Warning: We have just read about studies that make parents worry, so an important warning is required. No study in this book should be interpreted to mean that a student or his or her child is destined to avoid or have difficulties. All the studies presented talk about greater or lesser likelihood of particular outcomes, and interventions or environmental actions can change the probability of outcomes. Even when we talk about genetic effects on behavior, as we reviewed in an earlier section, environmental influences can affect outcomes even with regard to highly heritable traits.

Even without enormous effort, adults change according to the circumstances of adult life. For example, longitudinal researchers who followed children through adolescence into adulthood and compared late adolescent IQs with IQs obtained in middle age found that the group as a whole made modest gains. More striking, 11 percent of the sample gained more than thirteen IQ points. These tended to be people who were married to spouses whose IQs were ten points more than study members when they were adolescents.

Similarly, parents may shift their parenting styles under the influence of a partner. When a parent with an insecure attachment to his or her parents in childhood marries someone with a secure history, the insecure partner takes on the parenting style of the more secure partner and becomes warmer, calmer, and more positive.[93]

As you proceed with this book, take the information as guidelines for identifying factors that lead to the effective and satisfying parenting you wish to do.

INTERVIEW
with Sylvia Hewlett

Sylvia Ann Hewlett is chair of the National Parenting Association and, with Cornel West, coauthor of The War against Parents.

The Parents' Bill of Rights in *War Against Parents* describes laws and government changes to help parents. Are there other ways society can support parents?
Having a place for parents is important. There is no place for parents in our public life. That is so easy to change, and the symbolism of those changes is so powerful. It shows that we are supporting and celebrating parents' doing things with children. One of the ridiculous examples of how shortsighted our public places are is the newly designed children's center in Central Park. It is a beautiful place for the under-five crowd. It has all kinds of wonderful hands-on stuff—little story-time corners as well as the petting zoo.

But look at the fee structure going in; it is typical of many children's museums and children's parks around the country. If you are over two, you have to pay three dollars— not an insignificant amount—a parent pays seven dollars, but senior citizens get massive discounts. So what you see outside on any nice afternoon is a row of mothers having designated one mother to go in with the children because they cannot all afford to go in. If we are serious about encouraging parent-child recreational time, the first thing we have to do is make the fee structure reflect that. We should be encouraging single parents to take their children there. It is educational and absolutely something mothers should be doing with children. Yet when it is ten dollars a visit, they cannot do that. You stand there and look at the fees, and your jaw drops, because the group that does not need the subsidy in this context at all is the one that is privileged.

Another thing that makes me crazy in this city and is typical of other cities is that there is no place on buses for parents and young children and their strollers and other equipment. I take the bus across town to get one of my children at school. I go with my toddler, and there is no place to sit, no place to put the stroller. Now, buses have learned to recognize the needs of the elderly and the disabled. Right up front there are nice seats for them but no seats for pregnant mothers or parents with babies or young children. You get on a New York City bus, clutching your toddler, your equipment, and a stroller, and the first thing you do is feel apologetic about being there. The bus driver scowls at you, and no one wants to sit near you. It's a ridiculous situation, and it doesn't happen in other countries.

I also think there should be a parents' room in every school. At present there is no place to go, to hang out, to have coffee and read a little literature about developing reading skills or something. I think the whole thing about having a place for parents, an honored place in our public squares and in our schools and on our transportation system, is so critical. There is a tiny movement to create parking spaces in suburban malls for mothers with young children, but the efforts for programs like that are few and far between. That could spread like wildfire if a few communities did it. You need leadership. You need political leaders to take the issues seriously.

MAIN POINTS

Parenting is

- nourishing, protecting, and guiding new life
- providing resources to meet basic needs, love, attention, and values

Reasons for having children include

- love, affection, and stimulation
- creative outlet, proof of maturity, and sense of achievement
- proof of virtue and economic advantage

Joys of parenting

- arise from everyday experiences
- are generally what parents hope for
- far outweigh the effort and frustrations involved

The process of parenting involves

- ongoing interaction among children, parents, and society
- children who have their own needs and temperaments and at the same time meet important needs of parents
- parents who have responsibilities to rear their children and meet their children's needs while also maintaining marriages, work, and social relationships
- a society that defines roles, enforces basic requirements of parents, and serves as a powerful source of support or stress for children and parents

Changes in family life

- involve a shift from the nineteenth-century extended farm family to the nuclear family, which was the primary form for much of the twentieth century
- involve a shift from the primary form of the nuclear family to diverse families in the 1970s and, more recently, a shift to multigenerational families
- are in response to economic and social changes in society
- do not weaken bonds of solidarity between the generations

Parents are

- the single most important influence and resource in a child's life
- not the only influences on children's behaviors, for media, communities, and social events outside the family also influence children's behavior and development
- stimulators and providers of nourishing environments that enable children to achieve their maximal potential, even when genetic factors make special efforts necessary
- advocates who can make social changes to help children
- so influential that some suggest parents should be required to have a license to become parents
- difficult for state institutions to replace

Raising children changes parents, who

- become more perceptive, efficient, resilient, and socially skilled
- are motivated to correct bad habits
- feel new sense of awe and wonder in the world
- acquire greater understanding of themselves and others

When parents have difficult experiences early in life, they

- are not doomed to repeat them with their children
- can gain self-understanding and reparent themselves

EXERCISES

1. Interview your parent or parents, separately or together, about the joys they anticipated having with you before your birth. Did they experience them or others in addition to them? Were they surprised at any of the joys? If possible, interview a grandparent or grandparents about the joys they anticipated with your parents, and ask them the same questions. Were the joys the same for the two generations of parents? Were there differences, and if so, what were they?

2. From the year of your birth, trace the social influences acting on your parents as they raised you. For example, for the 1980s such influences might have included the increased rate of women's participation in the workforce, the high rate of divorce and remarriage, the drop in jobs for skilled labor. Look for the effects of social change on your daily life and the ways your parents cared for you. For example, if your mother worked, describe the day-care arrangements. If your parents divorced or remarried, describe how child care was affected.

3. Suppose that a person had to obtain a license in order to have a child, as David Lykken suggests. What would you require for such a license?

4. How do you think an adult's life would be different if he or she never had a child? How would remaining childless affect someone's psychological growth? Where would they seek the joys that children so readily supply to many adults?

5. Read the newspaper for one week, and cut out all the articles of interest to parents, including news and feature articles. The articles might cover a broad range of topics—solving children's behavioral problems, laws relating to parents' employment benefits or to the rights of parents in the workplace, laws regarding who is recognized as a parent at times of divorce or death. Describe what these articles tell you about the parenting experience at the beginning of the twenty-first century.

ADDITIONAL READINGS

Ellison, Katherine. *The Mommy Brain: How Motherhood Makes Us Smarter*. New York: Basic Books, 2005.

Kohl, Susan A. *The Best Things Parents Do*. Boston: Conari Press, 2004.

Marx, Jeffrey. *Season of Life*. New York: Simon & Schuster, 2003.

Siegel, Daniel J., and Hartzell, Mary. *Parenting from the Inside Out: How a Deeper Self-Understanding Can Help You Raise Children Who Thrive*. New York: Penguin, 2003.

Warner, Judith. *Perfect Madness: Motherhood in the Age of Anxiety*. New York: Penguin, 2005.

CHAPTER

2

Seeking Guidance

CHAPTER TOPICS	IN THE NEWS

In this chapter, you will learn about:

- The history of parent-child relationships

- Theories that emphasize the role of the environment in growth

- Theories that emphasize the role of internal stages and patterns of growth

- Theories that emphasize both environmental and internal causes of growth

- Parenting experts

- Research that supports parenting experts

New York Times, November 27: "Kids Gone Wild" describes advice to parents from different parenting experts. For experts' guidance to parents, see pages 68–73.[1]

Test Your Knowledge: Fact or Fiction?

1. Plato and Aristotle described the stages of childhood much as we do today.

2. It was not until the seventeenth century that parents' important role in forming children's habits and character was emphasized.

3. Theories of children's growth and development contradict each other and so are hard to use to deal with children's day-to-day behavior.

4. Parenting experts generally formulate advice for parents from their own practical experience as doctors and teachers and do not rely on psychological theories or research to support their advice.

5. Researchers and experts rely on parents' reports of what they do and do not go into the home to see what really happens there.

Providing loving care, attention, and opportunities for children to develop competence and self-esteem are challenging responsibilities. Where do parents turn for guidance? In this chapter, we explore four sources of guidance for parents: (1) what history tells us about parents' roles, (2) what current theories of children's growth and development tell us, (3) what parenting experts suggest, and (4) what research on parent-child relationships suggests is important.

We have seen the powerful role parents play in children's lives. How do parents learn what to do to carry out this role? A century and a half ago, when families were larger and relatives lived nearby, parents learned their roles from their experiences with their own parents and from their experiences helping to rear younger brothers and sisters or younger nieces and nephews.

Today, parents turn to other sources because, often, they do not live near relatives, have not grown up in large families, or have not learned from helping to rear younger relatives. They turn to what parents have done in the past, what theories about children's growth tell them is important to do, and what experts tell them they should do. We review here how all these sources can help parents go about the important job of rearing the next generation.

A BRIEF HISTORY OF PARENTS' ROLES

Understanding how parents reared children in the past has been difficult. Early writers focused on the politics, economics, diplomacy, and military history of their societies, and they did not include descriptions of the day-to-day life of families. Thus, family historians have had to draw conclusions from secondary sources of information, such as philosophical, religious, and medical writings, paintings, literature of the times, legal documents, and artifacts found in archaeological excavations.[2]

In the 1960s and 1970s, when historians first looked at the history of parent-child relationships, they focused narrowly on Western Europe and North America. Their initial impression was that, before the seventeenth century, there was little conception of childhood as a distinct stage, and when children were viewed as different from adults, they were seen mainly as innocents in need of strict training and discipline. Thus, historians had a dim view of parents' efforts through much of history, considering them indifferent or punishing. One historian stated that, the further back one went in history, the lower the level of regard and care for children, such that parenting in antiquity was described as the "Infanticidal Mode," with children abandoned, killed or brutalized, and the Middle Ages as the "Abandoning Mode."[3]

Later historians looked at many other civilizations and broadened our understanding of early parent-child relationships. A more detailed examination of parenting in early classical civilizations led to the conclusion that, although there were instances of infanticide and cruelty, in most instances classical parenting was much like our own.

According to one historian, in early Egypt "The pervasive social expectation was that parents would have large families, enjoy their children, and rear them with love and care. Egyptians also recognized stages of child development and had separate hieroglyphs designating infants, toddlers, youths, and adolescents."[4] Children were important parts of the family and were pictured with parents in state ceremonies. Both parents were warm and affectionate with children.

Early Egyptian infants received attentive care. They were carried in slings and nursed for about three years. Although mothers and older female relatives were the primary caregivers for young children, fathers spent leisure time with families, and happy family times were pictured with parents and children eating and playing together. Archaeological remains included such toys as dolls, balls, puppets, and board games, and paintings showed young children in many physical activities, such as swimming, wrestling, and roughhousing with each other.

At ages six and seven, children began preparation for their adult lives; girls learned household skills from mothers, and boys learned work skills from their fathers. Privileged boys and some girls attended school until age fourteen and learned to read, write, and do mathematical calculations.

In ancient Mesopotamia, wars and seasonal floods made life difficult.[5] Although having children was encouraged, children and family life were rarely depicted in paintings. Laws regarding parents and children reflected concerns about abuse and about disregard of children. Parents appeared more distant from their children, viewing parenting as difficult and demanding. Thus far, no scholars have been knowledgeable in the early languages of this area; greater linguistic understanding might change our view of parenting in early Mesopotamia.

The Israelites lived in multigenerational families that were self-sustaining units in an agrarian economy that encouraged having children. Like the Egyptians, families were warm and close, with both parents intimately involved in parenting. Children were nursed until they were about three, but mothers also had to integrate child care with work in the agrarian economy. Fathers were active in teaching older children. In contrast to other early civilizations, ordinary Israelites learned to read, write, and do mathematical calculations. As there did not appear to be schools, historians have assumed that parents passed these skills on to children at home.

As in Mesopotamia, life was hard, with wars and many losses. There were few toys, and few references to play have survived. Israelites seemed to have combined the positive parenting behaviors of the optimistic Egyptians with the stern outlook on life of the Mesopotamians.

The early Greeks and, following them, the Romans, took parenting very seriously because they wanted to develop good citizens.[6] The Greeks had a very definite view of children and childhood. Children were wanted—boys to continue the family line and girls to care for aging parents. Although children were thought to inherit physical and psychological characteristics from mothers and fathers, they were considered essentially unformed at birth and responsive to the influence of parents and other adults. Because children were born helpless and unable to express or meet their own needs, they were seen as fearful and in need of protection.

Plato and Aristotle, both Athenians, were the first to formulate organized ideas about the importance of parenting and effective ways to rear children. They believed, first, that children had specific needs that parents and other adults should meet. Second, because children were unformed at birth, the Greeks considered that parents had opportunities to shape children's behaviors into behaviors society needed and approved. Third, parents gave children freedom within the boundaries of safety. Finally, the Greeks believed that children required both parents' efforts as well as the support of the community.

Plato and Aristotle recognized stages of childhood similar to our infancy, early childhood (from ages two or three to five or six), childhood (ages five or six to puberty) and adolescence (puberty to young adulthood), but they also recognized individual differences in how children proceed through the stages. Both placed great importance on early childhood experiences. People were thought to learn long-lasting conceptions of good and evil, as well as the enjoyment of people, from the ways they were treated as babies. Parents were urged to provide gentle, nurturing experiences for them.

Girls became mothers in the teen years, so older female relatives often assisted in caregiving. Babies were nursed for two years by mothers or wet nurses. They were carried and rocked, and caregivers were encouraged to attend to their cries and figure out what babies needed. Caregivers protected babies from negative emotions such as pain, grief, and fear.

Early childhood was a period of games and play with age-mates. Children were supervised to ensure safety, but they were given freedom to play as they wished. Plato saw games as preparation for citizenship and for accepting authority from outside oneself. He lamented that adults did not recognize the long-term benefits of games when these activities were carefully supervised. Aristotle, too, saw games as preparation for adult activities. In childhood and adolescence, boys and girls grew in physical abilities and learned the skills needed for adult life. As in other cultures, fathers took a more active role with boys.

Roman families followed Greek views, with both parents involved in parenting and educating children, but fathers had more legal controls over children than in Greek culture.[7] They could sell children into slavery and could have adult children put to death. Before doing so, fathers had to seek approval from other family members, including mothers, and mothers were expected to soften fathers' harshness. Even though fathers had absolute control of children, Roman parents were more concerned about affection between parents and children than were the Greeks. They saw children as happy, affectionate, and outgoing, and wanted to have reciprocal relationships with them. The roles of mothers and fathers were more alike in Roman families than in Greek families. Mothers not only cared for infants and children but, like fathers, they were responsible for the education of older children. Both parents maintained strong bonds with their adolescent and adult children; and many Roman fathers had close relationships with their daughters as well as with their sons.

Like the Greeks, the Romans paid attention to teaching children because they considered children impressionable and quick to learn. They emphasized children's competitiveness, their memory skills, and their curiosity. But they saw children as noncompliant and so focused on discipline, which included more physical discipline than the Greeks used.

A noteworthy feature of Roman life in the upper classes was the frequency and number of divorces, many of which were friendly and preserved the alliances between the original families even after remarriage. The Roman family was then a somewhat flexible, shifting group of adults, all of whom looked after children.

In early civilizations, then, children were important members of the family. All the societies recognized that children went through stages of growth, and parents tried to tailor their behaviors to meet children's needs appropriately. Although infanticide and cruelty to children existed, exactly how much is not known, save that they were not the norm for these societies.

All these early societies protected children's health as best they could, and they were aware that children faced special dangers and required special treatments. The Israelites were very concerned about preventive care, urging parents to keep children out of the sun and to encourage healthy diets and careful chewing of food.

Parents were concerned about parasites, infections, and illnesses such as polio. The Romans were the most sophisticated physicians, producing discussions of obstetrics, care of the newborn, and medical problems according to the age of the child. These early societies had few treatments available for ailments. They relied on charms, prayers, diuretics, laxatives, and herbal remedies.

Historian Linda Pollock looked at parenting closer to our time. She studied actual parenting practices as revealed in almost five hundred diaries of parents and children, autobiographies, and newspaper accounts of court cases involving children, all taken from the years 1500 to 1900.[8] Based on more extensive evidence, she challenged and revised the earlier views of parent-child relationships of that period. "Nearly all children were wanted, such developmental stages as weaning and teething aroused interest and concern, and parents revealed anxiety and distress at the illness or death of a child. Parents, although they may have found their offspring troublesome at times, did seem to enjoy the company of their children. . . . It is also clear that the majority of children were not subjected to brutality. Physical punishment was used by a number of parents, usually infrequently and when all else had failed."[9] Restrained discipline was a consistent theme in diaries and newspaper accounts, so Pollock concluded that most parents did not batter children.

Relationships between parents and children were close. The writings Pollock studied offered many examples of parents who worried about children's health and education and were ready to help them as needed. Children also felt able to come to parents with their difficulties. Adolescence brought conflicts between the generations, but parents expected children to have independent thoughts and supported them and maintained contacts even when there were differences.

Parents in the seventeenth and eighteenth centuries were increasingly concerned with abstract questions about parenting—that is, the responsibilities of being a parent, the best methods of discipline, worrying whether they were competent enough to be parents. For centuries, then, parents have expressed anxiety about their competence as parents. As one nineteenth-century father wrote in his diary, "Often do I pray for more ability to guide and influence the dear dispositions of our dear children."[10] Despite writings advocating harshness and ridding children of evil influences, parents practiced more moderate discipline.

Although variations among parents existed at any given time and over time, Pollock describes a general continuity in parenting practices and concerns over the last five hundred years—given minor changes due to technological advances such as refrigeration, which affected feeding. She believes the limited variation in parenting practices is due to two fundamental features of child rearing: (1) parents' goal to protect and rear children to maturity, and (2) children's state of extended dependency.

"Children . . . make demands on their parents and parents are forced to operate within the context of these demands. The parents in every century studied accommodated to the needs of their offspring."[11]

Historical views of parent-child relationships tell us then that, from the dawn of civilization, parents have faced similar challenges in rearing children and, by and large, have responded with similar levels of care and concern to help their children grow, with similar worries about their own competence in carrying out the task. Contemporary parents share their level of concern, their fears and worries about their own competence, their challenges in helping children through stages of growth, with centuries of parents who have gone before them. Perhaps the survival and success of previous generations of parents and their children can give the present generation confidence that they, too, can do the job.

THEORIES OF GROWTH AND DEVELOPMENT

Theories describe children's growth and development and the factors thought to stimulate healthy growth. Although theories do not provide step-by-step directions for parents, they do help parents understand children's needs and the many ways parents meet them and contribute to children's growth. In most instances, theories are complementary, each contributing important information on different facets of children's growth.

In this section, we describe major theories of development and state in a paragraph how each is useful to parents. An adjoining box shows how each theory might view and respond to a common problem confronted by parents—namely, a child's difficulty in adjusting to the academic and social demands of the first grade. The child may be a boy who is overly active, won't stay in his seat, and doesn't do his work, or it may be a girl who is overly sociable, talks to others, gets out of her seat to help others, but does not do her own work. Such children have done well in preschool and are healthy and intellectually capable, but they are not completing their work, not following class rules, and not making expected academic progress.

Theories are grouped according to what each considers the primary source of growth: the environment, the internal qualities of the child, or both. For example, learning theories and Vygotsky's theory emphasize the role of the environment in stimulating growth, whereas Freud's theory and the work of Arnold Gesell emphasize the role of unfolding internal stages of development. Several theories, such as Bronfenbrenner's bioecological theory and Erikson's lifespan theory, emphasize the importance of both factors. The role of parents differs according to whether the primary source of growth is the environment or the child's own inner patterns.

THEORIES EMPHASIZING EXTERNAL STIMULATION FOR GROWTH

We look first at theories emphasizing the role of external stimulation in promoting growth.

Learning Theories

Learning theorists identify the specific forms of environmental stimulation that promote children's growth and give a very important and active role to parents, as it is parents who provide the child's environment. The child's role may vary from that of a blank slate who learns all behavior from external rewards and punishments to that of a more active learner who interprets the surrounding environment and selects goals and models to imitate. Despite this variation, the major force for development is seen as coming from outside forces that teach and produce behavior change.

Learning theories trace their origins to the work of Ivan Pavlov in the late nineteenth and early twentieth centuries.[12] His classical conditioning studies showed that animals could learn new behaviors when new signals were repeatedly linked to already-existing responses. For example, when Pavlov linked a neutral stimulus like a buzzer with the dog's salivation at the sight of food, the animal eventually salivated at the sound of the buzzer alone.

We see the process of classical conditioning in everyday life when people who experience a strong emotional feeling attach that feeling to other stimuli present at the time. Later, these stimuli alone may trigger that emotional response. For example, a child frightened by a dog that chased him may become frightened the next time he sees a dog running near him. A running dog alone triggers the fear the child felt when a dog actually chased him.

Whereas Pavlov concentrated on the association of stimuli that preceded the behavior of interest, American learning theorists focused on what happened *after* the behavior of interest. They looked at how behavior changed as a result of the positive or negative consequences of the behavior. They noted that behaviors increased when positive consequences followed consistently and decreased with consistent negative consequences. They identified kinds of rewards—material ones such as food or a toy, extra privileges such as staying up late, and social rewards such as attention or physical affection. They found that personal attention was a most important reward for children and adults alike. If children do not get attention for positive behaviors, they will seek attention through irritating behaviors such as whining and arguing.

Social learning theorists found that children learn even when there is no reward at all. They observe people around them and imitate them. For example, babies will not play with a toy if the mother has looked at it with disgust. Observation of behavior alone is enough to stimulate imitation. Children are most likely to imitate models who are warm, nurturing, and powerful. In extreme circumstances, when there is no model of warmth to copy, children will imitate a hostile, cold model.

Social learning theorists such as Albert Bandura focus on the active nature of the learner who chooses goals to pursue and reflects on performance. In our understanding of the process of learning, the learner's thoughts and interpretations of the environment are as important as environmental rewards and punishments.[13] Box 2-1 describes these theorists' views of the school problem.

Box 2-1
LEARNING THEORIES' VIEWS OF SCHOOL DIFFICULTIES

Learning theorists would focus first on the classroom and on the system of rewards and punishments that the child receives there. They may note that the teacher has established a pattern of paying attention to individual children only when they are not following the rules, such that a child is encouraged to break the rules because negative attention is better than no attention. The behavior in many classrooms has improved when teachers decided to comment only on children's approved responses and to give no attention, or a quick negative consequence, for disapproved behavior.

The teachers can arrange classroom and daily routine so that the child has fewer opportunities to engage in disapproved behavior. Regular in-class exercise breaks such as opportunities to sharpen pencils, get paper, and get water help children settle down. A child can be seated next to students who are less likely to answer when the child talks and more able to stay on task, to serve as a model for the child.

If changes in the classroom are not sufficient, the teachers can set up a daily ticket to take home, so that the child shows parents that he or she has completed the school work and has shown approved behavior and therefore has earned all his or her privileges for the afternoon and evening. Privileges might include television, GameBoys, or, if the child is older, talking to friends on the phone. Without the ticket indicating that work and behavior were approved, there are no privileges.

Parents then would be expected to look at study and work patterns at home and to set up structured routines, with positive consequences to increase approved behaviors and negative consequences for disapproved behaviors. Rewards of positive attention and privileges are more effective than material objects. Parents also serve as models for learning, with regular reading times and organized work patterns at home. They help children see the value of doing well in school and setting realistic goals with positive rewards.

Counseling for parents might be advised so that parents could use the most effective strategies to deal with the situation—avoiding yelling, nagging, or criticizing the child who will seek negative attention if that is the only kind available. A positive reward system that teaches the child approved behaviors is more effective. "Catch a child being good, and reward those behaviors," is the adage of many learning theorists.

Cognitive learning theorists, who believe that a person's interpretation of a situation will shape his or her response, would focus attention on the individual's assessment of his or her learning ability, as the self-perception may determine the behavioral response to the rewards. A child who does not think that he or she is capable may think a reward is an unearned one, and therefore efforts to change self-perceptions may lead to greater behavior change. We discuss this in greater detail in Chapter 5.

What Learning Theories Help Parents Understand   Learning theories help parents understand (1) their important role in modeling appropriate behaviors for children and structuring the consequences that teach children new behaviors; (2) that children watch and copy parents whether parents are carrying out approved or disapproved behaviors; (3) that children want parental attention and will seek it by negative means if they do not get it for positive behaviors; and (4) the conditions under which children learn best.

Lev Vygotsky's Theory

Lev Vygotsky, a Russian psychologist born in the late nineteenth century, gives parents a central role in supporting children's growth, but one that differs from the role accorded by learning theorists.[14] He believes that knowledge, thought, and mental processes such as memory all rest on social interactions with knowledgeable partners. Every culture has a view of the world and of the way to solve problems. Language, art, writing, and methods of problem solving all reflect this social worldview, which children learn from parents and daily experiences.

Whatever children learn, Vygotsky believes, they first experience at the social level in a social interaction with someone, often a parent, and then internalize the social interaction at the individual and psychological level. For example, a preschooler hears parents' speech to her: "Carrying the package was a help to me. Thank you for being such a good helper." Later, the child says the same phrase when she picks up her toys: "Good helper." Social interaction not only conveys societal knowledge of the world but also stimulates children to learn that knowledge.

Vygotsky describes a unique concept, *the zone of proximal development*. There is a range of actions a child can perform alone, demonstrating a capacity that is clearly internal. This is what we consider the child's level of ability. But Vygotsky points out that, when a more experienced person guides or prompts the child with questions, hints, or demonstrations, the child can respond at a more mature level not achieved when the child acts alone. So, a child has potential that emerges in social interaction guided by an experienced partner. For example, a child learning to talk may use a particular number of words spontaneously. That would be the child's verbal ability. A mother, however, might increase the number of words or the length of the sentence by prompting the child to use more words, saying, "The doggie?" and waiting for "runs" or "goes bow-wow." Adults' teaching has the greatest impact, Vygotsky believes, when it is directed to the child's learning potential at the high end of the zone of proximal development.

Language plays an important role in mental development, he believes. Language develops in social interaction and is a means of influencing others. Adults talk to children, influencing their reactions or behavior. Children initially guide their own behavior with external language similar to the words they hear; they then talk aloud to themselves as others have talked to them, and guide their own behavior with their speech. A toddler will say, "No, no," to herself as a way of stopping forbidden action, and gradually the speech becomes internal or inner speech. Such inner speech becomes thought in the older child. So language is the forerunner of thinking.

Box 2-2
LEV VYGOTSKY LOOKS AT SCHOOL DIFFICULTIES

Lev Vygotsky would see the teacher's role as critical in helping children settle down and acquire appropriate intellectual skills. He would encourage the teacher to be a warm, supportive figure who teaches the culture of the classroom and the behavior that is expected. The teacher helps the child progress through his or her personal zone of proximal development so that the child learns to do alone what, at first, he or she requires help to accomplish. This would require that the teacher or an aide spend extra time with the child in the beginning to help him or her master the skills, but then the child would be able to do the task alone.

Teachers would also encourage children to use language to guide their behavior, initially saying aloud as a whole class, or whispering to themselves, the steps they will take to accomplish the task. Words will become internalized as thoughts. To help this process, children can write themselves reminders of the definite steps they take. Teachers would also encourage parents to take these same steps.

What Vygotsky's Theory Helps Parents Understand   Vygotsky's theory helps parents understand (1) their important role in conveying their culture's view of the world and how to live in it; (2) their role as experienced partners in guiding children to more advanced behaviors; and (3) the very important role of language both in reflecting the culture's values and in advancing children's ability to think and reason. Box 2-2 describes how Vygotsky would look at the school problem.

STAGE THEORIES OF GROWTH

Let us turn now to theories that focus on the internal qualities of the person as the source of growth. These theories do not deny that the environment plays a role in growth, but inborn qualities, such as instinctual impulses, patterns of growth, or ways of thinking about the world, are considered the prime sources of growth.

Sigmund Freud and Psychoanalysis

Sigmund Freud, the founder of psychoanalysis, revolutionized the way we think about children's experiences in early childhood.[15] He treated individuals with emotional problems. In talking to patients, he noticed he could trace many adult symptoms to anxieties about experiences that had occurred in early childhood. Concluding that what happened in early childhood had lifelong effects on adults' personalities, he set about describing the significant dimensions of childhood. He focused on children's impulses, particularly sexual impulses and their sources of gratification. Children were viewed as pleasure-seeking creatures who had to tame their impulses to conform to parents' and society's demands.

Freud divided childhood into five psychosexual stages, which unfolded over time from birth to adolescence. The ways children attempt to gratify each stage's impulses, and others' reactions to their attempts, shape adult personality. Each stage is named after the area of the body that is the primary source of stimulation and gratification at that time. The stages are (1) the oral stage, associated with pleasures of nursing and taking in food; (2) the anal stage, during toilet training, associated with pleasures of tightening and releasing the anal musculature; (3) the phallic stage, during the pre-school years, when genital stimulation predominates over oral and anal gratifica-tions; (4) latency, in the early elementary school years, when sexual feelings were thought to be dormant; and (5) the genital stage, in adolescence, when sexual devel-opment and sexual feelings were thought to mature fully.

Freud believed that the outcome of the oedipal conflict, which he posited as occur-ring in the preschool years, was a major determiner of personality development. Just as children begin to feel competent and effective, he thought, they experience a failure that can permanently damage their self-regard. In these years, the child desires to be romantically involved with the parent of the opposite sex, to marry the parent, and to have a new family.

While this love flourishes, said Freud, preschoolers feel very competitive with the same-sex parent. They want to surpass and outperform the adult, and they talk a lot about how grown up and powerful they are. They are angry at the same-sex parent for standing in the way and wish that parent would leave or die. They feel guilty and anx-ious about their anger and seek reassurances that the same-sex parent has not been a victim of their aggressiveness. Eventually, the child deals with the anxiety by giving up the opposite-sex parent as love object and identifying with the same-sex parent as a model. As the child takes on the behaviors of the same-sex adult, the moral con-science and the commands of society become internalized in the form of what Freud calls the *superego,* which shapes the individual's response to authority and society.

Although Freud did not give direct advice to parents, he emphasized the impor-tance of appropriate gratification of children's natural impulses—feeding the child on demand, holding permissive attitudes about thumb sucking and toilet training, pro-viding acceptable outlets for aggressive impulses—without criticism or punishment.

What Freud's Theory Helps Parents Understand   Freud's theory helps parents understand (1) that children have internal needs that drive behavior, and neither they nor parents have complete control, and (2) that parents have a powerful role in understanding children's inner needs and helping them find acceptable ways to gratify their impulses. Parents are authoritative guides and supporters on the path to maturity, not generals commanding the course of growth. Box 2-3 illustrates Freud's approach to the school problem.

Piaget's Theory

Whereas Freud changed our views of children's emotional and personality develop-ment, Jean Piaget profoundly changed our views of children's intellectual growth by showing that children think about the world differently from adults.[16] Although dif-ferent, their thinking is understandable as it proceeds through a series of predictable stages. Piaget emphasized the child's active construction of knowledge. Learning about

---

Box 2-3
SIGMUND FREUD'S VIEW OF SCHOOL DIFFICULTIES

Sigmund Freud and his early followers would view a healthy child's inability to concentrate and follow school rules as a sign of anxiety due to an unresolved internal conflict. As this behavior appeared in the first grade, they would suspect that an underlying oedipal conflict may be delaying the development of age-appropriate behavior.

Children at five or six years of age are expected to have given up their preschool fantasies about romantic involvement with the parent of the opposite sex and to have formed an identification with the parent of the same sex. Internalizing socially approved behaviors and values occurs as the child identifies with the parent of the same sex and takes on the age-appropriate behaviors of this parent. A boy who identifies with his father may join him in running for exercise or reading bedtime stories to a younger sister. A girl who identifies with her mother may become very organized and eager to accomplish tasks and projects.

Since children are most likely to form positive identifications with same-sex parents and to internalize their values when parents are warm and trusted figures who do not arouse anxiety, a Freudian would assume that the problems lay in the relationship with the parents. When parents appear too threatening or too critical, or when they encourage children's immature romantic fantasies for the parents' own gratification, children fail to resolve these early fantasies by identifying with the appropriate parent and internalizing societal rules and standards. A Freudian also might think that the child is redirecting his or her feelings about a parent on to the teacher, treating the teacher as a substitute figure for the parent.

For a Freudian, the main way of dealing with the problem would be to recommend an informal discussion between teacher and parent about ways to increase the child's maturity at school. If that was not effective, some form of therapeutic counseling for the child would be sought to help him or her resolve the feelings.

---

the world is not a passive process of taking in what one sees and hears. Intellectual competence is a dynamic process in which the child explores the world, takes in information, and organizes it into internal structures called schemas. This process of taking in and organizing information is termed *assimilation*.

As children obtain new information, they find their internal schemas inadequate and modify them to account for the new information. The process of changing internal schemas to incorporate new information is called *accommodation*.

Intellectual growth is a constant interplay of taking in new information (assimilation) and modifying internal structures (accommodation) to achieve a balance or equilibrium between the individual's structure of the world and the world itself. *Equilibration* is the active process by which the individual achieves this effective balance.

An example of this process is seen in the child's growing understanding of what a dog is. Initially, a child may hear someone call a four-footed, hairy animal that barks "a dog." All four-footed, hairy animals may initially be called dogs, whether they are large or small and whether they bark, meow, roar, or whinny. The child's schema for animals will become more refined as he or she learns that some huge, hairy animals are called lions and horses, and other smaller, hairy animals, dogs and cats. Eventually, the child will have schemas of many different animals, and even within a schema of dog, there will be many kinds identified.

So it is with a young child's concept of persons. Initially, all adults are Mama and Dada. Eventually, the child will have an understanding of a world of adults with many different names—grandma, grandpa, auntie, uncle, teacher, coach, principal. Some are family members who will give you special consideration, and some are not.

Piaget described growth in terms of four major periods in which the child takes in and processes information in distinctive ways. In the first eighteen to twenty-four months of life, known as *the sensorimotor period,* the child's own body, perceptions, and actions are the focus of interest, and the schemas consist of action patterns. Initially, the child mainly repeats physical behaviors like kicking legs or opening and closing hands, but gradually, actions become more complex, and months later the child acts to achieve a purpose—reaches to grasp a toy or a piece of food. Toward the end of the first year, babies come to understand the permanence of objects—that is, that objects have an independent existence, even if the child cannot see them. The concept of permanence leads to exploration of these objects, how they work, and where they might be when they are out of sight.

Beginning at about eighteen to twenty-four months, children begin to move from immediate experience of objects, people, and whatever is present at the moment to representations or thoughts of what is not immediately present, and at about age two, children enter *the preoperational period,* which lasts until about age seven. They can represent what they see or hear with language that increases in the number of words and in the complexity of sentences to express thoughts. Symbolizing activity such as dreams and nightmares becomes more complex, as does imaginative play.

Although children are curious and ask many questions, Piaget believes that their concepts are limited because they pay attention only to a small number of characteristics of objects, usually sensory features. For example, they may think that a tall, thin glass holds more than a short, fat glass because they pay attention only to the height of the glass.

In the elementary school years, intellectual growth takes two leaps. At age seven, the child enters *the period of concrete operations.* The term *concrete operations* means that children can think more logically and are not so bound by the appearance of objects. They grasp relationships among objects and easily arrange a series of sticks by lengths with little trial and error. Children can think more logically and form classes (of objects, for example) because they have a keen interest in understanding how things work.

Between ages twelve and fourteen, children enter *the period of formal operations* and begin to think like adults. Not only can they think logically about tangible objects, they can think more abstractly about possible or hypothetical situations, about what might happen in the future. They can think about their own thoughts and about the thoughts and reactions of others. They become more concerned about abstract concepts such as justice and equality and engage in volunteer activities.

An example of the different ways of thinking in these stages is children's responses to the question "What do you think with?" Children of five or six say they think with their mouth or their ears because they speak thoughts with their mouths or hear others' thoughts with their ears. Children of eight or nine will say they think with their heads, but they describe thoughts as material things like little voices in their heads. Children of twelve will say they think with their heads and describe thoughts as immaterial, just present in their heads.[17]

What Piaget's Theory Helps Parents Understand   Piaget's theory helps parents understand (1) that they must take children's view of the world into account in their interactions with children; for example, parents will not expect the infant to understand in the middle of the night that the parent still exists even if the infant cannot see him or her, and parents will not expect their toddler to understand the abstract concept of danger—that if I run in the street, I will be hurt, or if I pull the pot off the stove, I will be hurt; and (2) that children need opportunities to explore and to think their own thoughts about the world in order to grow. Box 2-4 describes Piaget's approach to a school problem.

Arnold Gesell's Patterns of Growth

Arnold Gesell, a psychologist and pediatrician, carefully observed children's growth in all areas of behavior: physical, motor, perceptual, language, emotional, social, and adaptive.[18]

Gesell believed that growth in all areas involved the unfolding of inborn biological patterns but that individual differences in development were important as well. The inborn, hereditary core was especially important in the development of motor, language, and intellectual skills. In the area of social development, however, he believed that interactions with parents stimulated development. "For better or for worse, children and their elders must grow up with each other, which means in interrelation one to the other. The roots of the growth of the infant's personality reach into other human beings."[19]

Gesell wrote in his Foreword to *Child Behavior,*

> To understand a child, we try to understand his ways of growth, for growth is the prime essence of life, and above all child life. The child grows as a unit in mind, body, and personality. He is born into a culture, subject to the powerful influences of home, school, and community. But he is also subject to deep-seated growth forces which shape his individuality.[20]

The parent's role was to observe the child's growth, to understand the child's individual needs, and to provide appropriate experiences so that the process of growth could occur as naturally as possible. Gesell was optimistic that, even if parents erred, children would flourish, stating, "The inborn tendency to optimum development is so inveterate that he (the infant or child) benefits liberally from what is good in our practice, and suffers less than he logically should from our unenlightenment."[21]

Gesell drew "portraits" of children's behavior at monthly intervals in infancy and later at six-month intervals. He described periods of equilibrium and periods of

---

Box 2-4
JEAN PIAGET LOOKS AT SCHOOL DIFFICULTIES

Jean Piaget might look at the child's history of learning about the world and the organization of the classroom as sources of the child's problems.

In the first grade, children are in the process of moving from the preoperational period, with its limited focus on sensory aspects of objects, to the period of concrete operations, in which thinking is not confined to sensory aspects and reasoning is more logical. He might wonder whether the child has had sufficient active exploration to make this transition. Has the child been a passive television viewer or electronic game player, such that skills in assimilation, accommodation, and equilibration are not as developed as they need to be to master school material? He would ask, perhaps, whether children have developed adequate language skills to understand the concepts presented in class and to negotiate social relationships at recess and lunch.

Like a systems theorist, Piaget would have questions about the ways material is presented in the class. Does the learning material in the classroom encourage active exploration and hands-on learning so the child can more easily master the material? Is the teacher giving the child practice in looking at more than the sensory aspects of objects? Is he or she demonstrating concepts so the child can grasp them more easily? Can material first be presented in a way that someone in an early preoperational period can easily grasp—for example, allowing children to measure out equal amounts of water in tall, thin glasses and short, fat glasses to show that they are equal even when perception suggests that the tall, thin glass has more—and only then moving on to more complex reasoning tasks? For Piaget, children's growth from one period to another would be supported and respected without criticism.

---

rapid changes in abilities that could create stress for children and parents. Knowing the stages children go through helps parents to be patient, for they know difficult behaviors will not last forever, and also to avoid discouragement, for they know children will mature. The portraits inform and appeal to parents today. Gesell also described a process of developmental diagnosis to identify children in need of special attention.

What Gesell's Theory Helps Parents Understand   Gesell's theory helps parents understand (1) that growth occurs in many areas of behavior at the same time and that children can experience normal stress as skills unfold and become refined and organized, and (2) that parents have allies in the growth process itself, which tends toward optimal development, but that parents provide an environment so growth can proceed. Box 2-5 gives Gesell's approach to a school problem.

All theories emphasizing internal sources of growth remind parents that the growth process itself places demands on children—to balance pleasure-seeking impulses with social demands and to adjust to and integrate new behaviors and new ways of seeing the world. Thus, children respond not just to what parents or others teach and demand but to drives and changes making demands from within. These theories give children and parents active roles in growth. Children must find ways

---

🌳 **Box 2-5**
ARNOLD GESELL'S APPROACH TO SCHOOL DIFFICULTIES

To understand Gesell's view of a first-grader's problem, we have the words of two close collaborators who dealt with exactly that problem in their book, *Child Behavior.** Frances Ilg and Louise Bates Ames presented a variety of suggestions for understanding and dealing with the problem. First, they suggested that the mother meet with the teacher and a school psychologist to determine whether the child, though bright, was emotionally ready to meet the greater demands of first grade. If all agreed he was not, Ilg and Ames suggested he return to kindergarten. They felt that the average boy did better in first grade if he was closer to seven years of age.

If the child was intellectually and emotionally ready for first grade, then they wondered whether the child was physically sturdy enough for the longer day. Again, consultation with the teacher and school personnel could provide answers. If not ready for the longer day, then Ilg and Ames suggested that the child be allowed to reduce the number of hours in school each day until the child is able to adjust to the longer day. If school personnel were reluctant, they thought a letter from the pediatrician recommending such a modification would bring about the desired result.

If the child was ready in all respects for first grade, then parents could look to see if some one difficulty in the course of the day—a bully on the way to school, a fear of finding the bathroom at school, or anxiety about eating and the lunchtime routine—upset the child and disrupted his behavior at school. To find out about troubling events, parents could ask the child carefully about the day.

If all that failed, they suggested consulting a child specialist for expert help.

*Frances L. Ilg and Louise Bates Ames, *Child Behavior* (New York: Macmillan, 1928).

---

to gratify impulses and integrate new ways of behavior, and parents serve as knowledgeable and authoritative guides who support children's efforts to achieve balance, equilibrium, and integration.

THEORIES THAT EMPHASIZE BOTH EXTERNAL AND INTERNAL SOURCES OF GROWTH

We now turn to theories that emphasize the importance of both internal and external sources of growth. We look first at two psychoanalytic theories.

Erikson's Lifespan Theory of Development

Erik Erikson, a Freudian psychoanalyst with a strong belief in the importance of cultural and social influences on growth, devised a scheme for understanding lifespan development that focuses attention on the positive and healthy aspects of ego development.[22] Erikson focuses more on the positive environmental responses required for healthy growth than Freud did, so he is included in this section even though he posited unfolding stages of growth. The experience of parenting is a central feature of adult development, so he is an especially relevant theorist.

Erikson describes growth as a series of eight stages, as shown in Table 2-1. In each stage, physical and psychological capabilities appear and are the focus of development. At each stage, a developmental crisis or turning point occurs that leads, depending on the balance of positive and negative experiences, to the development of the positive or negative basic attitudes of that period—for example, trust or mistrust, autonomy or doubt/shame. Patterns of growth come from within but require support from the environment for healthy growth to occur.

Individuals have positive and negative experiences in the process of meeting needs, and both kinds of experience are important for optimal growth. Without some frustrations, we never learn how to cope with difficulties. However, for healthy growth, the balance should favor the positive. When this occurs, a strength or virtue develops.[23] Erikson does not believe that we resolve each crisis once and for all. Later experiences can change earlier resolutions for better or worse. Stress in adulthood, for example, can disrupt mature ways of coping such that a person may show immature behaviors. Positive experiences in adulthood can reverse mistrust or doubt developed in childhood.

Let us look briefly at the stages in Table 2-1. We focus on the qualities that develop when the appropriate experiences and positive environmental support occur; if experiences are primarily negative and support is lacking, negative qualities will develop. In the first year of life (stage 1), if caregiving is trustworthy, sensitive, and reliable, children develop a sense of trust and a feeling of hope about life. In the toddler years (stage 2), if children receive opportunities and encouragement for self-direction, they develop a sense of autonomy, the ability to act independently, and the strength of will to make free choices and act with self-control.

■ **TABLE 2-1**
ERIK ERIKSON'S EIGHT STAGES OF LIFE

Ages	Crisis	Virtue
0–1	Trust versus Mistrust	Hope
1–3	Autonomy versus Shame/Doubt	Will
3–5	Initiative versus Guilt	Purpose
5–12	Industry versus Inferiority	Competence
12–19	Identity versus Identity Diffusion	Fidelity
19+	Intimacy versus Isolation	Love
25+	Generativity versus Stagnation	Care
60+	Integrity versus Despair	Wisdom

Erik H. Erikson, *Childhood and Society*, 2nd ed. (New York: W. W. Norton, 1963); Erikson, *Insight and Responsibility* (New York; W. W. Norton, 1964).

In the preschool years (stage 3), children are more skillful and initiate more complex activities. If they receive encouragement for initiating and carrying through activities, they develop a sense of purpose and the ability to pursue goals free of fears of failure or criticism. In the elementary school years (stage 4), children attend school and are industrious and productive. If their skills are valued and encouraged with appropriate challenges, children's industry and sense of accomplishments outweigh feelings of inferiority, and they develop a sense of competence.

In adolescence, children incorporate sexuality into their expanding sense of self and develop an identity—a feeling of sameness and continuity of self. Individuals also incorporate society's views of who they are—as men, as women, as members of particular religions and ethnic groups. Individuals need to have their identities validated by their parents and society; otherwise, they remain confused, uncertain of who are and where they are heading. When positive identities are formed and validated, teens develop fidelity, which is defined as loyalty to one's choices, whether they be persons, goals, or ideals.

Adulthood is divided into three stages. The first (stage 6) is the establishment of intimate personal ties with an age-mate. Intimate relationships involve mutuality and surrender of the self to the relationship. The virtue that develops in this period is love, and it involves transferring the love experienced in the developing years of childhood to adult relationships.

The second stage of adulthood (stage 7) is a period of creating new life—generativity. In the past, women experienced generativity primarily in the family setting, creating a home and children; men in the past have done so in their work. Now, parenting and work are significant creative activities for both sexes. The virtue that develops is care—concern for and attention to what has been created, even if that requires sacrifice. This period is an extended one in the adult years.

In the final stage of life (stage 8), the focus returns to the individual's personal experience. Individuals must come to terms with their lives and be satisfied with who and what they are and what they have done. When this occurs, individuals develop a sense of integrity and wisdom about life. Erikson believes that children and grandchildren will be able to face life when parents can face death.

What Erikson's Theory Helps Parents Understand Erikson's theory helps parents understand (1) that psychological growth continues in adulthood and that resolutions of old conflicts are possible later in life, (2) that children are active, adaptive individuals who go through stages of growth to become independent, giving individuals concerned with other people and the world around them, and (3) that parenting is important both to the child who experiences it and to the parent who gives it. Box 2-6 describes Erikson's interpretation of the school problem.

Attachment Theory

Attachment theory is included here because it holds that the response of people in the environment determines the quality of the attachment, even though the push for attachment comes from within the baby. In 1958, the London psychoanalyst John Bowlby used the term *attachment* to describe the parent-infant relationship

---

Box 2-6
ERIK ERIKSON'S VIEW OF SCHOOL DIFFICULTIES

Like Sigmund Freud, Erik Erikson would look at children's behavior in terms of their present life situations as well as the history of their experiences leading up to that time. Although he would be guided by Freudian theory about children's romantic fantasies and the importance of positive identifications with the same-sex parent, he would also focus on the ego qualities and the virtues children have developed.

Examining the preschool period, Erikson would ask whether the child had had opportunities to develop initiative, confidence, and a sense of purpose about his or her activities. He would wonder whether parents had taken pleasure in their child's increasing mastery of activities and whether the parents' style of interaction encouraged the child's positive identification.

Like a systems theorist, Erikson would also attend to the teacher's qualities. He would wonder whether he or she was stimulating hard work and a growing sense of industry and competence in the child, or whether the teacher was arousing feelings of inferiority, leading the child to withdraw from the class work and engage, instead, in restless activity. He would also wonder whether the teacher and the school were valuing the child's growing skills and sense of cultural identity that begins to develop in these early elementary school years. For example, are girls' scientific and math skills encouraged? Do boys receive praise when they make up stories to express feelings?

Erikson would make the suggestions of the classical Freudian therapist but would also look at interventions that might change the teacher's style of teaching or the value system the school conveys to children.

---

and defined it as "an enduring affectional tie that unites one person to another, over time and across space."[24] He believed that it implied positive ties leading to healthy development, as opposed to the negative connotations of the term *dependency,* which Freudians used to characterize the child's relationship with the parent. The term *attachment* pointed to the positive functions of the tie for survival and preserving life. Although *attachment* initially referred to early parent-child relationships, its use has broadened to apply to parent-child relationships throughout the lifespan and to relationships with significant others such as friends, teachers, caregivers, and marital partners.[25]

Attachment refers to that aspect of the parent-child relationship that gives the infant feelings of safety, security, and protection and provides a safe base from which to explore the world. In infancy and childhood, the relationship is asymmetrical in that the infant derives security from the parents, but not vice versa. In adulthood, attachment involves a mutual, reciprocal relationship in which partners provide security and a safe base for each other.

Initially, attachment was measured in a laboratory situation in which observers noted the quality of the mother-child interactions during play (later, fathers were observed as well) and noted the child's reactions to the mother's leaving the room, a stranger's entering, and the mother's return.[26] Attachment has usually been measured at twelve months and at varying intervals thereafter. Attachment has also been measured by drawings, an Attachment Q-sort (a rating system used by observers to describe attachment behavior), and an attachment interview with teens and adults.

Infants and children differ not in whether attachment takes place—almost all children become attached as part of life—but in the quality of the attachment, depending on the behaviors of the adults.[27] The most common form of attachment is the *secure attachment,* which occurs when parents are accepting, emotionally available, and sensitive in meeting babies' needs. Securely attached infants are happy and secure with mothers, protest when mothers leave, and are happy and seek closeness when mothers return. About 60 to 70 percent of infants sampled in the United States have been described as securely attached.

There are three forms of *insecure attachment.* When parents are intrusive and overstimulating, infants are likely to form *anxious-avoidant* attachments, showing lack of concern when mothers leave and lack of interest in their return. About 20 percent of U.S. babies have such attachments. When parents are insensitive to babies' cues and often unavailable, babies are likely to form *anxious-resistant* attachments, protesting strongly when mothers leave and having difficulty establishing closeness when mothers return, alternately seeking the mother and resisting closeness. About 10 to 20 percent of U.S. babies have such attachments.

A third form of insecure attachment has been identified as *disorganized/disoriented* attachments. These attachments occur in families in which parents are frightened or traumatized and as a result may appear frightening to the child. Babies' behavior seems disorganized because, at times, they happily approach the mother as a securely attached infant would, and at other times they avoid the parent. They also appear disoriented, showing signs of confusion as to how to respond, sometimes "freezing" or "stilling" when near the parent. The percentage of such attachments is low in low-risk families (about 13 percent), but the percentage increases in high-risk families, to 82 percent in families whose members mistreat babies.[28]

Psychologists believe that strong attachments to parents and fear of strangers have survival value for the infant. Secure attachments ensure that the infant will stay close to the parent and remain responsive to guidance so the parent can continue to protect the child as the child becomes more independent.

Attachment relationships also provide a framework for babies' understanding of the world.[29] From these relationships, babies build internal models of how people relate to one another. Babies develop expectations of how well others will understand and respond to them, how much influence they will have on others, and what level of satisfaction they can expect from other people. They develop a sense of their own lovability when others respond positively to their overtures, and they anticipate similar responses from adults in new situations. When babies are ignored or rejected, they may develop a sense of unworthiness and helplessness. When interactions make up consistent patterns, babies acquire a sense of order and predictability in experience that generalizes to daily activities and to the world at large.

The benefits of early attachments extend to the future. Securely attached infants are more curious later in childhood than insecurely attached ones.[30] They attack a problem vigorously and persistently but accept help from others and are not aggressive. Children with early insecure attachments tend later to be more anxious and to have tantrums when presented with problems.

Attachment classifications vary in stability over time depending on the sample and length of time. Over short periods of time, say, twelve to eighteen months, stability is high;[31] two studies show substantial stability (about 70 percent) for the classification of security from one year to late adolescence and early adulthood.[32] However, two do not show long-term stability.[33] In general, when infants or older children live in families with many changes, especially negative changes such as divorce or loss of emotional support that change the nature of the parent-child relationship, stability of attachment is lower. However, the quality of attachment can change in a positive direction as well; mothers' increases in confidence and feelings of security improved the quality of their attachment to children.[34]

What Attachment Theory Helps Parents Understand   Attachment theory helps parents understand (1) that attachments are formed with important people throughout the lifespan, (2) that the way parents treat babies creates long-lasting expectations about the way the world will treat them, and (3) that attachments depend on the quality of the parent-child relationship at the time and will change as circumstances improve or damage the quality of the relationship. Box 2-7 describes what an attachment theorist might say about the school problem.

Systems Theories of Development

Systems theory is a broad term that applies to theories in many sciences, such as biology, psychology, and sociology. Systems theory emphasizes that the organism of interest—animal, person, family, organization—consists of many parts, all of which influence each other in important ways, and no part is more important than the others. Systems theories in developmental psychology look at several levels that influence the individual's behavior: genetic, neurophysiological, psychological, social, and sociological.[35]

In systems theory, there is no fixed, predetermined sequence of gene, neural pathways, behavior, effect on the environment, and the environment's response. Bidirectional transactions occur at all levels. For example, the effects of a parent's substance abuse on the genetic potential of the developing fetus, cited in Chapter 1, provide an example of how the environment of the organism can change genetic potential, which in turn shows up in the person's intellectual and social behavior, which can be passed along to the next generation.[36]

A dynamic relationship exists among all the levels such that the effect of any given event depends on the rest of the system. For example, a child's low birth weight may have different effects on the course of the child's development, depending on the social status of the family into which the child is born and the resources available to the family to help the child. When families have resources to get services, the effects of low birth weight are minimal or nonexistent; when families have few resources, effects are more marked.[37]

Recent research supports a systems perspective. Advances in imaging techniques have shown us that much supposed genetically determined brain development actually involves input from the environment. Beginning with conception and continuing throughout pregnancy, environmental factors such as nutrition, mother's health

> **Box 2-7**
> # ATTACHMENT THEORISTS' VIEW OF SCHOOL DIFFICULTIES
>
> Attachment theorists would look at school problems in several ways. First, they might expect that, unless there were some special physical or learning disability preventing mastery of the school difficulties, then the quality of the child's problem-solving abilities and self-control would be related to the quality of attachment relationships in the present and in the past. They would view interest in the world, curiosity, and self-control as emanating from secure attachment relationships.
>
> They would explore whether children have been consistently attached to parents since infancy. If so, they would expect that children would have an internal model of supportive, responsive adults and a history of confident, curious, problem-solving behavior. Thus, they would wonder whether a sudden stress—a family member's illness or marital troubles or some sort of traumatic event—had disrupted past effective functioning such that an otherwise well-functioning child is not able to focus and concentrate.
>
> They would expect that, if a child had an insecure avoidant or resistant attachment relationship with parents, the child might find it difficult to become attached to the teacher, settle down, and follow the teacher's requests. Most particularly, they would expect difficulties when children have disorganized/disoriented attachment relationships. Children would find it difficult to sustain attention, focus, and organization to learn material and complete work.
>
> In addition, however, to looking at past and present attachment relationships outside the classroom, they would look at the teacher's behavior. They would note whether he or she interacted with this particular child in a warm, sensitive, responsive way that established a secure attachment to the teacher so the child would cooperate with the teacher, follow directions, and learn.
>
> So, in the absence of any special disability or external stress in the child's life, they would see the attachment relationships with parents and the teacher as the engines of growth in the academic arena.

and experiences, physical surroundings, and stimulation influence "how the intricate circuitry of the human is wired."[38] After birth, environmental input and stimulation establish and strengthen connections among brain cells, thus shaping the architecture of the brain.

Systems theory insists that developmental action at any one of the levels can restrict development. We are very aware that genes place broad limitations on development, but as the Rochester Longitudinal Study showed in Chapter 1,[39] and as the behavior geneticist David Lykken[40] insists, the psychosocial environment can also place severe limitations on individual growth as well.

We now look at two systems theories that illustrate ways of seeing the relationships between the levels of experience and development. Box 2-8 shows how a systems theory would handle the school problem.

Box 2-8
A BROAD SYSTEMS VIEW OF SCHOOL DIFFICULTIES

A broad systems view would look at many possible reasons for children's difficulties in first grade and raise many questions that would be answered over time. Theorists might start at the genetic level. In Box 2-9, evolutionary developmental theory describes one way genetic influences can affect school behavior. A genetic contribution can arise from a marked family history of such behaviors, with fathers or mothers having similar problems when they were in school.

Systems theorists would also look at problems at the neurophysiological level of functioning as the reasons for school difficulties. They may see prematurity, birth complications, learning disabilities, or early exposure to domestic or community violence, all of which can change brain structure and wiring, as the cause of active, undercontrolled behaviors. In such cases, special tutoring or counseling, including behavioral interventions, might help the child to compensate for difficulties at the neurophysiological level.

Children's school difficulties may have many psychological origins varying in degree of seriousness. It may be hard for a child to separate from his or her mother for an extended day. Or family stresses, such as illness of a family member, a parent's loss of a job, or marital conflict leading to divorce, can increase nervousness and reduce children's abilities to sit still and think about what he or she is going to do. The child's undercontrolled school behavior could also be the result of the parents' long-standing difficulties in establishing control of the child's behavior at home. A community disaster, such as a natural disaster like a fire or flood, can decrease functioning and well-being.

Or it can be a combination of many factors—for instance, a flood triggers economic hardships for grandparents, who come to live with the family while plans are made to repair their home. Parents become stressed making arrangements for repairs and reorganizing household routines to include two older adults. A sensitive child may become overly excited and upset and find it hard to concentrate in school. Even when community events trigger stress, interventions occur most easily at the family level, as we shall see in Chapter 15.

Parents may seek first to handle the child's problems on their own or with the advice of relatives and friends, then consult with teachers or other school personnel or with family counselors as to how best to proceed. Teachers often can see the big picture and can give parents helpful guidance about the next and best steps to take to change the behaviors. Family therapists can give parents support and offer strategies for bringing about the changes they wish to see.

You can see that a systems theory looks at a child's behavior from many different perspectives and suggests many possible courses of action.

Evolutionary Developmental Theory

Evolutionary developmental psychologists look at how our genetic heritage influences our behavior today.[41] As its name suggests, the theory draws on Darwin's concepts of natural selection and reproductive fitness. *Natural selection* is the process whereby adaptive characteristics increase in frequency in a group because those behaviors that enable individuals to survive, to grow to maturity, and to reproduce—in brief, to adapt to their environments—are passed along to the next generation through the genes. Those who do not fit well in their environment die or reproduce fewer offspring.

Reproductive fitness refers to individuals' success in passing on their genes to the next generation. Contemporary evolutionary psychologists use the term *inclusive fitness* to describe individuals' success in reproducing their genes not only through their own children, who share 50 percent of their genes, but also through nurturing relatives such as younger siblings, who share 50 percent of the genes, or nieces and nephews, who share 25 percent of the genes.

Contrary to what one might expect, evolutionary developmental psychologists stress the importance of the genes as well as the environment in the development of human behavior. They believe we are flexible creatures who, with awareness, can change behavior patterns that were adaptive to a previous environment but are no longer effective in contemporary life. For example, in the past, mothers were infants' exclusive caregivers because only they could provide nourishment with breast milk. With the invention of refrigeration and modern formulas, fathers can participate equally in the care of infants. Our society now expects fathers to take a more active role in the care of young children.

The adaptive traits passed on through the genes are specialized abilities or *modules,* psychological mechanisms designed to solve problems in specific areas of expected experience. Language ability is an example of a module. Human beings appear preprogrammed to learn to speak. All societies have language. All children babble, and almost all children learn to speak, learning language in similar ways around the world, though the form of the language varies. If children are not presented with a language, they develop one of their own. Attachment behavior is an example of an inherited module or set of specialized skills that enable an infant to form a bond with a caregiver, who will protect the infant and ensure its survival.

Childhood behaviors that seem to have little direct relationship to survival or adult functioning are sometimes passed from one generation to another because they enable children either to survive childhood or to develop skills they will use in adulthood. Play is an example of such a behavior. Young animals and children around the world spend a lot of time in play, so we assume it serves an important function for the young. Many hypotheses are put forward about the function of play. Playful, rough-and-tumble activities may teach group members how to send social signals in a nonstressful situation. Play may give young members an opportunity to copy adult behaviors and experiment with variations on these behaviors, so it fosters creativity that may benefit adults. Active play also gives opportunities for developing and strengthening motor skills, and it may be a way of bonding members together in pleasurable experiences.

Evolutionary developmental psychologists trace the origins of family life back thousands of years to the time when we lived in small hunting-and-gathering tribes that depended upon organized, cooperative social behaviors. Such behaviors required a large brain capable of complex behaviors. A large brain meant that a child had to be born earlier, in a less mature state, so that the body of the mother could accommodate the size of the child's head in the birth process. Being born in a less mature state required an extended period of dependence on caregivers, and that, in turn, encouraged father's ongoing protection and support. Thus, a family system of mother, father, and children was born.

Early conditions of life also fostered the development of heavy parental investment in children. For immature children to survive, mature, and reproduce, caregiving had to extend over the long period of the child's dependency. The children of parents with minimal investments in caregiving were less likely to survive and reproduce, so natural selection resulted in increasing numbers of parents with heavy investments in rearing their children.

Evolutionary developmental theorists believe that the theory provides important insights about contemporary life and suggests new interventions at a social level.[42] For example, it can help us understand the conditions necessary for the development of parents who make heavy investments in their children. Research indicates that, when children grow up in harmonious families with the resources to provide many opportunities for development—lessons, trips, advanced schooling—children postpone sexual activity and mating, produce fewer children, and invest heavily in those they have. Conversely, when children grow up in conflicted families with limited resources and few opportunities for skill development, they reach puberty early, then invest heavily in sexual and mating behaviors and less in parenting behaviors.

Evolutionary developmental psychologists believe that a strong attachment and closeness to nurturing family members have had and continue to have survival value.

Evolutionary developmental theory suggests that one way to increase parental investment for those growing up in families with limited resources is to provide opportunities for growth and development—lessons, trips, academic help as needed, and opportunities for advanced education that encourage the postponement of sexual behavior as well as the parenting of few children but greater investment in each.

What Evolutionary Developmental Psychology Helps Parents Understand   This approach helps parents understand (1) that, as human beings, we have inborn tendencies based on our past history that make certain contemporary adaptations more or less difficult (see Box 2-9 for the ways that evolutionary developmental theory provides insight on school problems), and we must take heritage seriously as we make social interventions; and (2) that our strong attachment and closeness to nurturing family members has had and continues to have survival value.

The Bioecological Theory of Development

The most comprehensive system for understanding children's growth and the many factors affecting parents and children was developed by the late Urie Bronfenbrenner. He is a systems theorist who emphasizes the ecological context of development.[43] The term *ecology*, as Bronfenbrenner uses it, refers to the environments that human beings encounter in daily life as they grow and develop.

Bronfenbrenner describes a Process-Person-Context-Time (PPCT) framework for understanding development.[44] *Processes* are the daily interactions the child has with people, symbols, and objects in the environment and are the engines of development. A father's feeding a baby, a child's exploring a toy, and a child's learning a skill from a coach are examples of such processes or interactions. The *Person* has many characteristics, such as age, gender, ethnicity, temperamental disposition, abilities, and resources, which influence behavior and responses to others.

Bronfenbrenner's major contribution has been to expand our understanding of what makes up the child's environment, or *Context*. He describes several nested systems.[45] The *microsystem* is the pattern of daily activities and interactions the child has with symbols, objects, and people (primarily parents and siblings in the early period of life and then other caregivers, teachers, coaches, and friends). The *mesosystem* is the pattern of relationships and interactions between two or more settings in which a child participates—e.g., the interrelationships between parents at home and teachers at school, or between parents at home and caregivers at day care. The *exosystem* is a system that influences the child but with which the child does not have direct contact, such as parent's work and government agencies. For example, parent's work policies can determine parents' time with children after birth and, later, their participation in children's school activities.

Finally, the *macrosystem* refers to the broad, culturally shared beliefs about how things are done. It is the cultural context in which microsystems, mesosystems, and exosystems exist.

In addition to processes, persons, and context, Bronfenbrenner's system includes the concept of *Time*, which refers to the importance of regularity and stability in interactions and in the systems in the child's life.[46] Children need a sense of stability about

Box 2-9
EVOLUTIONARY DEVELOPMENTAL THEORY LOOKS AT SCHOOL DIFFICULTIES

Evolutionary developmental theorists distinguish between biologically primary abilities, such as language, that were selected through evolution, and biologically secondary skills, such as reading and writing, that build on primary abilities but are essentially societal inventions. Although human beings have been talking for thousands of years, are born with psychological mechanisms for learning language, and are motivated to learn, they have no innate mechanisms for learning to read or write. Reading and writing are skills humans have developed only in the last few thousand years, and until a century ago the majority of human beings around the world did not read or write. Reading and writing are cultural inventions that require high levels of attention and effort to learn.

Therefore, it is not surprising that many young children have difficulty settling into what is, in a sense, an "unnatural" situation in which they must sit all day and learn boring material. Their genetic structure is adapted to solving the problems of early human nomads, whose lifestyle required action and movement for survival. They are also built to spend long hours playing, rather than sustaining attention to written material. So, in the primary grades, especially kindergarten and first grade, children may need special interventions to help them learn.

What are the practical implications of these observations? There are several. First, it is possible to permit children to have more recesses during the school day, more rests from the effort. Such practices are already in place in schools in Taiwan and in Japan, where they have 10 minutes of recess for every 50 minutes of class work. Evolutionary developmental psychologists Anthony Pellegrini and David Bjorklund* recommend that students have many recesses scheduled throughout the day to increase their attention and learning in class following the breaks. Research evidence suggests that frequent breaks increase learning after the breaks, even if the breaks do not involve active physical exercise. The breaks appear to be more important for younger students, whose abilities to control and sustain attention are less developed than those of students in grades two and four. The nature of the break—physical activity, social games, or sedentary activity not related to learning—was not important; it was the fact of the break.

Two other recommendations are possible as well. More active forms of learning—through manipulating objects, for example, to learn math or reading—may increase children's abilities to learn. Another suggestion, one not made by evolutionary psychologists but one that follows from their theory, is to delay either school entrance or the introduction of material that requires such effort.

A parent, relying on evolutionary developmental theory, might take the child's school problems in stride, knowing that the effort of sitting long hours without a break and concentrating on material is hard for a first-grader. The parent can approach the first-grade teacher and suggest that the child's learning and behavior would improve with more opportunities for movement—going on class errands, having scheduled times for helping the janitor at school. Learning might improve with active manipulation of objects. At home, the parent can express understanding of the child's desire for activity and movement but also problem-solve with the child ways to settle

---

Box 2-9

---

more quickly into the class routine for learning. A parent with an interest in community action might encourage parent-teacher groups to look at the increases in learning that result when students have more frequent recesses.

*Anthony D. Pellegrini and David F. Bjorklund, "The Role of Recess in Children's Cognitive Performance," *Educational Psychologist* 32 (1997): 35–40.

---

where they live and what is expected of them in school. Many moves and changing school policies disrupt children's development.

Time also refers to the timing of events in a child's development. Poverty or divorce may have very different consequences for a toddler and for an adolescent. Finally, Time refers to the historical period, which exerts an influence on development. Children growing up in the Depression had a different attitude about work and savings from that of children who grew up during periods of economic abundance and security. And although historical time influences individuals and the contexts of their lives, people and their social lives can produce changes in history as well.

For the last decade of his life, Bronfenbrenner, who died in 2005, expressed concern about what he termed the "growing chaos" in children's and families' lives and the resulting decline in competence of those coming of age in the twenty-first century.[47] Compared with previous generations, children have less time and less involvement with parents because of family disruptions due to divorce and the fact that, in many families, both parents work long hours outside the home. Economic security has decreased, and almost 20 percent of children live in poverty. Children are emerging from schools less educated at a time when a technological economy demands intellectual skills. Youth express less trust in authorities and commit more crime; an increasing proportion of youth is spending their growing years in prison.

Bronfenbrenner believes that, as a society, we need to commit more resources to programs such as the G.I. Bill of Rights, which went into effect after World War II to help veterans get educations and families to own homes. He also points to Head Start as a program that strengthens and empowers children and families.

What Bioecological Theory Helps Parents Understand   Bioecological theory helps parents understand (1) that forces outside the family—historical events, economic factors, and social institutions such as work—impact parents' care of children; (2) that regularity and stability in children's lives are important; and (3) that help to improve parenting comes from changing not just what goes on in the home but also what goes on in the society. Box 2-10 presents what a bioecologist might say about a child's school problem.

Box 2-10
BIOECOLOGICAL THEORY'S VIEW OF SCHOOL DIFFICULTIES

Bioecological theory looks at four aspects of the situation: (1) the process, (2) the person, (3) the context, and (4) the time of the event(s).

So, in looking at the child's activity and inattention, bioecological theorists would look at many characteristics of the *person*—the child's dispositions, resources, and the demands the child's behavior places on others, as well as the child's age, gender, ethnicity—and would ask many questions. Is the child too young for first grade? Does he or she lack resources to cope with the everyday tasks of the classroom, or are these abilities just slow to develop? Is the child coping with a special stress, such as a new baby at home, that is making usual resources unavailable?

Bioecological theorists would look at the *process* of the child's interactions with teachers, peers, and parents. Are the interactions between the child and adult figures helpful in promoting new behaviors in the child? Do the interactions between the teacher and child occur irregularly and unpredictably such that the child has difficulty learning and moving on to more complex behaviors? Have parents been active in helping children develop the appropriate behaviors for the classroom?

More than most theorists, bioecological theorists would look at the *context* of the inattention and overactivity. What is the general culture of the school and its personnel regarding physical activity and attention to the requests of others? What is the attitude of the particular teacher in the classroom? Does the teacher present a model of the desired behavior? Is there sufficient structure in the school to promote self-control and attentiveness? Do children have adequate time for physical activities at school to drain off some of this energy? Are students monitored on playgrounds and in lunchrooms to ensure that school standards for self-control are being met? Are a large proportion of students living at the poverty level and coming to school hungry and restless? What is the culture of the community surrounding the school? Is there community disorganization due to special stresses, such as violence, that promote inattentiveness and inability to concentrate on work? Does the community provide recreational places and activities for youth?

Bioecological theorists would look at the *mesosystem*—the relationship between the parent and the teacher. Can they communicate and understand each other? Do they share common values about what is most important for students to learn, so they can work together to help the child adjust? A parent may feel that the teacher is unreasonable in his or her demands of the child. Do teacher and parent see each other as responsible for helping the child?

Bioecological theorists would also look at the *macrosystem*—the general cultural milieu of the child, which may encourage or discourage overactivity and inattention. They might point to the problems of too little time with two working parents and too much time with electronic games, videos, and TVs, which provide instant gratification and discourage the daily effort that much learning involves, at least at the beginning. They might point to the many responsibilities of parents, which reduce time for monitoring children and ensuring that they learn. These questions bear on the important dimension of historical *time*.

Box 2-10

Just as one would look in many places for the sources of the difficulties, one would look at several ways to address them. In addition to all the individual interventions parents and teachers could carry out with the child, bioecological theorists would encourage parents to get involved in parent-teacher-community organizations to provide resources that enable children to engage in many physical activities in a safe atmosphere. Parents can also encourage schools to adopt policies that guarantee physical education and physical activities at recesses, and they can carry such involvement into the political arena as necessary. It is through parent action, for example, that the culture and services for children with special needs have vastly improved. So, while parents and children are shaped by culture, they also shape the culture they inhabit.

Systems theories look at the many factors, from genes to governmental institutions to historical time, that shape children's growth, and the many factors that affect parents' behavior and their responses to children. Although parents do not control these forces, they do take active roles to manage the effects of these forces in their everyday lives.

Summary   Theories help us understand that changes in children's behavior come from the maturation or unfolding of internal stages of growth as well as from environmental stimulation. The parents' role varies from one of authoritative guidance and support, in the case of maturation, to one of active stimulation, in the case of theories that emphasize external sources of growth.

All these theories deepen parents' understanding of their role in children's lives and of the many factors that affect how parents carry out this role. Parents are not only models of behavior and providers of appropriate consequences for behavior; they are insightful, authoritative guides who understand the pressures children experience as they grow, and they provide support and direction for children. Parents are influenced by the historical time they live in, the social world they inhabit and bring to the child, the child's experience at the physical, emotional, social, and behavioral levels, the nourishing quality of the environment, and the lessons taught children by people outside the family. So, parents can rightly consider themselves the stabilizing and guiding center of a wide array of influences on children's lives.

Having looked at the ways the theories would approach a common childhood school problem, we see that each theory contributes insights about possible causes and remedies. Note that the insights are complementary rather than contradictory. That is, each theory looks at a slightly different facet of the problem; taken together, they present a multifaceted view of all the possible reasons and remedies for first-grade school difficulties. Probably no one child would require the insights of all these theories, unless the problem persisted over an extended time; yet all theories are useful to our understanding of the many different children who have first-grade problems. This illustrates an important point in parenting: There is no one reason and no one remedy for a child behavior of concern. All these theories help us understand some children.

CONSULTING EXPERTS

It is not surprising that parents consult experts. Parents want to do a good job at what matters most to them, and many experts, books, and television programs are available for advice. In this section, we review what experts have recommended and note areas of agreement and disagreement. We then consult two experts whose research supports the experts of the last forty years.

The experts available to parents are an impressive group. Most have been leading researchers or clinicians in fields such as medicine (pediatrics or psychiatry) or psychology. Their advice to parents in books, magazines, and newspaper columns has flowed from their academic or clinical work and has been only one aspect of their efforts to promote children's health and optimal development. In addition to parents, many experts have sought to influence educators and those responsible for public policy to improve children's education and community resources available to them.

Just as there has been general continuity in parents' behaviors with children over the centuries, so there has been much continuity in the beliefs of parenting experts. All experts see parents' role in children's lives as important, and many see parents' role in rearing the next generation as important in improving society and eliminating many of society's ills.

As with theories of development, experts have tended to stress parents' roles as teachers and molders of habits, as gentle guides and supports as inborn stages unfold, or as a combination of these roles.

John Watson

In the early part of the twentieth century, John Watson, the founder of behaviorism, applied learning theory to rearing children. Watson believed that children are blank slates who need to learn good habits. In his famous 1928 book, *Psychological Care of Infant and Child,* he advised parents to set strict and consistent daily schedules.[48] He was rigid in insisting that mothers not deviate from structured routines for eating, sleeping, and bathing.

Personality, he thought, developed from the early conditioning of emotions such as fear and anger. In his emphasis on the importance of early experiences and emotional development, he was like Freud and acknowledged his debt to Freud. Unlike Freud, however, he urged parents not to show or gratify children's desires for affection. He warned against too much love, which would make the child "a social 'invalid' wholly dependent on the attention and responses of others."[49] In a famous passage, he urged parents to treat children objectively. "Never hug and kiss them, never let them sit on your lap. If you must, kiss them once on the forehead when they say good night. Shake hands with them in the morning. Give them a pat on the head if they have made an extraordinarily good job of a difficult task. Try it out. In a week's time, you will find how easy it is to be perfectly objective with your child and at the same time kindly."[50]

Watson's stern advice was counterbalanced by the more optimistic view of Gesell, who said that parents' role was to understand, observe, and support children's individual patterns of growth. Recall the understanding way he would approach a child's school problem.

Benjamin Spock

The predominant expert advising the post–World War II generation of parents was Benjamin Spock, a Yale-trained pediatrician who had had several years of psychoanalytic training. His *Common Sense Book of Baby and Child Care* appeared in 1946 and underwent several revisions over the next fifty-five years.[51] In the first edition, Spock advocated a permissive approach to the challenges of feeding, toilet training, and aggressiveness. In subsequent editions, he increasingly emphasized the importance of helping children gain self-control and learn appropriate social behaviors along with a strong moral code and a commitment to helping others.

Spock initially addressed mothers and later both parents in a reassuring tone, urging them to trust themselves because they knew more than they thought they did about rearing their children. He minimized his role as expert, saying that ideas about what is correct change over time and that he was giving only commonsense ideas about how to care for children. Over time, he came to have more concerns about parents' anxieties and worries than about children's. He came to believe that children were resilient and survived the arguments and battles they had with parents but that parents tended to worry and brood about them.

Modesty about his influence as an expert was realistic, he discovered, when he carried out informal surveys of mothers' responses to the parenting advice they received. Generally, they ignored it, and he wrote to Anna Freud, "Despite the fact that we counselors considered ourselves mature, impressive, comfortable people, we were amazed at how resistant these young mothers were to following our advice, especially when it came to matters with an emotional charge."[52]

Experts who followed Spock have tended to be clinicians who drew on others' research and urged parents both to gratify children's needs and to set limits. They generally agree on certain basic principles: the goal of parenting as raising responsible, happy, caring, contributing individuals; the importance of parents' modeling approved behaviors, communicating positive feelings, and respecting children as individuals; the importance of praise and the avoidance of shaming and ridiculing children. They believe in consistent rules that are enforced, and they believe in limits.

These experts differ in three ways. They differ primarily in how to set and enforce limits and the role of punishments in limit setting. Some would give direct rewards and punishments, and others would rely on teaching children to control disapproved behaviors. They differ also in their focus or emphasis on certain areas of parent-child relationships and ways to translate common areas of agreement into action. For example, some experts focus on communication of feelings as a way to show love and aid growth, and others focus on respecting individuality by allowing children opportunities for growth through independent action and exploration.

Haim Ginott and Thomas Gordon

Psychologists Haim Ginott[53] and Thomas Gordon[54] focus on children's needs and are similar in emphasizing effective methods of communication to strengthen the parent-child bond and to attend to the child's individuality. Ginott establishes and enforces limits in an impersonal way, and Gordon encourages parent-child problem-solving sessions when conflicts arise. We discuss their methods of communicating with children in Chapter 4.

Rudolf Dreikurs

Rudolf Dreikurs, a child psychiatrist and one of the first to organize parents' groups, advises establishing close relationships as well as setting limits.[55] Dreikurs believes that children have built-in capacities to develop in healthy ways. Their strongest desire is to belong to a group, and from infancy they seek acceptance and importance within the family. Each child, however, develops a unique path to family acceptance. Parents influence children by gaining their cooperation, by using encouragement to stimulate development of children's inner resources, and by applying natural and logical consequences to provide limits for children's behavior. We discuss Dreikurs's concepts in greater detail in Chapters 4 and 5.

James Dobson

James Dobson stands in the tradition of experts who turn to the principles of learning theory to rear children.[56] Like Ginott and Gordon, however, he believes that parents should establish warm relationships with children. He recommends using positive rewards for approved behaviors and withholding rewards when disapproved behaviors occur. When conflicts arise, he suggests a parent-child contract with points for approved actions and loss of points for disapproved actions. When a child is clearly defiant of parents' authority, he would use physical punishment if all else has failed.

Dobson relates his views to a traditional religious perspective and worries about a contemporary society with increasing sexual freedom and secular values that destroy both close family life and moral child rearing.[57] He has founded organizations such as Focus on the Family and the Family Research Council to exert pressure on public officials to provide a social atmosphere that supports parents' teachings of traditional values by eliminating drugs, early sexual activity, and value-free education. Just as he wants parents to provide a healthy atmosphere for children's growth, he wants society to provide a healthy atmosphere for the family's growth. Although other experts, such as Spock, have made pronouncements on the social issues of the day, he is alone in the degree to which he has become a significant political force in the country by forming organizations to advance his point of view.

William Sears

William Sears, a pediatrician, developed what he calls *attachment parenting,* which encourages parents to accept their babies' dependency needs and meet them appropriately.[58] He describes the five 'B's of attachment parenting in infancy: (1) bonding with the infant at birth, (2) breast-feeding, (3) bed sharing (co-sleeping), (4) baby wearing (carrying the baby in a Snuggli or a sling), and (5) belief in the baby's cry as an important signal. The five Bs keep babies and parents physically connected so parents can learn who their child is and respond in a sensitive, caring way. We discuss this approach in greater detail in Chapter 6.

Stanley Greenspan

Toward the end of the twentieth century, child psychiatrist and psychoanalyst Stanley Greenspan emerged as a major expert.[59] Like Gesell, he is a careful observer who has described children's motor, language, intellectual, social, and particularly their emotional development from birth. He co-founded the organization Zero to Three to focus on the development and needs of children in this period. In addition, he has been concerned with children who have special developmental needs, for example, children with autism, discussed in greater detail in Chapter 8.

Greenspan has written a number of books describing patterns of development and parents' important role in helping children master the challenges in each area and develop appropriate skills. He has also turned his attention to advocating for social policies that support parents and children. With T. Berry Brazelton, he coauthored the book *The Irreducible Needs of Children* so that parents and public policy experts could lobby for reasonable supports.[60] He and Brazelton differ from Dobson in their social lobbying the same way they differ in parenting. They want society to pay attention to parents' needs by providing additional resources for families' growth, just as they urge parents to support their children's needs and growth. They focus on what society must give parents, whereas Dobson focuses on what society must eliminate to support parents.

Dr. Phil, *Nanny 911*, and *Supernanny*

The twenty-first century has brought us parenting experts on television. Dr. Phil[61] and the programs *Nanny 911*[62] and *Supernanny* offer parents guidance on child-rearing matters; like their predecessors, they are parent-centered as well as child-centered in their approaches. Dr. Phil is a psychologist, but the nannies are unique among experts because their expertise lies in their hands-on experience with many families, living in or spending long days with the children and their parents. In contrast to twentieth-century experts, these experts go into the homes and videotape parents and children interacting before the advice and after it. They observe how parents put the advice into practice and fine-tune parental behaviors. Perhaps because these experts go into people's homes and follow up, they are direct with their suggestions.

The nannies are among the most realistic experts, knowing the amount of effort change demands. They spend one day observing and drawing up a plan for change and the rest of the week modeling and guiding parents' interactions with children. They also show parents how to organize the home and daily routines.

Nannies Deborah Carroll and Stella Reid describe the "No-nonsense School of Parenting," which teaches parents how to "grow up and be parents,"[63] as follows:

> We believe that children need lots of love, but they also need lots of House Rules, giving structure to their days. This means strict limits tailored to children's personalities, and lots

and lots of positive reinforcement rather than constant nagging and negativity. We'll show you how to confront your family problems head-on with firm but loving discipline, clear and effective communication, and the implementation of family rules. We'll teach you how to stop making excuses, avoid tackling problems that may seem insurmountable, and how to stop giving in when your children are whining and crying.

Paradoxically, imposing *more* order on children allows them the freedom to thrive and stretch their wings and to grow up to be happy, healthy, and loved.[64]

Dr. Phil McGraw's comprehensive program helps parents make choices so they can have "a phenomenal family," defined as (1) a nurturing and accepting family system, (2) a unique family identity with a defined set of values and standards of conduct, (3) established rituals and traditions, (4) open communication, and (5) strategies for managing crises. To promote the phenomenal family, Dr. Phil recommends a behavioral system of rewards and consequences, time-outs, and contracts, as well as strategies for open communication.

Dr. Phil sees parenting as a "noble"[65] undertaking that is the center of the meaning of life. Both parents must work together to rear children, and although parents are not the only influences in children's lives, they do create an environment that enables family members "to rise above the noise of the world."[66]

Myla Kabat-Zinn and Jon Kabat-Zinn

Some experts come from religious or spiritual perspectives. We have noted Dobson's traditional Christian perspective.[67] Secular expert Dr. Phil talks of praying, making a pledge to God regarding his intentions as a parent, and encouraging parents to establish a set of values the family agrees upon.[68] At the end of the twentieth century, Myla and Jon Kabat-Zinn described a parenting approach based on the Buddhist tradition in *Everyday Blessings: The Inner Work of Mindful Parenting*.[69]

The three cardinal principles of mindful parenting are (1) sovereignty, by which the Kabat-Zinns mean respecting children's true inner nature and helping them to fulfill it; (2) empathy, that is, seeing and at times feeling events and situations from others' perspectives, including seeing ourselves as our children see us; and (3) acceptance of children and situations as they are, without demanding that they be something else.

Like other experts, they believe parents' role is to protect and guide children to maturity. Like other experts, they stress the uniqueness of each child, the importance of accepting and acknowledging their own and others' feelings, avoiding judgment and criticism, being strong and clear with children when that is required but with an attitude of love and an understanding of the child's needs.

The Kabat-Zinns' important contributions are their encouragement of parents to focus as much attention on controlling their own reactions to children as they do on controlling children's behaviors. They urge parents to live with tensions, to be still; to seek balance and understanding but not to rush in to attain them. They summarize mindful parenting:

> The challenge of mindful parenting is to find ways to nourish our children and ourselves, to remain true to the quest, the hero's journey that is a human life lived with awareness, across our entire life span, and so to grow into who we all are and can become for each other, for ourselves, and for the world.[70]

We have reviewed experts and seen that over the past hundred years there have been recurring themes that reflect theoretical perspectives as well. Some experts emphasize parents' teaching role, as learning theory suggests is important; other experts emphasize parents' role as guide and support in the process of maturation, as psychoanalytic and Piagetian theories suggest. In the last fifty years, these two perspectives have been viewed as complementary and equally important. Parents today can choose the expert whose emphasis and guidance most closely reflects their own values, for research supports both points of view, as we shall see.

RESEARCH THAT SUPPORTS EXPERTS

Few parents have heard the names Diana Baumrind or Gerald Patterson, yet the research work of both, carried out over decades, has provided a solid base of empirical evidence for experts who believe that love, nurturance, and understanding must be combined with firm, consistent limits if children are to flourish.

Diana Baumrind

In 1961, at a time when psychologists considered that permissive, democratic child rearing provided the most benefits for children, and parental control was defined as harsh, rejecting discipline, Diana Baumrind undertook research that has influenced experts for five decades. Her work was ground-breaking in many ways, and we detail her methods here because they account for the solidity of her findings.[71]

Baumrind observed a sample of 150 middle-class, predominantly white preschoolers in several settings—in nursery school, in laboratory sessions, alone and in teaching sessions with mothers, and at home from before dinner to bedtime. She developed measures of their positive behaviors rather than their problematic behaviors, which had so often been the focus of past research. She did not rely only on parents' verbal reports of their own behavior with children, although she did obtain reports via interview, as was typical of parenting research up to that time. She sent observers into the homes to record what occurred between parents and children, and she observed parents in the laboratory. Single-handedly, she followed her sample, observing the children again at ages ten, fifteen, and in their early twenties, to determine both the consistency and the long-term effects of her early parenting measures.

Baumrind began her work by first identifying preschoolers who showed positive behaviors in such categories as self-control, approach-avoidance tendency, self-reliance, vitality (mood varying from buoyant to dysphoric), and peer affiliation. Nursery-school teachers' quantified observations provided the measures of children's behaviors. From these descriptions, Baumrind identified competent children who had the capacity for socially responsible, independent behavior that included positive, cooperative relationships with parents and peers and purposive, achievement-oriented behavior in the world.

Baumrind also identified three patterns of parental behaviors associated with varying levels of children's competence: authoritative, authoritarian, and permissive.

Authoritative parents exercised firm control over the child's behavior but also emphasized independence and individuality in the child. Although the parents had a clear notion of present and future standards of behavior for the child, they were rational, flexible, and attentive to the needs and preferences of the child. Their children were self-reliant and self-confident and explored their worlds with excitement and pleasure.

Authoritarian parents employed similar firm control but in an arbitrary, power-oriented way without regard for the child's individuality. They emphasized control without nurturance or support to achieve it. Relative to other groups of children, the children of authoritarian parents were unhappy, withdrawn, inhibited, and distrustful.

Permissive parents set few limits on the child. They accepted the child's impulses, granting as much freedom as possible while still maintaining safety. They appeared cool and uninvolved. Permissive parents sometimes allowed behavior that angered them, but they did not feel sufficiently comfortable with their anger to express it. As a result, anger built up to unmanageable proportions. They then lashed out and were likely to harm the child more than they wished. Their children were the least independent and self-controlled and could best be classified as immature.

Baumrind described the conceptions of children held by the three groups of parents. Both authoritarian and permissive parents had unrealistic perceptions of children.

> Both Authoritarian and Permissive parents saw their child as dominated by egoistic and primitive forces. Authoritarian parents saw these characteristics in need of constraint, and Permissive parents (many citing Rousseau) tended to glorify these same characteristics. Few parents from either pattern took very much into account, on the one hand, the child's stage-appropriate desire to be good and to conform to parental expectations nor, on the other hand, the child's impulsivity and use of concrete reasoning which often interfered with his efforts to behave maturely. Thus, these parents appeared to construct a fiction about what their child was like and to relate to that fiction. . . . While Authoritarian parents tended to view children as having responsibilities similar to those of adults and Permissive parents tended to view children as having rights similar to those of adults, Authoritative . . . parents saw the balance between the responsibilities and rights of parents and the responsibilities and rights of children as a changing function of stage of development.[72]

Authoritative parents also interpreted the parental role as including the responsibility to teach children that, in their relationship, each had to treat the other as they wished to be treated, and children were expected to behave the same way in their relationships with others outside the family.

Baumrind's conclusions about the positive value of firm parental control and parental demands for mature behavior startled psychologists who associated parental control with parental rejection and children's behavior problems. Her findings that firm control and a family atmosphere of nurturance and understanding developed children's competence set her work apart from its predecessors and provided research support for all the experts who recommended understanding and nurturance as well as firm limits and consequences.

With regard to the debate about whether children's behavior is the result of maturational or learning processes, Baumrind wrote,

> Innate and maturational predispositions, present at birth, and mediated by neurophysiological processes, interact throughout the individual's life with environmental factors to

determine the course of development. Although maturation of the child's nervous system provides opportunities for development, these opportunities can be realized only in a facilitating environment designed by knowledgeable adults.[73]

Gerald Patterson

Gerald Patterson's research at the Oregon Social Learning Center also supports the experts who recommend both love and limits. We refer to his and his colleagues' work in later chapters as well, but here we point to the development of his ideas over decades. His research at the Oregon Social Learning Center, carried out at the same time as Baumrind's, initially focused on helping families with aggressive children who defied parents at home and teased and bullied other children at school.[74] Observers went to the homes to record and understand patterns of family interaction. Parents learned about behavior modification techniques. Then, parents and child drew up a contract of rewards and negative consequences to increase positive target behaviors and decrease negative behaviors. Families were followed over time, and their progress was noted. The program led to positive behavior change in the family and to fathers' taking more active roles in controlling children's behavior.

Over time, Patterson and his coworkers discerned a family pattern of interactions that led to aggressive behaviors. Several factors contributed to this process over time: children's temperamental qualities, parents' experiences with their own parents, the social conditions of family life (such as divorce), cultural factors, and parents' personal qualities, such as depression.

Combining their observations with insights from attachment research on the importance of sensitive caregiving and maternal warmth, Patterson and his coworkers sketched a process of development that leads to children's compliance or noncompliance, as follows:[75] Sensitive parents, responsive to their children's needs, form secure attachments to their children; they therefore create early in life a climate in which children are willing to comply because parents attend to their needs and wishes. The children act out of the commitment to the relationship with their parents. Throughout the learning process, parents give children the encouragement and support they need to persevere in the often-frustrating learning process.

As with mutual responsiveness, the process of coercion begins with the interactions between the mother/caregiver and the infant. Either partner can start the process, and both keep it going.[76] Typically, the infant is irritable and fussy, and the mother, for whatever reason, is negative and unpredictable in her response. This increases the infant's irritability. The infant comes to see the world as an unrewarding, unsupportive, unpredictable place. Or the mother may be depressed and pay little attention to the infant, who becomes irritable and negative and triggers further negativity on the mother's part.

The infant develops into a noncompliant, negative toddler who fails to follow rules. Crying, fussing, and whining give way to hitting, kicking, and breaking things to force parents to do what the toddler wants. The negative response of each partner in the parent-child dyad intensifies the other's response. Eventually, other family members are drawn into the negative cycle. The noncompliant toddler becomes the impulsive, defiant preschooler, who becomes the aggressive, bullying elementary school student.

To counter a negative cycle, Patterson and his colleagues have taught parents to use a supportive, consistent, positive reinforcement program to create a sensitive, caring relationship between parent and child. Once a warm relationship is established, then parents can actively teach desirable habits primarily through the use of positive statements and consistent consequences. Although they believe that temperamental qualities of parent and child affect the interactions between the two, Patterson and coworkers also believe that behavioral interventions can and do modify parents' and children's behavior.

Both Baumrind and Patterson and coworkers developed parenting recommendations from research based on observations of the daily lives of all family members. They have followed their study members over time and have noted the long-term effectiveness of the interventions they recommend. Coming from different perspectives, they have arrived at common ground in recommending nurturing, love, and consistent, firm limits.

Summary   The history of parent-child relationships over the centuries, much of the theory, most of the experts, and careful research all agree that parents' love, nurturance, consistent guidance, and limits are needed to support children's growth, which is determined by the maturation of the child's nervous system in a stimulating, supportive environment provided by parents. Following Chapter 3, "Cultural Influences on Parenting," we explore in greater detail how parents establish close relationships and support growth.

MAIN POINTS

The history of parent-child relationships over the centuries reveals that

- parenting in classical times resembled parenting today, with similar stages of childhood, similar concerns about children's needs, and the involvement of both parents
- parenting in the last five hundred years shows a general continuity with parenting today, valuing closeness and caring between parents and children as well as parents' concern for children's growth
- continuity in parenting is shaped by two factors: (1) parents' goal of helping children survive and flourish, and (2) children's needs

The theories reviewed here

- share many common features
- deepen parents' understanding of children's development and parents' role in promoting it
- focus on different aspects of development

Theories that emphasize the role of the environment in stimulating growth

- include learning theories as well as Vygotsky's view of the social nature of knowledge and growth

- give parents important roles as providers of the environment in terms of rewards and punishments to teach good habits or as partners in social interactions that stimulate growth
- view parents as positive models and knowledgeable guides who help children achieve their maximum potential
- see parents as transmitters of culture

Theories that emphasize internal stages or patterns of growth stimulating development

- emphasize that the growth process places demands on children
- view neither children nor parents as having complete control
- emphasize that parents and children have active roles in growth, as children must satisfy drives in socially acceptable ways and adjust to and integrate new behaviors
- view parents as authoritative guides who seek to understand children's experience and support children's growth by providing appropriate experiences

Theories that emphasize both external and internal sources of growth

- focus on all levels of experience, from genes to internal drives to societal organization to historical time
- stress the ways the environment supports internal growth patterns
- include genetic influences from our early human living conditions as well as numerous contemporary social influences, such as the economy
- give parents active roles in helping children integrate all the influences impinging on them

Parenting experts

- are primarily distinguished researchers, teachers, or clinicians who want to support parents' efforts in parenting
- agree on the goals of parenting, the importance of parents' attention, love, and concern for the child and the necessity of consistent limits
- more recently incorporate religious and spiritual values of many different perspectives
- in the twenty-first century include television advisors who videotape parents in the trenches and provide both direct suggestions and models of how to proceed in all areas to guide children

Careful researchers of parent-child relationships studied in the laboratory as well as at home find that

- authoritative parenting, which includes nurturance, attention to children's individuality and behavioral demands, and limit-setting, helps children develop social responsibility and competence
- authoritarian parenting, which makes many demands of children but gives little support to achieve these demands, is associated with unhappiness, inhibition, and distrust in children

- permissive parenting, which allows children freedom of impulse and expression but does not teach or support self-control and self-regulation, is associated with immaturity and dependence in children
- positive and negative cycles of parent-child interaction are established early in life, depend on the qualities of both parents and children, and require the actions of both to keep the processes going

EXERCISES

1. Which of the theories of children's development discussed in this chapter seems most useful to you in understanding children's growth and development? Why?

2. Which parenting expert seems most useful to you in helping parents? Why?

3. Erikson's theory of lifespan development focuses on the importance of positive experiences and strengths. Review your own life in terms of the strengths you have developed from positive experiences. For example, you may have developed a love of the outdoors, as well as independence and a love of the environment, from camping activities with your family.

4. Does the concept of attachment help you make sense of your experiences in life within and outside the family?

5. As a parent (or imagining yourself as a parent), do you think of your role as supporting the maturation of inborn qualities or as being responsible for what children learn and how they function?

ADDITIONAL READINGS

Brazelton, T. Berry, and Greenspan, Stanley I. *The Irreducible Needs of Children*. Cambridge, MA: Perseus, 2000.

Carroll, Deborah, and Reid, Stella, with Moline, Karen. *Nanny 911*. New York: Regan Books, 2005.

Dobson, James. *Parents' Answer Book*. Wheaton, IL: Tyndale House, 2003.

Hulbert, Ann. *Raising America: Experts, Parents, and a Century of Advice About Children*. New York: Alfred A. Knopf, 2003.

McGraw, Dr. Phil. *Family First*. New York: Free Press, 2004.

3

Cultural Influences on Parenting

CHAPTER TOPICS

In this chapter, you will learn about:

- A definition of culture and how it influences parenting

- How culture is transmitted from one generation to the next

- Celebrating cultural diversity

- Sources of cultural influences: race, ethnicity, socioeconomic status, religion

- Two cultural models of the parent-child relationship

- The characteristics, values, and parenting strategies of six ethnic groups

- The influence of socioeconomic status and economic hardship on parenting

IN THE NEWS

New York Times Magazine, November 21[1]: Early intervention program for children in need is related to children's long-term social gains. See pages 119–121.

Test Your Knowledge: Fact or Fiction?

1. Geneticists agree that the concept of race lacks validity and utility.
2. Individuals absorb culture from parents and authorities and incorporate it in their lives without thinking about it.
3. Social class plays a more important role in children's development than racial or ethnic background.
4. The self-esteem of people in different ethnic groups reflects the general regard accorded their group by society.
5. Parenting strategies have different effects in different ethnic groups.

Culture provides a nest for all the parent-child interactions we discuss throughout this book. In this chapter, we look at the many ways cultural forces shape the process of parenting. In discussing the broad trends in parenting within ethnic and social groups, we also learn about the great diversity within each group. We examine how socioeconomic status provides a context for the development of all members of our society. Finally, we look at how poverty and lack of social resources affect parenting.

Our country is a diverse society that has grown with waves of immigration that began twenty thousand years ago, when the first Native Americans trudged here from Siberia,[2] and that continue to the present, giving us twenty million new residents since 1980.[3]

In this chapter, we look at the diverse cultural influences that affect parents and children. We first define culture, then examine the many sources of cultural influence and the ways individuals incorporate cultural influences in their lives. We look at two models for understanding diverse cultural forces and then at the values and behaviors of people in specific ethnic and social groups.

WHAT IS CULTURE?

Culture is the set of values, beliefs, ways of thinking, rituals, and institutions of a group or population.[4] The group can be as small as a neighborhood, a school, or a community, or as large as a racial or ethnic group or a social class. Culture provides ways of seeing the world and, along with other influences, determines patterns of feelings and behavior in everyday life. As we saw in Chapter 1, it is a dynamic force responding to social, political, and economic events and shaping the meaning of these events for us.

Culture provides (1) the physical and social settings for parents and children, (2) the psychological characteristics valued in parents and children, and (3) recommended behaviors for family members.[5] So, culture shapes a broad range of parental behaviors, from the more general values taught by parents to the concrete aspects of daily life, such as where children eat and sleep.

To show the many ways culture influences parental behaviors, let us look at two groups of mothers—U.S. mothers and Italian mothers of infants four to sixteen months old—their goals for their children, and how these goals influenced their care of babies in the first year and a half of life.[6] The mothers and babies, all members of nuclear families, were interviewed and observed in their homes.

The two groups of mothers had different goals for their children. American mothers wanted their children to grow up to be (1) economically and emotionally independent, (2) happy, no matter what their financial status, and (3) honest and respectful with other people. Their immediate goal was to give babies the proper stimulation for healthy growth, which mothers feared they were not providing. Italian mothers' long-term goals focused on (1) good health for their children, (2) financial security, and (3) a good family life that included a spouse and children.

These mothers did not worry about being effective; they considered all mothers adequate simply because they were mothers. They did not feel responsible for the outcome of children's development, because they believed that children turn out as they will.

These goals shaped how infants and mothers spent their days. American mothers stimulated babies and gave them opportunities to be independent. Babies spent their time in one-on-one interactions with mothers (about one-third of the observation time) or alone in their rooms, sleeping or playing with toys. Although other people, including siblings, came in and out of the home, they did not usually care for the child. In Italy, infants were social. They had little direct interaction with mothers (10 percent of the observation time) and were almost never alone. They slept in the same room as their parents, often until the second birthday, and were regularly in the company of two or three people. For all but one baby, at least one grandparent lived nearby and visited daily.

As babies began to get around, U.S. parents babyproofed the environment, and at ten months, babies spent 52 percent of observation time crawling on the floor and exploring freely; mothers felt reassured that their children were developing well, because they were active and curious. Mothers taught infants at this age preliminary safety rules because they felt it was important for the child to accept some responsibility for safety. Italian mothers, on the other hand, believed free exploration was too dangerous—too cold, even in the summer—and involved too many hazards. Their ten-month-old infants spent only 26 percent of observation time crawling on the floor, and when it was time to walk, adults supported and held babies' hands. None of the Italian mothers felt concern that their children were not more independent.

American mothers worried about sleep habits, emphasizing and establishing healthy sleep patterns so that children got enough sleep even when they resisted nap time or bedtime. By four months of age, most babies slept in their own beds, often in their own rooms; several shared a room with a sibling but none did so with their parents. In contrast, Italian mothers rarely held to any sleeping schedule, and babies often dropped off to sleep in the midst of family activity without bedtime rituals or songs. One mother had no schedule, because she felt it was cruel to deprive the child of family time.

With regard to eating behaviors, however, the attitudes of the two groups of mothers were reversed. American mothers felt that their children could regulate their eating. Infants ate on demand and often at different times from the family, so eating was an activity involving mother and child, with the mother talking while she fed the infant. As children got older, they were encouraged to feed themselves. Italian infants, in contrast, were required to eat on four-hour schedules and to come to family meals even if they had to be awakened to do so. Solid foods were begun at four months, and infants had to eat certain amounts. They were expected to get used to eating rituals even if they did not like them, because eating was a social activity with the family.

So, cultural goals played a strong role in everyday caregiving activities, with American mothers emphasizing independence—in play, exploration, eating, and sleeping alone at bedtime—and Italian families enveloping their infants in complex social interactions that required adaptation on the part of the babies and gave few opportunities for independence.

Although these are differences in mothers in two different countries, within the United States we have similar differences, which we discuss in a later section.[7] Let us first look at how culture is transmitted.

HOW CULTURAL VALUES ARE TRANSMITTED FROM ONE GENERATION TO ANOTHER

Socialization is the term for the process whereby individuals learn the skills necessary for group life.[8] We used to think that parents and other authorities in society taught children and newcomers the beliefs, values, and feelings necessary to function competently in society, and children and newcomers passively absorbed them and lived by them.

Now we believe that children have an active role in the process of socialization.[9] Just as Piaget believes that children actively construct a view of the physical world, social scientists believe that individuals actively construct a view of their culture. Based on what parents teach, on what children experience, on what they see happen to those around them, and on what they learn from interactions with individuals outside their own group, children construct a cultural *schema* of the world. A cultural schema includes shared meanings and feelings about events and people, as well as ways to behave. The anthropologist Jean Briggs writes,

> The notion that meaning inheres in culture and that people receive it passively, as dough receives the cookie cutter, is rapidly being replaced by the idea that culture consists of ingredients, which people actively select, interpret, and use in various ways, as opportunities, capabilities, and experience allow.[10]

What role do parents play? William Corsaro and Katherine Brown Rosier describe a process in which the family is at the center of a web of cultural influences originating outside the family but sending strands of influence that end in the family.[11] Children first learn about their culture from interactions in the family, much as the American and Italian infants learned about the importance of independence and sociability from the earliest days of life in their daily routines of eating, sleeping, and play, and through rituals and stories about the culture. As children begin to move outside the family to the world of other caregivers, teachers, and peers and to other institutions such as schools, they learn about different cultures and gain new perspectives on the culture they learned at home.

Constructing a cultural schema is a process in which parents or others present expectations, and children become aware of them and evaluate them in positive and negative terms, resisting, refusing, or accepting them in part or in whole. Parents initially present cultural expectations in terms of behavioral expectations—sleeping alone, wakening for family meals, playing alone. Children signal their acceptance or resistance in their behavior—crying to sleep with parents, following parents, and refusing to play alone.[12]

Generational Differences in Culture

What happens when parents are raised in one culture and rear children to live in a different one? Studies of immigrants from Croatia showed that, even when families lived in self-contained communities stressing their traditional values, customs, and language, they were able to socialize their children to be more independent, questioning, and self-directed than the parents themselves had been raised to be, thus helping their children fit into the new culture.[13] The Croatian parents were able to Americanize their children as well as other Croatian parents did who themselves had become assimilated into the new culture. So, parents can encourage behaviors that are foreign to them.

First-generation immigrant families meet challenges in interfacing with the school system, which embodies the American values of independent effort to achieve knowledge, competition, questioning, and expressing opinions.[14] How do first-generation parents, those who came to this country, help their children achieve the school success that all immigrant parents want for their children? There is no easy route, and a variety of factors can help or hinder parents' efforts.

Chief among these factors is comfort with the language. Parents are more likely to become involved in school activities when they speak the adopted country's language or when school personnel speak their language of origin. Although many schools have personnel who speak Spanish, they are less likely to have staff fluent in languages of families from Cambodia, Thailand, or India. When local media carry school announcements in parents' languages, parents are more likely to know what is happening and to participate. When parents work only one day shift, they are more likely to have time to monitor children's homework and to become active in school programs.

Child Cultural Brokers

When parents do not speak the language, and other adult relatives are not available to serve as interpreters, children often interpret for parents in the outside world because they do speak the language.[15] They are termed *cultural brokers* because they serve as the link between the parents' culture and the European American culture. The psychological effects of taking on adult roles are not known. Children can gain self-esteem and feelings of confidence as they negotiate adult situations, gaining awareness of and sensitivity to parents' needs, which promotes closeness to parents.

On the other hand, in acting for parents children often take on parents' worries about money, living arrangements, job concerns, legal issues, and family members in the country of origin. They have often taken on adult roles in health-care situations, reporting symptoms, getting diagnoses of illnesses and directions for treatments and medications. Because children may misunderstand directions and can make errors with potentially serious consequences, California was the first state in the country to consider laws to prohibit the use of children as translators except in emergencies.[16] Experts are concerned also about the emotional burden on the child of being the first to learn of a parent's serious medical condition and the one to report it to parents.

Having served as authorities for their parents in public, children sometimes find it difficult to return to the role of inexperienced child at home. This is especially likely in adolescence, when teens want independence and can justify increased freedom in light of the responsibilities they already have taken on. If parents do not give it to them, teens may challenge and defy them.

MAJOR CULTURAL INFLUENCES

In rearing children, parents draw on the cultural values and behaviors of their racial, ethnic, and social groups. Sometimes, parents are blending two cultures.

Race

The term *race* refers to "phenotypic differences that arise from genetic or biological dispositions such as skin color and hair texture."[17] Geneticists identify five racial groups in the world: *sub-Saharan Africans; Caucasians,* which include Europeans, Middle Easterners, and those from the Indian continent; *Asians,* which include Chinese, Japanese, Filipinos, and peoples from Southeast Asia; *Native Americans;* and *Pacific Islanders.*

Scientists debate the usefulness of the concept of race because few genetic differences among races exist, and most of us carry genetic markers from more than one race. Even though race is a complex concept, other geneticists and epidemiologists want to maintain the distinction because fine-grained analysis of genetic markers does yield racial differences that can be useful in providing quality medical care.[18] Such racial designations are useful in seeking the origins of genetic diseases such as sickle-cell anemia, which is more common in African people, and in finding effective treatments for illnesses. For example, a medication not useful for Caucasians with congestive heart failure has been found to reduce fatal heart attacks by 43 percent in African Americans with congestive heart failure.

Ethnicity

The term *ethnicity* refers to "an individual's membership in a group sharing a common ancestral heritage based on nationality, language, and culture. Psychological attachment to the group is also a dimension of ethnicity, referred to as *ethnic identity.*"[19] Many ethnic groups exist within each racial group. For example, in the United States, Caucasians include people of German, Irish, Eastern European, or Italian descent. Native Americans include more than five hundred tribes, each with its own values. Asian Americans include Hmong, Filipino, Chinese, Japanese, and others. The Latina/o group includes people from many different countries in Central and South America as well as from the Caribbean Islands. Conversely, an ethnic group may have members in more than one racial group. For example, some Latinas/os fall into the Caucasian racial group, but others fall into the African racial group.

Many members of ethnic groups have experienced *prejudice,* defined as irrational, negative thoughts, feelings, and judgments about a person because of his or her race, religion, or nationality.[20] *Discrimination*—unfair treatment because of race, religion, or nationality—may accompany the prejudice but need not. Prejudice and discrimination against people because of their race is termed *racism.* Many other groups— religious groups as well as regional or social ones—also face prejudice and discrimination.

Immigrants to this country experience a process of *acculturation,* defined as "learning about a new culture and deciding what aspects are to be retained or sacrificed from the culture of origin."[21] Because culture is multidimensional, immigrants must attend to many new aspects of experience—language, food, customs, and social attitudes. Adaptation can be difficult.

Like the process of learning one's own culture, acculturation[22] occurs in stages. Initially, immigrants may feel relief at being here and may idolize the new culture; then, disillusionment may set in as the process brings frustrations and difficulties; and finally they come to a realistic acceptance of the new country with its positive and negative features. The host country also changes as it incorporates groups with new cultural traditions. When people retain aspects of and attachment to their cultures of origin and still feel comfortable with and attached to the customs of the new culture, they are described as having a *bicultural identity.* Today, members of ethnic groups usually have some form of bicultural identity or attachment to their culture of origin. Bicultural identity can occur when people of two different cultures marry and blend traditions. (See Box 3-1.) This stands in contrast to the past, when people coming to this country were expected to give up their previous customs and become assimilated into mainstream culture, becoming "like everyone else."

Social Status

Social status is perhaps the most powerful influence shaping parents' child-rearing behaviors. Belief in the American dream that ability and hard work determine success makes it hard to accept that social position can be such a force in children's experiences growing up, but several studies suggest this is so. Researchers who compared the home environments of four ethnic groups—European Americans, African Americans, Latinas/os, and Asian Americans—found that, although ethnic differences influenced what parents did, lack of resources overshadowed ethnic differences in the homes; parents of poor children provided fewer books, musical instruments, and lessons but also gave less attention and physical affection. Of the 124 items describing the homes and parenting, 88 percent were affected by poverty status, and only fifteen items (12 percent) were unaffected. The effects of few resources were similar across all ethnic groups.[23]

Annette Lareau, who intensively studied a small sample of European and African American families who differed in social status as well as ethnic background, also found that social class had a stronger influence than ethnic background on the lives of the nine- and ten-year-old children she studied. We discuss this study in greater detail in a later section, but here we highlight her conclusion that, although all individuals have both pleasures and difficulties in life, "Class position matters, every step of the way."[24]

Box 3-1
BLENDING PARENTING STYLES*

Marriage was not in Steve's plans when he met JoJo at his only friend's wedding. Steve had had a lonely time growing up in his family, and he had decided that marriage and family were not for him. His parents had married quickly after his mother became pregnant with his older brother but separated shortly after Steve's birth. His father died when Steve was nine, so Steve did not know him.

His mother had two more unsuccessful marriages and, as a single parent, moved a great deal, following her family's tradition of not laying down roots. In one school year, Steve moved three times. His mother did not believe in spending money on baby-sitters, so in the summer she would drop Steve off at the movies while she worked, and he would watch the same movie three or four times.

As a teen, Steve saved money and bought a car, and at sixteen he traveled through the Southwest by himself. He chose to go to college where he and his mother lived; he earned a degree and got a management job at K-Mart. He lived alone in his home, which had a pool, and he had only one college friend, whose wedding he attended. Steve was not close to his mother, but he talked with her on the phone about four times a year. His brother, who had become involved with drugs, died in a motorcycle accident.

In contrast, JoJo came from a large Filipino family in Chicago. She had fifty-two first cousins and hundreds of relatives around the world. As the oldest daughter, she was very attached to her extended family and its traditions.

Steve felt immediately comfortable with JoJo, and she with him. After a brief courtship, the two decided to get married. JoJo had one condition: that he first meet her family. She wanted their opinion of him because in past relationships she had failed to detect difficulties that her family sensed from the beginning.

Steve agreed, and when he changed planes on his way to Chicago, relatives appeared to guide him from one plane to the next. While clearly sizing him up as a potential relative, they were warm and accepting and telephoned ahead to Chicago with the news that he seemed a fine person. All the relatives in Chicago liked him—he was educated, had a good job, was kind and open, and he loved JoJo. They welcomed him with open arms even though he was not Filipino, and Steve responded to their genuine expressions of caring.

The priest who counseled them before marriage warned Steve, "You are not just marrying JoJo, son. You are marrying this family. They will become *your* family. They will be in your life, in your business, help raise your children, and expect you to care for them when they're in need" (p. 86).

Steve accepted the family. He loved them and felt they had saved him. "I've learned so much from them. They've given me an impression of what family can be. . . . I wish I'd had these ideas in my background. . . . What we have, as a family—despite the problems and rough patches—it's paradise for me. I consider this paradise. . . . They *care*. They genuinely care about each other. So when I walk in a room, they *light up*. They burst out of their chairs, their faces beam, they are enthusiastic. I have never had that in my family" (p. 88).

Box 3-1

When their daughter was born, JoJo's parents cared for her while JoJo worked, and a special bond formed between grandfather and granddaughter. Steve never worried about what would happen to the family if anything happened to him, as it had to Steve's own father. The extended family would step in and care for JoJo and their daughter.

Just as JoJo helped Steve grow, Steve helped JoJo grow by helping her set limits with her family. In the past, she had always done what they wished—going to Stanford University to study medicine, the field her father entered, even though she was more interested in music. She left college without finding direction in work, became a clerk in a store, and had not found work she liked.

When her parents baby-sat their daughter, Aubrey, JoJo observed that her parents were very indulgent and that Aubrey was becoming a spoiled princess. When they disciplined Aubrey, they used physical punishment. JoJo tried to teach them the things she and Steve had learned in parenting classes, but no matter what was said, they insisted on doing it their way.

Finally, Steve stepped in and told his in-laws that they could not visit and be with them until they were willing to follow his and JoJo's rules of child rearing. JoJo was grateful for his firm insistence. Although the families did not speak for a few months, JoJo and her family were there immediately when her father had a heart attack, and the relationships between the families resumed. Steve had asked the parents to telephone before they came to visit, and they followed that rule.

Both Steve and JoJo felt that their differences strengthened their family. Steve's experience in a family that stressed independence, self-reliance, and choice enabled him to demonstrate how to make choices and set boundaries. JoJo's warm and loving expressiveness and her commitment to family life provided a bedrock of security for the family. In speaking about their differences as strength, JoJo said, "We've never been able to fall into a pattern, never had a chance to fall asleep at the wheel. Our contrasts have made us conscious, made us pay attention" (p. 96).

As more and more families blend different ethnic and racial groups (in 2000, one-third of Latina/o and Asian American marriages were interracial), combining parenting styles from the families of origins will become more and more common. Steve and JoJo model how blending parenting styles creates a stronger family.

*From: Po Bronson, *Why Do I Love These People? Honest and Amazing Stories of Real Families* (New York: Random House, 2005), pp. 79–97.

Religions

Religions are are not discussed in detail here because they are so numerous in this country, but it is important to note that religious groups form cultures that provide niches for development and prescribe ways of life—no alcohol, no caffeine, prayers several times a day—that parents pass on to children.

Other Cultural Influences

Geographical areas with distinct cultures are found in areas of the North, South, East, and West. Rural and urban areas of residence also exert cultural influences.

CULTURAL MODELS OF PARENT-CHILD RELATIONSHIPS

Patricia Greenfield and Lalita Suzuki have surveyed differences among many ethnic groups and describe two cultural models—the independent and the interdependent—that provide a framework for organizing and understanding what parents think matters and what they do with children.[25] Table 3-1 outlines these two

■ **TABLE 3-1**
  CONTRASTING CULTURAL MODELS OF PARENT-CHILD RELATIONS

	Developmental Goals	
	Independence	**Interdependence**
Developmental trajectory	From dependent to independent self	From asocial to socially responsible self
Children's relations to parents	Personal choice concerning relationship to parents	Obligations to parents
Communication	Verbal emphasis	Nonverbal emphasis (empathy, observation, participation)
	Autonomous self-expression by child	Child comprehension, mother speaks for child
	Frequent parental questions to child	Frequent parental directives to child
	Frequent praise	Infrequent praise
	Child negotiation	Harmony, respect, obedience
Parenting style	Authoritative: controlling, demanding, warm, rational	Rigorous and responsible teaching, high involvement, physical closeness
Parents helping children	A matter of personal choice except under extreme need	A moral obligation under all circumstances

From Patricia M. Greenfield and Lalita K. Suzuki, "Culture and Human Development: Implications for Parenting, Education, Pediatrics, and Mental Health," in *Handbook of Child Psychology,* 5th ed., ed. William Damon, vol. 4: *Child Psychology in Practice,* ed. Irving E. Sigel and K. Ann Renninger (New York: Wiley, 1998), 1085. Reprinted by permission of John Wiley & Sons, Inc.

models, which apply to many different cultural and social groups rather than to any particular ethnic group.

In the independent model, parents help children become self-sustaining, productive adults who enter into relationships with other adults by choice. The child receives nurturance to develop autonomy, competence, and a freely chosen identity that in adulthood merges with others outside the family.

In the interdependent model, parents help children grow into socially responsible adults who take their place in a strong network of social relationships, often within the family, that place obligations on the adult. Parents indulge the young child, but as children grow older, they are expected to internalize and respect the rules of parents and other authorities. Parents and relatives are respected and obeyed, and family and group needs matter more than individual ones.

As we noted earlier, parents introduce children to cultural values at home, and children take these qualities with them into the larger society.[26] Children more easily adapt to the larger culture when the home culture is the same as or similar to that of the larger society.

THE CULTURAL INFLUENCES OF MAJOR ETHNIC GROUPS

We now focus our attention on six main ethnic groups, roughly in order of their arrival here: Native Americans, European Americans, African Americans, Latinas/os,

Children of different ethnic groups learn what is distinctive about their group and form a bicultural sense of identity that includes their ethnic group membership.

Asian Americans, and Middle Eastern Americans.[27] Each of these groups contains subgroups. Native Americans include representatives of over 500 tribes. European Americans come from all over Europe. The Latina/o group includes individuals from Central and South America as well as those from the Caribbean Islands. Asian Americans include people from a broad geographic area that ranges from Korea and Japan in the north to India, Pakistan, and the Philippine Islands in the south. Middle Eastern Americans include, among others, people from Lebanon, Syria, Egypt, Iraq, Iran, Jordan, Palestine, Afghanistan, Saudi Arabia, and Kuwait. Within each subgroup, diversity also exists among individuals because of social status, religious views, and personal experiences. Thus, any broad social trends we talk about will not apply to every person in the group or every subgroup.

Our knowledge of socialization in different ethnic groups is limited, for the reasons listed in Table 3-2. While current research tries to address these problems, we still have much to learn about the paths of development within these groups.

For each group, we shall look at current information about the group, a brief historical perspective, general values, contemporary families, and the socialization of children in the family. Table 3-3 presents demographic information on each group discussed.

■ **TABLE 3-2**
REASONS FOR LIMITED KNOWLEDGE OF CHILDREN'S SOCIALIZATION IN DIFFERENT ETHNIC GROUPS*

1. Only recently have social scientists sought out research subjects other than the readily available, European American, middle-class samples so frequently studied in the past.

2. When members of different ethnic groups have been included, study members are often children at risk because of a problem, and therefore results may not apply to the wide range of children in that ethnic group.

3. Most studies have compared children in a particular ethnic group with European American children and have focused on the ways they are different from European Americans. Few studies have examined the psychological paths of development of children within a particular ethnic group, looking for factors that influence differences among subgroups of the same ethnic group.

4. Few studies involve longitudinal samples of children of different ethnic groups, and such studies as there are rarely include in-home observations of family interactions with parents, which would yield the best information.

*The first three points are from Cynthia Garcia Coll and Lee M. Pachter, "Ethnic and Minority Parenting," in *Handbook of Parenting*, 2nd ed., ed. Marc H. Bornstein, vol. 4, *Social Conditions and Applied Parenting* (Mahwah, NJ: Erlbaum, 2002), 1–20; fourth point is from Vonnie C. McLoyd et al., "Marital Processes and Parental Socialization in Families of Color: A Decade Review of Research," *Journal of Marriage and Family* 62 (2000): 1070–1093.

■ **T A B L E 3-3**
DEMOGRAPHIC CHARACTERISTICS OF SIX ETHNIC GROUPS*

	Total Population	Native Americans	Whites† (European Americans)	African Americans	Latinas/os	Asian Americans	Middle Eastern Americans‡
Percentage of Total Population: 2004	—	1%	80%	13%	14%	4%	1%
Median Age: 2004	36	29	37.5	31	27	34	33
Education of Population over Age 25: 2003							
High School Graduate	84%	76%	86%	79%	59%	85%	84%
College Degree or Higher	27%	14%	28%	17%	12%	48%	41%
Median Household Income: 2003	$52,273	$34,641	$55,938	$34,608	$35,600	$63,883	$52,000§
Families below Poverty Level: 2003	9.8%	20.4%	7.3%	21.9%	20.1%	9.2%	17%
Children under 18 Living: 2004							
in Two-Parent Family	68%	—	74%	35%	65%	81%	85%
in Female-Headed Household	23%	—	18%	50%	25%	11%	8%
in Male-Headed Household	5%	—	4%	6%	5%	7%	7%
with Neither Parent	4%	—	3%	9%	5%	—	—
Average Number of Children per Household: 2004							
Married Couple	1.89	—	1.88	1.90	2.09	1.54	—
Female-Headed Household	1.72	—	1.59	1.90	2.00	1.41	—
Male-Headed Household	1.53	—	—	—	—	—	—
Percentage of Children Born 2002							
to Teen Mothers	11%	18%	10%	18%	15%	4%	—
to Single Mothers	34%	60%	28%	68%	44%	15%	—

*Despite the fact that the years are sometimes different, all statistics, unless otherwise noted, are from *Statistical Abstract of the United States: 2006*, 125th ed. (Washington, D.C.: U.S. Government Printing Office, 2005). Beginning in 2003, respondents could choose more than one race. The data are based on those persons who selected one race. Latinas/os can be of more than one race.
†Census category is "white"; not all are European Americans.
‡Data for Middle Eastern Americans come from Census 2000 Special Report. Augusta Brittingham and G. Patricia de la Cruz, "We the People of Arab Ancestry in the United States," U.S. Census Bureau, March 2005. Available on www.aaiusa.com.
§Income is based on data from 1999; income for other groups is based on data from 2003.

Native American Families

In 2004, approximately 2.8 million Native Americans lived in the United States—a 30 percent increase since 1990, when they numbered 2 million. They come from more than 500 tribes speaking more than a hundred languages. Approximately 60 percent live in urban settings; the remainder live near or on reservations.[28]

Historical Perspective Influencing the Group's View of Society   Native American history is distinctive because this group has experienced unique hardship as a minority culture. They have been forcibly removed from their land. At times they have been confined to reservations. Their children have been taken off to boarding schools, in which their language and cultural traditions were forbidden. Such mistreatment has stopped, but only fairly recently.

Although poorly treated, Native Americans have made notable contributions to mainstream American culture. The eminent historian Samuel Eliot Morison wrote in 1965,

> These natives first welcomed the Europeans, then fought them, and finally were subjugated by them. They gave the Europeans some of the world's most valuable agricultural products—maize, tobacco, the potato, cassava, and chocolate. They taught their conquerors hundreds of skills and so frequently mated with them that millions of people in the United States, Canada, Mexico, Central and South America have Indian blood in their veins.[29]

He concluded,

> In peace as in war the Indians have had a profound effect on later comers to America. Our culture has been enriched by their contribution. Our character is *very* different from what it would have been if this continent had been uninhabited when the Europeans arrived.[30]

To cite one example of their contribution, the Pennsylvania Iroquois' tribal constitution served as the model for the Constitution of the United States. Benjamin Franklin printed the tribal constitution with its protections for free speech and expression and its provision for impeachment of corrupt leaders along with other protective clauses. Franklin brought the treaty to the attention of colonial delegates when they met to write the Articles of Confederation, the forerunner of the Constitution. In 1987, the U.S. Senate passed "a resolution stating that the U.S. Constitution had been modeled on American Indian democracy."[31]

Native American child rearing, described in early settlers' accounts, meets many of the criteria of effective parenting in our times.[32] Native Americans were child centered. European settlers were surprised at how affectionate and caring they were with infants and young children. Native Americans nursed children for about two years and kept children physically close to them. When children reached age three and were mobile, parents gave them great freedom to move about and explore the world with only minimal restriction for safety reasons. Little or no physical punishment for children existed. Adults guided and supervised children, teaching them needed skills. Boys were reared to be hunters and warriors; girls, to be planters, gatherers, and nurturers of children. Both sexes had to be physically strong, hardy, and knowledgeable in survival skills. Parents encouraged children to develop independence, self-control, and stoicism. They also taught children to be grateful to a benevolent Spirit for giving them life and purpose. Although the government attempted to eliminate traditional Indian culture and language, a small number of Indian tribes, such as the Hopi, managed to maintain their traditions.[33]

Between 1890 and 1920, the government established boarding schools some distance from the reservations and forced Native American children to attend them for twelve years. Family members were not permitted to visit children during the school year, which dramatically reduced parental influence and socialization. Between 1920 and the 1970s, children usually attended these schools but were not forced to do so. Not having had models of parenting behavior for much of their childhood years, many Native Americans found rearing children a great challenge.

General Values   Themes of traditional Native American values include (1) strong identification with the social group and with the natural environment in which one lives, with little sense of self apart from the group and nature; (2) cooperation with the group to share the burdens of work; (3) focus on the present moment; (4) respect for the wisdom of the older generation; and (5) strong spiritual beliefs.[34] Many Native Americans have become Christians and see little contradiction in also continuing to uphold the spiritual values of their heritage.

Contemporary Families   The Native American population of 2.8 million is a young one, with 50 percent under the age of twenty-nine, in comparison with a median age of thirty-seven for the European American population. They have lower rates of high school and college graduation, but the majority do graduate.[35] See Table 3-3 for specific figures.

Current statistics indicate that Native American families face many challenges (see Table 3-3). Their median family income falls below that of European Americans and Asian Americans but is about the same as that of African Americans or Latinas/os. They have high rates of poverty, fewer children living in two-parent families, and a high rate of babies born to unmarried mothers. They also tend to have a higher rate of alcohol abuse, though the majority of Native Americans are not substance abusers.[36]

Parenting Children   We have less information about the socialization of children in this group than for children in the other groups because children make up a much smaller percentage of the Native American population. We do know, however, that Native Americans have retained their traditions of valuing children, keeping them close in the early years and giving them more independence as they grow older.

They have also continued the tradition of minimizing gender differences in socialization and respecting the contributions of both boys and girls. Researchers Walter Karamoto and Tamara Cheshire state, "Balance is an important factor in the socialization of boys and girls. The need to balance masculine and feminine characteristics, such as developing compassion in boys and strength in girls, is seen as vital to personal wholeness."[37] In tribal life, boys produce and play a creative role. Women are nurturers but are also encouraged to be leaders. Thus, an individual can embody many positive traits, as can be seen in this description of Wilma Mankiller, the former principal chief of the Cherokee Nation: "She is all those converged together. Like all of us can be. Warrior, peacemaker, mother, father, Beloved woman, the white and the red merged together, to take our story back."[38]

Native Americans also value creativity in children, including them in ceremonial traditions as well as music, dance, and art. Some children grow up to become writers, filmmakers, and artists. Many take an active part in preserving the languages and tribal traditions as they become adults. While maintaining traditions, Native Americans also feel the pressures of contemporary life. Often, both parents must work, but sometimes extended family lives in the home and can help care for the children. There appears to be a higher rate of child abuse in this group, perhaps because many grandparents spent years away from their parents in boarding schools and have not had models of parenting to rely on and pass on to children.[39] Community support has been important when parents cannot care for their children.

Americans of European Descent

The white population constitutes about 80 percent of the population of 293 million, but not all are European Americans; some are Latinas/os. Those who are European American trace their origins primarily to northern and western Europe, with Germany, Ireland, England, Italy, France, Poland, and Scotland providing the bulk of the immigrants to this country.[40]

Historical Perspective Influencing This Group's Views of Society   Like other groups, European Americans came to this country for many different reasons—to gain political and religious freedom, to escape persecution, and to seek a better way of life. Early settlers included indentured servants, who earned their passage and freedom by working for a predetermined period, and wealthy landowners with large grants of land. Within this group, enormous variation exists in cultural traditions, depending on when they came to this country and from what area of Europe. When we speak of European Americans, we frequently think of immigrants from northern Europe such as the English and the Scandinavians, who espouse the independent model of parenting, but millions of immigrants came from southern and eastern Europe with a model of parenting much more like the interdependent model.

General Values   We see the major values of European Americans in the American mothers described earlier in the chapter and in the independent model of culture. This culture emphasizes the importance of the individual, of the independent self, and of striving and attaining self-generated goals.

Contemporary Families   With a median age of thirty-seven, European Americans are the oldest population of all ethnic groups. They are an advantaged group, with high levels of education and income (see Table 3-3).

Families are generally stable. Seventy-four percent of children live in two-parent families, 18 percent in mother-headed families, 4 percent in father-headed families, and 3 percent live with neither parent. Twenty-eight percent of children are born to single mothers and 10 percent to teen mothers.

Parenting Children   Until 1990, most of what was known about children's socialization in the United States was based on middle-class European American families, so here is a brief summary.[41] As we saw in the study comparing U.S. mothers with Italian mothers, European American parents emphasize giving children encouragement and freedom to explore and learn about the environment and their world. Parents rely on verbal interactions with children to direct and guide behavior. The parents' role is to provide opportunities and support for growth, but children are expected to draw on their own abilities to improve and advance. This group gives less emphasis than other cultures on the active teaching of social skills and on emotional regulation in the family and with others.

Americans of African Descent

African Americans make up 13 percent of the U.S. population and, until the 2000 Census, were the second largest ethnic group in the United States. Now, they are third, as Latinas/os make up 14 percent of the population.

Historical Perspective Influencing This Group's View of Society   Most African Americans are descendants of slaves brought to this country against their will, indirectly via the West Indies or directly from West Africa, where family patterns differed from those of Europeans.[42] In comparison to European American families, which were nuclear families organized around marital ties, West African families were organized on the basis of kinship ties, and a husband and wife usually joined a compound of extended family members in either the bride's or groom's family.[43] There were also polygamous marriages, in which a husband and his wife or wives and relatives lived together. In African families, decisions were made by the head of the family and the rest of the male members of that generation. All the adults felt responsible for all the children, who lived together as brothers and sisters rather than as half-siblings or as cousins. Loosely supervised by the adults, the older children were often responsible for the care of younger children.

When they came to this country, African Americans brought this form of family life with them. The institution of slavery shaped African American families in this country. Slaves were encouraged to marry formally or informally and to have children, because children meant capital to the owner.[44] A small percentage of children were born out of wedlock, usually fathered by the owners. Slavery disrupted family life. Mothers often left their infants shortly after birth to work full-time. Other relatives and older siblings cared for the children. A theme of mutual longing of mother and infant prevailed in African American songs. The sale of one or more family members further destroyed the fabric of family life. African Americans valued marriage, as evidenced by their rushing to have their marriages officially registered in counties where they lived after the Civil War.[45] Many searched for family members who had been sold during slavery, in the hope of reuniting the family.

Immediately after the Civil War, when laws and the military enforced equal rights for African Americans, African Americans made gains in education and in financial and political power. These gains were short-lived, however, as segregation laws (often termed *Jim Crow laws*) were passed, enacted, and declared constitutional in the 1890s; such laws restricted where African Americans could live, go to school, eat, and shop.

Despite the fact that they had contributed to the country by fighting in all its major wars and had remained loyal to the country even when not given equal rights, African Americans faced limitations in all areas of life.[46] For example, soldiers who fought in both World Wars came home to be treated as unequal citizens. Not until the 1950s and 1960s did the courts declare the segregation laws unconstitutional.

Not only did African Americans face legal restrictions, many lived in an atmosphere of terror. From the latter parts of the nineteenth century to well into the mid-twentieth century, people used vicious attacks and lynching to incite fear and helplessness in African Americans. From 1882 to 1968, 4,743 people were lynched in this country; 3,446 were African American.[47] For almost thirty years, the government left lynching unpunished; the first government prosecution of lynching took place in 1919.[48] Vicious killings continued, as in 1955, when the mutilated body of Emmett Till was found. Following that period, guns predominated in the murders of African Americans such as Martin Luther King, Jr., and Medgar Evers for their actions in the community.

Through the days of segregation, the Great Depression, World War II, and the years following, family life continued to be strong, and three-quarters of children continued to live in two-parent families until the 1960s.[49] At that time, rapid urbanization and the disappearance of stable, unskilled employment for men led to a drop in the marriage rate but not the birthrate. That led to the increase in the number of one-parent families headed by women. This trend, first seen in African American families, has occurred to a lesser degree in other ethnic groups.

General Values   Andrew Billingsley believes that the following West African family values have survived and have been incorporated in contemporary life: (1) the primary importance of blood ties over all others, including marital ties; (2) the reliance on extended families rather than nuclear families; (3) the great value placed on children; (4) the importance of and respect for elders; (5) flexibility in role behaviors; (6) emphasis on balancing the needs of the individual with the needs of the family or group; and (7) the importance of obligations to other family members.[50] Reviewing research, Ross Parke and Raymond Buriel describe additional African American values that promote close families: (1) living near other family members and seeing relatives frequently, (2) including relatives and nonrelatives in the extended family and having "fictive" kin or close family friends who are called *auntie, uncle,* or *cousin,* and (3) having numerous gatherings, parties, and celebrations for holidays and other special occasions.[51]

Contemporary Families   With a median age of thirty-one, African Americans on average are younger than European Americans and Asian Americans (see Table 3-3).

Although their level of education is not that different from that of European Americans, their median household income is the lowest of all ethnic groups, and they have the highest family poverty rate.

African American families face challenges in rearing children. Sixty-eight percent of babies are born to single mothers and 18 percent to teen mothers. African American children are more likely to live in families headed by single parents than are children in other ethnic groups, and these families experience more financial pressures and the stresses that follow from that. Fifty percent of children live in single families headed by women, 35 percent in two-parent families, 9 percent with neither parent, and 6 percent in families headed by men. Still, 44 percent of children live in two-parent families.

Parenting Children   African American mothers are younger, have more children, and have them closer together, compared with European American mothers.[52] These patterns of childbearing may account for the fact that African American parents appear to make demands on children to be responsible and independent at an earlier age.

Although their family culture is warm and supportive, research suggests that African Americans may be harsh and parent centered in their approach to child rearing. Vonnie McLoyd writes, "Evidence from a number of studies based on observations, self-reports, and responses to vignettes suggests that black parents are more severe, punitive, and power assertive in the discipline of their children than white parents of similar socioeconomic status."[53] Though strict, they are not cold and rejecting in disciplining children. They, like parents in all other ethnic groups, make clear distinctions between punishment and physical abuse, and their forms of discipline do not result in higher rates of child abuse in the African American community when social class is controlled.[54]

Several factors may account for the greater harshness. First, African American families face greater economic stress; economic difficulties, as we shall see later in this chapter, account for greater strain and conflicts in parenting. Second, African Americans are more likely to live in poor neighborhoods where there *is* greater violence, making it important for children to follow parents' rules unquestioningly. Third, African Americans need to follow community rules because harsh punishments in the community could follow if they do not.

This group values education highly, even though de jure (by law) and de facto (in fact) segregation have placed major obstacles in their path.[55] A recent book, Peter Irons's *Jim Crow's Children*, describes the continuing impact of segregation laws in producing unequal access to quality education for African Americans in this country.[56]

The military has proven an important institution for African Americans.[57] Desegregated in 1948, it has provided greater access to education and occupational advancement than has been available in civilian life. Although they are only about 13 percent of the population, African Americans represented nearly 30 percent of the armed services personnel in 1985. In 2000, they represented about 22 percent of all enlisted military personnel, and African American women represented 35 percent of women enlistees.[58] Education, equal opportunity for advancement, belonging,

INTERVIEW
with Sherrie

Sherrie is a forty-eight-year-old African American woman who, at age forty-four, obtained a Master of Social Work degree and is in the process of obtaining her license as a clinical social worker. As part of her job working with children and families in an outpatient psychiatric clinic, she leads a parent-group for parents of out-of-control teens. Following her divorce, she raised her son from the age of three; at age twenty-eight, he is now a journalist.

Having worked with parents of many cultures, what do you see as the distinctive features of African American culture?

Born of adversity, African Americans are resilient. We are not as formal as Anglo-Saxons. We are more like Mediterraneans. I think our culture is warm, rhythmic, sensual but not sexual. We have rich traditions that are holdovers from African culture. Our celebrations are rich. We can make a celebration out of anything. I knew my husband's family was very poor. When I went there for dinner, there was very little, but it was a celebration, and we were happy. You knew who you were, and you knew you were loved.

We are very connected to each other. We have fictive kin—anyone can be a relative. Sometimes people say, "half-brother" or "half-sister." They are brothers and sisters. I think there is respect for ancestors and elders. Always call elders "Mr." or "Mrs." No matter how old I got, I would never call them by their first name.

We are religious and call on God in a lot of ways. My great-grandparents prayed every day. Church was important. There was no question. Black people went to church. There was a tradition and you knew you came from somewhere. I was always at home or at church. It gave me a sense of blessed assurance you belong. Not only are you a part of a church community, but you are a child of God. The black church organized voting rights. Martin Luther King came out of the church.

My great-grandparents never talked about slavery or sharecropping. They seemed almost to be ashamed of it, but I thought the shame wasn't on them, but on the people who enslaved them.

We grew up, hard-working people. There was pride in working. I knew the plant where my great-grandparents were janitors. I thought it was so cool there. My grandmother was the custodian at the Mint. My mother worked at a hospital for the elderly. As long as you were honest, any work was good.

Are there parenting strategies specific to African American parents?

When you are in the dominant culture, you don't have to think about safety and the things you have to face because of your color. African Americans have to be careful in the world. I heard stories about the South, and a great-great-uncle disappeared. I had to help my son think about issues of safety without feeling afraid.

How did you do that?

I taught him to be respectful, polite, not to set himself up in a negative way. I taught him that backing down to preserve his safety was acceptable and fine, and if he wanted to challenge something, he had to be prepared to pay a price. The world would look at him differently because he was a black male; he had to be aware of what it means to be black. There is a social reality, there is racism, but I didn't want him to be squelched. I wanted him to have dreams, to be creative. I never discouraged any of his dreams.

I felt the world did not have many expectations for a black boy. If someone asked him if he were going to grow up and be football player, I taught him to say, "I'm going to be a nuclear physicist." I gave him expectations. I would drive down Sacramento Street and show him the young men standing around on the street corner. I would ask him, "What are they doing?" He'd say, "Hanging out." I would drive up to the hills and show him the beautiful houses and ask him, "Do you want to live here?" He'd say, "Oh, yes." I'd tell him, "Well, if you hang out, you won't ever be able to live here."

In addition to teaching him about safety, I also had to help him when someone called him a name like "Nigger."

How did you do that?

I never felt there was any shame in slavery. If someone called him "Nigger," that was on them. My mom taught me, and I taught him, if someone called him "Nigger," "Shame on them. So, that's who you are. You are prejudiced." We walked away, and we didn't care.

People said, "Oh, Sherrie, you did such an excellent job with Jioni," but I had a lot of community support. None of my immediate friends had kids, so I enlisted people to help me. His godfather was my high school counselor. He bought his school clothes. I could call him and say, "Come and get him or you'll read about us in the newspaper." I had another friend at work who bought him his first baseball mitt, took him fishing and got him his first fishing pole. He also took him skiing.

The husband of my babysitter told me he was so active, a bundle of energy—get him into baseball. I got him into Little League. People liked having him around. He was curious. He had good manners, and he helped out. He went to visit the children of one of my coworkers, and she said, "How do you get him to eat his vegetables?" He cleared the table and her kids didn't do anything.

People would give me advice. When he was defiant, my boyfriend would say, "Sherrie, give him a task and leave him alone." I wanted him to do it on my time. I learned from professionals to tell him, "You do this, and then, you will get that." We went to counseling when he was nine, because I didn't like the way I was yelling and screaming. The counselor said, "Mom, you're the boss." I had never set a bedtime. He was my friend, and we were both night people so we stayed up and read. I learned to set consistent limits.

It was the hardest job I ever did, but I never felt I did it alone. He was a child of the community.

and safety are reasons cited for joining. One Chicago recruit described more fear on the streets of Chicago than in the Marines. "Being over in Baghdad, you've got a thousand people 100 percent behind you. Around here, who says you can't be going to McDonald's and that's it? Over there, you're part of everybody, you're with your friends and family, you're still safe."[59]

Churches are very important in the socialization of African American children. Between two-thirds and three-quarters of African Americans report that they belong to a church.[60] The church was a place of freedom and self-direction during slavery, and it has remained a source of inspiration, help, and reform to improve the lives of all African Americans. For example, it served as the home of the civil rights movement in the 1960s. A recent example of the church's prosocial activity is an organization of men in Oakland, California, where the murder rate greatly increased in 2002, with about 70 percent of victims being young African American men. Black Men First is made up of African American men from churches and mosques who go into high-crime areas to engage young men involved in drugs and crime and present them with another way of life.[61] Billingsley quotes C. Eric Lincoln's description of the African American church as "the mother of our culture, the champion of our freedom, and the hallmark of our civilization."[62]

Latina/o Families

Latinos and Latinas, defined as U.S. citizens of Latin American descent, numbered forty-one million in the 2004 census and are the second largest ethnic group, composing 14 percent of the population. About 58 percent of this group come from Mexico, 9 percent from Puerto Rico, 4 percent from Cuba, and 28 percent from all the other countries in Central and South America and the Caribbean Islands.[63]

Historical Perspective Influencing This Group's Views of Society   Many Latinas/os are born of the Spanish conquerors and the Native Americans who were already here. Mothers were Native Americans and relied on the teachings of that culture in rearing their children.[64]

Latinas/os were on this continent before the European Americans, but they were part of the Spanish empire that existed in St. Augustine, Florida, and extended across the southwest part of the United States.[65] Latinas/os in Texas and New Mexico became citizens of this country after those territories became part of the United States following the Mexican War in 1848. Waves of immigrants came from other countries and islands, particularly after the lessening of restrictions in 1965. Immigrants from Cuba and other Latin countries have come to escape political persecution, and some anticipate returning to their countries when there is greater freedom. Many immigrants, especially those from Mexico and other countries that are geographically close, retain strong ties to family members in their countries of origin, visit there frequently, and maintain strong attachment to their original cultures.

General Values   Because Latinas/os come from many countries, the group as a whole is quite varied. Nonetheless, they share many values. First, they value attachment to the family and group.[66] Like Native Americans, Latinas/os identify themselves with the family and see it as an extension of themselves. They feel obligated to help other family members, and they seek support, advice, and help from family members. They often live in extended family systems, with relatives coming to live for varying lengths of time. The extended family is a problem-solving unit that helps all members deal with the stresses of everyday life. Research suggests that the strong family support has positive benefits—more infants are breast-fed, and children receive more care from relatives.

Second, Latinas/os emphasize socially sensitive, considerate relationships with others. Children are expected to have a "proper demeanor" with others—courteous, mannerly behavior that reflects concern for others' feelings. Competitiveness may be discouraged if it interferes with positive feelings within the group. Third, respect for elders and authority is important.[67] Grandparents, for example, are looked up to and serve as models for younger children and adults. Even when children are grown and have families of their own, they must respect their parents and grandparents.

Fourth, more than 80 percent of Latina/o families are Roman Catholic, and their religion structures many rituals and family activities. According to researchers Parke and Buriel, "The cultural emphasis on respect, group harmony, and coopera-tion in interpersonal relations is in line with the religious themes of peace, commu-nity, and self-denial."[68]

Contemporary Families   Latina/o families are younger and larger than those of other groups. A large number of Latinos and Latinas were not born in this country (38 percent, by one estimate), and many have lacked educational opportunities, perhaps explaining the lower level of educational attainment in the Latina/o group.[69] Despite the lower educational level, their income is slightly greater than that of African Americans who, as a group, have more education. Like Native Americans and African Americans, Latinas/os face challenges in rearing children. A high percentage of children are born to teen and single mothers, and a large number live in single-parent families who have less income.

Parenting Children   Research comparing Latina/o families to European American families reveals many of the same differences that the European American–Italian comparison did. Comparisons of middle-class and working-class European American and Puerto Rican mothers of toddlers show that both groups of mothers want their toddlers to develop into loving, self-controlled individuals, but the groups differ in culturally significant ways.[70] European American mothers want children to become independent, self-confident, happy children who explore the world. Puerto Rican mothers want children to be quiet, attentive, and respectful of others' needs.

In these studies, European Americans stress individualism, and Puerto Ricans stress interdependent behaviors. These goals, then, shaped their ways of relating to their toddlers in day-to-day interactions. Both groups of mothers showed equal physical or verbal affection with children, except that Puerto Rican mothers were more affectionate during teaching tasks. Puerto Rican mothers were more likely to feed toddlers and more likely to structure their activities and to give directions for play than were European American mothers. In teaching activities, Puerto Rican mothers took an active role and were more likely than European American mothers to signal the child's attention, give commands, and give verbal affection in teaching a task. When toddlers were playing freely, Puerto Rican mothers continued to be active and gave more commands than did European American mothers. European American mothers were more likely than Puerto Rican mothers to encourage children to feed themselves and to play while mothers watched, and European American mothers spent more time teaching toddlers to learn tasks such as coloring and playing with blocks. They more often gave suggestions, rather than directions like the Puerto Rican mothers did.

Latina/o parents continue to be active and controlling as children grow older. Children absorb their parents' values. As adolescents, for example, Mexican American teens are more likely than European American teens to feel obligated to respect, help, and support their families.[71] Further, adolescents who have this value feel closer to their parents and siblings and have somewhat higher educational aspirations. Differences were large and consistent across socioeconomic groups within the ethnic group.

Like African American parents, Latina/o parents place a great emphasis on education and want their children to succeed.[72] Exactly why Latina/o children have performed less well, in the sense of lower rates of high school and college graduation, is not clear. Explanations fall into two main categories: (1) those that point to differences in the culture or in parenting beliefs and methods, and (2) those that point to poor schools, poor preparation, and few financial resources for college.

A recent survey from the Pew Hispanic Center indicates that finances are the main reason Latina/o students do not finish college.[73] Although poor preparation plays a role, Richard Frey, the survey's author, stated that lack of money is the main obstacle to college graduation. Latina/o students enroll in college, usually two-year colleges first, in higher numbers than do European American students, but they tend not to complete the four-year degree. Latinas/os receive less financial aid than European American students. Because they are older students and tend to have more obligations for family support, they can not borrow the large sums that the average student incurs by graduation—$17,000 in loans and $3,000 in credit card debt. The report concludes that increased financial aid for students already enrolled in college is an efficient way to boost the percentage of Latina/o college graduates. This problem affects not only the Latina/o population but society as a whole. "Over the next twenty-five years, the report said, the white working-age population will shrink by five million as baby boomers retire, while the Latina/o working-age population swells by eighteen million. These numbers make improved education of Latinas/os vitally important for the nation's workforce."[74]

Americans of Asian Descent

Asian Americans made up 4 percent of the population in the 2004 Census. They trace their origins to more than twenty-eight different countries in Asia.[75] In this brief space, we can discuss only broad trends among the national groups, which may have their own specific emphases. In addition, diversity exists within groups, depending on how many years the family has been in this country.

Historical Perspective Influencing This Group's View of Society   Asian Americans trace their attitudes toward children to Confucian and Buddhist philosophies that transcend national borders.[76] Young children are considered to be closely attached to the spiritual world because of their greater likelihood of mortality. They are regarded as pure, innocent, and good. These beliefs encourage parents to revere and protect their young. In this culture, just as plants require physical care in the form of watering and fertilizing as well as shaping in the form of pruning and directing growth, so children require physical care and direction.

The Chinese began coming to this country in the 1840s but were later restricted. The Philippine Islands became a commonwealth of the United States in 1898 and remained so until it became an independent republic following World War II. It has contributed a large number of immigrants and continues to do so.[77]

Japanese Americans began to come to Hawaii and to this country around the turn of the twentieth century because of economic conditions in Japan. The 1924 Immigration Act ended their immigration until after World War II. Japanese Americans prospered; by 1941, 40,000 Japanese adults lived on the West Coast with their 70,000 American-born children. At the beginning of World War II, most of these individuals were taken from their homes and sent to relocation camps in desert and mountain areas in the western states until the end of the war because of security concerns. Nonetheless, some Japanese Americans served with great distinction in the U.S. military. In the 1970s, the government gave compensation to each Japanese American who was incarcerated during World War II.[78]

Since the immigration laws changed in 1965, many immigrants have come from Asia, especially Southeast Asia. These people have often come to escape persecution at home or to find better economic prospects here. The most numerous subgroups in the 2000 Census were Chinese Americans, Filipino Americans, Asian Indians, Vietnamese Americans, and Korean Americans.[79]

General Values   Like many other groups, Asian Americans stress the interdependence of family members. The family is the focus of life; the self exists and is defined in relation to other family members, who are obligated to be close and supportive. Well-functioning adults feel required to discuss major decisions with other family members and get their support before proceeding. Outside the family, one has obligations to country and to work.[80]

Control is a second important value.[81] Families are organized with fathers as the figures in control and mothers subordinate to them. Mothers, however, take complete charge of children, and so from a child's point of view, mothers appear to be authorities as well. Children are obligated to respect and obey these authoritative figures.

Contemporary Families   Asian Americans exceed all other groups in educational attainment and income. Families are more stable, with more children in two-parent families and far fewer children born to teen and single mothers, compared with any other group.

Parenting Children   Asian cultures believe that infants and toddlers cannot reason, which makes parents totally responsible for their well-being.[82] The high level of care parents provide and their willingness to put the child's needs above their own reflect the responsibilities they feel toward children. They indulge young children and do all within their power to please them.

Asian American families emphasize family connectedness. Physical closeness is a way of promoting the infant's feeling of connection with family members. Mothers speak gently to young children and describe their own and others' feelings so infants can learn to empathize with others. Although children are often indulged in the early years, when they reach five or six they are expected to meet the demanding standards of parents and outside authorities.[83] Although Asian Americans value independence, they interpret the concept differently from European Americans, who define independence as freely expressing one's feelings and reactions and making decisions on one's own. Asian Americans view independence as expressed within the family. Children reflect their independence by becoming more able to meet family expectations. Asian American parents exert more control than European American parents, but it is not the cold, authoritarian control often seen in European American families.[84] Rather, it is control in the sense of teaching and governing the child in order to promote safety and growth. Parents monitor children closely and guide behavior in approved directions. When control *is* defined as governing the child, research finds no negative effects. Control defined as domination, as in the European American community, affects children more negatively.

Shaming has also been considered part of many Asian cultures. Children's attention is drawn to how their behavior affects and is regarded by others. The possible negative response from others then shapes the child's behavior. A form of teaching related to shaming is termed *opportunity education*. A parent points out another child's behavior, along with its positive or negative consequences, as an example that the child should copy or avoid, depending on the circumstances.

Asian Americans value education, and parents sometimes value themselves in terms of how well their children do in school and how much education they get.[85] Parents tend to see achievement as the result of the child's intense and prolonged effort rather than the result of innate ability. They expect children to work hard; as parents, they provide resources and tutoring as needed. As children go on in school, Asian American parents do not get as highly involved in volunteer activities as some other groups of parents do. Although achievement is important, Asian American parents also value the love of learning.

We have spoken of Asian Americans as a group, but a great deal of diversity exists among them. A study comparing the parenting of Filipino American, Japanese American, and European American mothers around eating behaviors highlights differences among these groups.[86] Mothers in each group defined slightly different goals in parenting. European American mothers wanted children to become happy, independent, creative adults. Japanese American mothers wanted children to develop into achieving adults who could manage life's demands while maintaining well-ordered lives that included close contact with families. Filipino American mothers had a slightly different emphasis. They wanted children to develop into responsible citizens who were well-mannered and respectful of authority.

The groups used slightly different ways to shape their children's mealtime behaviors. Both Japanese American and Filipino American mothers were more child centered in their interventions than European American mothers. Japanese American mothers, and fathers when they participated, focused all their attention on the toddler, engaging and feeding the child, and permitting the child to stop whenever full. Filipino American mothers were also child centered, but they kept babies on their laps during family mealtimes and spoon-fed children until they ate all that the parents thought they should. European American mealtimes were not toddler centered but focused on older children and fathers. Toddlers ate finger foods and sought attention as they needed it, and mothers responded to their needs. Filipino American mothers were more directive than Japanese American mothers, restricting babies' movements and insisting that babies do as the mothers requested. Japanese American mothers subtly directed children's behavior. They encouraged cooperation by making games of what the child wanted to do and gently guiding the child to do what the parent wanted. European American mothers were the least directive.

The study reports,

> Filipino- and Japanese-American mothers were highly attentive and affectionate toward their infants, but also either overtly (Filipino-American) or subtly (Japanese-American) controlling. Mothers conveyed the message that being a member of a tight family group involves both the warmth and attentiveness of belonging and also the obligation of conforming to adult wishes. The Caucasian-American mothers in this sample allowed more autonomy and were more relationally distant. They encouraged innovation as they focused on infants' completing their goal-directed actions—regardless of whether these disrupted the rest of the group.[87]

The groups differed in ways of relating to babies. European American mothers encouraged babies to engage others verbally—by talking and becoming part of mealtime conversations—whereas Japanese American mothers encouraged babies to seek contact by trying to accomplish a task and by obtaining help as needed.

Americans of Middle Eastern Descent

Middle Eastern Americans trace their origins to many different countries, including Lebanon, Syria, Egypt, Palestine, Iraq, Jordan, Yemen, Saudi Arabia, Afghanistan, and Kuwait. Like all other ethnic groups, this group includes several social and religious subgroups. The majority of Middle Eastern Americans are Christians (77 percent), with Muslims making up about 23 percent.[88] Middle Eastern Americans make up a small percentage of the population, estimated at $3^1/_2$ million (see Table 3-3), and living in predominantly urban areas.[89] A large majority are native-born Americans, and 82 percent are citizens.[90]

Historical Perspective Shaping This Group's View of Society   Middle Eastern Americans have immigrated in several waves.[91] The first wave, at the end of the nineteenth and early twentieth centuries, included agricultural workers from Lebanon who sought better economic conditions as the silk crop was failing. They became skilled laborers or owners of small stores. Christians came also, to escape the Ottoman practice of forcing military service on the children of Christians who did not convert to Islam. The common bond of religion eased their transition into American society. The early immigrants set up a "chain migration," in which the first member of a family established here saved money for the next member to come, so that eventually a broad network of family members was here and living close together. The restrictive immigration laws of the 1920s halted immigration until after World War II. At that time, and continuing since then, events in the Middle East have triggered waves of immigrants, most recently of Muslims. Their social backgrounds have varied; some were highly educated individuals who studied and remained here, and others were poor refugees fleeing conflicts there. Those who came as students and remained did not bring other relatives here and were more likely to marry Americans because they had more contact with American culture than did other subgroups.

General Values   Middle Eastern Americans place great value on religion and family. More than country of origin or skin color, religion defines people. Churches and mosques are centers of social as well as spiritual life. Marriage outside one's religion is frowned on.

In secular life, the most important value is the large, extended family formed by patrilineal descent lines. Middle Eastern Americans are raised to think of family interests before their own. Blood ties matter more than marital ties, but because cousin marriages are approved in this culture, many husbands and wives are of the same patrilineal family and can live close to both families.

Although patrilineality may include patriarchy, it entails a wider set of duties and obligations. Patrilineal rules give older generations power over younger, and men privileges over women. Yet it is necessary to mention that women have more power than Westerners think. Their power lies within their patrilineage, in their roles as mothers and sisters, and in their ability to influence relationships. It also lies in their potential to disrupt the social system by noncompliance with patriarchy.[92]

Obligations to family members are paramount, with financial as well as psychological support expected. When families bring relatives here from their countries of origin, they find jobs for them or help them start businesses. About 40 percent of Middle Eastern Americans report having landed their first job through a relative. Middle Eastern Americans also send money to relatives in their country of origin; in one study in Canada, 50 percent of foreign-born Middle Easterners and 22 percent born in Canada sent money home regularly.[93]

Upholding family honor is quite important. In this patrilineal culture, women's sexuality is of concern both before and after marriage. Women can be beaten, banished from the family, and in rare instances killed for having sexual relations outside of marriage and bringing shame on the family.

In return for the demands made on individuals, families provide protection, feelings of security, and closeness with others.

Contemporary Families   For this small ethnic group that lacks official minority status, statistics comparable to the other groups are hard to find. Middle Eastern American families are larger than those of other groups. In one study, 38 percent of women, half of whom were ages twenty to twenty-nine, had five or more children and presumably could have more.[94] The Middle Eastern median family income for 1999 was $52,000, higher than the median U.S. family income (see Table 3-3). The Middle Eastern American income continues to be higher than average, perhaps because women often work in family-owned stores and businesses.[95]

Middle Eastern Americans, on average, are highly educated, with 84 percent having a high school degree, 41 percent a college degree or higher education.[96] Seventy-two percent work in managerial, professional, technical, and administrative jobs;[97] yet Table 3-3 shows that there is still a high rate of poverty.

Middle Eastern American families immigrating to this country in the last decade have values that differ greatly from those in mainstream American culture. This makes rearing children difficult in many ways. In addition, these families must deal with Americans' lack of knowledge and understanding of their traditional culture and Islam. Since September 11, 2001, such families are also dealing with the suspicion and prejudice that have followed the terrorist attack in New York City by men from Saudi Arabia. Although groups of Muslims and Christians have met to increase understanding of each other's cultures, it is not an easy time for many Americans of Middle Eastern descent.

Parenting Children   Like all other ethnic groups, Middle Eastern Americans place a high value on children. Like many other groups, they indulge very young children. In extended families, many adults and older children look after and safeguard them.

As a patrilineal culture, Middle Eastern Americans emphasize respect for elders and privileges for boys.[98] Sons are highly valued and are given greater advantages and more freedom than girls. Even though many women contribute to family businesses, gender socialization is traditional. Girls are encouraged to help at home, to behave modestly in public, and to spend most of their social time with family and relatives. Early marriages are encouraged and make it harder for girls to obtain advanced education.

Particular tensions between parents and teens may arise when the teens want to spend time with peers and engage in school activities. Parents expect teens to continue to participate in religious activities and to visit and socialize with extended relatives, but teens in this country want to pursue their own activities. The resolution of such conflicts depends, in part, on the support teens and parents can bring to bear. If the family is an extended one in a large Middle Eastern community, the teens will have a harder time asserting their wishes, because parents have much support for theirs. If the family has few relatives and little communal support for parents, then teens may gain greater freedom.

Although boys are permitted to date before marriage, girls are not encouraged to do so. In one study, 80 percent of wives never dated before marriage and another 10 percent dated very little. Permitted to work before marriage, girls are encouraged to find teaching, clerical, secretarial, or other jobs in surroundings where there is not a high proportion of men.

As in many other ethnic groups, second-, third-, and fourth-generation Middle Eastern Americans are probably not so tied to the traditional ways of child rearing. However, recall that significant numbers of this ethnic group have immigrated since 1990, reflecting quite traditional orientations to families and children. Many Americans might disapprove of the Middle Eastern way of life. Yet, Palestinian American women in one survey believed their lives were better than those of most other American women; in another, 47 percent of Muslim women "felt they were treated as well [as] or better than the average American."[99] Only 33 percent of Muslim women born in the United States shared this opinion.

The Self-Esteem of Ethnic Groups

Researchers, concerned that prejudice and discrimination have led to both low levels of self-esteem and negative self-concepts in ethnic groups that society described negatively, compared the levels of self-esteem of European Americans and African Americans. They found that African American global self-esteem is as high as or higher than that of European Americans, despite the negative experiences many African Americans encounter in this society.

Jean Twenge and Jennifer Crocker carried out a meta-analysis of studies of self-esteem to determine whether other groups also scored as high as African Americans.[100] They looked at 712 comparisons of self-esteem among African Americans, European Americans, Native Americans, Latinas/os, and Asian Americans and found the rank ordering of these groups on inventories of self-esteem presented in Table 3-4. This table also presents the rank ordering of these groups in terms of society's positive regard, as measured in surveys of the national population.

The rank ordering of the groups on self-esteem does not follow the pattern of society's general regard for the group. Despite society's lower regard of their ethnic group, African Americans make positive statements about themselves and have

■ **TABLE 3-4**
RANK-ORDERING OF ETHNIC GROUPS WITH RESPECT TO SELF-ESTEEM SCORES AND POSITIVE REGARD BY SOCIETY*

Rank Order of Self-Esteem Scores (1 = Highest Self-Esteem)	Rank Order with Respect to Society's Positive Regard[†]
1. African Americans	1. European Americans
2. European Americans	2. Asian Americans
3. Latinas/os	3. Latinas/os
4. Native Americans	4. African Americans
5. Asian Americans	

*From: Jean M. Twenge and Jennifer Crocker, "Race and Self-Esteem: Meta-Analyses Comparing Whites, Blacks, Hispanics, Asians, and American Indians, and Comment on Gray-Little and Hafdahl," *Psychological Bulletin* 128 (2002): 371–408.

[†]Native Americans not included

Intially, children of all ethnic groups make positive statements about themselves, but as they grow older, they become more socialized in their cultural views of what is appropriate to say about themselves.

done so in studies over the past twenty years. In contrast, Asian Americans report the fewest positive self-perceptions although they have higher levels of education and income than all other ethnic groups and are considered most favorably of all other groups except European Americans. Of interest is the fact that the socio-economic status of the subjects reduced the differences among the groups. High-status individuals of all groups resembled each other in their levels of self-esteem.

With respect to age, the differences in self-esteem among the five groups were smallest in elementary school and grew larger through high school and into the adult years. This suggests that, initially, all children tend to make positive statements about themselves, but as they grow older, they become more socialized in their culture's views of what is appropriate to say about oneself. Self-esteem scores decreased with age in groups such as Asian Americans and Native Americans, which emphasize an interdependent self and minimize the importance of the self.

Interesting findings came from an examination of self-esteem in relation to the subjects' geographic area of residence and the years of data collection. The self-esteem of African Americans and Asian Americans was highest in areas where that group had greater concentrations of population. For example, African Americans' self-esteem was highest in Southern states, which had the greatest numbers of African Americans. This is similar to the finding that African American students at African American colleges have higher self-esteem than African Americans at European American colleges. Asian Americans living on the West Coast, where there are higher concentrations of Asian Americans, reported higher self-esteem than did Asian Americans in other parts of the country.

The subjects' cohort (year of birth) and the subjects' age at the time the data were collected also related to scores on self-esteem. In 1980, about twenty years after the civil rights movement began in the United States, African American scores on global self-esteem inventories began to rise. Twenge and Crocker speculate that the emphasis on the experiences and contributions of African Americans to this country, coupled with the civil rights movement's emphasis on group pride and self-respect, affected children who absorbed these messages in the 1960s and 1970s. As they got older, they retained the high self-esteem reflected by the data collected after 1980. Cohort differences are found for other groups as well. The most recently-born Asian Americans and Latinas/os have rising self-esteem scores and differ least from European Americans.

The authors conclude that a variety of cultural factors explain self-esteem in different ethnic groups. First, the cultural influence of the ethnic group itself plays a role. Scores are highest for groups that have an individualistic orientation that emphasizes independence, setting personal goals, taking control to achieve these goals, valuing uniqueness, and seeking to stand out from others. European Americans and African Americans emphasize these beliefs. Having an individualistic orientation does not mean that collectivist goals have to be ignored, although they usually are in the European American group. Asian American, Latina/o, and Native American groups, which stress an interdependent self that seeks harmony with others, not superiority to them, also are less likely to make positive self-statements and therefore score lower on measures of self-esteem.

Social factors also affect cultural groups' beliefs. First, as ethnic group members reside longer in this country and are exposed to its individualistic orientation, their reports of self-esteem begin to resemble those of European Americans. Second, self-esteem increases when groups receive positive messages from the communities in which they live. When political and social movements emphasize a group's contributions, and when groups feel support from large numbers who share their cultural orientation, then self-esteem increases. As individuals of higher status in all groups make positive comments about themselves, we can speculate that higher education, a major marker of status, brings with it an increasing appreciation of the self.

COMMONALITIES AMONG CULTURAL THEMES

While recognizing cultural differences in parents' behavior, we should not overlook the commonalities among parents in all groups in this country. All cultures place a high value on children and families, and most parents want their children to grow up to be effective adults, however they define effectiveness.

The majority of European Americans embrace the independent model of parent-child relationships. The other ethnic groups, including some subgroups of European Americans such as Italian Americans and Greek Americans, use a more interdependent model, emphasizing respect for elders and tradition, the importance of the extended family and family obligations, early indulgence of children followed (usually) by firm expectations, and a strong reliance on spiritual values. Because older European Americans, too, describe these values as the ones they were raised with, we can assume that large segments of the population endorse an interdependent model. If immigration continues as it has, and if ethnic groups continue to have larger numbers of children, this model may come to equal or replace the more dominant independent model of today.

Although ethnic groups may have special goals and concerns regarding children, parents' behavior has similar effects on children regardless of the ethnic group, family structure, social status, or gender of parents and children.[101] For example, parental support, monitoring of children, and avoidance of harsh punishment have been linked to children's positive growth and well-being in European American samples of parents and children. In national samples that include African American and Mexican American parents as well as European American parents of all educational and financial backgrounds, the same factors of parental support and avoidance of harsh punishment are associated with good grades, psychological adjustment, and rule-following behaviors in boys and girls aged five to eighteen in all groups.

In the adolescent years, parents' acceptance and involvement were related to teens' reports of academic achievement and general feeling of well-being in four ethnic groups—European Americans, African Americans, Latinas/os, and Asian Americans.[102] The greater the parents' involvement, supervision, and autonomy granting, the more teens reported competence and well-being.

A finding that initially emerged in African American samples has been found in European American and Latina/o samples as well. Nonabusive spanking that occurs in the context of warm family relationships is not related to an increase in children's behavior problems and aggression over time from ages four to eleven.[103] Spanking in the context of little emotional support is associated with increases in problem behaviors over time in the three ethnic groups.

We have now looked at differences in parenting goals and strategies among members of different ethnic groups and also at similarities in the effects of their strategies despite different goals. As Mary Kay DeGenova wrote in *Families in Cultural Context,*

> No matter how many differences there may be, beneath the surface there are even more similarities. It is important to try to identify the similarities among various cultures. Stripping away surface differences will uncover a multiplicity of similarities: people's hopes, aspirations, desire to survive, search for love, and need for family—to name just a few. While superficially we may be dissimilar, the essence of being human is very much the same for all of us. Experience the paradox of diversity: that "we are the same but in different ways."[104]

THE INFLUENCE OF SOCIOECONOMIC STATUS

Erika Hoff, Brett Laursen, and Twila Tardif believe that socioeconomic status (SES) provides a developmental niche for parent-child relations just as racial and ethnic backgrounds do.[105] Three factors—parents' occupation, education, and level of income—make up SES. Although income at or below the poverty level affects parenting (as we discuss in the next section), income closer to the average appears less influential than education and occupational status in shaping parenting beliefs.

The influence of social status, like that of culture, is not fixed. For example, parents' occupations may change as the result of increased education, or a family may find great success in some endeavor, and their income may rise sharply. Conversely, income and social status may drop as a result of unemployment. Further, parents can change their ideas about parenting as a result of new information rather than a change in educational level.

Summarizing the research on the influence of SES on parenting, Hoff, Laursen, and Tardif state that higher SES parents are *more likely than lower SES parents* to have a child-centered orientation to parenting. They seek to understand children's thoughts and feelings and to make them important partners in the process of parenting. They elicit opinions and encourage children's participation in making rules. Lower SES parents are more parent centered than higher-status parents are. They see themselves as authorities and want children to comply. When children do not obey, such parents may be harsh and punitive.

A second major finding is that differences in SES correlate with more differences in verbal interactions than nonverbal ones between parents and children. Higher-status parents talk more to children and elicit more speech from them. They also show more responsiveness when children do speak, and they encourage the development of verbal skills by supplying more labels that describe what children see and do.

Such differences may seem uninteresting and unimportant, but an unusual study has documented the profound impact of these verbal differences on young children's lives. Betty Hart and Todd Risley recorded the words spoken to and by children in their homes from the ages of one to three years.[106] For an hour each month, researchers visited the homes of forty-two European American and African American families of professional, working-class, and welfare backgrounds. Results indicated no gender or racial differences in language acquisition, but they did reveal large differences based on social group. All children in the study experienced quality interactions with their parents; all heard diverse forms of language spoken to and around them; all learned to speak by the age of three. However, the differing amounts and kinds of language heard in the homes surprised the investigators. First, professional parents spoke about three times as much to their children as did welfare parents and about one and a half times as much as did working-class parents. Children in professional families heard about 487 utterances per hour; children in working-class families, 301; children in welfare families, 178.

The emotional tone of the conversations also reflected startling differences. In professional families, children received affirmative feedback (confirming, elaborating, and giving explicit approval for what the child said) about thirty times an hour, or every other minute. In working-class families, children received affirmative feedback fifteen times an hour, or once every four minutes. In welfare families, children received positive feedback six times an hour, or once every ten minutes. Professional parents gave prohibitions about five times an hour, and welfare parents about eleven. Children in welfare families heard twice as many negative comments as positive ones, whereas children in professional families heard primarily positive comments and rarely any negative ones.

These findings have important implications for the development of self-concept and general mood as well as for language development. Language differences in the home at ages one to three strongly predicted vocabulary growth and intellectual development when the child was about nine years of age. The most important predictors of vocabulary and intellectual competence were the emotional tone of the feedback and the amount of linguistic diversity the child heard.

Encouragingly, the study shows that all parents have the capacity to promote language and intellectual development, because they already have the ability to speak and interact with children effectively. Increasing verbal interactions with children and providing more positive feedback to them will help language development and intellectual growth in homes where parents are inclined to say less and what they do say is negative.

Annette Lareau went into the homes of middle-class (those with managerial jobs or complex jobs requiring college-level skills), working-class (those with unskilled, lower-level, white-collar jobs with little or no managerial responsibility), and poor parents (those receiving public assistance) of European American and African American background.[107] She and her research assistants observed interactions occurring over many hours on about twenty occasions with each family, following the children and families at school events and doctor visits as well. Like Hart and Risley, Lareau found many elements of family life common to all social groups and found, too, that socioeconomic differences overshadowed the influence of ethnic background.

Table 3-5 presents the features common to families of all social levels. Table 3-6 describes the features of a parental philosophy of "concerted cultivation," which Lareau believes is characteristic of middle-class families, and features of the parental philosophy of "accomplishment of natural growth" characteristic of working class and poor families.

The children of all families had positive experiences, and all parents worked hard to rear their children, but parents in different classes exerted energy in different ways. Middle-class parents stimulated children with lessons, trips, and group activities. They helped children develop verbal and social skills; they encouraged children's sense of individuality. They taught their children how to interact with adults outside the home, how to present their own needs and to persist in an assertive but polite way until adults attended to these needs. They conveyed to children a sense of ease and confidence that the world would treat them well.

■ **TABLE 3-5**
CHARACTERISTICS OF ALL FAMILIES REGARDLESS OF SOCIOECONOMIC STATUS*

1. Enormous time and effort are expended by parents on parenting.

2. Children face challenges in the process of growing up.

3. Families experience times of fun, laughter, happiness, emotional closeness, and comfort.

4. Families have rituals regarding favorite meals, television shows, toys, games, and outings.

5. A large percentage of time is spent in routines such as eating, dressing, daily chores, and homework.

6. Families experience tragedies, such as premature deaths and auto accidents.

7. Family members have differing temperaments.

8. Families have differing levels of messiness and neatness.

9. Families provide a safe, secure, and homelike atmosphere.

*Adapted from: Annette Lareau, *Unequal Childhoods: Class, Race, and Family Life* (Berkeley, CA: University of California Press, 2003), pp. 237–238 and 274.

Children in working-class and poor families had advantages at home in the sense that they were less pressured and scheduled to attend lessons and activities. These children had more time for free play and often had much closer relationships with family members and cousins than children of the middle class. Still, these children longed to have some of the lessons and the trips. The real disadvantages of working-class and poor families came in their decrease in self-confidence as they moved outside the home. Many parents felt they did not meet the expectations of middle-class teachers and doctors, and some feared more severe criticism that might remove children from the home for failure to meet middle-class standards of discipline and punishment. Their children did not have the view that all would go well.

Parents from different social groups had different conceptions of both childhood and adulthood. Middle-class parents wanted children to have some fun in childhood, but childhood was seen as a period of preparation and skills development that would enable children to get good educations and good jobs in adulthood. Then, as adults, they could have fun and pleasure at work and with their families. The orientation was toward a future full of good experiences. Parents in working-class and poor families saw adulthood as a stressful time with uncertain jobs and little control of one's work and income. Childhood was the period of pleasure and freedom from stress.

Lareau believes the middle-class pressure for lessons and stimulating activities to develop each child's potential to the fullest comes from the changing nature of the country's economy, in which only outstanding performance will qualify a child for the shrinking number of well-paid jobs. This is what Judith Warner described in *The Perfect Madness*, discussed in Chapter 1.

■ **T A B L E 3-6**
TYPOLOGY OF DIFFERENCES IN CHILD REARING*

	Child-Rearing Approach	
	Concerted Cultivation	**Accomplishment of Natural Growth**
Key Elements	Parent actively fosters and assesses child's talents, opinions, and skills	Parent cares for child and allows child to grow
Organization of Daily Life	Multiple child leisure activities orchestrated by adults	"Hanging out," particularly with kin, by child
Language Use	Reasoning/Directives	Directives
	Child contestation of adult statements	Rare questioning or challenging of adults by child
	Extended negotiations between parents and child	General acceptance by child of directives
Interventions in Institutions	Criticisms and interventions on behalf of child	Dependence on institutions
	Training of child to take on this role	Sense of powerlessness and frustration
		Conflict between child-rearing practices at home and at school
Consequences	Emerging sense of entitlement on the part of the child	Emerging sense of constraint on the part of the child

*Annette Lareau, *Unequal Childhoods: Class, Race, and Family Life* (Berkeley, CA: University of California Press, 2003), p. 31.

Lareau also believes that well-funded community recreational programs can provide working-class and poor children with the athletic and musical lessons and the enriching experiences that middle-class parents provide, so that these children, too, can look forward to a bright future.

THE INFLUENCE OF ECONOMIC HARDSHIP

The previous section mentioned some families who received public assistance, but here we focus exclusively on what happens to families when income falls below the poverty level.

Parents who lack resources to care for their children experience increased stress in meeting the challenges of daily life. When experiencing economic hardship, parents become more irritable, depressed, and more easily frustrated.[108] Their psychological tension has a direct impact on their parenting and on their children. Such parents stimulate their children less, and they use less effective parenting practices. They do not communicate with children as openly or share power as much as they do in less stressful times. This tension affects children's schoolwork and behavior. When economic conditions improve, parenting skills improve, as does children's behavior.

In a study of parent-adolescent interactions in European American and African American families with single-parent or two-parent homes, financial strain was related to parents' having greater conflict with adolescents and less involvement in teens' schooling, and teens' receiving lower school grades.[109] Financial strain overrode the influence of ethnic background and family structure in predicting conflict with children and children's decreasing grades. Similar relationships between financial strain, changes in parents' behaviors, and decreases in children's adjustment also were found in European American and Mexican American families with early adolescents.[110]

Economic strain also had an indirect effect on children's behavior. When parents are upset and frustrated, they argue with each other and give each other less support, so parenting declines because parents are not working together.[111] When fathers remain supportive of mothers during economic hardship, mothers' parenting skills do not decrease at all.[112] Although social support from outside the family helps to reduce parents' low moods, it is support from the other parent that maintains parenting effectiveness.

Who Are the Poor?

The official federal index of poverty developed in the 1960s is the most common measure of poverty; it is based on pretax, cash income and the number of people in the family.[113] The index is determined by the estimated cost of food multiplied by three, as food was found in surveys to absorb about one-third of the family income. For example, the 2000 poverty threshold for two people was $11,569; for a family of three, $14,128; and for a family of four (two adults and two children), $18,104.[114]

Children, particularly the youngest, are the poorest individuals in the United States.[115] In 2003, the rate of poverty for children under eighteen was 18 percent (compared with 10 percent for those aged 65 and older).[116] Rates of poverty are higher for children in certain ethnic groups. In 2003, 34 percent of African American children and 30 percent of Latina/o children were living in poverty, compared with 14 percent of European American and 12 percent of Asian American children.

Many factors influence rates of poverty.[117] Poverty decreases when parental education increases and when the number of children in the family decreases. Poverty increases when children live in single-parent families, although living in a two-parent family is not a complete protection—in one study, almost half the years children spent in poverty occurred when they lived with two parents.

Three factors seem to push families into poverty: (1) decreases in the number of skilled jobs that can support families, (2) increases in the number of single-parent families, and (3) reductions in government benefits to families.[118]

Jeanne Brooks-Gunn and Greg Duncan refute the argument that the problems of the poor result from parents' genetic endowment or their work ethic.[119] They report that siblings reared in the same family with the same parental attitudes can differ in the age and duration of poverty in their lives and thus serve to control for the effects of parental characteristics on poverty. They found that sibling differences in income during childhood were related to siblings' years of completed schooling, suggesting that income does matter even when genes and work ethic are controlled for.

The Effects of Poverty on Children's Development

Brooks-Gunn and Duncan describe the effects of poverty on various aspects of children's functioning.[120]

Birth Outcomes and Physical Health   As compared to nonpoor children, poor children are twice as likely to suffer infant mortality, low birth weight (less than 2,500 grams), and growth stunting (less than the fifth percentile in height for one's age), often considered a measure of nutritional status. They are three and a half times more likely to suffer lead poisoning, which is often related to physical and cognitive impairments. Conversely, poor children are less often characterized as having excellent health and more often described as having fair or poor health.

Interventions to improve children's health also improve their test scores at school.[121] For example, an assistant superintendent of schools in Chula Vista, California, observed several years ago that the schools with the poorest academic progress were those with the greatest absenteeism for health reasons. He approached the director of the local medical clinic, who was also concerned about children's health care. Many of the children lacked health insurance and used expensive emergency room services for routine problems. Such bills went unpaid, and the clinic lost money. The school, the medical center, and the city organized a mobile medical clinic that went from school to school providing routine care for children. The clinic was linked with a family clinic on the school grounds, and parents were helped to fill out papers for federal health benefits.

Health improved. Children attended school more regularly. In class, they were alert and attentive. Academic performance and test scores improved. Clearly, health played a major role in this change.

Cognitive, Emotional, and Behavioral Development   Table 3-7 reveals that poor children are more likely to experience cognitive delays and learning disabilities than are nonpoor children. The poorer the child, the greater the delay. These differences appear on ability measures as early as two years of age and persist into the elementary school years. These differences persist even when mother's age, marital status, education, and ethnicity are controlled for.

■ **T A B L E 3-7**
SELECTED POPULATION-BASED INDICATORS OF WELL-BEING FOR POOR
AND NONPOOR CHILDREN IN THE UNITED STATES*

Indicator	Percentage of Poor Children (unless noted)	Percentage of Nonpoor Children (unless noted)	Ratio of Poor to Nonpoor Children
Cognitive Outcomes			
Developmental delay (includes both limited and long-term developmental deficits) (0 to 17 years)	5.0	3.8	1.3
Learning disability (defined as having exceptional difficulty in learning to read, write, and do arithmetic) (3 to 17 years)	8.3	6.1	1.4
School Achievement Outcomes (5 to 17 years)			
Grade repetition (reported to have ever repeated a grade)	28.8	14.1	2.0
Ever expelled or suspended	11.9	6.1	2.0
High school dropout (percentage 16- to 24-year-olds who were not in school or did not finish high school in 1994)	21.0	9.6	2.2
Emotional or Behavioral Outcomes (3 to 17 years unless noted)			
Parent reports child has ever had an emotional or behavioral problem that lasted three months or more	16.4	12.7	1.3
Parent reports child ever being treated for an emotional problem or behavioral problem	2.5	4.5	0.6
Parent reports child has experienced one or more of a list of typical child behavioral problems in the last three months (5 to 17 years)	57.4	57.3	1.0
Other			
Female teens who had an out-of-wedlock birth	11.0	3.6	3.1
Economically inactive at age 24 (not employed or in school)	15.9	8.3	1.9
Experienced hunger (food insufficiency) at least once in past year	15.9	1.6	9.9
Reported cases of child abuse and neglect	5.4	0.8	6.8
Violent crimes (experienced by poor families and nonpoor families)	5.4	2.6	2.1
Afraid to go out (percentage of family heads in poor and nonpoor families who report they are afraid to go out in their neighborhood)	19.5	8.7	2.2

Note: This list of child outcomes reflects findings from large, nationally representative surveys that collect data on child outcomes and family income. While most data come from the 1988 National Health Interview Survey Child Health Supplement, data from other nationally representative surveys are included. The rates presented are from simple cross-tabulations. In most cases, the data do not reflect factors that might be important to child outcomes other than poverty status at the time of data collection. The ratios reflect rounding.

*Jeanne Brooks-Gunn and Greg J. Duncan, "The Effects of Poverty on Children," *Future of Children* 7, no. 2 (1997): 58–59. Reprinted with permission of the David and Lucille Packard Foundation.

Poor children are twice as likely as nonpoor children to repeat a school grade or drop out of school. The duration and timing of poverty influence its effects on children's functioning. Those children who live in poverty thirteen years or longer have significantly lower scores on cognitive measures than do those who experience only short-term poverty. Poverty in the first five years of life is negatively associated with high school graduation, whereas poverty in the adolescent years is not.

Poverty is less clearly related to emotional outcomes than to physical and cognitive development. Parents of poor and nonpoor children report the same number of behavioral problems, with current poverty related to such behaviors as hyperactivity and peer difficulties. These differences are found even when mothers' age, education, and mental status are controlled for.

In addition to facing differences in health and cognitive skills, poor children are more likely to experience hunger, abuse, and neglect. They are more likely to experience violent crimes and to be afraid to go out in their neighborhoods. As teens, they are more likely to bear a child out of wedlock. Although Table 3-7 highlights increased stresses for poor children, compared with nonpoor children, it also suggests that poverty does not affect all children or all areas of functioning. Most poor children perform at grade level, almost 80 percent graduate from high school, and they are no more likely than nonpoor children to be described as having emotional problems.

Ways to Intervene

Effective interventions must address the effects of poverty on children's lives and development. Table 3-8 lists five ways poverty affects children's development. Prior to 1996, to help deal with these problems, parents could find two forms of assistance—cash-transfer programs that gave money directly to poor children through Aid to Families with Dependent Children (AFDC) and programs that

■ **T A B L E 3-8**
FIVE WAYS POVERTY AFFECTS CHILDREN'S EXPERIENCE AND DEVELOPMENT*

1. Low birth weight, poor nutrition, exposure to lead, and poorer health in turn predispose children to learning disabilities and school problems.

2. Fewer resources present in the home, such as books and musical instruments, to stimulate children; this factor is thought to account for as much as 50 percent of the effects of poverty on intellectual growth.

3. Economic hardship and stress decrease parents' skills with children and increase harsh behavior.

4. Parents have increasing psychological problems, such as depression and anxiety.

5. Stressful factors are present in neighborhoods, along with lack of positive resources for children.

*Greg J. Duncan and Jeanne Brooks-Gunn, "Family Poverty, Welfare Reform, and Child Development," *Child Development* 71 (2000): 188–196.

provided services such as Food Stamps and subsidized lunches. Food Stamps and AFDC, available to all families with a certain level of income, were termed *entitlement programs*. In 1996, however, the Personal Responsibility and Work Opportunity Reconciliation Act, more often called the Welfare Reform Bill, eliminated the sixty-year-old guaranteed AFDC program and replaced it with block grants to states, which could use the money in any way they wished to provide temporary assistance to poor families (Temporary Assistance to Needy Families, or TANF).[122] The Welfare Reform Bill and block grants have stimulated programs to help parents and children.

Increasing parenting skills as well as parents' ability to get health care and to stimulate children's learning addresses three of the areas listed in Table 3-8 that poverty impacts. Multifaceted Early Head Start programs, which target low-income parents with infants and toddlers, provide a full array of services to promote child development.[123] The services include health care, home visits, parent education, child care, and family support for twenty months in the first three years of life. In 2004, 62,000 families were enrolled in such programs around the country. In a preliminary study of the effects of the program on 3,000 children, investigators have found that such programs have increased parents' skills in the areas of (1) forming emotionally supportive relationships with children, (2) stimulating children's verbal and learning abilities, and (3) finding alternatives to physical punishment.

Three-year-old children in this program performed better on measures of verbal and intellectual abilities, on measures of attention span, and on measures of ability to emotionally engage parents than control children not enrolled in the program. They were also less aggressive. So, in the areas that parents increased in skills, children increased in performance.

A Wisconsin program titled New Hope provided many services to families with children aged thirteen months to eleven years and yielded improvements in children's functioning.[124] The program provided jobs for parents, financial supplements for the family, health care, and child care. When the children were assessed two years after the three-year program began, boys in the program had higher academic achievement, especially in the area of reading, and better study skills; they were more compliant with rules and more sensitive to others but at the same time more self-directed than boys in the control group. Girls in the program did not show as many increases in behavior. In comparison to girls in the control group, they had slightly higher academic achievement, but teachers rated them lower on study skills and social behaviors and higher on fearfulness and social withdrawal. Two years after the program ended, children continued to show academic increases, but boys' social advantages were not seen. The continued achievements even after the three-year program ended may have occurred because families in the program continued to use more center-based child care, and children continued to be more involved in community activities.

Follow-up studies of children attending an intensive, two-year preschool program found that the effects of such programs can last well into adulthood.[125] The High/Scope Perry Project developed and carried out in Ypsilanti, Michigan, in 1962 enrolled three-year-olds from a very poor neighborhood in a five-day-a-week, three-hour-a-day program that focused on helping children learn active problem-solving skills that included planning activities, doing them, and reviewing what they had done. In weekly home visits, parents got information on how to encourage learning in everyday life situations such as counting change at the grocery store.

Children in the program and in the control group have been followed into their forties. Although the initial differences between the groups at the ages of seven and eight were not impressive, significant differences have emerged in the quality of the lives of these two groups. Program children got higher grades in high school and were more likely to graduate from high school (66 percent as compared to 45 percent in the control group). Nearly twice as many have completed college. They are more likely to be employed (76 percent as compared to 62 percent), more likely to own a home and a car. They earn more ($20,800 as compared to $15,300).

Social achievements are significant as well. Only 28 percent of the preschool group have been sentenced to jail or prison, as compared to 52 percent of the control group. Men were more likely to marry, and almost twice as many were involved in raising their own children (50 percent compared to 30 percent).

The exact reasons for the long-lasting impact of the two-year program are not known, but one can speculate that parents increased their skills in relating to children and stimulating their learning, and children gained early problem-solving skills that set in motion a more positive cycle of behavior. Children had greater success in school, became more involved and found it rewarding, and attained more education, which enabled greater occupational success and social stability in adulthood.

One can only wonder how well children in all these programs might have done had the stimulation and extra support been provided not for two years but for fifteen to eighteen years, as occurs in middle-class families.

A PRACTICAL QUESTION: WHAT HAPPENS WHEN PARENT EDUCATORS AND PARENTS HAVE DIFFERENT VALUES?

Knowing that individuals within different ethnic and social groups may have particular values based on both culture and personal experiences makes us aware of the wide variety of beliefs about the goals and strategies of parenting. Tammy Mann, a parent educator, questions the effectiveness of parent educators when the mainstream philosophy of parenting they teach differs from the ideas and experiences of the parents they seek to influence.[126]

After the birth of her son, Mann became keenly aware of the discomfort parents can feel "when asked to abandon child-rearing practices and beliefs that may be intrinsic to their very definitions of themselves."[127] In rearing her own child, she realized how she treasured the authoritarian parenting strategies of her warm and giving parents, even though they did not meet the mainstream model of authoritative parenting (described in Chapter 2).

Mann lived in the South in a two-parent family. When she was two, the family moved to Detroit, accompanied by many aunts, uncles, and cousins, so she grew up with a large extended family who had frequent gatherings. The extended family periodically returned to the South for vacations, traveling together in "caravans."

Mann's parents shaped and controlled children's behavior without discussions of children's preferences or ideas. Children had to obey. Such control was to help children grow into accountable and responsible adults. Her parents expected children to help in the family from an early age. They emphasized respect for elders, manners, and polite behavior to others. Her mother had a strong religious faith, and the family participated regularly in church activities. Education was very important, and both parents wanted their children to go farther in school than they had.

As a parent, Mann finds herself maintaining her son's strong connections to the extended family. Although she, with her husband and son, lives far from other relatives, she makes sure her son visits the extended family in the summer and that all three travel to the South for family reunions. This does not substitute for the warm cocoon of the extended family she experienced as a child in Detroit, but she duplicates those childhood feelings for her son as best she can. Because religion has been so important to her and her parents, she delights in her son's spontaneous and easy reliance on prayer as a way of coping with the stress of waking up in the night alone.

Mann sometimes feels uncomfortable wanting to follow the values that have been such strengths for her and her brother and sisters, because they do not conform to what experts recommend. For example, she does not value independence, individual expressiveness, and achievement above all. Instead, she stresses family connectedness, responsibility to others, a strong religious faith, and educational achievement. She suspects that parents she has worked with in the past may have felt as alienated from mainstream parenting beliefs as she has, and she worries that rejecting "aspects of who we are, in an attempt to become something else deemed 'better,' can be more destructive than practitioners sometime imagine."[128]

She believes that parent educators and practitioners must first try to understand families and their values before intervening. Although the particular characteristics defining effective behaviors differ, most all parents share the common desire that their children become well-functioning adults. Parents are striving to do their best as they deal with issues of nurturance and setting limits. In rearing children, parents confront their own values regarding the importance of independence, compliance, respect, and achievement. Educators must help parents find the strategies and solutions that both help their children develop and fit with parents' values and earlier experiences.

Vivian Carlson and Robin Harwood describe a four-session program to help parent educators become aware of their own cultural orientations and values with respect to parenting and then to use their increased awareness to better understand and help parents.[129] Carlson and Harwood state that many educators are surprised to discover that cultural beliefs are more than a set of beliefs endorsed by a group. Groups pass on unspoken ways of viewing the world, but individuals interpret these beliefs uniquely in terms of their own experience. Thus, educators must pay attention to the unique beliefs, socialization goals, and values of the parents they work with. They also must be sensitive when parents' values differ from their own.

In this program, educators learn to ask questions to discover the long-term goals parents have for children, such as independence, social relatedness, respect and deference, and individual achievement. They also learn to identify parents' expectations about children's milestones, such as feeding themselves, becoming toilet trained, and sleeping by themselves.

During the course of the training, participants come to realize that knowledge of group history and characteristics is valuable but not sufficient for culturally sensitive practice. In particular, they appreciate the training emphasis on specific questioning strategies to use in exploring cultural beliefs and values with families; 95 percent of participants agreed or strongly agreed with the statement "I will use the information about socialization goal categories and questioning strategies in my work with families."[130] Such information enables educators to provide more effective and relevant services to parents.

MAIN POINTS

Culture provides

- ways of viewing the world
- goals and strategies for parenting
- a developmental niche for parent-child relations

The cultural models of parent-child relations include

- the independent model, which stresses children's independence, initiative, and the capacity for setting and achieving goals
- the interdependent model, which stresses children's becoming part of a strong social network that nourishes and supports them

Members of ethnic groups in this country

- have often experienced prejudice and rejection
- differ in values and strategies of parenting, with European Americans preferring the independent model and most other groups preferring the interdependent model
- differ in levels of self-esteem, with members of individualistic cultures reporting higher global self-esteem and members of interdependent cultures reporting lower global self-esteem
- report higher self-esteem when they feel supported and appreciated by their community
- are similar to each other in valuing children and wanting them to grow into effective adults
- appear to receive the same positive effects from supportive parenting

Parents of differing socioeconomic status have

- different views of their roles; higher-status parents are more child centered in their approach, and lower-status parents are more parent centered in their approach
- different goals and strategies; higher-status parents value verbal interactions with children, eliciting and understanding feelings, and negotiating differences, and lower-status parents value obedience and strict discipline for noncompliance
- similar forms of interactions with children but spend different amounts of time doing them

Poor children

- are more likely to suffer birth complications, cognitive delays, strict punishment, abuse, and neglect than are nonpoor children
- lack income that affects the quality of their health care, home environment, parenting, and neighborhoods
- profit from programs that provide support to parents
- profit from programs that provide stimulating activities for them

Parent educators benefit

- from exploring their own values about parenting
- from programs that help them to pay attention to parents' goals and preferred strategies

EXERCISES

1. Everyone receives many cultural messages from the groups to which they belong, whether determined by ethnicity, religion, geographic area of residence, age, or gender. What groups most strongly influence your views of the world and your general values?

2. Look at the ethnic influences that are part of your heritage. What values of these groups have you incorporated into your own life?

3. Recall the independent and interdependent models of parent-child relations. What are the advantages of each? Which of the two is more appealing to you? Why?

4. What are your short-term and long-term goals for parenting?

5. If you were a parent educator and were working with a parent who had a set of values that differed greatly from yours, how would you handle it?

ADDITIONAL READINGS

DeGenova, M. K., ed. *Families in Cultural Context: Strengths and Challenges in Diversity.* Mountain View, CA: Mayfield, 1997.

Demo, D. H., Allen, K. R., and Fine, M. A., ed. *Handbook of Family Diversity*. New York: Oxford University Press, 2000.

Hart, B., and Risley, T. R. *Meaningful Differences in the Everyday Experiences of Young American Children*. Baltimore: Brookes, 1995.

Illick, J. E. *American Childhoods*. Philadelphia: University of Pennsylvania Press, 2002.

Lareau, Annette. *Unequal Childhoods: Class, Race and Family Life*. Berkeley, CA: University of California Press, 2003.

McAdoo, H. P., ed. *Black Children*. 2nd ed. Thousand Oaks, CA: Sage, 2002.

4

Nurturing Close Emotional Relationships

CHAPTER TOPICS	IN THE NEWS
In this chapter, you will learn about:	*New York Times*, January 31[1]: Loved one's physical touch reduces stress. See pages 132–133.

In this chapter, you will learn about:

- Family systems and patterns of interaction
- The power of positive feelings
- Physical and emotional closeness
- Understanding and expressing feelings
- Family rituals
- Family Storytelling
- Identifying and managing negative feelings
- How parents under pressure can create and maintain positive feelings
- How children define the good parent

Test Your Knowledge: Fact or Fiction?

1. When parents have unhappy marriages, children function poorly even if parents develop good parenting skills.
2. Positive feelings such as joy and happiness are pleasurable in the moment, and they also contribute to the development of physical and psychological health.
3. Coaching children in understanding and expressing feelings helps them develop effective social skills and maintain physical health.
4. Children who observe angry silence between adults are not upset, because they do not understand the meaning of the silence.
5. Parents today have less free time than they have ever had, so it is hard for them to carry out all their tasks.

Parents in all ethnic groups give the same primary reason for wanting children: to love them and feel close to them.[2] Parenting experts agree that a primary task of parenting is nurturing close ties with children. How do parents do this? How do they create close bonds with children and at the same time manage the hassles and frustrations of everyday life so children feel loved and cherished?

In a 2002 national survey of sixteen hundred parents, 92 percent said it was crucial for parents to give children love and encouragement.[3] In this chapter, we look at how parents give children love and nurture close ties among family members while managing the daily frustrations that can interfere with closeness. We first look at patterns of family interactions from a systems point of view, to identify patterns that foster children's development and well-being, and then we look at more specific ways to increase emotional closeness and manage negative feelings.

FAMILY SYSTEMS AND PATTERNS OF INTERACTION

Parenting occurs in families. Whether families are small, with one parent and one child, or large, with several generations living together, family members form a system that cares for its members. Family systems theories developed in the 1960s, when therapists observed that many children's problems seemed to flow from parents' problems in their own lives or in their marriages. Therapists drew on insights from systems theory (explained in Chapter 2) to understand more precisely how parents' relationships to each other affected their children and their children's development.

The systems view emphasizes that a family, regardless of its structure, is a system made up of interdependent members who affect each other in a mutually responsive way.[4] An event in one family member's life has a ripple effect, touching all members, and their reactions, in turn, affect the person who initially experienced the event. Thus, a parent's loss of hours and pay at a job, or loss of a job altogether, affects the couple's relationship and their children, as we saw in Chapter 3 when we looked at the effects of economic hardship. The illness of a child or a parent touches everyone in the family. Brothers' and sisters' fighting affects parents, perhaps in different ways, and they react. When a child becomes a teenager, parents' lives and marriages are affected. Events touch everyone in the system, and everyone's reactions affect all the members in the system.

So, parenting behaviors and children's well-being depend on what happens between parents.

Negative Forms of Parental Interaction

When therapists first looked at family functioning, they identified several kinds of family interactions that increased children's behavior problems.[5] Parents could avoid recognizing their marital difficulties by "detouring" their feelings of tension in the marriage and focusing the feelings on a child who was described as "the problem." This was termed *scapegoating*.

Family therapists also described a process of *triangulation* in families. A parent forms a special bond or cross-generational alliance with a child as a way to get gratification that is not present in the marriage. The other parent is then left out. It is possible for both parents to form a triangulated relationship with the same child or to choose a different child for special closeness. In triangulated relationships, parents can become overinvolved and enmeshed with the child. A parent experiencing frustration in the marriage can disengage from the family and remain distant from all family members.

When researchers looked at families in the general population, they found the same patterns. In families researchers termed *enmeshed,* parents were angry, unable to agree on parenting rules, and overcontrolling and unaffectionate with children.[6] In families they termed *disengaged,* parents had high levels of hostility and provided little support for each other. Children in both enmeshed and disengaged families were more anxious, depressed, and angry than children in families where parents had average or greater marital satisfaction.

Researchers speculated that living with parental hostility, tensions, and difficulties decreased children's emotional security. Children felt more vulnerable in the world and, as a result, had symptoms of nervousness.

Positive Forms of Parental Interaction

When psychologists began to study forms of family interaction in healthy, representative samples, they found that parents in happy marriages generally had effective parenting skills, and their children functioned well. Mothers and fathers who were warm and sensitive marital partners were also warm and sensitive parents, and their children then functioned well. When parents were overwhelmed and disorganized, unable to spend time with family members and monitor children, their children had psychological difficulties in the areas of intellectual performance and social skills.[7]

A study of African American families has yielded typologies similar to those identified in national representative samples.[8] Families of African American adolescents were clustered into three types: *cohesive/authoritative, conflictive/authoritarian,* and *defensive/neglectful.* Parents in cohesive families were warm and sensitive yet authoritative with regard to rules and expectations; their teens were good-natured and trusting and had high self-esteem. Defensive/neglectful families were chaotic and disorganized. Parents, who were often single parents, exercised little discipline, and their children did what they pleased. Their children tended to be distrustful, uncooperative, and low in self-esteem. Conflicted/authoritarian parents were demanding, controlling, and insistent that children achieve; their children's self-esteem and social qualities were average, but teens did not perceive their own positive qualities of organization and hard work.

One study carried out on a large national sample of eight hundred families was able to identify a small cluster of families in which the quality of parenting and marital relationships differed.[9] Although 75 percent of the families had patterns of parenting skills that mirrored marital satisfactions, and children's functioning reflected the parents' effectiveness in these areas, 20 percent of the parents were described as having good parenting skills but unsatisfying marriages. Their children were less socially skilled and more aggressive than children whose parents had good marriages in addition to good parenting skills, but these children performed better on language and cognitive tests than children whose parents lacked parenting skills even if marriages were good. The children from families in which parents had good parenting skills but poor marriages were most similar in functioning to those children from families in which parents had moderately satisfying marriages and moderate parenting skills. So, good parenting skills enabled children to function at an average level even when parents were not satisfied with their marriages.

Coparenting

Coparenting focuses not on the marital relationship but on how two or more parenting figures relate to each other as they work together to rear children.[10] The concept is useful because it describes a relationship that is independent of the marital status of the parents and the family structure. Coparenting occurs whether parenting figures are married, separated, divorced, or remarried, whether extended family members are active parenting figures with or without the biological parent, and whether parenting occurs in periods of transition or periods of stability.

The principles of effective coparenting provide guidelines for establishing a stable family atmosphere so children can enjoy loving relationships with parents and other family members and can feel secure. James McHale and colleagues define effective coparenting:

> Effectively functioning coparenting units are those in which the significant adult figures collaborate to provide a family context that communicates to children solidarity and support between parenting figures, a consistent and predictable set of rules and standards (regardless of whether the child lives in a single household or in multiple ones), and a safe and secure home base.[11]

Research shows that parents' patterns of relating to each other as coparents are observable even before the child's birth, in their role playing of anticipated reactions to each other as they incorporate a baby into their family. Follow-ups of the parents' behaviors during the first year of the baby's life show patterns consistent with their role playing before the birth.[12]

Box 4-1 lists the basic ingredients of effective coparenting. The qualities suggest that, just as sensitive, responsive behavior with young children promotes emotional closeness and children's development, so do sensitive, responsive interactions between coparents build a strong alliance that promotes children's growth. The parental qualities of clear communication, cooperation, and coordinated working together to help children achieve agreed-upon goals, within definite boundaries of authority, create a calm, predictable family system. Within such a system, parents can then concentrate on nurturing emotional closeness and connections with children.

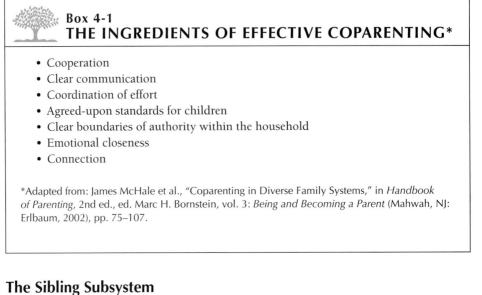

*Adapted from: James McHale et al., "Coparenting in Diverse Family Systems," in *Handbook of Parenting*, 2nd ed., ed. Marc H. Bornstein, vol. 3: *Being and Becoming a Parent* (Mahwah, NJ: Erlbaum, 2002), pp. 75–107.

The Sibling Subsystem

Families also include brothers and sisters, and parenting changes as the family grows larger. Parents want very much for their children to feel close and loving with each other as well as with them. What can they do to bring this about?

Parents first need to solidify their own relationship. Just as the quality of parents' marriages influences individual children's well-being, so does it influence sibling relationships. When parents get along with each other and relate positively to each child, brothers and sisters get long well. Conversely, when parents are angry with each other or are overwhelmed with stress, siblings are more likely to have negative relationships with each other.[13]

One might say, well, all brothers and sisters fight and dislike each other, and it doesn't matter; it's part of life. It does matter, though, because children learn social skills and patterns of negotiating with brothers and sisters that they may carry over into friendships with peers. Poor relationships between siblings can lead to sibling assaults. When brothers and sisters do not get along, older ones are more likely to lead younger ones into rule-breaking activity when they are both adolescents.[14]

When parents relate directly to children, the most important guideline is to avoid favoring one child over another. Parents do not always treat each child identically, as children of different ages and different temperaments have differing needs and rules, but parents must avoid making children feel that one child is more special or more valued than the others.[15]

Parents can also help children relate to new brothers and sisters by helping them form good relationships with other children prior to the birth of a new baby. When children can relate positively to other children, they bring these skills to the relationship with the new baby.[16]

So, sibling relationships are improved by positive relationships between the parents and by peer relationships where social skills are learned and practiced. We discuss this topic in later chapters as well but highlight it here to emphasize that family interactions among siblings affect the development of all siblings in a family.

THE POWER OF POSITIVE FEELINGS AND THOUGHTS

We have seen that, when there is a positive emotional tone in the family between parents and siblings, children develop in healthy ways. Recent research documents numerous benefits of positive feelings.

Researcher Barbara Fredrickson believes that each positive emotion broadens individuals' behavioral responses.[17] Joy stimulates play and creativity; interest encourages exploration and learning; contentment fosters appreciation of experiences and understanding of their importance to individuals' growth; pride builds connections with others to share what has been achieved, and love—described as an amalgam of all the positive emotions shared in relationship with others—stimulates play, creativity, exploration, and learning together. So, positive feelings broaden people's interactions and connect people more closely.

Further, positive emotions appear to undo the effects of negative feelings by calming the cardiovascular arousal triggered by negative feelings such as anger, sadness, or fear. When subjects watched films that aroused such positive feelings as contentment and mild joy after negative reactions, subjects' heart rates and blood pressure returned to normal more quickly. The arousal of positive feelings following negative experiences appears also to enable individuals to put negative experiences in broader perspective, minimizing their impact. The person is able to make plans and take action and does not become immobilized by the negative reactions. Although all these findings concern feelings induced in laboratory studies of representative samples of people, the findings on the benefits of positive feelings are similar to findings in studies of successful programs for the treatment of depression and anxiety, as we shall see in Chapter 11.

The list of good things connected with positive emotions is not complete. Positive emotions also contribute to the important psychological quality of *resilience*, defined as functioning effectively and achieving good outcomes when confronted with adversity and situations that decrease adaptation.[18] Positive feelings increase people's ability to function under stress.

We have discussed research with adults, but positive feelings are important in children's development as well. Research reveals that, if children simply think of some pleasant event for a short time, they resist temptation more successfully and respond to unfair treatment with fairness and generosity. Happy feelings inoculate children against the effects of negative events.[19] Further, a longitudinal study shows that how one spends leisure time in childhood, how one has fun in childhood, predicts psychological health at age thirty better than the presence or absence of anxieties and problems in childhood.[20]

Because so many benefits flow from positive feelings, we focus attention in this chapter and the next on ways to nurture these feelings in our homes with family members and in our daily lives with people we meet.

We talk first about physical and emotional closeness, about forms of communication that deepen relationships, and about activities such as routines, rituals, and storytelling that increase family closeness. In these experiences, we come to know one another most intimately—and intimate knowledge about children is what makes it possible for parents to relate effectively to them.

PHYSICAL TOUCH AND CLOSENESS

Physical closeness brings feelings of pleasure and relaxation. We have learned about the importance of physical contact from studies with animals and newborn infants. Rats whose caretakers handled and gentled them had great resistance to stress and survived surgeries that killed rats that did not have such handling.[21] Monkeys sought physical contact with a terry-cloth mother in preference to food. Preterm infants who received deep-pressure massages several times a day in the hospital gained weight faster, were awake and more active during the day, were more alert and responsive during a developmental assessment, and were discharged from the hospital sooner than infants who did not receive massages.[22]

Close physical contact with mothers serves to regulate infants' hormonal levels, sleeping patterns, eating patterns, heart rate, and vagal tone. (*Vagal tone* refers to the neural control of increases and decreases in the heartbeat and is considered a measure of individual differences in the expression and regulation of emotion.) In the first few weeks of life, infants who receive extra carrying and physical closeness cry less than babies who are not carried so much, and they are more visually and aurally alert.[23] When mothers are away or unavailable because of hospitalizations or trips, babies do not eat, sleep, or function physically and socially as well as they did before mothers' absence.[24]

The parents of colicky babies who were having trouble sleeping at three to six months of age were taught to massage their babies for fifteen minutes before bedtime.[25] Massaged babies, when compared to nonmassaged, colicky babies, were less irritable, fell asleep faster, and awoke fewer times during the night. During the day, they were more alert.

There is much less research on the importance of physical touch for older children, but we do know that physical contact helps adults.[26] Neuroscientists recently

Physical closeness and touch brings feelings of relaxation and emotional closeness for both participants.

used magnetic resonance imaging (MRI) on married women to document that holding their husbands' hands, as opposed to strangers' hands, can decrease stress from anticipated mild shocks and produce changes deep in the brain. Women in extremely close marriages experienced the greatest relief from stress.

Adults who have given infant massages have benefited from the massages as well.[27] Depressed mothers who massaged their infants were more alert and responsive in face-to-face interactions with their children. Elderly volunteers who were taught to give infant massages reported that they felt less anxious and depressed, slept better, and were more socially active. Improvements were greater after one month of giving infant massages than after one month of receiving massages themselves.

So, physical touch is important and can be maintained with toddlers and older children with nighttime massages, hugs, the physical play that fathers often engage in, pats on the shoulder. Recalling the relaxing power of holding a loved one's hand can encourage us to do that more at times of stress, for example, a parent's holding a child's hand on the way to a doctor's appointment or a laboratory test.

EMOTIONAL CLOSENESS

Parents form a close relationship when they love the child as a special person. Dorothy Briggs describes the psychological climate that enables children to feel their parents' love: "Nurturing love is tender caring—valuing a child just because he exists. It comes when you see your youngster as special and dear—even though you may not approve of all that he does."[28] Children are loved simply because they exist—no strings attached, no standards to meet. This is the "unconditional support" that Susan Harter refers to in her interview in Chapter 5 and Emmy Werner suggests in hers (see pages 134–135).

Parents form close relationships with children of all ages in two basic ways: by providing sensitive, responsive care that meets the child's individual needs and by becoming an interactive social partner who shares the child's response to life's experiences. Sensitive, responsive care fosters the child's feelings of security and closeness to the parent. Sensitive care changes with the age and individual qualities of the child. Becoming a social partner who provides appropriate stimulation and shares the child's experiences and pleasures in life takes many forms, depending on the age of the child, as we discuss in subsequent chapters.

Parents become aware of their child's unique qualities by observing the child's interests and behavior, listening to the child's thoughts and feelings, and responding to the child with open and appropriate expression of parental feelings. This may seem impossible with a baby, but as we shall see in Chapter 7, it is not. Understanding and communicating feelings are at the center of intimate relationships from the start.

UNDERSTANDING AND EXPRESSING FEELINGS

Babies come into the world with emotions and feelings that serve as signals to others of the infant's experiences and needs. Long before they have language, children express their feelings through smiles, laughs, cries, and frowns.

INTERVIEW
with Emmy E. Werner

Emmy E. Werner is a research professor of human development at the University of California, Davis. For three decades, she and her colleagues Jessie Bierman and Fern French at the University of California, Berkeley, and Ruth Smith, a clinical psychologist on the Hawaiian island of Kauai, have conducted the Kauai Longitudinal Study, resulting in books such as Vulnerable but Invincible, The Children of Kauai, Kauai's Children Come of Age, *and* Overcoming the Odds.

From your experience watching children at risk grow up on Kauai, what would you say parents can do to support children, to help maximize their child's potential? From your work with children at risk, what helps children survive and flourish even when faced with severe problems?

Let me say that, in our study, we studied the offspring of women whom we began to see at the end of the first trimester of pregnancy. We followed them during the pregnancy and delivery. We saw the children at ages one, two, and ten, late adolescence, and again at thirty-two and forty years. We have test scores, teachers' observations, and interview material at different times on these people. We have a group of children who were at high risk because of four or more factors. They were children who (1) experienced prenatal or perinatal complications, (2) grew up in poverty, (3) lived in a dysfunctional family with one or more problems, and (4) had a parent with alcohol or mental health problems.

You ask me to comment on parenting and what parents can do, but first I would like to urge that we redefine and extend the definition of parenting to cast a wider net and include people who provide love in the lives of children. I like to talk about *alloparenting,* the parenting of children by alternate people who are not the biological parents—they can be relatives, neighbors, siblings.

In our study of vulnerable but invincible children, we found that a major protective factor was that at least one person, perhaps a biological parent, or a grandparent, or an older sibling, accepted them unconditionally. That one person made the child feel special, very, very special. These parent figures made the child feel special through acts. They conveyed their love through deeds. They acted as models for the child. They didn't pretend the child had no handicap or problem, but what they conveyed was, "You matter to me, and you are special."

Now, another theme in our findings is that the parent figure, whoever he or she was, encouraged the child to reach out to others beyond the family—to seek out a friendly

A series of studies by John Gottman and his associates indicate that parents differ in their attitudes and thoughts about the importance of feelings.[29] Some parents have a heightened awareness of their own and their children's feelings and a strong conviction that feelings are a central part of life. Feelings signal that change is required. Anger serves to initiate action in frustrating situations, and sadness slows a person down to have time to cope with loss. These parents feel comfortable with their feelings, and they consider that a major parental task is to help their children live happily with their own emotional reactions. They do this by coaching children

neighbor, a parent of one of their boy or girl friends, and, thus, learn about normal parenting from other families.

The resilient child was temperamentally engaging. He or she encouraged interaction with others outside the home and was given the opportunity to relate to others.

I had no preconceptions about this protective factor, but what came through was that, somewhere along the line, in the face of poverty, in the face of a handicap, faith has an abiding power. I'm not referring to faith in a narrow, denominational sense, but having someone in the family or outside of it who was saying, "Hey, you are having ups and downs, this will pass, you will get through this, and things will get better."

Another thing was that these children had an opportunity to care for themselves or others. They became nurturant and concerned, perhaps about a parent or a sibling. They practiced "required helpfulness."

Now, another protective factor is whether the children were able to develop a hobby that was a refuge and gave them respect among their peers. One of our study members said later, "If I had any doubts about whether I could make it, that hobby turned me around." The hobby was especially important as a buffer between the person and the chaos in the family. But it was not a hobby that isolated you from others; it nourished something you could share with other people.

As many of the children looked back, they describe how a positive relationship with a sibling was enduring and important. As adults, they commented with surprise on how supportive the relationship was and how these relationships were maintained despite great distances and despite dissimilarities in life and interests.

What did adults say they wanted to pass on to their own children?

Looking back as adults, they felt that some sort of structure in their life was very important. Even though the family life was chaotic, if a parent imposed some reasonable rules and regulations, it was helpful.

They emphasized faith as something to hang on to and make this clear to their children. As parents now they are quite achievement motivated. They graduated from high school, and some went back and got additional training. They encourage their children to do well in school.

The main theme that runs through our data is the importance of a parent figure who says "you matter" and the child's ability to create his or her own environment. The children believed they could do it, someone gave them hope, and they succeeded against the odds.

to label their reactions, validating the importance of their feelings no matter what they are, and teaching their children strategies for expressing feelings appropriately. Feelings do not frighten these parents. Rather, parents see feelings as opportunities to become closer to their children through sharing strong reactions and teaching ways to handle them.

Other parents feel uncomfortable with feelings and seek one of three ways to handle the discomfort.[30] Dismissive parents minimize the importance of feelings, making light of them or ignoring them because they believe the feelings may make matters worse. Disapproving parents criticize, judge, and punish children for the expression of feelings. These parents usually disapprove of only a subgroup of feelings, such as anger and sadness, or only those feelings that arise under certain conditions, such as a "minor event." Children of dismissive and disapproving parents have a hard time trusting their own judgment. By learning that their feelings are wrong, children come to believe there is something basically wrong with *them* for having the feelings. Because they have little experience in acknowledging and dealing with their feelings, they often have difficulty controlling them and solving problems. Finally, *laissez-faire* parents accept all feelings and often comfort the child when the child experiences a negative emotional reaction, but they do little to teach or guide the child in expressing feelings appropriately. These parents seem to believe that expressing feelings in any form, appropriate or inappropriate, will take care of the problem. Their children do not learn to cope constructively with feelings and have difficulty concentrating, learning, and making friends.

So, the three types of response—ignoring feelings, criticizing feelings so they occur as little as possible, and accepting all expressions of feeling without providing guidance for expression—lead to similar kinds of problems for children, such as the inability to regulate feelings and to feel comfortable with themselves and others.

Gottman and his coworkers found that, when parents coached their five-year-old children to deal with feelings, the children functioned better physically and psychologically when they were eight years old. They performed better academically and were socially more competent with peers. They were physically healthier as well, perhaps because coaching helps children modulate their emotional reactions, which modulation in turn helps their physiological systems function better. Coaching involves listening to children's feelings, accepting and validating them, using I-messages (discussed later in this chapter) regarding one's own feelings, and helping children solve problems while maintaining acceptable limits concerning the expression of feelings. Coaching children not only helps them deal better with their feelings and with social and cognitive endeavors, it also frequently brings parents and children closer together because parents feel they really understand their children.

On the basis of their research, Gottman and his colleagues describe five key steps in emotion coaching:[31]

1. Parents recognize when they are having a feeling, what that feeling is, and when others are having feelings.
2. Parents consider feelings as opportunities for intimacy or teaching. When the child is upset, happy, or excited, parents see this as an opportunity to be close to the child and to teach the child how to express feelings appropriately.
3. Parents listen empathically and validate the child's feelings. They use active listening skills and validate what the child feels without trying to argue the child out of the feeling (see "Active Listening," following).
4. Parents help the child verbally label the feeling. The child may be confused about what he or she is feeling. Labeling the feeling is identifying the feeling, giving the child a word for the strong emotion; it is not telling the child how to feel. Labeling a feeling while the child is experiencing it appears to have a soothing effect on the child's nervous system. Labeling feelings also helps a child see that he or she can have two feelings at the same time.

5. Parents set limits while helping the child solve the problem. Parents limit the way feelings are expressed; they do not, however, limit the child's having the feeling itself. Anger, for example, is acceptable, but hitting a sibling is not. Parents help the child think of possible actions to express feelings and ways to achieve his or her goals in the situation.

Several additional strategies help parents implement these five steps. First, parents should avoid criticism, sarcasm, mockery, or humiliation when they talk to children about feelings. The importance of this advice cannot be overemphasized. In one study, parents' negative reactions (minimizing, becoming distressed, assigning punishment) to children's emotional reactions predicted poor emotional regulation and poor social functioning in children two to six years later.[32] No doubt the children's poor emotional regulation intensified parents' negative responses; nevertheless, parents' negative reactions predicted children's problem behaviors six to eight years later even when effects of early problem behavior and emotional regulation were controlled for.

Second, in emotion coaching, parents use scaffolding and praise in teaching. *Scaffolding* is giving basic information or other assistance to help the child begin problem solving. Parents also give specific positive feedback to the child at the beginning and then let the child take over and handle the situation.

Third, parents focus on the child's agenda, not on their own. If a child is upset while the parent is paying bills, the parent puts away the checks and focuses on the child or asks the child to wait a few minutes until the task is finished. Parents' use of these steps and strategies enables children to feel comfortable with their emotions and to find appropriate means of expressing them.

Gottman speculates that talking about emotional reactions has positive benefits for children because the verbal expression of feelings helps children plan appropriate actions and eliminates the consequences of inhibiting negative emotional reactions.[33] Negative emotions such as sadness and fear are usually processed in the right frontal part of the brain and are associated with withdrawal from stimulation and the arousal of internal physiological reactions, because the right hemisphere is connected with lower brain centers that are involved in physiological reactivity. Positive emotional reactions such as joy, interest, and even anger are processed in the left frontal area of the brain and are associated with engagement with the world. Language centers are also located in the left frontal area of the brain. Talking to children and helping them process their feelings activate the left frontal area of the brain, shifting stimulation away from the right frontal area so that children can calm their physiological reactions.

So, coaching children not only helps them deal better with their feelings and with social and cognitive endeavors; it also calms their physiological reactions and improves their health. In the process, coaching frequently brings parents and children closer together because parents feel they really understand their children.

Active Listening

One tool parents use in coaching is *active listening,* Thomas Gordon's term for what parents do when they reflect their children's feelings.[34] Parents listen to children's statements, pay careful attention to the feelings expressed, and then frame a response that restates what the child has said. Here is one of Gordon's examples of active listening:

CHILD: I don't want to go to Bobby's birthday party tomorrow.
PARENT: Sounds like you and Bobby have had a problem, maybe.
CHILD: I hate him, that's what. He's not fair.
PARENT: You really hate him because you feel he's been unfair somehow.
CHILD: Yeah. He never plays what I want to play.[35]

If the parent's response is accurate, the child confirms the feedback with a positive response. If the parent's interpretation is wrong, the child indicates that and can correct the misinterpretation by expanding on his feelings. The parent can continue active listening to understand what is happening to the child.

Active listening has several main advantages. First, it helps children express feelings in a direct, effective way. As feelings are expressed and parents accept them, children feel understood and learn that they are like everyone else.[36]

Second, as feelings are expressed, parents and children together learn that the apparent problem is not necessarily the real or basic problem. Like the rest of us, children use defenses and sometimes start by blaming a friend, a parent, or circumstances for what they are feeling. As parents focus on the feelings, children gradually come to identify the underlying problem and discover what they can do about it.

Third, listening to children's feelings is sometimes all that is needed to resolve the problem. Often, when we are upset, sad, or angry, we simply want to express the feeling and have someone respond: "It's really painful when a friend walks off with someone else and leaves you behind." The response validates the feeling as justified and important, and frequently that is all we want.

How can parents become active listeners? First, Gordon warns parents not to attempt active listening when they are hurried or preoccupied. Active listening requires persistence, patience, and a strong commitment to attend both to the child's words and to the accompanying behavioral clues. Furthermore, there are times when active listening is not appropriate. If a child asks for information, give the information. If a child does not want to talk about his feelings, respect the child's privacy and do not probe. Similarly, if active listening and the dialogue have gone as far as the child is willing to go, then a parent needs to recognize that it is time to stop.

One of the mothers in Haim Ginott's parenting group raised the question of reflecting back feelings of great sadness over a loss.[37] Is this wise? Does it help children? Ginott responded that parents must learn that suffering can strengthen a child's character. When a child is sad in response to a real loss, a parent need only empathize: "You are sad. I understand." The child learns that the parent is a person who understands and sympathizes.

I-Messages

When a parent is angry, frustrated, or irritated with a child, the parent can communicate his or her feelings constructively, with an I-message rather than by nagging, yelling, or criticizing. The I-message contains three parts: (1) a clear statement of how the parent feels, (2) a statement of the behavior that has caused the parent to feel that way, and (3) a statement describing why the behavior is upsetting to the parent. For example, a parent might say, "I feel frustrated when you don't empty the dishwasher at night, because I can't put the morning's dirty dishes in it."

Parents need to take time to analyze their feelings and to become more aware of exactly how they feel. Gordon points out that, often, when a parent communicates anger to a child, the parent may actually be feeling disappointment, fear, frustration, or hurt. When a child comes home an hour late, the parent may launch into a tirade. The worry that grew into fear during the hour of waiting is translated into angry words to prevent a recurrence of the event. The parent needs to express the fear and worry, not the anger.

What should a parent do if a child pays no attention to I-messages? First, be sure the child *can* pay attention to the I-message. Do not try to communicate feelings when the child is rushing out of the house or is already deeply immersed in some other activity. If an I-message is then ignored, send another, more forceful message in a firm tone of voice. Sometimes, a child responds to an I-message with an I-message. For example, when a parent expresses distress because the lawn is not mowed, the daughter may reply that she feels annoyed because mowing interferes with her after-school activities. At that point, the parent must "shift gears," as Gordon puts it, and reflect back the child's frustration by using active listening and then send another I-message.

I-messages have several benefits. First, when parents use I-messages, they begin to take their own needs seriously. This process benefits all family relationships because parents feel freer—more themselves—in all areas of life. Second, children learn about the parents' reaction, which they may not have understood until the I-message was spoken. Third, children have an opportunity to solve problems in response to I-messages. Even toddlers and preschoolers have ideas, not only for themselves but also for others. Siblings often have good ideas about what might be bothering another child in the family. They think of things that might have escaped the attention of parents.

I-messages can convey appreciation: "I feel pleased when you help me with the dishes, because then we have time to go to the store for your school supplies." I-messages are also useful in heading off problems and in helping children see that their parents have needs too. These messages, termed *preventive I-messages,* express parents' future wants or needs and give children an opportunity to respond positively. For example, if a parent says, "I need quiet so I can drive the car," the child learns what to do to be helpful.

Although closeness is enjoyable for and helpful to children, some parents do not feel good about themselves or some of their own qualities, which causes them to wonder whether their children might not be better off remaining distant from them. They fear that their children will pick up their bad qualities. Research on close and nonclose relationships among adolescents and their parents reveals that children who feel close to their parents are *less* likely to take on the parents' negative qualities than are children who feel distant. Parents' negative behaviors are a more potent influence on children when parents and children are not close.[38] Thus, even when parents have many self-doubts and self-criticism, closeness with them and all their failings is still a positive experience for their children.

FAMILY ROUTINES AND RITUALS

Family rituals and routines bring family members closer together. Family rituals were first studied to shed light on how troubled families preserved stability at times of stress. In studying families of alcoholics, Steven Wolin and Linda Bennett found that rituals provided a sense of rhythm and continuity to life that increase children's feelings of security and their capacity to communicate with adults.[39] Rituals provide stability by ensuring predictability in family life: No matter what else happens, the family eats dinner together, decorates the Christmas tree, and serves special meals for birthdays.

Children who grew up in alcoholic families who nevertheless maintained their family celebrations and rituals were less likely to develop alcoholic problems as adults than those who grew up with an alcoholic parent who did not maintain traditions.[40] The rituals served as protective, positive forces at times of stress, giving children feelings of security and closeness to others.

Recent work has focused on how family routines and rituals draw family members together in daily life, increase contact with family members across generations, and contribute to psychological health and well-being, especially at times of transition, such as the birth of a baby or marital dissolution.

Routines

Routines are defined as patterned interactions, occurring regularly on a daily, weekly, or monthly basis, that accomplish a practical goal—taking in food, getting sleep, carrying out chores.[41] There are no strong emotional investments in routines, and there is little thought about them after they are completed. They are ways to get things done, a means to an end, and can be changed if more efficient or useful ways present themselves.

Routines may not have symbolic or emotional investment for families, but they are still very important, because they represent structure and organization in family life. This is especially important at times of transition—to parenthood, for example. Household routines at that time help new mothers feel more competent and satisfied in their role as parents. Single parents who maintained routines around eating, bedtime, and doing things together felt more successful as single parents, and their children functioned better.[42]

Organized routines also increase children's academic competence.[43] For example, researchers studying young children's reading skills in a heterogeneous sample found that the routines of dinnertime meals, reading aloud, and homework made up what they termed the *intimate family culture*. The intimate family culture significantly predicted children's reading skills in third grade, accounting for most of the variance attributed to family income and ethnicity in predicting the sample's reading scores. In other words, intimate family routines appear to contribute strongly to the predictive power of social status and financial resources. When children from families with fewer resources have the intimate culture of families with middle-class resources, children achieve in reading at the same level as middle-class children.

Rituals

Rituals are defined as repeated patterns of behavior that have symbolic meaning for the family: "This says something important about us as a family."[44] Members invest emotion in routines and feel a sense of belonging when they carry them out. Recalling the ritual or anticipating it can arouse warm feelings, and not carrying it out can disrupt the cohesive feelings of the family. Rituals are major ways that cultural and ethnic groups pass their values on to the next generation. Rituals include family celebrations of major secular or religious holidays, and special family traditions such as vacations or birthday celebrations.

The drama and excitement of rituals and traditions encourage communication and increased involvement with other family members. Rituals draw generations close together and reduce the gap, for example, between parents and children, as everyone engages in rituals as equals—everyone in the family eats lots of food at holiday feasts, everyone in the family hits the piñata at a birthday.

Family therapist William Doherty categorizes rituals in terms of their purpose.[45] There are (1) connection rituals, which promote bonding between family members (family outings and vacations); (2) love rituals, for showing love to each member (birthdays, Mother's Day, Grandparent's Day); and (3) community rituals, which connect family members to the larger community (weddings, baptisms, other spiritual and ethnic celebrations). Box 4-2 includes Doherty's suggestions for creating rewarding family rituals.

Many routines, especially when children are young, can become family rituals. For example, bedtime routines can take on symbolic meaning and emotional investment when children are young; the bath, a story the child chooses, talking and cuddling, prayers, or being tucked in and kissed may be a routine parents and children cherish. As children get older, the activity may incorporate new features and remain a ritual—a talk with a teen in the kitchen before bedtime may replace the story and cuddling, but it still is a valued time together. Or as children get older, the

---

Box 4-2
MAJOR PRINCIPLES FOR ESTABLISHING REWARDING FAMILY RITUALS*

- Get agreement between adults in the family.
- Have as much participation as possible from all family members in planning and deciding what to do.
- Expect that cooperation from children will emerge slowly.
- Have clear expectations of what will happen and who will do what.
- Reduce conflict through open communication and respect for others' feelings.
- Protect rituals from the demands of other activities.
- Be willing to change or modify the rituals as needed.

*Adapted from William J. Doherty, *The Intentional Family* (New York: Avon, 1997), pp. 198–199.

ritual at bedtime may return to being a routine—a quick hug and kiss, and off to bed. We discuss routines again in Chapter 5, as they are important contributors to healthy eating, sleeping, and exercise habits.

STORYTELLING

Telling stories draws family members close to each other. As Susan Engel writes,

> We all want to know who we are and how we came into our world. We all want to know that we were recognized, that we are singular and special. And we each learn this, in part, through the stories we are told about our beginnings. We reencounter ourselves constantly throughout life and confirm what we already know by telling, over and over again, one version or one aspect of the story of our life.[46]

Storytelling begins at birth. "Babies are surrounded by the stories parents, siblings, and friends tell one another, and to them, a captive audience. By the time children are 2 and 3 years old, they begin adding their own voices to the stories that surround them."[47] Stories initially consist of only a few words about an event— "Played house. I was baby."

Observations reveal that mothers and toddlers tell about nine stories each hour.[48] In addition to telling stories to others, young children, as they play, often construct ongoing stories about what they are doing, monologues that will later develop into thoughts and daydreams. By the time children grow up and are in college, they tell from five to thirty-eight stories each day.

Engel gives parents tips for encouraging children to participate in storytelling. Children tell stories when they feel "confidence and joyousness in telling stories,"[49] and parents give that confidence when they listen attentively and express interest with smiles, gasps, facial expressions, repetitions. Parents collaborate in the stories by asking open-ended questions that encourage elaboration, and they expose children to a variety of stories and poems that stimulate their children's stories.

Stories serve several purposes.[50] They shape our views of ourselves, other people, and events in our lives. We often discover more about what we think, feel, or know in the course of telling someone about an experience. Stories tell us about the world, our cultures, and the values that hold our families together.

Recounting negative stories in a structured format has value too. Students were asked to write about either stressful or trivial events for four consecutive days.[51] Six months later, those students who chose to write about stressful events had fewer visits to the health center and reported better health than did those who chose to write about trivial life events. Adult workers who wrote about traumatic events once a week for four consecutive weeks missed fewer days from work than those in a control group. Putting upsetting events into words releases psychological tensions that cause physiological arousal when they are unexpressed.

Stories reflect important family themes that are expressed in other behaviors as well.[52] For example, researchers found that the content of stories parents tell about their families of origin reveals parents' underlying views about what to expect in relationships, and these expectations are related to parents' behavior at dinnertime and to their perceptions of their children. Mothers and fathers who told stories of rewarding, fulfilling relationships in their families of origin reported satisfactions in their marriages and showed more positive feelings at dinnertimes. They perceived their children as functioning well.

Conversely, mothers and fathers who told stories of unrewarding relationships in their families of origin expressed more negative affect at mealtimes and reported that their children had aggressive behavior problems. Continuity of positive and negative affect flowed across generations, with parents' reporting of affective relationships in their childhoods mirrored in their relationships with spouses, and children expressing affect similar to their parents'.

Reviewing the way parents interacted as they told a story to children, researchers noted that parents who coordinated their efforts and worked together, affirming each others' position, had more positive feelings in their dinnertime interactions, and their children had more positive affect as well.

In attempting to tell stories about their personal experiences, family members sometimes struggled to make sense of the experiences, but the effort was worth it because, in the researchers' words, "Families that are able to make sense of their experiences, pleasant or challenging, provide their children with a meaning-making system that can better prepare them for an unpredictable world."[53]

PROVIDING OPPORTUNITIES FOR SELF-EXPRESSION

Family relationships are most harmonious when both children and parents have outlets for expressing feelings. Activities such as daily physical exercise, drawing, modeling clay, painting, and cooking all serve as outlets to drain off tensions and irritations and provide individuals with additional sources of pleasure and feelings of competence. Wise parents provide children with a variety of outlets so that they develop many skills. Research indicates that childhood leisure activities, especially a wide variety—such as painting, reading, and sports—are more predictive of psychological health in adulthood than are the child's own personality characteristics. These activities promote self-confidence and self-esteem, which increase psychological health.[54]

IDENTIFYING AND DEALING WITH NEGATIVE FEELINGS

Active listening and I-messages help parents and children deal with negative feelings once they are aroused. But preventing stress is a major way to decrease negative feelings. To do this, we need to identify sources of stress in everyday life. Strategies to minimize hassles and negative feelings in the family include (1) creating family time, (2) developing a support system, (3) maintaining realistic expectations, and (4) learning ways to manage negative feelings.

Sources of Negative Feelings

We are aware that emotional extremes in parents, such as violent anger or clinical depression, affect children's behavior, but we may not know that even negative moods in the course of daily life—such as those caused by the overall challenges of parenting—can also adversely affect parents' interactions with children and children's behavior.

Lack of Time   Fifty-eight percent of parents worry about the small amount of time the family spends together.[55] Studies of time diaries over a thirty-year period and survey data on time use yield provocative findings. John Robinson and Geoffrey Godbey, summarizing their extensive work in their book *Time for Life,* point out that, according to time diaries recorded by participants, adults overestimate the number of hours they work.[56] They also underestimate the amount of free time they have (defined as time not spent in essential activities such as work, self-care, and family and household activities).

Robinson and Godbey argue that, of the 168 hours available each week, about 68 are spent sleeping and in necessary self-care such as eating and grooming. Of the 100 remaining hours, about 53, on average, are spent working and in direct family care, about 7 on discretionary self-care, and about 40 as free time. Parents of young children have less free time than adults in other age groups—about 30 hours per week, occurring mostly on weekends—but they still have about an hour more free time than was available to parents in 1965. According to the researchers, single parents have considerably less time with their children—about 3 hours less per week—so their children lose time with them, as well as daily time with the absent parent in the case of divorce.

Many would argue with these conclusions, but Robinson and Godbey's data and analysis of others' data do point to the fact that people may have more free time than they realize and that feelings of what they call *time-famine* have other causes, such as the accelerated pace of life. Robinson and Godbey write,

> Speed and brevity are more widely admired, whether in serving food, in the length of magazine articles, or in conversation. As the pace of life has speeded up, there has been a natural tendency to assume that other time elements have been reshaped as well. Primary among these assumptions is the notion that hours of work (duration) are increasing and that those who feel most rushed must work the longest hours.[57]

Feelings of lack of time may also come from the fact that Americans spend about 40 percent of their free time in an activity that gives them less satisfaction than most other leisure activities—namely, watching television. Thus, they do not take the time they have for more satisfying social activities and pursuits with family and friends.

Studies of time diaries reveal that children have less and less time for activities and conversations with parents.[58] A University of Michigan study found that, in 1981, children had about 63 hours per week for discretionary activities—free time when they were not eating, sleeping, in school, or engaged in self-care. In 1997, they had only 51 hours, a 16 percent decline in free time. Time in school increased from 21 hours per week to 29 hours per week, and time spent in self-care and getting ready to go places increased as well. Time spent talking to parents, however, decreased 100 percent. In addition, parents and children have less time with each other because about 50 percent of children experience divorce, and many go back and forth between two households and thus see less of each parent. So, time pressures exist for both parents and children.

Suggestions for Dealing with the Problem   First, Robinson and Godbey suggest that parents might feel less pressured if they realized that their feelings of time-famine, although genuine, are not related to the actual number of free-time hours available to them.[59] Free time is available in small chunks during the week and larger ones during the weekend, but parents must plan carefully to make good use of it.

Second, they advise parents to spend free time in activities that give them satisfaction. Television, as noted earlier, absorbs 40 percent of people's free time, despite the fact American adults do not rate it as satisfying as most other activities they engage in and list it as the first activity they would give up in a time crunch. What is the charm of television? "As an activity, television viewing requires no advance planning, costs next to nothing, requires no physical effort, seldom shocks or surprises, and can be done in the comfort of one's own home—with pizza only a telephone call away."[60]

Third, Robinson and Godbey voice their concern for what they term *time-deepening activities*—that is, doing two or more things at the same time to maximize one's use of time. Instead of time-saving efforts, Robinson and Godbey recommend cultivating time-savoring skills in order to appreciate

> . . . the simpler delights of life as they are occurring: the taste of good food, the presence of good company, and the delights of fun and silliness. To be happier and wiser, it is easier to increase appreciation levels more than efficiency levels. Only by appreciating more can we hope to have a sustainable society. While efficiency, at least as envisioned in American society, always starts with wanting more, appreciating may start both with valuing more what is already here and with wanting less.[61]

Box 4-3 presents additional suggestions for slowing down.

EVERYDAY NEGATIVE MOODS

Minor daily hassles at work or with children contribute to parents' negative moods, which in turn affect parenting and children's behavior. Negative moods bias parents' recall of children's past behaviors, shape parents' interpretations of current behavior, and cause parents to discipline children more harshly.[62]

Hassles do not have to be intense or prolonged. In one study, even a briefly induced negative mood reduced mothers' positive comments and verbal interactions with their children during play and laboratory tasks.[63] In another study, being distracted by a simple task involving anagrams resulted in parents' being less positive, more irritable, and more critical of and interfering with their preschoolers.[64]

The hassles that generally trigger a negative mood stem from the daily challenges of parenting rather than from major difficulties with children.[65] Hassles fall into two broad categories: (1) the effort required to rear children—continually

Box 4-3
PRAISING SLOWNESS*

Carl Honore, a Canadian foreign correspondent hurrying home to his family in London, waited impatiently for his plane in the Rome airport. A speedaholic who hated to waste a minute, he was using the time to glance through a newspaper, when an ad caught his eye—for a series of books titled *The One-Minute Bedtime Story,* condensed versions of classic fairy tales. "Perfect," he thought. His two-year-old son always wanted more bedtime stories, and he was in a hurry to get back to his chores. With this series, he could read six or seven and be back at work in less than ten minutes.

While he was calculating how fast he could get the books, he stopped, shocked at his willingness to shrink his time with his son down to a few minutes. On the plane, he thought to himself that his life had "turned into an exercise in hurry, in packing more and more into every hour. I am a Scrooge with a stopwatch, obsessed with saving every last scrap of time, a minute here, a few seconds there! And I am not alone. Everyone around me—colleagues, friends, family—is caught in the same vortex."

Honore found that this problem was not new. As long ago as 200 BC, the Roman playwright Plautus complained that sundials hacked and cut his days into small pieces. "I can't (even sit down to eat) unless the sun gives leave, the town's so full of these confounded dials."

Honore determined to slow down, to enjoy and savor the time with his family and friends. He began with little steps. He took off his watch and left it in a drawer. He cooked a meal from scratch. He read without turning on the television. He began to take walks, to do yoga and meditation. Eventually, he changed his work and became a free-lance writer, authoring the book *In Praise of Slowness.*

Does he ever hurry now? Yes, when he has something he must do quickly. But he does not hurry for the sake of hurrying. He seeks to do things at the right speed, the proper tempo. He does fewer things with less rushing.

He is happy to see that slowness movements are spreading around the world. The Slow Food Movement, begun in Italy, encourages the use of fresh, local produce consumed in a leisurely fashion with family and friends; the movement has attracted members around the globe. In 2004, Canberra, Australia, held a Slow Festival, with walks, long meals, and lectures on slowing down in all areas of life. In Canada, a group called SlowBiz encourages slowing down in the workplace, and in Poland, the Voluntary Slowness Movement has a website and a chat room that provide suggestions for slowing down.

Honore gives invited talks at conferences and organizations and interviews to magazines and television. Yes, at times, he works long hours extolling the benefits of slowness, but he has time for family, friends, and pleasure in life. He enjoys reading to his son at night, answering all his questions, and *The One-Minute Bedtime Story* is a dim memory.

*Carl Honore, *In Praise of Slowness* (New York: HarperCollins, 2004).

cleaning up messes, changing family plans, running errands to meet children's needs—and (2) the challenge of dealing with irritating behaviors such as whining, sibling fights, and constant demands.

Parents' personality characteristics, their coping styles, and the amount of support available to them can intensify or decrease stress.[66] Outgoing, sociable, optimistic parents are less likely to respond to hassles with negative moods. Parents who use avoidant coping styles, who wish stress would go away so they wouldn't have to deal with it, experience increased stress. Parents who use positive reappraisal of the situation, who feel they are learning from the situation and becoming more skilled, experience decreased stress and retain their self-confidence.

Everyday Anger   Many researchers have documented that, when children are exposed to different forms of anger, they respond with emotional arousal that triggers changes in heart rate and blood pressure[67] as well as the production of hormones.[68] Young children react in a variety of ways, regardless of whether the angry interaction is actually observed or only heard from another room or whether only angry silence is observed.

A majority of children show signs of anger, concern, sadness, and general distress that can disrupt play, lead to increased aggressiveness, or result in attempts to end the conflict or comfort the participant.[69] Almost half of children primarily feel distress, with a strong desire to end the fight. Slightly over a third of children are ambivalent, revealing both high emotional arousal and upset but at the same time reporting that they are happy. A small percentage (15 percent) give no response. The ambivalent child is the one whose behavior becomes more aggressive.

Not surprisingly, then, children exposed to parents' fighting at home have strong physiological and social reactions to anger.[70] In a laboratory setting, they tend to comfort the mother if she is involved in an angry exchange. With their friends, they characteristically play at a less involved level, and when anger occurs, they find it very hard to handle.

Children become particularly upset when arguments center on child-related issues or when parents imply that children are to blame for the argument.[71] If parents reassure them that they are not to blame, children are less distressed. When children feel that conflict is their fault, they are likely to intervene to try to stop it. Even children as young as four believe they can reduce parental anger, and, in part, they are right.[72] Parents say they are more likely to stop fighting when children aged four to six intervene. Older children believe there is less they can do to stop parents from fighting—and they are right, because parents pay less attention to their pleas.

Does this mean that parents should never fight or disagree in front of children? No. Conflict is a natural part of life when people live close together, and children may need to observe how conflicts are settled in order to learn these skills themselves. In their work, Mark Cummings and his associates discovered that children who viewed angry adults who found a compromise to a situation had emotional reactions that were indistinguishable from their responses when viewing friendly interactions.[73] They had the most negative reactions to continued fighting and the "silent treatment." Their responses to submissions or changes in the topic indicated that they did not consider the situation resolved. So, what matters most to children is whether adults achieve a fair compromise that settles conflicts after they erupt.

Even when there is no particular distress parents as well as children aged five to fifteen see themselves as major causes of angry feelings in others.[74] Children accurately perceive that they cause mothers' anger; mothers' diaries confirm that children's non-compliance and demands cause their anger.

Mothers, however, do not realize that they are the major source of children's anger. Mothers believe that children's anger comes from events outside the home and that happiness comes from within the home, but children report the opposite. They see their happiness coming from friends and personal accomplishments, and irritations and anger from the family.

In short, all family members see anger as very much a part of family life. Children appear the most accurate in seeing their behavior as a major cause of family anger—although on any given occasion they can be mistaken—and the family routines and demands as the main source of their own irritations.

Managing Negative Feelings

Because anger, stress, frustration, and guilt are all part of rearing children, parents need to find their own strategies for controlling the expression of these feelings. When these feelings lead to criticism, nagging, yelling, and hitting, both parents and children suffer. Children are hurt and discouraged; parents feel guilty and inadequate.

Nancy Samalin, who runs parent groups on dealing with anger, suggests that families compile lists of acceptable and unacceptable ways for parents and children to express anger.[75] Acceptable ways include such actions as crying, going for a walk, and yelling, "I'm mad." Unacceptable ways include destroying property, hitting, spitting, and swearing. Of course, I-messages are the most direct way to express anger, but sometimes people want physical outlets such as work or exercise. Table 4-1 lists a variety of ways to deal with anger.

■ **T A B L E 4-1**
EIGHT WAYS TO DEAL WITH PARENTAL ANGER

1. Exit or wait—taking time out is a way of maintaining and modeling self-control.

2. Make "I," not "you," statements to help the child understand your point of view.

3. Stay in the present—avoid talking about the past or future.

4. Avoid physical force and threats.

5. Be brief and to the point.

6. Put it in writing—a note or letter is a way of expressing your feelings in a way the other person can understand.

7. Focus on the essential—ask yourself whether what you are arguing about is really important and worth the energy involved.

8. Restore good feelings—calmly talk over what happened or give hugs or other indications that the fight is over.

Adapted from Nancy Samalin with Catherine Whitney, *Love and Anger: The Parental Dilemma* (New York: Penguin Books, 1992).

To parents who feel guilty about or frustrated with the mistakes they have made, Jane Nelson, using Dreikurs's guidelines (see Chapter 2, page 70), suggests following a three-step program: (1) recognize the mistake, (2) reconcile with the child by apologizing, and (3) resolve the problem with a mutually agreed-on solution.[76] Nelson advises parents to view mistakes as opportunities for learning. Seeing mistakes in that way reduces parents' self-criticism and their resistance to recognizing mistakes. Apologizing is a behavior children can emulate when they have made a mistake. It also enables parents to experience children's quickness to forgive. Dreikurs emphasizes that, like children, parents must develop the courage to be imperfect. He writes,

> The importance of courage in parents cannot be overemphasized. Whenever you feel dismayed or find yourselves thinking, "My gosh, I did it all wrong," be quick to recognize this symptom of your own discouragement; turn your attention to an academic and impersonal consideration of what can be done to make matters better. When you try a new technique and it works, be glad. When you fall back into old habits, don't reproach yourself. You need to constantly reinforce your own courage, and to do so, you need the "courage to be imperfect." Recall to your mind the times that you have succeeded, and try again. Dwelling on your mistakes saps your courage. Remember, one cannot build on weakness—only on strength. Admit humbly that you are bound to make mistakes and acknowledge them without a sense of loss in your personal value. This will do much to keep your own courage up. Above all, remember that we are not working for perfection, but only for improvement. Watch for the little improvements, and when you find them, relax and have faith in your ability to improve further.[77]

DEVELOPING A SUPPORT SYSTEM

When parents receive support from friends, relatives, and each other, they experience less stress and fewer negative moods. The support may come from organized parenting groups, which we discuss in Chapter 5. Or support may come from family members, such as grandparents.

Grandparents as Support

Outside the child's nuclear family, grandparents are the most important figures in most families. Grandparents influence grandchildren directly when they serve as caregivers, playmates, and family historians who pass on information that solidifies a sense of generational continuity. They are a direct influence when they act as mentors to their grandchildren and when they negotiate between parent and child. They influence grandchildren indirectly when they provide both psychological and material support to parents, who then have more resources for parenting.

Because minority families interact more with extended family members, more information on the role of grandparents in such families is available than for other families. For example, in 1984, 31 percent of African American children lived in extended families with one or both parents.[78] The extended family often includes one or both grandparents. Grandmothers help families nurture and care for children in a less structured, more spontaneous way than is possible when only two generations

When parents describe their own feelings and what causes them, children learn to be more sympathetic and understanding toward others.

are present. The grandparents' role depends on whether one or both parents live in the home. For example, grandmothers are less involved in parenting when both parents are present.[79]

In general, contacts between grandparents and grandchildren vary according to the age, health, and proximity of the grandparents.[80] Grandparents typically see their grandchildren monthly or a few times a month. Although a few studies suggest that only a small percentage of grandparents enjoy close, satisfying relationships with their grandchildren, many other studies indicate that young adults generally feel close to grandparents (averaging 4 on a 5-point scale of emotional closeness) and that "the grandchild-grandparent bond continues with surprising strength into adulthood."[81]

Geographic proximity is the most important predictor of the nature of the relationship.[82] When grandparents live close by, contact naturally increases. When grandparents are young and healthy enough to share activities, grandchildren feel close because of the shared fun. At the same time, when grandparents are older and in poorer health, grandchildren feel close because they can help them.

Gender plays a role in such relationships. Grandmothers are more likely to be involved with grandchildren than are grandfathers, and they appear to play a powerful role in children's well-being.[83] Anthropological research presented at an international conference on grandmothers indicates that the involvement of grandmothers and older female kin enhances the lives of their grandchildren.[84] In one study, the presence of the maternal grandmother increased childhood survival at age six to 96 percent from 83 percent, the survival figure for homes without grandmothers. The presence of the paternal grandmother did not change the childhood survival rates.

Evolutionary psychologists argue that maternal grandmothers provide more care and resources for grandchildren because they are absolutely certain that they have a genetic connection to the grandchild through their daughter. The survival of grandchildren means that their genes will survive. Maternal grandfathers and paternal grandparents cannot be as certain of the genetic connection, because a woman could bear a child not genetically related to them if she were unfaithful to her spouse. As a result, they have less motivation to nourish and support grandchildren.

Other psychologists point to psychological reasons for the greater impact of maternal grandmothers. Women may find the greatest support in help from their own mothers, who have long histories of providing loving care for them. When mothers feel cared for, they and their offspring fare better.

Other research indicates that some types of support given by maternal and paternal grandparents differ little.[85] A 1996 survey of Germans over age sixty five found that, on average, they gave 9 percent of their pensions to children and grandchildren, regardless of whether they were families of sons or daughters.

When grandchildren are very young, they see grandparents as sources of treats and gifts. When grandchildren are in elementary school, they look to grandparents to share fun activities with them, and in early adolescence, they also take pleasure in sharing a variety of activities with them. Grandchildren often see grandparents as more patient and understanding than their parents, and contemporary grandparents try to live up to this expectation.[86] They seek to be supportive to grandchildren rather than intrusive and critical. A grandparent can become particularly close at times of family change and can serve as confidant and advocate for the child who could become lost in the chaos of events (see Chapter 14).

Community Support for Parents

Most people in the community realize that raising children in today's world is a hard job. Over 70 percent of a national sample of fourteen hundred adults reported that adults in the community can play an important role by forming relationships with children, conversing with them, encouraging them to do well in school, and commenting on their positive behaviors. Only 5 percent, however, take any actions like this in their community.[87]

So parents have to organize their own community support networks for their children. Suggestions for how to do this are presented in Box 4-4. We discuss community support for parents in Chapters 9, 10, and 13 as well.

A PRACTICAL QUESTION: HOW DO YOU INCREASE POSITIVE FEELINGS WHEN PARENTS HAVE ECONOMIC STRESSES?

Experiencing positive feelings helps family members not only enjoy life and function more effectively but also handle problems. We saw in Chapter 3 that economic hardship creates stress and irritations. A program designed in Holland has had success in reinforcing positive family behaviors in welfare families. It focused on eight areas of positive parent-child communication, which are listed in Table 4-2.[88]

Box 4-4
BUILDING COMMUNITY SUPPORT FOR CHILDREN*

Parents and children profit when adults in the community take an interest in children, engage in relationships with them, and support them in their activities. When such support is not immediately available, parents can take the following actions:

- Encourage extended family members to take an interest in your children. Invite them to your children's special events, such as birthdays or school and athletic events. Invite them to join you and your family for events of mutual interest.

- Take an active role in supporting the friends of your children. Tell their parents about their special qualities or positive actions that you have observed. Ask the children about their interests and their views.

- In your neighborhood, set an example of ways you want adults to relate to your children by relating in that way to other children and their parents. Get to know children's names, their special interests—hire teenagers to do extra chores, organize and participate in block parties that include all generations. Organize families to accomplish a needed neighborhood chore, such as cleaning up debris after a storm or shoveling snow from sidewalks.

- As appropriate, encourage older children to ask parents of friends about career satisfactions, advice about specific colleges or graduate schools, or part-time jobs.

- Get to know your neighbors. Help them get to know your children, and have your children get to know them—for example, by speaking politely to them, offering to do favors for them. As appropriate, involve neighbors in your children's lives. Invite them to events in your home, such as a dinner or to watch a sporting event of interest to all. Invite them to school events of interest.

*Adapted from: Peter C. Scales, Peter L. Benson, and Eugene C. Roehlkepartain, *Grading Grown-Ups: American Adults Report on Their Real Relationships with Kids* (Minneapolis, MN: Lutheran Brotherhood and Search Institute, 2001), p. 57.

Increasing these positive forms of communication enabled families to improve their behaviors in all areas. For three to four months, social workers in Israel went into the homes of welfare families in which parents were having difficulties with preschool children. For the first ten or twenty minutes of the weekly hour-and-a-half visit, they videotaped family interactions. At the next visit, the workers and the family members watched the tape, which workers had already reviewed for positive interactions. Workers identified and reinforced one form of positive parent-child interaction at each visit. Occasionally, the workers modeled a positive interaction not yet observed in the family. Prior to the intervention, few of the families interacted positively with their children, rarely making positive comments to children about their behaviors or sharing

■ **T A B L E 4-2**
EIGHT FORMS OF POSITIVE PARENT-CHILD COMMUNICATION

1. *Naming with approval.* The parent provides a positive verbal description of what is occurring when the parent and child interact, so that the child understands the significance of the interaction.

2. *Taking turns.* All family members have an opportunity to express themselves and gain the appropriate attention from other members; no one is left out.

3. *Strengthening the weak link.* Any family member who is less interactive and assertive, whether child or adult, is encouraged to be more active.

4. *Following.* The parent makes verbal and nonverbal responses following an interaction with the child. The parent both comments on the interaction and looks at the child.

5. *Saying yes.* The parent phrases all directions to the child in terms of what the child is to do—"Carry your coat," not "Don't drag your coat on the floor."

6. *Supporting initiative.* Any initiative the child makes to learn something receives a positive response from the parent.

7. *Taking the lead.* The parent takes action and guides the child's behavior so that the child knows what is expected and that the parent is in charge.

8. *Sharing pleasant moments.* The parent takes time to enjoy the child and share in pleasurable moments.

These eight activities are broad enough to be adapted to interactions with growing children of any age, although there might be less saying yes and taking the lead with teenagers or older children than with younger ones.

Adapted from Anita Weiner, Haggai Kuppermintz, and David Guttmann, "Video Home Training (The Orion Project): A Short-Term Preventive and Treatment Intervention for Families of Young Children," *Family Process* 33 (1994): 441–453.

pleasurable times with them. The families receiving the intervention went from a mean of 1.83 on an index of positive parent-child communication at the start of the program to a mean of 8.04 at the end of the visits, and they maintained these changes six months after the program ended. The mean index of a group of control families who did not receive visits remained unchanged over a comparable period.

The intervention concentrated on positive behaviors, but an index of negative interactions—shouting at children, hitting them, and ignoring their attempts to get close—declined as well. Results included nonsignificant declines in shouting and hitting but significant declines in ignoring children's bids for closeness. When children cried or sought attention for a problem, parents were more likely to pick them up or give them some other form of attention. So, focusing on the positive increased the family closeness that was maintained over time and helped to decrease negative behavior as well.

HOW DO CHILDREN DEFINE THE "GOOD PARENT"?

Thus far, we have looked at close relationships from the point of view of how parents promote them. Let us look at the qualities children of different ages say they want in the "good parent" or "good mother."

Preschoolers interviewed about the qualities of a good and a bad mommy and daddy suggest that good parents are physically affectionate and nurturant, especially in providing food for children. In addition, good parents like to play games with their children and read to them, and they discipline them—that is, they keep children from doing things they should not do, but they do not spank them or slap them in the face. Bad parents have the opposite qualities. They do not hug or kiss, do not fix food, do not play games. They hit and do not let children go outside. Bad parents are also described as irresponsible—they go through red lights, throw chairs at people, and do not read the newspaper.[89]

As children grow older, they continue to value physical nurturing and affection, but they also appreciate qualities that reflect psychological nurturing. Mothers' good qualities include "understanding feelings and moods," "being there when I need her," and "sticking up for me." Children continue to emphasize the limit-setting behaviors in a good mother—"She makes us eat fruit and vegetables," "She yells at me when I need it"—but they want their mother to consider their needs and wishes in setting the rules. Older children still enjoy mutual recreational time—playing, joking, building things together. Finally, as children get older, they appreciate the teaching activities of the good mother.[90]

When early adolescents and their parents talked in a group about their definitions of a good parent, they agreed on several qualities.[91] Early adolescents' definitions touched on three main themes: attention to the child's feelings and individuality, spending time together, and parents' self-control. For early teens, the good parent is one who "listens," "respects you for who you are," "gives you a hug when you are sad." These teens emphasized spending time together, going places together, and having a parent who "knows when to be silly, not always serious." They saw the good parent as one who "manages their temper," "doesn't bark at you," "knows when to stop talking," and "tells you what they want you to do before you have to do it."

The parents of these teens focused first on qualities of responsibility. A good parent is one who "is a good role model," "teaches the child how to behave," and who is "consistent," "committed to being a good parent," and "firm but loving." They, too, focused on the good parent's self-control—"has patience," "manages their temper," is "nonreactive to bad behavior," and "never says 'I told you so.'" Although they focused less on the child's feelings and on time spent together, they did mention the importance of "listening" and "having a good time together."

In sum, children's descriptions of the good parent point to three main areas—being a sensitive caregiver, a social partner, and a person with self-control.

MAIN POINTS

Family systems theories emphasize that

- family members influence each other and are affected by events in each others' lives
- marital adjustment strongly influences children's development
- siblings form a subsystem that influences each others' social skills

Coparenting involves

- cooperation between caregiving, parenting figures whether married or not
- communication and coordination of effort
- agreed-upon rules and standards of behavior
- clear demarcation of power in the household

Positive feelings

- help people be more understanding and sympathetic
- contribute to later psychological health and physical health
- contribute to problem-solving skills and social skills

Physical touch and closeness

- help infants stabilize their functioning after birth
- help colicky babies with sleep problems develop longer sleep periods at night and greater alertness during the day
- help adults reduce anxiety and depression and reduce stress

Close emotional ties rest on the parent's love for the child

- as a unique person
- as expressed in sensitive daily care and in becoming a social partner
- in the sharing of feelings and thoughts

Understanding and expressing feelings

- involve listening to children's feelings and expressing one's own
- are avoided by parents who are dismissive, disapproving, or laissez-faire
- involve five steps of identifying, labeling, and validating feelings, helping the child find appropriate ways to express them, and setting limits.

Family rituals and routines

- differ from each other in that rituals have symbolic and emotional meaning and give a sense of identity, whereas routines are practical solutions to everyday tasks
- provide stability by ensuring predictability in family life
- encourage communication among family members
- link family members with the past and the future
- serve as protective factors in times of difficulty

Storytelling

- begins at birth and helps children discover who they are
- reinforces close relationships as parents and children share experiences

Disruptive negative feelings include

- stress from lack of time with family members
- daily hassles
- family anger

When adults express unresolved anger in the presence of a child, the anger

- produces feelings of sadness, anger, and guilt in the child
- makes it hard for the child to learn to express his or her own anger—some children become overly passive and others overly aggressive
- makes the child assume blame for the anger and feel responsible for fixing the situation
- has minimal impact when parents resolve conflict fairly

Strategies for dealing with negative feelings include

- using family time for satisfying activities
- using communication skills to express feelings appropriately
- developing a support system
- learning to deal with negative feelings

Positive forms of parenting can be encouraged in families experiencing economic hardship by

- focusing on family members' positive behaviors
- helping parents take turns with children and listen to children's comments
- helping parents guide the child's behavior
- sharing pleasurable times together

Children see the good parent as

- a sensitive caregiver
- a social partner
- a person with self-control

EXERCISES

1. Imagine a time when you were a child and felt very close to one of your parents (if you like, you can do this exercise for each of your parents). Describe your parent's behavior with you. What qualities of your parent created the closeness? Share these qualities with class members. Is there a common core? If you do this exercise with each of your parents, note gender differences. Have your mother and father at times shown different qualities of closeness with

you? Have your classmates experienced differences in their mothers' and fathers' behavior toward sons and daughters?

2. Imagine a time when you were a child and felt distant from one of your parents (again, you can do this for each of your parents), and describe your parent's behavior with you. What qualities of your parent created the distance? Again, share these qualities with class members and find the common core. Are these qualities the opposite of qualities that lead to closeness, or do they represent a variety of dimensions? Do the qualities you discovered in Exercises 1 and 2 support what clinicians and researchers say is important?

3. Take turns practicing active listening with a classmate. Have a partner listen actively as you describe one or several of the following situations, then listen actively to your partner as he or she does the same: (a) Describe a time when you were upset as a child. (b) Describe negative feelings in a recent exchange. (c) Describe scenes you have witnessed between parents and children in stores or restaurants. (d) Follow the directions your instructor hands out for what one child in a problem situation might say.

4. With a classmate, practice sending I-messages. Again, choose from a variety of situations: (a) Recall a situation when a parent was angry at you when you were growing up, and describe I-messages your parent might have sent. (b) Recall a recent disagreement with a friend or instructor, and give appropriate I-messages. (c) Describe public parent-child confrontations you have witnessed, and devise appropriate I-messages for the parents. (d) Devise I-messages for problem situations presented by your instructor.

5. Think back to the family rituals from your childhood. Which ones were most meaningful to you? The most enjoyable? Which ones do you want to pass on to your children? Which ones do you not want to pass on to your children? Is there a common theme in those you liked and disliked?

ADDITIONAL READINGS

Doherty, William J. *The Intentional Family*. New York: Avon, 1997.

Engel, Susan. *The Stories Children Tell*. New York: Freeman, 1999.

Gottman, John M., and DeClaire, Joan. *The Heart of Parenting: Raising an Emotionally Intelligent Child*. New York: Simon & Schuster, 1997.

Honore, Carl. *In Praise of Slowness*. New York: HarperCollins, 2004.

Robinson, John P., and Godbey, Geoffrey. *Time for Life*. University Park: Pennsylvania State University Press, 1997.

CHAPTER

5

Supporting Children's Growth and Development

<table>
<tr><td>

</td><td>

IN THE NEWS

New York Times, January 10:[1] Special mirror neurons in the brain help us understand and learn from others. See pages 159–161.

</td></tr>
</table>

Test Your Knowledge: Fact or Fiction?

1. Parents today believe they are doing as good a job raising their children as their parents did with them.
2. When individuals watch others' actions, neurons in the brain of the observer fire in the same pattern as neurons in the brain of the person carrying out the action.
3. Most parents who spank their children do it because they believe it is effective.
4. Children who watch the most television have time for few other activities.
5. Children have a natural interest in moral issues, so morality is not something we have to impose on them.

Parents want children to be healthy, responsible individuals, caring of others and themselves, and parents believe it is their responsibility to help children develop these qualities. With the hectic pressures of life today, however, parents report they are not doing as good a job as their parents did.[2] They would like more skills to do the job and to control outside influences, such as television, that interfere with what they are trying to teach children. This chapter focuses on how parents provide home environments that help children develop the qualities parents hope for, and how parents control social influences that are incompatible with their values.

Although the theories we discussed in Chapter 2 may differ about parents' role in children's development, parents believe it is their responsibility (1) to ensure the physical health and safety of the child, (2) to prepare the child to become an economically independent adult, and (3) to encourage positive personal and social behaviors such as psychological adjustment and self-esteem.[3] In this chapter, we look at how parents support children's growth and contribute to the development of their children's positive qualities. Table 5-1 lists tasks for parenting children of different ages. Although we will not cover all the parental tasks in this chapter, the table provides a useful framework for understanding parents' tasks in supporting children's growth and development.[4]

First, we focus on how parents model the behaviors they want children to develop, how they provide a home and way of life that encourage health and safety, and how they support emotional and moral competence and children's problem-solving skills. We look at possible actions to take when problems arise. We also review the actions parents take to provide the social climate that supports their value system. Finally, we look at the resources provided by parenting programs.

MODELING

Folk wisdom has long advised parents to be what they want their children to become—see Box 5-1. Now, research involving neuroimaging of the brain, usually done by means of functional magnetic resonance imaging (fMRI), supports such advice, as we appear to be preprogrammed to imitate others. Brain scans reveal that human beings are equipped with "mirror neurons" in many areas of the brain.[5] When individuals watch others' actions, mirror neurons in the brain fire in the same way as the neurons in the brain of the person carrying out the action. An unknown mechanism prevents the observer from actually making the same physical movements.[6]

So, when observers watch someone pick up a pen, throw a ball, or facially express disgust, the observers' brains light up in the same way as the brain of the person engaged in the action. Actions of the motor area of the brain are thought to trigger emotional reactions, so when we see disgusted expressions, the firing of our mirror neurons triggers reactions in the emotional areas of our brain, and we feel the disgust, sadness, or humiliation we witness in another.

Our mirror neurons serve several important functions. They help us understand what others are doing or are about to do and how they may feel, because we are having the same neurophysiological reactions. Some scientists think mirror neurons help us have empathy for others because, at a very real level, we feel their pain. Mirror neurons may also help us learn language, because the movements for language

■ **T A B L E 5-1**
DEVELOPMENTAL CHALLENGES FACED BY CHILDREN AND CAREGIVERS
FROM INFANCY THROUGH ADOLESCENCE*

Developmental Level	Children's Issues	Caregivers' Role
Infant	Physiological regulation	Sensitivity
	Attachment	Responsiveness
	Interactional synchrony	Availability
Toddler	Exploration of the world	Secure base
	Sense of mastery	Clear, realistic expectations
	Individuation	Consistent discipline
	Autonomous self	Use of internal state language
	Sense of right and wrong	Emotion regulation
Preschooler	Self-control	Clear roles and values
	Cooperation	Flexible management
	Sex-role identification	Organize/support peer relations
	Peer relations	
School-age child	Self-confidence	Open communication
	Peer group membership	Acceptance
	Close friendship	Indirect monitoring
	School adaptation	
Adolescent	Heterosexual peer relations	Psychological autonomy granting
	Dating	
	Autonomy	Indirect monitoring, especially early
	Occupational plans	
	Identity formation	Involvement and support
	Romantic relationships	

*From: E. Mark Cummings, Patrick T. Davies, and Susan B. Campbell, *Developmental Psychopathology and Family Process: Theory, Research, and Clinical Implications* (New York: Guilford, 2000), p. 207. Reprinted with permission.

are laid down as we watch others speak and gesture.[7] Difficulties in the functioning of mirror neurons may contribute to developmental disorders such as autism, in which children do not seem to understand other people's thinking and intentions.[8]

Box 5-1
WORDS HEARD ROUND THE WORLD*

In 1954, Dorothy Nolte needed material for her weekly newspaper column on family matters so she quickly penned a short poem encapsulating her child-rearing philosophy. The poem, initially thought to be anonymous, was translated into may languages and influenced millions of parents who never knew her name.

> If children live with criticism, they learn to condemn.
> If children live with hostility, they learn to fight.
> If children live with ridicule, they learn to feel shy.
> If children live with shame, they learn to feel guilty.
> If children live with encouragement, they learn confidence.
> If children live with tolerance, they learn patience.
> If children live with praise, they learn appreciation.
> If children live with acceptance, they learn to love.
> If children live with approval, they learn to like themselves.
> If children live with honesty, they learn truthfulness.
> If children live with security, they learn to have faith in
>   themselves and in those about them.
> If children live with friendliness, they learn the world is a
>   nice place in which to live.

The existence of mirror neurons has enormous implications for parenting because what children observe, they also experience at the neurological level. Parents' and siblings' behavior and other external influences, such as television, trigger templates in children's brains. Mirror neurons may account for such phenomena as the negative effects on children of witnessing domestic violence and others' arguing—it is as though they were experiencing the emotional turmoil of the participants.[9] Mirror neurons may account for the negative effects of mothers' depressive behavior, as children take on the behaviors they witness.[10]

Mirror neurons may help to explain the negative effects of witnessing violent television shows.[11] A study revealed that, when children watched violent television programs, mirror neurons in areas related to aggression fired, and children were more likely to behave in aggressive ways following the show.

Conversely, motor neurons may also account for the fact that mothers' positive moods and smiles are able to increase the smiles and moods of their infants,[12] and for the fact that toddlers and preschoolers imitate the caring behaviors of their caregivers.[13]

As we shall see when we talk about healthy eating and exercising habits and many other positive and negative behaviors, children copy what they see, so parents and all adults must be especially careful about their behavior around children.

HEALTHY LIFESTYLES

In the United States, life expectancy increased from forty-five years in 1900 to seventy-five years in 1999. This gain of thirty years resulted primarily from the prevention of illnesses rather than from increasingly successful treatments of illnesses like heart disease. Immunizations, improved nutrition, increased exercise, and better housing and drinking water all contributed to the gains.[14]

Establishing physically healthy environments and health-promoting behaviors are major parental tasks, although parents may not place them as high on their list of parental responsibilities as teaching social behaviors. For example, although 84 percent of parents say it is absolutely essential to teach courtesy and politeness, only 68 percent think it is essential to teach healthy eating habits,[15] and 51 percent think it essential to teach good exercise habits. Yet these areas of teaching are increasingly important, because healthy eating and exercise habits established in childhood can help protect children from heart disease, diabetes, and osteoporosis in adulthood. As one writer stated, "Childhood is actually the best time to start protecting an aging body, buckling it in for a lifetime of good health."[16]

Box 5-2 describes little steps that, taken together, can give your child a longer life. It indicates that factors involved in healthy lifestyles, such as proper eating and exercise, are not independent of each other but operate together to promote health. Further, a healthy lifestyle contributes broadly to psychological well-being and optimal intellectual functioning.

Safety

Safety measures are the first concern because injuries are the leading cause of death in children and teens. In the United States, injuries kill more children than all other diseases combined.[17] Not only do children die from injuries, they also suffer physical trauma requiring hospitalizations and extensive medical care, costing about

---

Box 5-2
WAYS TO PROMOTE CHILDREN'S HEALTH*

1. Provide healthy beverages—avoid juices and sodas.
2. Eat meals together as a family.
3. Encourage friendships with active peers.
4. Avoid eating while watching television.
5. Keep offering healthy foods even though they are initially rejected.
6. Control the kinds of food in the house rather than the child's eating behavior.
7. Impose strict rules for driving.
8. Set the example of healthy habits for your children.

*Adapted from: Tara Parker-Pope, "How to Give Your Child A Longer Life," *The Wall Street Journal,* 9 December 2003, p. R1.

twenty billion dollars annually. Initially, people thought injuries were the result of random accidents. About forty years ago, however, safety experts realized that, like illnesses, injuries could be prevented.

Figure 5-1 describes the major health hazards for children and teens and the actions parents take to reduce injuries. A recent survey of parenting books found that injury prevention was stressed for parents of young children, but books for parents of teens did not emphasize all areas of concern for teen safety.[18]

In the years from birth to age five, parents and other caregivers are the primary guardians of children's safety, but very early on, they teach children to take a more active role in preventing injury. As children grow older, parents share their role of guardian with other caregivers, parents of their children's friends, school authorities, and community officials who provide services for children. Parents have a daunting role here, but information from such medical and public health organizations as the Academy of Pediatrics and the National Center for Injury Prevention and Control gives parents guidance in how to carry out their role.

To provide a safe home, parents must monitor their own behavior so that their cigarette, alcohol, and drug use do not present a risk to children as well as to their caregiving abilities.[19]

Eating

Parents' tasks here are (1) to provide healthy food and nutrition to children, and (2) to help them develop healthy eating habits. These tasks are vitally important because good nutrition in early childhood promotes motor and cognitive development.[20] Poorly nourished children are less physically active, and they perform less well on measures of attention span and short-term memory, than well-nourished children. Although nutrient-rich diets can improve performance, adults who were poorly nourished over long periods of time in childhood continue to show lower performance on cognitive tests than well-nourished adults.

Good nutrition and eating habits are important as well. The number of overweight children has tripled from 5 percent in 1980 to almost 16 percent today.[21] Being overweight and the intake of fatty foods are related to the development of many physical problems, such as heart disease and diabetes, that compromise the quality of children's lives in adulthood.

Parents get guidance from medical and health personnel about nutrition, recommended foods, and sizes of portions, as these recommendations change from time to time. For example, the United States Department of Agriculture publishes a set of nutritional guidelines called the food pyramid, along with a booklet to help parents use the food pyramid with young children. When parents worry or have questions about their child's eating, they should discuss the problem with their pediatrician.

Box 5-2 includes many suggestions that contribute to better eating habits. Parents should establish regular mealtimes and meal routines so that eating becomes a happy social occasion.[22] If possible, the family eats dinner together each day or at least on the weekends. Meals are sit-down occasions focused on eating. Child-sized portions are served. The television is turned off, and conversation is encouraged.

■ **FIGURE 5-1**
WAYS TO PREVENT ACCIDENTS AND INJURIES*

Bedroom

1. Install devices that prevent windows from opening and child from getting out or falling out.
2. Cover electrical outlets.
3. Inspect toys for broken and jagged edges.

Bathroom

1. Keep safety caps on all bottles.
2. Keep medicines, aspirin, rubbing alcohol in locked cabinets.
3. Adjust water heater so water is not scalding hot.
4. Use rubber mats in bath and shower.
5. Keep bathmat next to tub and shower.
6. Do not allow young child alone in bath.

Living Room

1. Cover electrical outlets.
2. Check safety of plants.
3. Put rubber-backed pad under small scatter rugs.
4. Pad sharp edges of tables.
5. Have screen for fireplace.

Stairs

1. With young child, block off tops and bottoms of stairs.
2. If necessary, mark top and bottom steps.

Kitchen

1. Keep vomit-inducing syrup on hand.
2. Store soaps, cleaners, all poisonous chemicals in locked cabinet.
3. Have guard around burners or use back burners on stove so child cannot pull contents onto self.
4. Unplug all appliances when not in use.
5. Store sharp knives in safe place.
6. Store matches out of child's reach.

Dining Room

1. Cover electrical outlets.

Garage-Workroom

1. Keep tools out of child's reach.
2. Keep poisons locked up.
3. Store paints and other toxic materials out of child's reach.
4. Store nails and screws in safe place.

Have lock for door.

General

1. Install smoke alarms in house.
2. Have fire extinguishers in kitchen, most rooms in house, and garage.
3. Keep firearms out of home; if in the home, keep ammunition and unloaded guns in separate locked cabinets; become aware of firearms in homes the child visits and be sure they have same precautions.
4. Keep poison control, fire, and police department telephone numbers by the telephone.
5. Learn infant, child, and adult cardiopulmonary resuscitation and how to access 911.
6. Never allow buckets of water to remain after use when infants and young children are in home, as children can drown in them.
7. Discourage use of infant walkers.
8. Use currently approved automobile safety restraints for children of all ages and parents.
9. For all children and adolescents, use helmets for bicycling, skate boarding, and in-line skating; use appropriate padding and safety equipment for all sports.
10. Teach children pedestrian safety in parking lots, street corners; do not let children under six or seven cross the streets by themselves.
11. Have fire escape routes planned from home in event of fire, and make sure children know them well.
12. Never believe that children under five can be water safe, even if they have had lessons; be sure that children over five have swim lessons; but no child should swim alone, and even adults should always be encouraged to swim with another person present.
13. Discuss the role of alcohol in car and water accidents with early and late adolescents.

*From: The American Academy of Pediatrics Committee on Injury and Poison Prevention, "Office-Based Counseling for Injury Prevention," *Pediatrics* 94 (1994): 566–567.

When everyone is rushed in the morning, family members should rise earlier so children can sit down and eat breakfast without pleas to hurry. Family meals should include only pleasant conversation about the day's events that have taken place or are about to take place. Discussions of conflict or problems should be postponed, not brought up while eating. Families can discuss difficulties after everyone has eaten and cleaned up.

It is especially important to discourage eating in front of the television, because watching television while eating encourages eating high-calorie and fatty snacks. Children who reduced television time did not exercise more, but they reduced their eating in front of the television, and that led to slower weight gain.[23]

Parents should model moderate intake of healthy foods. Children are known to like the foods parents eat and encourage. When they introduce new foods, parents cannot expect children to like them the first time but must introduce foods as many as eight or ten times before children accept them.[24] Parents can also work with schools to eliminate high-fat, high-sugar foods in cafeteria meals and vending machines. Although recent studies indicate that school changes alone do not control children's weight, they can contribute to the healthy eating habits established at home.[25]

No one, simple change will encourage healthy eating, but many small ones, most of which are under parents' control, will.

Exercise

Physical activity contributes not only to children's physical fitness and skill but also increases children's self-esteem and self-image and decreases their anxiety and stress.[26] Physical well-being in childhood predicts overall long-term physical health, reducing the risk of heart disease, osteoporosis, and in women, breast cancer.

Our increasingly sedentary habits have resulted in decreasing levels of physical fitness. In 2001, 77 percent of California's fifth-, seventh-, and ninth-graders failed six aerobic strength tests, and performance levels decreased with age.[27] Although physical fitness was lowest in urban and poor areas of the state, even in California's wealthy Marin County 28 percent of children were described as physically unfit. Mark Dessauer, communications director of the organization Active Living by Design, commented, "Kids today are better at running a software program than running a mile. They have stronger thumbs than legs."[28]

Many influences, physical and social, contribute to physical activity. Genetic factors such as gender—boys are more active than girls—play a role.[29] Social factors, such as neighborhood safety and resources for physical activity, play a role. Friends who are physically active can encourage sports and outdoor activities.

Again, however, parents play a major role as models, and their influence is critically important. Physically active mothers tend to have children who are physically active. Parental inactivity is a strong predictor of children's inactivity. Families are strongly advised to begin exercising together to get the benefits of exercise and reduce the problems brought on by its lack.

Sleep

Sleep is necessary for life. Rats deprived of sleep die faster than rats deprived of food.[30] Sleep is so important that newborns spend sixteen to twenty hours a day sleeping, and by the time children are two years of age, more than half their lives—fourteen months—has been spent in sleep. Yet we are becoming a nation of sleep-deprived individuals. A recent headline in the *New York Times* stated, "Poll Finds Even Babies Don't Get Enough Rest."[31] The article went on to say that a survey by the National Sleep Foundation found that toddlers get, on average, two hours less than the minimum amount of sleep recommended, and preschoolers get four hours less, on average. Further, 18 to 21 percent of schoolchildren report feeling tired during the day, and 63 to 87 percent of adolescents report they do not get as much sleep as they need.[32] So, as in other areas of basic physiological functioning, we have problems.

Even though sleep is essential, its function is not clearly understood. Several theories exist. First, it is thought that, during sleep, the brain repairs itself, restoring depleted energy levels, repairing damaged cells, and growing new neurons.[33] Sleep is also thought to consolidate recent learning in long-term memory.[34] We know that children with intelligence quotients over 140 sleep thirty to forty minutes longer a night than children with IQs under 140.[35] Recent work indicates that, when children add one hour of sleep to their nightly patterns, whatever the pattern is, their improvement on cognitive measures is the equivalent of two years of growth.[36]

Helping children develop healthy sleep habits is a critical task for parents because poor sleep patterns are associated with lack of alertness, poor attention span, and poor memory, as well as learning problems.[37] As children get older, sleep problems are also associated with emotional problems.[38]

Because parents' actions differ according to the age of the child and the parents' values, we take up the topic of sleep in the appropriate age-related chapter. Here, we simply emphasize parents' critical role in ensuring that their children develop healthy sleep habits to prevent the behavioral, learning, and emotional problems associated with sleep deprivation, which is becoming increasingly common in our society.

Play

Every child's day should include some time to play, and part of that time should be play with parents. A longitudinal study of children's activities and behavior in the first six years of life found that those children who in infancy and early childhood had opportunities to engage in productive play developed greater self-control and were less likely to have behavior problems in first grade.[39] The exact reasons for the positive effects of play are not known. It may be that play creates feelings of pleasure and joy that enable children to adjust to demands more easily, as we saw in Chapter 4. It may be that play drains off tension so there is less negative emotion to control. Further, it may give children feelings of relaxation that increase ease of adjustment to others' requests.

Play with parents may be only twenty minutes, but it should be a time during which parents do not make demands on children or insist on some behavior, a time during which parents follow children's leads and engage with children under their direction. Children spend so much time during the day doing what parents or other caregivers request that it is important to have a time simply to play and interact for fun. The exact nature of the play will depend on the age of the child and the child's interests. With older children, the playtime may be just conversation, but it is nevertheless time set aside for pleasurable activity. Within safety limits, children can do what they want, and parents engage with them without correcting or criticizing.

INCLUDING MEDIA IN THE HOME

Families live in a media-rich world that includes books, magazines, television, tape and CD players, VCRs and DVD players, video games, and computers. The average home with children from eight to eighteen has 3.6 CD or tape players, 3.5 television sets, 3.3 radios, 2.9 VCRs or DVD players, 2.1 video game consoles, and 1.5 computers. Two-thirds of children this age have televisions in their bedrooms, and 30 percent have computers as well.[40] Thirty-three percent of children under six years have televisions in their bedrooms, 23 percent have VCR or DVD players, and 5 percent have computers.[41] Children spend more time in media activities than in any other activity except sleeping. They will likely spend more media time with the advent of BabyFirstTV, a cable channel with around-the-clock programs for children aged six months to six years.

   Parents' behaviors powerfully shape children's media use, but many parents feel uncertain how to use their power to manage media use. In this section, we first look at family media use, then at media's impact on children's lives, and finally at specific actions parents can take to control the media's influence on their families.

Media Availability and Use

Children under Six   Table 5-2 presents the results of a 2005 telephone survey of a nationally representative sample of 1,000 parents of children from six months to six years of age regarding their children's media use.[42] Focus groups with parents supplemented the information from the telephone survey. As can be seen, media use starts early and grows throughout the toddler years. Although the American Academy of Pediatrics recommends no screen time for children under two, the average child that age has about an hour of screen time per day, rising to two hours per day at age two and remaining there. Screen activities are the most frequent activity of young children, and twice as much time is spent in them as in reading activities. Children with televisions and VCRs in their rooms spend about half an hour more per day on screen activities than children who do not have bedroom media access.

Children between Eight and Eighteen   In 2005, a representative national sample of 2,032 children answered detailed questionnaires about the availability and daily recreational use of media.[43] Table 5-3 shows that they devote an average of six and a half hours a day, seven days a week, to recreational media use, primarily television and listening to music. Since children use more than one medium at a time, they

TABLE 5-2
TIME SPENT USING MEDIA AND IN OTHER ACTIVITIES, BY AGE

	In typical day, percent who did each activity				Average time among those who did activity				Average time among all children			
	Total	0–1	2–3	4–6	Total	0–1	2–3	4–6	Total	0–1	2–3	4–6
Reading or being read to	83%	77%	81%	87%*^	0:48	0:44	0:52*	0:48	0:40	0:33	0:42*	0:42*
Listening to music	82%	88%‡	84%‡	78%	0:58	1:04‡	1:00	0:53	0:48	0:57‡	0:50‡	0:41
Watching TV	75%	56%	81%*	79%*	1:19	1:02	1:28*	1:19*	0:59	0:34	1:11*	1:02*
Playing outside	74%	55%	80%*	81%*	1:51	1:43	1:47	1:56	1:22	0:56	1:26*	1:34*
Watching a video or DVD	32%	24%	41%*‡	32%*	1:18	†	1:20	1:23	0:24	0:13	0:32*	0:25*
Reading an electronic book	14%	11%	18%*	13%	0:42	†	†	†	0:05	0:05	0:06	0:04
Using a computer**	16%	2%	12%*	26%*^	0:50	†	†	0:50	0:07	0:01	0:05*	0:12*^
Playing video games***	11%	1%	8%*	18%*^	0:55	†	†	†	0:06	0:00	0:03*	0:10*^
Total used any screen media†	83%	61%	88%*	90%*	1:57	1:20	2:07	2:03	1:36	0:49	1:51*	1:50*

*Significantly higher than ages 0–1; ^Significantly higher than ages 2–3; ‡Significantly higher than ages 4–6; **Including for games and other purposes; ***Console or handheld; †Screen media includes TV, videos/DVDs, video games, or computers. It does not include electronic books; ‡Sample size too small to report.

From: Victoria Rideout and Elizabeth Hamel, "The Media Family: Electronic Media in the Lives of Infants, Toddlers, Preschoolers, and Their Parents" (#7500), Henry J. Kaiser Family Foundation, May 2006, p. 9.

■ **T A B L E** 5-3
TIME SPENT WITH MEDIA

Average Amount of Time 8- to 18-Year-Olds Spend per Day

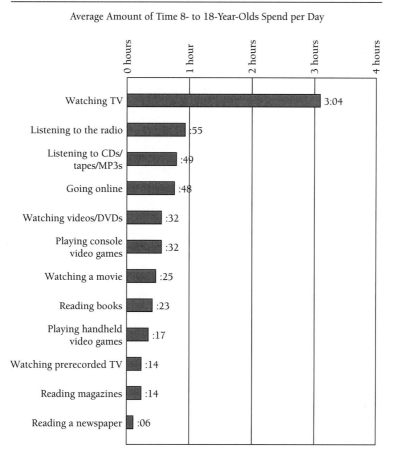

From: Victoria Rideout, Donald F. Roberts, and Ulla G. Foehr, "Generation M: Media in the Lives of 8–18-year-olds" (#7250), Henry J. Kaiser Family Foundation, March 2005, www.kff.org. p. 7.

put the equivalent of eight and a half hours of media use into six and a half hours a day—in the course of a week, about the equivalent of a full-time job with some overtime.

Table 5-4 presents the time spent in nonmedia activities, to help us understand media's place in the overall pattern of children's activities. Children who report extensive media use also report spending a significant amount of time hanging out with parents and friends, pursuing hobbies, and reading for pleasure, so media use does not appear to displace these activities. However, media use may affect amount

■ **T A B L E 5-4**
TIME SPENT IN NON-MEDIA ACTIVITIES

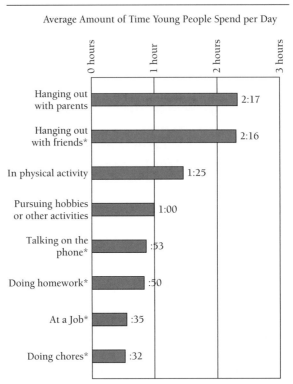

Average Amount of Time Young People Spend per Day

	0 hours	1 hour	2 hours	3 hours
Hanging out with parents				2:17
Hanging out with friends*				2:16
In physical activity			1:25	
Pursuing hobbies or other activities		1:00		
Talking on the phone*		:53		
Doing homework*		:50		
At a Job*	:35			
Doing chores*	:32			

*Data collected among 7th- to 12th-graders only. All other result are among all 8- to 18-year-olds.

From: Victoria Rideout, Donald F. Roberts, and Ulla G. Foehr, "Generation M: Media in the Lives of 8–18-Year-Olds" (#7250), Henry J. Kaiser Family Foundation, March 2005, www.kff.org. p. 8.

of time spent on homework and chores, as children spend a comparatively small amount of time in these activities. Media use is three to six times more frequent than any other activity in their lives.

There are gender, age, social, and ethnic differences in screen use. Teens spend more time listening to music and using the computer than younger children, who spend more time with television. Boys spend more time playing video games, an average of seventy-two minutes each day, compared to twenty-five minutes for girls. Girls listen to more music than boys do. African American children watch more television and movies and play more video games than Latina/o or European American children. European American children watch less television and fewer movies and play fewer video games, but they read more and use the computer more.[44] Latina/o children fall between these two groups. Children of higher social status read more, use the computer more, and watch less television.[45]

Parents' Media Use   Parents of young children report an average of two and a quarter hours of screen use per day.[46] Thirty percent report none or less than an hour per day, and 42 percent report more than two hours per day. Children whose parents have more than two hours a day of screen time also have increased screen use (thirty minutes more), compared to children whose parents have less than an hour of screen use.

Parents of children under six also report encouraging children's media use for several reasons. A main reason given is that, when children are focused on media, parents have uninterrupted time for chores, needed relaxation, and their own media use. Media use also provides a way to interrupt children's bickering and rule breaking. Some parents find that media calm children down and help them sleep. Some believe that video games provide a way for sons and fathers to bond.

In many homes, parents have the television on even if no one is watching. In almost one-third of children's homes, the TV is on all or most of the time, and in an additional 30 percent of homes, television is on during all or most meals. Not surprisingly, children in families with background television watch more television and are less likely to read and be read to.

Parents' Attitudes about Media   Parents' attitudes about the media vary.[47] They view computers as generally helpful to children (69 percent of parents say this), and view video games rather negatively, with 49 percent believing they mostly hurt children. About television, parents appear ambivalent. Although 70 percent believe children have learned information and positive behaviors from television, about a third of parents have seen children imitate negative, mostly aggressive behaviors from it.[48]

Media's Impact on Children's Activities and Development

When children read more, especially when they read for pleasure, they develop literacy skills that are related to academic success in school. The concern here is that children do not do enough reading, in part because other media displace such activity.[49] As noted above, when television is a constant presence in family life, reading occurs less frequently.

Of audiovisual media, television has been the primary focus of research on the effect of children's media use on growth and development. Television affects viewers powerfully. For example, one-year-old infants reacted to TV actresses' emotional preferences for toys just as they copied a mother's emotional responses to toys. They avoided the toys when the actress reacted negatively to them, and played with the ones for which she expressed positive feelings.[50]

Although television does not displace activities with parents and friends and other activities (see Table 5-4), its impact depends on the nature of the programs watched.

Positive Impact of Viewing Educational Programs   Watching educational programs can increase children's literacy and number skills and their knowledge of science and history. Studies that followed children whose viewing habits were first recorded in the preschool years and noted their behavior, interests, and viewing habits when they were teens found that children who viewed educational and informative programs as preschoolers reported higher grades, reading more books, greater creativity, valuing achievement more, and less aggression than students who watched general entertainment fare.[51]

The amount of time preschoolers watched was not predictive of adolescent qualities, but content was. The results were more consistent for boys than for girls and appeared when intelligence, family variables and adolescent media use were controlled.

Children's Sleep, Attention Spans, School Performance, and Weight   Television viewing in children under three years of age is related to several problems. First, it is related to irregular nap and bedtime schedules[52] in a sample of two thousand families, independent of the family's social status, the mother's health, the family's functioning, and parenting behavior in getting the child to bed. As noted earlier, poor sleep has negative consequences for children.

Second, in a longitudinal study of twenty-five hundred children, amount of television exposure when children were ages one to three was related to mothers' reports of their poor concentration, impulsivity, and restlessness at age seven.[53] Even when controlling for the child's gestational age and characteristics of the family, such as social status, parents' substance use, maternal mental health, and social status, the findings remained: The more television the child watched, the more likely the mother was to describe the child as having attention problems.

Third, television viewing before age three was also associated with poorer performance on tests of reading and math achievement when children were six and seven[54]; television viewing between ages three and five did not have similar negative consequences. It is possible that watching television at very early ages displaces other activities.

The placement of the television set matters. Children with bedroom sets scored less well on tests of achievement in math, reading, and language arts than children without bedroom sets.[55]

Television viewing has an indirect effect on weight. Television viewing appears to stimulate eating high-calorie snacks; decreasing school-aged children's viewing time was related to decreases in body-mass index.[56]

Aggression   According to researchers John Coie and Kenneth Dodge, reviews of the most careful studies

... indicate that the effects of TV violence are robust and account for about 10 percent of the variance in child aggression, which approximately equals the magnitude of effect of cigarette smoking on lung cancer. The finding appears to be one of the most rigorously tested and robust effects in all of developmental psychology.[57]

Viewing violent television is related not only to childhood aggression but also to adult aggression for both boys and girls. Longitudinal follow-up of two hundred children whose viewing habits were studied when they were in elementary school found that both boys and girls who watched violent television programs as children showed serious adult anger and violence with spouses and other individuals.[58] For example, 40 percent of men and 35 percent of women who were high TV-violence watchers as children pushed or shoved a spouse, and almost two-thirds of men and half the women self-reported a crime in the previous year. Controlling for the child's initial level of aggression, intellectual level, family social status, and parenting style did not change the results.

Recently, the American Psychological Association has called for more research on the effects of violence in video games. Their concern was fueled by an incident in which a teen grabbed an officer's gun and killed three officers after being arrested on suspicion of car theft. The boy, who frequently played the video game *Grand Theft Auto,* commented, "Life is like a video game. You have to die sometimes." The APA believes video games may be more harmful than other media because of the interactive nature of such games and has adopted "a resolution calling for the reduction of all violence in video games and interactive media marketed to children and youth."[59]

Sexual Attitudes and Behavior   Accumulating research suggests that teens who are exposed to media with high sexual content initiate sexual activity at younger ages.

Sexual content occurs on 83 percent of the most popular adolescent TV shows, about seven times per hour. Sexual intercourse is implicitly or explicitly depicted in 20 percent of the encounters.[60] It is rare that serious negative consequences of sexual behavior (pregnancy or sexually transmitted diseases) are shown. Teens who view more television with sexual content tend to overestimate the occurrence of sexual behaviors in everyday life and to develop more permissive attitudes about premarital sex than teens who watch shows with less sexual content.

A longitudinal study relating teen viewing to teen behavior over the course of the next year found that teens who watched more shows with sexual content were more likely to initiate sexual intercourse during the year than those who watched fewer shows.[61] Hearing talk about sexual actions had the same effects on behavior as witnessing a scene.

Sexual activity naturally increases in the course of adolescence, but viewing shows with sexual content seemed to "age" teens because they took on the sexual behaviors of teens one to two years older. For example, a twelve-year-old who watched the most sexual content on television behaved like a fourteen- or fifteen-year-old who saw the least.

Similar findings occurred when the sexual content of several media—music, movies, television, and magazines—was related to teens' sexual behavior over a two-year period.[62] Teens with the highest sexual-media diet were twice as likely to initiate sexual intercourse in the next two years as teens with the lowest exposure to sexual media. These results were significant for European American teens when other factors were controlled, but were not significant for African American teens because other control variables such as parental and peer attitudes were more powerful predictors of their sexual activity.

The Internet poses another challenge for parents. It contains images with sexual content and the possibility of sexual solicitations. Twenty percent of teens reported having stumbled onto explicit sexual images accidentally in the last year, and 19 percent reported having received an unwanted sexual solicitation in the last year. Most of these instances (73 percent) occurred while the teen was surfing the Net at home.[63]

Rules about Media Use   In general, parents have fewer rules about media use than might be expected. Parents of younger children under six years of age are more likely to have rules about media use than parents of older children. Sixty percent of parents with children under six have rules about how much their children can watch, and 85 percent have rules about the content of programming.[64] These rules seem to have an effect, as children in households with rules watch fifteen minutes less television a day than children in homes with no rules.

Fewer than half the children eight to eighteen (46 percent) report they have rules about television watching, and of those who do, only half report that the rules are usually enforced—the other half report they are enforced some, a little, or none of the time.[65] Yet for children twelve to eighteen, rules reduced television viewing one hour per day.

When it comes to computers and video games, only a small percentage of children report having rules—about 20 percent for computer use and about 17 percent for video games—and having rules makes little difference in the amount of time children spend with these media.

Whereas about 25 percent of parents use some form of filter or control on computer use, about 30 percent of teens say they have claimed to be older to get into websites and have succeeded.[66]

Parents' interactions with children around media use have effects.[67] Reading with children and talking about what is being read increase children's reading and comprehension. Parents' discussions with children about TV and movies influence children's interpretations of what they see. School programs that increase children's awareness of media use and encourage reductions in their use have reduced use in elementary school children, in turn reducing their aggressiveness on school playgrounds and their weight gain.[68] So, interactions with children around media use are effective.

Parental Actions to Manage Media

Currently, the American Academy of Pediatrics makes three recommendations:[69]

1. Discourage any television viewing for children under the age of two, and encourage more interactive pursuits, such as talking, singing, and building.

2. Limit total media time for children to one to two hours per day of good-quality programs.

3. Encourage alternative, more active pursuits, such as athletics, hobbies, reading for pleasure; recall that, when parents enforced limits, children did decrease media time.

Parents can take many additional actions to get the positive benefits of media use and reduce its negative ones:

1. Parents can limit the number of media in the home (e.g., televisions, Game-Boys) and locate them in places to reduce their use. For example, remove television sets and computers from the bedroom and place them in the family living area.

2. Turn media off during mealtimes and when no one is watching, and avoid eating while watching TV or videos.

3. Interact with children around media use. Watch programs with them, talk about shows or videos, play video games, and surf the Internet together. Use these interactions as opportunities to learn about your child's thinking and have the child learn about yours; have media used as family entertainment.

4. Use V-chips, video game ratings, and computer filters to control programming.

5. Set media rules for children, and enforce them.

6. Model appropriate media use.

7. Use media most often for learning and family interaction rather than relaxation, and use board games and reading together to relax.

When you and your children can bond together around media use, your children will understand your concerns about the media and may be more willing to follow rules and share upsetting experiences they have had with other people on the Internet.

Although it is understandable to use television or videos sometimes to make life easier for everyone, children will benefit when the main source of gratification each day is real relationships and real activities rather than those viewed on a screen.

Recall that parents' behavior serves as models for children. Use media judiciously, and do not permit it to interfere with interactions with children and other family members. The temptations are great, as parents are wired and busy much of the day. Parents' cell phones enable them to do business on the way to the grocery store or while driving children to lessons or sports, so actual conversation has disappeared. Especially for young children who are learning about the world from sharing experiences with parents, it is of concern that parents are engrossed in phone conversations during a walk or drive, while the child, essentially alone, stares out of the window or the stroller.

Parents can also take broader community action, with other parents, to get the kinds of programs they want for their children on television or to find ways to block unacceptable sites or solicitations on the Internet.

Parents move television sets and computers to a central family area and enjoy these media together, playing video games and surfing the Net with children.

CREATING A COLLABORATIVE FAMILY ATMOSPHERE

Psychologists have identified a family atmosphere of collaboration that enhances children's growth and enables them to learn the lessons parents most want to teach.

An Emotional Climate of Mutual Responsiveness

Parents create a family culture of cooperation and mutual responsiveness from the earliest days of the child's life. Sensitive parents provide responsive care that meets children's individual needs. Such care creates harmonious parent-child relationships and helps to establish a secure attachment between parent and child.[70] That attachment, in turn, encourages cooperation and willingness to attend to parents' requests as parents attend to children's.

When children have secure attachments to parents, they respond to such gentle parenting techniques as reasoning, so parents need not rely on assertive power strategies such as threatening and spanking. Reasoning with children helps children develop internal moral standards that then determine their conduct. Children with insecure attachments are not responsive to gentle discipline.

For several reasons, secure attachments may create a climate of receptive compliance.[71] First, when children feel secure with caregivers, they may be better able to understand and remember parents' messages because they are not anxious about their parents' acceptance of them. Second, when children feel secure with parents, they are happy and enjoy carrying out parents' requests. Third, secure attachments may increase children's attention and orientation to their parents' presence and their parents' wants.

Although it is easier to establish an atmosphere of receptive compliance when children are infants, it is possible to create such an atmosphere when children are in elementary school and in their teen years.[72] Recall the discussion of Gerald Patterson's work, in Chapter 2, which indicated that parents can create a positive atmosphere of collaboration with school-age children by paying positive atten- ~~3~~ tion to their behavior, spending time in enjoyable activities, encouraging them in their activities (discussed on page 178), and engaging in problem-solving when problems arise. All these actions increase children's willingness to listen and com- ply with rules.

Making children partners in routines as soon as they can participate contributes ~~4~~ to a collaborative atmosphere.[73] Parents can show infants how to help dress them- selves by guiding them through the actions in a playful way, letting them push their arms through sleeves or stick their heads out of the tops of shirts. Toddlers like to help, and many parents discourage their participation because everything takes longer, but finding small tasks to include young children in routines helps them de- velop a clearer idea or a script of the behaviors that make up the family routines around eating, picking up, and cleaning.

Conversations

A second step in establishing a collaborative family atmosphere is to talk—about ~~5~~ what people are doing, what they are thinking, feeling, whatever is happening.[74] In a world in which communication is becoming increasingly electronic, direct talking time is decreasing. As we noted in Chapter 4, storytelling is important because it talks about what has happened and creates closeness. Conversations as we discuss them here are about routine events and are more informational, conferring on what is happening now and may happen in the future. For example, a mother can have a conversation about what she and other family members will be doing on a Saturday morning. "We have to stop at the store to pick up the snacks for the picnic we're all going to after Jimmy's soccer game." Such conversations help children see how dif- ferent activities fit into the whole family's needs and schedule. See Box 5-3 for sug- gestions on more general conversations.

Parents also can talk about the rules and the reasons for them so children can understand why rules are important. Even when children are young and cannot un- derstand the exact words, the tone of voice indicates that there is a routine to fol- low. As children gain greater verbal understanding, clarity about the purpose of the rules and the effects on others when rules are not followed help children remember the rules and follow them. Talking when everyone's emotions are calm increases the likelihood that children will hear and take in what parents are saying. Conversation in the midst of conflict is not as useful.

When parents explain their reasons for rules in detail, expressing their concern in their body language as well as with words, children (especially young children), better understand what is required and why.[75] Talking about rules in a telegraphic fashion, saying only a few words, does not have as great an impact on children. When conversations describe how rules help everyone, children gain a richer understanding of how people relate to one another in a caring and considerate way.

At times of actual misbehavior and rule breaking, verbal strategies of discipline have many benefits. When mothers remain calm, use reasoning, and avoid threats and physical force, children's social and emotional competence grows, and they are able to internalize the rules. Forcing children with yelling and angry gestures increases children's frustration and defiance. In a later section in this chapter, we discuss mutual problem-solving, which helps parents verbally express themselves in positive ways at times of frustration and irritation.

Reading stories that illustrate the behaviors parents want to see in their children reinforces parental values in a way that appeals to children. For example, *The Little Engine That Could* illustrates for young children the value of courage and persistence.[76] For older children, adventure stories or stories about historical events can serve as springboards for longer discussions about approved behaviors.

Encouragement

Drawing on the insights of Alfred Adler, the first of Freud's followers to modify psychoanalytic theory to focus on individuals' healthy, purposive, and social behavior, Rudolf Dreikurs proposed positive child-rearing strategies.[77] He suggested that parents rely on encouragement to stimulate children's built-in capacity to develop healthy, effective behaviors. Because children naturally seek both to develop their abilities and to become competent, important members of their families, parents' main task is to provide an environment for growth to occur, not to use parental power to force or punish children.

A central feature of the growth-promoting environment is encouragement, which Dreikurs defined as "a continuous process aimed at giving the child a sense of self-respect and a sense of accomplishment."[78] Parents' tone of voice in speaking to children, along with their gestures, affection, and willingness to play with children, all communicate that children are valued and well-loved family members. Parents provide encouragement in three principal ways: (1) by allowing children the freedom to act on their own—even babies can have opportunities to amuse themselves and feed themselves, and as toddlers, they can share in family chores so they learn their own capabilities; (2) by identifying the child's positive contributions and help—"It's a real help when you empty the waste baskets," or "Thank you for taking the napkins to the table"; (3) by teaching children to ask for what they need so parents can better meet the needs—"Tell me what is upsetting you so we can see what can be done."

Parents encourage children by teaching them how to do basic self-care routines and chores, such as dressing themselves or making a bed. Parents anticipate that children will need time to develop skills, and they do not criticize or tear down children's confidence with statements such as "I can do it for you faster" or "You are

Box 5-3
CONVERSATIONS

Conversation, the verbal communication of thoughts and feelings*, serves many purposes in everyday life. It conveys factual information. As we saw in Chapter 3, it can boost the confidence of children who hear many positive responses to their comments and behavior. Conversations can bring us closer to others as we share our thoughts and feelings. As we saw in Chapter 4 when we talked about coaching children about feelings, conversations can help us identify and understand our feelings. In this chapter, we have seen that conversations about rules and routines and activities in everyday life help children manage their behavior more effectively.

It is easy to converse with young children because they are eager to share their experiences and reactions, and they do not worry as much as older children about criticism and negative reaction. With interested listeners who don't push them to talk, they will talk, ask many questions, and give their listeners fascinating insights into their worlds.

Older children may be more cautious, involved in their own activities, reluctant to give opinions that may trigger criticism. Educational psychologist Jane Healy has always urged parents to talk to children to stimulate children's thinking and reasoning abilities. One frustrated father came up to her after a lecture and said, "Tell us how . . .[†] Give us some practical ideas, not just vague prescriptions."[‡]

Healy had no immediate answers for the father, but she began to think about specific suggestions. A few months later, when working with an eleven-year-old boy who could not "think," yet had no disabilities to account for the problem, she devised a series of imaginative questions to spark family discussions and ground rules to keep the conversations going.

Here are imaginative questions to engage the whole family:

1. If you could talk to animals, what would you try to find out?
2. Try to imagine what life would be like if you were the size of a mouse.
3. Imagine a world in which everyone looked alike.
4. What if suddenly all the people in the country woke up speaking different languages and no one could understand anyone else?
5. How would the world be different if people were born with wheels instead of feet?

The rules of conversation are that everyone has to listen to what each person says without interrupting, criticizing, or putting down others' responses. One can ask for clarification, but there is no response that is wrong. One person serves as a facilitator. These questions get people talking, but it is up to parents to keep the conversations going in day-to-day life. Remember, it is through conversations and really listening that you know about your child's world.

Harvard psychologist David Heller has talked with children of many religions about their conceptions of religion and God. In his book *Talking to Your Child about God: A Book for Families of All Faiths*[†], he gives examples of questions parents can use to start conversations with children about their views of creation, God, and different religions, and—most important—ways parents can talk to children about parents' own beliefs.

(continued)

**Box 5-3
CONTINUED**

If you are a good listener with young children, you may not have to ask questions; they will ask you. From his personal collection of children's letters to God, Heller gives the following example of a nine-year-old boy who has many questions and some answers too.

Dear God,
How do you find a mom and dad for each kid? Do you match them up by their religions, what colors they are or by cities? Or maybe something else very different. Maybe you just use a big lottery. I must have won but my friend Billy did not do so good. Please help him. Love, Paul (p. 3)

Many wonderful conversations await you on all kinds of topics, so start talking—but spend more time listening.

*William Morris, ed., *The American Heritage Dictionary of the English Language* (Boston: American Heritage Publishing Co. and Houghton Mifflin, 1969).
†Jane M. Healy, *Is Your Bed Still There When You Close The Door?* (New York: Doubleday, 1992).
‡David Heller, *Talking to Your Child about God: A Book for Families of All Faiths* (New York: Bantam, 1988).

too little to set the table." When children are frustrated with the process of learning, parents call attention to the challenge of the task and to the gains the child is making. "Practicing the piano is hard in the beginning, but you are learning all the scales, and you are able to play more pieces."

In all families, children make mistakes. Dreikurs describes parents' tendencies to overemphasize these errors by pointing out every minor mistake and continually telling children what they must do to improve. Under such a regime, children may feel they have to be perfect in order to gain acceptance; such fears can keep children from trying activities because mistakes are so painful. As Dreikurs observed,

We all make mistakes. Very few are disastrous. Many times we won't even know that a given action is a mistake until after it is done and we see the results! Sometimes we even have to make the mistake in order to find out that it is a mistake. *We must have the courage to be imperfect*—and to allow our children to be imperfect. Only in this way can we function, progress, and grow. Our children will maintain their courage and learn more readily if we minimize the mistakes and direct their attention toward the positive. "What is to be done now that the mistake is made" leads to progress forward and stimulates courage. Making a mistake is not nearly as important as what we do about it afterwards.[79]

According to Dreikurs, mistakes are incompletions, not failures. They are signs that the child is trying to do something, is exerting effort, but is not quite ready to

INTERVIEW
with Susan Harter

Susan Harter, a professor of psychology at the University of Denver, has spent twenty years studying the development of the self and self-esteem and has written numerous articles and chapters on the subject.

You have done a great deal of research on self-esteem. More than any other quality, I would say, parents hope to help children develop self-esteem. What can they do to promote it in their children?

We have identified two broad themes that impact children's self-esteem. First, the unconditional support and positive regard of parents and others in the child's world are particularly critical during the early years. What do we mean by support? It is communicating to children that you like them as people for who or what they are.

That sounds relatively easy but is in fact extremely difficult. Most of us as parents are far more skilled at providing conditional regard or support for children even though we are unaware we are doing it. We approve of our child if he cleans up his room or shares or doesn't hit his brother. So our support is conditional on his conduct. However, it isn't perceived by children as supportive at all. Basically it specifies how the child can please the parents. That does not feel good to children.

Unconditional regard validates children as worthy people and lets them know they are appreciated for who they are, for their strengths and weaknesses. It also involves listening to them, which is very validating to children as well as adults. So many well-meaning parents, and I make the same mistake, preach at their kids because we think we have a lot to say. We think we're teaching when we are really preaching. We don't refrain from talking; we don't shut up, listen well, and take the child's point of view seriously.

With unconditional support early on, children internalize positive regard so that when they are older, they can approve of themselves, pat themselves on the back, give themselves psychological hugs—all of which contribute to high self-esteem.

Another major part of self-esteem, beginning at about age eight, is feeling competent and adequate across the various domains of life. One does not have to feel competent in every domain in order to experience high self-esteem. Rather, one needs to feel competent in those domains that he or she judges to be *important*. Profiles of competence for two children in the different areas of athletic, social, and intellectual competence can look very similar, but one child can have high self-esteem while the other can have low self-esteem. They both can feel competent in the same areas and feel inadequate in the same other areas. What distinguishes the *low*-self-esteem child is the fact that areas of incompetence are very important to his or her feeling of being worthwhile; thus the child doesn't feel good about himself or herself. The *high*-self-esteem child feels the low areas are very unimportant and so still feels good about himself or herself.

do the task completely. The child may need more time to learn or practice a skill. Although mistakes are unfortunate in that they take up time and sometimes cost money, they are valuable because a child learns what is not effective. In addition, many warm family memories center on mistakes that were overcome. So, parents help children figure out what the next step is.

PROMOTING COMPETENCIES

When parents are asked what they believe it is absolutely essential to teach their children, they respond: to be honest and truthful (91 percent of parents), to be courteous and polite (84 percent of parents), to have self-control and self-discipline (83 percent of parents), and always to do their very best in school (82 percent of parents).[80] In focusing on competencies in this chapter, we emphasize emotional and moral competence and problem-solving skills, because we discussed intellectual competence in broad terms in Chapter 2 and because social competence rests in many ways on emotional regulation and moral behaviors with others. We take up these topics in greater detail in the chapters on the appropriate developmental periods.

Promoting Emotional Regulation

When a child or teen can accept a parent's refusal to take him or her someplace without arguing, persist at a boring but important task, or seek out another group to play with when denied entry to a lunchtime game, we say the child has managed feelings well. Learning to modulate the intensity of emotional reactions and to control their behavioral expression is a major task of the growing years, and is necessary if children are to persist in frustrating school tasks, learn problem-solving skills, and exhibit acceptable social and moral behavior. Further, the ability to control one's feelings and pay attention to others' feelings is an important ingredient for successful social relationships with others. Parents play a central role in helping children learn emotional regulation.

As Haim Ginott wrote, "Emotions are part of our genetic heritage. Fish swim, birds fly, and people feel."[81] Babies come into the world with emotional responses, which are the main ways they tell parents what they want. Babies' cries tell parents to take action to end the distress. In the early weeks of life, babies' peaceful sleeping tells parents to relax, that everything is fine; and their alert interest tells parents to continue what they are doing, that their activity is noteworthy.

In the first few months of life, babies have a limited repertoire of feelings: distress, relaxation after such gratifications as nursing, and interest. But by the end of the first year, they will express such emotions as joy, pleasure, delight, wariness, sadness, anxiety, fear, and anger. In the second and third years of life, they express embarrassment, pride, and shame; still later, in the fourth and fifth years, guilt.[82]

Children are intensely interested in emotions. Babies as young as three months respond to the happy or sad faces of their mothers, imitating happy feelings, turning away from sad expressions. As soon as they can talk, children talk about feelings. Children as young as twenty-eight months have a beginning sense of what causes feelings and how to cope with them: "I scared of the shark. I close my eyes." "I give a big hug. Baby be happy." "Grandma mad. I write on walls."[83]

Modulating Feelings and Coaching Children in Their Expression   Children's temperaments influence the intensity of their emotional reactions from the beginning of life, but even in the case of irritable and fussy babies, parents' efforts over time can help children regulate feelings.[84] Parents take many actions to help children regulate their emotions.[85] First, they provide sensitive care with daily routines that meet children's individual needs and thus reduce negative reactions. Second, when children are upset, parents seek many ways to soothe and handle negative feelings.

When children develop language, parents verbally coach children to identify and communicate feelings, as we discussed in Chapter 4. Throughout childhood and adolescence, parents' talking with children about feelings and coaching children to understand and communicate feelings are the major ways in which children learn to identify and express feelings appropriately.

Parents also guide children to select appropriate forms of expression of feelings, but the ways they do this depend somewhat (although not completely) on the age of the child. To distract a toddler from her anger at having to take a bath, a parent may offer a favorite toy for play in the bath, but the parent of an early adolescent who argues about taking a shower might use problem-solving strategies (which we discuss in a later section).

Structuring the Environment to Help Emotional Regulation   Structuring daily routines, time, and space improves children's physical well-being and prevents them from becoming overwhelmed with feelings.[86]

Consistent daily routines regarding mealtimes, exercise, and sleeping promote physical well-being, which in turn promotes emotional regulation. When children are hungry, tired, and restricted in activity, they are more likely to have emotional outbursts.[87] Consistent times for sleeping, eating, studying, chores, exercise, and leisure give children a sense of stability and a sense of control; they can anticipate what they will be doing and reduce the frustration of irregular routines.

Children's frustration and outbursts at following household rules decrease when the organization of space and time promotes order and cooperation. Even in crowded households, designating boxes or shelves for children's toys and drawers for clothes reduces the frustrations of cleaning up because places are available for children's possessions. Setting a definite time to do homework reduces struggles over homework and school projects. Placing bulletin boards in the kitchen and bedrooms, with family schedules and reminders in the kitchen and personal reminders in the bedrooms, keeps each family member aware of the flow of family and personal activities. Scheduling times for individual and family chores reduces arguments and increases the likelihood that the chores will get done.

Organizing the refrigerator, filling it with fruits and vegetables instead of sodas and ice cream with little nutritional value, reduces arguments about eating these foods, because they are not there to consume.

All the steps listed here are preventive steps, and although they do not eliminate all arguments and temper outbursts, they increase the likelihood that life will be easier for all family members.

Modeling Emotional Regulation   Most important in helping children regulate their feelings, parents serve as models of emotional regulation. They remain calm with children, making requests in normal tones of voice, not yelling and screaming. They give children time to comply with routines, not swooping down on children with demands for immediate behavioral change. Parents remain conscious that their children are observing them at all times, and the ways they speak to extended family, brothers and sisters, and clerks in stores all model appropriate control for children.

Promoting Problem-Solving and Decision-Making Skills

Life contains challenges and frustrations. To live happily and effectively, children must develop problem-solving and decision-making skills. Problem solving consists of finding strategies with which to overcome or go around barriers and obstacles to achieve a desired goal. Problem solving also requires making choices: choosing one or more possible actions to achieve the goal and then evaluating the success of each in achieving the goal.[88] Parents want to help children learn to make the right choices. As one father said, "If you teach somebody how to make good decisions and to rely on themselves, they're going to manage pretty well later on. . . . You're not always going to be there."[89]

We appear to be born with the motivation and abilities to solve problems.[90] Babies just two months old show that they are capable of changing their behavior to achieve a desired goal. When given the opportunity to pull a lever to see a baby's face and hear a song, they quickly learn to pull the lever. When the lever pulling no longer produces the face and the song, they become angry and stop pulling the lever. Slightly older infants find ways to grab a desired object that is out of reach or to get help from a parent who can obtain it for them.

Preschoolers can plan and carry out simple tasks that they are familiar with. For example, they can plan a "shopping route" in a grocery store to get breakfast foods, but they find it harder to plan when the shopping list contains several kinds of items, such as breakfast foods and party foods. In addition to knowledge in the area of the problem to be solved, children must have the ability to manage the emotional reactions of frustration and anger and to delay action while they make plans. Thus, the emotional regulation just discussed is critical for developing skills in solving problems. Problem solving and planning also require time to think, and so parents must give children that time and not rush them through the task.

Parents guide children's problem solving by giving information and possible suggestions. Recall Vygotsky's views, described in Chapter 2, that parents' questions and support enable children to perform activities that they cannot perform alone. When children are young, parents' guidance is more active, directly suggesting or moving the child through the most effective actions, but as children get older and enter elementary school, parents may primarily use verbal questions and suggestions from the sidelines, letting the child make choices.[91]

Many very young children can solve problems in their own area of experience if a parent asks them what they think should be done. "What would help you get ready for bed more quickly?" Getting in the habit of soliciting their opinions and advice helps children think about strategies for solving problems. When they are older, they can learn a seven-step process they can use anywhere. This process is slightly modified from a program developed by Roger Weissberg[92] and his coworkers and described in Daniel Goleman's book, *Emotional Intelligence*.[93] Their six-step method of problem solving led to improved behavioral controls in elementary school children in a two-year school program designed to prevent problem behaviors. It did not include the last step, evaluating actions taken.

Red light

    1. Stop, calm down, and think before you act.

Yellow light

    2. Say the problem and how you feel.

    3. Set a positive goal.

    4. Think of lots of solutions.

    5. Think ahead to the consequence.

Green light

    6. Go ahead and try the best plan.

    7. Evaluate the results.

Parents can guide the child with questions if the child gets stuck. If the goal or alternative actions seem unsafe, parents can ask how wise such a goal or action is. Parents have to be careful not to be critical or to stifle their child's efforts at solving the problem. Sometimes, in the course of trying to solve the problem, the goal as stated is impossible to reach, and so the goal is changed. For example, an eight-year-old is frustrated because her friend, who was going to spend the night, had to cancel because family relatives suddenly came for a visit. The goal becomes to find another time her friend can spend the night and to find a way to be happy doing something else that evening—not to have the friend stay that night.

A longitudinal study of family planning discussions reveals that preschoolers begin to engage in conversations about future plans in the family and are especially likely to do so when there are many children in the family.[94] Child-initiated planning discussions increase with age and parenting style. Adolescents initiate more family planning discussions when parents have an authoritative style of parenting (see Chapter 2), which encourages children's choices, when parents withdraw because of lack of involvement, or when parents are permissive and leave planning up to children. Adolescents engage less in planning discussions when parents are directive and issue orders.

As parents observe children's goal setting, parents may believe it is their job to give their children accurate appraisals of their abilities and goals. Parents may fear giving children too much confidence, giving them unrealistic and inflated self-esteem that will lead children to misjudge situations and make serious and possibly harmful mistakes.

Albert Bandura, who has studied people's beliefs about their abilities to take effective action, states that, in hazardous situations, accurate self-perception of abilities is essential.[95] For example, if you overestimate your ability to swim in heavy surf, you are in trouble and may not have a chance to correct the perception. In nonhazardous situations, which make up most of life's situations, however, people are more effective when they *overrate* their abilities and set very high goals. Why? Because life is full of problems and challenges, and to overcome them, we have to persevere. People are most likely to persist when they believe in themselves and their abilities to achieve their goals. When people lack that confidence, they give up at the first setback interpreting the setback as a sign they are not competent to gain their objective.

Confident people, in contrast, see a failure or setback as an opportunity to learn something positive that they can use to obtain their goals. They are described as "hardy" individuals who are able to cope with negative events because they see them as one step on the way to success.[96] Confident people are not only able to achieve their goals in everyday life, but they are able to face trauma and loss and continue to function effectively. They do this by focusing on the positive side of the situation, building in positive experiences with friends and family to sustain them.

In his 2005 autobiography *Mirror to America,* noted historian John Hope Franklin gives an example of how his parents' "unrealistic" confidence in him helped him. He wrote,

> In my early years there was never a moment in any contact I had with white people that I was not reminded that society as a whole had sentenced me to abject humiliation for the sole reason that I was not white. Small wonder that some black boys and girls, having no one else to blame for the cruel disadvantage of being black, have grown to maturity hating themselves.
>
> Happily for me, my parents always insisted that race was irrelevant as far as one's personal development was concerned. They even taught me to believe that I could be, as they then articulated it, the first Negro president of the United States; if as a youth I had tongue in cheek when I declared my intent of realizing that ambition, it had the effect of establishing a measure of self-confidence that permitted me to pursue more realistic goals, if only more realistic by matter of degree.[97]

With that self-confidence, Franklin graduated from college, went on to earn a Ph.D. in history from Harvard University, authored numerous books and articles, including the best-seller *From Slavery to Freedom,* taught at major universities in this country and around the world, participated in civil rights activities and commissions, and in 1995, won the Presidential Medal of Freedom. Franklin's parents gave him the confidence to pursue his desire for education and achievement even when society's treatment implied they were unrealistic goals for him.

Promoting Moral Behavior and Judgment

Parents' hearts warm when they see their children offer an irritating cousin their favorite toy or tell the truth even when a negative consequence may follow. Such actions tell parents that children are learning right from wrong and learning to carry out what society believes are good actions. In brief, they are becoming moral individuals.

Moral competence refers to several aspects of children's behavior: (1) voluntarily carrying out positive acts that are helpful and beneficial to others—comforting a crying child, giving up a favorite television show so a sick brother can watch his favorite; (2) avoiding disapproved actions such as lying, cheating, stealing, and physical aggression; (3) developing a conscience or internal standards that direct behavior even when no authority is present; and (4) acquiring the capacity to make moral judgments.[98] Moral competence rests on the capacity for emotional regulation and self-control and on the capacity for empathy and concern for others, and so it is related to emotional regulation and social skills.

Children learn how to solve problems at early ages, and parents can help them develop skills by asking children what they think are solutions to a given problem.

Parents want to promote moral behaviors and the development of conscience and moral judgment. Fortunately, they have motivated partners to work with: children. Children are intensely interested in moral questions from the early days of life. As William Damon writes,

> It is a mistake to think of morality as a set of external standards that adults somehow foist upon an unknowing or unwilling child. Such an assumption distorts our view of the very real and intense moral feelings that children experience on their own accord. It overlooks the spontaneous expressions of moral sentiments that children frequently display in both peer and family settings. . . . Morality arises naturally out of social relationships, and children's morality is no exception. Wherever there is human discourse and interpersonal exchange there will follow rules of conduct, feelings of care, and sense of obligation. Children participate in social relations very early, practically at birth. Their moral

thoughts and feelings are an inevitable consequence of these early relations and others that will arise throughout life.[99]

Researchers have identified five core actions parents can take to promote moral behavior. These parental behaviors stimulate not only moral behavior but social behavior and emotional regulation as well. (See Box 5-4.) Modeling has a central role in transmitting values from one generation to another. Robert Coles, a psychiatrist who has studied children's moral and spiritual development for five decades, writes,

> The child is a witness; the child is an ever-attentive witness of grown-up morality—or lack thereof; the child looks and looks for cues as to how one ought to behave, and finds them galore as we parents and teachers go about our lives, making choices, addressing people, showing in action our rock-bottom assumptions, desires, and values, and thereby telling those young observers much more than we may realize.[100]

We have already discussed the importance of nurturing care and discussions of rules and the reasons for them. Holding children to high standards appropriate to their age and temperamental qualities, and giving children the support they need to achieve the standards, stimulate the growth of competent moral and social behaviors.

Connecting Children with Parents' Spiritual and Religious Values

To give children their parents' value system is to provide them with a framework for understanding life experiences. Children feel more secure when they feel that there

---

Box 5-4
PARENTING STRATEGIES TO HELP CHILDREN DEVELOP MORAL BEHAVIOR*

1. Model the actions and ways of thinking you want your child to develop.
2. Practice nurturant caregiving so children develop self-esteem and a sense of belonging.
3. Reason with children to help them understand the consequences of their actions and their effects on others.
4. Have high but realistic standards for children and provide support for children to meet the standards.
5. Involve children in family decision-making and problem-solving sessions so children can contribute their views and understand others' points of view.

*Adapted from: Marvin W. Berkowitz et al., "Educating for Positive Youth Development," in *Handbook of Moral Development*, ed. Melanie Killen and Judith Smetana (Mahwah, NJ: Erlbaum, 2006), p. 694.

is an order to the world and that they have a definite place in that order. If parents participate regularly in a church program, it is easy to incorporate children in services and activities that present a worldview that is meaningful to parents and children alike. Parents who do not belong to any spiritual or religious group can have discussions with children as they get older about parental beliefs and how they translate beliefs into actions. It is important to include children in activities to make the community a better place. Children learn social responsibility this way. It is important that parents' actions mirror values; otherwise, children regard values as just so much talk.

A TOOL CHEST FOR DEALING WITH PROBLEM BEHAVIORS

No matter how skilled the parent or how good the parent-child relationship, problems arise, and parents must deal with them. Verbal strategies of dealing with problems are preferred because they enable children to learn the reasons for consequences and to understand principles that can be used in other situations. For example, if parents talk about why it is important for children to be ready to go to school in the morning, they can then generalize the importance of promptness to other situations in school or with friends.

We give a number of strategies for parents to use according to the situation and their values. These tools should all be used in a family atmosphere in which good behavior receives attention and appreciation. Attention alone is enough reward for some children to increase the desired positive behaviors. Sometimes in the rush of everyday life, parents rush from one problem to another and pay attention only when the child is not doing what is requested. Thus, the child hears only what requires changing. So, parents first must be sure they are giving attention to the many ways their child follows their requests.

When actions are required, the following choices exist. We begin with natural and logical consequences because they require primarily that parents let children learn from the consequences of their actions.

Natural and Logical Consequences

Rudolf Dreikurs described the method of natural and logical consequences as an alternative to parents' use of power and punishment. The terms *natural consequences* and *logical consequences*[101] are used jointly and interchangeably but have slightly different meanings. Natural consequences are the direct result of a physical act. For example, if you do not eat dinner, you experience hunger. If you do not get your dirty clothes in the laundry, they are not washed. Parents mainly have to stand aside and let the natural consequences occur—let the child remain hungry until the next meal or wear dirty clothes.

Logical consequences are events that follow a social act. For example, if you lie, other people will not believe you. If you misuse the family car, your parents will not trust you with it. Natural and logical consequences are directly related to the act itself and are not usually imposed by others. Exceptions exist, however. If a natural consequence presents a risk to a child—e.g., running out into a busy street could result in being hit by a car—parents generally use a logical consequence. If a child starts toward the street, the child is restricted to playing in the house.

Logical consequences differ from punishment in several ways. Logical consequences are directly related to what the child has done—no clothes in the laundry basket results in having no clean clothes. A punishment may have no logical relationship to what the child has done—a spanking is not the direct result of being late for a meal but is the result of the parent's authority. The method of logical consequences does not place moral blame or pass moral judgment on the child. The child has made a mistake and pays the price. The parent stands by as an adviser rather than a judge.

When a parent establishes a logical consequence, it has to be one that he or she can accept when the child experiences it. For example, if a teen is told that the logical consequence of not getting homework turned in is that she will have to stay in on the weekend and complete it even though there is a desirable party on Friday night, then the parent has to stand by the consequence even though the child is sad and angry and the parent would like to see the child go the party.

Mutual Problem Solving

Thomas Gordon describes mutual problem solving as a useful technique when parents feel a situation must change.[102] Using an I-statement (described in Chapter 4), parents describe their feelings of frustration or worry and identify the problem behavior from their point of view. A mother may say, "I get frustrated on weekday mornings when I am driving children to school and they are not ready to go on time, because I am late for work and my supervisor yells at me. What do you think can be done to solve the problem?" Children can then give their suggestions. One might say he cannot get into the bathroom because his sister stays in there so long blow-drying her hair that he is always late, and even if he gets up earlier, he won't be able to get into the bathroom. His sister may agree that it is she who slows things down for him, and she volunteers to shower and then eat breakfast so he can get in the bathroom before she dries her hair. They all agree to try this solution for a week and see what happens. The aim of problem solving is to find a win-win solution agreeable to all concerned. There are six steps in the problem-solving process that children and parents can perform together:

1. Defining the problem; parents and children make I-statements.
2. Generating possible solutions; parents and children think of possible actions to solve problem.
3. Evaluating possible solutions; parents and children think about how each solution would work out.
4. Deciding on the best solution; parents and children make a joint decision.
5. Implementing the decision; each person does his or her part.
6. Doing a follow-up evaluation.

When an agreed-on solution is not followed, parents must send a strong I-message of disappointment and surprise as soon as possible. Perhaps the child can be helped to keep the agreement. Or perhaps another problem-solving session is needed. Gordon advises against the use of penalties to enforce agreements. Parents should assume that children will cooperate instead of starting with a negative expectation expressed in the threat of punishment. Children frequently respond well to trust.

Parents can also use a behavioral contracting system. Just as parents want children to perform certain behaviors, so children want to attain certain objects, activities, and privileges. Parents offer desired rewards in exchange for the performance of certain activities. For example, if a child does his chores (making his bed, clearing the table) without reminders, he earns an extra fifteen minutes of time for playing. Likewise, an older child may be given use of the family car on the weekends if she maintains acceptable school grades and arrives home at the prescribed times. Contracting is similar to mutual problem solving but differs in that parents act more as authorities who agree to dispense privileges and rewards in exchange for actions rather than as joint problem solvers.

Negative Consequences

Recall our discussion of learning theories in Chapter 2. Negative consequences are used to decrease behaviors that are not desired. If attention to positive behaviors and the methods discussed in the preceding section have not worked, parents can institute a negative consequence to decrease the likelihood of the behavior's recurrence. There are six general principles for using negative consequences:

1. Intervene early. Do not let the situation get out of control. As soon as the rule is violated, begin to take action.

2. Stay as calm and objective as possible. Sometimes, parents' upset and frustration are rewarding to the child. Parents' emotions can also distract the child from thinking about the rule violation.

3. State the rule that was violated. State it simply, and do not argue about it.

4. Use a *mild* negative consequence. The advantage is that the child often devalues the activity itself and seems more likely to resist temptation and follow the rule in the future.

5. Use negative consequences consistently. Misbehaviors continue when they are sometimes punished and sometimes not.

6. Reinforce positive social behaviors as they occur afterward; parents do not want children to receive more negative consequences than positive ones.

The following negative consequences range from mild to severe. First, *ignoring* might seem the easiest; the parent simply pays no attention to what the child says or does. It requires effort, however, because the parent must keep a neutral facial expression, look away, move away from the child, and give no verbal response or attention to what the child says or does. Ignoring is best for behaviors that are not harmful to anyone. For example, children's whining, sulking, or pouting can be ignored.

A second is *social disapproval*. Parents express in a few words, spoken in a firm voice with a disapproving facial expression, that they do not like the behavior. When children continue the disapproved behavior, parents can institute a consequence—removing a privilege, using the time-out strategy, or imposing extra work. When families have contracts, children agree to carry out specified chores or behaviors in exchange for privileges. When certain behaviors do not occur, children lose privileges.

Finally, *time out* is a method best reserved for aggressive, destructive, or dangerous behaviors. It serves to stop the disapproved behavior and to give the child a chance to cool off and think about the rule violation. The time-out method has many variations. The child can be requested to sit in a chair in the corner, but many children get up. If the child is required to face the corner, parents can keep a young child in the corner for the stated time. With older children, parents may want to add the rule that, if the child does not comply with time out for one parent during the day, making the presence of both parents necessary, then the child will spend twice the amount of time in time out. The time need not be long. For young children, the number of minutes in time out should equal the number of years in age. It is best to have only two or three behaviors requiring time out at any one time. Otherwise, a child may spend a great deal of time in the corner for too many different things. Further, both parents and all caregivers need to agree on the two or three things that will lead to time out so the child receives punishment consistently.

When children get older and have many toys and recreational pleasures in their rooms, such as stereos and computers, restriction to their rooms is not an effective punishment. For these children, it is better to substitute extra work or chores that have a constructive outcome, such as cleaning the garage or devoting time to a community activity.

Ineffective Forms of Discipline

A review of more than three hundred studies[103] identifies four kinds of problems in disciplining children: (1) inconsistent discipline, referring to inconsistency both on the part of one parent and between two parents; (2) irritable, harsh, explosive discipline (frequent hitting and threatening); (3) low supervision and low involvement on the part of the parent with the child; and (4) inflexible, rigid discipline (use of a single form of discipline for all transgressions, regardless of seriousness). All four forms of ineffective discipline are related to increases in children's aggressive, rule-breaking behavior that then frequently leads to social difficulties with peers.

THE USE OF PHYSICAL DISCIPLINE

Parents do not like to spank, and they do not consider it effective discipline.[104] Children believe parents have a right to spank, but they do not like it; it hurts their feelings and makes them feel angry and upset.[105] Health-care professionals and social scientists recommend against it.[106] Yet, the majority of parents have spanked children at one time or another.[107] How can we decrease or eliminate this behavior that no one wants to continue?

Definition of Levels of Physical Discipline

First, we must distinguish among forms of physical discipline. Physical discipline is often divided into two categories: (1) mild spanking, defined as a slap or two with the flat of the hand on the buttocks or extremities without causing any physical injury to the child and normatively used with young children between ages two and six, and (2) abuse, including beating, kicking, and punching that results in injury to the child.[108]

Even though these two categories seem clear cut, researchers face many difficulties in classifying parents with regard to their use of physical discipline, and therefore, understanding its use is more difficult than we would like.[109] First, as self-reporters of physical discipline, parents may not be accurate. Second, parents are often asked only whether and how often they spank within a specified period of time, such as the preceding week. Some parents who rarely spank but did that week may be identified as using physical punishment in the same category with others who rely more heavily on spanking. Also, a frequent user of physical punishment who did not happen to use physical means that week would be classified as a nonuser. Although researchers think that these errors cancel each other out, they do not know for sure. Third, parents are rarely asked how severely they spank their child, so whether the physical punishment is mild, harsh, or abusive remains unclear.

Prevalence and Frequency of Physical Discipline

Keeping in mind all the difficulties of identifying those who use different levels of physical discipline, let us look at the prevalence and frequency of spanking. When asked whether they have ever spanked their child, between 63 percent and 94 percent of parents say they have.[110] Although spanking has decreased over the past three decades, still, the vast majority have spanked a child.[111] In two large-scale studies, about two-thirds of parents of preschoolers aged three to five had spanked their child in the previous week, with an average of one to three spankings depending on the sample and subgroup.[112]

In a survey of parents of children five to fifteen years of age, 63 percent said they had used physical punishment. In a telephone survey, caregivers for 60 percent of children reported that they used physical punishment and minor physical violence (pushing, grabbing, shoving, and slapping), and 10 percent reported one or more instances of physical abuse or severe violence consisting of kicking, biting, or hitting with a fist.[113]

In a 1993 survey of middle-class families that included interviews with parents and children separately, 83 percent of parents reported using physical discipline.[114] Although most spanked a few times a month or less at mild to moderate intensity, researchers were concerned that about a third of the parents were reported by their children to use objects to hit them, and many said this occurred in about half the punishments. About 17 percent of children said they were hit a few times a week, and 4 percent said they were hit daily.

Spanking starts early in life. About 50 percent of parents report that they had spanked their child of less than a year old one or more times in the preceding week.[115] Spanking increases in the years from two to five, when between 60 and 65 percent of parents report having spanked a child. Beginning at age five, spanking decreases, so only about one-third of parents report having spanked their child in the previous week; by age nine or ten, that number drops to about 20 percent. Parents also report giving preschoolers, on average, more spankings per week (three) than they give older children (two).[116]

Characteristics of Parents Who Use Physical Discipline

Parents who are young, single, and under financial stress are more likely to spank than are older, married parents who have financial resources.[117] Parents who experience daily frustrations with children and have psychological problems report more spanking; still, as noted, 83 percent of middle-class parents in one study and 94 percent of middle-class parents in another used physical punishment.[118]

Mothers are more likely to use physical means of discipline than are fathers, perhaps because they do more of the daily child care.[119] African American parents are more likely to use physical punishment than are European American or Latina/o parents.[120] People who live in rural areas and in the southern part of the United States are more likely to use physical means of discipline than are parents in urban areas and the northern part of the United States.[121] Parents who identify themselves as religiously conservative report more frequent physical discipline than do those who do not identify themselves as religious conservatives,[122] and Catholics report less spanking than do Protestants.[123] Physical discipline is more likely, then, when parents are under stress or when they hold more traditional or more conservative values.

Characteristics of Children Who Receive Physical Discipline

As noted, preschool children are more likely to receive physical discipline than are elementary and high school students. Boys are more likely to be spanked than girls—in one study, 67 percent of boys received spankings, compared with 57 percent of girls.[124] Children described as having difficult temperaments and being noncompliant received more spankings than did other children.[125] Spankings also occurred more frequently in families in which parents and children argued and in which parents had fewer supports.

Reasons Given for Spanking

Seventy percent of parents nominated as outstanding parents by teachers of the year reported spanking, giving such reasons as the need to get children's attention in the face of a dangerous act.[126] A middle-class sample of parents gave a variety of reasons for spanking: "Nonphysical punishment is not effective." "Children learn better from punishment than from rewards." "Young children don't understand reasoning." "Physical punishment builds character and prepares children for the outside world, which can be cruel if children have not learned the consequences of their behavior." A common reason was, "It worked for me when I was growing up."[127]

Parents in this study were most likely to use spanking and hitting when children were out of control, disobedient, or disrespectful. Four factors were related to parents' spanking: (1) parents' belief in its usefulness, (2) parents' own experience with it as a child, (3) an authoritarian style of parenting, and (4) children's problems of aggressiveness and acting out. Although 93 percent justified its use, 85 percent of those who used it said they would rather not. They felt they were angry when they did it and that it upset the children; they wished they had alternatives.

Of concern to the researchers was the fact that parents continued the use of spanking despite their discomfort with it and its doubtful value. Parents seemed to rely on it as a continuation of their own childhood experiences of physical punishment instead of instituting change and learning new methods. The investigators were concerned that the children in the sample would continue the practice for the same reason.

The Effects of Physical Discipline

There is no doubt that physical abuse is related to many difficulties for children (see Chapter 15). Here, we focus on the effects of mild physical discipline. As just noted, parents and children alike feel angry and upset at the use of physical discipline. Children tend not to learn from it, so it seems more effective to find other ways to deal with problems. Experts agree that parents will have the best results in modifying children's behavior if they first use mild negative consequences along with reasoning.

Diana Baumrind believes that the effects of a spanking, which she defines as a slap or two with the flat of the hand on the buttocks or the extremities, depends on the context of the parent-child relationship.[128] Much research supports this position. The most recent study involved data collected from 1,990 children over a six-year period as part of the National Longitudinal Survey of Youth. The study included a sizable number of African American and Latina/o parents as well as European American parents.[129]

In this study, mothers were separated into three groups—no spanking in the last week, spanking once in the last week, and spanking more than once in the last week—when their children were four years of age and at two-year intervals over the next six years. When children were four, there was no relationship between the use and frequency of spanking and the child's behavior problems. Some children with few behavioral problems received many spankings, and some children with many behavioral difficulties received no spankings.

Spanking, however, increased behavioral difficulties over time. Although the behavior problems of all children increased from ages four to ten, those whose mothers continued to spank had more behavior problems than those who had not been spanked, unless moderating influences were present. When parents increased their spanking in these years, the increase in problems was greater than when spanking decreased or stayed the same. The findings were the same for all groups, so the effects of spanking did not differ as a result of ethnicity.

Children's mothers were also described in terms of their emotional warmth and supportiveness. Children with warm and supportive mothers had fewer behavior problems. Further, as the authors concluded,

> Although spanking can have a negative impact on children's socioemotional functioning over time, this effect is moderated by the emotional context in which such spanking occurs. When spanking occurs in a context of strong overall emotional support for the child, it does not appear to contribute to a significant increase in behavior problems.[130]

This finding was consistent in all three ethnic groups. It suggests that, when physical punishment is accompanied by warmth and reasoning, children interpret the punishment as a caring parent's response to misbehavior and not as rejection.

Review of studies from 1974 to 1995 on the effects of nonabusive or customary physical punishment found that nonabusive spanking led to a decrease in noncompliant behaviors.[131] Physical discipline was associated with no detrimental effects when it

1. was not severe
2. did not involve any implement
3. was used less than weekly
4. was used with young children two to six and possibly with children seven to twelve
5. was accompanied by reasoning
6. was used as a backup to other strategies
7. was used by parents who were not violent with other family members

Parents had the best results using nonabusive physical discipline when they were positively involved with children, were acting in terms of children's needs rather than their own motivations, did not arouse fear in children, provided consistent discipline, did not use verbal put-downs, and changed their main discipline to grounding as children grew older.

Although a large review of studies in 2002[132] revealed difficulties with aggressive behavior and social relationships, that review included moderate and abusive physical discipline that led to more serious concerns. When that review focused on mild physical punishment, the connection with difficulties disappeared.[133] We can conclude, then, that parents who have positive, warm relationships with their children and who use reasoning and mild physical discipline with young children from ages eighteen months to about five years do not appear to be placing these children at risk of long-term harm. Physical punishment in the absence of a warm relationship appears to contribute to an increase in children's behavior problems. Beyond age five, parents are well advised to find other disciplinary strategies.

Should We Ban or Outlaw Physical Discipline?

Social scientist Murray Straus wishes to ban physical discipline in schools and at home because of the potential for abuse and because it is related to aggressiveness among children and to a more violent society.[134] He cites statistics from a national representative sample of children revealing that the more corporal punishment a child receives in middle childhood and early adolescence, the greater the probability of the child's being a delinquent. Other social scientists such as Baumrind believe that research does not support a blanket injunction against spanking, as there are "no documented harmful long-term effects."[135] Further, she points out, in Sweden, where physical punishment was outlawed at home and at school in 1979, parental physical abuse of children as well as violent acts by teenagers increased.

How Can We Decrease Physical Discipline?

Gerald Patterson and Philip Fisher describe a vicious behavioral cycle that physical discipline reinforces.[136] When children do not comply, parents argue and then use physical discipline. When children comply, parents see that such discipline "works" and are therefore encouraged to use it again. Sometimes, though, during arguments, parents threaten physical punishment but do not carry out the threat because of children's loud protests. Thus, children are encouraged to protest loudly in the next encounter. In this way, parents and children train each other to escalate to a maximal level of protests and punishments. So, physical punishment is not easy to discontinue unless both parents and children change their behavior.

Parents start the process of change by using positive disciplinary techniques that create a collaborative family atmosphere, as described in Chapter 2 and earlier in this chapter. Parents pay attention to children's positive behaviors, give affection, and devote time to playing games. When parents discipline children, they use the nonphysical means of contracting, earning privileges, and time outs for behaviors that must be stopped. They use these techniques consistently, without anger or criticism or belittling the child, and they supervise children to make sure children follow through with the expected behaviors. Even if children protest loudly, parents do not back down; they persist with nonphysical discipline. Gradually, parents and children emerge from their vicious cycle of escalating conflict and physical discipline.

Discouraging the use of physical discipline, while a useful first step, does not automatically put in place the strategies of supportive parenting unless parents follow Patterson and Fisher's suggestions. The pediatrician Robert Chamberlin identifies the use of physical punishment as just one risk factor related to poor outcome for children. Because it is the accumulation of risk factors that causes the most damage, he believes that communities and professionals need to join with parents to promote the "affectionate and cognitively stimulating types of parenting behavior that appear more directly related to positive developmental outcomes rather than focus on whether or not parents use physical punishment."[137] Baumrind also cautions professionals,

> It should be the concern of professionals who work with parents to respectfully offer them alternative disciplinary strategies, using carefully evaluated intervention programs, rather than to condemn parents for using methods consonant with their own, but not with the counselor's, beliefs and values. Parents who choose to use punishment often seek guidance in using it efficaciously. Efficacious punishment is contingent upon the child's misbehavior, as well as upon the parents' responding in a prompt, rational, nonexplosive manner and with knowledge and consideration of the child's developmental level and temperament.[138]

PARENTING PROGRAMS

Just as people take courses in driving to get a license or in cooking to master basic skills, parents seek to learn skills in parenting programs. Parenting programs can be divided into those targeted for the general population of parents and those directed to parents with special needs, such as parents of twins or multiples, parents of premature children, or parents of children with attention-deficit hyperactivity problems. In this chapter, we review programs designed for parents in general and note the more specialized programs throughout the book.

Many programs are available for parents, some of which present programs of particular experts, such as Thomas Gordon's Parent Effectiveness Training; Rudolf Dreikurs's method and its adaptation, STEP (Systematic Training for Effective Parenting); and behavioral modification training. Analyses and reviews of more than fifty studies of Gordon's and Dreikurs's programs reveal that parents who attend these programs are more likely to listen to children, to encourage them, and to be more supportive and trusting of them. Some studies indicate children have higher self-esteem.[139]

Studies of parent behavioral training indicate that such training has its greatest success in decreasing problem behaviors such as infant crying, bed-wetting, bedtime fears, and noncompliant behavior.[140] Gerald Patterson and Carla Narrett point out that the benefits of behavioral training are greatest for parents of young, defiant children and are limited with older, more severely disturbed adolescents.[141] Patterson and Narrett consider children's behavioral change the most important marker for parent effectiveness; parents report children's behavioral change at home, but such change is not so often demonstrated in children's behavior at school.

Even a brief intervention of four sessions with parents can be helpful in preventing problems with infants.[142] First-time parents attending childbirth classes were routinely assigned to one of two groups. During pregnancy, one group received four sessions of behavioral training in helping newborns develop healthy sleep patterns. The control group had equal discussion time with instructors but no behavioral training. When infants were six to nine weeks old, investigators measured sleep patterns in infants over several nights. Infants of trained parents had longer sleep episodes, fewer night awakenings, and fewer night feedings. Trained parents experienced fewer difficulties with their babies and felt more competent and confident in managing babies' sleep patterns. In contrast, nontrained parents reported a greater number of difficulties in caring for their infants.

More recently, researchers have organized parenting programs based on their own research. These programs have been more successful in impacting both parents' and children's behavior, but they are not readily available to the general public. University researchers Philip Cowan and Carolyn Cowan have organized parent groups that do not seek to develop specific skills as much as give parents opportunities to discuss their own parenting experiences.[143] The Cowans first organized discussion groups for parents who were expecting their first child. The groups, which consisted of four couples and two professionals, began in the last trimester of pregnancy and continued for six months, to provide support for parents as they created their families. Parents talked about sources of stress, well-being and ways to increase closeness between the couple. Following the couples over five years, the Cowans found that those who participated in the couples groups were still together at the end of three years, whereas those in the control group experienced a divorce rate of 15 percent. At the end of five years, the divorce rate was similar for the two groups.

Impressed with the effects of the six-month groups, the Cowans began another intervention study at the time of the child's entrance into elementary school. Groups began when the child was four years old and about to enter school within a year.[144] The groups met for two hours a week for sixteen weeks. Although the parents were well-functioning volunteers who had not sought mental health services, still, their scores on measures of depression and marital satisfaction suggested they were experiencing stress in their daily lives.

Parent groups consisted of four couples and two mental health professionals and focused on five topics central to parents' and children's adjustment: (1) parents' sense of self, (2) their relationships with each other, (3) their relationships with their parents, (4) their relationships with their children, and (5) the life stresses and supports they experienced. In each session, parents had time to raise questions or problems. Researchers devised two forms of the parenting groups. In one group, leaders were told to focus on marital issues and parents' relationship as a couple in the open-ended discussion periods; in the other group, leaders emphasized parents' relationships with their children.

The control group consisted of parents who were offered a consultation with the staff couple who did their initial interview once a year for three years—the year before children entered kindergarten, once during kindergarten, and then once during first grade. Compared to children whose parents were in the control group, children of the parents in the intervention groups were more competent in kindergarten and first grade. They had higher academic achievement, fewer behavior problems, and more positive self-concepts. Both forms of intervention group were related to positive behaviors in children in kindergarten and first grade.

Gene Brody and his coworkers at the University of Georgia surveyed rural African American families' concerns.[145] The families identified two: Early sexual activity and adolescent substance use were areas of great concern to them. Researchers set up a training program to help parents and their eleven-year-old, early-adolescent children develop skills to avoid these behaviors. Titled the Strong African American Family Program, the program consisted of weekly two-hour sessions for seven weeks. Parents and children met separately for an hour and then jointly for an hour to practice the skills they learned.

Parents learned nurturing parenting skills, ways of monitoring and controlling children's behavior, adaptive strategies of racial socialization, and strategies for communicating information about sex and substances, as well as parents' expectations in these areas. Children learned the value of following household rules and doing chores, adaptive ways to counter racism, the importance of having a future orientation toward setting and achieving goals, ways to counter and resist the temptations of substance abuse and early sexual activity, and ways in which they who did not engage in these activities differed from those who did. Families in the control group received three pamphlets in the mail, on early adolescent development, on ways to manage stress, and on ways to encourage exercise.

Seven months after the parenting program, parents and children who received training demonstrated more behaviors associated with protective factors against substance use and early sexual activity than did those in the control group. Parents were more communicative of general information on early sexual activity and substance abuse, as well as their own expectations of children in these areas, and were more positive and supportive with children in this age period. Compared to youth in the control group, youth in the program had greater acceptance of parents' rules, a greater orientation to the future and to setting goals, and a more negative view of those who used substances and engaged in early sexual activity. The future behavior of these early adolescents will be tracked to see whether parents' and children's attendance in the programs and their development of protective factors against substance use and early sexual activity reduced the rates of these behaviors in children as they progress through adolescence.

The evidence from parenting programs, then, is that they help develop useful skills. The Cowans' programs have been highly successful in impacting children's behaviors when other programs have been less so. It may be that practice in communication skills and setting limits is most useful in a group where there is extended time for talking about one's own frustrations and needs in marital and extended family relationships as well as in interactions with children.

Camille Smith, Ruth Perou, and Catherine Lesesne reviewed the history and present state of parent education and concluded,

> Parenting is open to change, but it is not easy to change. . . . What has become clear from the research over many years is that the fundamental principle that parenting education programs (both universal and targeted) must stress is the importance of relationships. Relationships are among the most significant influences on healthy growth and psychological well-being. The quality of the parent-child relationship has long been acknowledged to be one of the most powerful predictors of optimal child development. Warm, responsive parenting is associated with later child language development, cognitive development, school success, and behavioral adjustment. Conversely, parents who are less involved and affectionate with their children are more likely to experience many more academic and behavioral problems with those children as they grow in years. . . . It is imperative that we stress the key component that should be a part of every parent education program: the importance and significance of the parent-child relationship.[146]

Even when parents and children have good relationships, problems arise, and parents often whish they had a single solution to each kind of problem they encounter in child rearing—one way to handle temper tantrums, one way to deal with teenagers' rebelliousness. Unfortunately, there is no one formula that all parents can use to raise all children. Each child, as well as each parent, is a unique individual.

When parents have difficulties, a seven-step problem-solving approach seems most useful. This approach allows parents to choose *interventions* (actions to change a problem behavior, such as holding a mutual problem-solving session or setting up a reward system) that take into account the child's age and temperament as well as the family's social values and living circumstances. It also enables parents to encourage the qualities that they and their ethnic group value. Here are the seven steps:

1. Spend pleasurable time daily with the child.
2. Specifically identify any problem; observe when and how often it occurs.
3. Question yourself on the reality of the problem.
4. Get the child's point of view.
5. Carry out an intervention.
6. Evaluate the results of the intervention.
7. Start over again if necessary.

As we conclude this chapter on supporting children's growth, it is good to keep in mind the words of Arnold Gesell and Frances Ilg:

> When asked to give the shortest definition of life, Claude Bernard, a great physiologist, answered, "Life is creation." A newborn baby is the consummate product of such creation. And he in turn is endowed with capacities for continuing creation. These capacities are expressed not only in the growth of his physique, but in the simultaneous growth of a psychological self. From the sheer standpoint of creation this psychological self must be regarded as his masterpiece. It will take a lifetime to finish, and in the first ten years he will need a great deal of help, but it will be his own product.[147]

Parents have the privilege of serving as guides and resources as their children create unique "psychological selves."

MAIN POINTS

Modeling
- is natural to us, as we have mirror neurons built into our nervous systems
- is an important behavior in all aspects of parenting

Healthy lifestyles
- prevent injuries and illnesses
- require parents' efforts to model and structure daily routines for eating, exercise, and sleeping
- influence intellectual performance and psychological adjustment

Children's media use
- occupies six and a half hours a day for children between the ages of eight and eighteen, and up to four hours for children under six
- does not prevent their enjoying and participating in other activities
- when it includes quality programming, has positive benefits of teaching children, giving them literacy and number skills, and modeling examples of positive actions

- can be related to negative consequences, such as increased aggression in childhood and adulthood, early initiation of sexual behaviors, and irregular sleep and reduced attention span, when children use too much media or media of poor quality
- can be shared with parents who regulate use

A collaborative family atmosphere

- rests on responsive, sensitive parental care of children
- rests on secure attachment of child to parents
- is never too late to establish
- includes children as partners in routines
- involves conversations about rules and future events
- includes the process of encouragement

Promoting competencies includes helping children develop

- emotional regulation through sensitive care, soothing and modulating of negative moods, structuring routines, and coaching children in expressing emotions as described in Chapter 4
- problem-solving skills: identifying the problem, developing strategies to reach goals, and evaluating the results of actions
- moral competence through modeling, nurturing care, reasoning with children, having high but realistic standards for children, involving them in family decision making, and connecting to parents' value system

The tool chest for dealing with problem behaviors includes

- natural and logical consequences
- mutual problem solving and contracting
- use of negative consequences like ignoring, loss of privileges, social disapproval, and time out

Nonabusive spanking

- is not approved by parents, children, or professionals
- is used by most parents at one time or another but most often by young parents under stress
- may or may not have detrimental effects, depending on the context of the parent-child relationship
- is best supplanted by other forms of negative consequence

Ineffective forms of discipline are

- inconsistent discipline
- harsh, explosive discipline
- low supervision of the child
- rigid, inflexible discipline

Parenting programs

- can provide support groups for parents and reduce the stress of parenting
- teach specific skills to parents
- enable parents to reduce children's behavioral difficulties
- increase parents' self-confidence and feelings of competence
- whatever else they include, must focus on the importance of the quality of the parent-child relationship and ways to improve and nourish it

EXERCISES

1. Observe parents and children together in a grocery store or at a playground or other public place. Try to find parents and children of different ages to observe. Are parents on a cell phone? Are parents and children talking to each other? If they are not, are they still having a good time together? What is the nature of their conversation? Is it about dos and don'ts? Is it about something they will be doing in the future? What theories of growth do parents seem to be using? What conclusions do you come to after observing three or four pairs of parents and children?

2. Write a description of the disciplinary techniques you recall your parents using with you during the elementary school years. How would you characterize your parents' methods of child rearing and your response to them?

3. Watch the television show *American Idol* or any other popular show of your choosing. What messages does that show convey about the meaning of life, the values of daily living, moral behaviors? Does that show teach or model positive or negative behaviors or both? If you have teenagers, would you want them to watch it?

4. The next time you feel frustrated about something, try out the problem-solving process described on page 185. Did it help you figure out what to do or help you to persist in what you knew you had to do? Why or why not?

5. Investigate the parenting programs available in your area. What is the range of programs in terms of cost, length, content? If possible, attend one meeting and give your evaluation of the class.

ADDITIONAL READINGS

Coles, Robert. *The Moral Intelligence of Children.* New York: Random House, 1997.

Goleman, Daniel. *Emotional Intelligence.* New York: Bantam, 1995.

Johnson, Simon. *Keep Your Kids Safe on the Internet.* New York: McGraw-Hill/Osborn, 2004.

Nelson, Jane. *Positive Discipline U.* New York: Ballantine, 1987.

Severe, Sal. *How to Behave So Your Children Will, Too!* New York: Viking Penguin, 2000.

6

Becoming Parents

IN THE NEWS

New York Times, June 27:[1] Parents become part of a team caring for premature babies in intensive care units. See pages 239–240.

Test Your Knowledge: Fact or Fiction?

1. About 50 percent of pregnancies in the United States are unintended.
2. When couples jointly make a decision about having a child, marital satisfaction remains high over time, even when they do not have a child.
3. Because of their youth, adolescent mothers have fewer complications during pregnancy and healthier babies than women who have children in their twenties and thirties.
4. Adoption is still restricted to two-parent families with at least average incomes.
5. Differences that emerge in comparisons of parents who use assisted reproductive technology and parents who naturally conceive their child favor parents who have used reproductive technology, as they tend to be more emotionally involved with and supportive of children.

Each individual who becomes a parent does so within unique circumstances. This chapter describes the many paths to parenthood in our contemporary society. We look at how parents decide to become parents and how the decision process itself affects parenting. We examine alternatives open to prospective parents who have difficulties conceiving. We look at the many factors in parents' lives—their age, their marital satisfaction, their relationships with extended family members, their work and economic situation, and their support system—that influence the experiences they will have in the transition to parenthood and as parents when the baby arrives. We also look at how parents can ease the transition through the most profound change they will experience in life: assuming responsibility for a new life.

The ways parents come to parenthood reflect many of the changes that have occurred in our contemporary society in the last thirty years. Forty years ago, almost all babies went home to married couples who either had reproduced their own child or had adopted a child born to an unmarried mother living in this country. Although artificial insemination of the father's or another's sperm could assist conception, such assistance was a rare occurrence. Today, a third of babies are born to unmarried mothers who may or may not marry the fathers.[2] Many persons unable to adopt in the past—lesbian, gay, single, and disabled individuals—are now able to adopt children, who come from many different countries. Couples who were infertile, or single people who wish to have a child, are able to conceive and bear a child with assisted reproductive technology. One of the most basic desires in life—to have a child—meets the most advanced technological changes in assisted reproductive technology.

As we noted in Chapter 1, parents want children to love, to care for, and to participate in their growth. Babies not only connect parents to the next generation and the future, they also draw families closer together, as grandparents, aunts, uncles, and sometimes great-grandparents provide an admiring and loving circle that surrounds both baby and parents. Family ties are strengthened as all work together to support the baby in its growth and the parents in their care-giving activities.

From the very beginning of pregnancy, the whole family system is involved. Philip Cowan, Douglas Powell, and Carolyn Cowan identify six aspects of the family system supporting parenting.[3] We have added a seventh to include all those individuals who play a role in bringing the child to life for parents who adopt or use assisted reproductive technology, because in many instances they are part of the family system that parents and child inhabit. The family system includes these aspects:

1. Each parent and already-existing children with their individual traits

2. The quality of each parent's relationships, both now and in the past, with members of the family of origin

3. Parents' relationship with each other, along with their abilities to communicate with each other and solve problems together

4. The quality of the relationships between brothers and sisters, if they exist

5. Relationships between parents and other important people in their lives—coworkers, work supervisors, friends

6. The relationship between each parent and each child in the family

7. Individuals such as birth parents, who give birth to children and give them to adopting parents, and those who donate eggs, sperm, or surrogate wombs to help bring the child to life. They, too, can be a part of the parenting process in open adoptions or ongoing relations with donors. See Box 6-1 for examples of such extended family systems.

We look first at factors related to readiness to parent, the decision to become parents, then at the process of transition to parenting and the factors that ease or complicate the process.

READINESS TO PARENT

When are people ready to have children? Recall David Lykken's parenting license requirements described in Chapter 1. He considered adults ready when they were over eighteen, married, employed, and without a history of violence.[4] Currently, parenting has few requirements; even those imposed in the past by such physical characteristics as age are being altered by medical technology, as women in their fifties and sixties can now have children. Even so, age does make it harder for older women to conceive. Boys and men can become fathers from adolescence and throughout life.

Social characteristics, such as education and employment of parents, are important because they enable parents to support a child. Parents' psychological characteristics appear to be the most important of all, because they impact parents' abilities to provide high-quality care once the child is born. Reviewing research, Christoph Heinicke identifies three psychological qualities of parents that provide "an optimal parenting environment": (1) parents' feelings of self-esteem; (2) their capacity for positive, mutually satisfying relationships with others, especially with the partner; and (3) their capacity for flexible problem solving.[5] We keep these three qualities in mind as we look at how various groups of parents decide to parent and make the transition to parenthood.

THE DECISION TO PARENT

Groups of parents do not differ as to their reasons for wanting children, but they differ in their readiness, their initial resources in providing for children, and the efforts they must make to become parents. The way one decides to become a parent reflects one's problem-solving and planning skills. It also sets the stage for the child's prenatal development and birth. When children are intended, mothers are more likely to live healthy lifestyles, to get early prenatal care, to have fewer pregnancy and delivery complications, and, as a result, to have healthier babies.[6] You might think that, in this age of highly effective contraceptives, all pregnancies are planned. Wrong—only half of all pregnancies are intended.[7] Pregnancies are defined as unintended when no child was wanted or was not wanted at this time; half are terminated through miscarriage or abortion, so about two-thirds of babies born are intended.

Box 6-1
EXTENDED FAMILIES

Because families are created in many ways, we now have new family members. In open adoption, the birth parent or parents have shared knowledge and some form of continuing contact with their child and the adoptive parents. It creates ties that can meet everyone's needs and removes many of the mysteries of adoption, to the benefit of all. Birth parents know what is happening in the child's life, the child knows who the biological parent is, how he or she resembles that parent, and why the parent chose adoption for the child. The adoptive parents can answer children's questions about their family histories. Adoptive parents also gain a clearer understanding of their own role in their child's life and have less fear that the biological parent wants to come and take the child away. In many ways, adoptive parents gain confidence in their own importance to their child.

A major advantage is that birth parents emerge from the shadows and become real individuals who had difficulties and made the best choice they could to give their child a happy, healthy life. Adam Pertman, who adopted two children and wrote the book *Adoption Nation*,* described his family's experiences with two open adoptions:

> The kids are delighted and so are Judy and I. We now have a way of getting answers to medical and genealogical questions (among others), and most wonderfully, we all care about one another and feel we're members of an extended family. Counterintuitive as it may seem—and true to the research into open adoption—there's no role confusion, no divided loyalty, or any of those sorts of concerns. Some parents may have different experiences, but I'm deeply grateful for this transformation in our lives. (pp. 213–214)

Even if birth parents remain unknown, adoptive parents may include them in their mental pictures of family. Christina Frank describes her many thoughts about the birth mother of her Vietnamese daughter, Lucy. When Lucy's birth mother left the child at a clinic, she left only a short note giving Lucy's birth date and the brief explanation, "A family situation."**

As Mrs. Frank walked the streets of Hanoi, she looked at every woman, wondering if she were the one. When she returned to the United States with the baby, and people commented, "How could a mother give up her child?" Mrs. Frank felt fiercely protective of the mother, thinking that Americans could not understand the poverty and desperate circumstances in some countries that would lead a mother to give up her child. She said nothing the first time someone made that remark, but she later would reply that only a "fool would question the reasons behind *my* daughter's birth mother's decision." She wrote, "By then, Lucy was not the only new member of my family. I had come to think of her birth mother and all her biological relatives as family too."[†]

Assisted reproductive technologies also create new families. Men can donate sperm to a sperm bank many times. Many different women can use batches of the sperm and can sometimes buy and freeze several batches to create full siblings later. While the sperm banks generally keep no records of whether or how many children are born of the sperm, families have organized Internet registries so that siblings and donors can

(continued)

Box 6-1
CONTINUED

sign up to locate each other by the donor's number. Although only a few hundred donors have signed up, seven thousand siblings have signed up. More than a thousand siblings have connected with each other, as have a much smaller number of donors and their offspring.[‡]

In one instance, a donor was found to have fathered twenty-one children under the age of three living in very diverse families—four in lesbian-couple families, three in heterosexual-couple families, and six in single-parent families. These families post pictures of all the children on a website they created and describe children's ongoing development and their responses to such demands as toilet training. The families hope to take a vacation together in 2007.

The Donor Siblings Registry enables older children and mothers to connect and share experiences via e-mail. One sixteen-year-old, who had learned only three years earlier that her parents used donor sperm to conceive her, felt angry that her parents lied to her for so many years. She shared this with her fifteen-year-old half-sister, who had known for years. Both girls confided that, in crowds, they always looked to see if there was a six-foot-tall, blond-haired man with blue eyes.

When siblings get together, many feel a great sense of familiarity. They introduce them to others as half-brothers or half-sisters, whereas they use the word *donor* to refer to the biological father.

One mother, who corresponds with eight other women who used the same man's sperm, feels that knowing other children has helped her son feel more connected to a man who has been a very shadowy figure. Knowing the other children has helped him to see his father as a person. "It's not a phantom person out there any more."[§]

Another mother, whose daughter is one of the twenty-one siblings, feels thrilled, for she wants her daughter to have "family," which she cannot provide. She plans to go on the vacation with the other families and hopes to become close to one or two other families so that, should she die of high blood pressure (which she developed during the pregnancy), perhaps one of the other mothers or couples would be guardians for her daughter.

As more and more matches are made between siblings and between donors and offspring, we may create the kind of extended family situations that are possible with open adoptions. Desire for a connection to our biological roots is a powerful force that draws people together.

*Adam Pertman, "And Then Everything Changed," in *Like No Other Love*, ed. Pamela Kruger and Jill Smolowe (New York: Riverhead, 2005), 213–214.
**Christina Frank, "She Is Among Us," in *Like No Other Love,* ed. Kruger and Smolowe, p. 15.
†Ibid., p. 19.
‡Jennifer Egan, "Wanted: A Few Good Sperm," *New York Times Magazine,* 19 March 2006, p. 44.
§Amy Harmon, "Hello, I'm Your Sister: Our Father Is Donor 150," *New York Times,* 20 November 2005, p. A20.

You also might think that married couples have planned or intended births and unmarried couples have unplanned or unintended births. Wrong again. About 70 to 80 percent of births to married couples are intended, and about 45 percent of births to unmarried women are from intended pregnancies.[8] About 15 to 19 percent of unmarried teens intended to get pregnant and have babies. So, let us look at how subgroups of prospective parents make the decision to parent.

Married Couples

When couples become parents, the most important factor in understanding their decision and its effects is whether the partners agree on the decision. Carolyn Cowan and Philip Cowan identified four decision-making patterns.[9] *Planners* (52 percent) discussed the question and made a definite decision to have or not have a child. *Acceptance of fate* couples (14 percent of those expecting) had unplanned pregnancies that they accepted quietly or, in many cases, enthusiastically. *Ambivalent* couples (about 26 percent) expressed both positive and negative feelings about being parents, with one parent leaning in one direction and the other parent leaning in the other direction. *Yes-no* couples (about 10 percent) were in marked conflict about having or not having a child.

The couples' decision-making processes regarding pregnancy were related to their problem-solving skills in other areas. Yes-no couples were less effective in solving everyday problems, just as they were less effective in deciding about the pregnancy. The decision-making process regarding pregnancy influenced marital satisfaction over time and after the baby's birth. When couples plan the decision, regardless of whether they do or do not have a child, their marital satisfaction remains high following the birth or for an equivalent time period. Couples who accept an unplanned pregnancy experience a drop in marital satisfaction, but their initial level is so high that they are still as satisfied as the parents who plan the decision.

Marital dissatisfaction is greatest among couples who are ambivalent or in conflict but still have a baby. Ambivalent couples who do not have a child retain a high satisfaction level, but these levels drop when they have a baby they do not agree on. The yes-no couples have the least satisfaction. Of nine yes-no couples who have a child, seven divorce by the time the child enters kindergarten. In all seven cases, the husband did not want a child. The two women who did not want to have children seem better able to adjust, and their marriages continue.

So, using problem-solving skills and arriving at an agreed-upon solution helped parents maintain a satisfying relationship after the baby's arrival.

Unmarried Parents

In the 1960s, only 5 or 6 percent of births were to unmarried women.[10] This figure gradually rose to 32 percent in 1995. It has remained at this level, with the latest figure being 34 percent in 2002.[11]

Many factors account for the increase in births to unmarried women.[12] Economic factors play a role. In the past, men's role was thought to be that of economic provider, and with the decreasing earning power of potential working-class husbands and fathers, the number of marriages declined. As men's incomes decreased, women's incomes increased because of their entry into the workforce, and they postponed marriage. As a result, a greater number of women were left in their later childbearing years without a husband but with the desire for a child. Also, in the past, public assistance enabled young, single women to support children; such assistance has decreased over the last ten years.

In addition to economic factors, changing social attitudes and values play a role, with increasing acceptance of forms of family life other than the nuclear family. Our society is more accepting of divorce, single parenthood, couples' living together, and births occurring outside of marriage. We also now have the reproductive technology to enable single parents to have children who are at least partially genetically related to them.

With greater social acceptance of alternate family forms, psychological motivations appear to play a role in nonmarital births.[13] Children, whether born within or outside of marriage, bring social capital to parents, increasing parents' interactions with family members, neighbors, and people in the community and creating a social network of support for parents. Parents gain status as mature adults deserving of respect. Examining large survey data over a period of years reveals that women who have less education and less income and who view children as social capital are more likely to have a child outside of marriage than women who have more education, are more involved in their work lives, and do not want a child outside of marriage.

So, today, parents who have never been married form a heterogeneous group that includes (1) cohabiting parents who may or may not marry after the birth of the child, (2) single women who may or may not have been in relationships at the time of conception but now live alone, (3) unmarried lesbian and gay couples who choose to have children by adoption or by ART, and (4) single fathers who raise their own child, adopt, or have a child by ART. We know much less about single fathers than we do about the other groups. The largest group of unmarried parents are unmarried heterosexual mothers, and so we turn to them first.

Single Mothers   Many people think of unmarried mothers as young teens or economically advantaged professional women like television's Murphy Brown. The average unmarried mother is, in fact, a woman in her late twenties or thirties who had her first birth outside of marriage when she was a teenager and is now having her second or third nonmarital birth.[14] Births to unmarried women occur more often when mothers have low socioeconomic status and less education and when they have lived in single-parent homes in disadvantaged neighborhoods.

Births to unmarried mothers are twice as likely for African American women and Latinas as for European American women. Cohabiting with the child's father increases intended and unintended pregnancies for all three groups, but Latinas are more likely to plan births with cohabiting husbands than the other two groups, and European American women are more likely to marry the fathers than African American or Latina mothers. African American women are more likely than the other two groups to have births when not cohabiting with fathers.

Adolescent Single Mothers   Although only about 19 percent of teen mothers plan their pregnancies, their decision to continue the pregnancy is related to the value they place on having children. Like adults, adolescent mothers want children because they see children as sources of love, fun, stimulation, and achievement. Adolescent mothers are more likely to view children positively when they have few ways to get needs met.[15] For example, adolescent mothers who did not work or who did not feel very independent or self-sufficient were likely to have a high desire for children. These feelings, combined with the examples of their own mothers, who also had children early, increased the value they placed on children. Viewing children positively, however, was related only weakly to subsequent parenting.

Once pregnant, adolescent mothers must decide whether to continue the pregnancy, and we know little about the role of fathers in this decision. About half of adolescent mothers decide to terminate. Those most likely to make such a decision come from middle-class families; they feel support from family and friends for their decision.[16] Adolescent mothers who release a child for adoption—in one study, 4 percent—come from small, financially stable families. They have had academic success and see other alternatives for themselves. They have positive views of adoption and believe their mothers support their decisions.[17]

Single Mothers Who Plan   An increasing number of women are making the conscious choice to have a child alone. Slightly under 5 percent of babies are born to unmarried women with college educations, but these are the mothers who make very deliberate decisions.[18] Strong desires for a child, along with the feeling that they have lost the opportunity to do this under the ideal circumstances of marriage to a loved partner, spur women to consider this option.

We do not know the precise stages single mothers go through in making their decision to have a child. Merle Bombardieri, a social worker who holds workshops and counsels prospective single mothers, believes that a third of the women later decide not to have a child.[19] She believes that feelings of loss may cause the desire for a child, and she encourages women to discover and mourn any unresolved grief. When the loss is mourned, the desire for a child may well decrease.

A national organization, Single Mothers by Choice (SMC), holds sessions for prospective mothers and urges them to consider a variety of issues: their ability to support a child financially, to mesh family life and work, to face rearing a child on their own, and to provide a loving home for a child in the absence of a father.[20] Like Bombardieri, the group also urges women to mourn the loss of the ideal pregnancy prior to conception. One study in the 1970s indicated that single women are most likely to become parents when they can build support systems that enable them to combine work with rearing children.

Unmarried Heterosexual Couples   Almost 40 percent of babies born to unmarried women are born to women living with the baby's father; almost half of these babies are planned,[21] and the births increase the rate of marriage. Though these unions are less stable than marriages, research shows that, within five years, 60 percent of such parents will marry, 12 percent will continue to live together, and 28 percent will separate.[22]

These couples have less education and lower earnings than married couples but higher education and greater earnings than single mothers. Compared with married couples, cohabiting men and women have more egalitarian attitudes toward gender and share both the workload at home and responsibilities for earnings more equally,[23] but cohabiting couples are not as happy as married couples. They report more feelings of insecurity and hostility in the relationship, and they appear less positive and stimulating with the babies than married parents do.[24]

Lesbian and Gay Unmarried Couples   Three or four decades ago, most lesbian and gay parents were parents from heterosexual marriages that had ended in divorce. They maintained relationships with their children when they formed same-sex partnerships.

More recently, through adoption or with the aid of assisted reproductive technology, lesbian and gay partners can choose to become parents.[25] Like heterosexual couples, lesbian and gay parents consider whether they have the economic resources and psychological readiness to provide care. In addition, they must plan strategies for dealing with negative reactions and prejudice against their sexual orientation. So these births are carefully planned. Although research in this area is limited, as many as 50 percent of gay men would like to become fathers.[26] Men who became fathers through adoption or surrogacy had higher self-esteem and fewer negative attitudes about homosexuality than did men who were not fathers.

To become parents, lesbian and gay couples need information about available resources on adoption or assisted reproductive technology. They also must consider the legal aspects of parenthood when one parent is the biological parent and the other is not and may therefore have no legally recognized bond to the child. Such disagreements about parenthood have resulted in bitter custody battles. These issues are best handled prior to the child's arrival.

Unintended and Unwanted Parenting

A large study of four thousand mothers found that approximately one-third of all births were *unintended*, meaning the births were mistimed or not wanted. Unintended births are of concern because mothers are less likely to seek prenatal care in the first three months and more likely to continue habits such as smoking and drinking alcohol. They are more likely than mothers who planned babies to have babies who are premature, of low birth weight, or small for their gestational age, and they are also less likely to breast-feed their babies. When mothers get appropriate care throughout pregnancy, differences in the two groups of babies disappear.[27]

When mothers have *unwanted* children, defined as the mother's not wanting to have any children or not wanting to have more than she has, mothers are less happy, more prone to depression and to greater difficulties rearing not only the unwanted child but also their siblings.[28] Mothers who bear unwanted children are less likely to spend time with them when they are young and more likely to spank them. Difficulties in mother-child relationships continue; hence, even in adolescence and young adulthood, mothers are less affectionate and less supportive with their children.

In a long-term study carried out in Czechoslovakia, children whose mothers had twice requested but were twice denied abortions had significantly more problems and less enjoyment in life than did children whose parents wanted them.[29] In elementary school, the unwanted children had fewer friends, more behavior problems, and poorer school performance, even though they had equal intelligence. In adolescence, the differences between the two groups widened, and in young adulthood, individuals unwanted before birth were less happy with their jobs and their marriages. They had more conflict with coworkers and supervisors and less satisfaction with friends. They were discouraged about themselves and their lives, but many took the positive step of getting help for their problems.

At age thirty, there were still differences between unwanted and wanted children, but the gap had narrowed. Women who were unwanted, however, were more likely to be single or divorced, unemployed, and having difficulties in parenting than women who had been wanted. There were few differences between the two groups of men. At age thirty-five, unwanted children continued to seek more psychiatric treatment than wanted children. Adults who were unwanted as children did not develop such problems as alcoholism or criminality, but they were underrepresented on indicators of well-being and excellence.

Although the average tendency is to have some difficulties when a child is unwanted, the following excerpt represents the love many children experience despite being unwanted initially.

> My twin brother and I were born in postwar Poland, at a time when my parents—both Holocaust survivors whose families were decimated by the Nazis—felt neither emotionally nor financially capable of raising more than the two children they already had. But my mother became pregnant and a doctor told her an abortion might kill her, so here I am. Knowing why I was born has never made me feel insecure or unwanted. My life is so filled with blessings and difficulties like everybody else's, and I have two devoted parents who would move mountains for me.[30]

THE TRANSITION TO PARENTING

Nine months of pregnancy give parents time to prepare for the baby's arrival, even though a month or two of that time may have elapsed before the pregnancy is confirmed. Here, we sketch the transition process for several groups of parents: parents who planned children, young parents, older parents, parents who use assisted reproductive technology (ART), and parents who decided to adopt children.

A Healthy Lifestyle

When parents plan a birth, they can establish a healthy lifestyle months in advance of conception. A healthy lifestyle is important because, by the time parents know the mother is pregnant, four to eight weeks of important prenatal development have occurred, and mother's exposure to medications or environmental toxins can affect the growing child before she is aware of the pregnancy.

Pregnancy is described as a critical period of development for the growing fetus because events that affect development at this time may be difficult or impossible to reverse or remedy after birth.[31] Prevention of problems becomes the main aim. So, the first act of parenting is to adopt a healthy lifestyle that consists of appropriate levels of exercise, healthy eating habits, and avoidance of damaging substances such as tobacco, alcohol, and environmental toxins. Although in many ways mother and child form a symbiotic unit during the pregnancy, it is also important to realize that, even in the early months, they are two separate organisms, and substances that may not harm the mother in any way (e.g., the medication tetracycline) may harm the growing baby.

We cannot address all lifestyle changes, as some may depend on the individual parent's health and physical problems, and we cannot go into detail about each one. We list major groups of hazards to mother and child in Table 6-1. In addition to infections and nonprescription drugs, we list environmental toxins. Numerous prescription drugs affect pregnant women, and pregnant women are advised to check all drugs with their physicians, including any herbal or nutritional supplements, as they too can have damaging effects on the fetus.

■ **T A B L E 6-1**
RISKS IN PREGNANCY*

Infections	Sexually Transmitted Diseases
Chicken pox	Chlamydia
Cytomegalovirus	Genital herpes
German measles, or rubella	Gonorrhea
Hepatitis B	Human papillomavirus (HPV)
Human Immunodeficiency Virus (HIV)	Monilial vulvovaginitis
Listeriosis	Trichomonal vaginitis
Toxoplasmosis	
Varicella	

Drugs	Environmental Toxins
Alcohol	Lead
Amphetamines	Mercury
Caffeine	Polychlorinated biphenyls (PCBs)
Cocaine	Glues and solvents
Ecstasy	Pesticides
Marijuana	X-rays
Nicotine	

*Adapted from: Glade B. Curtis and Judith Schuler, *Your Pregnancy Week by Week*, 5th ed. (Cambridge, MA: DeCapo, 2004).

At the same time parents avoid hazardous substances, they should practice healthy habits, chief among which is healthy eating. Good nutrition not only promotes a healthy pregnancy for mother and child, it also affects the child's development after birth.[32] Studies in developing countries and in low-income groups in the United States have found that nutritional supplements taken by mothers during pregnancy have increased birth weights of babies and have also improved babies' performance on cognitive measures after birth.

Maintaining positive emotional moods and managing stress during pregnancy are important as well, because high levels of stress have been found to be related to increased fetal motor movements[33] and, later, to the child's hyperactivity and irritability.

Experiences in the Transition

Parents who have a committed relationship and plan to become parents are more likely to come to the experience with the resources of education and work that supports the family.[34] When parents, single or married, have planned the pregnancy and conception has followed within a matter of months, they come to pregnancy with great anticipation and few stressful feelings from trying to conceive. When the pregnancy is unplanned, the stress of the transition is increased by the difficulty of making a decision about the pregnancy and the conflict that may occur between the parents. Such stress makes it hard for the parent or parents to use the time of the transition to prepare psychologically for the baby's arrival.

Pregnancy involves many physiological and psychological changes. Physical changes include changes in levels of fatigue, sleep and eating patterns, size, shape, and emotional reactivity, to mention only a few. Parents begin to accommodate to the demands of the life growing within the mother. The changes are easier to adapt to when parents have deliberately taken on the challenges rather than being forced to adjust to them.

Ellen Galinsky, whose work is discussed in greater detail at the end of the chapter, has interviewed parents regarding their psychological reactions to becoming parents and caring for children.[35] She describes pregnancy as the period of image making. Parents form ideas of what they will be like as parents and what the baby will be like. In the first three months of the pregnancy, parents may feel elated about the coming baby but also fearful about the possibility of miscarriage. Even in the early months, their images may clash with reality. Parents may not feel as excited as they hoped to, even though they planned the baby. Maybe there was more morning sickness or tiredness than anticipated. Throughout parenthood, parents must adjust their images and expectations to fit the reality. That process starts in pregnancy and continues.

In the next three months, Galinsky believes, parents prepare for parenthood. They think of the changes in their roles that will occur after the baby comes. They look at their own childhoods and think how they want their child's life to be similar to or different from what they experienced. If they already have a child, they wonder how a brother or sister will adjust or how they will be able to love more than one child. Parents often look at their relationship with each other and how they as a couple are managing. Are they supportive of each other? What will it be like after the baby comes? They may form new friendships with other parents-to-be, and older friendships may fade into the background.

In the last three months of the pregnancy, parents' thoughts turn to the birth, and they begin to worry about what it will be like. During this time, childbirth classes help parents make realistic preparations for the birth and arrival of the baby. Parents in the classes often form ongoing support groups to talk about worries and stresses.

With all the changes occurring inside their bodies, women may become more dependent on help from their partners and their extended family. When relationships among family members have been positive and mothers feel family members accept them, they function more effectively. Although prospective fathers may feel excited about the birth, they are beginning to get a taste of feeling that they are on the sidelines, as they do not really know what it is like to have a life growing inside them. During pregnancy, women may be more preoccupied with the growing child and so have less time for their partners, as will happen also after the birth. So fathers-to-be have adjustments to make as well.

Single parents must begin to build the support group that will sustain them after the birth. They must accept that they will be exhausted with the care of a newborn or young child, and friends or family members must be organized to help.

When Parents Are Young

Adolescent parents typically come to parenting having experienced many difficulties over a number of years. Still, there is great diversity of outcome for these parents, and experiencing difficulties does not prevent some from organizing their lives and becoming effective parents. As researchers wrote,

> The invidious stereotype of the adolescent childbearer underestimates young mothers' chances of recovery. . . . Ironically, part of the handicap of being a teenage mother may come from a widespread perception that failure is virtually inevitable—a belief that may become a self-fulfilling prophecy.[36]

The difficulties teen parents have experienced and bring to parenting fall into four main categories: (1) the teens' social backgrounds, (2) early family relationships with their own parents, (3) their own personality characteristics, and (4) their relationships with peers.[37] The social backgrounds of adolescents who become teen parents contain such risk factors as being the child of an adolescent mother, living in a single-parent home with a parent who has little education, living in poverty, and living in a community with a high level of poverty and welfare assistance.

The family relationships of adolescent parents often embody change and conflict. Their parents are less involved and less affectionate than parents of teens who do not have teen pregnancies, and they provide less monitoring as well. With parental supervision, teens headed in the direction of deviant behavior tend to stay involved in school and avoid pregnancy.[38]

Teen parents' own personality characteristics in childhood predict later teen pregnancy. First—and very important—they have experienced more sexual abuse in childhood or early adolescence; in one study, 65 percent had been sexually abused—61 percent by several perpetrators.[39] As early as eight years of age, teen mothers were seen as different from those who would not become teen mothers.

Following a sample of low-income children, researchers found that eight-year-old girls who were described by peers as "aggressive" or "aggressive and withdrawn" were more likely to be teen mothers than were those girls who were low or average on aggression and withdrawal.[40] In addition, the prospective mothers were more likely to have school and conduct problems in elementary and high school and were more likely to drop out. In grade school, they were more likely to be rejected by peers, and in high school more likely to have deviant friends who broke rules and engaged in high-risk behaviors.

Early maturation and high rates of sexual activity increase girls' chances of becoming pregnant as teens.[41] Girls with these risk factors have more gynecological problems and sexually transmitted diseases. Studies comparing adolescent mothers with teens who did not have babies have found that adolescent mothers are less independent, less certain of themselves, and less trusting of others.[42] They have a diffuse sense of identity and greater susceptibility to depression.

Most studies of adolescent parents have focused on mothers, because the fathers of their babies, in about 50 percent of cases, are in their twenties or older.[43] Recent work has followed samples of boys to determine the characteristics of those who become adolescent fathers. In many instances, they share the qualities of the mothers.[44] They are from low-income families in which parents often have problems with antisocial behavior. Their parents use ineffective disciplinary techniques and do not monitor the boys well. By early adolescence, these boys begin to engage in deviant, rule-breaking activities. They also have little academic success. Another study identified similar risk factors but concluded that the accumulation of risks, not any single risk, was most predictive of adolescent fatherhood.[45]

Although teenage mothers experience few difficulties becoming pregnant, they suffer more pregnancy complications and have babies with problems more often than do mothers in their twenties or early thirties. Prematurity and low birth weight, which increase the likelihood of cerebral palsy, mental retardation, and epilepsy in babies, occur most often in the babies of teenage mothers.[46]

Teenage mothers are also less effective in parenting. Compared with older mothers, they are less able to provide stable living arrangements, so their children experience more moves and changes in caretakers and male support figures.[47] Single parenthood increases the risk of poverty, but adolescent single motherhood confers an additional disadvantage on mother and child.[48] The exact reasons are not known, but lower educational attainment and the smaller likelihood of entering a stable, supportive marriage are two important factors. Ethnic origin also makes a difference. One study found that delaying parenthood to age twenty-five resulted in economic gain for European American women but not for African American women.[49] Further studies found that African American mothers receive more support from family and friends than do Latina mothers.[50]

It is not surprising, then, that children of adolescent mothers are at greater risk for problems in development even if they are later-born children of teenage mothers. They are more likely to suffer from illnesses and to be seen in emergency rooms, even when families have medical coverage.[51] Infants and toddlers of teenage mothers do not differ from children of older mothers in cognitive measures; however, by the time they reach preschool age, differences begin to emerge and continue into the elementary school years, when they face a greater likelihood of academic difficulties, school failure, and behavior problems.[52] Teens of adolescent mothers are more likely than others to become teen parents (in one study, 40 percent of girls and 21 percent of boys); still, the majority of children of teenage mothers do not themselves become teen parents. Even when they delay childbearing, however, they are not as competent and well adjusted in early adulthood as are the children of those mothers who delayed pregnancy until their twenties.[53]

Although adolescent mothers and their children have many problems, diversity of outcome, as we noted earlier, is a striking finding of many studies. Table 6-2 lists the protective factors that increase success for these mothers, along with risk factors that impede success. Indeed, many adolescent mothers in the United States and New Zealand[54] overcome their problems.

Having reviewed the many difficulties associated with teen parenting of today, it is important to emphasize that it is not youth per se that creates the difficulties, but young parents who have lived in unstable families having babies who, in turn, live in unstable circumstances.[55] Follow-up studies of teens who gave birth in the early 1980s, when 55 percent of the teen mothers were married, indicate that income and psychological adjustment of these mothers are comparable to those mothers who married in their twenties.

■ **T A B L E 6-2**
RISK AND PROTECTIVE FACTORS FOR CHILDREN OF ADOLESCENT MOTHERS*

Risk Factors

1. Living in poverty, with attendant problems of frequent residence changes, living in high-crime and high-violence areas, and experiencing changes in caretakers and male support

2. Birth complications: prematurity, low birth weight

3. Poor parenting from mothers

4. Behavior and school problems

5. Less social support from relatives and friends

Protective Factors

1. Being a boy

2. Having an easy, adaptable temperament

3. Having intelligence and problem-solving skills that lead to better coping

4. Mother continuing her education

5. Mother limiting the number of subsequent children

6. Mother entering a stable marriage

7. Mother having high self-esteem

*Adapted from: Joy D. Osofsky, Delia M. Hann, and Claire Peebles, "Adolescent Parenthood: Risks and Opportunities for Mothers and Infants," in *Handbook of Infant Mental Health,* ed. Charles H. Zeanah, Jr. (New York: Guilford Press, 1993), 106–119.

■ **T A B L E 6-3**
GUIDELINES FOR OLDER PARENTS*

---

1. Be open with children about your age and your reasons for postponing children. Lying and avoiding the issue cause children to feel shame or embarrassment about your age.

2. Make a special effort to understand your children's world, as it may seem very different from the one in which you grew up.

3. Connect your children to extended family members. If this is not possible, provide an extended support network of friends who serve as uncles, aunts, or grandparents.

4. Stay physically fit and energetic so you can share physical activities such as hiking and camping with your children. If you cannot participate, then see that children join friends and other adults in these activities.

5. Most important, balance the time you spend on work and nonfamily commitments with your family's needs so your children feel they are an important part of your life.

---

*Adapted from Andrew Yarrow, *Latecomers* (New York: Free Press, 1991).

When Parents Are Older

The age of first-time mothers has been increasing. In the past, women over thirty-five who had babies were usually having the last of their children; now, many mothers are having their first. In 2004, approximately 600,000 babies were born to women over thirty-five, many to first-time mothers.[56] Factors that account for the growing number of older first-time mothers include feminism, a general postponement of childbearing, the large number of Baby Boomers of childbearing age, advances in contraception, better health among women, advances in reproductive technologies, and better obstetrical care.

Still, women over thirty-five more often have difficulties with a first pregnancy. Spontaneous abortions increase from 25 percent at age thirty-five to 50 percent at forty-five,[57] and mothers over thirty-five have a greater percentage of genetic abnormalities in the fetus, so screening for such abnormalities is routine for them. Like teenage mothers, older mothers have a greater likelihood of pregnancy complications such as diabetes and low-birth-weight babies, but these can be treated, as they can be with younger women.

Although older mothers face difficulties in conception, they have many advantages as parents. Compared with younger mothers, they have more education, higher-status jobs, and, as a result, greater incomes and more money available to spend on their children.[58] Further, older parents tend to be in more stable marriages and to be more attentive and sensitive parents. Because they are older and have had more experience in life, they find it easier to put children's behavior in perspective and not become frustrated over little things. Yet older parents' work and community responsibilities make it more difficult to incorporate an unpredictable, time-consuming young child into their lives. (Table 6-3 lists some suggestions for older parents.)

When Parents Are Single

Single parents can be young or older, women or men, with advantages or with very few advantages; it is hard to describe a general process of transition. When women are young and single, they are very much like the adolescent parents described in the preceding section. When they have planned for a child and have sources of help, they resemble parents who have prepared for a child.

A new group of single parents is less studied, and that is single men who raise children on their own.[59] They may have adopted a child, or they may have impregnated a woman who wants to give the child for adoption. The biological father wishes to have custody and raise the child as his, but laws in many states set a very narrow window of time in which fathers can register to claim paternal rights to adopt the child. Currently, fathers have brought suits to obtain custody in several states.

State registries have increased in the last ten years to protect the rights of the child to permanent placement, to protect adoptive parents from having a child taken from them after several years as happened in the early 1990s, and to give fathers rights too. The registries, however, are little publicized, hard to locate, and have varying windows of time for registration, some as little as five days from birth and others until the adoption petition is filed. Further, registries may give fathers

Single fathers are getting more help in learning parenting skills. Many are attending parenting groups and learning the joys of fatherhood.

rights only within a county or state, so if the mother takes the child out of state, the father has no rights. Fathers are at a disadvantage in knowing about registries and registering within the time limits.

One single father in Texas fought for paternal rights after his son had been adopted, and arrived at a compromise with the adoptive parents. The adoptive parents are raising the boy, who is now thirteen, and the noncustodial father has visiting rights.

Balancing everyone's rights in these complex situations is difficult. We want fathers to be attached to and responsible for children, yet at times mothers want the right to have children in situations of their choosing. Adoptive parents want security for themselves and the baby so that close ties will not be severed abruptly to protect the rights of a biological parent who has just learned he is a father.

Another group of fathers being helped to become parents are young men who have fathered children outside of marriage, who sometimes have a relationship with the mother and sometimes do not.[60] Although programs have been available for mothers for a long time, there are few programs around the country for single young men who want to be responsible parents. More single fathers are identified now, as Congress passed a law in 1993 encouraging paternity establishment, and many states have inaugurated hospital programs to enable fathers to establish paternity at the time of the birth of the child.

Data from a national sample of nonmarital births between 1998 and 2000 reveals that 69 percent of fathers establish paternity, most often in hospital programs.[61] Establishing paternity is related both to formal child support payments and to psychological and social support following the birth.[62] Increasing contact with the fathers benefits the child, but only if the father is a reliable, supportive figure. If fathers engage in antisocial activity, then the more time they spend with children, the more likely children are to have conduct problems.[63]

These fathers need parenting programs that provide life skills, parenting information, and psychological support as they seek to be more active and responsible figures in their children's lives. In 2002, only six such programs were available nationwide. See comments in Box 6-2 regarding the positive force such programs can be in men's lives.

When Parents Use Assisted Reproductive Technology (ART)

Prospective couples can turn to special interventions if they have not been able to conceive a child. Infertility was long assumed to be caused by the mother's reproductive problems, but in 40 to 50 percent of cases, it results from men's problems. Infertility has traditionally been defined as the failure to conceive after a year of unprotected sex, although a recent international study of fertility in 782 couples suggests that 91 percent of couples will conceive by the end of the second year of trying to conceive if there is no specific cause for infertility.[64] Although infertility is the major reason parents seek assistance, single women and gay and lesbian couples also seek assisted reproductive services.

Box 6-2
PROGRAM FOR SINGLE FATHERS*

In 2002, the Fathers at Work Program in Richmond, California, was one of only six programs nationwide to provide single fathers with services to help them become productive parents who could support their children and be responsible fathers. To qualify, men had to be under the age of thirty and have at least one biological child with whom they did not live. Most had not finished high school and had low incomes. They received help with schooling, managing finances, getting work, learning skills in conflict management, negotiating, and most important, parenting.

The lead counselor said, "In their environment, they didn't get positive role models. That's why these guys turn to programs like ours." The men want to be good fathers but do not know how. When they begin to learn skills, they live up to their potential as fathers.

The men got support from each other in twice-weekly peer support groups. They were able to share what was happening in their lives and to take advice from each other. When one father said that it was okay for him to sell drugs as long as he told his son not to, the other men argued with him, saying, "They don't even listen to the words—they watch what you do."

Another man in the group said that, in these sessions, he learned that the world "doesn't revolve around me." He had to learn to stop blaming everyone else for his problems. "I wasn't taking any responsibility for it. This shows a lot of fathers what they're capable of doing. We all want to be good fathers."

Another man described unpredictable living arrangements as a child, staying with grandparents, his mother, then his father, his father's girlfriend and seven children, seeing his father very irregularly. He was able to get job training and a $35,000-a-year job so he could make his monthly support payment of almost $1,000 for his two children. He was able to obtain joint custody for one and to see both each week.

*Jason B. Johnson, "Father Grows Up," *San Francisco Chronicle*, 3 September 2002, p. A15.

Interventions   Interventions available to help couples range from intrauterine insemination using the father's or another man's sperm, to surgery and the highly complex methods of assisted reproductive technologies.[65] The interventions can result in a child that is genetically related to both parents (when the parents' eggs and sperm are used), to one parent (when either the egg or the sperm is used), or to neither parent (when both donor egg and donor sperm are used).

Initially, ART takes the form of supporting natural processes by insemination and by chemically stimulating the ovaries to produce more eggs. In a more advanced method, the egg can be removed and fertilized in a petri dish and then implanted in the uterus. This technique is used for many reasons, for example, for women who have blocked fallopian tubes. In 2003, there were more than 120,000 *in vitro* fertilizations; between 30 and 40 percent resulted in pregnancies.[66] More advanced techniques include *introcytoplasmic sperm injection (ICSI),* or injecting a sperm directly into the egg and then transferring the fertilized egg into the uterus. This has enabled many infertile men to become fathers.

Then there is donor assistance, which can take several forms. There are sperm and egg donations and, more recently, fertilized embryo donations. Further, a surrogate mother (or birth mother) may carry the fertilized embryo to term for the mother. See the interview with Michelle and Steve on page 227. The surrogate may also, but not necessarily, donate an egg for fertilization.

Sperm donations were the first form of donation. Stored in sperm banks, the donations provided healthy sperm that could be matched with the characteristics of the prospective parents. Traditionally, the donors were anonymous, but more recently, banks have asked donors whether they would be willing to be contacted when the child reaches age eighteen. Since the early 1980s, egg donations have also been available through clinics. Because medications are used to stimulate and remove the eggs, egg donation is a more complicated procedure than sperm donation. Perhaps for that reason, egg donors are sometimes friends or relatives of the parents rather than anonymous donors, and they may well sustain an ongoing relationship with the parents.

Donor embryos have raised concerns. These are embryos that couples had frozen, reserved for their use in the event that they did not conceive from the embryos that were implanted. The couples had the children they wanted and no longer needed the embryos. There are approximately 400,000 such embryos in the country, but only about 2 percent have been donated to other couples.[67] Although couples originally felt they would be willing to donate, they decline to do so years later, saying they would feel too uncomfortable knowing they had children being raised by others, and that their children had brothers and sisters they might not know.[68]

A religious organization called Snowflakes has encouraged couples to release these embryos to other parents for adoption and to keep some form of contact with the families after the birth, as in open adoption.[69] The organization insists that receiving families get counseling about doing this, and the two families can set criteria for an ongoing relationship. Other organizations have concerns that the term *embryo adoption* means that the embryo has the same status as a child; thus far that is not true, as some are donated for research.

Advances in ART have enabled scientists to diagnose genetic disorders prior to the implantation of the fertilized egg in the uterus.[70] Known as *preimplantation genetic diagnosis* (PGD), the procedure of taking one cell from the eight-celled embryo, testing it for genetic diseases such as Tay-Sachs, and implanting only embryos without the genetic defect permits parents to know that the embryo is healthy at the start of the pregnancy. Parents do not have to wait several months to have amniocentesis done to determine that the fetus is healthy.

Preimplantation genetic diagnosis has also been used to identify embryos with genetic makeup that could, at birth, provide a genetic match to save the life of an existing sibling with an incurable genetic disease. For example, a child with Fanconia anemia, a genetic disorder that leads to the child's early death, can be saved with a perfectly matched bone marrow transplant. Parents have successfully sought help to produce siblings with genetic makeup that saves the life of an existing one.

Although most would agree to the use of PGD to prevent or cure illness, there are concerns that it can be used to create "designer babies" with the preferred sex, height, intelligence, or hair color. Lori Andrews, a lawyer specializing in the legal aspects of reproductive technologies, worries about polls that indicate that 43 percent of responders think it is acceptable for parents to select the physical characteristics of their children, and 42 percent believe it is acceptable to select intellectual traits. She worries that, down the road, people may shop for a baby like they shop for a car. She writes,

> If anything is clear to me as a mother, it is that parenting involves dealing with surprises. Some bring joy: for instance, the discovery of wonderful characteristics you probably never would have thought to program into your child. And yes, other surprises—an illness or accidents—can bring terror.
>
>   But, especially where children are concerned, it is the job of the family to provide unconditional love and acceptance, regardless of those surprises. Parents, above all, should not be saddling their babies with admission standards for birth.[71]

Assisted reproductive technology and donor assistance were originally used to help infertile married couples, but these procedures have also enabled single women and lesbian and gay couples to have children. When donor eggs and surrogate mothers are involved, the methods can also help single men become parents of a child to whom they are genetically related.

Parenting   Major studies carried out primarily in Europe found that, whether parents rely on *in vitro* fertilization or donor sperm, their parenting behaviors resemble those of parents who naturally conceived their children.[72] Even though parents have experienced numerous anxieties about having children and numerous medical procedures, these difficulties do not detract from their parenting. In fact, when compared with parents who naturally conceived children, mothers in donor insemination families were described as warmer, more sensitive, and more responsive when children were in early elementary school and again at age twelve. Children in these families thought their mothers were as warm as other mothers. Interviewers described fathers in donor insemination families as more detached in matters of discipline when children were twelve, but mothers and children did not perceive any differences in these fathers' behaviors.

Teachers' ratings and psychiatric assessment of the records revealed that the children in all these groups were equally competent and as socially skilled as children reared by parents who had had no difficulties in conceiving.

In studies comparing the parents who used sperm and egg donors and parents who naturally conceived their children, the differences between parents favored the parents using egg and sperm donations.[73] These parents had more positive parent-child relationships and were more emotionally involved with the child than parents who naturally conceived their children. Similar findings occurred when parents who used surrogate-mother arrangements were compared with parents who naturally conceived their children; parents who used surrogate arrangements were found to have higher psychological well-being and more positive parent-child relationships than parents who naturally conceived their children.[74]

A major hypothesis accounting for the positive differences in families using donor and surrogate arrangements is that those seeking parenthood through those means are highly motivated parents who planned carefully, truly enjoy their children, and parent them in a sensitive and effective way.

INTERVIEW
with Michelle and Steve

Michelle and Steve, already the parents of a four-year-old boy, had twins, a boy and a girl, with the help of a gestational surrogate mother. They were delighted to be interviewed about their experiences doing this. Their son was three years old, and Michelle was eight and a half months pregnant with a girl when the placenta ruptured, after which they lost the baby, and the operation to save her life eliminated the possibility of carrying another child.

Steve: We were devastated and had grief counseling that gradually transitioned into counseling about how to have another child. We explored adoption and went to seminars about adopting children from China, South America, and we also explored surrogacy. We went to two different agencies and had interviews and decided to try surrogacy, and if that was unworkable, then adoption.

Michelle: We chose an agency in which all the women in charge—the owner, the lawyer who drew up the contract—had children by surrogate parenting. It was a very carefully run place. All the surrogate mothers and their husbands—most were married—had to be screened psychologically. The surrogate mothers had to have given birth to at least one child and had a smooth pregnancy and delivery. They were paid to do it, but if money were the primary goal, then they could not be surrogate mothers. They could not have big debts either. We also were screened for psychological stability.

Steve: We almost balked about the way the owner wanted to choose the mother, but we went along with it. We could look at a book of surrogate mothers and pick a few we definitely liked and a few we did not want, but the owner would make the final match for the first interview. If we didn't think the person would work, she would choose someone else. The reason she did this was so prospective parents would not be interviewing a number of people trying to decide on a person. When we questioned her about this method, she said, "Trust me," and she hit a home run. She picked Anisa. We all had dinner together—the owner and her husband, Michelle and I, and Anisa and her husband. It was a social occasion, and there was almost no discussion of surrogacy.

Anisa was charming, and she was a dream surrogate. She was from a Seventh Day Adventist family so she was a vegetarian, only occasionally had any caffeine, and she had a healthy lifestyle. Also, she was a billing clerk in the obstetrics and gynecology office of a husband-and-wife team, so she had constant access to a medical support network. The woman M.D. was her best friend, and she took a great interest in the pregnancy, too.

Most surrogates are picky about the couple they do this for, and most want a "virgin" couple. They want to bring the first child into the world for a childless couple, to provide them something they could not have otherwise. We already had a child, but Anisa wanted to help us have a sibling for our son. She has been very close to her sister, and she wanted to provide that kind of relationship for our son. After the dinner, we all felt positive about going ahead, so we had a meeting to settle the parameters of the relationship. We had to decide how many times to try, how many babies she would carry. The cost of one child would be $15,000, with an additional charge of $5,000 for twins. We knew we would be happy with twins, as twins run in the family, and Anisa agreed, but we all left any more than that for later discussion.

We also had to decide what kind of relationship we would have afterward. All of us wanted an ongoing relationship. She is an important person in our lives. We see her a

(continued)

INTERVIEW with Michelle and Steve

(continued)

few times a year, and every holiday she sends the children gifts, and we always send her flowers or gifts at holidays.

Michelle: We had to go through the process of *in vitro* fertilization. I had to take fertility drugs to stimulate the ovulation of eggs, but I had done that with our son. Anisa had to take drugs to suppress her cycle so it matched mine, and she had to take drugs so that she could be receptive after my eggs were harvested, fertilized, and ready for the transfer to Anisa. If there are too many embryos that survive after the transfer, you have to decide what to do. Three embryos were seen on the first ultrasound, but a week later there were only two, so we were very happy with twins.

During the pregnancy, I talked regularly on the phone with Anisa. She lives about 200 miles from here. I would call and see how things were going. I never had any worry about her taking care of herself, as she worked in a medical atmosphere and knew how important diet and sleep were. Sometimes I'd tell her, "Oh, go out and get a new maternity outfit." Her husband was such a low-key guy. I don't know that a lot of guys would go along with her carrying someone else's children. He was an unsung hero. We never worried she would want to keep the children. She had two girls, and the babies were always referred to as "Michelle's babies," and she was carrying them because I could not.

Steve: The labor and delivery were very smooth. About a month before, she had to go to the hospital for a day, but she carried the twins to eight and a half months. She was in the delivery room, our parents were there, our aunt, Anisa's parents were there, and her husband. We drove down, and David, our son, was with us, but he had been exposed to chicken pox and could not go into the maternity ward. So, someone was always with him.

Michelle: With David, I had a painful labor of fifty hours, but Anisa was sitting in the labor room, calm, with an occasional "Ooh." Then the doctor said, "You're ready," and she hadn't moaned or screamed or anything. She was completely calm and casual, like it was nothing. It was so amazing to me how easy it was for her. That first night, Anisa and I spent the night with the twins in the hospital. The next morning, I went to the motel and got a nap, and David and Steve were at the hospital. When I went back, the doctor said, "Everything is perfect. Do you want to take the babies home?" Anisa's daughters came and saw the babies, and we took pictures.

Steve: It was an emotional time for everyone. Anisa was happy because it was so successful. It was a risk to offer someone that. We were thrilled to have the twins, and they slept all the way home.

Michelle: We were on an emotional high for a year because it was such an amazing thing, and we wanted everyone to know about it. And there is more use of surrogacy than you would think. Once you begin to talk about it, you find that many people have been involved. I was talking to someone at work who was visiting here, and he made the comment, "Ever since my wife did surrogacy for a neighbor," and went on to describe something. Friends offered to be surrogate mothers, but we decided to get an objective third party.

How do the twins, now five, understand Anisa's role?

Steve: The counselor told us that young children understand helping, and we told them that Mommy made the babies, but she needed help to get them to birth—her tummy could not carry them so Anisa helped us and carried the twins to birth.

A paramount issue is whether children of donor conception have the right to know this fact and learn about their biological origins.[75] Initially, few were told. The American Fertility Society recommends telling children about their origins. Britain and the Netherlands have recently banned anonymous donations of sperm, and any child at age eighteen now has the right to look up and seek the donor father.[76] In Sweden, individuals conceived by donor eggs or donor sperm have the right to identifying information at age eighteen and can contact the donor if they wish. In the United States, the tendency in the past has been not to tell children, and records have been destroyed, but currently there is a move to adopt the policies of Sweden. The Sperm Bank of California, for example, already requests permission from donors to give children identifying information when they are eighteen, and 80 percent of donors have agreed. The first children have recently reached eighteen, so we shall soon see how this works out.[77] The Internet, as we saw in Box 6-1, is making connections with half-siblings possible, as well as some donor-child connections.

The desire for greater openness is supported by studies of open adoption, which reveal that a lack of secrecy and a better understanding of one's biological parents have improved the adjustment of adoptive children.[78] The situation of children of donor eggs and donor sperm is not exactly comparable to that of adopted children, as a biological parent did not "give them up" but instead helped create them for their rearing parents. Still, knowing about a donor and the fact that one can have contact with this person later in life may eliminate the anger, confusion, and the sense of a missing biological connection felt by some children and adults of donor sperm or donor eggs.

Assisted reproductive technology has created legal and ethical dilemmas that are currently solved on a case-by-case basis in the courts.[79] Who owns eggs, sperm, and fertilized embryos? Can eggs, sperm, or fertilized embryos be used after divorce to create children? Should unused fertilized embryos be given to couples seeking to have children? Is it baby selling if models or Harvard students advertise their eggs for fifty thousand dollars? Should clinics help women in their sixties become pregnant even though they may not live long enough to raise the children? Is it ethical to use PGD to create tall, smart, or curly-haired children, or children of a certain sex, to meet parents' requests? At present, the United States has few recognized guidelines to resolve these issues. As Debora Spar documents in her book *The Baby Business*,[80] creating babies is the only three-billion-dollar industry in the country without guidelines.

When Parents Adopt

Like many aspects of parenting, adoption has undergone changes in the last two or three decades.[81] Between 2 and 4 percent of children in the United States are adopted, about half are adopted by biological relatives and other kin such as stepparents, and about half are adopted by adults not biologically related to them. This section focuses on children adopted by people not related to them.

Changes in the Nature of Adoption   Historically, adopted children were the offspring of single women, but in the last three decades, fewer babies were available for adoption, because abortions decreased births to single women, and more single women kept their babies.

Parents wanting to adopt a child looked to other sources for children. They looked at transracial adoptions within the United States (discouraged in the 1970s and 1980s but less so in the 1990s); they considered adopting children with special needs, defined as older children or children with special physical or emotional needs. Adopting parents also began to look to orphanages in Europe, Latin America, and Asia. The number of visas issued for immigrant orphans rose from 8,000 in 1989 to 19,000 in 2001.[82] Asia and Latin America are the areas from which adopted children most often come today.

Adults previously excluded from adoption—older, single, gay, lesbian, disabled, or poor adults—are now approved for adoption.[83] Preliminary research indicates that these adoptive parents experience great satisfaction in their roles as parents and have good placement outcomes. Children adopted by single parents do as well as those adopted by young couples, even though single people tend to adopt more difficult children. In addition, legislation has enabled foster parents to adopt children in their care.

Open Adoption   In the past, adopting parents had limited or no information or contact with biological or birth parents. Currently, adoptive and birth parents have been allowed greater access to information about and more contact with each other. In some instances, the birth mother selects the adopting parents and maintains ongoing contact with the child and the family; this is referred to as *open adoption*. The adopted child is sometimes included in the birth mother's family and activities as well. Open adoption has helped remove the element of secrecy from the adoption process. *All* the child's parents can know what is happening to the child, and the child can know them all as well. Children learn that birth parents love them even though they cannot provide for them.

Research on open adoptions suggests that the birth mothers show better adjustment after placement than birth mothers who do not maintain contact.[84] Adoptive parents also seem to feel better because they are less fearful of losing children, and they have a better understanding of birth parents, so they can answer children's questions more completely. As rated by adoptive parents, children in open adoptions appear to have fewer problems than other adopted children.

Transracial and International Adoptions   Studies of children adopted in the United States who grew up with parents of different ethnic backgrounds than their own find that many children function well, but some report identity confusion.[85] This is greatly reduced when parents provide experiences that enable children to develop a positive racial identity, as parents adopting children from other countries are required to do.

When parents adopt children from other countries, they must meet all the criteria for adoption in that country as well as those of the state in which they live. Currently, the Hague Convention on International Adoption is seeking an internationally agreed-on set of criteria to safeguard children's rights.

A major concern of adopting parents centers on the emotional trauma children may have experienced in orphanages or other settings prior to adoption and the effects of such trauma on attachment and later psychological development.[86] Research shows that the longer the children have spent in institutional care, the more likely they are to have intellectual and emotional problems; nonetheless, with major support from parents and professional help, these children improve substantially over time.

In families with transracial or international adoption, children's adjustment is eased when parents form a new family ethnic identity.[87] Parents provide experiences that connect not just the child but the whole family to the child's ethnic group of origin. This may mean learning a new language or new customs, celebrating new holidays, or living in new areas where there are more families of the child's origins. Such a child needs models of the culture and opportunities to have friends of his or her group of origin. Currently, organizations form tours to countries where children were adopted, to acquaint children with the geographical regions and, in some instances, with birth families, although this is rare because usually records do not exist.

Greater openness about adoption, along with greater awareness of the adoption process because of the adoption of children from other countries, has improved people's perceptions of adoption and adoptive parents. Some companies now offer parental leave for adoption. Celebrities talk about their own experiences as adopting parents or adopted children, and children from other countries talk about their two cultures of origin. Children are now less likely to be teased and made to feel different because they are adopted.

We deal with the special issues of adoption as they arise in the course of development—for example, the transition to parenting later in this chapter, and forming positive identities in Chapters 9 and 11.

Talking about Adoption and Children's Understanding of It   When parents feel secure, they neither overemphasize the fact of adoption nor hide it. They can explain the different ways to form a family, and they accept that their child has links to two families—to them and to biological parents.

The general advice is to tell children sometime in the toddler and preschool years.[88] Adoption, however, is not something you explain once or twice when the child is young and then forget about. Recent research evidence suggests that most preschoolers are unlikely to understand what adoption is even when parents have explained it to them and they refer to themselves as adopted. Preschoolers confuse adoption and birth, making no distinction between the two ways of having children. By the age of six, most children can understand that there are two paths to parenthood—birth and adoption—and they understand that adoption makes the child a permanent member of the family.

Between ages eight and eleven, children begin to understand that adoption is not the usual way families grow.[89] They become more aware that their biological parents exist somewhere, and many children become concerned that their biological parents may return and take them away from their adoptive families. By the end of this period, children return to a belief in the permanence of adoption, even though it is not until early or middle adolescence that they understand it as a legal process.

Young children think adoption occurs because adoptive parents have strong needs to love and care for children and provide them a good home, but in elementary school, children recognize that parents adopt children for additional reasons, such as infertility, family-planning needs, and the welfare of children. Very young children do not wonder why they needed to be removed from their biological parents. With increasing age, children distinguish financial reasons, parental death, and their biological parents' inability to provide care as reasons for adoption.

In the school years, children may become confused about where their loyalties lie—to the family they live with or to their biological parents. They become more aware of reciprocity in relationships and focus more carefully on the reasons their biological parents relinquished them.

When children become teenagers, their questions about adoption may focus on identity issues. "What was my biological family like?" "What are my roots in this world?" "How am I like my biological parents?" As sexual interest increases in adolescence, children's interest in their own conception and birth may also increase. They fantasize about their biological parents. Although the fantasies start in early childhood, they become more specific and tied to real possibilities, for example, being the product of an affair with a married man. Adolescent girls may worry that they are going to follow their biological mothers' paths and conceive children who will be put up for adoption.

Adoption can color feelings and changes in adolescence for some children but not for others. Just as biological parents must try to understand and listen, send active I-messages, and set limits, adoptive parents must act similarly with each child as an individual. It is especially upsetting to have a teen scream, "You can't tell me—you're not my real parent." Parents' best protection and soundest guide is self-confidence in their own parenting skills and the wisdom to know when to listen and when to set limits.

As adopted children get older, parents may face the possibility that at some point their children will want to seek out their biological parents. Many do this not because they are unhappy with their adoptive parents but because they want a greater sense of their genetic history and an understanding of the social roots they inherited from the biological parents. They want to understand their biological connections in the world. Adoptive parents cope best when they can sympathize with their children's desires, when they see the search as a reflection of the child's basic need for as complete a sense of identity as possible. Parents have the greatest difficulty coping when they see the search as a reflection on their adequacy as parents. Sometimes parents discourage the search for fear children will learn unpleasant facts. But in many instances, actual knowledge, even of an unpleasant sort, is more welcome than the unknown or imagined.

Parenting Behaviors of Adoptive Parents   Many adopting parents come to parenthood sad because they could not have a biological child and anxious from the intense scrutiny they have undergone to determine their suitability as parents. One can imagine their feeling self-conscious and uncertain in their parenting behaviors.

However, a study comparing the parenting strategies of parents who adopted a child at birth, parents who relied on donor insemination and ART, and parents who naturally conceived a child found few differences among the parenting behaviors of the three groups.[90] When children were between four and eight, adopting mothers did not differ from mothers of naturally conceived children in warmth, sensitivity, or attachment to their children. Mothers who used donor insemination and ART were warmer and more involved than the other two groups. Teachers and psychiatric evaluation judged children in the three groups as functioning equally well, with no problems.

When these children were twelve, the adopting parents continued to demonstrate warmth and control similar to that of parents of naturally conceived children. Again, psychiatric evaluation and teachers' assessments indicated that children, too, continued to function well in all three groups, with no significant differences among them. Mothers of adopted children, however, described their children as having problems of rule breaking and aggressiveness, but a more objective assessment did not present such a picture. Thus, the parenting behaviors of parents who adopted a child at birth seem quite similar to those of parents who have naturally conceived a child.

There are some suggestions that adopted children may have more problems in the school years in the United States, that teachers see them as less mature socially and emotionally[91], and that they are overrepresented in clinics for psychological problems such as aggressiveness and academic problems (they constitute 5 percent of clinic populations but only 2 percent of the general population). Several causes are suggested for these statistics. Children may be more vulnerable because of genetic predispositions of biological parents, as well as prenatal and immediate postnatal environments, and adoptive parents may be more alert to difficulties and want to see them addressed.

Studies of adult functioning of adopted children reveal that, by early and middle adulthood, they resemble adults reared in biological families.[92] In a study comparing adopted adults with friends, the two groups were similar with respect to life satisfaction, purpose in life, intimacy, and substance use.[93] The adopted adults, however, reported lower self-esteem than did friends, although the difference of 1.5 points was small, and greater depression. More of the adopted sample (30 percent) fell into the clinical range of depression than did the sample of friends (19 percent), but 70 percent of the adopted adults fell within the normal range when the figure for the average sample was 80 to 85 percent. A factor in the findings was the greater variability among the adopted sample, in part related to whether the adult was seeking his or her biological family. Adopted adults seeking their biological families reported lower self-esteem and greater depression than did other adopted adults. Still, all adopted adults expressed insecurity about adult attachments. They formed relationships with peers but expressed greater discomfort in the relationships than did their friends.

David Brodzinsky and Ellen Pinderhughes caution that focusing on the problems of adopted children obscures the real benefits of adoption for children.[94] Recall from Chapter 1 that the biological children of parents at risk for petty criminality who were adopted early in life and reared by adopted parents not at risk for petty criminality had less than one-third the risk of these behaviors in adulthood as did children reared by their at-risk biological parents.[95]

Other studies comparing adopted children with children who were reared by parents who had considered giving them up or were ambivalent about keeping them found that adopted children functioned better.[96] Adopted children also functioned more effectively than children living in institutions, long-term foster care, or poverty.

Adoption clearly provides benefits to children, even though children will have to deal with whatever mysteries exist about biological parents or have a more complex path to identity formation, as we shall see in later chapters.

Summary   All the studies on the decision to parent and the transition to parenthood indicate that Heinicke's three qualities for parenting[97] are the important ones. Regardless of whether parents naturally conceive their child, use assisted reproductive technology, adopt, have children at a young age or older, parents will be more effective and more satisfied and their babies will flourish when parents have good feelings about themselves, their families of origin and their partners, and use problem-solving strategies to reach their goals.

ADJUSTMENT TO PARENTHOOD

The arrival of a baby changes every aspect of adults' lives, from finances to sex, sleeping habits, and social life. Although many first-time parents report that nothing could have adequately prepared them for the experience, knowing what to expect can still help parents cope.

The Power of Positive Relationships

Throughout this book, we shall see that positive relationships sustain parents as they care for their children. Positive relationships with their own parents[98] and with each other enable parents to be more loving and effective parents. Further, positive relationships with children are related to children's healthy growth.

When mothers and fathers feel support from each other, their competence as parents grows, and interaction with the baby becomes more effective. Father-infant interactions and fathers' competence, particularly, are related to feeling support from mothers (see the interview with James Levine on page 235). Even basic activities are influenced by the quality of the marriage. Mothers experience fewer feeding difficulties when their husbands are supportive and view them positively, whereas marital distress is related to inept feeding by the mother.[99]

What constitutes a positive marital relationship? One contributor to marital satisfaction is parents' agreement on role arrangements.[100] It does not matter whether couples are traditional or egalitarian in their division of tasks; satisfaction increases when couples have similar ideologies. A second contributor to marital satisfaction is a couple's ability to communicate with each other—to express thoughts, feelings, and needs in ways each partner can hear and respond to. Communication does not have to be verbal. A look, a gesture, a touch, or an action can communicate support, agreement, or the need for further conversation.

Parents who focus on what is good about the situation or the action of the other person, who avoid negative criticism and angry exchanges, feel less stress and create less stress for each other. These parents discuss different points of view and express themselves forcefully, but they stay focused on making needed changes to improve the situation, and they avoid assigning blame for problems.

These qualities are possible to develop even if parents live separately and care for the child alone. Making agreeable care arrangements, respecting the other parent as

INTERVIEW
with James Levine

James Levine is the director of the Fatherhood Project at the Families and Work Institute. He served as a principal consultant to vice president Al Gore in drafting the federal initiative on fatherhood, created by executive order in 1995.

What are the best ways to get men involved in parenting?

There are several issues. I think the absolute key is the couple's expectations of what the father's role will be. If the mom doesn't expect the dad to be involved, and the dad doesn't expect to be involved, that's a prescription for noninvolvement. If Mom doesn't expect Dad to be involved, and Dad might want to be involved, he won't be involved. The mother is the gatekeeper in the relationship. Many women say they want husbands to be involved, but in effect, they want them to be involved as a sort of Mom's subordinate or assistant. Mom's the manager, telling Dad how to be involved, as opposed to assuming Dad will be involved and will learn the skills to be a father. It is important for mothers to back off and be in the background, and let fathers be with children.

So, one key to involvement is the couple's dynamics. I don't mean to blame Mom, but there is a system here—men and women as a system—and one starts here in terms of making a supportive system for fathers' involvement.

Then let's look at men in terms of men and the system outside the couple. All the research we've done shows that men today define success on two dimensions—being a good provider and, equally important, having good relationships with children. So, if you look at the values men bring to parenthood, there are generally agreed-on desires to have close relationships with their children. But, aside from the couple relationship, there are two obstacles. Men sometimes feel incompetent as to how to do this; they need skills. And, second, their work sucks them up in spite of their best intentions to give time to relationships with children. They spend a lot of time working, not to avoid forming relationships with children but as a way of caring for children.

A key to change is changing the cultural cues men get about being fathers. Looking at this from an ecological and systems point of view, we can ask, "What are the cues that men get about parenting across the life cycle?" The expectations others have about them have a lot to do with shaping their behavior. For example, prenatally, if men get expectations from the health care system that they are expected to be at prenatal visits, they will be there. Mostly, however, they get the message they have no role during the pregnancy. Yet, research has shown that one of the best predictors of good prenatal care for the mother is whether the partner is involved with prenatal care.

We have found in our work with low-income men that, when men understand how vital their role is even before the child is born, they can change their level of involvement. Knowing how important their role is with their babies increases the motivation of low-income men to be involved.

So at the time of birth and afterwards, if the pediatrician sends messages that he or she wants both parents at visits—"I need to know both of the baby's parents. I want to see you both, not just the mother"—that message shapes the father's behavior. Same thing at preschools or day care. They can also send messages that they want both parents, not just mothers, to be involved.

So it is the expectations that are embedded in daily interactions that are the real keys to fathers' involvement. If you look at the face-to-face interactions with maternity nurses

(continued)

INTERVIEW with James Levine

(continued)

and pediatricians, embedded in dialogues with doctors, health-care providers, and teachers are messages about expected involvement. If more messages expect fathers to be involved, and daily interactions offer support for fathers' involvement, fathers will be involved.

To give a specific example, West Virginia wanted to increase the rate at which fathers established paternity of children born to single mothers, and the question was how to do that. One could think about a big public-information campaign with messages to encourage involvement, but the key was the maternity nurse, who had the most influence on both the young man and the young woman. The father would come and look at the baby, and if the nurse assumed he was some bad guy and chased him away, if she did not invite him in to be involved with the baby, he would disengage and disappear. They increased the rate of paternity establishment by increasing the dialogue with fathers and also by changing what the nurse said to mothers. The nurse told mothers it is important for children to be involved with their fathers even if mothers decide not to marry the fathers. In two years, the rate of establishing paternity went from 15 percent to 60 percent of fathers who claimed paternity of babies born to single mothers.

The overall message to fathers was we want you here, we want you to establish paternity and be fathers to your children. Changing expectations encoded in daily interactions are the important elements in increasing fathers' involvement with their children.

---

a person, and cooperating in coparenting, as we discussed in Chapter 4, can promote parents' effectiveness and babies' growth even when marital satisfaction is not possible.

A single parent develops a support group of extended family or friends who help with the caregiving activities and also share the mother's or father's delight in the baby's growing engagement with her and the world. A support group plays a powerful role by being available when a single parent needs to talk over a problem or needs encouragement when sleepless or frustrated or lonely.

Changes the Baby Brings

A great deal goes on during the early months. Parents are highly involved in the nurturing stage of parenthood,[101] caring for the child and accepting their new role as parents. They worry, "Am I doing okay?" "Am I the kind of parent I want to be?" Gradually, parents incorporate other parts of their lives—work, extended family, friends—into their caretaking activities.

Parents may find it difficult, however, to give each other the support that is so crucial in coping during this period. A significant number of new mothers report specific problems, including (1) tiredness and exhaustion; (2) loss of sleep, especially in the first two months; (3) concern about ignoring husband's needs; (4) feeling inadequate as a mother; (5) inability to keep up with housework; and (6) feeling tied down.[102] Mothers did not anticipate the many changes that would occur in their lives when their babies arrived, in part because they did not realize how much work is involved in caring for an infant. Fathers had a similar ordering of complaints: (1) loss of sleep for up to six weeks; (2) the need to adjust to new responsibilities and routines; (3) the disruption of daily routines; (4) ignorance of the amount of work the baby requires; and (5) financial worries (62 percent of the wives were employed prior to the child's arrival and only 12 percent afterward). Husbands make such comments as "My wife has less time for me" and "Getting used to being tied down is hard."

The new father may see the infant as a threat to his relationship with his wife and to their lifestyle. Concern about the amount of time, money, and freedom the baby will surely consume can obscure the joy he expects—and is expected—to feel. No more candlelit dinners or even impromptu decisions to go to a movie or to make love, not for a while. The father has not had the physical experience of carrying the baby for nine months, nor is he as likely to be as involved as the mother in the care of the newborn. For a while, at least, the needs of the baby will come before the wishes of the husband—and those needs will be frequent and unpredictable, delaying meals and interrupting sleep. Almost all fathers and mothers, however, find that emotional attachment to their babies grows and deepens if they are patient and caring.

Dimensions Underlying the Adjustment

Two longitudinal studies—one carried out by Carolyn Pape Cowan and Philip Cowan[103] and the other by Jay Belsky[104]—have yielded remarkably similar findings on the basic dimensions underlying the adjustment process. First, a major determiner of the ease of the adjustment process is parents' ability to balance their needs for autonomy and self-care with the need to be close to other people, particularly their spouse and child. Parents have an easier time when they can create an "us" relationship that has priority over individual needs. They put aside immediate individual wants in order to help their partner, because that improves their relationship. A husband may put aside his desire to go visiting as a family, because his wife is tired and needs to rest, and he wants them both to feel good about the outing. Or a wife may not ask her husband to skip his evening jog to help with the baby, because she feels he needs to unwind from work, and she wants a relaxed family atmosphere when he is with the baby. Other dimensions are listed in Table 6-4.

Those parents most at risk for difficulties are unrealistic about the changes a baby will bring, have negative views of their partner and their marriage, and are pessimistic about solving problems. They take no action to arrive at mutually satisfying solutions to their difficulties. Table 6-5 lists many actions parents can take to ease the transition for themselves and their partners.

Both Belsky and the Cowans agree that transitions vary by gender. Although men and women have many common experiences—both find the baby irresistible, both worry about bills and the increased work, and both feel better about themselves as a result of parenthood—they experience the transition in different ways. For one, the experience is much more physical for women than for men. Because women have a biological connection with the child during pregnancy, labor, and delivery, the child is a greater reality to them, and many maintain the intimate physical

■ **TABLE 6-4**
DIMENSIONS UNDERLYING THE TRANSITION TO PARENTHOOD

---

1. The capacity to balance individuality and mutuality

2. The communication skills of both parents

3. Attitude (positive and negative) in confronting situations and people

4. Expectations about what the baby will bring

5. The ability to devise a sharing of workload that is compatible with couple's beliefs and ideologies concerning appropriate behavior for men and women

6. The ability to come to terms with patterns of behavior learned in the families of origin

7. The ability to manage conflict effectively

Adapted from Jay Belsky and John Kelly, *The Transition to Parenthood* (New York: Delacorte, 1994); Carolyn Pape Cowan and Philip Cowan, *When Partners Become Parents* (New York: Basic Books, 1992).

■ **TABLE 6-5**
RECOMMENDATIONS TO COUPLES FOR EASING THE TRANSITION TO PARENTHOOD

---

1. Share expectations.

2. Give yourselves regular checkups on how each is doing.

3. Make time to talk to each other.

4. Negotiate an agenda of important issues; if one partner thinks there is a problem, there is.

5. Adopt an experimental attitude; see how solutions work, and make modifications as necessary.

6. Don't ignore sex and intimacy.

7. Line up support for the early stages after the birth.

8. Talk with a friend or coworker.

9. Find the delicate balance between meeting your needs and the baby's needs; children grow best when parents maintain a strong positive relationship.

Adapted from Carolyn Pape Cowan and Philip Cowan, *When Partners Become Parents* (New York: Basic Books, 1992).

connection with the child by breast-feeding. Men experience the pregnancy and the early months after birth from a greater distance and often feel left out. Lacking the close physical connection with the child, fathers often need more time to form a strong attachment with the baby.

In most instances, couples navigate the transition well, not because they have fewer or less serious problems than the couples who experience difficulties, but because they have developed effective ways to cope with changes and resolve conflicts.

These domains were identified through studies of couples, but they apply to the transitions of single parents as well. Single parents have to form a supportive network of individuals who can help. Whether their support group is made up of friends or family, single parents have to share with these individuals their expectations and feelings; they must all find ways to divide the workload, manage conflict, and avoid negative outbursts.

Adjustments of Parents Who Adopt or Who Have Premature Children

In addition to the usual stresses of the birth of a baby, parents who adopt or have premature children face additional challenges. Unlike most parents, who have nine months of preparation for parenthood, parents who adopt or have premature births are often plunged into parenthood in unpredictable ways. Adopting parents may have waited months or even years for a child, when suddenly the child arrives with little warning, perhaps ill or stressed at all the changes. Workplaces may be unaccommodating, and friends may ask many questions. Adopting parents may also worry that the birth mother will change her mind.

Fortunately, adopting parents have buffers. These parents tend to be older, with all the advantages of older parents described earlier in this chapter. Compared with younger parents, they are more settled in their work, have greater financial resources, have been married longer, and have developed better coping skills.

Parents of premature children may have little or much to manage. If children are only a few weeks premature, parents may have no problems. If a child is born at twenty-four or twenty-six weeks after conception, however, the child might stay in the hospital for an extended period of time. His or her parents must consider whether the child will survive and whether long-term problems will develop. They also face the ongoing stress of dealing with hospital and medical personnel and the changing medical status of their child. Further, when the child comes home, they may need to make many changes to address the special needs of their child.[105]

Parents of premature children are advised to interact with them and to take over as much care of their children as possible in the hospital.[106] A recent hospital intervention, Kangaroo Care (KC), benefited the infant and the whole family.[107] Kangaroo Care consisted of skin-to-skin care between mother and infant; for at least an hour a day for a period of two weeks, the infant, wearing only a diaper, lay between the mother's breasts. Observations of the families' interaction patterns when infants were three months of age revealed that Kangaroo Care was related to increases in mothers' sensitivity to their infants and in their ability to adjust their stimulation to the babies' needs. Kangaroo Care was also related to increases in affectionate touching between parents and between parents and child. At three months of age, infants were less irritable than infants in a control group who did not receive Kangaroo Care, and there was greater reciprocity in the relationships between parent and child. It is thought that the physical contact helped the mother understand the baby's needs better and give more sensitive care; as a result she felt more confident and positive toward both the baby and her husband. Mother's positive touching of her husband increased his positive touches with her and the baby.

A very brief version of this intervention has proved useful for full-term infants as well.[108] Infants who received one hour of Kangaroo Care with mothers about twenty minutes after birth were found to have more organized motor movements, to sleep better, and to have less crying following the Kangaroo Care. The benefits were observed for up to four hours. For full-term infants, Kangaroo Care helped to reduce the stress associated with all the physiological changes at birth and appeared to help newborns achieve greater regulation of their physiological state. The authors encourage further research to study "the issue of continued KC during the first postnatal weeks and the possible effects on mother-infant interaction, infant temperament, and attention-related skills during early life."[109]

In the special circumstances of adoption and premature birth, all the ways listed for couples to ease the transition to parenthood are important. Support from friends or from new friends dealing with similar situations, and clear communication between parents and between parents and professional workers, are especially essential.

A PRACTICAL QUESTION: WHAT CHANGES CAN PARENTS ANTICIPATE FOR THEMSELVES?

Parents continually develop new behaviors as they rear their children and as they deal with their frustrations as parents. So, it is not surprising that creating these new responses leads to permanent changes in parents themselves. Yet, there has been relatively little research on parents' changes as a result of parenting.

Ellen Galinsky, a consultant and lecturer on child development, found herself changing after her children were born. Curious about the meaning of her feelings, she consulted books and research reports to see what other parents were describing. Finding little to inform her, she began forming groups of parents of young children. She then interviewed 228 parents with different experiences of parenthood—married, divorced, step-, foster, and adoptive parents. These parents did not represent a random sampling but were a broad cross section of the population.

Galinsky has divided parenthood into six stages, in each of which parents focus their emotional and intellectual energy on the task of that period.[110] These stages differ from most in that a parent can be in more than one stage at a time with children of different ages. The first stage, occurring in pregnancy, Galinsky terms the *image-making* stage. It is a time when parents prepare for changes in themselves and in their relationships to others. The second stage, *nurturing,* goes from birth to the time when the child starts to say "No," about eighteen to twenty-four months. As parents become attached to the new baby, they arrange their lives to be caregivers, balancing their own and their child's needs and setting priorities. The third stage, *authority,* lasts from the time the child is two to four or five. Parents become rule givers and enforcers as they learn that love for children goes hand in hand with structure and order. From the child's preschool years through adolescence, parents are in the *interpretive* stage. Children are more skilled and independent, and parents establish a way of life for them, interpret outside authorities such as teachers, and teach values and morals. In brief, they teach children what life is all about.

When their children are adolescents, parents enter the *interdependent* stage. They form new relationships with children, and, although they are still authorities, their power becomes shared with children in ways it was not in past years. In the sixth stage, *departure,* parents evaluate themselves as their children prepare to leave home. They see where they have succeeded and where they might have acted differently.

Galinsky summarizes her views of how parenthood changes adults:

> Taking care of a small, dependent, growing person is transforming, because it brings us in touch with our baser side, it exposes our vulnerabilities as well as our nobility. We lose our sense of self, only to find it and have it change again and again. We learn to nurture and care. We struggle through defining our own rules and our own brand of being an authority. We figure out how we want to interpret the wider world, and we learn to interact with all those who affect our children. When our children are teenagers, we redefine our relationships, and then we launch them into life.
>
> Often our fantasies are laid bare, our dreams are in a constant tug of war with realities. And perhaps we grow. In the end, we have learned more about ourselves, about the cycles of life, and humanity itself. Most parents describe themselves as more responsible, more accepting, more generous than before they had children.[111]

SUPPORT FOR PARENTS

Various kinds of support can help parents adjust to parenting. When parents successfully meet the demands of their new roles, they feel competent and effective. These feelings of self-efficacy can continue, influencing ongoing parenting in beneficial ways. Family and friends provide informal sources of support as well as information, advice, and direct help in the form of shopping, cleaning, and cooking so parents can get some rest. Other, more formal sources of support consist of classes and support groups.

Classes

Most couples are referred to classes at hospitals or in the community prior to the arrival of the baby. Even programs given in hospitals at the time of the birth can provide information that increases parents' competence in caring for their babies. Such information focuses on babies' states and their repertoire of behaviors, the ways they send signals to parents, and how parents learn to understand and respond to the signals. Especially helpful are tips on when to "engage" with babies (when they are fed and alert), when to "disengage" (when babies turn away, fall into a drowsy state), how to feed infants, and how to deal with crying.[112] As we noted in Chapter 5, a brief behavioral parent training[113] enables parents to help their newborn develop healthy sleep patterns.

Support Groups

As we noted in Chapter 5, the Cowans found that couples groups were very helpful to new parents.[114] Couples discussed the stresses of adjusting to parenting and found reassurance in learning that others had similar problems. The couples discussed activities or attitudes that reduced stress and produced well-being and closeness between parents. The Cowans found that all the couples who were in the six-month groups at the time of the birth were still together when the child was three years old, whereas 15 percent of couples who had not been in the groups were divorced. When children were five years old, the divorce rate was the same for the two groups.

When parents conceive a child and bring him or her into the world, they embark on possibly the most life-changing experience of their lives. Whether well or poorly planned, the child elicits new behaviors from parents and at the same time brings a host of new pleasures to them. When parents can work together with each other or with supportive friends and relatives, when they communicate expectations, experiences, and feelings as they care for the baby, the baby brings parents, friends, and relatives closer together to share life experiences in a more intense, meaningful way than previously known. Babies demand a great deal, but they give much in return.

MAIN POINTS

The decision to be a parent involves

- assessing parental readiness in terms of time and psychological resources
- couples' planning children and resolving differences
- single adults' planning children
- accepting a child if unplanned
- resolving ambivalence so the child is wanted, not rejected

Changes in adoption policies and assisted reproductive technologies

- mean that people who would have been childless in the past can now have children
- raise questions about children's rights to know their biological roots

Timing of children

- depends on the psychological qualities of parents rather than their age
- affects a child's later adjustment; if parents are not mature, a child may develop later problems
- has resulted in negative stereotypes of teenage mothers and positive views of older ones

The means of becoming parents

- has little effect on parenting strategies
- has no documented effect on children's functioning and competence

Babies bring

- new routines and responsibilities
- great pleasures
- a special appreciation in parents who have experienced infertility

Dimensions underlying a parent's transition to parenthood include

- balancing individuality and mutuality
- communication skills

- positive attitudes
- agreed-on division of labor
- parents coming to terms with their own childhood experiences

Parents experience greater ease in the transition when they

- maintain intimate bonds with their partner or a supportive friend or relative
- share expectations, feelings, and workload with partners
- line up support from friends, relatives, or groups of other parents
- adopt an experimental attitude toward solutions—trying them and seeing what works

EXERCISES

1. Imagine that you and your partner are discussing your readiness to have a baby. What factors would make you feel that you are ready? How would you handle a disagreement between the two of you about whether to have a baby? Suppose you both felt strongly about your opinion; what would you do?

2. Describe your expectations of parenthood. What changes will it require of you? Do you think your expectations are realistic? Describe the activities that you do now that might prepare you for being a parent—taking a course in parenting, learning to solve conflicts in a positive way, practicing communication skills with friends, learning about children and their needs. Are there other things you could be doing?

3. Plan out the support system you would organize for yourself and your partner if you were having a baby in three months. Whom would you include? How involved would your relatives be? How much extra expense would such a system create?

4. Imagine you are a fifteen-year-old girl who becomes pregnant and wants to keep her child. Investigate the resources in your community that would enable you to keep the child, remain in school, get a job. Visit the programs or day-care center where your child would be cared for. Are the services adequate?

5. Imagine you and your partner required donor insemination or egg donors. Investigate the resources in your area and the requirements for people using them.

ADDITIONAL READINGS

Belsky, Jay, and Kelly, John. *The Transition to Parenthood.* New York: Delacorte, 1994.

Cowan, Carolyn Pape, and Cowan, Philip. *When Partners Become Parents.* New York: Basic Books, 1992.

Kruger, Pamela, and Smolowe, Jill, ed. *Like No Other Love.* New York: Riverhead, 2005.

Pertman, Adam, *Adoption Nation.* New York: Basic Books, 2000.

Yarrow, Andrew. *Latecomers: Children of Parents over 35.* New York: Free Press, 1991.

7

Parenting Infants: The Years from Birth to Two

IN THE NEWS

New York Times, December 29[1]: More parents sleep with infants than ever before. See pages 260–263.

Test Your Knowledge: Fact or Fiction?

1. Despite the advances in medical technology, the number of babies born prematurely rose to a twenty-year high of 12 percent in 2001.
2. Though mothers and fathers relate differently to infants, they are equally competent caregivers.
3. Duplicating conditions in the womb helps calm and soothe newborns so that they can settle into their new world more easily.
4. Massage helps calm and soothe the infants of depressed mothers.
5. Parents of two-year-olds intervene eight to ten times per hour in order to gain children's compliance with rules.

What are babies like? How do they relate to parents and shape what parents do? How do parents encourage babies' development and competence? Who and what support parents in their important roles as caregivers of the next generation?

Babies depend completely on adults for their survival. Reflexes, such as sucking and grasping, enable babies to adapt to their new world, but they rely on caregivers to provide the food, warmth, and soothing that they need to grow in their new environment. This chapter describes the parent-child interactions promoting growth in the first two years of life.

THE NEWBORN

During the first three months, babies' body rhythms and states are not organized. Their irregular systems gradually settle into a more organized pattern.[2]

The average newborn sleeps about eighteen hours a day, waking every three or four hours to eat. However, some babies sleep up to twenty-two hours, and some as little as ten hours. Sleep is of two kinds. Infants spend about 50 percent of their sleep time in active, *REM sleep* (rapid eye movement sleep, sometimes termed *dreaming sleep*), and 50 percent in *non-REM quiet sleep* (when the body is relaxed and still). Over time, the percentage of REM sleep decreases, so that by age two, only 35 percent of sleep is of this kind. Over the first six to twelve months, sleep becomes organized into a longer period of eight to twelve hours at night, with two naps during the day, totaling about sixteen hours per twenty-four-hour day, on average.

Babies also cry and appear distressed. Great individual differences exist, however. In newborn nurseries, babies cried from one to eleven minutes per hour, with a daily average of about two hours. Hunger and wet diapers were significant causes, but the largest single category of causes was "unknown." The crying may have expressed a social need for cuddling, warmth, or rhythmic motion.[3]

Infants' crying increases to about three hours per day at six weeks, mostly concentrated in the late afternoon or evening hours.[4] Crying decreases to an average of one hour a day at three months. Although hunger seems to be the predominant cause, "unknown" remains the second-highest category for this age.

Early Social Reactions

Babies come into the world preprogrammed to respond to human beings.[5] They see most clearly at a distance of 8 to 10 inches, the average distance of a parent's face from the baby when being held. Babies show an early preference for objects that in any way resemble a human face—even a circle with a dot or two for "eyes." They hear best in the range of the human voice. Infants a few hours old respond to the cry of another newborn and then often cry themselves. Babies also move in rhythm to human speech.

Newborns are observant. When less than a week old, they can imitate an adult's facial expression of sticking out a tongue, fluttering the eyelids, or opening and closing the mouth.[6] This suggests that a newborn has a rudimentary sense of self as a human being capable of imitating a person and has the motor control to do it.

Early Parent-Child Relationships

In addition to feeding babies, keeping them warm, and seeing that they sleep, parents soothe babies and regulate their physical system. A major way to do this is through physical contact with the infant.[7] As noted in Chapter 4, physical contact with mothers regulates infants' hormonal levels, sleeping and eating patterns, and heart rate. Increased physical contact, such as mothers' using Snugglis to carry newborns, also promotes mothers' sensitivity and responsiveness to their babies and contributes to secure attachments between infants and mothers.

Infant-directed speech and music provide another way to soothe and regulate babies' arousal states.[8] In recent research with premature babies in neonatal

Box 7-1
WOMB SERVICE*

Dr. Harvey Karp, a pediatrician, has written a book, *The Happiest Baby on the Block,* that will transform many parents' lives by giving them tools to calm and soothe their newborns. Dr. Karp describes a five-step method that will help newborns settle into their new world more easily, especially those newborns with intense temperaments who find it difficult to soothe themselves.

Dr. Karp believes that newborns would really benefit from another trimester in the womb because at birth their neurological systems are still immature and easily overwhelmed with the forms of stimulation they find here. They need the "womb service" they are used to. In the womb, babies are folded up in tight quarters with much uterine support surrounding them; they hear the sound of blood coursing through arteries and veins, the sounds of stomachs gurgling, and sometimes background voices. They move in many different ways as mothers go about their daily activities.

When they are born, their little bodies are out in space, with arms and legs moving wildly; they miss the enfolding support of the uterine walls, especially when lying on their backs. Often, it is deadly quiet and dark, like a cave. And they can only lie there; they can't move around on their own. So, until the nervous system develops and gives babies greater ability to regulate themselves, as it gradually does in the first three months, babies find it hard to settle in, and many cry.

Dr. Karp's method is to duplicate as closely as possible the characteristics of life in the womb because reminders of that time trigger a child's powerful calming reflex. This reflex, Dr. Karp believes, is essential to a healthy pregnancy and delivery. If fetuses had tantrums and frenzies of activity and flailed around forcefully, they would increase the risk of causing the umbilical cord to wrap around their necks or wedging themselves into odd positions that would be difficult to change in the uterus or birth canal.

His five-step program is to be done a specific way:

1. Swaddling—very tightly wrapping the baby in a receiving blanket
2. Side/stomach position for holding the child—in the stomach position, the baby is held against the body so he or she feels pressure on the stomach—always laying the baby on his or her back for sleeping
3. Providing a "shhhh" sound that duplicates noise in the womb helps babies— some parents use a vacuum cleaner or dust buster, but parents can also make "shhhh" or shushing noises
4. Swinging or some form of rhythmic motion, such as jiggling, dancing, rocking, or carrying the child in a sling
5. Sucking on a pacifier, breast, or finger

These five steps together make up what Dr. Karp calls the Cuddle Cure to soothe babies. He believes these steps copy what many other societies do naturally to calm babies. In some societies, babies are continually held or carried by someone. He points to an interesting custom in Bali. For the first one hundred and five days of life, babies are thought to belong to the gods. They are held most of the time. At the end of that time, a ceremony takes place in which they receive their first sip of water; an egg is rubbed on their arms and legs to give them strength; their feet are allowed to touch Mother Earth; and they are welcomed as new members of the human race. At about

---

Box 7-1

---

this same time, American babies have settled in and become socially outgoing, responsive babies, and many parents feel their newborns are now the babies parents imagined they would be at birth.

Innovations in neonatal nurseries have had success in creating more womblike experiences for premature babies born two to three months early.[†] It is a complicated process to create an individualized care plan for each baby while he or she is in the hospital, to train staff and parents to carry it out, and to monitor the child's response, but research indicates great benefits from the program. The program, begun within seventy-two hours of birth, lasted until the child reached the corrected age of two weeks. (*Corrected age* is the child's age from the date of expected arrival, not from the date of actual birth.) Parents and staff did everything possible to reduce stress and to physically support the child, with much Kangaroo Care time; often two nurses carried out a procedure—one held and supported the baby while the other did the procedure.

At the corrected age of two weeks, babies who had the experimental treatments had better neurobehavioral functioning and increased coherence between frontal and other brain regions. At the corrected age of nine months, the experimental babies' development was significantly advanced. They scored in the 73rd percentile for overall development, and the control babies scored at the 39th percentile. The sample was small, but the results very impressive.

*Adapted from: Harvey Karp, *The Happiest Baby on the Block* (New York: Bantam, 2002).
[†]Heideliese Als et al., "Early Experience Alters Brain Function and Structure," *Pediatrics* 113 (2004): 846–857.

---

intensive care units, playing lullabies for brief periods during the day reduced babies' stress by masking hospital noises. With less stress, babies' sucking rates, weight gain, and oxygen saturation increased, and they left the hospital sooner. Music therapists' or mothers' singing or talking directly to babies reduced stress more effectively than did recorded music.

Shortly after birth, full-term babies also respond to the lyrical qualities of mothers' speech directed to them, and to the rhythms of human conversation, as well as songs sung directly to them.[9] Music seems to promote not only an optimal level of arousal but social communication and closeness as well.

In their early interactions, parents shape infants' emotional reactions, encouraging positive moods and smiling and discouraging negative moods with phrases such as, "Don't cry" or "Don't fret."[10] Babies respond to parents' emotional reactions and pattern their own after what they see parents do. Infants as young as ten weeks mirror mothers' emotional expressions; they respond with joy and interest to mothers' happy faces, with anger and a form of fear to mothers' angry faces, and with sadness to mothers' sad faces.[11] Babies pattern their moods after mothers' moods on a more ongoing basis as well. Over time, mothers' positive expressions are related to increases in babies' smiling and laughter.[12]

As the infant's system settles down in the first two to three months of life, parents begin to engage their baby in a social dialogue during face-to-face interactions.[13]

VOICES OF EXPERIENCE

What I Wish I Had Known about the First Two Years

"I remember when we brought him home from the hospital, and we had him on the changing table for a minute, and I realized, 'I don't know how to keep the engine running.' I wondered how could they let him go home with us, this little package weighing seven or eight pounds. I had no idea of what to do. I kind of knew you fed him, and you cleaned him and kept him warm; but I didn't have any hands-on experience, anything practical. In a way, I would have liked them to watch me for a day or two in the hospital while I change him, to make sure I knew how to do it. It's kind of like giving me a car without seeing whether I could drive it around the block."   FATHER

"I wish we had known a little more about establishing her first habits about sleeping. The way you set it up in the beginning is the way it is going to be. Having enough sleep is so important. We went too long before we decided to let her cry for five minutes. Then she got into good sleep habits."   FATHER

"I wish I had known how it would change things between me and my husband. The baby comes first, and by the time the day is over and he is in bed, we have two hours together, but I just want to curl up and take care of myself."   MOTHER

"I wish I had known about how much time babies take. It is like he needs twenty-four-hour attention. For an older parent who is used to having his own life and is very set in his ways, it is hard to make the changes and still have some time for your own life."   FATHER

"She had this periodic crying at night in the beginning, and you are caught in the raging hormones and somehow I thought if I just read Dr. Spock again or if I read more, I'd understand it better. And we joked about reading the same paragraph in the book over and over. We needed reassurance it would end, and at three months it ended. That was the hardest part."   MOTHER

"Someone said, when you have a child, it's like two appointment books—his appointment book and yours. And first you do everything in the kid's appointment book; and then when you're done, you do everything in the kid's appointment book again. I wish I had known they weren't joking. I knew that it would be a challenge, and in some ways I wish I had known more. But in other ways I think if I had really known exactly how hard it would be sometimes, I might have been more reluctant or waited longer, and that I would really have regretted—not doing it."   FATHER

"I wasn't prepared for all the decisions. Is it okay if he does this or not? He's trying to do something; shall I step in so he doesn't hurt himself, or shall I let him go? It's making all those choices, making sure what I feel."   MOTHER

"I wish I had known what to do about climbing. He climbs all over everything. I have the living room stripped bare, but I wonder if this is the right thing."   MOTHER

"I wish I had known how much time they needed between one and two. They are mobile, but they are clueless about judgment. I think it was one of the most difficult times. Even though she did not get into a lot of trouble, sticking her finger in the light sockets, still she takes a lot of time and watching, so the transition to two was great."   MOTHER

Sensitive parents adjust their behavior to the rhythm and tempo of the baby, looking for periods of alertness and readiness to respond. In face-to-face interactions, parents wait for their baby to look at them before they talk, tickle, or play games. Babies as young as three months develop expectations about how interactions proceed, and they become distressed if these expectations are not met. For example, when a parent of a three-month-old adopts a still, impassive facial expression, the baby responds negatively and often tries to elicit the anticipated reaction by smiling or vocalizing.[14] If this does not work, the baby turns away. Similarly, if a parent arrives when the baby is distressed over a routine such as a diaper change and does not attempt to soothe the child, the baby protests.

Influencing the behavior of others who respond in return establishes babies as social partners with parents. At the same time, parents recognize babies' increasing role as active participants who have individual preferences and unique behavioral preferences. As partners, parents and babies interact and adjust to each other; they create mutual understanding and *intersubjectivity,* or a shared state of meaning.[15] In the state of shared meaning, the baby uses the parent as a *social reference* for responding to experience. For example, babies will not play with a toy if the mother has looked at the toy with disgust.[16]

Babies' temperaments and emotional reactivity influence the social dialogue between parent and child. When babies adjust well to change and are easily soothed when upset, parents can regulate the babies' environments and conditions reliably and consistently. However, when babies are fretful, easily upset by change, and difficult to soothe, parents find it harder to provide this consistent regulation, and both partners in the dialogue become frustrated.

DEVELOPMENT IN THE FIRST TWO YEARS OF LIFE

Observers have identified three periods of major reorganization in babies' development over the first two years of life.[17] They occur at about three months, seven to nine months, and eighteen to twenty months and are related to neural changes that enable babies to become more efficient learners and more effective social partners. In this section, we discuss babies' physical, intellectual, language, and emotional development, as well as development of self, at these stages.

Physical Development

On average, the baby grows from about 21 inches at birth to about 33 inches at the end of two years, and birth weight increases to about 29 pounds. Growth, however, involves more than an increase in size and weight; it includes increasing organization of behavior as well.

As just noted, at about three months changes occur in the nervous system. Increased myelination of nerves in cortical and subcortical neural pathways and an increase in the number of neurons improve the child's sensory abilities and bring greater stability and control of behavior. The nervous system appears more integrated. Babies seem to settle down, with greater organization of bodily functioning. Voluntary, coordinated behaviors replace reflexes as the latter gradually disappear. Babies are more awake during the day and at night drop into a quiet sleep before dreaming.

Eight months brings changes in physical development that underlie several changes in behavior. Increased myelination of neurons occurs in the motor area, in areas of the brain controlling coordination of movement, and in areas responsible for organization of behavior. At about this same time, most babies develop the capacity to sit alone. Next comes control of the trunk, which leads to creeping and crawling. Babies now can move rapidly in all directions. Finally, walking replaces crawling sometime between ten and eighteen months.

Locomotion enormously affects babies' exploratory and social behavior.[18] When babies crawl and move around their environment, they can look at, touch, and manipulate objects. Exploration triggers new social reactions to babies. When infants reach out for objects, mothers often begin to name what they are touching and to describe features of the objects, and so babies' language increases. Because babies can now initiate interactions with others more easily, locomotion also brings social changes. Crawling babies often get close to adults, crawl into their laps, and smile and vocalize more at them.

After the first year, motor abilities become more finely tuned. Walking and running become automatic; reaching and grasping, more refined. This increase in skills enables toddlers to explore the environment more carefully than before.

Intellectual Development

Physical and intellectual development are closely intertwined in the early months and years. To learn about the world, the child must be able to come in contact with it by getting around, exploring objects, and seeing how they work.

As noted in Chapter 2, Jean Piaget believed that, in the first two years of life, the child is in the sensorimotor period of development, in which perceptions and motor activity are the sources of knowledge.[19] Infants gradually move from interest in their own bodies and actions to interest in actions involving people and objects in the environment. Toward the end of the first year, they begin to imitate others in simple actions, such as waving bye-bye. Imitation becomes more sophisticated in the second year. At about eighteen to twenty-four months, toddlers develop representational thought, which leads to greater language development and more complex responses to the environment. L. S. Vygotsky, too, emphasizes the importance of language for intellectual development. Children guide their behavior with words that, with age, become inner speech, which becomes thought.[20]

Parents' main role in their children's intellectual development is to provide a stimulating environment children can explore, the freedom to act and learn, and models that guide children and help them reach their full potential.

Language Development

Lois Bloom believes that language enables people to express their intentions (their thoughts, feelings, and desires) to achieve intersubjectivity with others important to them.[21] In her view, the child's drive for expression is what motivates language development. Because language involves the communication of thoughts and feelings important to people, language is closely intertwined with social, emotional, and cognitive development.

The earliest forms of communication are infants' emotional reactions—their smiles, frowns, cries. Parents who read these signals can, for example, distinguish a cry of anger from one of pain or hunger. Gradually, babies develop cooing, then babbling and the repetition of syllables as in *ma-ma* or *da-da-da.* Parents and infants develop a social dialogue. Even before they have words, babies capture adults' attention, take turns, and communicate when they babble and coo with adults. Their sounds have inflections that express happiness, requests, commands, and questions. A single word, such as *mama,* can be a question, an order, an endearment, or a request.

Children's first words pertain to objects, people, and experiences important to them. Words describe what their feelings are about. They also usually refer to events in the present. With advances in cognitive development, their words refer to past and future experiences as well.[22]

From the beginning, children use words to explain feelings, but they do not label their feelings until about age two. By the beginning of the third year, toddlers talk about positive feelings such as being happy, having a good time, feeling good, and being proud. They talk about negative emotions as well—being sad, scared, or angry. They talk about uncomfortable physical states—being hungry, hot, cold, sleepy, and in pain.[23] Aware of others' feelings as well, toddlers develop ideas about what actions cause feelings and what actions change feelings. Here are some comments from twenty-eight-month-olds: "I give a big hug, Baby be happy." "I'm hurting your feelings 'cause I mean to you." Toddlers also learn that one person's feelings can stimulate another person's actions. "I cry. Lady pick me up."[24]

Cognitive development in the second year provides children with more complex thoughts to communicate. Thus, Bloom believes, the two-word sentence emerges to enable children to communicate their intentions and reactions to the world.[25]

Emotional Development

Emotional reactions are a central part of babies' lives; even in the earliest months, infants have a range of facial expressions that change every seven to nine seconds.[26] Infants also have characteristic emotional responses, such as joy or irritability, some of which persist over time.

As noted earlier, mothers begin to guide and shape babies' emotional reactions in the first three months of life. Mothers of boys appear more responsive to them than to daughters and match their sons' behaviors more often as well.[27]

Babies respond to others' emotional reactions and pattern their own after what they observe. They not only pattern their moods after parents' reactions but also modify their behavior on the basis of adults' emotional reactions. Confronting what appears to be a visual cliff, ten-month-old babies look to mothers' facial expressions for guidance. When mothers smile, babies continue to crawl, but when mothers look fearful, they stop.[28] As we have seen, when mothers look at toys in a disgusted manner, babies refuse to play with them.[29]

By the end of the first year, babies express interest, surprise, joy, sadness, anger, fear, and disgust.[30] In the second year, feelings become refined and stronger in all areas.

Self-Regard   Toddlers gain a clearer sense of themselves as individuals. They enjoy their activities and take pleasure in their accomplishments. Unconcerned with others' reactions, they do not appear to make value judgments about their own actions.[31] Children have a beginning sense of standards, as seen in their looking for recognition when they have done something well, turning away when they have not succeeded, and showing distress and making repairs when they have broken something, even accidentally. Still, their main response is one of delight in what they do.[32]

Empathy   Toddlers go beyond the infant's crying at others' distress—they take action.[33] They touch, cuddle, and rub the injured party or try to bring the child something he or she would like. Many go through a process of referring the pain to themselves. If a mother bumps her arm, the child rubs the mother's elbow and then his own. Compassionate action follows self-referencing behavior. Investigators suggest that true kindness may depend on the ability to relate others' distress to one's own.

Toddlers do not express as much concern when they are the cause of distress. They intervene to help or remedy the situation, but they do not feel guilty for causing the problem. Toddlers' concern is most frequently directed to family members, particularly to mothers, who receive much of their toddlers' comforting and helping.

Anger   Parents want most to understand children's anger. Florence Goodenough found that many factors influence the occurrence of anger.[34] Outbursts peak in the second year and are most likely to occur when children are hungry or tired (just before meals and at bedtime) or when they are ill. Thus, when reserves are down for physical reasons, tempers flare. Outbursts are usually short-lived—most last less than five minutes—and, with young children under two, the aftereffects are minimal. With increasing age, children tend to sulk and to hold on to their angry feelings. From one to two years, the immediate causes of anger seem to be conflict with authority, difficulties over the establishment of habits (eating, baths, bedtime), and problems with social relationships (wanting more attention, wanting a possession someone else has).

In the study, parents of the children who had the fewest outbursts were consistent, used a daily schedule as a means to an end, and had a tolerant, positive home atmosphere. They established consistent and fair rules. With realistic expectations that children would be independent, curious, and stubborn, they anticipated problems and found ways to prevent them. These parents tried to help children conform by preparing them for changes in activities. They announced mealtimes or bathtimes in advance so children had ten minutes or so to get ready. In these homes, parents focused on the individuality of the child. When a real conflict arose, however, they were firm.[35]

Parents of children with many outbursts were inconsistent and unpredictable, basing decisions on their own wants rather than the child's needs. These parents tended to ignore children's needs until a problem forced them to respond. In some of these families, parents imposed a routine regardless of the child's activity of the moment and forced the child to act quickly in terms of their own desire. Criticism and disapproval characterized the home atmosphere.

In short, when children are tired, hungry, or sick, they tend to respond with anger. Parental behaviors that reinforce attachment—acceptance, sensitivity to children's needs, and cooperativeness—minimize temper outbursts.

Ways to Handle Negative Feelings   Toddlers have several ways to handle negative feelings. They use words to express their feelings and to get feedback from parents about how to manage them.[36] They enlist parents' and caregivers' help in resolving the negative feelings and different situations they cannot handle. They call or pull parents to whatever they want fixed. Toddlers also use objects to handle negative feelings. They frequently use transitional objects such as stuffed animals, blankets, pieces of cloth, or dolls to provide comfort in times of distress. The use of such objects peaks in the middle of the second year, when as many as 30 to 60 percent of children have them.[37]

Happiness and Affection   Toddlers feel joy in learning and in the free use of their abilities. Although they most enjoy pursuing their own goals, they also enjoy meeting adults' expectations. In one laboratory study, toddlers played in a mildly interested way with toys, but when adults asked them to do easy, interesting tasks, such as arranging the toys in a certain way, the toddlers did so quickly and enthusiastically.[38] Later, when allowed to play freely with no adult involved, they happily repeated the tasks. The researchers concluded that toddlers derive great pleasure from matching their actions to the words of another, and the pleasure of accomplishing a goal is a powerful motive for their obeying commands.

Affection also increases in this period. Toddlers pat, stroke, and kiss their parents, particularly mothers. They are also affectionate to animals and younger children.

Development of the Self

Integrating current research and theory, Susan Harter describes how the self begins to evolve in the first years of life.[39] From birth to four months, the infant gradually establishes predictable, satisfying patterns of eating, sleeping, quieting, and arousal. In responding to caregivers and reacting to the surrounding world, the infant develops a rudimentary organization and integration of the perceptual and sensorimotor systems and gains a first sense of self and others.

In the period from four to ten months, the infant becomes more differentiated from the caregiver in social interplay and begins to develop an interpersonal self. As this period progresses, infants form attachments to caregivers, thus experiencing an increasing connectedness to others. At the same time, infants act on the world in more complex ways and begin to get a sense of their own ability to affect objects—make a mobile move, shake a rattle. Caregivers who react positively to babies' bids for attention increase babies' sense of control over events. The regularity and consistency of babies' feelings in response to others' behaviors—for example, delight from tickles and being thrown in the air—or in sharing emotional states with others help babies develop a sense of themselves and what they can expect in interactions with others.

From ten to fifteen months, babies become increasingly differentiated from caregivers and find a greater sense of themselves as agents who make things happen. Though attached to parents, they move off, using parents as secure bases for exploration in the world.

From fifteen to eighteen months, a "me-self" develops. Toddlers begin to internalize how others respond to them—that is, they start to react to themselves as others do. Children at this age recognize themselves in a mirror, identify photographs of themselves, and respond strongly to others' responses to them.

From eighteen to thirty months, toddlers develop a greater understanding of what influences others to act; as a result, they gain a greater sense of the separation between the self and others. Developing language enables toddlers to describe themselves and what they do. By age two, they use pronouns such as *I, me,* and *mine,* and they describe their physical appearance and actions—"I run," "I play," "I have brown hair." Besides reflecting a growing self-awareness, describing looks and actions also actually increases self-awareness.

Development of Self-Regulation

As we have seen, self-control begins to develop in the earliest days of life.[40] In the first three months of life, infants regulate arousal states of wake and sleep and the amount of stimulation they get. They also soothe themselves.

From three to nine months, infants modulate sensory and motor activities. Although they possess no conscious self-control yet, they do use motor skills to gain parental attention and social interaction. As they reach out, form intentions, and develop a rudimentary sense of self, their capacity for control begins to emerge.

From nine to eighteen months, infants show awareness of social or task demands and begin to comply with their parents' requests. As infants act, investigate, and explore, their sense of conscious awareness begins to appear. These trends continue in the second year.

Researchers observing year-old babies' obedience to their mothers' commands in the home found that babies obey their mothers' commands when the mothers accept and are sensitive to babies' needs.[41] Mothers who establish harmonious relationships with their babies, who respect them as separate individuals and tailor daily routines to harmonize with the children's needs, have babies who are affectionate and independent, able to play alone, and (even at one year) able to follow their mothers' requests. Thus, at this early age, a system of mutual cooperation between mother and child is established and maintained as each acts to meet the requests of the other.

Although children first show control by following the requests of others, they soon begin to inhibit their activities on their own volition.[42] For example, a toddler of fifteen or sixteen months may reach for an object, shake her head, and say, "No, no." Toddlers are most successful in avoiding forbidden activities when they direct their attention away from these objects or activities—looking elsewhere, playing with their hands, finding an acceptable substitute toy. A substantial number of two-year-olds can wait alone as long as four minutes before receiving permission to touch.[43]

THE PROCESS OF ATTACHMENT

In Chapter 2, we described attachment as an enduring tie that binds the child to the parent, who is a source of security for the child. We also saw that secure attachments promote a variety of positive behaviors. How do parents establish such bonds?

An analysis of sixty-six studies on infants' attachments to mothers (as mothers were the focus of most studies) found that *sensitivity,* defined as the ability to perceive the infant's signals accurately and respond appropriately and promptly to the child's needs, was a major but not the only contributor to the infant's secure attachment.[44] *Mutuality* (positive harmony and mutuality in relationship), *synchronicity* (coordinated social interactions), and *positive attitude* (emotional expressiveness, acceptance, and delight in the child) all contributed to the formation of secure attachments. So, when parents are sensitive, responsive, warm, accepting, and attentive to the rhythms of the child's behavior and individuality, they create a state of mutual understanding that fosters a secure parent-child attachment.

As children become toddlers, parents maintain a state of mutual understanding through continuing sensitivity and availability as a secure base for exploration. In this state of mutual understanding, parents go on to teach and guide children, balancing support and guidance with increasing independence for the child. The effective parent observes the child's level of interaction in a situation and stays, in a sense, one step ahead. When the child confronts a new barrier, the parent steps in to give just the amount of help that enables the child to solve the problem and move on. This form of guidance is termed *scaffolding,* or balancing the child's weakness (see Chapter 4).[45]

Research shows that mothers and fathers relate differently to infants in terms of both quantity of time spent and the kinds of activities engaged in with infants.[46] Data collected in the 1980s and 1990s showed that, even though many mothers had jobs, they spent more time with children. In these studies, fathers spent, on average, only 40 percent as much time with children as mothers did.[47]

Data collected from a national representative sample in 1997 reveal that fathers in intact families now spend more time with children.[48] On weekdays, fathers of infants spent 60 percent as much time as mothers in activities and in being available for activities with infants, but on weekends, they spent 80 percent as much time. Fathers do proportionately less caregiving than mothers, but they spend exactly the same amount of time in social activities. In addition to caregiving, play, and social activities, fathers also do household activities and teach children.

Though they show different amounts of involvement, mothers and fathers are equally competent as caregivers.[49] Fathers can be as sensitive as mothers in their interactions with infants, reading and responding accurately to babies' cues. Babies drink as much milk in fathers' care as in mothers'. Mothers are more likely to hold babies in caregiving activities and to verbalize than are fathers. In fact, the mother's role has been described as providing a "holding environment" for infants as they regulate their system and develop increasing skills in interactions with people and objects in the environment.[50]

Fathers are more attentive visually and more playful in physically active ways than are mothers.[51] Fathers are most likely to be highly involved in caregiving and playing when the marital relationship is satisfying and their wives are relaxed and outgoing. Both fathers and mothers give mostly care and physical affection in the first three months, when babies are settling in. As babies become less fussy and more alert at three months, both parents become more stimulating and reactive.[52]

Box 7-2
INTERVENTIONS TO INCREASE SECURE ATTACHMENTS FOR IRRITABLE BABIES AND THEIR MOTHERS

Concerned that irritable temperament put babies at risk for insecure attachments with their mothers, Dymphna van den Boom recruited a sample of one hundred irritable babies and their mothers to carry out an intervention to decrease that risk. Babies were assessed at the tenth and fifteenth days after birth with Brazelton's Neonatal Behavioral Assessment Scale to identify irritable infants. The babies were all first-born children in low-status, primarily two-parent families (only three families were headed by single mothers) in The Netherlands.

The irritable infants were randomly assigned to a control or experimental group.[*] When infants were between six and nine months, the experimental group received three home visits, in which Dr. van den Boom observed mother-infant interactions and made suggestions to increase mothers' sensitivity and responsiveness. She increased mothers' attentiveness to infants' signals and appropriate responses to them. She also suggested effective ways for mothers to soothe babies when they cried, and explained why it was important to do so. She encouraged mothers to play with their babies to increase pleasurable interactions and reduce the negative quality of interactions. Each visit lasted two hours and was focused on the individual behaviors of each mother-infant pair.

After the intervention, when infants were nine months old, experimental-group mothers were significantly more sensitive, more stimulating, and more attentive to their children, and their babies were more sociable, more able to soothe themselves, and cried less. They also explored more. All infants and mothers were seen again when infants were twelve months of age, and level of attachment was assessed. In the control group, 22 percent of infants had secure attachments, and 78 percent had insecure attachments. In the experimental group, 62 percent had secure attachments, and 38 percent had insecure attachments.

These children and their mothers were seen again when children were eighteen months, twenty-four months, and forty-two months.[†] Mothers in the experimental group continued to be more attentive, more responsive, and more supportive, and their children more cooperative and more involved with peers than children in the control group.

In speculating about the reasons for the long-lasting benefits of the brief intervention, van den Boom attributed the effects to mothers' learning how to attend to and interpret children's behaviors and then how to respond to them in a sensitive way. Increases in mothers' sensitivity increased the security of the attachments, and that security also contributed to positive behaviors as children began to move outside the immediate family. One suspects that part of the success was the very personal attention and specific suggestions tailored to each mother-infant pair.

[*]Dymphna C. van den Boom, "The Influence of Temperament and Mothering on Attachment and Exploration: An Experimental Manipulation of Sensitive Responsiveness among Lower-Class Mothers," *Child Development* 65 (1994): 1457–1477.
[†]Dymphna C. van den Boom, "Do First-Year Intervention Effects Endure? Follow-up During Toddlerhood of a Sample of Dutch Irritable Infants," *Child Development* 66 (1995): 1798–1816.

TASKS AND CONCERNS FOR PARENTS OF INFANTS

Marc Bornstein describes four main tasks for the parents of infants:[53]

- Nurturant caregiving: providing food, protection, warmth, and affection
- Material caregiving: providing and organizing the babies' world with inanimate objects, stimulation, and opportunities for exploration
- Social caregiving: engaging and interacting with infants—hugging, soothing, comforting, vocalizing, playing
- Didactic caregiving: stimulating infants' interest in and understanding of the world outside the parent-child relationship by introducing objects, interpreting the surrounding world, and giving information

T. Berry Brazelton and Stanley Greenspan add that experiences must be tailored to the individual characteristics of the child and that both parents and children require a community that supports parents' efforts and children's growth.[54]

We look here at two main tasks of parenting: (1) establishing an optimal state of arousal for infants and (2) promoting infants' self-regulation.

Establishing an Optimal Level of Arousal

Reducing time spent in crying and establishing healthy sleep patterns promote a state of arousal that enables babies to respond to people and to the world around them. We saw in Chapter 3 that parents achieve these ends in ways that vary by culture. The interdependent model of parenting emphasizes close physical contact and a close relationship between parent and child, and the independent model emphasizes the child's growing independence and interest in the world.[55]

Although parents in the United States most often rely on the independent model of caregiving, emphasis on behaviors characteristic of the interdependent model has grown. Many U.S. mothers are following recommendations of the medical community to breast-feed babies for at least a year, and more parents are using Snugglis and slings to carry their children, as do parents in other parts of the world. So, let us look at which strategies work best to reduce crying and promote healthy sleep patterns.

Crying   As noted, crying increases at about six weeks and decreases at about three months of age. A thorough study of crying in the first year of life found that babies had as many crying episodes at the end of the year as at the beginning, but they spent much less time in each episode.[56]

In the first quarter, there was no relationship between the baby's crying and the mother's behavior. In the second quarter, a trend appeared that became significant in the third and fourth quarters. Those mothers who responded immediately to the cries of the baby had babies who cried less. Conversely, ignoring a baby's cries seemed to increase the amount of crying, measured by frequency and duration. Those mothers who responded most at the beginning of the year had less to respond to at the end of the year.

INTERVIEW
with Jacqueline Lerner and Richard Lerner

Richard Lerner holds the Anita L. Brennan Professor of Education position at Boston College, and Jacqueline V. Lerner is a professor of education at Boston College.

Parents are interested in temperament and what this means for them as parents. What happens if they have a baby with a difficult temperament that is hard for them to deal with? Is this fixed? Will they have to keep coping with it?

R. Lerner: We don't believe temperament necessarily is fixed. We believe that temperament is a behavioral style and can, and typically does, show variation across a person's life. We're interested in the meaning of temperament for the person and the family in daily life.

J. Lerner: Although we know temperament is present at birth, we don't say that it is exclusively constitutionally derived. Temperament interacts with the environment. We find children who do seem to stay fairly difficult and children who stay fairly easy. Most children change, even from year to year. Given this, we can't possibly believe that temperament ever becomes fixed unless what happens in the family becomes fixed.

R. Lerner: What we are concerned with are individual differences. They are identifiable at birth, but they change, we believe, in relation to the child's living situation. We find that what one parent might call difficult is well below the threshold of another parent's level of tolerance for difficulty. What some people find easy, others find quite annoying.

In fact, you can find in our case studies examples of how difficult children ended up developing in a particular context that reinterpreted their difficulty as artistic creativity. One girl picked up a musical instrument at age thirteen or fourteen and began playing. She had a gift for that. Prior to that, she had a difficult relation with her father, who found her temperamental style totally abhorrent to him. As soon as she had this emerging talent, he said, "Oh, my daughter is an artist. This is an artistic temperament." They reinterpreted the first thirteen years of their relationship, believing they had always been close.

We believe the importance of temperament lies in what we call "goodness of fit" between the child's qualities and what the environment demands. The child brings characteristics to the parent-child relationship, but parents have to understand what they bring and how they create the meaning of the child's individuality by their own temperaments and their demands, attitudes, and evaluations. Moreover, I think parents should understand that both they and the child have many other influences on them—friends, work, or school.

When you think about the fit with the environment, how do you think about the environment; what is it?

R. Lerner: We have divided demands from the environment into three broad categories: the physical characteristics of the setting, the behavioral characteristics of the environment, and the behavioral and psychological characteristics of the other important people in the child's life.

J. Lerner: The setting has physical characteristics, and the people have behavioral characteristics and demands, attitudes, and values.

R. Lerner: Parents need to understand the demands of the context (the living situation) they present to the child by means of their own values and behavioral style. Even the features of the physical environment the parents provide can affect the child's fit with the context. Parents need to understand there are numerous features of the context; because of the child's individuality, a better or lesser fit will emerge. For example, if your child has a low threshold of reactivity and a high intensity of reactions, you don't want to put that child's bedroom next to a busy street. If you have a choice, you'll put that child's bedroom in the back of the house or won't let the child study in any part of the house where he or she will get distracted.

A poor fit also occurs if you have a child who is very arrhythmic and you demand regularity, not necessarily as a verbal demand but perhaps in the way you schedule your life. You begin to prepare breakfast every morning at 8:00, the bagel comes out at 8:05 and disappears at 8:15, and some days the child makes it and some days not. The parents have to see how they may be doing things that create poorness of fit. It's not just their verbal demands but also their behavioral demands and the physical setup of the house.

J. Lerner: Some parents don't see what they are reinforcing and what they are teaching their child through their demands. There has to be consistency between the demands and the reinforcements. Sometimes you don't want to be too flexible. I learned this the hard way. My nine-year-old tells me about what I have done in the past. "But when I did this last week, it was okay and now it isn't."

In actively trying to get the child to behave or in trying to change a temperamental quality, parents need to focus themselves on what behaviors they want reinforced and what ones they don't. They need to be perceptive on both ends of the response—the demands they are setting up and what they are actually reinforcing. If you know a child is irregular in eating in the morning and you want to change the pattern because you know he'll get cranky and won't learn well if he doesn't have a full stomach, be consistent. "You don't walk out the door unless you have had at least three bites of cereal and a glass of juice." But if you let it go one morning, you can expect the child to say, "Well, yesterday you didn't make me do that."

From your research, do you see potential supports for children as they are growing up?

R. Lerner: More and more children experience alternative-care settings, and this has to become a major support. The socialization of the child is moving out of the family more and more, and we are charging the schools with more of the socialization duties. Throughout infancy and childhood, the alternative caregiving setting is the day care, the preschool, and, obviously, the school. These settings have to be evaluated in terms of enhancing the child's fit and the ability to meet the demands of the context.

What strategy is most effective in terminating crying? Picking up and holding the baby stopped the crying 80 percent of the time. Feeding, which involves physical contact, was almost as effective. The least effective method was to stand at a distance and talk to the child.

In reviewing ways of providing comfort to crying babies, Judy Dunn found that caregivers around the world soothe by "rocking, patting, cuddling, swaddling, giving suck on breast or pacifier."[57] Monitoring the crying of the babies from three to twelve weeks, investigators found that supplemental carrying in a Snuggli for three extra hours per day eliminated the peak of crying that usually occurs at six weeks, reduced crying overall, and modified the daily pattern of the crying so there was less in the evening hours.[58] Equally important, babies who were carried more were more content and more visually and aurally alert. Supplemental carrying provides all the kinds of stimulation that we know soothe babies—rhythmic, repetitive movement with postural changes. Close physical contact also enables mothers to understand and respond to their infants better.

Another recent suggestion for soothing crying babies takes a different approach. In his clinical and research training, William Sammons has observed many different kinds of babies and gradually developed the belief that babies have the ability to calm themselves, given the opportunity to develop this skill.[59] Babies suck on fingers, wrists, or arms; get into a certain body position; or focus on certain visual forms such as walls, objects, or light to soothe themselves. In his pediatric practice, Sammons has encouraged parents to engage in a mutual partnership with babies so that the infants can find their own ways to calm themselves.

Parents can combine these two latest solutions to the crying problem by increasing the amount of carrying they do and, at the same time, letting the infants find ways to calm themselves when they do cry and fuss without an identifiable cause.

Sleep   Changes are occurring in the ways parents establish sleep patterns. In most parts of the world, infants sleep with a parent (co-sleeping), and most toddlers and older children sleep with or near a parent. Surveys reveal that, in the United States, infants in middle-class families sleep alone or in bassinets or cribs near a parent, and by six months of age, most sleep in their own rooms.[60] In families of lower social status, however, a significant number of babies co-sleep with parents—in one sample, 80 percent of African American infants and 23 percent of European American infants slept with their parent or parents.[61] And now a growing number of middle- to upper-class parents sleep with their babies, perhaps to make breast-feeding easier at night, to reduce babies' crying, or to stay connected with the child at night.

As we noted in Chapter 3, babies' sleep is a matter of great importance to American parents. There are two general approaches to helping babies sleep. The first and more traditional one in the United States was put forth by Richard Ferber in 1985[62] and by Athleen Godfrey and Anne Kilgore in 1998.[63] According to this approach, as babies mature, most learn to put themselves back to sleep at night. So, babies need to develop habits of going to sleep that they can duplicate in the middle of the night to put themselves back to sleep. If they develop the habit of falling asleep while nursing or being rocked, they will be unable to duplicate those conditions in the middle of the night and will cry. The parents' job is to develop a regular

VOICES OF EXPERIENCE

The Joys of Parenting Children in the First Two Years

"I love babies. There is something about that bond between mother and baby. I love the way they look and smell and the way they hunker up to your neck. To me it's a magic time. I didn't like to baby-sit particularly growing up, and I wasn't wild about other people's babies, but there was something about having my own; I just love it. And every one, we used to wonder, how are we going to love another as much as the one before; and that is ridiculous, because you love every one." MOTHER

"There is joy in just watching her change, seeing her individualize. From the beginning it seemed she had her own personality—we see that this is not just a little blob of protoplasm here; this is a little individual already from the beginning. She has always had a real specialness about her. It was exciting to see her change." FATHER

"I think it's wonderful to have a baby in the house, to hear the baby laugh, sitting in the high chair, banging spoons, all the fun things babies do. They seem to me to light up a household. When there's a baby here, a lot of the aggravations in the household somehow disappear. Everyone looks at the baby, plays with the baby, and even if people are in a bad mood, they just light up when the baby comes in the room. I think there is something magical about having a baby in the house." MOTHER

"There is the excitement of baby talk becoming real words." MOTHER

"I enjoy that she directs me more than I could sense. Before, there was a 'yes' or 'no' response, but now there is more back and forth. If I dress her, she shows me she wants to sit or stand—'Do it this way' is what she seems to say. Before, she was tired or not tired, hungry or not hungry, okay or not okay. Now there is much more variation." FATHER

"I've heard of this, and it's true; it's rediscovering the child in yourself. Sometimes, it's the joy that he and I hop around the couch like two frogs on our hands and knees. Or we're in the bathtub pretending we are submarines and alligators. Sometimes he likes to ride around on my shoulders, and I run and make noises like an airplane or a bird. And I am not just doing it for him, but we are doing it together, playing together." FATHER

"I was just blown away by the way he tries to help other children. From a very young age, he has done this. Now, when a little girl he sees every day cries, he takes her one toy after another and says, 'This is? This is?' meaning, 'Is this what you want?' until he gets her to stop crying by giving her something she wants. He's very people oriented, very affectionate, and seems so secure." MOTHER

"Watching her grow, seeing her grow, seeing the different stages, I just take pleasure in everything she does now, because I know she will be on to a new stage soon." MOTHER

"As he gets older, I relate more, play more. He is more of a joy. Some of the joys are so unexpected. I would stop myself and open up and think, 'Oh, this is my son, he's so joyful. He's smiling for no particular reason.' I am not that joyful, but he's joyful for no reason. He reminds me of joy." FATHER

(continued)

VOICES OF EXPERIENCE

The Joys of Parenting Children in the First Two Years

(continued)

"It's the first time in my life, I know what the term 'unconditional love' means. The wonder of this little girl and nature! I have never experienced anything like that. It is 'Yes,' without any 'Buts.' " FATHER

"When I was ten years old, my school had a program in which we spent a few hours a week with babies and toddlers. I will never forget the eyes of the babies. They were so clear and trusting. I felt good every time I looked in their eyes." PROSPECTIVE FATHER

---

routine that soothes the child, who is then put in the crib to fall asleep alone. Parents respond to crying with verbal soothing but no picking up. Parents then increase the length of time each night before providing the soothing, and the child's crying gradually decreases. When mothers in other countries are told of this method, however, they consider it abusive or neglectful to leave the child alone to sleep.[64] The other approach to helping babies sleep is that followed by the rest of the world—namely, having babies sleep with mothers or both parents. The babies may fall asleep near the parents or in the parents' bed, but they sleep most of the night with the parents.

Controversy attends the wisdom of co-sleeping. A recent report identified more than 800 deaths associated with co-sleeping over the past eight years, either because of the parent's rolling over on the child or the child's being wedged between the mattress and the wall or the headboard.[65] The counterargument is that many more babies die of sudden infant death syndrome (SIDS) when sleeping alone, and that by co-sleeping, a nearby parent could perhaps detect breathing difficulties before death. Moreover, when babies co-sleep with mothers, they nurse more, and breast-feeding is thought to be protective against SIDS. Thus, environmental factors that promote breast-feeding are thought to reduce infant vulnerability to SIDS.[66] Those parents who want to co-sleep are advised to use an attachment to their bed where the child can sleep without risk of rollover or being wedged.[67]

Although many consider Ferber to be a staunch supporter of sleeping alone, he stated in a recent interview that his children slept in the same bed with him and his wife and had to be trained to sleep in their own beds.[68] In general, his feeling is that children can sleep with or without parents. "What's really important is that the parents work out what they want to do."

James McKenna, a biological anthropologist and the director of the Mother-Baby Behavioral Sleep Laboratory at Notre Dame, believes that co-sleeping regulates the infant's physiological system. "Biologically and psychologically, infants, children, and their parents are designed to sleep close."[69] He acknowledges that there are no systematic studies of the relationship of sleeping arrangements to children's developing personality characteristics, but studies are beginning to produce evidence of the benefits of co-sleeping. For example, one study described co-sleeping children as less fearful and better behaved than children who slept alone. A study of adults who, as children, co-slept with their parents suggested the adults had a feeling of satisfaction with life. They came from Latina/o and African American families in New York and Chicago. The study, however, found no simple outcome of co-sleeping; rather, co-sleeping as a child was seen as part of a relationship embedded in a cultural and social system related to adult characteristics.

In contemporary society, co-sleeping is one facet of a larger system of *attachment parenting,* which incorporates many aspects of the interdependent model of caregiving. The pediatrician William Sears encourages parents to accept their babies' dependency needs and meet them appropriately. He describes the five Bs of attachment parenting in infancy: (1) bonding with the infant at birth, (2) breast-feeding, (3) bed sharing (co-sleeping), (4) baby wearing (carrying the baby in a Snuggli or a sling), and (5) belief in the baby's cry as an important signal. The five Bs keep baby and parents physically connected so parents can learn who their child is and be able to respond in a sensitive, caring way.[70]

Sears raised his own children this way and has been counseling parents for over three decades. The number of attachment parenting advocates is on the increase, perhaps because, as more mothers work outside the home, they want to find ways to stay connected to their infants and young children. Advocates of attachment parenting believe it (1) simplifies life (parents have no bottles, cribs, or strollers to manage), (2) increases parents' sensitivity and responsiveness as they get to know their babies better, (3) promotes gentle discipline, because children's natural tendencies to independence and self-control are allowed to develop slowly and gradually over time, and (4) focuses on the family's needs, not just the needs of parent or infant.[71]

> With attachment parenting, parents and children find their needs in cooperation with one another, thus creating a family-centered lifestyle. A key benefit of this responsive style of caregiving is that both parents and children feel that they are getting their "cup filled," as some parents say. Children feel whole and secure, while parents feel more relaxed and confident.[72]

Attachment parenting does not require that a caregiver be at home full-time, and there is much advice on how to combine attachment parenting and working. Parents are advised to create a community of caregivers who share the parents' values and will behave in the same way toward the baby when the parents are not there. Such caregivers would give breast milk the mothers have pumped, carry the children during the day, and respond quickly and attentively to children's cries.

Advocates believe that "experienced attachment parents who have seen their children through early childhood and beyond describe this gentle nurturing style as a completely fulfilling way of life."[73] Research evidence certainly supports elements of attachment parenting—the importance of sensitive, responsive care and the decrease in crying that comes from increased early carrying—but it is not clear that co-sleeping and prolonged carrying of the child are beneficial, nor is it clear that immediate gratification of desires is essential or wise for all babies. Recall that soothed fearful and inhibited children maintained those behaviors when firm support to learn self-soothing appeared more useful in helping them overcome the behaviors (see Chapter 1).

Parents do many things to encourage children's compliance; they persuade children and guide them in what to do.

Promoting Self-Regulation

In children's first eight or nine months of life, parents nourish and give physical care to babies, meet their needs, and help them regulate their functioning. Babies cooperate in the care, but parents are the more active partners, relying on their own sensitivity to understand what babies want. Now we turn to a task that parents find challenging and demanding: helping children develop the ability to control their own behavior.

Encouraging Compliance   Toward the end of the first year, babies' increasing motor and cognitive skills enable them to plan and carry out actions that do not meet parents' approval, so even in the first year, parents begin guiding and modifying children's behavior. Babies also have the capacity to comply with simple requests. The way parents go about shaping children's behavior to meet standards establishes behavioral patterns that children use in interactions with others.

In the second year of life, toddlers gain increasing control of their behavior. The goal is not simple compliance with rules but autonomy, or *self-regulation*—the capacity to monitor and control behavior flexibly and adaptively even when an adult is not present.[74] Self-regulation is achieved by age three to four.

Parents take many actions to encourage children's cooperation with parental requests. First, they create an atmosphere of receptive compliance, described in Chapter 5.[75] When parents have secure attachments to children and are sensitive and responsive to their needs, they create a climate in which children are more likely to comply. When noncompliance occurs, parents use reasoning and explanations— low-power techniques—that result in a sharing of power. Sharing power with children has a strong impact because it communicates essential respect for the child as a person.[76]

In addition to creating an atmosphere for receptive compliance, parents often take preventive action to head off conflicts before they arise. Parents divert children's attention from tempting but forbidden activities by suggesting interesting substitutes. For example, in grocery stores, they suggest that children pick out items, or they make a game of identifying products or colors or items to prevent whining for candy.[77]

Establishing Rules   Parents generally introduce rules that dovetail with the toddler's increasing abilities;[78] Table 7-1 lists sample behavior standards. A detailed study of mothers' rules and toddlers' compliance reveals that the major rules at thirteen months center on safety for the child, for other people (no hitting, kicking, or biting), and for possessions. At about eighteen months, the rules expand to include behavior during meals, requests to inhibit behavior and delay activity, and early self-care. At about twenty-four months, more is expected in terms of polite behavior and helping with family chores (putting toys away). By thirty-six months, children are expected to do more self-care, such as dressing themselves.[79]

Children's compliance with safety rules is high and increases with age. The time and involvement required for promoting all areas of self-regulation are enormous, and parents of two-year-olds intervene eight to ten times per hour to gain compliance. Such parents need a great deal of energy and support.[80]

PARENTS WHO FACE SPECIAL DIFFICULTIES

Which parents have the most difficulty in parenting infants and young children? In this section we look at (1) the special difficulties adolescent, depressed, and substance-abusing parents face as they rear their young children and (2) ways to help these parents.

■ **TABLE 7-1**
SPECIFIC BEHAVIOR STANDARDS, BY CATEGORY

Category	Category Items
Child safety	Not touching things that are dangerous Not climbing on furniture Not going into the street
Protection of personal property	Keeping away from prohibited objects Not tearing up books Not getting into prohibited drawers or rooms Not coloring on walls or furniture
Respect for others	Not taking toys away from other children Not being too rough with other children
Food and mealtime routines	Not playing with food Not leaving table in the middle of a meal Not spilling drinks, juice
Delay	Waiting when Mom is on the telephone Not interrupting others' conversations Waiting for a meal
Manners	Saying "please" Saying "thank you"
Self-care	Dressing oneself Asking to use the toilet Washing up when requested Brushing teeth when requested Going to bed when requested
Family routines	Helping with chores when requested Putting toys away Keeping room neat

J. Heidi Gralinski and Claire B. Kopp, "Everyday Rules for Behavior: Mothers' Requests to Young Children," *Developmental Psychology* 29 (1993): 576–584. Copyright © 1993 by the American Psychological Association. Reprinted with permission.

Adolescent Parents

Adolescent Mothers Adolescent mothers' psychological immaturity creates difficulty in caregiving. Although they can be as warm as older mothers, adolescent mothers view their infants as more difficult, and they are less realistic in their expectations of children.[81] They foster premature independence in their infants, pushing them to hold their bottles, sit up too early, and scramble for toys before they can get them; however, as infants become toddlers, these mothers reverse their behavior and become overly controlling, not letting toddlers explore freely or have choices in activities.[82] Adolescent mothers also fail to provide a stimulating home environment conducive to learning, and they offer less verbal stimulation.[83]

Children of adolescent mothers face a greater likelihood of academic difficulties, school failure, and behavioral problems.[84] Factors that promote positive development include the mothers' improved circumstances. If a mother goes off welfare between her child's preschool and adolescent years, she reduces the risk of her child's being retained a grade. When a male figure is present, adolescent offspring have fewer behavioral problems than those with no such figure.

Although these findings come largely from studies of African American teenage mothers, work with other samples in the United States and New Zealand yields similar findings.[85] Samples with a broader representation of poor adolescent mothers of African American, Latina, and European American backgrounds find similar difficulties in the maturity level of all the mothers and in their abilities to translate their love for their children into supportive, nurturing care.[86] Diversity of outcome, with some mothers making heroic efforts to raise their children under very difficult circumstances, characterizes the samples.

Many teen mothers have had to face early sexual abuse. These young girls feel helpless, unprotected, inferior, and unworthy of care; as a result, they fail to develop self-protection skills and are vulnerable to predatory or uncaring men. Further, they carry these feelings and difficulties into their role as parent and often cannot protect their own children from sexual abuse. In Chapter 15, we explore the effects of sexual abuse in greater detail.

Most findings about teen mothers cut across all ethnic groups. However, African American adolescent mothers receive more support from family and friends and are less strict than Latina mothers.[87]

Although they undoubtedly face many problems, adolescent mothers are often committed to their children, and many raise them successfully. Unfortunately, we pay less attention to the successes than to the failures. For example, 75 percent of teen mothers studied in Baltimore were employed and not involved with social services, yet we focus on the 25 percent who received services.[88]

Adolescent Fathers Although adolescent fathers are typically less involved with their children than are older fathers, adolescent fathers are often not completely absent. About 25 percent of adolescent fathers live with their infants, and a national survey suggests that about 57 percent visit weekly in the first two years of life. The percentage of those visiting drops as the children grow older—40 percent when the child is between two and four and a half, 27 percent when the child is four and a half to seven, and 22 percent when the child is over seven.[89]

African American fathers are more likely to be involved than are European American and Latino fathers. Only 12 percent of African American fathers have no contact with their children, whereas 30 percent of European American fathers and 37 percent of Latino fathers have no contact.[90]

Adolescent fathers are more likely to be involved when other people in the environment support their involvement. (See the interview in Chapter 6 with James Levine.) When adolescent fathers do remain involved, however, they use many directives and negative comments, as do the mothers. Adolescent fathers were observed in one study while solving problems and tasks with their children. The fathers offered strategies for completing the tasks, but they also gave many commands and made many negative comments as the children worked on the tasks. The fathers' negative ways of relating to their children encouraged negativity and resistance in their children, thus creating a vicious cycle. Researchers concluded, "Through their fathers' early entry into parenting and their parents' lack of resources and use of negative control, these children may be shaped, like their parents before them, into the next generation of antisocial children."[91]

Help for Teenage Mothers and Fathers   Two kinds of programs attack the problems of teenage pregnancies: (1) those that postpone the birth of the first child by means of effective education and birth control and (2) those that help parents once they have had children. Both programs emphasize effective birth control while encouraging teens to develop a sense of confidence about their ability to make and carry out future goals for themselves.[92] Teen mothers also benefit from programs that help them sustain positive relationships with their children and their families.

There are also programs to encourage active parenting for adolescent fathers, as detailed in Chapter 6.

Depressed Parents

Studies of depressed parents have focused on mothers, as they are the ones who interact most frequently with their babies.[93] As a group, depressed mothers look at their infants less often, touch them less often, have fewer positive facial expressions, and vocalize with infants less often than do nondepressed mothers. They are also less affectionate and play less with their babies. They see their babies in a more negative light than do nondepressed mothers. In addition, depressed mothers rate themselves more positively than others see them.

Depressed mothers' affect seems contagious, because babies of depressed mothers are fussier, more irritable, and less active than are babies of nondepressed mothers. Further, babies of depressed mothers show these behaviors with adult nondepressed strangers, who, in turn, respond with negative affect, setting up a vicious cycle. Depression in babies is observed at birth. They have higher sensory thresholds and therefore need more stimulation to respond. They already show flat affect and low activity levels. They also have some of the same physiological characteristics that distinguish their depressed mothers from nondepressed mothers, such as elevated levels of norepinephrine and cortisol, which contribute to irritability. Moreover, by three months of age, they have EEGs that show right frontal activation similar to their mothers'.

Babies of mothers who are successfully treated for depression show no longterm adverse effects of their infant experience. Preschool children of mothers who continue to be depressed, however, show the same physiological characteristics as earlier. Further, depressed mothers continue to report having more behavior problems with their children than nondepressed mothers report with their children.

Because the effects of mothers' depression on infants' behavior are reversible, interventions to help depressed mothers and their infants are essential. Effective interventions are directed to the mother and the child and their patterns of interaction.[94] In addition to the usual psychiatric treatments of medication and psychotherapy, interventions to alter mothers' mood include massage therapy and relaxation therapy, which have been found to lower mothers' scores on measures of anxiety and depression. Further, music therapy sessions, during which mothers listen to their preferred music, appear to temporarily reduce right frontal EEG activation.

Massage therapy—provided by mothers and professional therapists—can also help infants of depressed mothers. It reduces infants' fussiness, improves their sleeping patterns, increases their ability to soothe themselves, increases their activity level, and results in more positive patterns of interaction with mothers. In one study, just rubbing an infant's legs while the child gazed at the still face of the mother reduced the infant's distress. In another study, an adult's rubbing the infant's legs while smiling and cooing increased the infant's eye contact more than did smiling and cooing alone.

Coaching also improved the interaction between mothers and children. Withdrawn, depressed mothers were encouraged to keep their infants' attention. When mothers played more games and had more positive facial expressions, their babies responded with more activity and more positive moods. Depressed mothers who were intrusive and overstimulating were thought to be more effective when they imitated their infants' behavior. Imitating babies seemed to slow mothers' responses, enabling them to react more appropriately to their infants.

Interventions that seek to change depressed mothers' lifestyles have also helped decrease depression. Becoming more active and returning to school or work improves mothers' interactions with their babies; they are less negative than depressed mothers who remain at home. In one study, mothers who were encouraged to return to school where infants were cared for in a center improved in mood and positive interactions with their infants. While there, infants received optimal stimulation and regulation of moods for significant periods of time during the day and related to their mothers better.

Substance-Abusing Parents

Although systematic research has not yet detailed the specific ways in which substance abuse affects parent-child interactions, we can make general observations on how parents' substance abuse affects children. It is difficult, however, to disentangle the effects of the substance abuse itself from the effects of the preexisting psychological and social problems of the parents and the poor living conditions that often accompany substance abuse once the child is born.

Substance abuse is associated with pregnancy and birth complications. Compared with nonabusers, pregnant women who abuse substances are less likely to be in good health and less likely to seek prenatal care, compounding potential problems with pregnancy and delivery. Their babies may be born prematurely and be small for their gestational age. Substance abuse during pregnancy affects children's prenatal development directly and can lead to fetal damage and to on-going health problems after birth.[95]

Infants born to heroin and morphine addicts are themselves addicted, further complicating the process of nurturing these children. Preliminary research indicates that these children are more likely to have impairments in arousal, activity level, attention modulation, and motor and cognitive development. The kind and severity of impairment depends on the type, amount, and timing of the substance abuse during pregnancy.[96]

Fetal alcohol syndrome (FAS) exemplifies the kind of damage a substance, even a legal one, can do. FAS is a congenital condition acquired by some children of alcoholic mothers. These babies are stunted in growth and development and are hyperactive. Their faces are often deformed, with asymmetrical features, low-set eyes, and small ears, and their intellectual growth is retarded. Worst of all, the damage is not reversible. When FAS was first identified, experts believed that a steady, daily consumption of 3 to 6 ounces of alcohol by the mother was necessary to produce abnormalities. More recent research suggests that smaller doses have been related to such problems as low birth weight, sucking difficulties, and developmental delays.

Observational studies of substance-abusing mothers and their infants indicate that these mothers are more negative and are at times more withdrawn but at other times more interfering and directive than are non-substance-abusing mothers.[97] They have difficulty being sensitive, responsive caregivers. Insecure attachments are more likely between substance-abusing mothers and their infants and toddlers than between non-substance-abusing mothers and their children. Similarly, alcoholic fathers are more negative in interactions with their one-year-olds and more directive than fathers who have few or no problems with alcohol.[98]

Parents' substance abuse can not only produce long-lasting physical and intellectual impairments in children but also put them at risk for other problems.[99] Parents who abuse substances are more prone to violence—toward both adults and children. They are more likely to physically or sexually abuse, neglect, or abandon their children. Even if their behavior is not that extreme, they have more angry arguments in their families; high levels of anger, as noted in Chapter 4, are damaging to children.

Programs to help parents eliminate substance abuse must pay attention to the needs of the children of these parents as well.[100] First, drug-exposed infants with vulnerability to stress may be especially affected by parents' chaotic living arrangements. Effort must be directed to helping these parents establish stable and nonviolent households. Second, because their arousal and regulatory systems are altered, these children need help on a continuing basis. They experience difficulties as they enter group situations and the demanding environment of school. More information is needed on the medications and educational interventions that would help such children. Third, psychological assistance must be available to parents and children on an ongoing basis to help them cope with a variety of everyday problems that their circumstances compound. Children of substance-abusing parents face an increased risk of developing mood problems as well as substance-abuse problems. Mental health professionals, however, must be aware of the complicated interactions of biological, genetic, and environmental factors in order to break "the continued cycle of substance use, poverty, and environmental chaos that so often tracks the lives of so many children from substance-using homes."[101]

Non-substance-abusing adults who grew up in a home where a parent was a substance abuser tend to have difficulties as a parent. Philip Cowan and Carolyn Cowan report that, to their surprise, 20 percent of the parents in their study of couples becoming parents grew up with an alcoholic parent. Although none reported current problems with alcohol, "on *every* index of adjustment to parenthood—symptoms of depression, self-esteem, parenting stress, role dissatisfaction, and decline in satisfaction with marriage—men and women whose parents had abused alcohol had significantly greater difficulty."[102]

Even more distressing was the generational legacy of the children (the grandchildren of the alcoholics) in their study. Parents saw their preschoolers as less successful, though objective measures suggested that these children functioned as well as others. "This suggests that parents who grow up with troubled and ineffective parenting develop unrealistic expectations . . . of their children, and as a result, have difficulty seeing their children's behavior in a positive light."[103] (In Chapter 15, we look at how parents have dealt with growing up in abusive homes.)

A PRACTICAL QUESTION: HOW DO PARENTS MANAGE WHEN CHILDREN ARE BORN PREMATURELY?

A news article reported that, in 2001, one of every eight children was born prematurely, defined as less than thirty-seven weeks' gestation, and one in twelve was born "dangerously little."[104] This is the highest rate of premature births in the twenty years of record keeping. The cause is thought to be the increasing use of fertility drugs, which tend to produce multiple births, which are in turn more likely to be delivered prematurely.

The term *premature* covers a wide variety of newborns—from the child born at thirty-five weeks gestation who weighs five pounds and can go home in a few days to the low-birth-weight babies weighing between three pounds, five ounces and five pounds, eight ounces, and the very low birth weight babies weighing less than three pounds, five ounces. The outcomes for premature births depend on the degree of prematurity, medical problems at birth, and health status of the child in the course of early development.[105]

In the previous chapter, we discussed the experiences of most parents at birth and in the hospital; here, we discuss the special challenges caregivers face when they have had a premature baby. For example, caregivers need to remember that, in at least the first two years of life, the child's age should be measured from the time of the due date, not the actual date of birth.

Premature babies lack the special "baby" features that draw adults to them—the big heads, broad cheeks, flattened nose, and large eyes.[106] They may make little noise initially, because they may lack the strength to cry; when they do cry, their cries differ from those of healthy babies and are quite arousing. Parents also miss the pleasure of babies' smiles, because smiles appear approximately six weeks after the due date and therefore can occur months after the premature baby is born.

INTERVIEW
with Anneliese Korner

Anneliese F. Korner is emeritus professor of psychiatry and the behavioral sciences research at Stanford University School of Medicine. She has studied infant development for the last forty years and in the last seven has collected data and developed a test, the Neurobehavioral Assessment of the Pre-term Infant. This test assesses a premature baby's progress in the early weeks of life.

You have done research with infants, particularly premature infants, for many years. What would you say are the important things for parents to do that will be helpful for their premature child?

To hang in there! One of the things that many, many studies have shown, not mine because I do not follow the infants beyond the hospital, is that when preemies go home, they usually are not as rewarding to parents, in the sense that they get easily disorganized with too much stimulation, and they are not as responsive as full-term babies. Particularly if a mother has already had a full-term baby, she will find that the preemie whom she is bringing home, who may have been very sick, may not give her the rewards that a full-term would. Sometimes parents begin to feel rejected, and a vicious cycle is set up. The less the baby responds, the more the mother tries; she overstimulates the child further, and the baby turns away even more. It takes sometimes as much as five to eight months for a baby to become more responsive; by that time many parents have become rather discouraged. It is exactly at that time when they really should be responding to the baby. One can't blame them because they have had this history of trying so hard and not getting anywhere and feeling discouraged. Kathy Barnard, for example, has said this is when parents need help. They are turned off, unrewarded, and the baby really needs them at that age, so parents need encouragement to get reinvolved.

Can a parent spoil a child with a lot of picking up?

Certainly not in the early months. In the early months, the parents are a shield for the baby, and certainly if the baby is very uncomfortable, restless, or is crying, the idea of picking him up also gives him the feeling of being able to have an effect on people. He's not spinning his wheels; he's trying to communicate, and he is successful. One hears less about spoiling babies these days.

One of the most important things for a relationship is to enjoy each other. It is infinitely more important than pushing a child to achieve. In other words, there is so much richness in the parent's responding with joy to what a baby does and in the normal give-and-take that is part of the early relationships that the interchange is a rich source of stimulation and gratification for both participants. A mother is an infinitely complicated stimulus for a baby. Enjoying the child, being reciprocal, just being there, is what it is all about.

In addition, parenting a "preemie" is more demanding, both physically and emotionally.[107] Because preterm babies left the protective womb early, their systems are not ready for the level of stimulation they have encountered in the world, especially the world of the intensive care unit. They may be unresponsive much of the time, or they may react intensely to stimuli full-term babies can absorb. So, parents have a very narrow range of behaviors that will be intense enough to stimulate but not overwhelm the baby. Thus, clinicians have described the premature baby as "more work and less fun" than full-term babies.[108]

Both mothers and fathers naturally adapt their behaviors to meet preterm babies' needs. Compared with other parents, they are more active in holding and touching babies, directing their attention. They may appear to be overstimulating as they try to compensate for their child's special needs. Over time, preterm babies come to resemble full-term babies in their development, but mothers of preterm babies may use different strategies to achieve these ends. For example, they may hold babies more to encourage mutual gaze and responsiveness, because preterm babies respond with more gazing when being held. Despite all the differences in early experiences and early parent-child interactions, preterm babies are as securely attached to parents at twelve and eighteen months as are full-term babies.[109]

Looking at preterm infants' cognitive development over time and the supports that facilitate it emphasizes the powerful effect of the mother's attitude on the baby's growth. Attitudes that mothers of full-term babies had about themselves, their babies, and their husbands were only moderately related to their babies' growth, but in the preterm sample, mothers' attitudes were very strongly related to the baby's progress.[110] When mothers in this sample felt that their role was important and that they were doing a good job, and when they felt positively about the baby, their husband, and life in general, their babies developed well. Parents' responsiveness and social stimulation are related to children's academic and social success through young adulthood.[111]

Parents of premature babies need to understand their strong and important role and the child's capacity for healthy growth, for our culture seems to hold subtle negative beliefs about preterms. When mothers were told an unfamiliar six-month-old baby was premature, they were more likely to rate the child as smaller, less cute, and less likable, even when the child was actually full term.[112] In brief interactions, they touched the child less and offered a more immature toy for play. What is startling is that the babies' behavior changed with these women, and they became less active. College students watching videos of the interactions could tell immediately whether the child was described as full term or preterm.

This negative view of premature babies may not affect the parents directly, because they are influenced by their daily contact with the child. Such stereotypes, however, may influence friends and relatives of the parents, who in turn affect the parents.[113] Mothers who do well tend to adopt and nurture an optimistic attitude about the long-term outcome for the child. Professional support that discusses possible difficulties and coping strategies is at times disruptive for these mothers, although such help is useful to women who feel under stress with their infants.[114]

Because preemie babies start life with special problems, parental overprotectiveness is not unusual in the first several months, as the child grows and becomes stronger. If overprotectiveness persists after the first year or exceeds what the pediatrician considers reasonable, however, parents have developed a problem. Parents must learn to grit their teeth and let their initially vulnerable babies take a few tumbles and some hurts. Giving children freedom to grow also gives parents free time to spend with each other. Sometimes they may choose to get a baby-sitter and go out. This is important. As we have discussed in Chapter 6, parents must make time to nourish the marital relationship if they are to develop a close, satisfying family life.

Many programs help mothers of preterm babies in the first three years of life. Multifaceted interventions working with mothers and children at home and in centers over a three-year period increase cognitive and behavioral functioning more effectively than do programs giving only medical care and routine services for parents.[115] Although differences in children's behavior resulting from participation in these programs disappear at ages five and eight, it is clear that added services can promote preterm babies' development and would likely continue to do so if programs were extended into the preschool and elementary school years.

Of course, all parents face certain transitions as they raise their children. The next two sections discuss the main stages of such transitions and the types of programs that can help parents through them.

PARENTS' EXPERIENCES IN FACING TRANSITIONS

As we saw in Chapter 6, when parents move from the image-making stage of pregnancy to the nurturing stage of infancy,[116] they must adjust the images they created of their anticipated baby and of themselves as parents to the reality of their infant and their actual skill in caring for the baby. When expectations have been unrealistic, adjustments are painful. At the end of Chapter 6, suggestions for easing the transition to parenthood emphasized parents' need for support and self-care while they focus on meeting infants' needs for physical care and nurturing.

Parents of toddlers face another transition—to Galinsky's authority stage (see Chapter 6). This lasts from the child's second to fourth or fifth year. In dealing with their own feelings about having power, setting rules, and enforcing them, parents have to decide what is reasonable when children mobilize all their energy to oppose them and gain their way. In the nurturing stage, parents were primarily concerned with meeting babies' needs and coordinating their own with caregiving activities. Usually, the appropriate child-care behavior was clear—the baby had to be fed, changed, bathed, and put to bed. Although judgment was required in deciding about letting the child cry or timing sleep patterns, still the desired aim was clear.

In the authority stage, parents must develop clear rules and have the confidence not only to enforce them but also to deal with the tantrums that follow. Parents require self-assurance so they can act calmly and neutrally when they meet with opposition from their children.

SUPPORT FOR PARENTS

Parents have undertaken the most demanding and time-consuming job of their lives. However, they receive only the support and education that families provide on an informal basis and professionals offer in pregnancy and birth classes. In our contemporary society, with fewer intact families and more working grandmothers, the vast majority of parents need more help. The middle-class couples in the Cowans' study described in Chapter 6 benefited from an ongoing parents' group. Many new parents with resources find that "doulas," or pregnancy and childbirth companions, provide vital help and information. They sensitize parents to their children's needs and to effective responses.[117]

Many programs are available for parents who face special challenges or have few resources. We saw a sampling of these in the discussion of teen and depressed parents and parents of premature children. The Yale Child Study Center has organized a broad array of programs for parents and their children from birth to the early school-age years.[118] These interdisciplinary programs serve as models for presenting services that can benefit all families. They offer parent groups and professional consultations on parenting. Home visit interventions help parents attend to the physical and emotional needs of children. Special services exist for groups with particular problems, such as parents with a history of infant loss.

All these programs enable parents to learn effective responses for their particular child and contribute to parents' feelings of competency and parental self-efficacy, defined as the belief that one can perform appropriate parental behaviors and influence the child's development.[119] Parental self-efficacy is positively related to parents' satisfaction in the parenting role and to the quality of care parents give children. It also serves as a buffer against stressful factors in the social environment and in the child's development. When difficulties arise, parents believe their behaviors make a difference, and they act. As we saw with the parents of premature children, their actions trigger a self-fulfilling prophecy. Parents who thought their actions were important were socially stimulating and responsive, and their behaviors predicted later academic and social success for their children.

MAIN POINTS

In the first two years, infants

- gain control over their bodies and learn to sit alone, stand, walk, and run
- take a lively interest in the world around them, reaching out to grasp and explore objects and the world
- develop language gradually from cooing, babbling in the early months, to words at one year and the two-word sentence by age two
- develop a wide range of emotional reactions; at the end of the first year, they express anger, fear, joy, pleasure, curiosity, and surprise, and by the end of the second year, they show more affection, more eagerness to please, greater resistance to parents' directives, and great delight in their accomplishments

Successful parents

- are nurturant, material, social, and didactic caregivers
- are available, attentive, sensitive partners who synchronize their behavior with the child's individual needs

- soothe babies and help them regulate their physiological states
- form enduring attachments with their children
- stimulate development when they play and converse with children
- interact with infants in different ways, with mothers holding babies more and doing more caregiving and fathers being more playful and physically stimulating

Parents regulate children's behavior effectively when they

- establish an atmosphere of mutual understanding
- act to prevent problems
- introduce safety rules before other rules
- use low-power techniques such as reasoning and explanation when non-compliance occurs

Parents likely to have trouble establishing secure attachments with infants

- have a negative, critical approach to children because they are teens, are depressed, or abuse substances
- have difficulty effectively timing responses to children, either withdrawing or overstimulating them
- can be helped with interventions that provide education, opportunities for the parent to get to know the child, and support

Preterm babies

- make special physical and psychological demands on parents
- have a narrow range of optimal stimulation that is neither over- nor under-stimulating
- receive long-term benefits from parents' attention and stimulation

As they incorporate infants into family life, parents

- often do not anticipate the stress produced by the number of changes needed
- seek support from each other and their social network
- experience many joys

EXERCISES

1. Recalling the father's comment on page 248 that he knew so little about babies that he should not have been permitted to take one home from the hospital, work in small groups to devise an exam for new parents. Compare suggestions among the different groups.

2. Go to a toy store and spend an imaginary $150 on toys for an infant or toddler. Justify your choices.

3. Go to a supermarket or a park on a weekend, and observe parents and infants or parents and toddlers. Note how the children respond to the environment

around them, to parents, and to passersby. Try to find children about the same age to see how individual differences among children determine responses to the same environment. Observe parenting behaviors, and describe their effects on the children.

4. Go to local hospitals and agencies to determine what kinds of instruction or hands-on training is given to parents to provide safe environments for infants and toddlers.

5. Interview mothers or fathers about how much time they spend with their infants and toddlers each day. What is the family schedule? Who does what? What do they most enjoy doing with their young child? What do they see as the greatest joys and stresses of having children?

ADDITIONAL READINGS

Bing, Elizabeth, and Colman, Libby. *Laughter and Tears: The Emotional Lives of New Mothers.* New York: Holt, 1997.

Brazelton, T. Berry, and Greenspan, Stanley I. *The Irreducible Needs of Children.* Cambridge, MA: Perseus, 2000.

Karp, Harvey. *The Happiest Baby on the Block.* New York: Bantam, 2002.

Levine, James, with Pitt, Edward W. *New Expectations: Community Strategies for Responsible Fatherhood.* New York: Families and Work Institute, 1995.

Saarni, Carolyn. *The Development of Emotional Competence.* New York: Guilford, 1999.

C H A P T E R

8

Parenting in Early Childhood: The Years from Two to Five

CHAPTER TOPICS	IN THE NEWS

CHAPTER TOPICS

In this chapter, you will learn about:

- Children's development
- Relationships with parents, siblings, and peers
- Managing sleep, aggression, withdrawal, with developmental delays
- Parents' experiences and supports

IN THE NEWS

New York Times, April 4[1]: Brothers and sisters of children with special needs also have special needs. See pages 303–304.

Test Your Knowledge: Fact or Fiction?

1. Poverty not only reduces physical resources like books and toys in the home, but also affects the amount of positive attention poor children receive.
2. Between 10 and 30 percent of children are thought to be sleep-deprived.
3. To help children manage aggressive feelings, parents are advised to avoid anger and punishment and use positive parenting instead.
4. The moment with the most potential for causing emotional trauma for a child with special needs is when the child realizes that society views his or her differences as signs of inferiority.
5. Parent-child interactions account for about 70 percent of the emotional distress preschoolers experience at home.

How does parenting change in these years? Does parenting become easier as children's skills and competence increase? How do parents support children's growing sense of self and help children relate to peers and others outside the home? Where do parents get support as they raise their children?

The years from two to five are exciting. By age two, children have learned the basic skills of walking and talking, and have gained a sense of personal identity and a greater understanding of others' needs and feelings. In the years from two to five, they develop all these skills further. Their thinking becomes more complex, allowing them to consider others' wishes and act in positive ways to help them. They have greater self-control and relate to people and the world around them in more complex ways.

PHYSICAL DEVELOPMENT

Between ages two and five, children grow more slowly than before. However, they grow rapidly enough—from about 34 inches and 29 pounds at age two to 42 inches and 42 to 45 pounds at age five. The brains of these children are active and primed for learning. Compared with an adult brain, the brain of a three-year-old has twice as many synapses (connections) among brain cells and is two and a half times more active, requiring more glucose and having more neurotransmitters (chemicals that facilitate the transmission of information from one cell to another). When young children reach puberty, they will begin to get rid of old, little-needed connections in a process called *pruning,* and the number of synaptic connections is reduced to that found in adult brains.[2] Brain development helps the child control voluntary movements and increases alertness and memory, which in turn underlie observable advances in motor, cognitive, and personal-social functioning.

INTELLECTUAL DEVELOPMENT

Greater motor coordination enables children at this age to interact with objects in the environment in more complex ways than were possible at a younger age. Increased attention span allows the child to pursue activities for a longer time, and increased memory enables her to recall more-detailed sequences.

Thinking becomes more complex. Children can distinguish real events from imagined ones and from dreams and nightmares.[3] Their understanding of people increases.[4] Toddlers understand that others' desires determine their actions, but preschoolers go beyond this and see that others' thoughts often determine both feelings and actions. For example, children learn that, when a parent believes that the child pushed a younger sibling by accident, the parent's feelings and responses differ greatly from those of a parent who thinks the child pushed the sibling on purpose.

LANGUAGE DEVELOPMENT

Children progress from having about 50 words at nineteen months to having 10,000 words at age six, in the first grade, learning an average of 5.5 words per day.[5] The length of sentences grows from 2 words at age two to complex sentences of several words, with clauses.

Parents influence children's acquisition of language, as we saw in discussing social class differences and language in Chapter 3, but Lois Bloom believes that the child initiates conversations and learns not only language from parents' responses

VOICES OF EXPERIENCE

What I Wish I Had Known about the Years from Two to Five

"I wish I'd known how to react when they lied. You know kids lie, but it hurts me terribly. It was a very painful experience even though I know I did it." MOTHER

"I wish I had known how much frustration comes just because kids are kids and you have to be tolerant. They don't have the attention span for some things. They might want to do something with you, but they can only do it for about fifteen minutes. You have to go places prepared with all his things or with things to keep him entertained. In the car on a trip, we have a lot of things for him to do. When you plan ahead, you can still be spontaneous at times. You learn that if you are prepared, things really don't have to be a hassle." FATHER

"Everything. I wish I'd known more about communication, how to talk to your children, and the most effective way to help them grow with a strong ego, a good sense of self. We were raised with a lot of 'Do this and don't do that,' a lot of demanding and dictatorial things as opposed to trying to solicit participation in the process of decision making, trying to get in touch with your child's feelings so you really do understand how they feel about things. That's really hard to learn, and I don't know how you can learn it without the experience of actually having the child. But I'm continually learning how to understand her feelings about things." MOTHER

"I think it is incredible that we don't teach anything about being a parent. I have to learn it as I go along, because I want things to be different for them than they were for me growing up. I can't use my own experiences as a guide." FATHER

"I wish I had known how to handle them so they could be spontaneous and feel good about the things they did. How to be spontaneous with them is one of the hardest things for me." FATHER

"I wish I had known how to handle things like believing in Santa Claus. I didn't know whether to encourage it or not or when to tell her there was none. She learned gradually, I think, but she doesn't want to tell her little brother yet." MOTHER

"[I] wasn't prepared for all the decisions. Is it okay if he does this or not? He's trying to do something; shall I step in so he doesn't hurt himself or shall I let him go? It's making all those choices, making sure what I feel." MOTHER

"There is anxiety, a feeling of vulnerability I have never felt before. If he gets sick, what are we going to do? If he has a little sickness, we just hope the doctor is doing the right thing. We went through a great deal in the past few weeks choosing a nursery school for him, and we hope we have done the right thing, but is this the one for him?" FATHER

"I wish we had—because he is our first child—more of a sense of the norms. What is okay versus what is a problem and what is really bad? Is this normal, is this just kids being kids? He pushed someone at school three times; is this par for the course or is this a problem? We don't know when we are reacting and when we are overreacting." FATHER

but also social rules, others' expectations of him or her, and general guidelines for solving social problems.[6]

EMOTIONAL DEVELOPMENT

Preschoolers' understanding of and expression of feelings grow in breadth and complexity. Preschoolers become increasingly accurate in understanding the connections between feelings and the events and social interactions that produce them. Though they at first believe that feelings are temporary, by the end of the preschool period, they recognize that feelings can persist and are influenced by what one thinks.[7]

Children can accurately identify what triggers emotions, especially when there is a social cause for the feelings. In one study, preschoolers agreed 91 percent of the time with adults in giving reasons for other preschoolers' feelings as they occurred in the course of everyday activity.[8] Preschoolers were most accurate in understanding anger and distress and less accurate in regarding happy and sad reactions.

Even so, because differences exist between preschoolers' and adults' understanding of feelings, parents often do not understand their children's reactions. Preschoolers evaluate events by their outcomes. If wrongdoers successfully achieve their ends, the preschooler assumes that they feel good about that. The preschooler may know an act is wrong but not necessarily feel wrong or bad for doing it.[9] Children of this age are particularly happy to evade punishment while still getting what they want.[10] However, they are highly sensitive to punishment, feeling angry or sad whether the punishment is deserved or not.

Preschoolers' most common form of emotional upset is crying, which accounts for 74 percent of the disruptions at home.[11] Anger represents about 23 percent of these incidents. Parent-child interactions account for 71 percent of the upsets, with sibling conflicts accounting for only 13 percent and peer conflicts for 6 percent of the distress.

Parents' usual response to the distress is not to comfort but to give the child a practical, problem-solving response so that the child can deal with the situation. When parents encourage children to take action with problems, children are better able to plan and are more effective in social activities and other areas.

By age three, children judge their behaviors by internal standards and show pride and pleasure when they meet their standards and are upset and ashamed when they do not.[12] They hide their feelings of disappointment and guilt,[13] with girls more likely than boys to hide the negative feelings.[14]

Anger

As just noted, children continue to battle with parents about daily routines, and peers become a source of frustration as well. Increasing age reduces the outbursts of undirected physical energy and increases purposeful activity to achieve goals. The most competent children handle anger in direct ways that reduce further conflict and maintain social relationships. Boys express their feelings and take no action; girls assert themselves to obtain their wishes.[15]

When children were exposed to strangers' arguing in the next room, three emotional styles of responding to anger were identified.[16] Concerned emotional

The relationships among siblings are emotional, intense, affectionate—and sometimes aggressive. How well siblings get along is partly determined by the parent-child relationship.

responders (46 percent of children) showed negative feelings of upset during the episode and later said they felt sad and wanted to leave when they heard anger. Unresponsive children, who showed no emotional reaction, were only a small percentage of the group (15 percent). They were least likely to respond to aggressiveness in play with friends. Ambivalent responders (35 percent) showed both positive and negative feelings during the anger episode. They were upset, but later said they were happy during the episode. These children were most likely to become physically aggressive in play following the anger episode and were most responsive to aggressiveness in peers. Their behavior accounted for almost all the increased aggressiveness in play following the episode of anger. If these children had been able to handle their ambivalent feelings, they might have had no need to be aggressive.

Fear

Fears are a natural part of life as children grow up. In the early years of infancy, fears of noise, loss of support, and strangers are most evident, but these anxieties gradually fade. In the preschool years, children experience fears of animals, the dark, harm from imaginary creatures, and natural disasters such as fires and storms. Anxiety and fear in response to unfamiliar people and strange situations may result from temperamental qualities. Some individuals demonstrate marked physiological excitability when confronted with the unfamiliar.[17] Such excitability is identified in infancy and manifests itself in inhibited, avoidant behavior that persists through the toddler and preschool years.[18] As the child becomes familiar with the person or place in question, fear of the unknown sometimes dissipates. Still, many inhibited children play less freely with peers at home and in alternative care settings. They have difficulty in taking turns and in engaging in fantasy play. As we saw in Chapter 1, by not rewarding the overreactivity and by providing structure for their child, parents can help the child overcome these reactions.

Realistic concerns about dangers such as falling out of a tree and hurting oneself can motivate the child to be cautious when appropriate. Intense fears, however, can prevent the child from exploring the world and interacting with other people. Research suggests further that intense fears at this time have a long-term impact: Preschool boys who experienced intense fears of bodily harm were, as adults, anxious about sexuality, uninvolved with traditional masculine activities, and concerned with intellectual performance.[19]

Empathy

Children's ability to respond sensitively to others' needs increases as they grow. Preschoolers appear more able than toddlers to adopt the perspective of the other person and respond to him or her. Because preschoolers are better able to understand the sources of emotional reactions, their strategies for helping go more directly to the source of the problem. When another child is angry, they are likely to give some material thing to the child or share with him or her.[20] When another child is sad or distressed, they are more likely to do something positive for the child, playing with or comforting the child.

Sharing with and giving to friends occurs most frequently in an atmosphere of comfort and optimism. Best friends continue to share when happy, appreciative responses follow. When sharing does not occur but the friend remains happy and smiling, the conflict does not escalate, and sharing resumes.[21]

What qualities in parents stimulate empathy in young children? Children who are kind and helpful in response to the suffering of others have mothers who are warm, caring individuals concerned with the well-being of others. These mothers expect children to control aggression, and when they do not, the mothers show disappointment—"Children are not for hitting," "Stop! You're hurting him." Mothers of empathetic children model kindness, but they go beyond that to teach children how to do what is expected. They maintain high standards and continue a warm, caring relationship with children.[22]

Children also learn empathy from books and stories that have moral themes. Fairy tales, universal favorites of children, present models of kind, caring behavior that triumphs, often after many tribulations, over evil and cruelty.

THE DEVELOPMENT OF THE SELF

In early childhood, children continue to define themselves in terms of their physical characteristics and their actions. While they continue to use concrete descriptions, they are beginning to organize their self-perceptions and see themselves in more general though dichotomous terms such as good or bad, smart or dumb.[23] Most children continue to focus on their positive qualities and see themselves as "all good," but preschoolers who have experienced abuse are more likely than other children to consider themselves as bad.

Children are beginning to evaluate their behavior, as noted earlier, but still they are optimistic in approaching new tasks.[24] They believe that, when they want something, they will be able to achieve it, and they ignore any failures on their way. The reason is not cognitive immaturity, for they can pay attention to others' failures and make realistic predictions about their chances for success. When success matters, they believe they will be able to exert whatever effort is necessary to achieve their ends. As we shall see in later chapters, such optimism is an aid to accomplishment rather than an obstacle to it.

Gender Identity

Babies are born into a gender-typed world. In the days prior to routine ultrasounds during pregnancy, the baby's sex was usually the first fact known about a baby after birth. Today, however, the fetus's sex is often the first fact known during the pregnancy. Once delivered, babies enter an environment in which gender shapes the furniture, colors, clothing, and toys available for the child. Parents often select dolls and pink bedding and clothing for girls and sports equipment, vehicles, and blue clothing for boys.[25] Adults perceive babies identified as boys as tough and sturdy and the same babies identified as girls as frail and sweet.[26]

An important part of one's self concept is *gender identity,* defined as an individual's personal experience of what it means to be a boy or girl, man or woman.[27] Physical, social, and psychological factors contribute to gender differentiation. Physical factors include genes, which, in turn, trigger hormones that lead to the development of internal and external sexual characteristics and also influence behavior.[28] Societies and their subcultures transmit beliefs about what is appropriate for boys and girls through prescriptions of child rearing, and parents contribute their influence as well. Gender identity, however, "is not simply something imposed on children; at all points of development, children are actively constructing for themselves what it means to be female or male."[29]

From infancy, the child begins to evolve a sense of gender differences.[30] At seven months, infants respond differently to the voices of men and women; by nine months, they respond differently to men's and women's faces. By one year, infants can link men's voices with men's faces and women's voices with women's faces. In this way, they begin to develop a sense of gender categories.

Perhaps without realizing it, parents begin gender-typing behavior by responding in emotionally positive ways to the child's appropriate gender-stereotyped activities and choices.[31] For example, they often encourage boys to manipulate objects and explore the world and discourage them from expressing feelings and asking for help. Parents encourage girls to ask for help and to help with tasks. Through parents' emotional responses, children learn the appropriate gender labels and begin to develop a gender schema.

A *gender schema* is an organized body of knowledge of what it means to be a boy or girl. By age two, toddlers have learned to label men, women, boys, and girls and have begun to associate gender labels with objects, activities, tasks, and roles. Twenty-five-month-old boys, for example, are more likely to recall and imitate gender-related activities like shaving a teddy bear than an activity associated with women—namely, diapering a teddy.[32] Toddlers also indicate awareness of gender-appropriate toys and activities. In the preschool years, they take pride in playing with gender-appropriate toys and feel self-critical when they do not.

Between two and two and a half, children identify their own gender and proudly announce, "I am a boy" or "I am a girl."[33] They gradually learn that gender is stable across time—they will always be male or female. They also learn that gender persists in different situations—a girl remains a girl whether she has short or long hair, wears pants or a dress, drives a truck or takes care of a baby. Children learn first about their own gender and then about the other. Generally, girls have greater gender knowledge than do boys, but they are less tied to stereotyped play than are boys. Because children appear most prone to gender stereotyping while they are in the process of learning, stereotyped activity tends to peak in the preschool years.

By age three, boys and girls agree on the roles for boys and girls, men and women. They also see that both sexes have a common core of positive qualities.[34] Both boys and girls are strong, kind, unafraid, messy, dirty, smart, and quiet. They hold positive beliefs about their own sex, valuing the qualities associated with being a boy or a girl.

Up to about eighteen months of age, boys and girls show no differences in such behaviors as aggressiveness, toy play, large motor activity, and communication attempts, all of which exhibit gender differences in the next year.[35] Beginning at age two, boys prefer active pursuits and building activities, and girls prefer arts and crafts and reading. In the third year, boys and girls begin to play in same-gender groups, and this continues into the school years.

On average, boys tend to be more active and aggressive than girls. Girls are found to be more helpful and sometimes more fearful. Caroline Zahn-Waxler refers to the gender issues in problem behaviors as the problems of the warriors and the worriers.[36] We discuss parents' behavior in encouraging gender differences in children's behavior in a later section.

Ethnic Identity

Ethnic identity begins to be laid down in the preschool years, when children first learn to identify themselves as members of an ethnic group. They initially use skin color as a marker. In one study, African American and Native American preschoolers could correctly identify pictures of their racial groups, but when shown dolls, they preferred and identified with white dolls. Although these same children measured high in self-esteem, researchers speculated that their preference for white dolls showed they knew that white figures are preferred and, feeling good about themselves, chose white dolls.[37]

As they proceed through these early years and on into school, children gradually learn what is distinctive about their own ethnic group. Ethnic identity becomes more firmly established by age seven, when children of different groups realize they cannot change their ethnic identities.[38] We discuss ethnic identity formation in greater detail in Chapters 9 and 10.

THE DEVELOPMENT OF SELF-REGULATION

A two-year-old cannot wait or delay action well and is less flexible in adapting behavior to the social situation than is a three-year-old.[39] Even though children understand routines and rules, any strong stimulus can tempt them to forbidden behavior—a two-year-old, for example, may run into the street to pursue a prized ball.

Overall compliance appears to increase up to thirty months; after that, children increasingly can comply without help from parents. Still, by age four, parents remind or guide about 40 percent of the time.[40]

Although resistance to parents' requests continues for years, children of different ages adopt varying strategies for expressing their resistance.[41] Initially, toddlers rely on direct, often angry, defiance and passive noncompliance. These methods decrease somewhat with age as toddlers develop more skill in bargaining and negotiating. Despite a change in resistant strategies as the child ages, children's general choice of behavior tends to remain stable. Those children who use the most unskilled forms of resistance as toddlers use the most unskilled forms as five-year-olds. Those who use simple refusal and negotiating as toddlers are most likely to use bargaining at age five.

Children often adopt similar methods in resisting parents and in influencing them to get their own way. Children who use outright defiance to resist parents use forceful methods, such as demanding and whining, to get what they want. Children who resist by bargaining and negotiating use persuasion to influence parents.

Defiance occurs most frequently when parents use high-power strategies such as commands, criticisms, threats, and physical punishments to control children's behavior. Suggestions and guidance in the form of explaining, persuading, directing, and verbally assisting the child to do what is wanted all increase compliance. Giving feedback about difficulties is also helpful.[42] Verbal methods make requests clear to the child. When children understand what is wanted, compliance is high; noncompliance occurs most frequently when requests are not understood.[43]

Positive feelings increase children's compliance. In one study, mothers were trained to play with children for ten to fifteen minutes per day for a week in a nondirective, responsive manner—following the child's lead, when possible being a partner in the play, avoiding comments and questions.[44] In the laboratory, the children had more positive moods after playing in this way with mothers than did children whose mothers received no special play instructions.

In another part of the same study, when children were instructed to recall a happy, positive mood for fifteen seconds, they were more compliant in picking up blocks than were children who were instructed to recall a negative mood such as anger or fear for fifteen seconds. Although we cannot conclude from this study that responsive play leads directly to compliance—as the differences in positive mood between the two groups of children were not significant after a week of play—we can say that responsive play leads to pleasurable feelings and that a pleasurable, good mood leads to compliance.

SOCIAL DEVELOPMENT

Social development in preschoolers involves interactions with parents, siblings, and peers. Here, we look at all three in turn.

Parent-Child Relationships

As children grow, verbal interactions play an increasingly important role in parents' interventions to promote close relationships and to help children learn to regulate their behavior.

Ross Parke and Raymond Buriel believe that parents meet role expectations and socialize children in three ways: (1) as an interactive partner with the child, (2) as a direct instructor, and (3) as a provider of activities and opportunities that stimulate children's growth.[45] These three ways involve direct and indirect socialization. Parents directly model and teach children such behaviors as kindness, consideration, and emotional regulation. Parents also provide an indirect influence when they encourage children's interests and activities. Let us look at parents' activities in terms of these three roles.

Attachment   Parents are interactive partners, providing sensitive, involved, flexible parenting to maintain the attachment that supports children's sense of security and their trusting relationships with other people. Although attachment quality in the first two years influences preschool attachment, preschoolers' present circumstances and the quality of the current relationship are what most influence preschoolers' sense of security and social adaptation.[46]

Socializing Gender Roles   Socializing boys' and girls' gender roles illustrates Parke and Buriel's three forms of parental influence. First, parents model gender behaviors in their direct interactions with children.[47] Mothers carry out more caregiving activities and are more nurturant in everyday activities; fathers are often more direct and assertive. These behaviors occur in casual interactions as well as in caretaking activities. In an observational study of parents' and preschoolers' play together, mothers were more affiliative and supportive in playing with trucks than were fathers, who were more assertive and direct than mothers. These differences were seen in European American and Latina/o parents and in parents of multiethnic backgrounds.[48]

As interactive partners, parents may stimulate gender-stereotyped behavior indirectly when they respond to boys and girls differently. Although mothers and fathers treat boys and girls alike in many ways—they are equally attached to sons and daughters and use authoritative strategies with both[49]—they also reveal subtle differences in how they respond to boys and girls.[50] For example, mothers are more responsive to irritable infant sons than daughters; they talk more to daughters than to sons and use more supportive speech. Such differences in behavior may indirectly reinforce the gender-related behaviors of assertiveness in boys and verbal skills in girls.

Second, as educators, parents teach children directly about gender-appropriate behaviors. When given a truck to play with, one little girl commented, "My mommy would want me to play with this, but I don't want to."[51] So such teaching does not always succeed.

Third, and most important, parents teach children gender-appropriate behavior through their encouragement of different activities and interests.[52] Until recently, boys were encouraged to be more active in sports than were girls, and such activities were thought to build boys' skills in teamwork and cooperation. When girls were highly active like boys, they received more negative responses from adults. Today, both boys and girls receive more encouragement for physical activity.

Children receive similar socialization from peers and teachers in school. As noted earlier, peers beyond the age of two or three spend their playtime in same-gender groups, and their interactions there may have a strong influence on gender-related behaviors.

Parents' Stimulation of Children's Competence   Parents provide homes, objects, activities, and interactions that facilitate growth in competent functioning in all areas. Using data from the National Longitudinal Survey of Youth (NLSY), a national sample of families in which ethnic groups were oversampled to obtain data on these groups, Robert Bradley and his coworkers described the homes and daily routines of children from birth to age fourteen in four ethnic groups (European American, African American, Latina/o, and Asian American).[53] They noted the poverty and nonpoverty status of the family as well.

The findings reveal great diversity in the home environments and activities that parents provide for children. The overriding influence on home environment is poverty status. Regardless of ethnic group, poverty reduced not only the physical objects such as books, tape recorders, and musical instruments available to children, but also—and more profoundly—the quality of parent-child interactions in *all* ethnic groups at *all* ages. For example, poor children were less likely to be hugged and kissed, less likely to be spoken to, and more likely to be spanked than were nonpoor children. Poverty status affected 88 percent of the variables used to describe the homes.

Parents vary stimulation depending on their children's age. Parents are more likely to kiss and hug infants than older children. They are more likely to respond to the attention bids of preschoolers than children of other ages. Younger children are less likely to be taken places like museums than are children over six.

Stimulation of learning in the family—as measured by such things as the number of books available for children; access to tape recorders, musical instruments, lessons, and sports activities; and encouragement of hobbies—predicted motor and social competence, language development, and academic achievement of children in three ethnic groups—European Americans, African Americans, and Latinas/os.[54] (Asian Americans were not included, because their numbers were too few for statistical purposes.) These results were found for almost all age groups and for poor and nonpoor children alike.

Interestingly, learning stimulation was related to a greater number of children's problem behaviors from early childhood to adolescence in the three ethnic groups, as reported by mothers. Possibly, mothers who stimulate learning are quick to note and report children's problem behaviors as they would like to change those behaviors. Also, the pressure to learn may produce stress for children, causing them to act out.

In addition to providing books and activities that stimulate learning and competence, parents also stimulate growth when they play with children. In these years, parents engage in two forms of play—interactional play and object play.[55] Initially, parents structure and facilitate the play, but they give children an ever-larger role. In the preschool years, children become the primary initiators and directors. Interactional play includes the rough and tumble play that fathers and children enjoy. Families in the United States engage in such play more than do families in other countries. It peaks when children are one to four and, for boys, is related to social competence and popularity with peers in the preschool years. Such play, however, is related to abrasive peer relationships for girls. Interactional and object play involve more verbal interactions and more symbolic pretend play as children grow older. In pretend play, children learn the routines of everyday life; as in earlier years, parents emphasize turn-taking and other kinds of reciprocity.

Both forms of play help children develop emotional, social, verbal, and intellectual skills. For example, for children between twenty-one months and four years of age, symbolic play with mothers predicted social skills at five and a half years.

The Processes of Mutual Responsiveness and of Coercion   In previous chapters, we described the importance of *reciprocity,* mutually rewarding interactions between parent and child, which plays a fundamental role in socializing the child and helping the child to internalize the family's values and standards of behavior. Studies of mothers and their children between ages two and five indicate that a system of reciprocity consists of two primary components: (1) cooperation between mother and child and (2) positive emotional tone in the mother-child interactions.[56]

Claire Kopp, who has extensively studied the development of self-regulation, emphasizes the important role of love for parents. She writes,

> Where does self-control come from? It comes from a desire to be part of a social order, a desire to have love and affection. Children do not follow rules because they think the rules are wonderful. Children are not like that. They want love and affection, and they see that by following the rules, they get love and positive reinforcement. I am concerned about children being in a situation where they are not rewarded for following the rules, where they are not given reasons for rules, and where they do not get techniques or strategies that help them develop cognitive understanding of the rules.[57]

Gerald Patterson describes the kind of process Kopp worries about.[58] He details a process of coercion that begins early in life and has consequences for the parent-child relationship and the child's behavior over time. This process is almost the mirror image of mutual reward and illustrates what happens when parents are negative and give little or no positive reinforcement for following the rules.

Like mutual responsiveness, the process of coercion begins with the interactions between mother or caregiver and infant. Either partner can start the process, and both keep it going. Typically, the infant is irritable and fussy, and the mother, for whatever reasons, is negative and unpredictable in her response. That increases the infant's irritability. The infant comes to see the world as an unrewarding, unsupportive, and unpredictable place. Or the mother may be depressed and pay little attention to the infant, who then becomes irritable and negative and triggers further negativity on the mother's part.

Patterson and his coworkers have taught parents to use consistent, positive rewards to modify children's behavior. They believe that parents' use of a supportive, consistent, and positive reinforcement program creates the sensitive, caring relationship between parent and child that attachment theorists advocate. Though they believe that the temperamental qualities of parent and child affect the interactions between the two, they also believe that behavioral interventions can and do modify parents' and children's behavior. Consistent use of negative consequences, such as ignoring, loss of privileges, and time-outs, can reduce the noncompliant behaviors that occur even in the best of parent-child relationships. Like systems theorists, they also identify contextual factors, such as low income and parental divorce, that can intensify the coercive process. A two-year longitudinal study of boys from ages one to three documents the gradual development of this coercive process.[59]

Clearly, coercion can arise in any family, especially when children become preschoolers and gain new skills for noncompliance. The benefits of mutual rewards, however, can last well beyond these years.

Cultural Influences on Parenting   As described in Chapter 3, different cultures emphasize different goals in parenting. Those following the interdependent model want preschoolers to learn to value close and harmonious family relationships and to take their appropriate place in the traditional social hierarchy.[60]

Besides uncovering differences in goals, research has revealed differences in how parents communicate and teach children.[61] Parents following the independent model most often use verbal instructions to influence their preschoolers, who are moving away from them physically. They use verbal praise to encourage approved behaviors and teach verbal self-expression as a means of encouraging curiosity and thinking. Such teaching and encouragement help children in a culture where verbal instruction is such a central part of schooling and education.

Parents stressing the interdependent model rely on empathy and the close parent-child bond to teach the child; they give little verbal instruction, because the child knows through empathy what the parent wants the child to do.[62] Children's learning occurs in an apprenticeship role, in which the child is close to the parent or teacher and gradually takes on the adult's behaviors. Verbal instruction consists of short directives with little encouragement for self-expression.

Relationships with Siblings

Because siblings are usually born within a few years of each other, many young children must deal with the introduction of another child into the family. Parents want their children to love and care for each other. The question is, How do parents promote positive relationships within the family?

Although most firstborn children get upset and often misbehave after a sibling's birth, particularly when the mother is interacting with the baby, the vast majority (82 percent) of two- to four-year-old firstborns have positive feelings about being a brother or sister. At the end of the first year, 63 percent reported wanting another sibling.[63]

Parents use various strategies to integrate a new child into the family.[64] In some families, fathers attend to the needs of the firstborn, and mothers care for the newborn; in others, the father takes on more household tasks, leaving the mother time to care for both children; and in still others, both parents do all tasks. When parents are warm and responsive with both children and have secure attachments to each child, the children tend to get along with each other. When parents have a positive relationship with each other, less sibling conflict usually arises. Conversely, when parents have more conflict with each other or when parents use physical punishment with children, sibling conflicts increase.

When parents maintain high standards for behavior and have warm and caring relationships with their children, they help young children adopt kind and helpful behavior in response to others' suffering.[65] Parents not only model kindness but also teach children how to do what is expected. For instance, parents expect children to control aggression, and they show disappointment if children do not. They make clear but nonangry comments such as, "Children are not for hitting" or "Stop, you are hurting him."

Though many older siblings feel that mothers favor younger siblings,[66] longitudinal studies of mothers' behavior with their two children when each is one or two reveal that mothers are quite consistent in the amount of affection and verbal responsiveness they direct to each child at that age.[67] Because their behavior toward each child changes as the child grows, one can see a difference in how they treat the two when the two are different ages. Mothers are, however, less consistent in their

INTERVIEW
with Judy Dunn

Judy Dunn is a professor at the Institute of Psychiatry in London.

What are the most important ways to help children have satisfying relationships with brothers and sisters?

It is reassuring for parents to learn how common it is for brothers and sisters not to get on. They fight a great deal. The main variable is the children's personality. This child is one way and that child is another, and they don't get along. They don't have any choice about living together, and so it's easy to see why they don't get on. It is such a no-holds-barred relationship. There are no inhibitions, and both boys and girls can be very aggressive.

It is reassuring for parents to know that fights occur not just in their family. No one really knows what goes on in other families, and so you think it is just in your own. But children can fight a lot and still end up with a close relationship.

When there is the birth of a new sibling, keep the level of attention and affection as high as possible for the firstborn. I think it's almost impossible to give too much attention to the first child at this time.

Also, keep their life as similar as possible [to the way it was before the arrival of the new baby]. Routine things matter a lot to little children. They like predictability. The mother structures their whole world, so that after a baby comes, they can be upset just by any changes Mother makes in their routine.

In middle childhood, there is a strong association between sibling fights and feelings that the other child is favored by the parent or parents. It is important to be aware how early and how sensitive children are to what goes on between parents and children. It is never too early for parents to think about the effects of what they are doing on the other child. So always be aware of how sensitive children are and avoid favoritism.

ways of controlling different children at a given age, probably because they have learned from experience.

Peer Relationships

Two-year-olds play with peers, taking turns and sharing. They form stable relationships that can last beyond a year, and such friendships are important emotional attachments that enable them to adapt more easily to changes at preschool or day care.[68]

Preschoolers engage in more cooperative play and in more fantasy play than do toddlers.[69] They like friends who share their activities, and they want to have fun with minimum friction, so they dislike those who disrupt play.[70] Although friends have as many fights as do casual acquaintances, friends handle them differently, disengaging and finding a solution that gives each partner something equal, whereas casual acquaintances fight until someone wins.[71] The majority of encounters are friendly—in one study, 81 percent—and children return friendly overtures, preferring playmates who reach out to others.[72]

Even in early childhood, some children are more socially skilled than others, as they are outgoing and able to regulate their emotional reactions in peer interactions.[73] Secure attachments to parents help children feel trusting and confident in social relationships, whereas insecure attachments increase children's feelings that others are rejecting and neglectful.[74] Parents' monitoring of young children's social interactions and guiding children to join in and play with others also increase social skills.

TASKS AND CONCERNS OF PARENTS

Parents of children aged two to five face new tasks as well as old. Parenting in this age period includes the following:

- Being a sensitive, responsive caregiver who provides feelings of security to the child
- Balancing acceptance of the child's individuality with control of his or her behavior
- Providing stimulating experiences with toys and people
- Helping children face challenges so they feel successful
- Serving as coach to foster the child's increasing competence in self-control and social relationships
- Helping the child to conform to rules outside the home
- Providing companionship and play

The years from two to five can bring frustration for parents and children in the daily routines of sleeping, eating, and so forth. Problems at home can lead to trouble for the child at school or at day care. This section emphasizes ways to help children maintain self-regulation through getting optimal amounts of sleep, managing temper outbursts and high activity, and reducing sibling rivalries, aggressiveness, and social inhibition.

Sleeping

A *USA Weekend* article begins, "In an on-the-go nation that prides itself on 'getting by' on very little sleep, children are the latest victims of this cultural disinclination toward rest."[75] As we discussed in Chapter 5, sleep serves several important functions.

Sleep problems, as measured by parent report, are high in the preschool years and decrease with age.[76] Still, there is modest stability in problems across time and, even at this young age, sleep problems are related to emotional and behavioral problems and to high activity, so it is important for parents to ensure that children get sufficient sleep. Between eighteen months and three years, children usually need between eleven and thirteen hours per night, and from four to twelve, about ten hours per night.[77] Between 10 and 30 percent of children are thought to be sleep deprived.

Because everyone goes to bed together, parents who practice co-sleeping may have few difficulties getting children to go and to stay there. Still, many parents who co-sleep do not want to go to bed as early as their children, so they may have trouble getting children to bed.

Parents promote good sleep habits by establishing a regular, enjoyable, nighttime ritual that prepares the child for going to bed. It may include a bath, songs, stories, and a brief massage to relax the child. The activities should be restful and relaxing and not stimulating.

Children have to learn to fall asleep in ways they can duplicate in the middle of the night when they awake as we all do. Older infants, toddlers, and preschoolers often develop sleep routines that they cannot duplicate on their own. When they wake up in the night and cannot go back to sleep, they cry, wanting comfort, or, if older, they crawl into their parents' bed for the rest of the night. Parents can change children's sleep associations, if they feel the change is important. Children will be very uncomfortable in the beginning but will gradually learn new associations.

Sleep expert Richard Ferber describes his progressive waiting approach to help children fall and stay asleep.[78] Ferber's approach takes account of the child's feelings and provides emotional support as children develop new sleep habits. Parents should start his method only when they can commit the time to carry out the approach for several nights.

Parents first establish a relaxing bedtime routine. They then put the child to bed at the time the child usually *falls asleep,* to maximize the chance that the child is sleepy. The child is awake and alone in the bedroom. If the child cries, parents wait a specified time and then enter the room to reassure the child that he or she is not being abandoned. Parents can speak to the child for a minute and pat the child but must leave within a minute or two while the child is awake. Parents enter *not* to stop the crying or get the child to sleep but only to reassure the child there is no abandonment.

Each night, the periods of waiting increase on the first, second, and third entries but remain at the third level for subsequent entries. Each night for seven nights, the waiting times for each entry increase. On the first night, for example, parents wait three, five, and ten minutes, and ten minutes for each entry thereafter; the second night, five, ten, and twelve minutes; the third night, ten, twelve, and fifteen minutes, and so on, working up in small increments to twenty, twenty-five, and thirty minutes on the seventh and subsequent nights. Ferber encourages parents to establish briefer wait times if they feel uncomfortable with these times. The important features are that parents increase wait times progressively and carry them out consistently.

If the child wakes during the night, the same method is used again, starting with the minimum time until the child falls asleep. Parents also use the system at nap times, with the modification that if the child has not fallen asleep after thirty minutes, he or she is allowed to get up. Parents do not permit children to make up for lost sleep by sleeping later in the morning or at nap time.

Ferber modifies the method for parents who co-sleep with children. Parents put the child to bed in the same way and enter at similar times to reassure the crying child. In the middle of the night, parents remain unresponsive to the child's requests for patting or playing, even if that means getting out of bed and going to another room, again returning to reassure the child at the designated times.

Many children in the preschool years are afraid to go to bed because of monsters or robbers. Ferber believes such fears reflect anxieties about loss of behavior control around issues such as toilet training, anger regarding siblings, and peer aggression. These anxieties are then expressed as fears of monsters. He urges parents to give the child reassurance.

> She needs to know that nothing bad will happen if she soils, has a temper tantrum, or gets angry at her brother or sister. At such times she can best be reassured by knowing that you are in control of yourself and—to the extent that she needs it—of her, and that you can and will protect her. . . . The monsters are in your child's mind, and it is there you should focus your efforts.[79]

If the child seems very frightened at night, parents are advised to do whatever is necessary to help the child feel safe and able to sleep, because each night of good sleep makes the next night easier. Parents can spend enjoyable time with the child in the bedroom, move the child's bedtime later so the child will be sleepier, offer rewards for staying in bed until sleep comes. Parents may check in on the child until the child falls asleep to show that they are available. Parents may lie down with the child briefly and may even sleep in the child's room if anxiety is severe. If nighttime fears are the result of a family problem or part of the generalized anxiety seen in many situations, counseling is advised.

Sometimes children will awake in the night crying and upset from scary dreams. If they have had a nightmare, they will be awake and can often tell parents about the dream. Although these dreams occur at night, they are related to the conflicts, feelings, and stresses of the day. Nightmares are a part of growing up. They peak at about the time children enter school and again at ages nine through eleven. A child waking up from a nightmare is afraid and needs reassurance rather than logical arguments. A parent can remain with the child until he or she falls back to sleep, or perhaps can lie down with the child, but it is best not to make the latter practice a habit.

If nightmares occur frequently, parents can begin to examine what in the child's daylight hours is causing the trouble. There may be an adjustment to a new brother or sister, or a change to a new preschool group. Helping the child cope with stress during the day is the surest way to prevent nightmares.

It is important not to confuse nightmares with night terrors. In both cases the child awakes in the night, appearing very frightened. The causes for these two behaviors, however, differ. Nightmares are scary dreams that occur during light REM sleep, and they result in full awakening, often with the child's having some memory of the dream. The child will call and want comfort. Night terrors, however, occur during a partial awakening after a very deep state of sleep. They take place during the first few hours of sleep at night—about one and a half to three or four hours after the child goes to sleep—just as he is entering a light state of sleep. The child is not fully awake when he calls or cries. The cry may sound like a scream, and so the parents assume the child has had a nightmare. In this case, however, if a parent tries to hold the child, he pushes the parent away; comforting does not help. The child may drop back to sleep automatically and have no memory of the night terror the next day.

For nightmares, reassurance and comfort are the effective parental response. For night terrors, parents should not attempt to wake the child or offer comfort. They should avoid interacting with the child unless she requests it and let her fall back to sleep. If they believe it was a night terror, they should not make too much of it with the child, who may be frightened to hear how terrified and out of control she felt. Night terrors disappear as children get older.

Temper Tantrums

Temper tantrums are common responses to parents' requests. Recalling Florence Goodenough's study on anger from Chapter 7, let us examine what Haim Ginott, Thomas Gordon, Rudolph Dreikurs, and the behaviorists suggest about parental management of children's temper tantrums. Ginott recommends accepting all angry feelings but directing children's behavior into acceptable channels. Parents can do this verbally by saying, "People are not for hitting; pillows are for hitting" or "Scribble on the paper, not on the wall." Neither parent nor child is permitted to hit. If verbal statements do not end the tantrums, parents take action, even in public. Mothers have reported stopping the car until the fighting stopped in the back seat, or returning home if a child has a tantrum in a store.[80] These methods require time, but the mothers report success and say they felt better as a result of taking action.

Gordon suggests finding substitute activities to head off trouble. If no jumping is permitted on the sofa, parents can allow children to jump on pillows on the floor. Once anger surfaces, Gordon suggests that parents listen actively and provide feedback about the frustration and irritation the child feels—sometimes children need nothing more than acceptance of what they are feeling.

Gordon recommends mutual problem solving to find a solution agreeable to both parent and child.[81] Even when a compromise is not possible and a child is still upset, active listening may be useful. He cites the example of a child who could not go swimming because he had a cold. When the child's mother commented that it was hard for him to wait until the next day, he calmed down.

Dreikurs recommends many of the techniques that Goodenough found were used by parents whose children had few tantrums. In establishing routines, Dreikurs suggests being flexible with children, concerned with their needs and interests, but firm in enforcing the routines.[82] When tantrums occur, parents are urged to ignore them and leave the room. Ignoring a child is appropriate in public as well as at home.

The behaviorists use a similar method of ignoring. John Krumboltz and Helen Krumboltz tell of a little boy who learned that, if he cried and had a tantrum, his parents would pick him up instead of paying attention to the new baby.[83] When they realized that their actions were creating the tantrums, they agreed to ignore the outbursts. When the boy learned that he gained nothing by banging his head and demanding what he wanted, the tantrums stopped. The behaviorists insist that parents must be firm and consistent. Otherwise, tantrums will continue, and each time, children will hold out longer because they have learned that they can win by outlasting the parents.

VOICES OF EXPERIENCE

The Joys of Parenting Children Ages Two to Five

"When she was four, she was the only girl on an all-boy soccer team. Her mother thought she was signing her up for a coed team, but she was the only girl, and she enjoyed it and liked it even though she is not a natural athlete. She watched and learned and got good at it, and we got a lot of joy out of watching her." FATHER

"Well, every night we have a bedtime ritual of telling a story and singing to her. This is probably beyond the time she needs it, but we need it." MOTHER

"He's very inventive, and it's fun for both of us when he tells stories or figures out ways to communicate something he's learned or heard. When his mother had morning sickness, he heard the baby was in her tummy so he figured out the baby is making the morning sickness, pushing the food out." FATHER

"It's fun to get home in the evening; he comes running out and jumps up, which is really fun. It's a wonderful greeting." FATHER

"One of the delights that comes up is reading him stories, telling him the adventure of John Muir, at the four-year-old level. We were talking about places to go, and I said, 'Maybe we could go visit the home of John Muir.' He said, 'Oh, great, then I could go up there and have a cup of tea.' And I remembered I had told him a story about Muir's having tea in a blizzard, and he remembered that. He put that together, and it came out of nowhere. It knocked me over that he remembered that image." FATHER

"I enjoy her because I can talk to her; we have these wonderful conversations, and she can tell me about something that happened to her today at school that was really neat for her, and I just love to hear about it." MOTHER

"It's fun to hear him looking forward to doing things with us. He'll ask how many days until Saturday or Sunday because on those days I wait for him to get up before I have breakfast. Usually I'm up and gone before he gets up. He likes to come out and get up in my lap and share my breakfast, and it's a ritual. He looks forward to that and counts the days." FATHER

"She's really affectionate, always has been, but now out of nowhere, she'll tell you she loves you. She likes to do things with you, and when you give her special attention, one on one, she really likes it. We play games—Candy Land or Cinderella—or just one of us goes with her to the supermarket or to the park. We read stories every night and do some talking. Sometimes I put a record on and we dance." FATHER

"The joy comes from the things we do as a family, the three of us—going to see Santa Claus together or to see miniature trains and take a ride. Early in the morning we have a ritual. When he gets up early, he has a bottle of milk and gets in bed with us; the lights are out, and we are lying in bed, and he tells us his dreams and we watch the light outside and see the trees and see the sun come up. We do that in the morning, and it is a quiet joy." FATHER

(continued)

VOICES OF EXPERIENCE

The Joys of Parenting Children Ages Two to Five

(continued)

"The things that children do, you know they understand, but they haven't got the words to say what they want, so they tell you in the other things they do. They let you know they understand. It is so exciting to see her grow, and say, 'Yes, Daddy.' At thirty-one months, they are so smart, they comprehend so much; but they cannot convey it in words. You see it in their actions."   FATHER

"The time I like best with her is hanging out together, and she loves doing projects with me. She likes to help me with a project when I am working in the garage, and I'll show her how to use tools, and it's a special time with Dad."   MOTHER

"One night at dinner, he was watching his little sister who's one, and he said, 'Do you think when she gets to be a big girl she'll remember what she did as a baby?'"   FATHER

"I like going for a walk with her, and we went skipping rocks at the reservoir. I was going to show her how to skip rocks because she had never seen that before. Of course, she wanted to try it, and I didn't think she was old enough to do it. I had found the best skipping rock; it was just perfect. I was going to hold her hand and do it with her. She said, 'No, I want to do it myself.' I thought, it is more important to just let it go. So I said, 'Here let me show you how.' So I showed her, and she said, 'No, I can do it.' She threw it and it skipped three times! The first time she ever threw one! She wanted to stay till she did it again, and we did a little; but it will be a while before she does that again, I think."   FATHER

Stanley Turecki and Leslie Tonner distinguish between the manipulative tantrum and the temperamental tantrum.[84] Some children use tantrums to manipulate the parents into getting them what they want. In the case of a manipulative outburst, Turecki recommends firm refusal to give in. Distracting the child, ignoring the outburst, and sending the child to his or her room are all techniques for handling that kind of tantrum.

In the more intense temperamental tantrum, children seem out of control. Some aspect of their temperament has been violated, and they are reacting to that. For example, the poorly adaptable child who is compelled suddenly to switch activities may have an outburst, or a child sensitive to material may do so when he or she has to wear a wool sweater. In these instances, Turecki advises a calm and sympathetic approach; parents can reflect the child's feelings of irritation or upset: "I know you don't like this, but it will be okay." Parents can then put their arms around the child, if permitted, or just stay near the child. No long discussion of what is upsetting the child takes place unless the child wants to talk. If the situation can be corrected, it should be. For example, if the wool sweater feels scratchy, let the child remove it and wear a soft sweatshirt. This is not giving in, but just correcting a mistake. All parents can do then is wait out the tantrum.

Throughout a display of the temperamental tantrum, parents convey the attitude that they will help the child deal with this situation. Though parents change their minds when good reasons are presented, they are generally consistent in waiting out the tantrum and insisting on behavior change when necessary.

Sibling Rivalry

When a younger sibling is born, the older child feels jealousy and anger, as well as caring, warmth, and protectiveness. As children grow and become mobile and verbal, new kinds of problems arise.

In applying Ginott's principles to sibling rivalry, Adele Faber and Elaine Mazlish suggest that parents consider themselves negotiators in these situations.[85] They can recognize that each child's feelings are unique and justified and can accept the feelings without necessarily approving them. As long as neither child is in danger, parents need not feel they must settle the differences. A parent can always interrupt and say, "Hitting doesn't solve problems." If that fails to stop physical aggression, parents can step in and calmly separate the children.

Gordon advocates the use of active listening. This enables children to express their feelings and grants them freedom to resolve differences. When children listen actively to each other, a climate is created in which children can work out their own problems. One mother whose children were four, six, and eight found that the children, including the four-year-old, devised rules that decreased fighting and name calling. The children were upset by verbal insults and decided they would try to send I-messages. If the situation became too heated, they would go to their rooms to cool off.

Dreikurs considers sibling rivalry in detail. He believes that parents can reduce the jealousy among children by making it clear to all that each child in the family is loved for his or her individual qualities and that it is not important whether one child does something better than another. Parents love each child, but a child's trust of that love can be diminished when parents use one sibling's behavior to humiliate another child: "Why can't you be more like Jimmy—he ate everything on his plate."

When siblings bicker or fight, Dreikurs recommends treating all children the same. They are all sent to their rooms if play becomes noisy. If one child complains about another, parents can react so that children feel a responsibility to live in peace. Parents can point out that a child who acts up today may only be trying to retaliate for an incident that happened yesterday. Misbehavior involves all children in the family, and they can learn to take care of each other. Cooperation can be fostered by taking children on family expeditions and having all the children play together. When they see that life is more fun when they cooperate and get along with each other, children learn to settle their differences.

Behaviorists also suggest that parents withdraw from the sibling fights and reward cooperation as a way to increase positive interactions. Children blossom when they hear praise for their good points. Once a fight breaks out, however, parents are encouraged to say as little as possible and to offer a reward for good behavior.

All these techniques are important. Parents must decide which ones will work best in a particular situation: helping children become aware of each other's feelings, increasing verbal communication, ignoring fights, or administering punishments while making sure to reward positive interactions.

High Activity Levels

As the brain develops from birth to age three, a child's motor activity increases. From age three to nine, as the brain matures, the child's attention span increases, focusing improves, and motor activity decreases. The inability to inhibit motor behavior is, perhaps, the biggest single behavior problem in boys and often is identified as a problem in the preschool years. The child may always have been active, but problems arise when a great interest in activity continues after mastery of motor skills occurs in the toddler period and is accompanied by such other qualities as excessive restlessness, short attention span, and demanding behavior that permits no delay in gratification. A child who experiences these problems is not necessarily hyperactive. Even children with high levels of activity still within the normal range are perceived negatively by preschool teachers, parents, and peers.[86] They are restless, fidgety, poorly controlled, and impulsive. They do not respond well to limits and are often seen as uncooperative and disobedient. With peers, they are outgoing and self-assertive, aggressive, competitive, and dominant. Children described this way at ages three and four are viewed similarly at ages seven and seven and a half.

Both mothers and fathers of highly active children often possess qualities similar to those of their children.[87] They tend to be directive, intrusive, and rather authoritarian with children. They engage in power struggles and competition with their children.

What can parents do? First, parents must get out of the vicious negative cycle that has been created. They must begin to spend some positive time with their children, enjoying them.

At the same time, parents establish structure and daily routines in which the child takes an active role and puts to constructive use the high energy level that might otherwise be disruptive. The structure need not be rigid, but a general schedule of many daily activities will help a child. If, for example, the child has a simple breakfast that he or she can help fix—cereal, juice, toast—confidence and independence are encouraged, energy is consumed, and structure is accepted.

Donald Meichenbaum and Joseph Goodman have found that impulsive children can be taught to guide their behavior and achieve greater control by using a form of self-instruction.[88] Parents show the child what they want done and at the same time talk about what they are doing. The child then acts and talks out loud to describe the actions—"First I take off my pajamas, then I hang them up, then I put on my shirt and pants."

The behaviorists Robert Eimers and Robert Aitchison advise parents to be alert and consistent in providing rewards for positive behaviors.[89] Highly active children often feel rewarded by the attention they receive for misdeeds. "Try to catch the child being good," they suggest, and give rewards of praise and social approval. These seem to be more important than material rewards to active children.

To increase attention span, Eimers and Aitchison recommend helping children with puzzles and other games that require concentration. They urge parents to praise the child for completion of the task rather than for correctness. Poorly coordinated active children benefit from opportunities to develop physical skills. Games that involve running, balancing, and gymnastic movements are helpful. Drawing and playing with Legos or other construction toys also facilitate the development of fine motor coordination.

Aggression

Temper outbursts and hyperactivity reflect anger, lack of control, and noncompliance, but they do not necessarily involve aggression.[90] *Aggression* is out-of-control behavior that is destructive and hurts others or their possessions. Concerned at their preschooler's aggression, some parents respond with anger and impulsive behavior. In their frustration, they try to force the child to change through power-assertive strategies that prove to be ineffective. They do not, however, take consistent, ongoing action to change the child's behavior, because they consider it a temporary phase the child is going through. This is the coercive family process described by Patterson.[91]

His research, however, suggests many actions parents can take to decrease aggressive behavior, even aggression that has developed over a length of time. First, parents must control their own angry responses to their children. These responses present a negative model of response to frustration that children copy. Their anger also creates an atmosphere of high emotional arousal that keeps children from taking in what parents are trying to teach.

Second, parents need to use a consistent set of positive rewards for nonaggressive behaviors and negative consequences like time-outs for aggression to teach children control.

Third, parents teach children specific social skills and skills of emotional control, as described in Chapters 4 and 5. Research indicates that aggressive and disruptive preschoolers retain strong interests in and concerns for others and want to get along. These concerns decrease as disruptive children get into elementary school.[92] At this earlier age, then, parents can rely on children's desire for good relationships with others to teach the positive skills necessary to get along with them. In teaching nonaggression, such parents have to take a more active role than they might wish. Research shows that parents of aggressive children expect that they can issue directives and commands, and children's social behaviors will change. As we have seen, however, it is not that simple.

From beginning to end, parents must become more positive in their view of their child and in the emotional tone of their interactions. Parents often reject the aggressive child as Patterson described, but children need parents' positive regard and the feeling of being special to them.

Social Withdrawal and Inhibition

Like aggressive behaviors, social withdrawal and inhibition may have many origins—in the temperamental qualities of child and parent, attachment experiences, parenting techniques, and contextual factors.[93] As described in Chapters 1 and 7, physiological reactivity and arousal in infancy are related to fearful and inhibited behavior in toddlers. Children who have anxious and insecure attachments to mothers at one year are more likely to be inhibited toddlers who become more withdrawn as they get older. When parents are critical and use authoritarian, high-power strategies to control children's behaviors, their preschoolers tend to be fearful and inhibited. Parental and family qualities such as maternal depression and economic stress can reduce parents' effectiveness, leading to withdrawal and inhibition in their children.

Even though withdrawal causes significant problems for children, parents are generally more concerned about aggressiveness. Parents of withdrawn children are often surprised and puzzled at their children's behavior, often feeling embarrassed and guilty about it. Believing that shyness is an inborn quality, they tend to use high-power, directive strategies with children to change the behavior. These usually do not work. Such parents can, however, take many positive actions that resemble the effective strategies parents of aggressive children use.

First, they can express a positive attitude toward their child as a person. Parents of withdrawn children tend to be negative in their comments about them, expressing the view that parents have to step in and help children function, but this is not a helpful attitude.

Second, they can be supportive in teaching social skills and encouraging play with others. At the same time, they have to stand back and permit the child to act independently. In their zeal to help their physiologically reactive child, they may have become overprotective, too worried about an upsetting interaction, and therefore too controlling. The child does not have a chance to learn that he or she can succeed independently.

Third, parents have to look at their own behaviors. Do they model a fearful, inhibited approach to new situations and people? Do their own problems interfere with their ability to be positive and to support their child? If so, they need to try to change themselves as part of their attempt to help their children.

A PRACTICAL QUESTION: HOW CAN PARENTS HELP WHEN CHILDREN HAVE DISABILITIES OR DEVELOPMENTAL DELAYS?

These early years involve rapid development in children's skills and abilities. Some children show clear signs at birth that they will have developmental delays. Perhaps a genetic disorder or birth difficulties have resulted in significant problems for the child. Sometimes, however, the delay is identified later, when the child fails to develop certain skills. For example, a language disorder may show up in the second or third year of life when the child does not learn to talk at the same rate as other children. More pervasive developmental delays in language and the capacity for social relationships with others may also become identified over time.

How can parents help such children psychologically? As soon as disabilities or delays are detected, parents must seek professional consultation if not already provided. Research indicates that, for most disabilities and delays, the earlier the diagnosis and

Box 8-1
PARENTING BROTHERS AND SISTERS OF CHILDREN WITH SPECIAL NEEDS

Nothing so clearly reveals the strong connections between family members as the fact that, when one member has an ongoing health or developmental problem, everyone in the family is touched and reacts. Parents direct their efforts to getting and providing the best possible care for the child, and they organize family and work life to include the additional activities. They get psychological support for the child with special needs and sometimes for themselves from organizations and professionals. In the stress and pressure of all these activities, it is not surprising that the needs of the brothers and sisters of affected children are often overlooked.

Yet brothers and sisters of children have special stresses and needs, and parents can help in many ways. The exact nature of siblings' responses depends on the specific nature and the effects of the special problem confronting the family. In many ways, siblings' reactions are similar to those of parents. Like parents, they too love and often admire the child with a special problem and feel sad at the special difficulties or limitations that child experiences; they wish there were something they could do to make things better. Like parents, they share the restrictions or burdens that a physical or developmental problem places on family activities, and they too experience the general public's reactions to unusual behaviors. Sometimes, they feel guilty they are healthy and were spared special problems. And sometimes, they feel angry at lack of attention and the burdens of intense feelings that appear to have no outlet.

Adult brothers and sisters of children with special needs have organized several suggestions for parents to ease the stress for siblings.[*] Doing so is important, according to Don Meyer, founder of the Sibling Support Project, because "these brothers and sisters will likely have the longest relationships of anyone, relationships in excess of 65 years. They should be remembered at every turn."[†]

First, parents must sit down and talk to siblings in age-appropriate terms about the child's special problems—what the problem is, what causes it, what the interventions do to help—giving as much information as is appropriate for siblings' ages. Parents must provide many opportunities for children to ask questions, and they must be sure there are no misinterpretations of what they have said. Parents should try to see whether brothers and sisters have special fears that they too will develop the problem.

Second, parents need to encourage brothers and sisters to express their feelings about what happens in the family and about their relationships with the child with special needs. Parents must be especially accepting of all feelings, giving children permission to express them, especially negative ones, as many children fear burdening their already-stressed parents. One mother of a withdrawing thirteen-year-old sibling asked several times about any upsetting feelings. The girl always denied any, but before giving up, the mother commented, "It must be difficult being the sister to . . . ." Her daughter began to cry, and a host of feelings poured out. Parents can sometimes elicit feelings with their own I-statements: "I wish we didn't have to have all these physical therapy appointments, and I am sure your sister wishes that too. How about you?"[‡]

Third, include siblings in discussions and plans for treatments insofar as is possible. Much as one includes even very young children in the plans for a family event such as a new baby or a grandparent's visit, brothers and sisters should be included in what is happening—a proposed new diagnostic test, new specialist, or new treatment.

(continued)

Box 8-1
CONTINUED

Siblings' suggestions for helping to care for a child with special needs, as well as their actual help, enable them to feel like important members of the family. Parents need to acknowledge children's help too.

Fourth, give brothers and sisters their special time with parents. It may not be a large amount of time, but regular time that a child can count on indicates that that child is important too. If that is impossible because a child is in the hospital, recruit a family member who can take siblings for special time. Give siblings time, too, when their needs come before those of the child with special problems. Regardless of the problem, at certain points a baby-sitter can be enlisted to care for that child while brothers and sisters have some special activity with parents.

Fifth, help brothers and sisters develop their own activities and interests that give them pleasure. Again, if parents cannot drive for lessons or sports teams, have a friend or relative who can take siblings. Developing interests helps children increase their skills and make new friends, giving brothers and sisters confidence and a sense that parents care about their development too.

Sixth, model the ways you want brothers and sisters to relate to the child with special needs; think and talk about the problem, explain the situation to others, and accept help from others. Brothers and sisters copy what you say and do. When parents cry and feel helpless or hopeless, children feel sad and hopeless too. One mother reported that, after her daughter had a seizure at a store, she found her four-year-old sister answering shoppers' questions with the same words the mother had used in explaining it to her.

Seventh, get brothers and sisters involved with sibling support groups that enable them to talk to other brothers and sisters who live with a child with special needs. Their age-mates can bring special understanding that parents may not have. In Seattle, Washington, Don Meyer has started a support group that gives information and has discussion groups for children around the country. People from other countries have used it as a model for groups in their own countries.

*Kate Strohm, *Being the Other One* (Boston: Shambala, 2005).
†Gretchen Cook, "Siblings of Disabled Have Troubles of Their Own," *New York Times*, 4 April 2006, p. D5.
‡Strohm, *Being the Other One*, p. 170.

intervention, the greater the child's progress. Because of individual differences in children's rates of growth, accurate diagnosis is sometimes complicated. If delays or disabilities are mild, telling a significant delay from slow growth within the average range can be difficult. In any case, professional consultation is essential and provides directions for parents.

Parents must first obtain all appropriate services for children and arrange the family routines to include them. This can be a full-time job. Once this is done, these parents' tasks are the same as those of other parents—to provide feelings of acceptance, appreciation, and security through sensitive, responsive interactions with the child and to support the child's own motivation to grow and function effectively.

A child's disability or delay affects all family members.[94] Mothers and fathers confront experiences they never anticipated. Their lives include many professionals and numerous activities that come on top of all the usual child-rearing tasks. Yet, the family and family support are the most valuable aids in helping children achieve their maximal potential. This book cannot detail the many physical, cognitive, language, and social disabilities and delays that occur or the many therapies for them. Here, we focus on parents' care and the family's emotional atmosphere as engines for development.

Linda Gilkerson and Frances Stott write,

> Children who have a congenital disability may experience disability as an inherent part of their body and self. Like other aspects of the child, the disability contributes to a sense of identity and is in need of acceptance, appreciation, and affirmation. . . . Infants initially develop unimpeded by an awareness of their disability. However, the moment with the most potential for emotional trauma comes not when the child realizes that he or she is different but when the child discovers that the differences are perceived by society as inferior.[95]

As the child grows and develops, the disability takes on different meanings. At all ages, parents must convey that the child's worth lies in being who she or he is, not in becoming "normal" or like others. The authors review the "fix-it model of disability" in which the child's value lies in working hard and making progress to become "normal." According to one therapist, children with disabilities must come to see themselves as both intact and disabled at the same time, and to do this they require their families' love and acceptance. Supportive relationships within the family help children develop a sense of themselves as willing, purposive individuals who can act.

A ten-year longitudinal study of children with motor and other disabilities and delays supports the importance of family emotional atmosphere and parents' sensitive and responsive caretaking.[96] The child's disability predicted growth in intellectual, social, and adaptive skills over this period. Beyond the disability, however, personal characteristics of the child and the family predicted progress in development. Children's ability to regulate feelings and behavior and express them appropriately, as rated by teachers, and children's ability to remain motivated to learn predicted progress. Sensitive and responsive mother-child interactions predicted growth in social and communication skills.

Parents' stress was related to the extent of the disability and to their child's level of stress as reflected in behavior problems. When children did not develop behavior problems, mothers' stress remained stable and low over the period. Social support and good problem-solving skills reduced parents' stress.

Early intervention programs for children from birth to age three generally include psychological services for the entire family. When these programs are delivered in school at age three, however, family members are usually no longer included, and the emotional functioning of all family members is often ignored. From the results of the longitudinal study, one can see that reducing parents' stress and children's emotional problems would aid development and would be worthwhile additions to such programs.

PARENTS' EXPERIENCES IN FACING TRANSITIONS

In these years, parents continue in what Ellen Galinsky terms the *authority stage*.[97] Many parents, bogged down in battle with their young children, find themselves doing and saying things they vowed they never would—the very words they hated to hear from their own parents when they were children. Parents are shaken and upset as their ideal images of themselves as parents collide with the reality of rearing children.

Parents' images of themselves undergo revision in light of the way they actually behave. Because it involves change, this can be a painful process. Parents must change either their ideal image or their behavior to come closer to living up to their own standards. Their images of children change as well. Parents discover that children are not always nice, loving, cooperative, and affectionate. Children can be extremely aggressive—breaking things, hitting parents, pulling their hair.

One father described how he coped with these feelings by revising the kind of parent he wanted to be and by finding new ways to relate to children so that he met the images he wanted to keep of himself as a parent:

> Stanley and his wife have one son, eighteen months old. Stanley is a doctor. "In my family, growing up, when someone got angry at someone, they'd stop loving them—which made me feel abandoned as a child. . . .
>
> "When my son gets angry, the easiest thing for me to do would be the same—walk out and slam the door.
>
> "I tell him that even though I've said no, I still love him. I hold him while he's having a temper tantrum, and I tell him it's okay for him to be angry with me.
>
> "Being able to do this is recent, new, and learned, and it's hard work. In the past, I couldn't see beyond my own feelings. What I've now learned is that I have to see past them.
>
> "Another thing I've learned is that if I've gotten angry at my son or if I've done something that I feel I shouldn't have, I'm not the Loch Ness monster or the worst person in the world. I learned the reparability of a mistake."[98]

Parents must also deal with each other as authorities. Both parents' agreeing on how and when to enforce rules is wonderful, but this frequently does not happen. One parent is often stricter or less consistent; one may dislike any physical punishment, but the other may believe it is the only technique to handle serious rule breaking. Communicating with each other, finding ways to handle differences, matters for all parents. They may, for instance, agree to back each other up on all occasions. Other times, they may agree to discuss in private any serious misgivings they have about the other's discipline; then the original rule setter can revise the rule. Still other times, one parent may decide to let the other handle discipline completely. This is a less desirable solution because it means one parent is withdrawn from interaction with the child. Parents need to find ways to resolve differences so they support each other in child rearing. Mutual support is the most important source of strength in parenting.

Single parents and employed parents must work with other authorities, such as day care providers or relatives who provide major care, to develop consistent ways of handling discipline. Again, communicating with other caregivers helps provide consistent solutions to problems. When authorities do not agree, children become confused and are less able to meet expectations.

As parents become aware of their personal feelings about being an authority and learn to deal with them, they can put these misgivings aside and deal more neutrally with rule enforcement. As with handling infancy, a range of preparation, such as gaining information from books, groups, parenting courses, and other parents, helps parents handle the demands of conflicting feelings in the authority stage.

SUPPORT FOR PARENTS

Recall from Chapters 1 and 5 the parents' support groups that Philip and Carolyn Cowan organized to help parents cope with the transition to parenting and then with the transition to the child's being in school.[99] Such groups help parents develop realistic expectations for their children and themselves. As one parent stated, in these early years, one is not exactly sure of what the limits or expectations should be, and these groups can provide information, discuss what the range of individual differences are, and which strategies work with various children. Parents can then more easily manage problems and enjoy the time with their children.

MAIN POINTS

As their motor, cognitive, language, and social skills increase, toddlers and preschoolers

- develop a greater sense of self and independence
- take pleasure and delight in their new accomplishments
- express new emotions of pride, embarrassment, and shame
- refuse to do what parents want if it conflicts with their own goals
- gradually learn control of their behavior through internalizing rules and standards

As their independence grows, children also develop closer relationships with others, and they

- become more physically affectionate with family, friends, and pets
- become more concerned about others
- are kinder and try to resolve angry interactions
- delight in complying with some adult requests and meeting a standard of behavior
- are more likely than not to follow parents' requests

As they develop a greater sense of individuality, toddlers develop a sense of gender identity that

- is proudly announced at two to two-and-a-half years
- initially is based on parents' positive and negative emotional responses to gender-appropriate activities
- organizes activities so that boys manipulate objects and explore the world more and girls express feelings, ask for help, and give help more

Parents whose children function well and have secure attachments

- are available, attentive, and sensitive to the child's individual needs
- grant the child as much independence as possible within safety limits
- provide models of kind, caring, controlled behavior
- talk with the child to explain reasons for what is done, to understand the child's view of what is happening and to let the child express himself or herself
- play with the child to increase the child's positive mood and desire to cooperate in routines and activities

Parents regulate children's behavior effectively when they

- establish a process of mutual reward
- act to prevent problems
- avoid coercive reciprocity
- introduce rules that dovetail with the child's abilities
- use low-power techniques, such as reasoning and explanation, when noncompliance occurs
- work together so children get a set of consistent limits
- do not abuse their power

Problems discussed center on

- sleep
- sibling rivalry
- handling temper tantrums and high activity levels
- dealing with aggression and withdrawal
- helping children with disabilities feel accepted

Joys include the child's

- delight in increasing skills and personal achievements
- helping behaviors
- greater communicativeness

EXERCISES

1. Interview two couples who have preschoolers. Ask them about their children's daily routines and their worries and pleasures regarding their children. What are the sources of stress and support for the parents? Are the stresses and supports similar in the two families?

2. In groups, recall early experiences of gender learning. (a) Did the teachings deal with activities, appearances, feelings? (b) Who was teaching you about gender-appropriate behavior—parents, siblings, peers, relatives, teachers? (c) Were you more likely to accept the teachings of adults or of peers? Make a

group list of the kinds of experiences members had. (d) Are similar experiences occurring today?

3. In groups, recall early experiences with siblings. Was there much fighting? Did parents teach children how to get along? Did parents punish children for not getting along? What seems to make for the best relationships with siblings? What roles do siblings play in your lives as you get older?

4. Watch Saturday morning television programs for children and decide how much time and what specific programs you, if you were parents, would permit your toddler and preschooler to watch. Justify your choices.

5. Interview three preschoolers about their joys in life. What do they like best to do? Do they get to do it as much as they want? How can parents make their lives happier? Are their requests reasonable? Do you think parents are aware of what makes their children happy?

ADDITIONAL READINGS

Eisenberg, Nancy. *The Caring Child.* Cambridge, MA: Harvard University Press, 1992.

Golombok, Susan, and Fivush, Robin. *Gender Development.* New York: Cambridge University Press, 1994.

Gottman, John. *Raising an Emotionally Intelligent Child.* New York: Simon & Schuster, 1994.

Greenspan, Stanley I., and Wiedner, Serena. *The Child with Special Needs.* Reading, MA: Addison-Wesley, 1998.

Murphy, Tim, and Oberlin, Loriann Hoff. *The Angry Child.* New York: Three Rivers Press, 2001.

9

Parenting Elementary School Children

IN THE NEWS

San Francisco Chronicle, November 26:[1]
Parents are one of many factors in children's academic success. See pages 314–315 and 338.

Test Your Knowledge: Fact or Fiction

1. Adding an hour of sleep to a child's existing pattern increases memory and reaction time on cognitive tests equivalent to two years of chronological age.
2. Early school success serves as a protective factor against the development of high-risk behaviors—delinquency, substance abuse in adolescence.
3. Children around the world, regardless of sex or socioeconomic status, agree with each other on what is upsetting even more so than do adults and children within the same culture.
4. Children believe it is wrong to violate a moral rule even if an adult tells them to do it.
5. Pediatricians report a three-fold increase in the number of children they judge need psychological help—18.7 of those seen in 1996 compared to 6.8 in 1979.

School launches a child on a sea of opportunity for learning, but stress accompanies the greater independence. Parents' roles change as they encourage independence, continue to guide the child's behavior and interpret the outside influences the child confronts. How do parents foster the child's success at school and with peers? How do they help children deal with upsetting experiences and disappointments that lie beyond parental control?

Children have learned the routines of living—eating, dressing, toileting—and can take care of many of their own needs. They express themselves easily. Their world enlarges as they go off to school, meet new friends, and adjust to more demanding tasks. Stress increases because they now compare themselves with others and against external standards, they worry about their competence in many areas and feel vulnerable to embarrassment and feelings of inadequacy.

Learning in a structured setting is a central focus of activity in the years from five to ten. It takes up most of the daytime and some evening hours as well, and it draws on all children's skills and abilities—their motor skills, their verbal skills, their planning and intellectual skills, their emotional control, and their social skills. Learning also depends on family stability and a calm, stress-free atmosphere at home so that children's energies can be directed to learning about the world.

Why is it important to devote so much time and effort to learning?[2] Children's intellectual and academic achievements prepare them for higher education, better jobs, and greater income throughout life; but equally important, school success, beginning in the first grade, serves as a buffer and protective factor against deviant activities such as delinquency and substance abuse in adolescence and adulthood. Academic success seems to provide alternative means of gratification. And it increases social competence and social acceptance, which in turn reinforce academic success.[3]

Parents play a powerful role in encouraging and supporting children's school success. Parents' intellectual stimulation and their beliefs about children's abilities strongly influence students' aspirations and levels of achievement. Their positive remarks can be great support, and their criticisms can be remembered for life. Although the role is powerful, many actions can be simple. As we saw in Chapter 5, the simple family rituals of regular meals together and regular reading time, along with an hour more of sleep a night, produced significant academic gains for children.

Parents play an active role in helping children learn basic skills.

Parents also have the daunting task of ensuring that schools and school personnel carry out their parts in the educational process. Recent longitudinal studies document that the quality of the schools and teachers plays a major role in supporting children's intellectual growth in the years from five to eighteen. When these institutions are of poor quality, children's abilities, though adequate at age five, fail to develop as they would in a stimulating atmosphere.[4]

PHYSICAL DEVELOPMENT

We discussed in Chapter 5 the steps parents take to ensure healthy physical growth.

From ages five to ten, girls and boys have approximately the same height, weight, and general physical measurements. At five, they are about 42 inches tall and weigh about 40 to 45 pounds. By age ten, they stand at about 52 inches and weigh about 75 to 80 pounds. In the elementary school years, children's coordination is well developed. They ride bikes, skate, swim, play team sports, draw, and play musical instruments. Nearly all the basic skills in the area of gross (running, skipping) and fine (cutting with scissors, drawing) motor coordination are laid down by age seven, and further development consists of refining these skills.

Recent studies of neurophysiological functioning and brain development indicate that high levels of emotionality may play a role in organizing neuronal groups in the neocortex and in building connections between the cortex and emotional centers in the brain.[5] High levels of emotion also affect learning, and parents' role is to help children regulate their feelings. If children go to school with heightened fear and anxiety, they may not be able to focus and learn. If they go to school with heightened impulsivity and emotional arousal, they may have difficulty attending to and learning new material.

INTELLECTUAL DEVELOPMENT

Three major cognitive changes occur in the elementary school years.[6] First, children learn to reason generally. At about age seven, children become less focused on their own perceptions and more involved in the objective properties of what they observe. They organize their perceptions and reason about a broader range of objects and situations. Because they also more easily adopt the other person's point of view, they understand other people and their reactions better. At the end of this age period, around ten to twelve, thinking becomes more abstract and more closely resembles adults' ways of reasoning.

Second, children at this age organize tasks and function more independently than before. They observe their own behavior and their thinking processes as well as set and pursue their own goals. Third, they acquire knowledge in an organized learning environment—school—that sets standards by which they and others evaluate their performance.

VOICES OF EXPERIENCE

What I Wish I Had Known about the Elementary School Years

"I wish I'd known how much you need to be an advocate for your child with the school. When we grew up, our parents put us in public school and that was it. Now, you have a lot more options, and the public schools aren't always great; so you realize how active you need to be in order to ensure a good education for your children." MOTHER

"The main thing, I think, is how important temperament is. My daughter was in one school that was very noncompetitive; that's a wonderful philosophy, but it wasn't right for her. She is very competitive, and in that atmosphere she did not do as well. So with the second child, we are going to be more careful to see that there is a good fit between her temperament and what she is doing." FATHER

"I was surprised that, even though the children are older, they take as much time as when they were younger; but you spend the time in different ways. I thought when they started school, I would have a little more time. Instead of giving them baths at night and rocking them, I supervise homework and argue about taking baths. Knowing that things were going to take as much time would have made me less impatient in the beginning, and I would have planned better." MOTHER

"I learned that, especially from five to eight, say, children are not as competent as they look. They really can't do a lot of things that on the surface you think they can. They have language, and they look like they're reasoning, and they look like their motor skills are okay. So you say, 'When you get up in the morning, I want you to make your cereal,' and they can't do it consistently. And so because we didn't know that with the first child, I think we made excessive demands on her, which led to her being a little harsher on herself. Now with the second one, if she can't tie her shoes by herself today, even though she could two weeks ago, we're more likely to say, 'Okay,' instead of, 'Well, you can tie your shoes; go ahead and do it.' If you give them a little help, it doesn't mean you are making babies of them; it means they have room to take it from there." FATHER

"I wish I'd known more about their abilities and work readiness. My daughter had some special needs in school. In preschool, she did well, although I could see there were immaturities in her drawings and writing, but she got lots of happy faces. I was misled by the positive comments they always wanted to make to her, and I thought she was doing better than she was. When she got to school, it came as quite a shock that she was having problems. With my son, I have been more on top, and I ask more questions about how he is really doing, because I want to get any special needs he has addressed. My advice to any parent is that, if at all possible, volunteer in your child's school. I gave up half a day's pay, and in my financial situation that was a real hardship. It is very, very important to keep a handle on not just what is happening educationally, but also who the peers are and what is going on." MOTHER

SCHOOL

School is a major organizing force in parents' and children's lives. School provides opportunities for learning, but it also places demands and stress on both parents and children. School occupies five to six hours of children's day throughout much of the year, and it determines their evening activities as well. Children must function in large groups of initially unknown children and adults. They also must meet standards of behavior and achievement.

Influences within the Home

Jacquelynne Eccles, Allan Wigfield, and Ulrich Schiefele list four parental factors that contribute to children's motivation and outcomes in school: parents' social characteristics, their general beliefs and behaviors, their specific beliefs about their child, and their specific behaviors.[7]

Parents' Social Characteristics   Parents' education, income, marital status, and number of children, as well as neighborhood characteristics, determine the resources available to parents to encourage their children's achievement at school. Nonetheless, a parent's limited resources need not determine what happens with children. Ben Carson, an internationally recognized African American pediatric neurosurgeon at Johns Hopkins University, describes how his mother—married at thirteen years of age to a man who, she later learned, had another family—raised her two sons.[8] She worked as a domestic, sometimes holding two or three jobs to make ends meet. When Ben was in the fifth grade, he was at the bottom of his class and nicknamed "Dummy." Very concerned, his mother insisted the two boys turn off the television. She required that they read two books per week from the Detroit Public Library and give her a written report on each book. The boys did not know for some years that she could not read the reports.

Ben read books about animals, plants, and rocks. Later that year, he was the only student in his class able to identify a particular rock. He suddenly realized, "The reason you knew the answer was because you were reading those books. What if you read books about all your subjects—science, math, history, geography, social studies? Couldn't you then know more than all those students who tease you and call you a dummy?"[9] Within a year and a half, he went from the bottom of his class to the top. With relatively few external resources, his mother took action that promoted her son's success.

Parents' General Beliefs and Behaviors   Parents' general beliefs and behaviors create an emotional climate in the home that influences children's achievement. By forming secure attachments with their children, balancing independence and structure, and providing appropriate adult models for learning, parents help their children develop competence and motivation to achieve.

Parents' general beliefs about gender-appropriate behaviors shape what they provide for their sons and daughters. For example, they tend to provide boys with manipulative toys that develop spatial abilities. They are less likely to enroll daughters in computer programs and competitive athletics, and they are more likely to direct sons toward gifted programs. These behaviors in turn influence their children's achievement.

Cultural values about the sources of achievement influence what parents expect of children and themselves. In the United States, European American parents view the child's innate ability as the main determiner of achievement. They consider it their role to give children emotional support in schoolwork. Failure is seen as a sign of limited ability. Asian American parents, however, believe hard work and effort determine success. They take an active role in seeing that their child exerts the necessary work and effort to achieve high standards. Failures are seen as remediable with increased effort.

Parents' Beliefs about Their Child Parents' beliefs about a child's skills and abilities and reasons for success shape children's achievement. Parents can encourage or discourage academic work by saying a child has ability or, conversely, has no skill at a task. They can soften a failure by identifying it as remediable through further work.

Parents' expectations regarding school achievement predict children's academic success more accurately than do the child's ability scores.[10]

Parents' Specific Behaviors As noted in the previous chapter, parents' stimulation through books and activities predicts achievement. Providing stimulating toys and opportunities for exploration; reading to children, encouraging conversation, verbal expression, and curiosity; providing lessons and activities that develop children's skills—all contribute to children's academic success. Further, although we do not often think of emotional regulation as an important skill for school success,[11] it is essential if children are to deal with the frustrations of learning new material and getting along with others.

Parents also organize the home and the daily routine so the child has a time and place to do schoolwork. Parents also spend time giving spelling words and listening to reading.

Influences within the School

The staff's expectations of students, the organization of the school, the cohesiveness of the staff, the staff's sensitivity to students' needs, and the staff's recognition of performance do appear important for student achievement. Further, teachers' skills in managing conflict can reduce or increase children's behavior problems, such as aggressiveness.[12]

Children develop strong attachments to teachers and their schools when they are actively involved in the learning process and have opportunities and rewards for developing competencies. Effective teachers, like effective parents, have clear, fair, and realistic expectations of students.[13] Teachers emphasize mastery-based learning in a cooperative atmosphere in which students teach each other.

Influences within Students

Children who have personal maturity when they enter school adjust relatively easily.[14] Children who enter school with friends or who have a stable group of friends outside school also adjust relatively easily.[15]

Most children start school with positive beliefs about their abilities and capacities to learn. Children in first grade believe that all children can learn and that all they need is effort—those who do best have worked the hardest.[16] Another group of children react strongly to failure and criticism.[17] When they fail a task or receive criticism, they feel bad, blame themselves, and see themselves as bad people who deserve punishment, even at young ages. They feel unworthy and inadequate, helpless to change the situation. Such children see failure as a sign they lack some innate quality. Because they believe that no amount of effort or hard work will lead to achievement, they abandon any attempts to improve. They avoid challenging tasks and give up at the first sign of difficulty. In contrast, children who persist see criticism or failure as signs to look for a different solution or ways to improve some aspect of their work. They feel good about what they have done and anticipate that others will appreciate their efforts as well.

Some training programs give children strategies for goal setting and interpreting failure in different ways, as well as encouraging these children to enjoy the process of learning rather than focusing on the achievements of learning. Such programs reduce feelings of helplessness.[18] We talk about this further in a later section.

Children from certain cultural backgrounds may feel at a loss to achieve in what seems a strange environment.[19] They may be used to working in cooperative ways, focusing on the effects of objects on people, learning from traditions, and obeying standards. The school atmosphere of competition, objective knowledge gained from reference books, and questioning teachers may require adjustment.

Despite such cultural differences, children of different ethnic groups enjoy school, feel good about themselves and their achievements, and expect to do well in the future. They work hard and are self-disciplined.[20]

EMOTIONAL DEVELOPMENT

Elementary school children understand their feelings better than preschoolers do and realize that feelings depend, in part, on what led up to the event and how the event is interpreted.[21] For example, at ages six and seven, children are pleased with their success, whether it comes from luck or effort. When they are nine and ten, children feel proud only if they believe their effort produced the success.

Children are most likely to express their inner feelings when they are alone with a person who they believe will respond in a positive, understanding way.[22] Unfortunately, as children—particularly boys—grow older, they anticipate a less positive response from others, even from parents. Thus, older boys are much less likely to express their feelings than are girls or younger boys.

Common Feelings of Schoolchildren

Elementary school children experience many common feelings, which parents can help them handle. Children's ability to regulate their emotions appears related to temperamental qualities,[23] but parents' understanding helps guide them toward achieving self-control.

Empathy   Because children's awareness of others' feelings increases in elementary school, they are better helpers and are more likely to offer social strategies rather than material ones to change distress when they see it in other people, for example, suggesting playing with a friend rather than giving a toy.[24] Children are most likely to help others when they feel happy, competent, and effective themselves. They are also most likely to help if they like the person and that person has helped them in the past. So, positive feelings about oneself and others lead to generosity at this age.[25]

Aggressiveness   Aggression decreases during this period, but consistent individual differences emerge and tend to persist over time. Further, aggressive children often have problems such as poor peer relations and difficulty in acquiring academic skills. See the section on peer relationships for more on aggression.

Fearfulness   With age, children grow less fearful. Many of the fears of the preschool period—of animals, of the dark—decrease. Some specific ones remain, however—fear of snakes, of storms. These fears appear related to temperamental qualities involving general timidity. Up to age five, fears are equally prevalent in boys and girls, but beginning with the school-age years, sex differences increase. Fears and phobias are more prevalent in girls at all ages.

Loneliness   For a long time, social scientists thought that children could not experience loneliness prior to adolescence, when they became more separate from the family. Recent research, however, finds that five- and six-year-old children have conceptions of loneliness as clear as those of adults.[26] They describe feelings of being sad and alone, having no one to play with. The remedy, they report, is to find a playmate. Older elementary school children give even more poignant descriptions of loneliness—"feeling unneeded," "like you're the only one on the moon," "always in the dark," "like you have no one that really likes you and you're all alone."

Extreme loneliness is related to lack of friends, shy and submissive behavior, and a tendency to attribute social failure to one's own internal inadequacies. Such loneliness, in turn, prevents the child from interacting with others and intensifies the problem.

Unhappiness   In one study, parents and teachers described 10 to 12 percent of a representative sample of ten-year-olds as often appearing miserable, unhappy, tearful, or distressed.[27] The children themselves reported similar depressive feelings. Boys and girls were equally as likely to report such feelings.

INTERVIEW
with Barbara Keogh

Barbara K. Keogh is professor emeritus of educational psychology at the University of California, Los Angeles. Her research interests include the role of children's temperament in children's adjustment to school.

For many parents with children in the elementary school years, issues concerning school are quite important—how to get children ready for school on time, how to help them behave in school, how to get them to do schoolwork. You have done a great deal of research on children's temperament and school, and I think temperament plays a role in many children's adjustment.

It intrigued me when I started work in this area, a long time ago, that most of the work with temperament had been done with interactions in families, and yet when you think of the number of interactions that teachers have with children per hour, per day, in a classroom and add that up over the school year, temperament is an enormous potential influence.

When we began our research, we found that teachers have a very clear picture of what teachable children are like. One of the very important contributors to teachability is the stylistic variables or temperament variables that characterize children. Some children are easy to teach. They settle down better, they are not as active, they are not as intense, their mood is good, they adapt well, they like novelty, they are curious. All those things make teachers think, "Gee, I am a great teacher," when they have a whole classroom full of children with those characteristics.

So we are really operating on the assumption that children's experiences in school are influenced by individual variations in temperament. We have tried to document and understand the kind of impact these variations have on the teachers. We have used the concept of "goodness of fit" in a loose way.

I am convinced, and this is not a new idea, that teachers do not operate at random. They make decisions based on how they attribute the reasons for the behavior. They may think that active, distractible children are mischievous and need to be restricted and punished, and that children who are very slow to warm up or are withdrawn are lazy and uninterested. When we work with teachers and make them aware of temperamental characteristics, we get a very consistent response: "Oh, I never thought of that." Making teachers sensitive to temperament variations helps them reframe the child's behavior, and it makes the behavior much less upsetting to teachers.

It also carries planning implications. If you know a youngster is very distractible, very active, and very intense, then you can predict that every time you have a long wait in line, there's going to be a problem with him. It's predictable.

Children around the world, regardless of sex or socioeconomic status, agree with each other on what is upsetting even more than do adults and children within the same culture.[28] The loss of a parent is the most devastating occurrence, and the birth of a sibling the least upsetting. Parental fights are highly stressful. Children reveal their sensitivity in their distress at embarrassing situations—wetting their

When teachers begin to think of the individual variations on a temperamental rather than motivational basis, they begin to manipulate the environment more effectively. Temperament helps teachers reframe the problem behavior so it is not viewed as purposeful. This is true for both temperamentally "difficult" and "slow to warm up" children.

Another example I like is that most of the youngsters in an elementary class are delighted by novelty. The teacher says, "Oh, we are going to have a wonderful surprise today. At ten o'clock the fire department is coming." Most of the kids are excited. There will be a few "slow to warm up" youngsters who will say, "But at ten o'clock we are supposed to do our reading." They are upset because the usual routine is not followed. The teacher thinks, "What's the matter with that child? Why isn't he interested?" The child has a need for routine and a tendency to withdraw from newness or change. These children can profit from advance preparation. If they know a day in advance, they get a little forewarning.

Do you have any advice for parents as to how to help their children adjust to school?
Certainly parents have to be advocates for their child. That is absolutely necessary even if it means being confrontational, which is often not too productive. But certainly parents need to be aware when their child is unhappy at school, when their child is having problems, and address the problem with school people.

It has to be recognized that when we are working on a ratio of twenty-five youngsters to one teacher, there are going to be good matches and poor matches in any class. In no sense does that demean the quality of the teacher or the nature of the child. But there are differences in style, and some styles match better than others.

One thing parents can do is to provide teachers with some recognition that their child might not be a good match for this classroom. It helps the teacher to know that the parents are aware of that. So they can direct their mutual efforts to modify the class so the demands are more reasonable, or they can give the child extra help in modifying his or her behavior so it is more compatible with what is going on in that class.

Do you feel that most teachers are willing to change?
Yes, I do. We have worked with a lot of teachers in our research, and I think it helps them to think of ways that they can structure the situation so it is more compatible with the student without loss of educational goals. Yes, we have found teachers to be very open, and they were able to relate what we were saying to different children they have known: "Oh, yes, that's like Joey."

pants, being caught in a theft, being ridiculed in class. Although many students like school, it also causes them anxiety, frustration, and unhappiness, with many children worrying about grades, being retained, and making mistakes. Adults may be surprised at children's sensitivity to embarrassing situations and their concern about school. The data emphasize that children can have perspectives on life that are quite different from those of their parents and often not immediately apparent to parents.

Daily journals of elementary school students in the United States reveal that boys are more likely to cite external situations and demands, such as school, chores, interruptions, and environmental factors, as sources of stress.[29] Girls report disappointments with self and others and failure to live up to responsibilities as sources of stress in their lives.

Coping with Stress

In facing stress, children adapt in many ways. First, they use their own resources and the tools their parents give them. Second, they turn to trusted people for further support and guidance.

Strategies   Children are most likely to strike at the roots of the difficulty when the problem stems from peers or school, where they feel they have more control. Children tend to use distraction strategies to adjust to situations they cannot control, such as doctors' visits.[30] Children also tend to use enjoyable activities to buffer themselves from stress. Athletics, being at home with families, and special treats of food or surprises all help children to deal with stressors.[31]

Supportive People   When dealing with stressful or negative situations, children often seek others to help them. Children "perceive mothers as being the best multipurpose social provider available, in contrast to friends and teachers, who are relatively specialized in their social value."[32] Friends provide companionship and emotional support second only to parents. Teachers provide information but little companionship. Fathers are excellent providers of information, but are generally less available for direct help. Figure 9-1 illustrates where children of different ages and ethnic groups seek support.[33] Until early adolescence, parents and extended family provide the primary sources of support. Extended family are more important for African American and Latina/o children than for European Americans.

THE DEVELOPMENT OF THE SELF

In elementary school, children become capable of integrating behaviors and forming a more balanced view of themselves that takes into account both positive and negative qualities.[34] They are no longer limited to thinking of themselves in extreme terms—instead of smart or dumb, they think of themselves as smart at some things and not so smart in others.

Children also begin to evaluate their behavior in comparison to their peers. In the early grades, comparisons may be overt and direct—"I can finish the work faster than you"—but as children grow older, comparisons become subtler and less direct—"I have more friends than the other girls in my class."

We discussed in Chapter 6 that adopted children view themselves and their adoptive status in different terms as their thinking becomes more complex during

■ **FIGURE 9-1**
CONVOYS OF SUPPORT BY AGE AND ETHNICITY

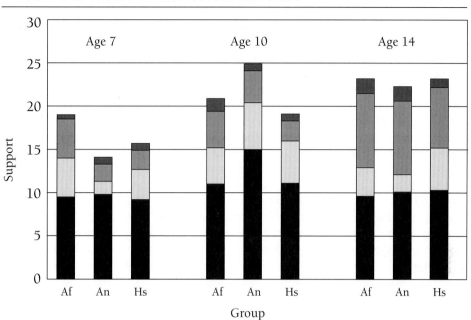

Af = African American, An = Anglo (European) American, Hs = Hispanic

Mary J. Levitt, Nathalie Guacci-Franco, and Jerome L. Levitt, "Convoys of Social Support in Childhood and Early Adolescence: Structure and Function," *Developmental Psychology* 29 (1993), p. 815. Copyright © 1993 American Psychological Association. Reprinted with permission.

this period.[35] Children become more curious about their biological origins and what led parents to give them up. They also begin to experience the loss of their biological family. "It is the experience of loss that ultimately leads to a sense of ambivalence about being adopted, as well as the emergence of adoption adjustment problems."[36]

Parents must provide a supportive family atmosphere and acknowledge that the child's experience of himself or herself is different from that of most children because the child comes from two families. On the other hand, parents must not overemphasize this difference. Ongoing communication of the child's feelings can help parents understand the child's experiences and feelings and permit the child to hear the parents' points of view.

Gender Identity

Psychologists used to think that gender development was largely completed in the preschool years. Studies of older children, however, reveal that gender identity continues to develop over a long time; in fact, it never truly ends.[37]

Children in elementary school reason about the constancy of gender identity in more advanced ways than before.[38] Preschoolers comprehend the stability of gender over time, and many comprehend the stability across situations. In the elementary school years, though, fewer children explain the constancy in terms of gender norms and external appearances, such as clothing, than do younger children. Further, an increasing number of children explain gender constancy in unchangeable, operational terms such as physical characteristics—"I have a penis"—or concepts such as "God made me a girl." Although one might expect that a greater realization of the constancy of gender identity would lead to more gender-stereotyped interests and behaviors, children in these years, particularly girls, are more flexible in their preferences for activities, chores, and future occupations than they were as preschoolers, and this flexibility increases with age.

Children develop a set of attitudes about what is gender appropriate, and, as noted in the previous chapter, these gender-appropriate schema motivate children to engage in gender-appropriate activities. At the same time, however, personal experiences and interests shape children's views of what is gender appropriate for them as individuals.[39] Children show greater flexibility with regard to psychological traits than with regard to activities or occupations of the opposite gender. Those children who do endorse activities and occupations usually associated with the opposite gender do so because they believe these activities and occupations are appropriate for both genders.

The most flexible and tolerant children come from families where parents and same-sex siblings are flexible in their activities. Same-sex peers also play an important role in promoting flexibility and tolerance.

Ethnic Identity

Children learn about their own ethnic identities in a process similar to that involved in gender identity.[40] First, children learn to identify their ethnic group (label themselves white, African American, Latina/o). This occurs in the preschool years for European American and African American children, and a little later on for other groups such as Asian Americans. Children then learn what is distinctive about their own ethnic group. Children of all groups can do this by about age seven. Finally, again at about age seven, children learn ethnic consistency and constancy and realize they cannot change their ethnic identity. In this period, children learn what it means to be part of their culture. By age ten, they know their identity and prefer their own group.

While children learn about their ethnic identity from parents and the culture around them, they also learn about their ethnic identity indirectly from their daily activities, just as they learn about gender identity.

Collected in 1997, mothers' daily diaries of children's activities reveal significant ethnic differences in everyday routines that reflect the distinctive values of each group.[41] Compared with African American, Latina/o, and Asian American children, European American children spend more time playing, more time in sports activities, and less time studying. They spend more time reading than do African American and Latina/o children but less time than do Asian American children. This pattern of active, social pursuits fits well with European American mothers' beliefs that studying and academic skills are less important than the development of social skills and general cognitive skill.

African American children differ from the other three groups in spending more time in church and church activities; Latina/o children enjoy more household and family activities; Asian American children spend more time in educational activities. These patterns of behavior reflect the values of each ethnic group.

Children not only learn what it means to be part of their group, but they also come to prefer their own group, seeing it quite positively and viewing other groups less favorably. Studies indicate that in-group favoritism develops first in children by about age five.[42] Children initially prefer their own group without looking at the out-group negatively. Attitudes toward out-groups develop gradually in the early elementary school years. Out-group prejudice appears least likely to develop when children attend a multiethnic school where they have interactions with children of different groups and when they can describe negative qualities about the in-group. Children's ability to recognize negative qualities about their own group seems to enable them to see the positive qualities in other groups. Nevertheless, even when out-group attitudes are not negative, in-group favoritism is so great that out-group children suffer in comparison.

Self-Esteem

Susan Harter has carried out extensive research on self-development and self-esteem. Global feelings of self-worth are related to two independent factors: (1) one's feelings of competence in domains of importance and (2) the amount of social support one receives from others. Those highest in self-worth feel good about the abilities they value and also feel that others support and accept them. Those lowest in global self-worth feel they lack competence in domains deemed important and report that they receive little social support. Harter notes that no amount of social support can directly counteract one's perception of incompetence; conversely, no amount of competence can completely overcome feelings of lack of social support. So, to increase self-esteem, one has to increase both social support and feelings of competence in valued domains.

In Harter's studies, high-self-esteem children aged three to seven had two qualities—confidence in approaching situations and resilience when frustrated or upset.[43] These are also the qualities of children securely attached to their caregivers. Parental support, then, is a more important determinant of early self-esteem than is competence per se. In later childhood, both support and feelings of competence are important in determining self-worth.

The areas of competence that contribute most to feelings of self-worth are physical appearance and social acceptance by others—namely, parents and peers. Surprisingly, physical appearance and social support continue to be salient across the lifespan for individuals from eight to fifty-five years of age. Elementary school children also evaluate themselves in terms of their scholastic and athletic competence and their conduct.

Although self-esteem depends on the early positive regard given by parents and caregivers, this regard does not fix it for life. Levels of self-esteem can increase over time as individuals become more competent in areas of importance to them or as they receive increased support from others. Self-esteem decreases under the reverse conditions.

Times of change and transition, such as entrance into kindergarten, can trigger changes in self-esteem. New skills to develop, new reference groups for comparison, and new social groups for support provide the stimulus for change. Children maintain self-esteem most successfully when they join or create positive social support or when they increase in other areas of competence.

Recall from Chapter 3 that elementary school children of different ethnic groups resemble each other in self-esteem.[44] As they begin to take on culturally valued behaviors, self-esteem scores diverge, depending on the culture's values. When cultural values stress individualism, expressiveness, and self-assertion, then self-esteem scores stay high, as they do in African American and European American groups. When cultural values emphasize respect for tradition, interdependence with others, and critical self-evaluation, then self-esteem scores drop, as they do in Latina/o and Asian American groups.

In sum, self-esteem arises in elementary school children in much the same way as in adults. Factors such as social support, competence, and cultural values affect self-esteem at this age.

THE DEVELOPMENT OF SELF-REGULATION

Elementary school children distinguish between guilt (feeling you did something naughty, feeling very sorry, wanting to make amends, fearing others will not like you) and shame (feeling afraid of being laughed at, feeling embarrassed, wanting to run away).[45] Guilt comes when children feel they have broken a moral rule, whereas shame is related to both moral and social blunders.

By about age eight, children become more self-critical, and their self-esteem is related to their ability to control verbal and physical aggression and other negative emotions. They feel ashamed when they violate a rule, and they take pride in being able to regulate their behavior and do what is approved. This is a good reason for parents to help children meet approved standards. Children do not feel good about themselves when they engage in behaviors they know others their age do not do.[46]

Table 9-1 lists the parental behaviors associated with children's self-regulation and prosocial behavior. Self-control and caring emerge from mutually responsive interactions with parents, from direct teaching and guidance from parents, and from parents' modeling of caring behaviors.

Children begin to reason about social interactions at early ages and, even in the preschool years, distinguish between moral rules, which concern issues of harm and justice for others, and social rules, which are conventions people agree on.[47] They consider hurting others to be more serious than breaking social conventions.

In the early elementary school years, reasoning about moral and conventional behavior becomes more complex, and children take into account the context of an event. They look at social situations and distinguish certain behaviors as matters of personal choice, other behaviors as matters of social convention, and still others as moral issues. For example, it is morally wrong to deprive a person of a basic right such as access to schooling because of race or gender, but a person has the right of personal choice to choose friends even if someone of another race or gender is not

■ **TABLE 9-1**
PARENTAL QUALITIES ASSOCIATED WITH CHILDREN'S SELF-REGULATION AND
PROSOCIAL BEHAVIOR

1. Being warm and supportive with children

2. Developing mutually responsive relationships with children

3. Helping children understand others' feelings and the effects of their behaviors
   on others

4. Using reasoning and persuasion to gain children's compliance with rules

5. Including children in family decision making

6. Helping children develop an internal code of rules for behavior

7. Modeling caring and concern for others

Adapted from Nancy Eisenberg and Carlos Valiente, "Parenting and Children's Prosocial and Moral
Development," in *Handbook of Parenting*, 2nd ed., ed. Marc H. Bornstein, vol. 5: *Practical Issues in
Parenting* (Mahwah, NJ: Erlbaum, 2002), 111–142.

included.[48] Children consider it wrong to violate a moral rule even if an authoritative adult tells them to do it. For example, it is wrong to keep on fighting even if an adult tells you to do so.[49]

SOCIAL DEVELOPMENT

In this period, children begin to spend more time away from home. While parents and home remain the center of life activities, friends begin to claim more of children's time.

Parent-Child Relationships

Parents spend half as much time with elementary school children and give them less physical affection, compared with preschoolers. Even so, parents enjoy parenting as much as in earlier years, and they report as much caring and regard for children as earlier.[50]

Parents' Role in Positive Behaviors   Parents' acceptance of, involvement in, and sensitivity to children's needs continue as major forces in helping children become responsible, competent, happy individuals. Parents are still the number-one figures for schoolchildren, whose greatest fear is of losing their parents.

If problems occur, parents' actions can help improve behavior. In one study, when parents modeled appropriate social behaviors and gave positive reinforcement for skillful social behaviors or made extra efforts so children could be with peers, then children who experienced social rejection gained in social skills and friendships.[51] Children's cognitive and social-emotional competence increased for a sample of high- and low-risk children assessed at ages four and thirteen.[52] Mothers who valued children's thinking for themselves and not conforming to others had high-risk children who gained in cognitive status. For both high-risk and low-risk children, mothers' lack of depression and lack of criticism and dissatisfaction were related to children's increase in social-emotional competence. Mothers' positive statements were also related to high-risk children's growth in social-emotional competence.

Parents' Role in Negative Behaviors   Parents' behaviors contribute not only to success but to negative outcomes as well. Mothers' harsh discipline, rated by interviewers and spouses and reflected in parents' statements of choice of discipline methods, predicted children's aggressive, impulsive behavior problems at school from kindergarten through grade four.[53] Even when the initial level of problem behavior was controlled, harsh discipline—seen in yelling, threatening, pushing, and spanking—predicted increases in aggressive behaviors over the four years. These relationships are not explainable solely on genetic grounds, that is, by aggressive parents passing on these traits to children and then having to use harsh discipline. A study of adoptive parents and children found that genetic factors play a role, however, in that children at risk for aggressive behaviors (based on the behaviors shown by their biological parents) tended to evoke negative parenting, which in turn increased aggressive behavior.[54] Even so, many children who were not at risk for aggressive behavior developed aggressive behaviors when parents used harsh discipline. Thus, genetic risk is not necessary to developing aggressive behaviors when parents use harsh discipline.

Parents' Changing Roles   Because parents no longer have exclusive control of children, they tend to permit children to make decisions that the parents monitor, supervise, and approve. This coregulation or sharing of control with children serves as a bridge to the preadolescent and adolescent years, when children will assume more control.[55]

   Conflicts between parents and children center on children's interpersonal behavior with others (their fighting, teasing), children's personality characteristics (their irritability, stubbornness), and parents' regulating activities, like rules about TV watching, chores, bedtime, and curfews.[56] Parents tend to justify their point of view in terms of conventionality, practicality, and health issues. Children tend to listen to parents' rules that prevent harm and psychological damage to others. Children report that they have more conflicts with fathers than with mothers. Rather than physical punishment, effective discipline involves removal of privileges.

Mothers' and Fathers' Roles   In the elementary school period, mothers and fathers continue to relate to children in different ways.[57] Mothers take major responsibility for managing family tasks—scheduling homework and baths, for example. Mothers are both more directive with children and more positive in their reactions to them.

   Fathers, though more generally neutral in affect, continue to engage in more physical play and give more affection to both boys and girls. When fathers have high-status jobs, they have less time to spend with their children, and so low job salience is related to men's playfulness and caregiving.[58] Men are most likely to be involved as fathers when mothers do not take on all the caregiving and managing. Nevertheless, the more skillful the mothers are with children, the more skillful fathers become. Both parents are similar in being more demanding of boys than of girls and more disapproving of boys' misbehavior.[59]

Though mothers and fathers have different roles, children see them as having many qualities in common.[60] Both parents are described as loving, happy, honest, responsible, self-confident individuals. Fathers are more interested in learning and creativity than are mothers, and mothers are more concerned about others' feelings than are fathers. Children describe themselves less positively than they describe their parents but still see many similarities with them. They are loving, happy, and interested in learning and creativity, but they are far below parents in self-confidence, cooperativeness, responsibility, and honesty. Children described "having good family relationships" as the most important family goal of mothers and themselves, but feel fathers' most valued goals are "educational/vocational."

When parents make demands on the child, social responsibility increases in boys, self-assertiveness in girls. Diana Baumrind suggests that parents actively encourage characteristics outside the usual gender stereotypes. Unless they exert a specific effort to encourage a broader range of characteristics, the natural tendencies for both mothers and fathers is to encourage assertiveness in boys and cooperation and a more dependent role in girls.[61]

Socializers of Ethnic Identity   Parents play an important role in the formation of their children's ethnic identity. School-age children reason more logically and better understand parents' statements. Because they spend more time outside of parents' direct control, they are more likely to experience prejudice or, at least, confusion at the different values other people hold.

Parents serve as buffers between children and the larger society, interpreting social experiences for their children and helping them deal with them. To socialize children with regard to racial and ethnic issues, parents first teach children (1) their own cultural values, (2) the values of the majority culture, and (3) the realities of being a member of their own group in the majority culture and how people cope with the realities.[62] Successful socialization goes beyond this to teach pride in one's ethnic group and the importance of one's own self-development.

We focus here on how African American parents socialize children, because more research is available on this group; other groups may experience a similar process.[63] African American parents think that teaching about their racial identity is important but is not *the* most important information to pass on to children. To parents, being African American means children should learn how to deal with prejudice, feel pride and self-respect, learn the value of a good education, and recognize that their fair and moral behavior is not always reciprocated.

Many African American parents do not discuss ethnic issues with their children. In a national sample, over one-third of parents reported making no statements, and few of the two-thirds who reported making a statement touched on more than one area. Which parents are most likely to talk to their children? Older, married parents who live in racially mixed neighborhoods with a sizable white population are most likely to talk to children. Mothers are more likely to socialize children than are fathers. Parents living in the Northeast tend to discuss racial matters, perhaps because, as in mixed neighborhoods, there is more contact among races.

Table 9-2 summarizes socialization messages that African American parents share with their children. Only about 22 percent teach racial pride and a positive self-image, yet this is the area parents are most uniquely fitted to address. Both majority and minority children evaluate themselves the way others close to them do,

■ **T A B L E 9-2**
SOCIALIZATION MESSAGES AFRICAN AMERICAN PARENTS IMPART
TO CHILDREN*

Message	% Parents
Achieving and working hard: *"Work hard and get a good education."*	22
Racial pride: *"Be proud of being black."*	17
Themes of black heritage: *"Taught what happened in the past and how people coped."*	9
Focus on intergroup relations: *Summary category of many responses—accommodate whites, use collective action to help blacks*	9
Presence of racial restrictions and barriers: *"Blacks don't have the opportunities whites have."*	8
Good citizenship: *"Be honest, fair."*	7
Recognition and acceptance of racial background: *"Realize you are black."*	7
Fundamental equality of blacks and whites: *"Recognize all races as equal."*	6
Maintenance of a positive self-image: *"Instruct children to stay away from whites."*	5 3[†]

*Information from the National Survey of Black Americans, a representative national sample of 2,107 men and women. Statements tabulated from the answers to two questions: "In raising children, have you told them things to help them know what it is to be black?" and "What are the most important things you have said?"

[†]Remaining categories of 1 or 2 percent include a variety of responses having to do with emphasizing religious principles, discussing personal traits, and stressing general self-acceptance.

From Michael C. Thornton, Linda M. Chatters, Robert Joseph Taylor, and Walter R. Allen, "Sociodemographic and Environmental Correlates of Racial Socialization by Black Parents," *Child Development* 61 (1990): 401–409.

and so what parents convey strongly affects the children's self-esteem. Because a minority child may get inaccurate and negative messages from other children, the media, and authority figures such as coaches or teachers, it is even more important for minority parents to encourage a positive self-image and racial pride. When parents emphasize awareness of social restrictions and barriers but at the same time encourage self-development and ethnic pride and help children develop strategies for dealing with barriers, children are happy, high in self-esteem, and successful in school.[64]

Relationships with Siblings

Siblings frequently spend more time with each other than they do with parents.[65] Their relationships improve in the elementary school years and become more enjoyable. The degree of satisfaction depends on the emotional climate in the family, because sibling relationships tend to mirror the ways parents treat each other and the ways they relate to children.[66] When parents are responsive to children and treat them fairly, then siblings have good relationships.

Conversely, when mothers and fathers are angry with each other, they are more hostile with their children, who, in turn, show anger at their siblings and their peers.[67] Children's behavior may be disruptive for a variety of reasons. They may model parents' fighting with siblings and peers, or they may be so upset and irritable that they lack emotional control and become angry. They may even blame themselves for the marital conflict. Because conflict in sibling relationships during these years predicts a child's level of anxiety, depression, and acting out in early adolescence, improving these relationships when tension arises is important.[68]

Although most research on sibling relationships has been carried out on European American families, research with rural African American families has yielded similar results.[69] When parents have good relationships with each other and positive relationships with their children, the older siblings develop good emotional control and are supportive and caring with younger siblings. Even though these parents work long hours and have financial pressures, when parents are caring with them, the older children also show care with younger siblings.

Peer Relationships

In the elementary school years, children have more contact with peers, spending about 30 percent or more of their time with them in a wide variety of settings—school, sports, and interest groups—with less adult supervision than before. As in the preschool years, children are attracted to peers whose interests are similar to theirs.[70] They continue to prefer positive interactions and to work problems out so that everyone's needs are met. Relationships grow when children can express thoughts and feelings clearly.

In these years, children begin to compare their social behaviors with those of peers.[71] Some children are identified as popular and sought after as friends. These children are socially skilled and enter new activities or relationships in quiet ways, not drawing attention to themselves. Friendly, cooperative, sensitive to others' needs, and helpful, they rarely interfere with others' actions or plans.

Aggressive Children   Some children are rejected. This occurs mostly when they show aggressive behavior, which takes many forms. Children may physically hit or hurt others, or they may be verbally assaultive—taunting, teasing, humiliating others. This type of aggression is overt, noticeable, and more characteristic of boys than of girls.[72] Another form of aggression, termed *relational aggression,* is more subtle, not easily detectable, and more characteristic of girls. It consists of acts designed to deprive children of friends—spreading untrue rumors about a target child, organizing other children to reject the target child, refusing to be a friend unless the target child does favors. These behaviors are considered aggressive because they are meant to hurt or damage another child.

In one study, about 27 percent of boys were described as aggressive, and of those boys 93 percent were overtly aggressive.[73] About 22 percent of girls were described as aggressive, and of those girls 95 percent were engaged in relational aggression. Only about one-quarter of aggressive children used both forms to hurt children; most relied on one or the other. Note that when relational aggression is assessed, girls are almost equal to boys in aggressive behavior.

Because both forms of aggressive behavior lead to peer rejection, ongoing social problems, feelings of loneliness, and low self-esteem, interventions are important so children can gain acceptance and avoid the problems of adolescence and adulthood associated with aggressiveness in childhood.[74]

Bullying   Bullying occurs when an aggressive child targets a single child or a small group and, though unprovoked, pursues the child(ren) and uses force in an unemotional way, divorced from conflict or disagreement. About two-thirds of aggressive children are overt bullies, and 10 to 15 percent of all children are victims of overt bullying.[75] As noted earlier, almost all aggressive girls engage in relational aggression, and about 8 percent of all girls are victims of relational aggression.[76] Victims of both forms of bullying share certain characteristics. They tend to be quiet, inhibited children with low self-esteem. They are sometimes physically weaker. A small subgroup of victims are impulsive, disruptive children who invite negative reactions from others. Victims accept the aggression, withdrawing or responding with immature behavior such as crying, thus rewarding the bully's behavior. As victims continue to experience bullying, their self-esteem decreases further, and over time they become depressed and develop behavior problems at home and at school.[77] When followed up in young adulthood, victims have as many social skills as young adults who were not bullied, but bullying has left its mark. Former victims are prone to feelings of depression and low self-esteem.

Research on ways to combat bullying indicate that those children who have confidence in their social skills and resist bullying with self-assertion are able to end the victimization, even if they are initially inhibited or physically weaker children.[78] They need not be physically aggressive, but they do not tolerate the attacks. Parents can help children combat bullying by enrolling children in social skills programs that teach and rehearse self-assertion. Victimization requires intervention to help both the victim and the bully, as both suffer in the present and the future. Unfortunately, bullying rarely fades away on its own.

TASKS AND CONCERNS OF PARENTS

Because elementary school children spend more time out of parents' direct care, parenting tasks include new activities as well as previous caregiving behaviors. In this age period, parenting tasks include the following:

- Being attentive, available, and responsive and modeling desired behavior
- Structuring the home and daily routines so children have healthy lifestyles
- Monitoring and guiding children's behavior from a distance
- Encouraging new skills, new activities, and growing interest in friends
- Participating in children's activities outside the home in supportive ways (room parent, den leader)
- Serving as an interpreter of children's experiences in the larger social world
- Serving as children's advocate with authorities outside the home
- Maintaining family rituals
- Sharing leisure activities and fun

As parents learn how to manage these tasks, they and their children face many concerns specific to this age. School is clearly a source of worry to children. Schoolwork is also a source of concern to parents, who pay great attention to promoting children's success in school. Other issues faced include isolation, aggression, lying, stealing, sibling rivalry, chores, and television watching.

Promoting Healthy Lifestyles

When their children were infants, parents of school-age children may have thought that, when their children could sleep through the night, feed themselves, and follow simple routines and rules, they would be finished dealing with issues of eating and sleeping. As we have seen, however, healthy sleep, eating, and exercise habits continue to affect children's physical well-being, and children do not establish and maintain them without parents' help. Poor sleep and poor eating habits are related to school inattentiveness and restlessness, which interfere with being able to concentrate and learn new material.

As we saw in Chapter 8, parents establish and monitor their children's sleep habits early on. This continues through the elementary years. Because each child is unique, parents have to determine the proper amount of sleep for their child and maintain bedtimes so the child gets it.

A recent study indicates that adding an hour's sleep each night to children's existing schedule improves memory and reaction times on cognitive tests; the increase is the equivalent of two years of chronological age on these tests.[79]

Parents have no control over what children eat when they are away from home, but they do control the food available at home. Parents can buy primarily healthy foods and model healthy eating habits. If potato chips and soda are at hand, children will consume them or beg to do so. If parents do not provide such snacks, children are less likely to argue for them.

Serving healthy meals and having positive conversations during meals encourage children to enjoy eating and to eat a reasonable amount of food. Although it can be difficult to plan and organize family meals with the television off, the effort is worth it.

Building regular exercise times into daily routines is difficult when both parents work, but pre-dinner calisthenics for all family members or post-dinner walks in good weather may work. Knowing how important exercise is can alert parents to opportunities at school or in the neighborhood for children, and perhaps the whole family, to exercise.

Daily family routines and rituals organized around sleeping and eating not only lead to better physical condition of all family members but also increase the psychological well-being of family members (see Chapter 4). A review of fifty years of research on family routines and rituals finds that routines draw family members together and improve relationships.[80]

Helping Children Regulate Feelings

Pediatricians report a growing number of children aged five to fifteen with psychological problems requiring help.[81] Research comparing the responses of pediatricians in 1979 with responses in 1996 finds that in 1979, 6.8 percent of children were identified in routine office visits as having psychological problems requiring help, and in 1996, the comparable figure was 18.7 percent. The largest increases were in attention-deficit hyperactivity problems, which went from 1.4 percent of children seen in the 1979 survey to 8.5 percent in 1996, and in emotional problems, which went from 0.2 percent in 1979 to 3.2 percent in 1996.

Chapter 4 talks about coaching children to identify their own and others' feelings and to deal with them in acceptable ways. Here we focus on two common feelings—anger and discouragement—because they can be so easily aroused as part of the school experience yet must be controlled.

Anger   Psychologist Tim Murphy has described a program for parents to help their out-of-control children.[82] In describing the angry child, he makes several important points. He defines *anger* in broad terms: a feeling of displeasure, as a result of a perceived injury, and a desire to retaliate against the source of the injury. This definition reflects what many parents see in the angry child.

He describes four stages of anger: the buildup, the spark, the explosion, and the aftermath. He also describes what he terms *microbursts* of anger—the sudden, brief outbursts that end almost as soon as they start. He urges parents to attend to these microbursts. Because the child is not extremely upset, parents can often use the episodes to help the child develop a better understanding of feelings and better problem-solving skills.

Murphy describes several important characteristics of the angry child. First, rather than distinguishing sadness, disappointment, and frustration, the angry child turns all negative experiences into anger. Second, the angry child sees the source of the difficulty as someone else's deliberate action against him or her. Frustration is seen as caused not by uncontrollable events or family needs or even the child's difficulty in accomplishing something but by the parent, particularly the mother. Third, and most important, angry children are not clear thinkers or effective problem solvers. Prone to negative self-talk that immobilizes them, they cannot figure out how to make things better. Sadly, they often equate anger with power and feelings of self-esteem.

According to Murphy, the meaning of anger is in part related to family patterns of interaction. In the hurried, busy family, anger is a sign of stress. In the troubled family dealing with problems of addiction, loss, parents' psychological problems, and marital discord, anger is a sign of pain. In the angry family, anger serves as a sign of power. In the indulging family, anger is a sign of desire. Indulging parents have led children to believe they should have what they want. Because they do not set many clear guidelines and do not reinforce the guidelines they do have, the child learns to persist as long and as angrily as necessary to win each battle.

Drawing on many of the anger-management strategies discussed in Chapters 4 and 5, Murphy describes positive parenting in terms of six healthy attitudes. Some of these resemble Rudolf Dreikurs' approach to the handling of children's mistakes (see Chapter 4):

1. Teach the child to be independent.

2. Emphasize the process of accomplishing the task, not just the end product.

3. Keep the childlike perspective alive in you so you can better understand and empathize with your child.

4. Choose what you say carefully; words of criticism can remain in a child's memory forever.

5. Learn to laugh at some of the difficulties and avoid taking them so seriously.

6. "Parent peacefully in an angry world;" teach the positive behaviors that will avoid the problems—for example, teach a child tolerance before the child becomes prejudiced; coach feeling expression before a child becomes angry.

Gerald Patterson's program also deals with children's angry outbursts (see Chapter 8).[83] It focuses on paying positive attention to children's behavior, engaging in fun activities, and then consistently rewarding behaviors with positive and negative consequences as necessary.

Discouragement   In these years of rapidly developing skills, meeting new friends, and learning in formal settings in comparison with others, discouragement is a common feeling, especially for the more cautious, less confident child. Martin Seligman offers a program quite useful for parents in his book *The Optimistic Child*.[84]

Seligman has documented the nature of pessimistic attitudes that lead to discouragement and withdrawal from challenging tasks. Pessimistic individuals consider difficulty a sign of a pervasive, permanent problem that is one's personal fault and is unchangeable. Pessimistic children see a poor math grade as the result of their own stupidity and inability to do math. They sometimes avoid studying because they are discouraged and feel they are no good at the subject.

Parents can supply new interpretations of the problem. Perhaps the child did not study enough, perhaps the child needs extra tutoring. Parents can encourage their children to look for solutions to problems and to exert effort to achieve them, as most problems will improve with such efforts from the child. Parents also must avoid critical personal comments, such as "You never learn at school—you just fool around," which can sap children's confidence.

Promoting Positive Social Relationships

Parents play an important role in helping children develop effective social skills.

Helping the Shy Child   Shy children hesitate to approach others, are often uncertain of what to say to others, and are uncertain how to join games. They worry about rejection. Philip Zimbardo and Shirley Radl offer many suggestions for the parent of the shy child. These measures focus on increasing the child's expressiveness (smiling, talking more), interactions with others (starting conversations), and opportunities for social contact.[85] All these actions are designed to increase self-esteem, confidence, and socially outgoing behavior. This behavior, along with coaching about group interactions, minimizes the likelihood of a child's being bullied and enables the child to deal more effectively with bullies.

Behaviorists coach children in effective ways of interacting and provide opportunities to practice (1) participating in group activities (getting started, paying attention to the game), (2) cooperating in play (sharing, taking turns), (3) communicating with the peer (talking or listening), and (4) validating and supporting the peer (giving attention and help). The benefits are found to persist a year.[86]

Several factors are related to improvement in children's social status.[87] Children who got involved in extracurricular activities improved in social status. Whether it was the development of new skills, the opportunities for making new friends, or increased confidence and self-esteem that led to improved social status is not known. Children who took some responsibility for peer difficulties and whose parents believed good social skills were important, modeled them, and gave appropriate rewards for skillful actions also improved in status. Boys who felt self-confident and socially skilled improved their status as well.

Helping the Aggressive Child   A major form of intervention for aggressive children is to help them develop positive social skills. Much like group programs for shy children, behavioral programs for aggressive children focus on positive behaviors. These programs encourage cooperation, offer positive techniques to support peers, develop verbal skills to make requests and suggestions, teach positive techniques for anger management (as outlined in the preceding section),

Box 9-1
RICHARD LAVOIE'S STRATEGIES TO DEVELOP SOCIAL COMPETENCE*

Richard Lavoie has long worked with children who have learning disabilities of many kinds. He observed that social difficulties can be closely linked to the difficulties in learning. If a person cannot process auditory material, she may not follow conversations well; if he has expressive language problems, he may be slow and awkward in expressing himself or explaining his feelings to a friend.

Lavoie points out that, if you have trouble in school, you can always enjoy athletic activities and all the social activities away from school. "But if your child has poor social skills, he simply cannot avoid situations that require these skills. Any and all activities that involve two or more people require the use of social skills."[†]

There is no technology to help a child compensate for social difficulties as there are for learning disabilities (e.g., word processors and calculators).

Lavoie has developed a system that parents, teachers, and counselors can use to help a child with learning disabilities develop social competence. It is a system any parent can use with a child with social difficulties.

Lavoie's basic belief is that children's social missteps are unintentional—they want to have friends, but they don't know how to "tune in" to social situations, join groups, make and keep friends, and resolve conflicts. They need help in all these areas, and each area requires many different skills.

To assist the child, parents take several steps. Most important, they remain calm, nonjudgmental helpers who serve as coaches and mutual problem-solvers. As coaches, they help children prepare for difficult situations. If children are going to new classes or new programs, parents may go to the buildings or places in advance and become familiar with them. They help children rehearse for new social situations such as sleepovers or birthdays. They go over appropriate conversations for upcoming situations such as meeting new people or giving a gift.

At times of isolation, friction, or conflict, the adult and child together, in a calm, nonblaming way, review what happened and carry out what is called a *social skills autopsy*—so termed because it is an attempt to determine the cause and effect of a "social error" in order to prevent its happening again. The social skills autopsy consists of five steps:

1. Ask the child to describe what happened.

2. Ask the child to identify what he or she thinks was the social mistake responsible for the difficulty; often, the child fails to identify what went wrong in the situation.

3. Help the child identify the particular social error accurately. Put forward alternative options in the situation, and let the child choose an appropriate one.

4. Create a social scenario with the same basic error or moral and see if the child recognizes the problem. For example, if the child got interested in his or her activities and went late to a birthday party, resulting in everyone's waiting to go to a movie, a similar scene is made up in which the parent is late and delays everyone, and the child is expected to identify the error. If he or she fails, another scenario is made up.

(continued)

Box 9-1
CONTINUED

---

5. The child practices the remedy at least once in the coming week—for example, being on time for all social activities or sports.

The adult and child are collaborators; the adult asks questions and leads in much the same way that Vygotsky suggests in Chapter 2. This process is carried out over and over, helping the child gradually build up successful strategies. The process is unending because, as a child masters a certain set, he or she may be on to a more advanced level of social interaction and have to learn a new set. But parents are always there as consultants and coaches.

Lavoie's book is a treasury of useful suggestions for parents whose children can have many different kinds of specific problems.

*Richard Lavoie, *It's So Much Work to Be Your Friend* (New York: Touchstone Books, 2005).
†Ibid., p. XXIX.

---

and provide opportunities for children to rehearse the skills that increase social competence and peer acceptance. In follow-up studies, children who attended such programs achieved greater peer acceptance and reduced their aggressive responses.

Helping the Bully   Dan Olweus has studied bullying extensively in Norway and developed a school-based program to decrease it.[88] This program requires the involvement and commitment of school administrators, teachers, parents, and students. Adults create, at school and at home, an environment in which children experience warm, positive attention and firm limits against negative behaviors. Negative behaviors receive consistent, nonhostile, nonphysical consequences, and monitoring occurs in and out of school.

Interventions occur at the school, class, and individual level and include the formation of a coordinating group, meetings with staff and parents, better supervision during recess, class rules against bullying, and class meetings. At the individual level, parents, teachers, and students meet to discuss specific incidents and to develop strategies to handle them. Emphasis is on developing effective forms of communication and positive behaviors in all students, not just in bullies or victims.

Evaluated by 2,500 students and their teachers, the intervention program was found to reduce bullying by 50 percent and decrease other antisocial acts as well. Moreover, bullying away from the school did not increase. Students expressed greater satisfaction with their schoolwork, and their social relationships with children increased. The benefits were in some instances more marked after two years than after one year.

In all areas of social difficulties—shyness, aggressiveness, victimization—taking action to learn social skills, to engage in activities that increase confidence, and to assert

VOICES OF EXPERIENCE

The Joys of Parenting Elementary School Children

"He's nine, and for the last several months, maybe because I'm the dad, he's come and said, 'Now there's this girl who's written me a note, what do I do?' Or, 'I have an interest here, how do I act?' I never heard any of this from my daughters. Then he says, 'What were you doing in the third grade? How did you deal with this when you were in the third grade?'" FATHER

"Being able to see life through their eyes is fun, sharing the way they see things, the questions they ask." MOTHER

"They are very loving kids. They'll give me a kiss good night and say, 'I'll love you forever.' That's a tradition." FATHER

"It was fun to see him learn to read. First, he knew the letters and then he read a little, and by the end of the year, he could read a lot." MOTHER

"I like watching them when they don't know I'm watching. They're playing or taking something apart. That's when you see how well you've transferred your values to them." FATHER

"It's fun to see the children join in with other kids. They went with their cousins to a July 4th celebration. They got right into a game with children they didn't know." MOTHER

"She wrote poems in school this year. It's amazing. She's quiet, and yet when you see the poems, you realize how much goes on in her head, how observant she is." FATHER

"I like seeing how important family is to them. They enjoy seeing their cousins, they like family to visit." MOTHER

"I'm a kid again. I get to do everything I liked to do all over again." FATHER

"It's fun when she says, 'Mommy, smile at me, make me laugh.'" MOTHER

"I enjoy watching their relationship grow. They are nineteen months apart. They play together a lot. She said to me, 'Sometimes, he's fun to play with and I love him, but sometimes he's a rascal.' They do a lot of imaginary play." MOTHER

"Every night we have a talking time just before he goes to bed, either he and his Dad or he and I. He's a real deep thinker, and he likes to get advice or get a response, and he just needs that verbal connection. So a few years ago when he was five, he was talking about being afraid of death and that he might not be married and he might not have children and that would be the worst. I can hear parts of what he might hear at church or other places like school, and he takes it all very seriously; when it collides, he wants to know what the answer is. They are always things we don't know the answer to, either." MOTHER

"I can say, as a father of two girls between five and ten, that to be a father to girls is delightful. It's nice being looked on as a combination of God and Robert Redford. They have a little glow in their eyes when they look at Dad, and it's great. The younger one said, 'When I'm ticklish, you know why? Because I love you so much.'" FATHER

oneself when attacked help children improve their social status. Parents play an important role here—to ensure that children have opportunities to increase their social competence and to ensure that the school atmosphere is a safe place for all children.

The Partnership of Families and Schools

In the past, people looked on the school as a separate social entity that carried the primary responsibility for educating children. Parents played a secondary role—raising funds, volunteering in the school, and enriching the curriculum with their input and values. Recently, a partnership model for families and schools has been advanced.[89] Acknowledging the powerful impact of parents' involvement and encouragement on children's educational progress, the partnership model seeks to forge a strong link between parents and the schools. This model rests on six major kinds of involvement:

1. Parents provide a home that allows children to (a) be healthy and attend school, (b) be calm and confident enough to pay attention in class and do their work, (c) receive encouragement to perform well, and (d) have home settings that support doing homework and educational projects. Schools provide families with information on effective parenting and school-related issues; they sometimes also provide supportive programs or workshops.

2. Schools communicate and keep parents informed of school matters and students' progress and behavior. This includes notices on students' current performance, any difficulties that arise, and any noteworthy behaviors of students, as well as information on school programs, school needs, and opportunities for parental involvement in projects. Effective communication also involves channels for parents' input on programs.

3. Parents, children, and other community members contribute their own special skills to promote children's education, as in cleaning, painting, and giving cultural information of interest.

4. Teachers help parents monitor and help children learn at home. Schools make educational goals and curricula available, show parents how to assist their children, and even give joint assignments that parents and student carry out together.

5. Parents participate in school organizations and in formal or informal groups that advise educators on school priorities, school improvement programs, and parents' and students' perceptions of problems in the school environment.

6. Finally, parents and schools work with business organizations, local government agencies, and volunteer groups to form partnerships that support school programs.

Lying and Stealing

When parents create a supportive atmosphere in which children can talk about mistakes and misdeeds, and when they offer encouragement rather than criticism, lying and stealing are reduced. Still, almost every child has told a lie at one time or another, and all parents have concerns about lying and stealing, because trust in others is such an important part of close relationships.

Parents are wise to express their feelings of concern about dishonesty, accept matter-of-factly that the child has lied or stolen, and problem-solve with the child ways to be more truthful and honest. If a child lies about schoolwork, they should find out if there are special problems at school. If a child brags about false exploits, they do well to focus on why he or she needs to do this to feel good. Parents express their belief that their child wants to be honest, and as partners, they need to figure out how to bring this about. Mutual problem-solving, as discussed in Chapter 5, is very useful. In this process, the parent becomes an ally and a resource, not an accuser and a judge. The child learns that one can get help when in trouble and that one need not be perfect to be loved.

A PRACTICAL QUESTION: WHAT CAN PARENTS DO WHEN SCHOOL AND PSYCHOLOGICAL DIFFICULTIES INTERFERE WITH ACADEMIC ACHIEVEMENT?

Children may forget homework or resist doing it because it is hard. They may be anxious and have few friends at school. Such problems frustrate children and parents and require action, but they usually do not interfere with school performance and achievement. Sometimes, however, children's school difficulties are so marked that they prevent learning and successful school performance, and they require parents' and teachers' actions to remedy the situation. For example, forgetfulness on a daily basis may be part of a larger picture of general inattention, hyperactivity, and impulsivity, the core symptoms of attention-deficit hyperactivity disorder (ADHD). Or children may have learning disabilities involving difficulties regarding reading, writing, or carrying out actions in the correct sequence.

These problems may not have appeared at home, and they may not be immediately apparent at school. A child may seem a little slow in "settling down" at school or a little slow in learning and printing letters, but parents and teachers may initially consider the child able to attend or do the work. When difficulties persist over time and result in lowered performance or failure to learn material, parents and teachers together must consider what to do. Space does not permit detailed discussions of attention-deficit hyperactivity disorder, learning disabilities, or the great variety of emotional disorders that interfere with achievement, but a general plan for dealing with these kinds of problems is described.

School difficulties require accurate diagnosis as the first step in the process of remedying them. Learning disabilities and ADHD are common sources of problems, but they are not easy to separate, because the two significantly overlap. School study teams and school psychologists observe and test children and provide vital information in identifying sources of the problems. If difficulties do not fall into certain categories or meet certain criteria of delays, schools might not do assessments, in which case parents have to seek assessments privately. If they cannot afford such services, which can be quite expensive, parents can seek help from agencies or local colleges that provide services on a sliding-scale basis.

When specific difficulties are identified, then parents, teachers, and children meet to plan how to remedy them. It is important to involve children in the process, as they need to understand specifically what they need to change, and they may have good ideas about how to produce change. In encouraging new behaviors and skills, parents and teachers identify the specific positive behaviors they want from children. Sometimes, thinking that children know what to do, adults give general directions: "Be good in school today" or "Get your work done." Instead, they need to be specific: "When I give you a work sheet, stay in your seat until you finish it, and then you can bring it to my desk." "When you write, use a finger's width between each word." "Go slowly so you read each word."

The level of work expected must be tailored to children's abilities. When children are performing below grade level, tutoring and special assignments are required so that children are able and motivated to practice and increase their levels of performance. If assignments are too difficult at the age-appropriate level but are expected nonetheless, then children will grow discouraged and resist doing them. Levels of work difficulty can change as children learn basic skills. As with other kinds of school problems, daily contracts can be made with children regarding their behavior and the amount and kind of work they must complete to earn privileges.

Emotional problems such as extreme anxiety or depression can also decrease school performance and are usually addressed in consultation with mental health professionals. Clinicians can provide parents and schools with realistic expectations and work demands for children and help parents and teachers make plans to control the effects of the emotional reactions. They can suggest school interventions and modify them, depending on their level of effectiveness.

Serious problems at school impact family life as well. Children might hate and resist schoolwork. They might insist they cannot do the work, so parents must be sure they can. Once parents know that the work is appropriate, they must provide an atmosphere of encouragement that motivates children to strive for improvement. Parents must be sure that children continue to get all the help and support they need at school and at home.

At the same time that parents help children deal with difficulties, parents also identify children's strengths, inside and outside of school, and help children gain pleasure and satisfaction from them to balance the effort and frustration required by problem areas. For example, sports of different kinds can channel the energy and frustration of athletic children, and artistic activities such as music or drawing provide important outlets for creative children. As children progress through school, they have greater opportunities for choice in subjects, and parents can help them select courses that draw on their abilities.

Siblings may use school difficulties as a means of teasing or for comparisons that enable them to feel better about themselves and their skills. Parents must stop such behavior and teach family members that all children have their own special strengths, and everyone has one or more areas in which they must strive for improvement. Parents can express empathy for children who must spend long hours, year after year, in an atmosphere and activity that brings frustration.

Having daily fun with family members, perhaps after dinner, relaxes everyone and increases good feelings that sustain effort and motivation for the work. School difficulty is not easy for parents, children, or school personnel, but working together as a team, focusing on solutions, helps everyone feel better and leads to greater success.

PARENTS' EXPERIENCES IN FACING TRANSITIONS

Children's entrance into school marks a new stage in parenthood. Children spend more time away from their parents in school and with peers. They are absorbing new information and are exposed to new values. Ellen Galinsky describes this parental stage as the *interpretive stage*.[90] Parents share facts and information about the world, teach values, and guide children's behavior in certain directions. They decide how they will handle the child's greater independence and involvement with people who may not share similar values.

At this point, parents have a more realistic view of themselves as parents than before and a greater understanding of their children as individuals. Parents have been through the sleepless nights and crying of infancy, the temper tantrums of the toddler, and the instruction of their children in basic routines and habits. They have a sense of how they and their child will react in any given situation. Though some carry a negative view of themselves as parents, most have developed a sense of their strengths and difficulties and a confidence that, by and large, they and their children are okay. Children, however, leave the parents' control and enter a structured environment with rules and regulations. Children are evaluated in terms of their ability to control their behavior and learn skills that will help them as adults. For the first time, external standards and grades compare children with each other. Parents must deal with, and help their children deal with, these external evaluations, which may differ from those parents have formed at home.

For parents, bridging the gap between the way they treat their children and the way their children are treated by teachers, group leaders, and peers may be a constant struggle. Parents develop strategies for dealing with teachers, doctors, and principals who do not see the child as they do. An attitude that stresses cooperation among adults seems most effective. When parents share their knowledge about their child, when they seek to understand the child's behaviors that demand change, they can form a coalition with adults outside the home to produce a positive experience for their child.

In the process of explaining the world and people's behavior, parents refine their beliefs and values, discarding some and adding others. Children often prompt changes when they discover inconsistencies and hypocrisies in what parents say. If lying is bad, why do parents tell relatives they are busy when they are not? If parents care about the world and want to make it a safer place, why are they not doing something to make it safe? In the process of answering these questions, parents grow as well as children.

SUPPORT FOR PARENTS

There are many forms of support for parents of elementary school children. Parents work together with teachers and school personnel in Parent Teacher Associations or local organizations to provide the most effective schools possible. Specialized parent support groups also offer valuable information and resources. For example, Children and Adults with Attention Deficit Disorders (CHADD) provides support for families dealing with ADHD; the Orton Dyslexia Society helps with problems of reading; the Learning Disabilities Association of America, with learning disabilities. In addition, local and state organizations can be helpful.

Parent training programs also provide support. Extensive and effective programs to decrease children's aggressiveness and improve social behavior have been devised at the Oregon Social Learning Center. Patterson and his colleagues have worked with married parents, divorced single parents, foster parents, and parent-teacher partnerships to establish structure as well as positive and consistent rewards to help children learn to control aggressive behavior and develop prosocial behaviors at home and at school. These programs have found success and are being refined and expanded.

These are secular forms of support. At all age levels, parents and children find moral support and strength from religious activities as well. This source of support becomes important at this stage, because children begin to explore moral and ethical issues and are exposed to more ideas about these issues than before. Religious participation provides opportunities for discussing moral principles and applying them to everyday life.

Parents involved in religion can easily include their children. When parents have no affiliation, Joan Beck recommends that parents develop an individual belief system that they share with children as they grow.[91] The process of developing an agreed-on source of spiritual or secular meaning in life can enrich the entire family.

Religious faith also contributes to feelings of confidence and security. In their study of resilient children who overcame the difficulties of growing up in troubled families, Emmy Werner and Ruth Smith point to the importance of faith:

> A potent protective factor among high-risk individuals who grew into successful adulthood was a faith that life made sense, that the odds could be overcome. This faith was tied to active involvement in church activities, whether Buddhist, Catholic, mainstream Protestant, or fundamentalist.[92]

Children's conception of God adds security to life by providing fallible parents with a backup expert who helps them.

"God is my parents' parent and mine, too," said one girl.[93]

MAIN POINTS

As children's competence increases, by the end of this period they have

- acquired all the basic skills in gross and fine motor coordination
- developed more logical thinking abilities so that they can grasp the relations between objects
- learned greater understanding of their own and others' emotional reactions

- gained greater control of their aggressiveness and become less fearful
- learned to remedy situations they control and adjust to situations others control
- come to value themselves for their physical, intellectual, and social competence, developing an overall sense of self-worth

Schools

- are the main socializing force outside the family
- create stress in children's lives because children worry about making mistakes, being ridiculed, and failing
- promote a strong bond with children by encouraging active participation in learning and activities
- promote learning when they provide a calm, controlled environment and when teachers are gentle disciplinarians with high expectations for students
- often do not reward the values of ethnic groups that emphasize cooperation and sharing among their members
- are highly valued by many ethnic group members who wish their children to spend more time there, do more homework, and have more proficiency tests
- provide opportunities for social experiences

With peers, children

- interact in an egalitarian, give-and-take fashion
- prefer those who are outgoing and supportive of other children
- interact more effectively when parents have been affectionate, warm, and accepting with them and less effectively when there is stress in the family
- can improve relationships when they learn new skills

Parenting tasks in this period include

- monitoring and guiding children from a distance as children move into new activities on their own
- interacting in a warm, accepting, yet firm manner when children are present
- strengthening children's abilities to monitor their own behavior and develop new skills
- structuring the home environment so the child can meet school responsibilities
- serving as an advocate for the child in activities outside the home—for example, with schools, with sports teams, in organized activities
- providing opportunities for children to develop new skills and positive identities
- becoming active in school and community organizations to provide positive environments for children

In Galinsky's interpretive stage, parents

- have achieved greater understanding of themselves as parents and of their children

- develop strategies for helping children cope with new authorities such as teachers and coaches

Problems discussed center on

- helping children meet school responsibilities
- helping children regulate anger and discouragement
- dealing with social problems such as social isolation, aggression, and bullying
- changing rule-breaking behavior such as lying

Parents' joys include

- observing increasing motor, cognitive, and social skills in children
- reexperiencing their own childhood pleasure through their child's experience

EXERCISES

1. Break into small groups of four or five. Take turns recalling (a) how your parents prepared you for school, (b) how you felt the first days you can remember, (c) what your early experiences were, and (d) how confident or shaky you felt about your abilities. Then identify ways parents and teachers could have helped more. Share your group's experiences with the class and come up with recommendations for parents and teachers.

2. In small groups, take turns recalling the pleasurable events you experienced during the years from five to ten. Then come up with a class list of twenty common pleasurable events for that period.

3. Take the list of twenty pleasurable events developed in Exercise 2 and rate each event on a scale of 1 to 7, with 1 being least pleasurable and 7 being most pleasurable, as you would have when you were a child of nine or ten. What are the most pleasurable events? How do parents contribute to them?

4. In small groups, recall the fears you had as a child from five to ten. How could parents or teachers have helped you cope with those fears?

5. In small groups, discuss major activities that built sources of self-esteem in this period. Were these athletic activities? group activities like Scouts or Brownies? school activities? Come up with recommendations for parents as to the kinds of activities children find the most confidence building.

ADDITIONAL READINGS

Lavoie, Richard. *It's So Much Work to Be Your Friend.* New York: Touchstone Books, 2005.

Levine, Mel. *A Mind at a Time.* New York: Simon & Schuster, 2002.

Murphy, Tim, and Oberlin, Loriann. *The Angry Child.* New York: Three Rivers Press, 2001.

Seligman, Martin E. P. *The Optimistic Child.* New York: Houghton Mifflin, 1995.

Steyer, James. *The Other Parent.* New York: Atria, 2002.

10

Parenting Early Adolescents

IN THE NEWS

New York Times, September 7[1]: Author believes early adolescents need interaction with parents and parental monitoring. See pages 358–359.

Test Your Knowledge: Fact or Fiction?

1. Students face a mismatch between their developmental needs and the opportunities offered in the school environment.
2. Brain changes occurring in early adolesence influence teens' ability to organize and plan actions.
3. Early adolescents report siblings are more of a problem than parents or peers.
4. The ways to help aggressive early teens are similar to the ways to help inhibited shy teens.
5. To help children develop, parents are advised to stay more closely connected to their boys and to encourage more independence in thought and action for girls.

In this period, changes in physical form, in ways of thinking, in time spent away from parents, in school settings, and in the importance of peers all demand adaptation from both parents and teenagers. How do parents maintain close relationships while teenagers are becoming more independent? How do parents of different ethnic groups help their teenagers deal with the specific problems youth confront while establishing their identity? How do parents grant autonomy while continuing to monitor their children's behavior?

Leaving the childhood years of stable growth, children experience all the stresses of rapid physical growth, a changing hormonal system, and physical development that results in sexual and reproductive maturity. Thinking matures as well; as a result, they may think about situations and feelings in new ways. Most early adolescents enter the more demanding and less supportive environment of middle or junior high school. Peer relations take on a new importance and provide both great pleasure and stress.

Throughout such change, early teenagers seek a stable sense of identity—who they are, what goals they will pursue. They question parents' authority and argue their own points of view. Parents have to find ways to encourage independence and self-esteem, helping children become more competent; yet parents must continue to monitor the teenagers' behavior and not permit so much freedom that children get into trouble they cannot handle. Though taxing for parents, this is an exciting time to watch children blossom as they take their first steps out of childhood into a new life.

PHYSICAL DEVELOPMENT

Adolescence begins with biological change. From five to ten, boys and girls have about the same height, weight, and general body composition. The physical changes of puberty, the age at which sexual reproduction is possible, begin at about eight or nine and extend to the end of the second decade.[2]

The brain triggers endocrine organs to release hormones that affect children's physical growth and secondary sexual characteristics (breasts, body and facial hair), resulting in reproductive maturity. Hormonal changes occur before any outward indications of puberty, so parents do not know at first that puberty has begun. For girls, these changes take place from about age eight to seventeen; for boys, on average, from eleven to twenty. Although children vary in the age at which the changes take place and the rapidity of the changes, the sequence remains consistent. Maturational timing appears stable across ethnic groups with adequate nutrition.[3]

For girls, a spurt in height accompanies the growth of secondary sexual characteristics such as body hair and breast development. Sexual organs, such as the uterus and vagina, grow and vaginal secretions appear. By the time menstruation occurs, on average at twelve and a half, the breasts and body are well developed. When girls first menstruate, they do not ovulate (send an egg to the uterus) with each period.

Boys' sexual hormonal secretions begin at about eleven and a half; the first visible sign of puberty is growth of the testes and the scrotum that holds the testes. The growth spurt begins about a year later along with the growth of the penis and facial and body hair. Boys' voices change later in puberty.

The timing of the changes matters.[4] Early-maturing girls have greater difficulties than later-maturing girls. They experience more conflicts with parents, perhaps because they want more freedom, and with peers—both boys and girls—because their bodies and interests are more advanced. Research suggests that early-maturing girls, defined as menstruating before eleven and a half, were more prone to depression and substance abuse than later-menstruating girls.[5] Early-maturing boys have an advantage because of increased height, weight, and muscular strength, which are valued in sports.[6]

Puberty also brings changes in sleep patterns.[7] With physical maturation, the timing of melatonin secretion changes, and there is later onset of sleep, so adolescents frequently delay going to bed for physical as well as school reasons, and parents have to help them maintain regular sleep schedules to avoid excessive daytime sleepiness.

In addition to sexual maturation, brain reorganization is occurring as well.[8] We do not know as much as we would like to know about all the changes in structure and in neurotransmitters and chemicals in the brain. We do know that, from one year to early adolescence, the child's brain contains an abundance of connections and requires more glucose than that of the adult brain. At puberty, however, "pruning," or reduction in the number of connections, occurs and the least-used connections are eliminated. A smaller number of connections may help the brain become more efficient. At the same time, brain functioning appears to become less diffuse, and basic cortical functions such as speech are localized predominantly on one side of the brain.

For parents, perhaps the most significant development in this period is the increased development of the prefrontal and frontal areas of the brain, which are involved in the higher cortical functions of reasoning, planning, and problem-solving. The myelination of nerves in these areas occurs over many years of adolescence. It should not be surprising, then, that teenagers are not as consistent, organized, and structured as parents might wish. Parents need to listen to teens' thoughts and feelings and encourage them in their problem-solving activities, as described on page 365, but knowing all the physiological changes that are occurring can increase parents' patience with their adolescent children.

Psychological Reactions to Growth and Development

Physical qualities play an important role in how children evaluate themselves. Of the things adolescents like least about themselves, they cite physical characteristics most.[9] Areas of concern include skin problems, height, weight, and overall figure. Early adolescents are most dissatisfied with their bodies, whereas older adolescents feel better about their bodies, and college students feel best of all. With time, adolescents adjust to all the changes that have taken place and eventually feel good about themselves.

Family conditions affect the timing of puberty. For example, mothers with a history of mood disorders have a greater likelihood of family stress, and when biological fathers are absent, these factors together predict early timing of girls' puberty.[10] In addition, mothers with a history of mood disorders who also experience stress from relationships with boyfriends or second husbands are more likely to have daughters with early puberty. When mothers' primary romantic involvement was with biological fathers, no relationship existed between stress and early puberty. So, family stress from different sources is related to early menarche for girls. Stresses related to early puberty for boys have not been identified.

Puberty triggers the beginning of a gender difference in moods. Prior to puberty, boys and girls are equally likely to get depressed, but following pubertal changes, girls show significantly more depressive symptoms.[11] The difference is small but significant at ages thirteen and fourteen, and it increases to a larger difference in adulthood.

VOICES OF EXPERIENCE

What I Wish I Had Known about Early Adolescence

"They seem to get caught up in fads in junior high. They do certain things to the max to be part of the crowd. I wish I'd known how to handle that. At what point are these fads okay, because it's important to identify with your peer group, and at what point do you say no? If they are really dangerous, then it's easy; but with a lot of them, it's a gray area, and I wish I'd known what to do better." FATHER

"I wish I had realized that she needed more structure and control. Because she had always been a good student and done her work, I thought I could trust her to manage the school tasks without my checking. But she lost interest in school, and I learned only very gradually that I had to be more of a monitor with her work than I had been in the past." MOTHER

"I wish I had known more about mood swings. When the girls became thirteen, they each got moody for a while, and I stopped taking it personally. I just relaxed. The youngest one said, 'Do I have to go through that? Can't I just skip that?' Sure enough, when she became thirteen, she was moody too." MOTHER

"I wish I'd known how to help the boys get along a little better. They have real fights at times, and while they have a lot of fun together and help each other out, I wish I knew how to cut down on the fighting." FATHER

"I wish I knew what to expect. They are all so different, and they don't necessarily do what the books say. Sometimes, I'm waiting for a stage; now I'm waiting for adolescent rebellion, and there is none." MOTHER

"I wish I had known about their indecisiveness. He wants to do this; no, he doesn't. He gets pressure from peers and from what we think is right, and sometimes he goes back and forth. I am more patient about that now." MOTHER

"I wish I had known that if we had dealt with some behaviors when they were younger, we would not have had a problem from eleven to fourteen. He was always a little stubborn and hardheaded, wanting to do what he wanted. But right now, I wish we had done something about the stubbornness because it is a problem. He does not take responsibility, and it gets him into trouble at school. Looking back it has always been a problem, but we did not deal with it." MOTHER

Pubertal changes at ages ten to fourteen are associated with increases in family conflict. Several factors may play a role in the increase.[12] Hormonal changes leading to greater irritability and to negative emotionality may intensify conflict. With all the physical changes, children may assume that they are now mature and demand more freedom than parents feel is appropriate.

Information and preparation about puberty and all the changes it brings help reduce anxiety and worry. Many parents, however, feel uncomfortable talking to their children on this subject. We discuss ways to do this in a later section.

Changes in physical form, in ways of thinking, in time spent with peers, and in school away from parents demand adaptation from parents and early adolescents.

INTELLECTUAL DEVELOPMENT

Jean Piaget describes the years from twelve to fourteen as the period when adolescents begin to think like adults.[13] They enter the *formal operations period,* during which they come to think more abstractly than previously. Although children can reason logically when confronted with tangible objects and change during the period of concrete operations, Piaget believes they still cannot reason logically about verbal propositions or hypothetical situations. In this period, adolescents can freely speculate and arrive at solutions without having the objects or people directly at hand; that is, they can analyze a problem in their heads. Further, they can enumerate all possible combinations of events and take action to see what possibilities actually exist.

Their increased capacity for abstract thought enables adolescents to think about their own thoughts. They become introspective, analyzing themselves and their reactions. They are also able to think about other people's reactions and anticipate them. They think of the future, imagining what they might be doing as adults, what might be happening in the world. They can think of ideal situations or solutions and become impatient with the present because it does not meet the ideal they have pictured. Their introspection, concern about the future, idealism, and impatience with the present all affect parent-child relationships, as we shall see. Adolescents also begin to think more complexly about other people and their actions. They see people more realistically and may cease to idolize their parents.

SCHOOL

Many early adolescents make transitions to middle or junior high school in this period.[14] These school settings do not meet the psychological needs of their students, and academic achievement and interest in school decrease. Research shows increases in test anxiety and learned helplessness in response to failure. Both truancy and dropping out increase.

Today's schools are larger than before and organized so that teachers know students less well, but they are also more demanding. Larger schools with less individual attention require a level of responsibility and self-direction that many early adolescents do not have. As a result, students face what Jacquelynne Eccles and colleagues call a "mismatch" between the developmental needs of early adolescents and the opportunities offered in the school environment.[15] The pressures from school affect girls and boys of all ethnic groups in similar ways.

Parental involvement is a major determiner of positive or negative school outcome in all ethnic groups and in economically disadvantaged conditions.[16] When parents are involved and set positive expectations for children, early adolescents have more positive views of their own abilities, become engaged in schoolwork and school activities, and have better attendance and grades.[17] Parents provide a context of beliefs that shape the child's self-system, which in turn motivates action that has a positive outcome.

When parents fail to counteract students' natural discouragement with school changes and stress, students develop negative beliefs about their own abilities and self-worth, fail to attend and to do the work, and receive poor grades.[18] In even the poorest and least advantaged economic situations, parents' involvement and optimism about children's abilities enable students to achieve academic competence. Parents' actions help students to develop increased capacity for self-regulation, which then leads to achievement.[19]

For early adolescents, schools that support competence continue to have the same qualities as effective elementary schools.[20] When students view teachers as academically and emotionally supportive, then they experience less stress and less alienation at school; conversely, when they view teachers as unfair or biased, students' stress increases. When schools encourage students to focus on effort, self-improvement, and task mastery, rather than competition, students feel increased motivation and well-being. Students' needs for autonomy are met when schools encourage choice whenever possible—such as in choice of seating and work partners—and emphasize active participation in learning.

EMOTIONAL DEVELOPMENT

Reed Larson and Maryse Richards gathered extensive data on the experiences and daily lives of children aged nine to fifteen years and their parents.[21] In addition to a core sample of fifty-five Midwestern, European American, working- or middle-class families of mother, father, and early adolescent as well as other siblings, Larson and Richards sampled 483 early adolescents. In their research, they gave electronic pagers to parents and their children and to children in the larger sample. They systematically beeped them eight times a day for seven days—all family members were beeped at the same time even if they were not together. At the end of the week, they also interviewed the participants about the week. From the 24,000 "snapshots" of daily life—7,000 from family members and 18,000 from children in the larger sample—Larson and Richards constructed a portrait of the daily emotional lives of young adolescents and their families. This section draws on this study in describing the emotional experiences and parent-child relationships of this age period.

Emotional life becomes more intense and complex during adolescence. Elementary school children rarely experience two different feelings at the same time; they rarely worry about the future or brood about others' reactions to them.[22] They live in the present, and when a difficult situation passes, they cease to think about it. So, they are more likely than early adolescents to describe themselves as very happy.

Although early adolescents' overall mood resembles that of their parents, they tend to have more emotional variability—more highs and more lows—than do their parents.[23] Part of their emotional variability stems from their heightened self-consciousness and concerns about how they appear to others. In one study, about a quarter of normal fourteen-year-olds reported feelings of being looked at, laughed at, or talked about.[24] David Elkind believes that the early adolescent "is continually constructing or reacting to an imaginary audience."[25]

Despite all the physical, social, and psychological changes of adolescence, as well as the heightened sensitivity, two-thirds of early teens report low to medium stress. The one-third who report high levels appear to be dealing with additional stress from such family events as marital arguing and divorce.[26]

Larson reports concern, however, that 27 percent of early teens reported boredom when beeped, much of the time at school and in study activities.[27] Honor students report boredom as often as do acting-out early teens. Early adolescents, Larson writes, "Communicate an ennui of being trapped in the present, waiting for someone to prove to them that life is worth living."[28] He believes that positive development requires that teens develop initiative, defined as a feeling of internal motivation to engage in challenging, effortful activities that are pursued over an extended period of time. Later in this chapter, we discuss how parents promote this quality in children.

Depressed and negative moods also increase over the early adolescent years. Although the increase seems slight for the majority of young teens, 10 to 20 percent of parents say their children have experienced some depressed mood—sad, unhappy feelings—in the past six months, and 20 to 40 percent of early adolescents report the same.[29] Depressed mood increases from age thirteen to fifteen, peaks at seventeen to eighteen, and then drops to adult levels. As noted, girls are more likely than boys to report depressed mood, particularly early-maturing girls. We take up depression in greater detail in Chapter 11.

Positive experiences can serve as a buffer against the effects of stress. Such experiences provide an "arena of comfort" in which early teens can escape stress, relax, and feel good.[30] When early adolescents from various ethnic backgrounds were asked about their sources of support, all pointed to the importance of close family relationships.[31] Friends are very important as well.

THE DEVELOPMENT OF THE SELF

Early adolescents now think more abstractly than before, and they describe themselves in terms of more general traits.[32] Though they may think of themselves as stupid because of poor grades and low creativity, they do not yet integrate this negative quality into their overall picture of themselves. The negative and positive qualities remain isolated as separate traits. This separation may serve as a psychological buffer so the negative traits from one sphere do not influence the overall view of the self.

In this period of change, adolescents begin to explore who they are, what they believe, what they want. They are in the process of forming what Erik Erikson calls a *sense of identity,* a sense of a differentiated and distinct self that is the real inner "me."[33]

The process of achieving a sense of identity occurs gradually over several years. Adolescents explore new experiences and ideas, form new friendships, and make a commitment to values, goals, and behavior. This can cause conflict and crisis as the choices get worked out. On the other hand, some adolescents choose traditional values without even considering for themselves what they want to do with their lives. They face no crisis or conflict, because they do not want to deal with issues. James Marcia terms commitment without exploration *identity foreclosure* to indicate that possibilities have been closed off prematurely.[34]

A different path is taken by adolescents who experience a *moratorium,* or an exploration without commitment. This is essentially a crisis about what they want to do. They have ideas they explore, but they have not yet made a commitment to act. Finally, some adolescents experience *identity diffusion,* in which they can make no choices at all. They drift without direction.

One study found that adolescent boys who rank high in identity exploration come from families in which they can express their own opinions yet receive support from parents even when they disagree with them.[35] Boys are encouraged to be both independent and connected to family members. Adolescent girls who rate high in identity exploration come from families in which they are challenged and receive little support from parents who are contentious with each other. Girls may need this slightly abrasive atmosphere in order to pursue a heightened sense of individuality rather than follow the path of intensifying social relationships. However, these girls do feel connected to at least one parent.

Personal Identity and Reference Group Orientation

William Cross describes two aspects of identity or self-concept: *personal identity* (PI), which includes such factors as self-esteem and general personality traits, and *reference group orientation* (RGO), which includes group identity, group awareness, and group attitudes (see Figure 10-1).[36] He discusses RGO primarily in terms of racial identity, to explain why people of the same ethnic group with equal commitments to that group may have very different attitudes about ethnic identity—that is, they have very different RGOs.

He states that RGO may be prominent in some groups and not in others—for example, some European Americans think of themselves only as Americans whereas others have a strong ethnic identity as Italian Americans or Irish Americans. Cross shows the usefulness of these concepts in understanding gender identity. Two women might be similar with regard to self-esteem and self-worth, but one may

■ **FIGURE 10-1**
SCHEMATIC OF THE TWO-FACTOR THEORY OF BLACK IDENTITY

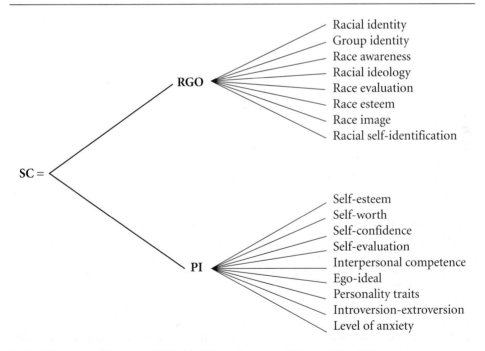

Note: Self-concept (SC) = personal identity (PI) + reference group orientation (RGO)

From William E. Cross, Jr., "A Two-Factor Theory of Black Identity," in *Children's Ethnic Socialization*, ed. Jean S. Phinney and Mary Jane Rotheram (Beverly Hills, CA: 1987), Figure 6.1, p. 122. Copyright © 1987 Sage Publications, Inc. Reprinted by permission of Sage Publications.

have a strong RGO as a feminist and interpret much of her experience in the light of that group identity, while another woman might not.

Gender Identity

In these early adolescent years, gender identity intensifies, with boys taking on a more masculine attitude and girls becoming more egalitarian regarding sex roles.[37] Although both sexes are aware of gender-appropriate activities, gender flexibility, in terms of self-choices for activities, and tolerance of others' gender choices continue to grow.[38]

Ethnic Identity

Achieving a sense of identity is a more complicated task for minority than for majority youth. They have two cultures to explore, understand, and integrate in their quest for identity. They begin with a diffused view of their ethnic background. They talk to parents, family friends, and other adults about ethnic issues. They read books and share experiences with friends. Aware of prejudice, they think about its effects on their work and life goals. In the eighth grade, about a third of African American students are actively involved in this exploration. By age fifteen, about half of such students are actively exploring their cultural roots and traditions, and an additional one-fourth have already achieved a sense of identity.[39]

Two difficulties arise.[40] First, many parents do not talk with their children about their cultural background, and they do not share their own experiences in the majority culture. Perhaps because they do not want to burden their children with experiences that no longer occur, or perhaps because they are uncomfortable with issues of culture and race, many parents remain silent and offer no models. As such, children have to seek information elsewhere and cannot consciously pattern themselves after their parents.

Second, such adolescents have to explore and integrate two cultures. Integrating one set of cultural traditions with the realities of everyday life is difficult enough. With two cultures that sometimes conflict with each other, the task becomes quite complicated.

Which values does one select? Children and adolescents ideally should be permitted a bicultural identification that includes both cultures. Youth of ethnic backgrounds who combine, for example, the emphasis on cooperation and sharing found in many ethnic cultures with the assertive independence of the majority culture are effective in a wider range of situations than are those attached to just one set of values. Because peers or family may pressure the adolescent to adopt only the traditional cultural values, a bicultural orientation is not easy to achieve.

The process of achieving identity is even more difficult when the ethnic culture is devalued and adolescents experience negative stereotyping. Youth may then refuse to explore their ethnic roots and may seek a foreclosed identity. Evidence suggests that this happened more frequently among minority than majority adolescents.[41] Some adolescents internalize the negative images, feel deficient and worthless, and develop what Erikson calls a *negative identity*. Currently, more minority youth develop a positive cultural identity and feel high self-esteem, compared with adolescents in past years. A positive ethnic identity enables youth to replace tension and defensiveness with self-confidence about the future.

THE DEVELOPMENT OF SELF-REGULATION

In this time of change, adolescents develop ways of handling impulses, which they will continue to use as they grow older. Longitudinal studies of early adolescents that have followed them into adulthood through their thirties and forties find adult impulse control is well predicted from behavior during this period.[42]

Jack Block has looked at family characteristics associated with under- and over-control.[43] He found that poorly controlled men and women come from families who, in their early adolescent years, did not give children models of effective control. The parents were not able to put aside their own concerns and interests and provide the necessary consistency in discipline. They did not reward and punish children's behavior in a logical way that teaches children how to control themselves. Instead, they used discipline only when they themselves were extremely angry. The child, fearful and panicked by the rage, could not absorb the lesson and thus never received the teaching necessary to achieve good control of impulses.

Overcontrol in men seems to come from having authoritarian and highly controlling parents. The dominant mother who sets high standards and arouses guilt to punish the child for misdeeds is a powerful figure in establishing overcontrol. Fathers in these families withdraw from the parenting role and support their wives' domination. Together, the parents so overcontrol the son that he remains fearful of impulse expression, even of pleasure, as an adult. The average girl is so well controlled that Block found it difficult to isolate any one group of overcontrolled girls to study the qualities of the family.

Although enduring modes of impulse control appear by the early adolescent years, not every impulsive act forebodes a future of impulsivity. Even the most responsible, dependable young teenager will engage in forbidden acts—partly to test the limits, partly to savor the experience, partly to impress friends. Such acts include drinking, smoking, driving the car without permission, and cutting school. How to distinguish an isolated forbidden act from a more serious problem with impulse control is a skill parents must develop.

SOCIAL DEVELOPMENT

Parent-Child Relationships

Young adolescents spend about half as much time with parents as they did in the elementary school years.[44] Parent and child are alone as often, but family activities at home and with relatives decrease.

Parent-Child Conflict   In the early adolescent years, any time with parents may well be spent in arguments. As noted earlier, parent-child conflicts increase and provide stress to children, though parents appear less aware of them.

This disparity between children's and parents' impressions exemplifies the divergent realities that can exist in families and that Larson and Richards consider as the source of difficulties at this age. "Once we go inside family life we find that it is an illusion to talk about 'the family,' as though it were a single entity. The family is the meeting ground of multiple realities."[45] The authors believe that parents' and offspring's inability to understand and deal with their different realities creates problems for all family members.

In their sample, fathers worked hard and viewed time at home as leisure. They brought home their work stress, which affected all family members. Mothers, whether employed or not, felt they should be able to create a harmonious home atmosphere; when frustrated, they sought pleasure in activities outside the home. When parents were available and responsive, adolescents' negative feelings decreased.

Parents and children agree that mundane, routine behaviors cause the most conflicts. Schoolwork and grades become a more frequent topic as early adolescents move into junior high school. As they move into high school, chores become a focus and remain a major topic during later adolescence.[46]

Though they understand parents' insistence on following conventions, young adolescents simply do not agree with them. Early adolescents insist that many of these issues should be matters under their personal control. Though aware of their children's points of view, parents usually do not accept them as valid. Early adolescents do, however, recognize certain moral issues that they will not challenge—for example, hitting others, not sharing.

Parents and children agree that most of the time conflicts end because children follow parents' wishes. In only 18 percent of conflicts do parents follow children's requests, and joint discussion and decisions settle just 13 percent of the disagreements. So although there are conflicts, children acquiesce.[47] The basic relationship between parents and children remains solid.

Mothers, however, bear the burden of the increasing disagreements,[48] perhaps because they are more involved than fathers in routine household management and scheduling. It also may be that mothers are more emotionally reactive with adolescents, so both boys and girls argue with them more. When fathers are present as a third party in disagreements, boys are more respectful and mother-son relations improve. Father-adolescent relations are more open and interactive when mothers are not present as a third party.[49] Mothers seem to dominate the relationship, and fathers withdraw.

When parents insist on retaining power and control and refuse to give children opportunities to share decision making, children become highly peer oriented.[50] They seem to seek egalitarian relationships and mutuality with peers because they are denied these experiences with parents. When parents monitor the behavior of early adolescents but permit them input in making decisions, the adolescents are better adjusted.

Parents may find themselves especially upset when their children argue with them, because it violates their expectations of compliance and communicativeness. While the conflicts at this age do increase, children usually acquiesce to parents' requests, as we have seen. Only about 10 percent of families face serious relationship problems during adolescence, and these difficulties often precede the

INTERVIEW
with Anne Petersen

Anne C. Petersen is senior vice president at W. K. Kellogg Foundation in Battle Creek, Michigan. Her research interests center on adolescence; with John Janeway Conger, she is the author of Adolescence and Youth: Psychological Development in a Changing World.

What do parents of adolescents need to know?
The societal view of adolescents is negative. I collect cartoons, and they portray an extreme view of adolescents as having hormone attacks, being difficult, impossible.

This belief in our country that adolescents are difficult and want to be independent is one of the biggest pitfalls for parents. We know that, though adolescents want to be autonomous, they need parents. We know that young adolescents are argumentative, sometimes obnoxious. Parents throw in the towel, and that is the worst thing they can do. Adolescents need to know that parental support is there. There have been historical changes in the family, increasing the possibility for kids to be independent with cars and to have more time away from home; all these changes have exacerbated the trend toward independence and separation. Too much freedom is detrimental to adolescents' development.

Parents need to know that when you ask adolescents, especially young adolescents, who is most important to them, they say the parents, even if the parents are reporting conflict. We find, then, that parents are less positive about their adolescents than their adolescents are about them. Adolescents' off-putting behavior—telling parents to get lost because the adolescents are mature—is not really the message they want to send. They are asking for a little more space; they are asking for help in becoming autonomous and interdependent rather than independent.

Research shows that conflicts are about little things, not big things. The conflicts are not about values, but largely about doing dishes, taking out the garbage. They are a way of relieving tensions. Parents ought to be a safe source for venting tensions. If they cease to be a safe source, then young adolescents are really lost; they have no one.

Parents sometimes believe that they need to be their child's buddy, but that's not true. They need to be parents. They need to provide unconditional love, firm guidelines, and strong expectations.

Puberty and all the change that accompanies it is a difficult time for boys and girls, especially when they have to change schools. It seems to work slightly differently for boys than for girls. In general, boys seem less influenced by what is going on with parents, but basic support is pretty important. If parental support is not there, it is very bad for girls. Those girls who have a lot of family conflict or lack support are the ones who become the most depressed.

How would you say your own research has influenced the way you rear your children?
I think it has changed a lot of things. That my daughter rebelled was a big shock. I remember vividly the day she refused to do something. There was no door banging, but she said she would not do something I had just assumed she would do. I immediately had the stereotypic reaction, "'Oh, my heavens, what is going on here?" All of a sudden I realized that this was what I had been talking about for a long time. Knowing all the data, why should I be surprised that my kid goes through this too?

(continued)

INTERVIEW with Anne Petersen

(continued)

It helped a lot to know what could be effective in dealing with this. We had a family conference. What she was saying was, "How about taking my needs into account?" She was upset that we just assumed she would be a part of some activity. It is enlightening to realize that we don't treat an adult, a colleague, or a friend like that. It makes sense to change your behavior toward young adolescents. Well, we worked it out. There are still occasional lapses of communication, and that's where the problems really are. Somebody assumes that somebody else is going to do something, and there is either a conflict of schedules or wishes. But at least saying, "Yes, you are right, you ought to have an increasing role in family decision making" and have a forum within which to do it made a lot of difference to her. She did not have to explode. She could put her two cents in.

When there is a good reason, we change our plans to meet her needs. It is important for us to show that we do not need to be controlling things, that we do respect her views, that she does have a voice. I am sure if you were to ask both our children, they would say they do not have as much say as they would like. That is because we still do believe that we are the parents and there are some things that we need to decide.

We believe that it is important to let them see how we are thinking about things and to understand decision-making processes. So, we talk in the family about money and about vacation plans, and we really try to include them—not just out of respect for them to increasingly become a part, but also to let them see how we think about things so they have the benefit of knowing how adults make decisions. That seems to work pretty well.

---

age period.[51] The more usual arguing reflects not dysfunction but rather the many changes parents and children are undergoing.

Harmonious Parent-Child Relations   When parents use an authoritative style of parenting—being accepting, responding sensitively to needs while still maintaining reasonable limits—teens show effective, responsible behavior.[52] Sensitive acceptance and responsiveness promote self-esteem and social connectedness; firm standards promote self-control. Parents must also be flexible and willing to modify their practices as their child receives growing responsibility for decision making. Recall that in Chapter 9 we talked about parents' monitoring children from a distance. As they move into early adolescence, children receive even greater opportunities for decision making under parents' decreasing supervision. The art lies in knowing when to keep control of children's behavior and when to relinquish it.

Monitoring   Research shows that parental monitoring is related to children's effective functioning. As such, parents are advised to monitor children. Hakan Stattin and Margaret Kerr, however, urge a new interpretation of the findings.[53] They point out that monitoring is frequently measured by parents' report of knowledge of their children's activities and friends rather than parents' tracking and observing children's activities. Stattin and Kerr find that parents have such knowledge because children tell them what they are doing. Thus, Stattin and Kerr believe, measures of monitoring may actually measure good communication, trust, and family closeness rather than direct monitoring. When monitoring is measured by parents' control of children's activities, it appears unrelated to children's positive behaviors, even though in the same research parental knowledge predicts effective functioning. So, creating close family ties, trust, and good communication appears more important than close surveillance and tracking.

Creating Mutually Responsive Dialogues with Early Adolescents   Parents' ability to engage children in conversation and mutual problem solving is critical for family functioning during these years. What promotes parents' skills in talking to children? Mothers of fifteen-year-old girls were coached for two one-and-a-half-hour sessions to listen more, ask open-ended questions, encourage children to talk, and avoid lecturing.[54] Mothers practiced role playing and applied the skills to discussing issues of sexuality and AIDS with their daughters. Mothers who were coached spoke less, asked more open-ended questions, and were less judgmental than were uncoached mothers. Teens of mothers who were coached did not talk more than teens of mothers who were not coached, but the former did feel more comfortable in talking to mothers about sexuality, and they did report more discussion about birth control than did the other teens.

When parenting strategies were assessed and related to twelve-year-olds' problem-solving skills over a two-year period, researchers found that when parents were negative and harsh in parenting, early adolescents were negative and resistant in problem-solving sessions.[55] Early adolescents who were positive and skilled problem solvers could not change parents' harsh strategies. Supportive and nurturant parents who persisted in positive parenting, even when dealing with resistant and negative teens, helped children become more flexible, effective problem solvers. When parents avoided engaging in teens' negative overtures, teens' behavior eventually changed.

Promoting Ethnic Identity   Parents continue to serve as models and sources of information about ethnic cultures and ethnic identity. Table 10-1 presents ways parents can encourage positive ethnic identity. Controversy has arisen about whether parents are wise to teach children that difficulties and failures are due to society's prejudice against them. Research suggests that such messages may be related to children's social withdrawal and peer conflict rather than self-esteem.[56] Research with fourteen- to sixteen-year-old African Americans indicates that both children's racial identity and their self-concept appear strong and positive when parents teach recognition of African American achievements, proactive strategies for dealing with the racism that African Americans encounter, and responsibility to the community as a whole.[57]

Taking Time   David Elkind has described the stress children experience when parents press them to grow up and take on adult characteristics. He writes that parents who experience extreme pressure in their own lives want their children to grow up quickly, eliminating that source of stress.[58] Children are pressured to achieve, to take

■ **T A B L E 10-1**
METHODS TO ENHANCE IDENTITY FORMATION
OF ETHNIC MINORITY YOUTH

1. Methods should be proposed to keep minority youth in school and academically oriented, since lack of education increases the risk of poverty and disadvantage.

2. Efforts are required to heighten health consciousness, because poor health interferes with identity processes. The physical health of many minority youth lags behind that of majority youth.

3. Importance of social networks should be affirmed. As they socialize children, churches and extended families are important resources for minority families.

4. Methods should be proposed to support parents as cultural transmitters. Many ethnic group parents do not discuss their distinctive values and experiences, and such parents must receive support as they begin to do this.

5. Proposals are needed to offer a media-focused, cultural emphasis that affirms positive group identity for all youth to combat negative stereotyping.

6. Methods are needed to promote teaching of native languages and cultures, particularly for Native Americans at risk of losing their cultural heritage. Creativity is required to encourage biculturalism while preserving cultural traditions.

7. Programs are required for the special training of teachers so that they will be sensitive to cultural traditions, communicative patterns, and sometimes the language of minority students.

8. Child-rearing support by way of teaching parenting skills is required to promote parents' sense of ethnic pride and enhance the home-school partnership.

9. Improved training is required for mental health workers serving ethnic minority populations.

Adapted from Margaret Beale Spencer and Carol Markstrom-Adams, "Identity Processes among Racial and Ethnic Minority Children in America," *Child Development* 61 (1990): 305–306.

on more chores and responsibilities, without too much participation on the parents' part. The push to turn children quickly into adults can be very detrimental at this age, however, because many early adolescents seem to like the greater freedom but cannot handle it yet. Elkind regrets this pressure on children, because it robs them of the childhood they need to grow, learn, and develop fully.

Family Events   Both parents and children respond to the distress they see in those close to them.[59] When a family member develops psychological symptoms as a result of life events, and daily hassles in the home increase, then other family members are affected. When family members can deal with their individual problems without developing symptoms or becoming overly stressed, then other family members are not drawn in and upset. It is not the occurrence of a major life event that disrupts the family; it is how the individual involved copes with it.

VOICES OF EXPERIENCE

The Joys of Parenting Early Adolescents

"Seeing him care for younger children and babies is a great pleasure. He's a great nurturer with small children. He has endless patience." MOTHER

"He is a talented athlete, and his soccer team got to a championship game. He scored the winning goal, and when he took off with the ball down the field, I was very proud of him. It was a unique feeling of being proud that someone I had helped to create was doing that. He had felt a lot of pressure in the game, so to see how incredibly pleased he was gave me great joy." FATHER

"I enjoy the fact that she is very independent and makes up her own mind about things. She is not caught up in fads or with cliques, and I can trust her not to follow other people's ideas. The down side of that is that she resists some of my ideas as well." MOTHER

"I enjoy her sense of humor. She jokes about everyday events, and I laugh a lot around her." MOTHER

"I like that he does things I did, like play the trumpet. He started at the same age I did, and since he took it up, it has rekindled my interest and I started practicing again. This last weekend, we played together. He also brings new interests too. Because he likes sailing, I have started that and really like it." FATHER

"She is in that dreamy preteen state where she writes things. She wrote a poem about the difference between being alone and loneliness. She has a real appreciation of time on her own and how nice being alone can be. I like that because I had that at her age." MOTHER

"It's nice just being able to help them, feeling good because they are being helped out and benefited." FATHER

"It's nice to see her being able to analyze situations with friends or with her teachers and come to conclusions. She said about one of her teachers, 'Well, she gets excited and she never follows through with what she says, so you know you don't have to take her seriously.'" MOTHER

"I really enjoy being in the Scouts with the boys. Once a month we go on a camping weekend, and I really look forward to that." FATHER

"I was so impressed and pleased that after the earthquake, he and a friend decided to go door to door and offer to sell drawings they made of Teenage Mutant Ninja Turtles. He raised $150 that he gave for earthquake relief. I was very proud that he thought this up all by himself." FATHER

"I was very happy one day when I found this note she left on my desk. It said, 'Hello!!! Have a happy day! Don't worry about home, everyone's fine! Do your work the very best you can. But most important, have a fruitful life!!!' I saved that note because it made me feel so good." MOTHER

"He enjoys life. He has a sense of humor. He's like a butterfly enjoying everything; eventually he'll settle in." MOTHER

(continued)

VOICES OF EXPERIENCE

The Joys of Parenting Early Adolescents

(continued)

"He's very sensitive, and his cousins two years older than he is ask his advice about boys. They may not take it, but they ask him even though he's younger." FATHER

"It's very rewarding to see them in their school activities. My daughter sings in the school chorus, and I enjoy that, and my son is in school plays." FATHER

"I am very pleased that she is less moody now than she used to be. We used to refer to her lows as 'Puddles of Frustration,' but she has got past that now." MOTHER

"Well, they have their friends over, and we have ping-pong, pool, cards, and we stressed having these things available. I enjoy playing all these games with them." FATHER

Happy family times are important, because they provide a reservoir of good feeling that sustains all family members through times of conflict and crisis. Family life focuses so heavily on routine chores that outings often provide the best means for members to share fun. Family card games, mealtime rituals, and watching certain TV programs together can also provide a sense of sharing and solidarity that adolescents report as highly meaningful to them. Making time for fun and games in a busy schedule may save time in the long run as conflicts and arguing decrease.

Relationships with Siblings

As in previous age periods, young adolescents show a great deal of ambivalence toward siblings. Ninety-seven percent of a large group of teens say they sometimes, or usually, do like their brothers and sisters, and only 3 percent say they do not like them. However, they rank brothers and sisters as one of their biggest problems, more of a problem than parents or peers.[60]

What do siblings do that is so upsetting? Primarily, they invade the early adolescent's privacy. They go into their rooms, take their possessions, try to be part of their activities. A second major complaint is that younger brothers and sisters get privileges older ones did not get at that age. Adolescents feel their brothers and sisters are getting away with something. Teasing is a third source of complaint. Sometimes teasing is not meant to be cruel but is a way of having a kind of conversation. A fourth reason for resentment is that parents favor another child. Sometimes early teens feel that older siblings get more respect and trust, and younger ones get more attention. Sibling conflict may be fueled by tensions from other areas. For example, if a teen has had a hard day with teachers and a fight with friends, she cannot come home and yell at her parents, but she can yell at a bratty brother or sister who made a face at her.[61]

Siblings can become close during these years for the same reasons that peers are close—they can understand the emotional ups and downs, the problems that early adolescents are feeling, in ways that parents may not. They may become allies in asking parents for privileges or rule changes. Sibling relationships usually improve as older siblings become more independent and no longer compete for parental attention or resources.

Peer Relationships

Young adolescents report fewer close friends than do elementary school children, but they gain more support from these relationships than do younger children (see Figure 9-1 in the previous chapter).[62] Friends have equal status, and they often understand what the other is experiencing in ways parents cannot.

In these years, children form cliques, small groups of five to nine members who choose each other as friends.[63] The most common activities are hanging out, talking, walking around school, talking on the phone, watching TV, and playing physical games. Girls spend more time than boys talking and shopping, and boys more time than girls playing contact sports. Group activities serve several purposes: They provide sociability and a sense of belonging, promote exploration of the self and achievements, and provide opportunities for learning and instruction. Hanging around and talking promote closer social relationships, whereas competitive games promote achievements and greater understanding of the self. Both kinds of activities contribute to psychological growth and give children the kinds of experiences they need to form a stable sense of identity.

In the beginning of early adolescence, teens spend most of their time in same-sex groups.[64] Girls spend only about an hour a week in the presence of a boy, and boys spend even less time in the presence of a girl. However, in the seventh and eighth grades, children spend four to six hours a week thinking about the opposite sex, but only about an average of one-half to one-and-one-third hours actually with them. As teens move through high school, they spend more time with the opposite sex.

Parents worry that their children will rely on peers for advice and guidance. As in earlier years, though, children usually pick friends who are like themselves and reflect their parents' values. Parents can relax a little when they read this conclusion of psychologists: "Although the influence of peer groups and friendships increases across adolescence, parents retain their primary influence over major decisions regarding life values, goals, and future decisions."[65]

TASKS AND CONCERNS OF PARENTS

Parents' tasks expand as they become not only caregivers and interpreters of the social world but also models for an increasing number of behaviors in the world outside the home. Parenting tasks include the following:

- Continuing to be the single most important influence in the child's life
- Being sensitive to the child's needs and open to discussion of the child's viewpoint

- Modeling self-controlled, responsible daily behavior in all areas of life and in discussions with children
- Monitoring children's activities and behavior
- Communicating information and values on important but difficult-to-discuss topics such as sexuality, substance use, and discrimination
- Making time, being available for conversation when the child is ready to talk
- Giving children more decision-making power
- Providing support as children undergo many physical changes and social challenges, so home is an understanding place
- Sharing pleasurable time

This section describes how parents use active listening skills and behavioral methods to work effectively with young adolescents. It also emphasizes parenting strategies that help children develop initiative and problem-solving skills so they can resolve intense feelings and engage in activities and peer relations that bring good feelings.

Communicating with the Noncommunicative Early Adolescent

Noncommunication is a common problem for parents, though children do not see it this way. Parents complain that children come home, go to their rooms, and shut the door. When they emerge for meals or snacks, they say little, answering any question with only a word or two. They do not talk about what they are doing, thinking, or feeling. Children do not seem unhappy, but parents feel they do not know them anymore. Parents may feel hurt when children say little to them but talk for hours on the phone to their friends.

Parents can interact with children to promote conversation. Don Dinkmeyer and Gary McKay advise three strategies: (1) comment on nonverbal behavior, (2) ask for comments, and (3) be a model of conversing.[66] For example, parents can try commenting on facial expressions or body language: "Looks like you had a good day today," or "You look happy." Teens may not follow up with any comments, but parents have made an effort.

Parents can ask for comments: "How's school going?" or "What are you and Jenny doing tonight?" If the child answers with one word or two, parents should drop the conversation and wait for another time. Parents can remain good models of communication by talking about their own day, friends, and plans.

Once teens begin to talk, parents can listen and communicate their feelings. If parents jump in with criticism, judgments of the child or others, blame, or sarcasm, children clam up. Reflecting the teenagers' feelings helps teens to continue to talk. If teens talk about problems they are trying to work out and want to discuss them, parents can ask open-ended questions and listen.

There are many "don'ts" to the process of encouraging conversation. Don't force the child to reveal her feelings. Don't give advice once the teen has begun to talk.

Don't rush to find the solution. Don't hurry to answer questions; delaying an answer can stimulate thinking. Adele Faber and Elaine Mazlish give the example of a girl who asked her mother, "Why don't we ever go to any place good on vacation like Bermuda or Florida?"

The mother answered, "Why don't we?"

The girl replied, "I know, I know. Because it's too expensive. . . . Well, at least can we go to the zoo?"[67]

Faber and Mazlish describe useful techniques when teens begin to talk about discouragement or frustration. They suggest showing respect for the child's struggle with comments like "That can be hard," It's not easy," or "Sometimes it helps when . . ." then giving a piece of information: "It helps, when you're rushed, to concentrate on the most important item." Teens are free to use the information or not. Parents have to watch their tone of voice so the information does not sound like advice.

Faber and Mazlish also present interesting alternatives to saying "no." Because teens are sensitive to control and may not like to ask if they often hear "no" in response, having other ways to respond is useful and will encourage greater talkativeness. Suppose a teen wants his mother to take him to the store at 5:30 while she is cooking dinner. Instead of giving a flat "no," she can say, "I'll take you after dinner." If she cannot do it, she can say, "I'd like to be able to help you out, but I have to get dinner on the table and get to that meeting at 7:00." A parent can leave out the "no" and just give information. For example, if a teen asks for an extra, expensive piece of clothing, the parent can say, "The budget just won't take it this month." If there are ways the teen can get the item, the parent can pass that information on: "If you want that as a birthday present at the end of the month, that would be fine."

All strategies recommend fostering self-esteem and autonomy by focusing on the positive things teens do. When children feel good about themselves, they talk more. Dinkmeyer and McKay describe how parents use encouragement to foster self-esteem at times of frustration. Encouragement focuses on effort, improvement, and interest and is reflected in phrases like "You really worked hard on that" or "I can see a lot of progress" or "You were really a big help to your brother in cleaning his room." Though using all these different strategies does not guarantee a talkative teenager in the home, it does increase the likelihood of conversation.

Encouraging Problem-Solving Skills

In this age period, parents confront children's resistance on many issues. Teens often nag and demand what parents are unwilling or unable to provide. Further, teens refuse to do what parents consider reasonable, such as clean their rooms. In Chapter 5, we examined mutual problem-solving sessions with children to resolve conflicts within the home. Now we discuss how parents can help children apply these strategies not only to impulsive disagreements at home but also to relationships with peers and others at school.

Problem solving requires the child to define the problem, become aware of his or her feelings and others' feelings and reactions, generate solutions to the problem, choose a solution and carry it out, then evaluate the results, starting over if necessary. Problem solving requires that parents remain calm so that children have opportunities to think and develop their skills. Parents can ask open-ended questions and encourage the child to continue to think of solutions.

Myrna Shure has developed "I Can Problem Solve" programs to teach children from four to thirteen to learn to find their own solutions to the problems that bother them.[68] Combining many of the communication skills discussed in this chapter and in Chapter 4 with an emphasis on having children think of alternative actions, these programs help parents avoid highly emotional battles that interfere with good communication and effective solutions.

To solve problems, Shure believes, children must (1) understand others' feelings and underlying motivations, (2) generate new solutions to the problem, (3) anticipate the consequences of each potential solution, and (4) plan behaviors in advance to avoid potential problems. Shure recommends working on only one or two of these skills at a time. Because they are often locked into their own thoughts and feelings of the moment and have trouble seeing different options for action, early adolescents need special help with all of the steps.

If the problem involves them, parents send an I-message that expresses their needs and feelings; otherwise parents are supportive, refusing to dictate or force solutions. Shure recommends doing this with questions such as "How will the other person feel or react?" "What will happen if you do that?" "What is your plan?" "How will that work?" If children have no answers, parents do not push but instead let children figure the problem out, provided no danger is involved. Where parents have concerns about safety or the necessity of solving the problem now, they engage in mutual problem solving, as described in Chapter 5.

Shure's method helps early adolescents develop the independence and ability to plan that are so necessary for children of this age. Developing initiative has similar aims.

Promoting Initiative

Based on his research with early adolescents and their families, Larson believes that, for positive development in these years, early adolescents must develop initiative, which "consists of the ability to be motivated from within to direct attention and effort toward a challenging goal."[69] An important quality in itself, initiative also serves as the foundation for important qualities such as creativity and leadership. Teens, however, experience effort and challenge in activities in which they lack interest, such as schoolwork, and they lack effort and challenge in activities that interest them, such as activities with friends. The task is to find activities that both interest and challenge teens.

Larson believes that structured voluntary activities, pursued over time, do just this. The experience of setting goals, organizing activities (often in collaboration with peers), and accomplishing goals leads to the development of independence, decision-making skills, and self-control. These, then, carry over to other activities.

For example, participation in voluntary activities in grade ten predicted increase in grade point average in grades ten to twelve. Participants in outdoor adventure programs gained in assertiveness, locus of control, and independence. Furthermore, positive changes continued for as long as two years after the program ended.

Larson speculates that voluntary activities, broadly structured by adults but with direct responsibility given to children for organizing and carrying out the activities, "provided an environment of possibilities for planful action, for initiative."[70] Children develop a language and way of thinking that gives them a sense of agency, of being able to accomplish what they set out to. "Children and adolescents come alive in these activities, they become active agents in ways that rarely happen in other parts of their lives."[71]

Voluntary school activities draw on the problem-solving skills that Shure encourages. Adult leaders in the activities raise open-ended questions that prompt teens to analyze and think through the consequences of actions. They are supportive and nonjudgmental. Research shows that when Little League coaches adopt an encouraging attitude, give information on how to improve, provide positive reinforcement for effort as well as for accomplishments, and stress fun and self-improvement rather than winning, players report more enjoyment in playing and greater self-esteem, and they are more likely to sign up for the team the next year than are players whose coaches are not so supportive.[72] Interestingly, positive coaches learned these skills in one three-hour session, and the techniques had the biggest effects on boys with low self-esteem.

Promoting Positive Peer Relationships

Peer acceptance involves both a cognitive understanding of others and oneself and appropriate peer behavior.[73] When children have difficulties—either being too inhibited or too aggressive—problems may exist in how they view people as well as how they behave. Aggressive children, for example, are quick to see others' negative behavior as intentional and therefore worthy of retaliation.[74] Part of the way to help such children is to encourage them to examine their interpretations of others' behavior and adopt more benign views of others' intentions. When they view negative behavior as accidental, children reduce their aggression. Similarly, shy, inhibited children should be encouraged to review their positive traits and identify the positive contributions they can make to social activities. Peer acceptance requires outgoing behavior that shows respect for others and oneself by listening to others, being open and friendly, having a positive attitude, initiating interactions, and avoiding aggressive, negative behaviors.[75]

Philip Zimbardo and Shirley Radl make several suggestions specifically geared for ages twelve to seventeen.[76] Because appearance matters so much to adolescents, Zimbardo and Radl suggest working from the outside in, concentrating first on appearance so that teenagers look as good as possible from their point of view. Skin problems should be attended to immediately. Parents must consult a dermatologist if skin problems cause any distress for teens. Weight, too, can be a problem. Zimbardo and Radl recommend first seeing a pediatrician who can discuss weight and the means to achieve ideal weight. Parents then should have suitable foods available

Parents model appropriate behaviors for teenagers—exercising, not smoking, not drinking excessively.

and serve as models of good eating patterns. Teeth sometimes need attention. Because many children and adults now wear braces, they are not the source of embarrassment they once were.

Grooming and clothes also aid appearance. Most early adolescents will take lengthy showers and shampoo their hair daily. When it comes to clothing, parents should allow the teen to follow the current fashion as far as the budget allows. When clothes are more expensive than parents can afford, possible solutions include buying, for example, one or two pairs of expensive pants rather than four or five cheaper ones. Or teens can earn money to make up the difference between what the parents can afford and what the clothes cost.

At home, parents can do all the things that increase children's sense of security and self-worth. Respecting privacy, treating the child with respect, keeping lines of communication open, giving responsibility, giving appropriate praise, not prying into the child's thoughts and feelings, and having rules and structure—these all contribute to a sense of security that enables the child to reach out to others in these sensitive years.

Handling School Problems

Experts are divided on the handling of school problems. Some give all the responsibility to the early adolescent to handle the problem; others encourage the parent to take an active role.

Haim Ginott cites the example of a thirteen-year-old boy who brought home a note from the teacher about his poor behavior.[77] His mother said, "You must have felt terrible to have to bring home a note like that." He agreed he did. His mother wrote the school that she was sure he would handle the problem. (In the past she would have yelled and screamed.) The next day, she met with the principal, but her son had already begun to improve his behavior. However, it is rarely that easy.

Thomas Gordon, as well as Dinkmeyer and McKay, considers that the child has the problem, an issue he or she must deal with. A parent can be a model of effective work habits and can be interested in the child's feelings about school, but essentially schoolwork is up to the child.

Not so with the behaviorists. Robert Eimers and Robert Aitchison describe recommendations to help an eleven-year-old boy who was failing school.[78] Testing revealed he was bright and had no special learning problem. He simply misbehaved in class and did not do homework. Eimers and Aitchison described the problem as the boy's not getting sufficient rewards for doing work. Parents found a suitable place to work, in the dining room, and the boy was given a choice of rewards for spending specified amounts of time on his homework. Initially, the amount of time he put in was brief, but gradually it was increased so that he could obtain the reward.

To improve his classroom behavior, the boy received points for working predetermined amounts of time at his desk. When he clowned in class, he was put in a brief time out. The teacher also praised the boy for on-task behavior. We can see here that parents and teachers can do many things to change school behavior—organizing the environment, giving praise and rewards for appropriate behavior, and punishing for inappropriate behavior.

Research suggests that parents should take an active role in dealing with school problems. Given the age of early adolescents, mutual problem-solving sessions and sending strong I-statements of concern might be appropriate tactics. If these do not lead to an effective plan for change, then parents can try the behavioral system. If children fall behind in school because they are not doing the work, they can find it very hard to catch up when they finally decide to take action. For this reason, the behaviorists' approach has merit.

Parents clearly have many ways to help young adolescents deal with various issues. Table 10-2 reflects many of the strategies this section has discussed.

A PRACTICAL QUESTION: WHAT SPECIAL NEEDS DO ADOLESCENT GIRLS AND BOYS HAVE?

Girls

Mary Pipher, who has worked closely with adolescent girls, believes that, in the teenage years, girls lose their sense of themselves as individuals and become overfocused on the needs, feelings, and approval of other people. Girls have to develop "identities based on talents or interests, rather than appearance, popularity or sexuality. They need good habits for coping with stress, self-nurturing skills and a sense of purpose and perspective."[78] She believes that homes that offer both protection and challenges help girls find and sustain a sense of identity.

■ **T A B L E 10-2**
TEN STEPS TO HELP CHILDREN DEVELOP THEIR ABILITIES

1.	Understand children's special skills and areas of difficulties.
2.	Provide appropriate levels of stimulation that neither bore nor overwhelm children.
3.	Teach children that their biggest limitations are the ones they place on themselves and what they can do.
4.	Help children learn to ask questions and seek answers.
5.	Help children identify what really interests and motivates them.
6.	Encourage children to take sensible risks even though there is no guarantee of success.
7.	Help children take responsibility for their behaviors—both positive and negative.
8.	Teach children to tolerate and deal with frustration, delay, and uncertainty.
9.	Help children understand other people's feelings and points of view.
10.	Remember that, in helping children realize their abilities, what counts is not financial resources, but the way you interact with children and the kinds of experiences children have in everyday life.

Adapted from Wendy M. Williams and Robert J. Sternberg, "How Parents Can Maximize Children's Cognitive Abilities," in *Handbook of Parenting*, 2nd ed., ed. Marc H. Bornstein, vol. 5: *Practical Issues in Parenting* (Mahwah, NJ: Erlbaum, 2002), 169–194.

Parents need to listen to daughters and encourage independent thought and rational decision-making skills and to encourage friendships with boys and girls and a wide variety of activities that build skills in many areas—artistic, athletic, intellectual, and social. As a therapist, Pipher teaches adolescent girls to separate thinking from feeling and to combine these two aspects of experience in making decisions. She also teaches girls to manage pain in a positive way.

> All the craziness in the world comes from people trying to escape suffering. All mixed-up behavior comes from unprocessed pain. I teach girls to sit with their pain, to listen to it for messages about their lives, to acknowledge and describe it rather than run from it.[79]

She also encourages altruism to counter the self-absorption that is characteristic of adolescence. Helping others leads to good feelings and to greater maturity.

Boys

The clinical psychologist William Pollack believes that boys are socialized from childhood to conform to what he calls the Boy Code.[80] This code requires boys (1) to be strong, tough, and independent, even when they may feel shaky and in need of support; (2) to be aggressive, daring, and energetic; (3) to achieve status and power; and (4) to avoid the expression of tender feelings, such as warmth and empathy. He believes that boys are forced to separate from parents too early and that, if they protest, they are ridiculed and shamed. He writes,

> I believe that boys, feeling ashamed of their vulnerability, mask their emotions and ulti- mately their true selves. This unnecessary disconnection—from family and then from self—causes many boys to feel alone, helpless, and fearful. . . . Over time, his sensitivity is submerged almost without thinking, until he loses touch with it himself. And so a boy has been "hardened," just as society thinks he should be.[81]

Pollack advises parents to get behind the masks that boys develop by (1) becom- ing aware of signs that sons are hiding their feelings, (2) talking to sons about feel- ings and listening to what they say, (3) accepting sons' emotional schedules for revealing feelings (boys may be slower than girls), (4) connecting with sons through joint activities that can bring parents and sons closer together, and (5) sharing their own growing-up experiences with their sons. He calls for the development of "a New Boy code that respects what today's boys and men are about—one that will be based on honesty rather than fear, communication rather than repression, connec- tion rather than disconnection."[82] Boys need to stay connected to those who love and support them and encourage them to express all their feelings. "They need to be convinced, above all, that both their strengths and their vulnerabilities are good, that all sides of them will be celebrated, that we'll love them through and through for being just the boys they really are."[83]

So, parents need to help both boys and girls find and express their own true selves. This means staying more closely connected to sons than in the past and encouraging more independence of thought and action in girls than in the past.

PARENTS' EXPERIENCES IN FACING TRANSITIONS

Many parents report that they do not feel ready to have teenage children. The child- hood years have gone so fast, it seems too soon to have a daughter with a mature figure and sons with bulging muscles and low voices. Parents also find their chil- dren's sexual maturity disconcerting. They are surprised to see sons with *Playboy* magazines and hear girls talking about the sexual attractiveness of boys.

Their adolescents' mood swings and desires for greater freedom throw parents back to some of the same conflicts of the toddler and preschool years. The elemen- tary school years were stable because parents could talk and reason with children, but now they are back to dealing with screaming, crying, moody creatures who sometimes act young but at the same time want more freedom. Parents may feel that they themselves have grown and matured as parents, able to handle crises, only to find themselves back at square one, yelling and feeling uncontrolled with their children.

Though it is difficult to give up certain images of themselves and their children, parents must do so. Children are no longer children; they are physically and sexu- ally mature. They are not psychologically mature, however, so they still need the guidance parents can give. Parents often have to give up images of themselves as the perfect parent of an adolescent. They recall their own adolescence, the ways their parents handled them, and in many cases they want to improve on that. Sometimes they find they are not doing as well as they want and have to step back and see where they went off track.

As they mature, early adolescents gain the physical glow and psychological vitality that comes from feeling the world is a magical place. At the same time, parents are marching to or through middle age. It is hard to live with offspring who present a physical contrast to how parents themselves feel. Further, the world is opening up to adolescents just as some parents feel it is weighing them down. Parents have heavy responsibilities, often taking care of aging parents as well as growing children. Parents feel they have little time and money at their own disposal, yet they live with young people who seem to have a great deal of both.

Thus, parents have to be careful not to let resentment of the freedom and excitement of their teenagers get in the way of being effective parents. As parents develop reasonable expectations of the amount of freedom and responsibilities their children are to have, they must be careful not to overrestrict or overcriticize out of envy.

To highlight the greater freedom and control children have, Ellen Galinsky calls this the *interdependent stage* of parenting.[84] Parents have several years to work through these issues before their children are launched. When parents can become more separate from their children—can be available to help them grow yet not stifle them in the process—then parents' and children's relationships take on a new richness.

SUPPORT FOR PARENTS

Parents often feel overwhelmed by cultural forces that do not support their efforts to rear children well. For example, the media bombard teens with messages about sexuality that conform to few families' values. William Damon has developed the Youth Charter program to combat cultural forces that make rearing children more difficult.[85] Parents can initiate this program to organize teachers, clergy, police, and others who care about children to develop community practices and standards that promote children's healthy development. Parents' child-rearing efforts serve as a bridge to connect children to community activities at school, with peers, and in the neighborhood. Communities have to be organized to support parents' goals.

Damon outlines a way of organizing concerned adults to identify children's specific needs and work together to find ways to meet them. Standards and expectations are drawn up for children and for the community so that parents and concerned citizens and youth can control teen drinking, vandalism, and early pregnancy and build a community more supportive of children and families. Damon writes,

> Beneath the sense of isolation that has divided our communities, we all share a deep well of concern for the younger generation. If we can find a way to tap into that well, child rearing can become the secure and fulfilling joy that it should be, rather than the risky and nerve-wracking challenge that it has become for too many parents.[86]

MAIN POINTS

In early adolescence, sexual development
- begins and takes years to complete
- triggers psychological reactions in young people
- is related to increases in family conflicts

Early adolescents
- begin to think more abstractly and analyze themselves and other people
- find the transition to junior high difficult because the school environment is a mismatch with early adolescent needs
- worry about conflicts with parents, friends, and school authorities
- experience stress when many changes occur at the same time
- are more involved than previously in peer relationships and cliques

A sense of identity
- depends on exploring a variety of alternatives and making a commitment to values, goals, and behavior
- can be foreclosed if teens make a commitment without exploring their options
- is not achieved when early adolescents experience a moratorium, or explore without making a commitment
- is achieved in a complicated way by those youth who must integrate two cultures and deal with prejudice

Peers
- are sought as primary attachment figures when parents are uninterested and give little guidance
- are sought for different kinds of relationships by boys and girls—with girls wanting to talk and express their feelings and boys wanting to engage in group activities with little self-revelation

In this period, parents
- continue to be accepting, sensitive caregivers
- provide role models of ethical, principled behavior and provide accurate information on topics such as sexual behavior and substance abuse
- monitor children's activities and behavior
- give more decision-making power to adolescents
- add to children's stress when they cannot deal with problems in their own lives

Problems discussed center on
- developing problem-solving skills
- controlling emotional reactions and dealing with social difficulties

- failures in communication
- the special needs of girls and boys

Joys include

- observing accomplishments in physical, artistic, and intellectual endeavors
- feeling good because the parent has helped the child in a specific way
- observing the child's capacity to take responsibility for self
- emotional closeness

EXERCISES

1. See the video or DVD of the movie *Akila and the Bee* and compare socializing experiences in the three ethnic groups depicted in the movie. What are the roles of parents and community in the different groups? How do adults and the community socialize children for success in the different groups?

2. In small groups, take a survey of students' school experience in the years when they were eleven to fifteen. What size was the school and what grades were included? Have each student rate that school experience from 1, very dissatisfied, to 7, very satisfied. Tabulate the average ratings for each kind of school setting and note whether students were happier when older students were included.

3. Break into small groups and have students list the kinds of experiences that increased their self-esteem in early adolescent years. With input from the whole class, write suggestions for parents who want to increase the self-esteem of their early teenagers.

4. Divide into pairs. In the first exercise, have one partner take the role of a parent who wants to talk to his or her early adolescent about appropriate sexual behavior for the teenager, while the other partner takes the role of the teen who wants more freedom. Then reverse roles, and have the second "parent" try to convey values about appropriate uses of substances in adolescent years to the second "teen." In doing this, practice active listening and sending I-messages.

5. Discuss with other students the importance of peers in their early adolescent years. Did you experience peer pressure? Did parents let you spend time with your friends? What do you think are reasonable rules with regard to time spent with peers? At what age do you think dating should begin? Why that age?

ADDITIONAL READINGS

Damon, William. *The Youth Charter: How Communities Can Work Together to Raise Standards for All Our Children.* New York: Free Press, 1997.

Elkind, David. *The Hurried Child.* Cambridge, MA: Perseus Books, 2001.

Garbarino, James. *See Jane Hit: Why Girls Are Growing More Violent and What Can Be Done about It*. New York: Penguin, 2006.

Pipher, Mary. *Reviving Ophelia*. New York: Ballantine, 1994.

Pollack, William. *Real Boys*. New York: Holt, 1998.

Shure, Myrna B., with Israeloff, Roberta. *Raising a Thinking Preteen*. New York: Holt, 2000.

Strauch, Barbara. *The Primal Teen*. New York: Random House, 2003.

11

Parenting Late Adolescents

IN THE NEWS

New York Times, December 10:[1] Study looks at genetic factors in depression. For discussion of causes of depression, see pages 398–401.

Test Your Knowledge: Fact or Fiction?

1. There is no one way for teens of different ethnic groups to harmonize ethnic identity and identity with the larger American culture.
2. The typical teen has zero to one partner with whom they had sex, usually less than a couple of times a month.
3. 85 percent of girls and 88 percent of boys report that the primary reason for dating someone is his or her positive personality traits.
4. Girls with depressive symptoms are more at risk for smoking, drinking, and drug use.
5. 45 percent of aggressive boys have symptoms of depression as well.

How do late adolescents use their parents and families as a secure base when they venture farther away from home in activities, schooling, and jobs? How do they stay safe when so many risks abound? We look at how parents give information and support to benefit their children when they become independent.

Late adolescents have matured physically and sexually. Having adjusted to many changes, they are ready to look to the future. They envision careers, future lifestyles, and romantic relationships. They also balance pleasure with work at school or in jobs.

Parents, too, are adjusting to their children's many changes. As adolescents make choices, parents stand by to provide information and to help if problems develop. Parents sense their child's impending departure from home with mixed feelings.

PHYSICAL DEVELOPMENT

As the physical changes of maturation near completion, adolescents must integrate them. They must learn to practice healthy behaviors, such as eating a good diet, exercising, and avoiding risky behaviors such as smoking, drinking, using illegal substances, and engaging in high-risk sexual activity. Psychosocial factors are intimately related to physical health: The leading causes of death in these years, accounting for 75 percent of deaths among adolescents, are accidents, suicide, and homicide—all potentially preventable.[2]

Health Concerns

In the high school years, girls rate their physical health as less good than that of boys their age and that of girls ten to fourteen.[3] They appear accurate in their self-assessments, as high school girls exercise less and diet more. Girls are more likely than boys to make physicians' visits and be hospitalized, primarily because of reproductive health needs. While boys give themselves a better health rating than girls give themselves, boys are twice as likely to die because they are more often involved in motor vehicle accidents.

A socioeconomically mixed group of 1,400 teens listed their health concerns as follows: acne, obesity, menstruation, headaches, sexuality, sexually transmitted diseases, substance use, "nervousness," and dental problems.[4] Concerns are similar in samples of European Americans, African Americans, and Latinas/os. In large measure, these are the same concerns that adults have for teens' health.

Both boys and girls have concerns about engaging in high-risk behaviors. Because these behaviors are the main source of mortality for teens, such concerns are realistic. Figure 11-1 presents questionnaire data gathered from 3,000 high school students in 1996 and 1997.[5] More worrisome figures about alcohol use indicate that in a large-scale study of high school seniors, one out of three boys and one out of five girls indicated that they had consumed five or more drinks in a row in the past two weeks.[6] Dangerous in itself, such behavior is also related to both injuries and deaths from motor vehicle accidents.

High-risk behaviors are related to current mood and life experiences. For example, girls who have depressive symptoms are twice as likely as those with no or few depressive symptoms to smoke, drink, or take drugs, and three times as likely to have eating disorders.[7] Girls who have been physically or sexually abused or forced to have sex on dates are at risk in the same ways.

Adolescent Sexual Activity

Before they become sexual with a partner, adolescents engage in self-stimulating sexual activities like fantasizing and masturbation. These may occur separately or

■ **F I G U R E 11-1**
RISKY BEHAVIORS: SMOKING, DRINKING, USING DRUGS; OLDER GIRLS AND
BOYS REPORT SIMILAR RATES

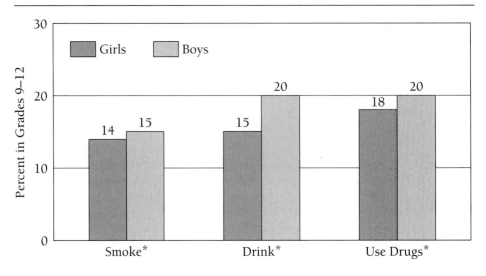

*Smoke = Smoked several cigarettes or a pack or more in the past week
Drink = Drink at least once a month or once a week
Use Drugs = Used illegal drugs in the past month

Cathy Schoen et al., *The Commonwealth Fund Survey of the Health of Adolescent Girls* (New York:
Commonwealth Fund, 1997), p. 25. Reprinted with permission from The Commonwealth Fund.

together—fantasies are used by half the teens who masturbate. Masturbation,
which often begins between age twelve and fourteen for boys and girls, is the most
common form of orgasm in both sexes in the adolescent years.[8]

Heterosexual activity usually proceeds from kissing to petting above the waist to
petting below the waist, and then to intercourse.[9] Figures vary for the exact percentages
of adolescents experiencing sexual intercourse. Figures indicate that, on average, about
50 percent of ninth- through twelfth-graders have had sexual intercourse.[10]

Boys are more sexually active than are girls. In one study, almost 30 percent of
boys reported intercourse by age sixteen, but only 13 percent of girls.[11] At age eighteen, the comparable figures are 64 percent of boys and 44 percent of girls. Ethnic
groups vary. African American boys and girls tend to be more advanced than European Americans and Latinas/os. For example, by age seventeen, 92 percent of
African American boys report having had intercourse, while only 50 percent of
Latinos and 43 percent of European Americans make similar reports. By age seventeen, 40 percent of African American girls report having had intercourse, compared
with 25 percent of European American and 24 percent of Latina girls.

Among sexually active teenagers, intercourse may occur infrequently and with a
limited number of partners.[12] According to one survey, most teens had intercourse
again with the first partner, but the relationships were not long-lived. The typical
teen had zero to one partner with whom they had sex, usually less than a couple of
times a month. About two-thirds of adolescents in one study experienced their first

intercourse in the homes of parents or friends. Their partners were most often people they knew well—a steady date or close friend.

Many mothers underestimate their teens' sexual activity; though 58 percent of teens fourteen to seventeen report sexual activity, only 34 percent of mothers report that their children are engaged in sexual activity.[13] Though very responsive to perceived parental values, teens often misperceive the strength of the mother's disapproval of sexual activity, in part because they share little conversation about sex.

It is important for parents to recognize that children need to hear parents' personal views expressed, that they do not automatically know what matters to parents. When they do know, many are willing to conform. Half of adolescents who do not have sexual relations say that the main reason they do not is that they fear their parents would find out about it.[14]

Though teens want to avoid pregnancy and sexually transmitted diseases,[15] rates of contraceptive use are very low in the early adolescent years—in one study 23 percent of girls under fifteen used contraceptives within the month of first intercourse but 42 percent delayed use for the first year. In contrast, among older adolescent girls, 50 percent used contraception at first intercourse.[16] Forty-eight percent of boys age twelve to fourteen used condoms at first intercourse, compared with 60 percent of those fifteen to nineteen years old.[17]

The condom is the most popular birth control method reported by unmarried teen girls, of all ethnic groups, when they first have sex.[18] Latina/o teenagers are less likely than other groups to use contraceptives, perhaps because many are recent immigrants who have language difficulties, limited access to health care, and a cultural tradition of not preventing pregnancy.

Sexually transmitted diseases (STDs) are a major risk for adolescents because of early age of intercourse and a lack of regular contraceptive use. Next to homosexual men and prostitutes, adolescent girls have the highest rates for any age group of gonorrhea, cytomegalovirus, and pelvic inflammatory disease. Now they face the added specter of AIDS (acquired immunodeficiency syndrome).[19]

Because of the disease's long incubation period, the precise risk that AIDS presents to teenagers is not known. Many people coming down with it in their twenties presumably contracted it as teenagers. However, adolescents may be at high risk, because the number of teen cases is increasing and because teens often do not use contraceptives. Unprotected sex with drug-using individuals is a major form of transmission in the heterosexual population. Further, teens are more susceptible than adults to all STDs, so they may be more vulnerable to AIDS as well.[20]

INTELLECTUAL DEVELOPMENT

Late adolescents' thinking advances and becomes more abstract than before. Teenagers can keep in mind several dimensions of a problem, generate more options for action, and evaluate more facts. They think in relative rather than absolute terms.

Though revealed in laboratory research studies, adolescent abstract reasoning capacities are not always seen in the decisions adolescents make in their everyday lives. For example, driver training improves the knowledge and driving skills of sixteen- to eighteen-year-olds, but increased knowledge and skill have not reduced

---

VOICES OF EXPERIENCE

What I Wish I Had Known about Late Adolescence

"I wish that I had got my children involved in more family activities. When they were mostly through adolescence, I heard a talk by a child psychiatrist who said that often when teenagers say they don't want to do something with the family, at times you have to insist because they do go along and enjoy the event. I wish I had known that sooner, because I accepted their first 'No,' when I perhaps should have pushed more."   MOTHER

"This may begin earlier, but it goes through adolescence. I had always heard they look for their own independence, their own things to participate in, but until you really experience it with your own, it's hard to deal with it. When you read about independence, it sounds like it's carefully planned out. When it actually happens, all of a sudden they want to do something that they have never done before and which you firmly believe they have no idea how to do. It can be driving for the first time or suddenly announcing they want to go somewhere with friends. I knew it was going to happen, but exactly how to handle it myself and handle it with them so they got a chance to do something new without it being dangerous has been a challenge to me."   FATHER

"I wish that I had known that I had to listen more to them in order to understand what they were experiencing. I sort of assumed that I knew what adolescence was about from my own experience, but things had a different meaning to them. What was important to me was not that important to them, and I wish I had realized that in the beginning."   MOTHER

"I wish I knew how to raise children in adolescence when you have traditional values and many of the people around you do not. It's very hard to do here in California compared to the South, where we came from. There, everyone reinforces the same values, and it is a lot easier for parents."   MOTHER

"I wish I had known to be more attentive, to really listen, because kids have a lot of worthwhile things to say and you come to find out they hold a lot of your viewpoints."   FATHER

"I wish I had known it was important to spend time with the children individually. We did things as a family, but the children are so different, and I think I would have understood them better if I had spent time with them alone."   MOTHER

---

the number of teenage driving accidents. So, teenagers have knowledge but do not necessarily have the maturity to put it to use in day-to-day actions. Applying abstract thought depends on social and emotional factors as well.[21]

Karen Bartsch focuses on another factor that affects children's and adolescents' knowledge and thinking: their individual theories about the material at hand.[22] Increasing knowledge is not accomplished by just feeding new facts into a receptive learner. First, one must dispel inaccurate theories and then present new facts when the person is receptive and ready to absorb the information. For example, as long as some teenagers hold the false belief that they can get pregnant only if they want a child, they will not take in contraceptive information, because they believe it is not relevant to them. It does not fit with their idea of how one gets pregnant. In discussing factual information with teens, parents are wise to get the teen's beliefs or underlying assumptions out in the open before presenting new facts.

SCHOOL

The transition to high school brings problems similar to those experienced in the transition to junior high school.[23] High schools are larger and more impersonal than junior high schools. The increased bureaucratic structure reduces interactions between students and teachers, so that teachers cannot easily become mentors.

In adolescence, peers play a more important role in scholastic achievements than they have in earlier years.[24] Because young teens want to gain peer acceptance, they are vulnerable to their friends' views of them. If new friends devalue academic achievement, adolescents may shift away from academic pursuits to concentrate on social activities or sports.

Parents' practices affect students' achievement. Students who describe their parents as authoritative perform well in school and are actively engaged in school activities. Students who report their parents as authoritarian or permissive have the lowest grades.[25]

Students' achievement is related also to how they feel about themselves and their abilities. Underachievement in high school, defined as getting grades significantly below what would be expected on the basis of students' ability tests, occurs in all socioeconomic and ethnic groups.[26] Compared with students of the same ability who achieved grades appropriate to their ability, underachieving boys and girls had lower opinions of their abilities, lower feelings of competence, less involvement in academic and extracurricular activities, lower educational and occupational aspirations, and more involvement in heterosexual relationships. Additionally, underachieving girls had fewer friends and less family support for their occupational desires and tended to be the youngest children.

To prevent dropping out, school interventions must occur early in students' careers so that their frustration and low self-esteem do not accumulate. Students do not drop out at the first hint of trouble; they usually have had difficulties for a long time and see little hope of reversing the process. Early interventions can enable them in some small measure to experience success and pleasure at school.

WORKING

In the school year 1998–1999, 62 percent of boys and 57 percent of girls held jobs.[27] While there have been concerns that working decreases school grades and educational motivation, the effects of working depend primarily on the nature of the job. When teens work long hours in stressful environments with little adult supervision, the likelihood of negative effects increases.[28] Employment in a favorable work environment where teens can gain skills and get to know people, however, can promote understanding of people and give experience in the responsibilities of work.[29]

EMOTIONAL DEVELOPMENT

Teens' feelings about themselves and their lives tend to remain the same from early to late adolescence.[30] Those who were happy in the first year of high school are happy as juniors. They show more stability in their feelings about friends and school, however, than they do in their feelings about family and solitude. Feelings about family tend to improve—52 percent say they are happier with family as juniors, 12 percent say less happy, and 36 percent report no change. This greater happiness appears to derive from late adolescents' broader perspective. They interpret experiences in a new light and as a result become more accepting both of family and of solitude.

Stressful life events include family loss such as the death of a parent; relationship loss such as the loss of boyfriend or girlfriend; physical problems such as having acne, needing to wear glasses or braces, or being overweight; and school problems such as failing one or more subjects or going to a new school.[31] The more stresses a middle-class teen experiences, the more likely he or she is to develop problems such as depression, alcohol use, or delinquent acting out. Family support helps girls under high stress avoid difficulties. For boys under stress, the support of friends rather than family helps to reduce problem behaviors to a slight degree.

Inner-city youth who experience stress cope best with negative life events when they have high self-esteem and are socially expressive with peers.[32] While they may report more anxiety than do teens with low stress, these adolescents get good grades and relate well to others despite the stress in their lives.

Adolescents who reported many negative events not only felt depressed but also experienced poor physical health following the events. Hormonal changes may also play a role in depressed mood or aggressiveness.[33] As we have seen, positive events can serve as protection against the effects of negative events when they do occur.

A sense of self-efficacy, or belief in one's abilities to take decisive action, plays a more important role in adolescence than before. Teens make many choices, some of which will have long-term implications.[34] Beliefs in their abilities to face challenges improve adolescents' emotional well-being and protect against depression at this vulnerable time. Thus, belief in one's abilities plus support from parents and peers are major deterrents to low mood. (We discuss depressive symptoms in greater detail later in the chapter.)

THE DEVELOPMENT OF THE SELF

Mid-adolescents speak of the many different "me's"—the self with my mother, the self with my father, the self with my best friend, the self with my boyfriend.[35] Seeing their behavior change with circumstances intensifies mid-adolescents' concerns about "the real me." They feel they express their true selves when they discuss their inner thoughts, feelings, and reactions to events; they express false selves when they put on an act and say what they do not mean. Teens report acting falsely (1) to make a good impression, (2) to experiment with different selves, and (3) to avoid others' low opinions of them. When they believe they have parents' support, adolescents can voice their opinions and express their true selves. The higher the level of support, the more adolescents can express themselves and the higher their self-esteem.

In late adolescence, teens come to terms with contradictory qualities by finding a more general abstraction that explains the contradiction. For example, they explain changes in mood—cheerfulness with friends and discouragement with parents—by describing themselves as moody. They also come to accept the contradictions as normal—"It's normal to be different ways with different people." As they observe their changing behaviors, late adolescents note the situations in which they show the traits they value and in which they feel support, and they come to seek out these situations.

Gender Identity

Differences Differences in gender identity at this age appear mainly in the content of the identity, not in the process by which identity is formed. In the past, boys' identity has been linked with independence and achievement at work and girls' identity with close relationships with others. Boys have been socialized to get ahead and girls to get along.[36] These traits are expressed in their self-descriptions. Boys see themselves as more daring, rebellious, and playful in life than girls and, at the same time, more logical, curious, and calm. Girls see themselves as more attuned to people than are boys (more sympathetic, social, considerate, and affectionate) and more emotionally reactive (more worrisome, more easily upset, more needing of approval).[37]

Gay/Lesbian Identity In adolescence, a small percentage of teens identify themselves as gay, lesbian, or bisexual.[38] For boys, the mean age of awareness of same-gender attraction is thirteen, with self-description as "homosexual" occurring between fourteen and twenty-one. For lesbians, the average age of awareness is sixteen, with self-description occurring around twenty-one years of age.

Society's negative view of homosexuality and lesbianism creates pressure and self-doubt in adolescents attracted to same-sex partners. In one study, adolescents reported strong negative reactions from parents (43 percent) and friends (41 percent) on revealing their same-sex preference. They reported discrimination by peers (37 percent), verbal abuse (55 percent), and physical assault (30 percent).[39] Because such discrimination and rejection create additional psychological problems, it is not surprising that gay adolescents are two to three times more likely to attempt suicide than are other adolescents and may make up as much as 30 percent of all completed youth suicides.[40]

In spite of others' negative views, many homosexual and lesbian adolescents evolve a positive self-concept of themselves as lovable, respectable, competent individuals. As with ethnic minority youth, support from family and others may be especially critical in forming a positive self-concept and combating the social disapproval they may encounter.

Ethnic Identity

By late adolescence, most teens have achieved a sense of ethnic identity. Ethnic identity and high self-esteem are mutually related. High self-esteem promotes exploration of ethnic identity, and ethnic identity promotes a sense of self-esteem.[41]

Studies of African American and Mexican American adolescents in schools where they were the major groups and had positive status found that all students formed a positive ethnic identity, but they differed in the degree to which they valued and identified with the broader American culture.[42] *Blended bicultural* students positively identified with both the majority and their own ethnic group. For example, they saw themselves as African and American and saw no conflict between the identities. *Alternating bicultural* students identified with the majority culture when at school or at other places but primarily identified with their own ethnic group. A third, smaller group were termed *separated* students, as they did not identify at all with the majority culture, which they felt rejected and devalued them. Among African American students, slightly over half were classified as blended biculturals, about a quarter as alternating biculturals, and 17 percent as separated. Among Mexican American students, about one-third were classified as blended biculturals, almost two-thirds as alternating biculturals, and only 2 percent as separated.

Although a positive identification with both cultures is thought to be important for personal adjustment, the three groups of students did not differ on measures of self-concept, academic grades, and level of anxiety. Thus, there appear to be three pathways to integrating the experience of having two cultures, and the pathways all seem equally related to measures of effectiveness.

THE DEVELOPMENT OF SELF-REGULATION

Because of new capacities for abstract thought and the ability to see more options, adolescents can attain higher levels of moral reasoning. They have internalized the rules. At the same time, they can better understand others' points of view, so they can reason in a more sympathetic way, emphasizing general reciprocity between people.[43]

A major task of this age period is to engage in healthy behaviors and avoid high-risk activities such as smoking, drinking, drugs, and early sexual intercourse. Parents' support and monitoring contribute to teens' development of internal restraint or the internalization of standards that, in turn, guide their behavior onto positive paths.[44] In the next section, we deal in detail with the parents' role. Here, we focus on adolescents' qualities that enable them to pursue healthy activities.

Adolescents' positive orientation to school and their intolerance of harmful behaviors such as physical aggression, stealing, and property damage predict avoidance of problem behaviors such as drinking, drugs, and precocious sexual intercourse for both boys and girls in three different ethnic groups.[45] Low self-esteem, low expectations of success, and having friends who model problem behaviors all predict adolescents' engagement in these disapproved behaviors.

Other individual qualities predicting drug use include a large time commitment to part-time work, higher income, and more evening recreational time.[46] Drug use tends to be lower among those with religious commitments. Further, a significant number of adolescents give up drugs such as marijuana and cocaine as more accurate information on their harmful effects becomes available.

While parents and social scientists have long worried about the negative influence of peers, less attention is paid to the positive influence of a high-achieving, competent friend who may shift a teen's behavior in a more positive direction. In the next section, we examine peer relationships more closely.

SOCIAL DEVELOPMENT

Parent-Child Relationships

Although parents see less of their adolescents, the dimensions of parenting that predict competence in the preschool years continue to predict adolescent competence reflected in self-reliant, independent behavior and in the capacity for meaningful relationships with others. Diana Baumrind identified three dimensions of parenting: parental *commitment,* along with the balance between *demandingness* (establishing rules, monitoring compliance, and enforcing rules) and *responsiveness* (being supportive of the child and paying attention to the child's needs and interests).[47] How parents relate to children during adolescence is more important in determining adolescent competence than are earlier parenting techniques.

Parenting Styles Baumrind describes six different parenting patterns and relates them to children's drug use. *Authoritative* parents have strong commitments to children and balance demands with responsiveness to children's needs: "Unlike any other pattern, authoritative upbringing *consistently* generated competence and deterred problem behavior in both boys and girls, at *all* stages."[48] *Democratic* parents, who are strongly committed to children and highly responsive to their needs, are only average in demandingness. Their children are highly competent as well but are freer to explore drugs.

Nonauthoritarian-directive parents, who emphasize conventional control and value conformity, have children with the least drug use, but this is accomplished by strict obedience to rules so that children are conforming and dependent on adult approval. *Authoritarian-directive* parents are even more restrictive and less supportive and have less competent children. Parents of both types are moderately committed to their children.

Unengaged parents are neither demanding nor responsive, nor are they committed to children. They either actively reject or neglect parenting responsibilities. Free of adult authority, children from these families have little direction and are described as immature. These adolescents have had problems dating back to the preschool years, and they lack competence in many areas of adolescent functioning. *Good enough* parents are about average on the different dimensions, and their children are about average in competence.

Although Baumrind's sample was relatively small, primarily white, and middle class, her family classifications applied equally to a large, ethnically diverse sample of 4,100 adolescents between the ages of fourteen and eighteen who were followed for two years.[49] Regardless of the adolescent's sex and socioeconomic or ethnic background, authoritative parenting was related to adolescent self-confidence, competency, self-reliance, avoidance of delinquent activity, and general good mood. In European American and Hispanic families, authoritative parenting was also related to school achievement, but African American and Asian American students did not show increased school performance. "In no cases were adolescents from nonauthoritative homes better off than those reared in authoritative families."[50] Even if only one parent is authoritative and the other is not, their adolescents achieve better grades than do those who grew up with two nonauthoritative parents.[51]

Authoritative parenting is also related to adolescent personality and peer group membership in European American students who seek out crowds who reinforce academic achievement and school involvement. These students receive the same message about values and behavior from parents and peers.

Among minority youth, no relationship exists between authoritative parenting and peer group membership. This appears to result from ethnic minority members' not having equal access to all peer groups. For example, an Asian American may be excluded from the "jocks" or the "druggies," and an African American may be excluded from the "brains" (see the section on peers later in this chapter).

Authoritative parenting exerts an even greater influence when the teenager's friends' parents also rely on authoritative parenting. Friends tend to be more competent, and such peers help to maintain high levels of adjustment.

Neglectful or unengaged parenting is consistently associated with low competence, psychological distress, and acting out. Adolescents from indulgent and authoritarian homes fall somewhere between those from authoritative and those from neglectful homes.

Serving as Consultants   A parent serves as a reliable resource and consultant for children in areas of importance not only by providing factual information and values, as described in Chapter 10, but also by helping teens develop the confidence to carry out effective behaviors. In addition to giving information about reproduction and the consequences of early sexual activity, parents promote the postponement of sexual activity by encouraging teens to have interests and activities that absorb their time and attention and give them satisfaction.[52]

Parents also help adolescents develop the social skills to withstand pressure for sexual activity and to insist on safe-sex practices when they are sexually active. Further, parents provide supervision and, as far as possible, do not permit teens to be in situations that can lead to spontaneous sexual activity. For example, because first intercourse most often happens at home, parents should not go away for the weekend and leave teenagers alone at home.[53]

Parents serve as consultants in a similar way when teenagers enter the world of work.[54] They provide information about the pros and cons of different jobs and possible occupations children can consider, and they help children develop interpersonal skills to pursue vocational goals.

Encouraging Autonomy   Although conflicts about everyday issues continue, late teens accept and respect their parents' conventional views on situations and thus please their parents. Teens do not necessarily give in, but parents are more likely to grant their requests now, perhaps because teens seem to understand their reasoning.[55]

When adolescents struggle less over power with their parents, they become more self-governing and independent without giving up warm family relationships. Parents and adolescents then form a partnership directed toward establishing such autonomy.[56] When attachment is secure, parents and teens can regulate emotional responses and engage in problem-solving behaviors with relatively little anger and frustration.[57] With secure attachments, both parents and teens can discuss differences and arrive at compromises. Anger appears to motivate securely attached family members to overcome differences and restore harmony. When the attachment is secure, a balance exists between the needs of the individual and the needs of the relationship.

Relationships with Siblings

Sibling relationships improve in later adolescence, compared with those same relationships in the elementary school years and early adolescence.[58] Relationships become more egalitarian and less intense. Egalitarian relationships may occur in the context of either support or growing distance.

The standing in the family constellation partly determines the perception of the relationship. Older adolescent siblings are less likely to dominate younger siblings than before, but they also report less companionship and affection than younger siblings want. Younger siblings look up to older ones and report less conflict than older siblings report. Even though adolescents and other family members spend less time together, the attachment among siblings remains moderately strong.

Peer Relationships

In the United States in a typical week, high school students spend twice as much time with peers as with parents.[59] Relationships with same-sex and opposite-sex peers provide adolescents with similar forms of support that differ from those given by parents. Adolescents report that their relationships with friends provide intimacy, companionship, and understanding, whereas relationships with parents provide affection, instrumental help, and a sense of reliability in relationships.[60]

Three changes occur in peer relationships in these years.[61] First, peer interactions are generally unsupervised by adults. Second, they are more likely to include larger numbers of peers, who form crowds. Finally, peers gravitate to members of the opposite sex.

In adolescence, intimacy increases because friendships involve more self-disclosure, expression of feelings, and support for friends as needed.[62] Friends are expected to tell each other their honest opinions and to express satisfactions and dissatisfactions with the other person. Friends also have to learn to resolve conflicts as they arise. So, friendships promote the development of social skills that, in turn, enrich friendships. Intimacy in friendships is related to adolescents' sociability, self-esteem, and overall interpersonal competence.

Adolescents feel quite loyal to their friends—in continuing friendships despite parents' disapproval and in not revealing details of the relationships to others. Although overall 56 percent would report that a friend was considering suicide, far fewer (17–20 percent) would break a confidence about drugs and alcohol, and almost none (6 percent) would reveal that a friend was shoplifting.[63]

Peer groups that form in adolescence are larger than the cliques of the early adolescent years. Bradford Brown refers to these as *crowds*.[64] As noted in Chapter 10, cliques form out of mutual choice. Crowds, though, are based on judgments of personal characteristics, and a person must be invited to join. Through time we have seen slight shifts in the kinds of crowds that exist, but generally studies find groups of "jocks" (athletes), "brains," popular kids, "druggies" or delinquents, and "nerds."

Parents' behavior indirectly influences the kinds of group friendships adolescent children form.[65] Members of four groups—"brains," popular crowd, "jocks," and "druggies"—described their parents' child-rearing practices. When parents stress achievement and monitor children closely, children tend to get high grades and belong to the "brains" group. When parents fail to monitor and do not encourage joint decision making, children tend to become part of the popular crowd and/or may be exposed to the drug crowd. Peer group norms are most likely to reinforce those behaviors that parenting strategies have encouraged.

Different ethnic groups were more likely to belong to certain groups. European American students tended to be part of the popular crowd or the "druggies." Asian Americans were more likely to belong to the "brains," and African Americans were more likely to belong to the "jocks."

Dating

By the time teens graduate from high school, most, though not all, have dated.[66] Dating gives practice in developing feelings of trust and enjoyment with the opposite sex and provides the basis for later romantic attachments. Because there are almost no studies of same-sex dating, we discuss only heterosexual dating here.

The social process of dating begins in earlier years when same-sex friendships give practice in establishing egalitarian, cooperative, supportive relationships with age-mates. In junior high school years, opposite-sex friendships increase and give early adolescents greater understanding and ease with the opposite sex. Dating and, eventually, romantic relationships develop from opposite-sex friendships and peer contacts in large-group social activities.[67]

Although most mid-adolescents have had one dating experience, most teens are not dating at any one time. A study of middle-class, European American adolescents indicates that dating relationships are casual, short-lived, and intense.[68] When dating,

The quality of parental relationships influences teens' relationships with friends, but it is the quality of teens' friendships that predict their relationships with romantic partners.

teens see and talk to each other on the phone almost every day, but the relationships last, on average, four months. Dating usually occurs in public settings, and movies, hanging out, and parties are common dating activities. In late adolescence, couple-only dating increases and occurs in more private settings.

Eighty-five percent of girls and 88 percent of boys report that positive personality traits are the primary reason for dating a person, with physical attraction being the second, though less prominent reason, reported by 46 percent of girls and 68 percent of boys. Intimacy, support, and companionship are major satisfactions in dating. Negative aspects of the relationship are also similar for boys and girls, with both disliking the level of commitment involved or some negative qualities of the person.[69]

While parent-child attachments have been considered major determiners of the quality of dating and romantic relationships, recent work indicates that the quality of dating relationships is more closely related to the quality of peer friendships.[70] When asked to describe attachment, care received, and affiliation in relationships with parents, friends, and romantic partners, adolescents' perceptions of their relationships with romantic partners were related to their perceptions of their relationships with friends but unrelated to their perceptions of relationships with parents. The quality of peer friendships appears to play a pivotal role in the development of romantic relationships. Parents influence the quality of friendships, and the nature of the friendships in turn affects dating and romantic relationships.

TASKS AND CONCERNS OF PARENTS

In this age period, parents remain caregivers but also grant their teens greater autonomy. Parenting tasks include these:

- Continuing their commitment to children by monitoring and enforcing rules while supporting and accepting their children's individuality
- Being available, responsive caregivers
- Serving as models of responsible behavior
- Communicating information and values in an atmosphere of open discussion
- Serving as consultant to children as they make important decisions
- Allowing children to separate in an atmosphere of acceptance
- Sharing enjoyable times together

The problems encountered during adolescence relate to physical and emotional functioning, social behavior, and family interactions. We now discuss how parents help their children deal with these problems.

Promoting Healthy Behaviors

Starting from the birth of their child, parents have been concerned about the child's health and safety. They have provided a healthy diet and opportunities for exercise, taken the child for vaccinations and medical and dental checkups, and done all they can to achieve this primary goal of parenting. In adolescence, parents' concerns about health and safety issues increase, as three of five deaths in the second decade of life are related to social factors such as unintentional injuries, homicides, and suicides.[71] Parents, however, lack the power to take direct action to ensure children's well-being; they must rely on teens' ability to avoid high-risk behaviors. So, adolescence is a time of worry and limited responses. Nonetheless, parents can rely on information and awareness as their most effective deterrents of high-risk behavior in teens.

Parents' Healthy Behaviors   As parents seek to promote teens' healthy behaviors and discourage high-risk ones, they need to turn first to their own behaviors. When parents promote good nutrition, exercise, good dental care, and abstinence from smoking, and when they use reasoning and grant children autonomy, their children have good health.[72]

On the negative side, when parents use substances such as alcohol, cigarettes, and marijuana, children are likely to adopt these behaviors as well, especially if there is a good relationship between parent and child.[73] In two other longitudinal studies following children from the preschool years to young adulthood, substance abusers came from families in which parents abused substances as well.[74] Recognizing the long-standing nature of the serious substance abuser's problems and the person's need for extensive help is important.

So, a first step for parents in promoting adolescents' healthy behaviors is to adopt such behaviors themselves. Then, parents must reinforce the children's behaviors that protect against risks.

Protective Factors   Protective factors in the family, the individual child, and the social environment can increase the likelihood of healthy behaviors and reduce the likelihood of high-risk ones. In a national sample of 12,000 high school students, adolescents who said their parents cared about them and spent time with them in joint activities reported fewer high-risk behaviors.[75] Parents' supervision and granting of autonomy have also been found to predict fewer health problems and adolescents' avoidance of drug use, with parents' supervision of teens' behavior being the single most powerful predictor of drug avoidance.[76] These findings occur in other studies as well; both parents' involvement and interest in their teens predict avoidance of smoking, drinking, and drug use. So, parents' involvement, interest, supervision, and granting of psychological autonomy are primary protective factors in avoiding high-risk behaviors.[77] There is also evidence that parents' expectations about socially acceptable behavior in other arenas such as school serve as protective factors.[78] Parents can provide these protective family factors.

Adolescents' personal qualities also serve as protective factors. Teens with a positive orientation to school, a commitment to socially approved activities and avoidance of deviancy, and good relationships with adults avoid problem behaviors.[79]

Social influences such as peer groups, school atmosphere, and religious affiliation also serve as protective factors against high-risk behaviors. Of the 88 percent of high school students who reported an affiliation with a religion, those who said religion and prayer were important to them reported a later age of first sexual intercourse and were less likely to use substances of any kind.[80]

To deal effectively with potential high-risk behaviors, parents must be aware of what their child is doing and feeling in order to both provide information and monitor behavior effectively. In the next few sections, we focus on eating problems, early sexual activity, and drinking.

Promoting Healthy Eating   A minority of adolescents develop problems in eating that result in obesity (gross overweight), *anorexia nervosa* (severe underweight), or *bulimia nervosa* (binge eating following by self-induced vomiting or purging with laxatives). In contrast to obesity and anorexia, which are observable because they change physical appearance, bulimia may be difficult to detect, because the bulimic frequently maintains average weight.

These three eating problems are not entirely distinct from each other.[81] Anorexics and bulimics may, at one point, have been obese, or they may become obese as they grow older. It is difficult to know the exact numbers of adolescents suffering from these eating disorders. Though anorexia and bulimia are rare, they do appear to be increasing. These two disorders are more commonly seen in girls than boys, most probably because physical attractiveness, defined as thinness, is so valued for girls in U.S. society.

Although the three eating problems have different outcomes in terms of physical appearance, they have several features in common. Each condition can be caused by a variety of factors: hereditary factors play a role in weight gain; physical factors such as metabolism or feedback control mechanisms may be related to anorexia nervosa; family patterns of eating and interacting influence eating behavior. Though physical and biological factors play a role, psychological and social factors contribute the most to these disorders.

In the case of obesity, families may equate love with food; adolescents may then use food to buffer themselves in times of disappointment. In the case of all three eating disorders, problems in identity formation may underlie the behavior. Teenagers who have found it difficult to establish separate identities for themselves as worthwhile, valued individuals may overeat, starve, or purge themselves. Anorexics often succeed in many areas but do not feel competent and independent, even though others believe they are. Underlying concerns about sexuality and interactions with opposite-sex peers can spur eating problems that prevent appropriate dating and sexual behavior because the child's appearance is so deviant.

Eating problems in turn create difficulties. People with eating disorders often feel self-conscious, depressed, and discouraged about their pattern of eating. Bulimics often fear being discovered in their purging, while anorexics fear their weight loss will be noted. Not only do psychological problems result, but serious medical conditions can follow as well. Bulimia can lead to metabolic changes, electrolyte imbalances, ulcers, and bowel problems. Severe overweight can result in heart and blood pressure problems and diabetes. Anorexia can result in electrolyte imbalances, malnutrition, cessation of menstruation, and heart problems. Anorexics have twelve times the risk of dying as nonanorexics.[82]

Besides obtaining medical and psychological help for their child, parents can take many specific actions to ensure recovery. The nutritionist Marcia Herrin[83] believes that parents can help their children with eating disorders when (1) they move beyond anger and blame and focus on the problem at hand—namely, the eating habits; (2) both parents and the relatives involved in feeding children agree on the plan and present a united front; (3) parents form a collaborative alliance with the child to change the eating behaviors, though parents remain in charge; (4) parents expect refusals and resistance and do not take them personally; (5) parents remain flexible; and (6) parents fight the problem, not the child. Parents can also promote secure attachments with children, responding in positive and caring ways. Finally, parents should not let the eating disorder dominate their view of the child or their own activities. By taking care of themselves and engaging in activities that give them pleasure, while making sure their child does things that he or she enjoys, they provide effective daily support.

VOICES OF EXPERIENCE

The Joys of Parenting Late Adolescents

"I think it's really fun to watch them grow up and mature. It's fun to see them discover things about themselves and their lives. The older ones have boyfriends, and I'm seeing them interact with the boyfriends."   MOTHER

"Sometimes the kids have friends over, and they all start to talk about things. It's nice to see them get along with their siblings as well as their friends. It gives you a good feeling to see them enjoying themselves."   FATHER

"I felt very pleased when my son at sixteen could get a summer job in the city and commute and be responsible for getting there and doing a good job."   MOTHER

"I like it when they sit around and reminisce about the things they or the family have done in the past. They all sit around the table and talk about an outing or a trip we took, saying 'Remember this?' It's always interesting what they remember. This last summer we took a long sight-seeing trip, and what stands out in their minds about it is funny. They remember Filene's basement in Boston or a chicken ranch where we stopped to see friends. One father took the Scouts on a ski trip. They got stuck in the snow on the highway for hours, and the car almost slid off the road. He said, 'Never again.' I said, 'Don't you realize that because of those things, the boys will probably remember that trip forever? You have given them wonderful memories.' "   MOTHER

"I really enjoy her happiness. She always sees the positive side to a situation. Things might bother her from time to time, but she has a good perspective on things."   FATHER

"I really like to see them taking responsibility. Yesterday they had a school holiday, and I was donating some time at an open house fundraiser. They got all dressed up and came along and helped too. The older one coaches a soccer team of four-year-olds, and the younger is a patrol leader in the Scouts, so they both have responsibility for children. They complain sometimes that it's hard to get the little kids' attention to show them things, but I think they like it."   MOTHER

"I enjoy that she is following in the family tradition of rowing. I rowed in college, and my brothers did, my father and grandfather did, and she saw a city team and signed up. She does it all on her own and has made a nice group of friends through it."   FATHER

"I can't believe that she has had her first boyfriend and it worked out so well. They met at a competition, and he lives some distance away, so they talk on the phone. He has a friend who lives here, and he comes for a visit sometimes and does lots of things with the family. We all like him, and it is nice for her to have a boyfriend like that."   MOTHER

"The joys are seeing them go from a totally disorganized state to a partially motivated, organized state. You can see their adult characteristics emerging."   FATHER

"I enjoy seeing my daughter develop musical ability, seeing her progression from beginning flute to an accomplished player who performs, and seeing how much pleasure she takes in her accomplishment."   MOTHER

(continued)

VOICES OF EXPERIENCE

The Joys of Parenting Late Adolescents

(continued)

"It really gives me a lot of pleasure to see the two of them help each other. They seem to have respect for each other. She is the brain and helps him with school, and he helps her too at times." FATHER

"I enjoy his maturity. He's so responsible. He tests us, but when we're firm, he accepts that. I'm real proud of him because he looks at the consequences of what he does." FATHER

"I enjoy his honesty and the relationship he has with his friends. He is real open with his feelings, and his friends look up to him. He's a leader." MOTHER

"He's not prejudiced. His best friends are of different ethnic groups. People trust him and like him because he's real concerned about people." FATHER

"I feel really pleased about the way the boys get along together. There is rivalry, but there is a lot of love. The older one takes the younger one under his wing, and the younger one looks up to him." FATHER

Promoting Later Sexual Activity   As noted earlier, about 50 percent of ninth-through twelfth-graders indicate they have had sexual intercourse. Teens are most likely to delay sexual activity when parents express and explain their disapproval of it and when students have interests and success at school.[84] When religious values and commitments support abstinence, teens are also likely to delay sexual activity. Teens under stress from early physiological changes, work pressures, or attraction to same-sex peers are more likely to engage in sexual activity.[85]

In a sample of 12,000 seventh- through twelfth-graders, about 20 percent of girls reported having gotten pregnant. Girls who did not get pregnant reported that they shared more activities with their parents and viewed their parents as disapproving of contraceptive use. They themselves recognized the many negative consequences of pregnancy and were more likely to use effective contraception at their first and most recent intercourse.[86]

Having expressed their values and shared information with their children, parents must minimize the possibility of early sexual activity by monitoring and supervising their children's time spent alone with the opposite sex. The most frequent place for first intercourse is the home of the parent or a friend. If pregnancy occurs, parents must get professional help. There are no easy answers, and parents and teens must work together to find solutions they can live with. Supportive communication with teens and medical and religious professionals can aid families in working out solutions that meet their needs.

Discouraging Alcohol Use   Although parents often are more concerned about their children's use of marijuana and other drugs, alcohol is the substance most frequently used. In 1994, alcohol was implicated in 29 percent of motor vehicle deaths of fifteen- to seventeen-year-olds and 44 percent of deaths of eighteen- to twenty-year-olds.[87]

Awareness of teens' alcohol use is essential for parents' effective management of this high-risk behavior, yet in one study, only about a third of mothers and fathers whose children reported regular alcohol use said it was possible that their child used alcohol.[88] Seventy-one percent of mothers and 69 percent of fathers were unaware that their children drank. Over 50 percent of mothers and fathers were aware that their children's friends drank, however. Parents seemed to be saying, "Other teens drink, but not my kid."

When aware, parents can take action. Minimizing household access to alcohol reduces the risk of teens' drinking. When teens are connected to parents and family members and when parents are active and available participants at home, the risk of frequent alcohol use among teens drops.[89] Teens are more likely to use alcohol when they have low self-esteem, earn low grades, work more than 20 hours per week, and experience or act on same-sex attractions. Religious beliefs and prayer also serve as protective factors.

Should problems arise, parents must seek help. Miller Newton's experience with his son provides an illuminating example. Newton served as the director of alcohol treatment programs in Florida, and his wife was a supervising counselor at a treatment agency. Both parents were knowledgeable about the use of at least one drug. Their two older children, nineteen and twenty, were both happy and competent people. The first time their fifteen-year-old son Mark came home drunk, the family rallied around him, gave him information about alcoholism in the family, and began to monitor his behavior more closely. He was a bright, curious boy with many interests and a passion for healthy living, so the family was unprepared for the next drunk episode, two months later. Mark was violent, threatening his father and brother. At that time he admitted he was using pot as well.

Close family supervision followed, and Mark was allowed to go to only certain places and had to be home at certain times. His parents said that if there were recurrences, Mark would go into a treatment program. When a fight erupted a few months later, the parents found evidence of much drug use. Mark entered a residential treatment program and has been free of drugs for several years.

In their book, Beth Polson and Miller Newton outline actions parents can take to promote a healthy, drug-free adolescence.[90] They insist that how families live day by day is the most important factor. Parents need to be involved family members who know what their children are doing and who their friends are. Then, they must make clear to adolescents that theirs is a drug-free family in which there is (1) no use of illegal drugs or misuse of any legal drugs or prescriptions, (2) no routine use of alcohol by parents, (3) no intoxication by adults, (4) no alcohol use by underage children, and (5) no use of drugs to lose weight, sleep, relax, or wake up. Every family member agrees to this contract. If a child is found to be using drugs, parents call the parents of all the child's friends to discuss ways of promoting organized student activities.

The family follows a similar plan for drug use. Casual drug use or experimentation are related to teen competence in many areas, as two longitudinal studies show,[91] but when parents have concerns about drug use, the child is taken to some additional form of counseling that deals with the child and the family. Because family members can help drug-oriented children, family counseling is important in addition to any individual therapy prescribed. As in many other areas, the family joins with other families to provide support and actions to promote a healthier, safer adolescence.

The Newtons' experiences make solving the substance abuse problem appear direct and straightforward—identify the problem and get the child into treatment. However, many families go through months and years of turmoil in dealing with their child's substance abuse.[92] Either because parents fail to recognize the seriousness of the problem or because teens refuse to enter and comply with treatment programs, parents and children can become entangled in a series of hostile arguments, threats, and chaotic scenes leading to teens' running away or police interventions.

Parents get help dealing with their own feelings of fear, anger, shame, and guilt concerning their child's substance abuse. They learn they did not cause nor can they cure the problem. Their child benefits from their support and encouragement.

Promoting Adolescents' Capacity for Emotional Regulation

In the adolescent years, boys are at high risk for poorly controlled aggressive behavior and girls are at risk for depression.

The Importance of Parents' Examples   The way parents handle their feelings impacts children's development and management of aggressive and depressed feelings. First, parents' handling of feelings serves as a model to children as to how or how not to regulate feelings. Second, the level of emotional arousal in the home, resulting in part from parents' handling of feelings and conflict with each other, may promote or interfere with teens' ability to manage their feelings.

Helping Children Control Aggressive Feelings   James Garbarino, an internationally recognized expert on the impact of violence on children, became concerned about the epidemic of youth killings, often in inner cities, and determined to discover the causes to help parents and society prevent them. Between 1996 and 1998, he interviewed young murderers and summarized his conclusions in *Lost Boys: Why Our Sons Turn Violent and How We Can Save Them*.[93] He compared his own early temperamental qualities to those of the boys who eventually killed and described all the supports and resources he had in gaining control over his early feelings.

> I myself was a difficult infant and toddler—cranky, troublesome, willful, and aggressive. At two I was found standing on the wall of the balcony outside our sixth-floor apartment and talking to the cats in the courtyard. When my mother ordered me in, I refused. That same year, I ran away from home one night and was found wandering the streets in my pajamas. When I was three, the neighbors routinely came to my mother to complain that

I was beating up their six- and seven-year-old children. When I was six I would stand at the top of the monkey bars on the playground, let go with my hands and challenge other children to try to shake me off.[94]

Garbarino describes himself as being impulsive and subject to sudden inner rages. At age twelve, he cruised the neighborhood on his bike, wondering what it would be like to commit the perfect crime, perhaps a murder. By later adolescence, however, he was president of the student council and editor of the yearbook. In 1964, the Lions Club of his city sent him to Washington, D.C., as a model youth.

Garbarino attributes his success to the tremendous help and support he received from his two loving parents, a safe neighborhood, and demanding schools.

My mother devoted her every minute to me, literally "taming" me as one would a wolf pup. My father was there for me, a positive force in my life. When I started elementary school, I was assigned to strong and effective teachers in the early grades who took charge of me and the rest of their students and made sure we behaved in a civilized manner.[95]

Although he lacked inner controls, Garbarino lived in a world

filled with people who cared for me, with opportunities to become involved with positive activities at school and in the community, and with cultural messages of stability and moral responsibility. And I believed in God. In other words, while I was still living with a stormy sea inside, I was solidly anchored.[96]

In *Lost Boys,* Garbarino contrasts his own early experiences against the accumulation of stresses that many young murderers confront in their childhoods—the lack of connection with parenting figures, the lack of caregivers' positive regard and reasonable limit setting, and stresses such as poverty, physical and sexual abuse, and family or community violence. As noted in Chapter 1, not any one stress but rather the accumulation of stresses is what leads to difficulties.

Garbarino believes that successful programs for violent boys provide (1) a safe, secure environment at home or in a community facility with people who can offer the support and positive daily messages that children require to learn to conform to adult standards, (2) techniques for promoting social skills and overall psychological development, and (3) discussions focused on moral reasoning and responsibility. Such programs have to be ongoing and continuous so children have opportunities to learn positive social skills and emotional regulation, which take years to develop.

The average aggressive adolescent boy with conduct problems does not murder someone or go to jail; still, aggressive, rule-breaking boys do continue to have problems through adolescence and into adulthood.[97] They are more apt to abuse substances, to drop out of school, to find getting and keeping a job difficult, and to have driving infractions. Further, they tend to date girls who are also aggressive and to start families early. "It is hard to overemphasize the importance of childhood conduct problems for adjustment failures in young adulthood for males. These failures are pervasive and severe, and the consequences for the young man, his intimate partners, and the children whom he fathers are profound."[98]

What do researchers recommend? As noted in earlier chapters, attentive, fair, supportive, consistent parenting helps boys learn new behaviors to replace the forcing, irritating, negative behaviors learned at home. Social skills programs with age-mates also decrease the aggressive, disruptive behaviors that drive others away.

A third kind of intervention focuses on helping boys learn emotional regulation. In one study, aggressive boys who were emotionally volatile—irritating, disruptive, and inattentive to others—had far more problems with peers than did boys who were only aggressive.[99] Adolescents are willing to accept the teen who is only aggressive and seeks what he wants. They reject, however, the aggressive boy who fails to pay attention to others and interferes with others' activities. Thus, this boy must learn to control overreactivity and attend to others' needs. Anger management and communication skills programs can help here.

A longitudinal study of rule-breaking boys noted that about 45 percent of boys with aggressive problems also had symptoms of depression that were likely to persist into adulthood.[100] The boys who were both angry and depressed were at risk for more severe problems in adulthood than were boys who were either angry or depressed. Thus, help must deal with both sets of problems for a large number of aggressive, rule-breaking boys.

Helping Children Manage Feelings of Depression   Depression varies along a spectrum. At the one end are depressed moods—feeling down, being unhappy over an upsetting event such as failing a test or fighting with a friend.[101] The feelings may last a brief or an extended time.

In some cases, depression is a normal response to a loss—the death of a parent, the divorce of parents, the loss of an important pet, moving to a new location.[102] Children may show signs of depression off and on for months following the event, depending on the severity of the loss. Gradually this depression will lift. Adolescence brings mood changes, and many boys and girls are occasionally blue. These temporary moods do not involve the global retreat from other people and decline in schoolwork that clinical depression does.

Depression can be accompanied by angry, rebellious, acting-out behavior that masks the underlying condition. Some children who are serious discipline problems in school and become involved in drugs, alcohol, and risk-taking behavior are depressed. They lack self-esteem and feel helpless about themselves and helpless to change.[103]

The most serious end of the spectrum, clinical depression, involves depressed mood and loss of interest or pleasure in usual pursuits. The depressed person may feel blue, down in the dumps, hopeless, or helpless in dealing with the mood. Disturbances in sleep, eating, and activity patterns may or may not accompany the mood. Sometimes people awake early in the morning and cannot return to sleep. Their appetite decreases, but some may eat compulsively and gain weight. Their energy level drops, and they move more slowly and accomplish less than they did formerly. Sometimes clinical depression is accompanied by loss of concentration and poor memory, so school performance may drop. Because they feel less interested and withdraw, depressed children may have fewer friends. These are the main markers of clinical depression.[104] Children may also have thoughts or plans to hurt themselves or, less often, someone else.

Studies suggest that between 10 and 15 percent of children and adolescents show some signs of depression.[105] Because this occurs less before puberty, the majority of

INTERVIEW
with Susan Harter

Susan Harter is a professor of psychology at the University of Denver and has carried out extensive studies on self-esteem. This interview is continued from Chapter 5.

Self-esteem seems very important because it gives the person a kind of confidence to try many new activities. How important is it to have self-esteem?
Self-esteem has powerful implications for mood. The correlation between how much you like yourself as a person and your self-reported mood on a scale from cheerful to depressed is typically about .80.

Low self-esteem is invariably accompanied by depressive affect. We have extended these findings in developing a model that helps us understand suicidal thinking in teenagers. We included Beck's concept of hopelessness and have measured specific hopelessnesses corresponding to the support and self-concept domains. We ask, "How hopeless are you about getting peer support, parent support, about ever looking the way you want in terms of appearance?" "How hopeless are you about your scholastic ability?" There are various separate domains.

The worst consequences occur if you feel inadequate in an area in which support is important and feel hopeless about ever turning that area around. Moreover, if you don't have support and feel there is nothing you can ever do to get that support, this feeds into a depression composite of low self-esteem, low mood, plus general hopelessness. Thus, the worst case scenario is the feeling that I am not getting support from people whose approval is important, I am not feeling confident in areas in which success is valued, I am hopeless about ever turning things around, I don't like myself as a person, I feel depressed, and my future looks bleak. That, in turn, causes kids to think of suicide as a solution to their problems, as an escape from painful self-perceptions leading to depression.

There is another scenario that may also lead to suicidal thinking, namely, the teen who has done extremely well in all these areas. Then they experience their first failure, for example, scholastically (they get their first B), athletically (they feel they are responsible for a key loss), or socially (they don't get invited to a major party). As a result, they consider suicide as a solution to their humiliation. These teens seem so puzzling, but we think that conditional support plays a role here. We saw kids whose support scores were reasonable, but when we interviewed them, they would say, "Well, my parent only cares about me if I make the varsity team or if I get all As" or whatever the formula is for that family. So conditionality of support is important.

I think it is important to point out that the reason people are spending so much energy and money on studying self-esteem is that low self-esteem has so many consequences, such as depressed mood, lack of energy to get up and do age-appropriate tasks and be productive, and, for some, thoughts of suicide. Most parents want their children to be happy, and self-esteem is an important pathway to happiness and the ability to function in today's world.

young people showing depression are teenagers. In any given year, 8.3 percent of adolescents show signs of depression, about 50 percent higher than the adult rate of 5.3 in a given year.[106] Twenty percent of teenagers report having experienced a major depression that was not treated. As noted in the previous chapter, before puberty, boys and girls are equally likely to be depressed, but after puberty, the rate for girls doubles.

Many factors are thought to cause depressive states, including biological factors. For example, a family history of depression in parents and close relatives indicates greater susceptibility to the disorder.[107] Life events such as divorce, family mistreatment resulting in abuse or neglect, and failures to learn healthy emotional expression in family settings can contribute to depression.[108]

Nevertheless, no one kind of circumstance produces depression. Some depressed children come from disorganized families that have experienced multiple stresses. Some depressed children lack friends and do poorly in school, but, as stated earlier, other depressed children are highly successful and seem to have many friends and enjoy much success.

As a result of any combination of factors, children can become depressed and develop the hopeless feeling that they are confronted with an unresolvable problem that will continue. They blame themselves as incompetent, inadequate, and unworthy in some way.[109]

Prior to puberty, suicide attempts are rare, but after puberty, the rate of suicide attempts skyrockets. Recent data from the Centers for Disease Control indicate that annually, 19 percent or 3 million teenagers had suicidal thoughts, 2 million made plans to carry it out, and 400,000 made suicide attempts that received medical attention.[110] Many attempts go undetected, as teens may hide cuts or throw up pills or sleep them off without telling anyone. Known figures reveal an average of more than a thousand attempts each day, every day of the year. Each year, about 2,500 teens, and approximately 5,000 in the age range of 15 to 24 years, kill themselves. More girls attempt suicide, but more boys die.[111]

When parents notice the signs of depression mentioned earlier in this section, they should seek qualified professional help. At the present time, there are several forms of help for depression.[112] Family therapy, individual therapy, and group therapy aimed at helping the child change negative self-evaluations are useful. Medications are often used as well. Medications are sometimes prescribed, but they require careful management. Research continues on the most effective combinations of treatments for teenagers.[113] If parents are uncertain whether their concerns about their child are justified, they can always consult a therapist by themselves to determine the severity of the depression and the need to bring the child in.

Once help has been obtained for the child and the family, parents can listen and accept all the child's feelings about being depressed. Many parents, eager to see their children feel better, try to argue the child out of the depression, pointing out all the reasons the child should not be depressed—"These are the best years of your life. Enjoy them." Trying to argue someone out of depression, however, can make the individual even more depressed. He or she comes to believe that the other person is right: "I must be really weird for feeling this way."

Further, some parents minimize the importance of talk about suicide, believing that those who talk about it do not do it or that they simply want attention. Parents should never consider such talk only an attention getter. Even attention getting can be fatal, as those attempting to get attention sometimes kill themselves by mistake.

In addition to getting professional help, parents can help depressed children in several ways. Parents can encourage problem solving when difficulties arise and express confidence that children will find acceptable solutions to problems. Programs that help prevent depressive symptoms in at-risk children are described in Martin Seligman's *The Optimistic Child*.[114]

Parents can also follow Harter's suggestions to boost children's self-esteem.

> We can intervene to improve self-esteem, by helping the individual to become more competent in areas in which he/she has aspirations, or by aiding the individual to discount the importance of domains in which high levels of success are unlikely. Self-esteem can also be improved by intervening to provide more opportunities for support and approval from significant others. Such interventions should not only enhance the individual's self-esteem, but prevent the more insidious cycles that involve hopelessness, depression, and associated suicidal thoughts and gestures that may serve as the ultimate path of escape.[115]

Promoting Positive Peer Relationships

Previous chapters' suggestions for promoting positive peer relations may apply to teens' problems as well. For example, parents can foster positive peer relationships by promoting teens' ability to regulate their feelings and resolve conflicts positively. Helping children develop communication skills and ways to manage anger so it does not spill out in uncontrolled ways with peers enables teens to have fewer conflicts and to resolve the ones they have in positive ways.

In the teen years, the quality of parent-child relationships influences the teens' orientation to peers.[116] When teens feel they have good relationships with parents and feel that parents allow them a growing role in decision making, teens are better adjusted, less likely to report extreme orientations toward peers, and less likely to seek peers' advice than are teens who feel that parents retain power and control. This latter group of teens seek the egalitarian relationship and mutuality they do not feel with parents. Relationships between fathers and teens are especially predictive of peer relationships, perhaps because fathers and children engage in many recreational activities, and skills learned there transfer to relationships with peers.[117]

Promoting School Success

Teenagers cut classes; they ignore homework assignments; they fail to complete courses; they pick courses that will not prepare them for what they say they want to do; they drop out of school. All strategists advise parents to move cautiously. Schoolwork and college and vocational choices are areas in which the children make choices. Parents, however, can serve as helpful consultants. They can place responsibility on children, question the source of the problem, seek remedies, and support children's coping techniques by reminding them of earlier successes. They can also communicate their feelings about the seriousness of the situation and the importance of dealing with it. This approach takes more time than does criticism or advice on how to improve.

When adolescents are achieving below their ability levels, studies have found two general approaches helpful.[118] The behavioral technique of regularly monitoring schoolwork by means of a progress report and giving positive consequences such as privileges and rewards helps students raise their performance level. A second strategy is a comprehensive approach to increase teens' study skills, their academic skills (by means of tutoring), and their social skills so they feel more at ease at school. Parents' involvement and use of consequences is also key to such a program. Addressing academic problems alone through tutoring or private therapy has not been as helpful as multifaceted approaches.

Fitzhugh Dodson cites an example of how parents can serve as consultants in helping children with courses of study. He received the following letter:

> My son is sixteen and he just despises the academic aspects of school (and 90 percent of it is academic). The only things he likes are wood shop, metal shop, auto mechanics, and P.E. He does poorly in all of his academic subjects. But he is very good with his hands. He loves to take his car apart and work on it, and he's terrific when it comes to fixing our TV set or tinkering with radios or CBs. But college is coming up soon, and I don't know what to do.[119]

Dodson advises getting information on community colleges or trade schools nearby, as the son seems to be suited for a skilled trade. He also says to show the young man the variety of skilled trades and how to get training in one that appeals to him. Dodson concludes with this comment: "Some parents have a snobbish resistance to the idea of their son or daughter learning a skilled trade instead of going to an academic college. I think this is a mistake. Better a good auto mechanic, happy at his job, than an unhappy and inept teacher or insurance salesman."[120]

A PRACTICAL QUESTION:
HOW CAN PARENTS TELL WHETHER
THEIR TEEN HAS A SIGNIFICANT PROBLEM?

Even when teens are doing well, parents worry. All parents know of an outgoing, academically successful, seemingly happy teen who suddenly took a handful of pills or who almost died of alcohol intoxication. Anxious parents want to know the signs of a serious problem. Generally, changes or decreases in teens' level of functioning at school, at home, and at work can indicate one or more of several possible problems.

Marcia Herrin outlines the early warning signs of an eating disorder: obvious increases and decreases in weight; a sudden and intense interest in diets, nutrition, and nonfat foods; skipping meals; drinking only noncaloric drinks; a frantic pace of exercise or athletic activity; discomfort around eating and meals; preoccupation with physical appearance; low self-esteem; and depression.[121] These behaviors have more meaning collectively than individually. A professional can help evaluate parents' concerns.

Harold Koplewicz helps parents identify depressed teens.[122] He describes the "moody" teen who has lost a boyfriend and is down for days or weeks but recovers and continues her activities and her relationships with friends and family.

> But if the sadness persists—if [she] has become a different person, if she's lost her sense of humor, if her sleeping and eating habits are disturbed, and if she's becoming socially isolated and is suddenly having trouble keeping up with school-work—it may be that the breakup was the triggering event of an underlying depression that needs to be treated.[123]

In addition to such classical signs of depression, Jane Brody points to tiredness, boredom, irritability, temper outbursts, sudden threats to leave home, physical symptoms such as headaches or stomachaches, and anxiety.[124]

Substance abuse may be harder to detect until it becomes a serious problem, because teens often engage in such behavior away from home with peers, and parents can only detect the consequences of it—coming home drunk, a ticket for driving under the influence, loss of interest in school, cutting, a drop in grades, a new group of friends, anger and irritability at parents, a decrease in responsible behaviors such as chores, and increasing difficulties with others at school or at work.[125] Changes in eating and sleeping and an increased number of physical complaints may accompany drug use as well.

All these problems share many of the same warning signs. With the help of school and professionals, parents can get the best assessment of what is happening to their child and the form of treatment needed.

As parents identify and seek treatment for their children's problems, they often learn that they themselves have the problem but have not recognized or accepted it. Parents of depressed teens may discover, for example, that they themselves have suffered from depression. Parents of a substance-abusing teen may realize that they are problem drinkers. Parents of children with eating disorders may see they have a problem in this area as well. As parents seek treatment for teens, the whole family benefits.

PARENTS' EXPERIENCES IN FACING TRANSITIONS

To understand how parents react and adapt to the changes and turmoil of their children's adolescence, Laurence Steinberg observed 204 families for three years.[126] He found six aspects of a child's adolescent behavior that trigger parents' emotional reactions: puberty and its associated physical changes, maturing sexuality, dating, increasing independence, emotional detachment, and increasing de-idealization of the parent.

Parents with the following risk factors were most likely to experience difficulty: (1) being the same sex as the child making the transition, (2) being divorced or remarried (especially true for women), (3) having fewer sources of satisfaction outside the parental role, and (4) having a negative view of adolescence. Protective factors that eased parents' adjustments to their teens' adolescence were having satisfying jobs, outside interests, and happy marriages. The positive supports buffered parents so that, in times of difficulty with children, they had other sources of satisfaction and self-esteem.

Steinberg found that about 40 percent of parents experienced difficulties, 40 percent responded to children's changes but were not personally affected, and 20 percent enjoyed the greater freedom as their children became more independent. Based on his research, Steinberg makes the following suggestions to parents for handling this stage of family development: (1) have genuine and satisfying interests outside of being a parent, (2) do not disengage from the child emotionally, (3) try to adopt a positive outlook about what adolescence is and how the child is changing, and (4) do not be afraid to discuss feelings with mates, friends, or a professional counselor.

SUPPORT FOR PARENTS

Numerous national and local organizations can supply parents with information and resources as well as direct them to professionals in the area. For example, Eating Disorder Awareness and Prevention serves parents in Seattle; Depression and Related Affective Disorders Association helps them in Washington, D.C. Al-Anon and other anonymous family groups are available nationally and locally for families dealing with alcohol and drug problems.

ToughLove is an organization started by parents in the late 1970s to help themselves and other parents cope with rebellious, out-of-control adolescents. Parents form support groups with other parents and develop communication with agencies and individuals to promote community responses to truancy, drug abuse, running away, and vandalism. Parents seek real consequences for this behavior so adolescents will learn to avoid the disapproved behaviors. Psychiatrist Dr. Ron Zodkevitch has updated this method to deal with current issues, such as body piercings and violence, and newer forms of treatment, such as medications. He believes the program has wide applications and is useful for all parents.

The founders of ToughLove, Phyllis and David York, are professionals who had difficulty with their impulsive, acting-out adolescents.[127] They found it hard to set firm, fair limits that they could enforce. Meeting and talking with other parents gave them feelings of support as they set limits and carried them out. In fact, when parents in the group find limit setting difficult, other parents will meet with the family or the teenager and back up the rules. Others offer to go to court hearings or other official meetings. By providing many sets of adults to help parents help children, the group becomes a community effort to establish and maintain a safe environment for all children.

MAIN POINTS

In this period, late adolescents

- reach sexual maturity
- engage in sexual activity, and many have their first sexual intercourse
- think more abstractly and can generate more options and possibilities
- get excited at school when permitted active participation in discussing or organizing experiments
- are stable in their feelings about friends and school but become more positive in their feelings about their parents
- are likely to become depressed or develop problems such as alcohol abuse if stress is high

- work in large numbers and can gain skills if the work environment is favorable

When late adolescents consider themselves, they

- describe themselves in psychological terms and, through introspection, begin to see patterns in their behavior
- need support from family and community
- reveal gender differences in their self-descriptions, with boys seeing themselves as more daring, logical, and calm than girls, and girls seeing themselves as more attuned to people and more emotionally reactive than boys

Peers

- are major sources of support and companionship and are sought out in times of trouble
- have dating relationships that are often intense but short lived
- want dating partners with positive psychological qualities and physical attractiveness

Parents

- continue their commitment to children by monitoring, supervising, and enforcing rules, yet at the same time supporting and accepting children's individuality
- serve as consultants and provide factual information on topics of importance to teens
- share more power in decision making with teens so that teens can be more self-governing in the context of warm family relationships and so they can separate with a sense of well-being

Parents' reactions to their children's growth

- stimulate their own growth, as parents often rediscover and rework feelings and conflicts from their childhoods
- often stimulate parents to find new possibilities in their own lives
- may bring parents closer to each other

Problems discussed center on

- eating problems
- substance use/abuse
- aggression
- school problems
- depression
- peer relationships

Joys include

- observing increasing social maturity and closeness with friends
- enjoying greater personal freedom
- seeing altruistic behavior
- watching adult traits emerge

EXERCISES

1. Break into small groups; discuss how parents can help their teenagers resist peer pressure to have sexual relations before they are ready.

2. Interview parents about their experience during adolescence: Did they grow up in a city or smaller town? How much freedom were they allowed? What were the rules for them? What stresses did adolescents at that time face? Whom did they go to for support? How did their parents discipline them? Return to class and break into small groups; discuss the ways that parents' experiences differ from those of adolescents of today and report to the class on four major differences.

3. In small groups, describe the most effective discipline techniques parents used with you and write ten suggestions for parents of adolescents.

4. Describe three ways you found to reduce stress as an adolescent. Work in small group to compile a list of the ten most popular ways to reduce stress, and come up with a class total.

5. In small groups, discuss ways that adolescent boys and girls can share experiences so they can come to understand how life experiences can differ and what the stresses are for each gender. Share ideas with the whole class.

ADDITIONAL READINGS

Babbit, Nikki. *Adolescent Drug and Alcohol Abuse: How to Spot It, Stop It, and Get Help for Your Family.* Sebastopol, CA: O'Reilly, 2000.

Garbarino, James and de Lara, Ellen. *And Words Can Hurt Forever: How to Protect Adolescents from Bullying.* New York: Free Press, 2002.

Herrin, Marcia, and Matsumoto, Nancy. *The Parent's Guide to Childhood Eating Disorders.* New York: Holt, 2002.

Levine, Madeline, *The Price of Privilege.* New York: HarperCollins, 2006.

Steinberg, Laurence, with Steinberg, Wendy. *Crossing Paths: How Your Child's Adolescence Triggers Your Own Crisis.* New York: Simon & Schuster, 1994.

Zodkevitch, Ron. *The Toughlove Prescription: How to Create and Enforce Boundaries for Your Teen.* New York: McGraw-Hill, 2006.

12

Parenting Adults

<table>
<tr><td>

CHAPTER TOPICS

In this chapter, you will learn about:

▇ Definitions of adulthood

▇ Theoretical perspectives

▇ The influence of historical time

▇ The diversity of parent-child ties

▇ Parenting children in transition to adulthood

▇ Parenting independent adult children, dependent adult children, and adult children moving between dependence and independence

▇ Parenting the adult parent

</td><td>

IN THE NEWS

Wall Street Journal, January 6[1]: Survey reveals most Americans say adulthood begins at age 26. See pages 408–410.

</td></tr>
</table>

Test Your Knowledge: Fact or Fiction?

1. When adolescents leave home at age eighteen, their identities are pretty well formed.
2. Even though the jobs of inner-city teens and young adults pay little and have little prestige, these teens get a sense of autonomy and control from their work.
3. Young adults who have developed maladaptive ways of coping have opportunities in their twenties to change and develop competence and resilience.
4. When parents of adults divorce, the divorce has little effect on children's relationships with their parents because they are now independent of them.
5. Aging adults have little opportunity to create better relationships with their adult children because they see little of them.

As all parents know, parenting is a lifelong endeavor. It continues well beyond the years the child lives at home until, finally, as the parent becomes old, the child becomes the parent to the parent. In this chapter, we look at how parents and children relate to each other as they grow older together.

A 1999 survey of Americans reveals that 91 percent consider family relationships extremely important, and another 9 percent report them to be somewhat important.[2] In the previous six chapters, we described ways to maximize the potential of these relationships from the child's conception through adolescence. We now turn our attention to ways parents can nourish these relationships when children are adults.

We continue this chapter by examining criteria for adulthood and theoretical perspectives on parent-child relationships in the adult years. We look at the diversity of family forms in these years. Then, we examine parent-child relationships in particular contexts—parenting in the transition to adulthood, parenting independent adult children, parenting dependent adult children, parenting children who move back and forth between independence and dependence, and, finally, parenting the parent.

CRITERIA FOR ADULTHOOD

No single event marks the arrival at adulthood the way puberty marks the beginning of sexual maturity. The legal system typically defines anyone under eighteen as a child and everyone over eighteen as an adult.[3] Adolescents can achieve adult status prior to age eighteen if they marry, have a child, enter the military, or petition the court to become emancipated minors after showing proof that they can support themselves financially and psychologically.

When you ask samples of adolescents (average age sixteen), twenty-year-olds emerging into adulthood (average age twenty-four and adults in their thirties and forties (average age forty-two to state what behaviors a person must achieve to be considered an adult, there is good agreement among these three age groups.[4] Table 12-1 lists the ten items most frequently endorsed as criteria for adulthood and the ten items least frequently endorsed. The items frequently used to define adulthood center on psychological characteristics—responsibility and independence. A second cluster of items refers to self-control and self-regulation—using contraceptives, not driving while drunk, not shoplifting; and a final group refers to the capacity to protect a family and manage a household. Items used less frequently to describe adulthood are what might be termed the "external role markers" of the adult role—marriage, having a child, buying a home. Compliance with social rules for such behaviors as language use and alcohol consumption is also among the infrequently endorsed items.

When the participants were asked whether they had achieved adulthood, the percentage of each age group who checked "Yes" increased with age (see Table 12-1). For the two younger age groups, however, about half the participants said they were adults in some ways and not in others. Still, once in their twenties, few thought they had not achieved some form of adulthood.

A sample of college students listed eight similar factors for determining their independence from parents: self-governance, emotional detachment, financial independence, separate residence, disengagement, school affiliation, starting a family, and graduation from school.[5]

■ **TABLE 12-1**
ITEMS MOST AND LEAST FREQUENTLY ENDORSED AS DESCRIBING AN ADULT*

Most Frequently Endorsed Items	Percentage Endorsing
Accepts responsibility for consequences of actions	90
Decides own beliefs/values independently of others	80
Establishes relationships with parents as equals	75
Financially independent of parents	71
Avoids committing petty crimes such as vandalism, shoplifting	70
Capable of running a household (women)	64
Uses contraception if sexually active and not trying to have child	63
Avoids drunk driving	63
Capable of keeping family physically safe	62.5
Capable of running a household (man)	61

Least Frequently Endorsed Items	Percentage Endorsing
Has had at least one child	9
Married	13
Committed to long-term love relationship	13
Purchased a home	14
Has had sexual intercourse	16
Not deeply tied to parents emotionally	22
Finished with education	26
Avoids using profanity/vulgar language	26
Avoids becoming drunk	29
Settled in a long-term career	30

For each item, participants were asked whether the behavior must be achieved before a person can be considered an adult; participants checked Yes or No. The percentage given is the average of all participants in the sample who checked Yes.

Have you achieved adulthood? Percentage:	Yes	No	Yes and No
Adolescents (average age 16)	19	33	48
Emerging adults (average age 24)	46	4	50
Young adults (average age 42)	86	2	12

*Adapted from: Jeffrey Jensen Arnett, "Conceptions of the Transition to Adulthood: Perspectives from Adolescence through Midlife," *Journal of Adult Development* 8 (2001): 133–143.

In reviewing all the criteria for adulthood, these basic criteria emerge: the ability to be psychologically and financially self-sustaining and to take on the work responsibilities of adulthood, but not necessarily marriage and parenthood.

THEORETICAL PERSPECTIVES

After describing important dimensions of childhood growth, Erik Erikson focused attention on adult development in his 1950 book, *Childhood and Society,* discussed in Chapter 2.[6] A major factor influencing growth in the adult years is the caregiving role that adults take on. Generating new life meets the basic human need to create and guide the next generation. Mature individuals need to be needed, and caring for children meets that need. Erikson primarily discussed parents in relation to their children in childhood; he did not detail parent-child relationships when both were adults.

John Bowlby's concept of attachment can help us understand parent-child relationships in adulthood. He wrote, "Whilst especially evident during childhood, attachment behavior is held to characterize human beings from the cradle to the grave,"[7] and "Availability of the attachment figure is the set-goal of the attachment system in older children and adults."[8]

To Bowlby, availability means three things: open communication with the attachment figure, that person's physical accessibility, and his or her help as needed.[9] For adults, the attachment figure may be only potentially physically available, and the forms of help may differ from those needed in childhood, but the attachment figure remains a source of security and protection. As we shall see, communication, physical proximity and contact, and the mutual exchange of help are aspects of adult parent-child relationships and so can be seen as a continuation of the attachment process begun in childhood.

Life-course theory points to the importance of historical time as an influence on parent-child relationships. Glen Elder writes, "Lives are lived interdependently and . . . social and historical influences are experienced through this network of shared relationships."[10] Social and economic events present successive generations with particular challenges.

Jeffrey Arnett believes that the cultural context of our times requires a new stage of psychological development that occurs in one's twenties.[11] He terms it *emerging adulthood.* In industrialized countries, in which many occupations require years of education for jobs in an information-based economy, entry into adult roles is postponed. Currently in our society, marriage and parenthood have been postponed, on average, to the mid-to-late twenties, leaving a block of ten years between the end of adolescence and the beginning of adult roles as Erikson described them.

Emerging adulthood is neither adolescence nor adulthood, but a period characterized by a "relative independence from social roles and from normative expectations."[12] Individuals are no longer dependent on parents but are not yet spousal partners or parents, so they are free to explore many possibilities—different kinds of work, different relationships, and new behaviors. Many use this time to seek stimulation and engage in more high-risk behaviors than they did in adolescence or will continue to do in their thirties or forties. Much of this exploration is done alone, as no age group except the elderly spends as much time alone as people aged nineteen to twenty-nine. In their searching, individuals are optimistic, and Arnett cites a poll indicating that 96 percent of eighteen- to twenty-four-year-olds expect to achieve their goals in life.

However, not all young people experience a period of emerging adulthood. In those developing countries in which adult roles of marriage, settled worker, and parenthood begin at age eighteen or twenty, there is no period of exploration. Within our own industrialized society, this period does not exist for those adolescents who are settled workers at sixteen or eighteen.

Research supports Arnett's assertions about a period of change and possibility in the twenties. As already noted, Table 12-1 documents that half the participants in their twenties see it as a period in which they have taken on some adult characteristics but lack others and subjectively do not consider themselves as adults. Other longitudinal research on coping and resilience finds that the twenties are a period of change, during which a group of planful, resourceful individuals are able to overcome maladaptive behaviors and go on to achieve greater competence and integration in young adulthood than they experienced in their twenties.[13]

DIVERSE FAMILY FORMS

Vern Bengtson and his colleagues have used the concept of *intergenerational solidarity* to describe the behavioral and emotional ties among family members who have been followed in the Longitudinal Study of Generations.[14] Bengtson has developed a typology of families differing in various levels of intimacy, closeness, and contact.

Table 12-2 presents five family types based on the patterns of responses on six dimensions of parent-child interactions. In a large, nationally representative sample, Bengtson and his colleagues found that 25 percent of the sample were categorized as tight-knit, 25 percent were sociable, 17 percent were detached, 16 percent were intimate but distant, and 16 percent were obligatory types. No one type stands out as the most common.

Women were found to be most likely to be closely attached and tight-knit with the next generation, with only 5 percent in the detached category. Men were most likely to have sociable and obligatory kinds of relationships with children.

Income, age, and gender of children did not affect the distribution of the types. There were ethnic differences, however. European Americans were more likely than African Americans and Latinas/os to have obligatory relationships with mothers, and more likely than African Americans to have detached relationships. This supports other research indicating greater closeness with mothers in the African American than in the European American community.

Clearly, such types offer a tool for understanding families. So, let us keep these types in mind as we look at parenting in different contexts.

■ **TABLE 12-2**
CONSTRUCTING A TYPOLOGY OF INTERGENERATIONAL RELATIONSHIPS USING FIVE
SOLIDARITY VARIABLES

Types of Relationships	Affect (Close)	Consensus (Agree)	Structure (Proximity)	Association (Contact)	Gives Help	Receives Help
Tight-knit	+	+	+	+	+	+
Sociable	+	+	+	+	−	−
Intimate but distant	+	+	−	−	−	−
Obligatory	−	−	+	+	(+)	(+)
Detached	−	−	−	−	−	−

Vern L. Bengtson, "Beyond the Nuclear Family: The Increasing Importance of Multigenerational Bonds," *Journal of Marriage and the Family* 63 (2001): 9. Reprinted with permission.

PARENTING DURING THE TRANSITION TO ADULTHOOD

There are numerous paths to adulthood, each with its own particular stresses and strains. Parenting strategies must therefore differ somewhat to provide children the support they need.

Supporting Growth and Development

Parenting in this period involves continuing the strategies of later adolescence—conveying acceptance and support of children, as well as recognizing their increasing capacity to care for themselves and to make appropriate decisions. Parents use problem-solving strategies that give children an increasing share of authority in determining solutions.

Yet as Bowlby has pointed out, attachment figures also serve as potential helpers and nurturers as needed. This support takes many forms. Financial or economic support can take the form of paying for further education or paying children's living expenses while they get further training.[15] Parents can offer loans or gifts for cars, deposits for apartments, down payments for homes. The amount of financial help depends on parents' resources and their willingness to use them for increasingly independent children.

A recent study reveals significant differences between mothers' and children's expectations regarding the support that mothers would give children in young adulthood.[16] Few mothers expect to provide the support that many children assume will be there. Young men expect more support than do young women, and they expect more support than mothers expect to give.

What mothers will support varies widely. Although most will help with attending college or getting further education, beyond that, there is much less agreement on helping single versus married young adults, or helping children who live at home versus those who live away from home. So, each family has to negotiate acceptable solutions.

Social support is divided into emotional, instrumental, and informational benefits.[17] Emotional benefits include feeling cared for, valued, encouraged, understood, and validated as a person. Instrumental benefits include help with certain tasks such as child care or repairing cars. Informational benefits include advice about school, referral to resources, or guidance about tasks.

The Steep Climb to Adulthood When Resources Are Scarce

Adolescents sometimes suddenly enter adulthood by taking on the roles of parent and worker. When families support this transition, they often reflect a closeness in which the adolescent contributes to the family's well-being.

The Role of Parent   After their babies are born, teen mothers usually continue to live with parents, sharing resources with parents in a mutual exchange of help. They may work while mothers care for their babies, or they may baby-sit younger siblings while they care for their own babies and the mothers work. In Chapter 14, we look at the effects of these living arrangements on children; here, we focus on the parent and "teen-adult" relationship. These families fall into what Bengtson calls *tight-knit* families. They involve closeness, frequent contact and proximity, and exchange of help. When parents and children agree on issues, they meet all the criteria for tight-knit families.

Early parenthood forces teen mothers, and fathers if involved, to become mature—to focus on others beside themselves, the usual focus of adolescent attention.

> For many poor adolescent girls, early motherhood promises to resolve salient developmental issues of identity, intimacy, and achievement. In the absence of other pathways to proficiency, childbearing represents a tangible achievement providing a new opportunity for mastery, and a new arena for experiencing oneself as competent. Some adolescents actually do succeed in realizing the goals that first led them to become parents. Among these young women, motherhood seems to serve as a psychological catalyst for these adolescents, a way to stop them from really destroying their lives—a sort of self-administered slap in the face. As one adolescent mother observed, "That's how I straightened myself out, by getting pregnant. After all the places that tried to help me, I ended up doing it myself. . . . I never went back to my old ways."[18]

The teens who succeed in achieving the adult roles of mother, partner, and student-worker are those who have emotional and practical support from their families, who participate in a good intervention program, and who receive further schooling and training for occupational success.

The Role of Worker   In inner-city areas, many families depend on young teens to support themselves and meet their own needs for clothing and entertainment through low-wage jobs. As high school ends, parents depend on children's working longer hours and contributing their earnings to the family. These families are tight knit when they agree on issues.

Katherine Newman has followed the careers of low-wage, teen, and young adult workers in New York City over a nine-month period. She described the positive growth in identity and self-esteem that teens and young adults in inner cities feel as they take on the role of responsible worker and learn disciplined work habits. While teen employment in low-wage jobs has been found to interfere with school and positive adjustment in middle-class samples, in inner cities, work appears to teach teens the importance of planning and further schooling. Teens learn that, without good school performance and more training, they will not be able to leave low-wage work.[19]

Even though teen jobs offer little prestige, and peers make fun of the low-paying work, young men and women can still gain a sense of autonomy and self-control from work. "I'm independent and I don't have to ask anyone for anything. You know, I can get things on my own, do things on my own, you know."[20]

Another benefit of work is feeling part of contemporary teen culture. Youth can buy some of the clothes and CDs that wealthier teens buy. They can make plans for future spending and enjoy achieving their goals. In working, they also join a social network that supports responsible behavior. They meet young people with a similar work ethic and avoid the street culture that encourages living in the present, hanging out, and dropping out of school. Employers sometimes serve as mentors; they reward positive work habits and encourage post–high school education.

Low-wage jobs will never enable a worker to move away from the family and live independently, but they will provide enough cash to pursue further training to climb the occupational ladder. When parents have sufficient resources and can allow children to keep some of their earnings, then young adults can live at home and attend technical schools or local colleges. As Newman concludes,

> Even in some of the poorest parts of New York City, a city with over 1 million people on welfare, adolescents are working in large numbers in low-wage jobs in order to escape the pressures of the streets, assist their parents in supporting the household, take responsibility for their own cash needs, and amass the capital it takes to invest in post-high-school training and educational opportunities. In the course of their work experience, an involvement that typically begins between 13 and 15 years of age, they acquire a set of values that place a high premium on personal responsibility as well as a set of personal contacts that, over time, become central to their social lives. . . . Engagement in the work world confers dignity, enhances a sense of independence and personal responsibility, and makes it possible for young people to make meaningful contributions to their households and the well-being of their own children.[21]

We do not know the level of agreement in these close families, nor do we know how parent and child are interacting with each other. We can nonetheless see that, at a time when many young adults are leaving home for college and becoming more distant from families, these youth remain close and involved with family members as equal contributors to family well-being.

A More Gradual Path to Adulthood

When the family has financial resources or when students earn scholarships and grants that enable them to go away to school, youth can enjoy certain areas of independence while still receiving parents' financial help and other support as needed. They are out of the home and making some decisions, but they have not taken on the adult roles of sustaining worker or parent.

College students who emphasize self-governance as a defining characteristic of becoming adult have high self-esteem and feel connected to others.[22] Boys who emphasize emotional detachment as a defining characteristic of adulthood, compared with boys who do not, report greater loneliness and lower self-esteem. In contrast, girls who emphasize emotional detachment feel higher self-esteem, greater life satisfaction, and less loneliness, compared with peers who do not emphasize detachment.

The quality of the parent-child relationship can ease or complicate children's entrance into adulthood. Parental values and encouragement of autonomy within the context of positive parent-child relationships promote young adults' success and well-being as they complete college and enter adulthood in their twenties.[23] College students also bring the effects of past family experiences into adulthood with them. A multinational survey of life satisfaction and positive moods in college students in thirty-nine countries found that young adults enter adulthood in good spirits when they come from families where parents have marriages with good or average agreement between partners.[24] When parents are married and argue or when they divorce and remarry and argue, young adults have lower life satisfaction and more negative moods. When parents argue and divorce, and children grow up in homes with no arguing, their levels of life satisfaction and positive moods resemble those of youth from average marriages.

Problems Encountered in the College Years

Although the college years are supposed to be happy times of fun and learning, several universities document increases in the number of students reporting depression, anxiety, learning disabilities, and attention problems.[25] Columbia University reported a 40 percent increase in the number of students coming to the Counseling Center between 1994 and 2002. In addition, alcohol and drug use have increased,[26] with 1,400 college students dying each year from alcohol-related accidents, including alcohol poisoning and car accidents. As in late adolescence, parents provide role models of healthy lifestyle and help college students get professional assistance as needed.

These college students appear much like the vulnerable early adolescent students identified by Suniya Luthar and Bronwyn Becker.[27] In their study of a wealthy northeastern community, they found that 22 percent of suburban girls reported depression and 26 percent clinical levels of anxiety, while 22 percent of boys reported similar levels of anxiety. In addition, both boys and girls reported elevated substance use. In adolescence, these problems were associated with distant relationships with parents and peers and strong feelings of pressure to achieve outstanding levels of academic achievement.

In studying the continuity of depression from adolescence to the early twenties, researchers found that different dynamics were at work in the depression of young men and young women.[28] Women's depression, both in adolescence and in the

Children who emphasize self-governance as a defining characteristic of becoming an adult have high self-esteem and feel connected to others.

early twenties, was related to their current relationships with family and friends. Girls and young women who felt less closeness with parents experienced more depression during both time periods. In young men, those who were most likely to feel depressed as young men were those who, in adolescence, experienced tensions with parents around discipline issues and less opportunity for sharing in decision making. When adolescent boys did share in making decisions with parents, they were less likely to be depressed as young adults, perhaps because they had developed greater independence. Both young men and women were affected by the nature of their peer relationships; both felt more depressed when peers were a negative influence.

In a study of substance use in children of alcoholics in their early twenties, researchers found that some who used drugs and alcohol at that time were continuing a pattern of behavior begun in adolescence, yet others were using for the first time.[29] There is some relationship between effective coping skills developed in adolescence and avoidance of problematic and impulsive substance use in the early twenties.

As in late adolescence, parents model healthy lifestyles during children's early twenties. When children show problem behaviors, parents help children get the help they need from appropriate individual providers and treatment programs.

The Path to Adulthood for Adolescents with Chronic Physical Health Problems

Data from the National Longitudinal Survey of Youth (NLSY) have enabled researchers to track the paths of a nationally representative sample of 251 adolescents with chronic health problems such as asthma, diabetes, arthritis, and cerebral palsy as they become adults.[30] David Gortmaker and his colleagues first speculated that poor health might interfere with success in being a worker and marital partner. However, when they compared the adult status of those 251 youth with the rest of the sample on measures of work and career histories, family income, marital status, and self-esteem, they found few differences.

When assessed in their twenties, the two groups "attain levels of education, income, marriage, and self-esteem that are average for their age group."[31] They show differences in rate of employment, with 73 percent of the healthy group and 67 percent of the group with chronic conditions working, as well as a difference of $1,700 in annual income. On years of education, marital status, and self-esteem, no significant differences between the groups appear.

This does not mean that youth with severe physical health conditions, such as youth who are technology dependent on wheelchairs or other equipment, face no obstacles to achieving adult status. Nonetheless, while they or others with severe conditions have added problems, the majority of teens with chronic physical health problems achieve adult status comparable to others in their age group.

General Parenting Strategies for the Transition Period

While theory and research have traditionally focused on the importance of separation from the family, current work indicates that whatever the path to adulthood, positive attachments to parents and parents' support ease the way.[32] At work and at college, mentors also play a role similar to that of parents. Positive attachments to these figures improve the youths' adjustment in young adulthood.

PARENTING INDEPENDENT ADULT CHILDREN

There are many contexts for parenting independent adult children, and each shapes parents' behavior. Some independent adult children are single and live away from home with their own friends and activities, seeing the family at intervals. Other independent single adult children continue to live with the family or nearby and remain part of all family activities. Other independent adult children have established their own families and have taken on the major life role of parents. Whether close by or far away, they relate to parents as colleagues.

Ongoing Nurturing

During this period, children are expected to be self-supporting, independent, and responsible. They need love and emotional support and sometimes information and instrumental support. As noted earlier, demographic changes in economic and family stability have resulted in independent adult children's often requiring more material assistance from parents than did young adults in the past.[33]

The majority of parents give some form of help, most often in the form of advice and child care. In one study, though, 25 percent of adult children reported receiving $500 or more from parents in the last year. As we shall see, this is significantly more money than parents receive from adult children. See Table 12-3 for a summary of who gives and, in older years, who receives help.

Generational Closeness

From the description of Bengtson's five types of families, recall that three of the five types, or about 60 percent of the sample, reported closeness between the two generations, and three of the five types also described joint activities. The birth of grandchildren increases this closeness between generations. As noted earlier, parents are more likely to be giving when a grandchild arrives, as there is more for them to do. They have information about child rearing and information about the new parent as a baby and growing child that is of interest to the new parent as he or she sees the new baby develop. Parents can also provide instrumental help in the form of household help, child care, and general support.

As grandparents, they also have the marvelous opportunity to reexperience the joys of childhood without the responsibilities, unless they become the primary caregivers. As Gail Sheehy writes, "At this stage of our lives, we can let a grandchild take us back to one of the biggest delights of childhood—becoming so absorbed in

■ **T A B L E 12-3**
GIVING AND RECEIVING IN THE FAMILY

Adult parents give to adult children when

- Parents have the resources to do so
- Parents and children are geographically close
- There is a good relationship between parents and child
- A grandchild arrives
- Grandchildren are young
- Women are the parents

Older parents who are more likely to receive help from children are

- Women who have many children
- Women who have been caregivers
- Widows

Adapted from Steven H. Zarit and David J. Eggebeen, "Parent-Child Relationships in Adulthood and Later Years," in *Handbook of Parenting,* 2nd ed., ed. Marc H. Bornstein, vol. 1: *Children and Parenting* (Mahwah, NJ: Erlbaum, 2002).

playing a game or flying a kite or blowing bubbles that time passes and we don't even notice it."[34]

Grandparents serve their grandchildren as storytellers, family historians, playmates, and patient coaches in life.[35] This greatly benefits the grandchildren (see Chapter 4), but it also serves grandparents. Grandchildren give grandparents a sense of purpose in life, opportunities to pass on values, and sometimes a chance to redo or undo some of the parenting mistakes of the past. Specifically, grandparenting can sometimes help the relationship between parents and adult child and heal wounds from the past. The parent can also be more giving and understanding of the adult child, and the adult child can enjoy and benefit from the greater closeness and understanding of the parent. (See the interview with Julie and Leon.)

Sheehy sums it up, "Grandchildren soften our hearts. They loosen the sludge of old resentments and regrets. It's a chance for reconciliation between ourselves and our children."[36] The best gift of all is having the love you feel recognized in your grandchild's smiling response to you.

Sheehy's rules for effective grandparenting include the following: (1) provide support to your children, not advice; (2) learn to wait your turn for time with grandchildren; and (3) have close relationships by modern means of communication—e-mail, video conferencing by means of a software package, or sending photos from a digital camera.

Generational closeness decreases when parents divorce and even more when divorced parents remarry.[37] Divorce appears to have a ripple effect across the generations, affecting the relationships between parents and adult children and between grandparents and grandchildren. Grandparents who divorce are more likely to live farther away from children and grandchildren, see them less often, and have weaker ties with grandchildren. The effects of divorce are more pronounced for grandfathers and for paternal grandparents and less pronounced for maternal grandmothers and their grandchildren.

Conflicts between Parents and Adult Children

When parents and adult children in the Longitudinal Study of Generations (LSOG) were asked to describe areas of conflict, about one-third could not list any conflict, and many made explicit statements about the satisfactory nature of the relationship.[38] About two-thirds described an average of one area of conflict. The two most frequent areas accounting for the majority of problems were similar for the two generations—communication/interaction style and lifestyle habits/personal choices—with about a third of the complaints falling into each category. A third prominent area, accounting for about 16 percent of complaints, concerned conflicts about child-rearing values and practices.

Complaints about communication include being critical, deceptive, indirect, and verbally abusive. Both generations complained about feeling rejected and abandoned because the other family member interacted little with them. Some disagreements here related to divorce and centered on the treatment of one spouse by the other. Conflicts over lifestyles included conflicts regarding living with partners, financial spending habits, style of dress, alcohol use, and choice of friends.

INTERVIEW
with Julie and Leon

Julie and Leon are a married couple in their late sixties. They have four children—two sons, forty-four and forty-three, and two daughters, thirty-eight and thirty-six. All are currently married with children, and one has had a previous divorce. Each family has three children, ranging in age from newborn to eighteen. One daughter lives fifteen minutes from her parents, the sons live about an hour away, and one daughter lives about three hours away. They are a tight-knit family, spending holidays, vacations, and weekend recreational time together. Family members exchange help, with Julie and Leon providing baby-sitting and emotional support for grandchildren, and the children giving them special recreational opportunities such as an extended two-week vacation. Not only are the children close to the parents, but the children are close to each other and spend time together without the parents.

Julie and Leon became parents in the late 1950s, when families were larger than they are now and when mothers stayed at home. Julie returned to work when her girls were ten and twelve, but she had a flexible job that enabled her to be home by three. She continued to work until her retirement two years ago. Leon retired the year before.

What do you think accounts for the fact that you have such a close-knit family and that your children get along with each other so well?

Julie: One of the secrets is, "Keep your mouth shut because so much is different now." Many of the things that we did in raising our children, especially in the first five years, are passé now.

Leon: For example, our children went to bed and stayed in their own beds all night. They could come in early in the morning, but they did not sleep with us at night. It's not right or wrong, but you adjust to differences.

We made sure our kids were active in sports, and when I came home from work, I played with them, practicing kicking for soccer or throwing for baseball. When the boys were in baseball, I was president of the Little League and scheduled all the games for a thousand kids in the league. We were just as active in the girls' sports. We made sure that, when possible, each of the kids attended the other kids' games or tournaments. The girls went to the boys' events, and even when the boys were in college, they attended the girls' games and competitions when they could.

I took time off from work to go to the games, in contrast to my father, who never came to see me play even if he was off work. He said it put too much pressure on me.

Julie: Having come from a divorced family, being involved with the children, being at home for them and not getting divorced were very important to me.

Child-rearing conflicts centered on the spacing of children, level of permissiveness or control, and the level of acceptance and approval of grandchildren. Other areas of conflict included conflicts over values, religion, and politics (12 percent), conflicts over work habits (6 percent), and conflicts over household standards/maintenance (2 percent).

An underlying theme of the verbal comments is that both parents and children want to feel close and get along, and both feel disappointed when this does not happen. There may be empty nests, but neither generation wants empty spaces in their hearts.

Leon: I wanted our home to be a place where the kids could bring their friends and play. My mother wouldn't let my friends in the house, and if she did, she criticized them so much afterwards that I never wanted her to see them. So I was determined to have the kids and their friends around and to spend a lot of time with them because I enjoyed it. I could relate to them, and it was easier than work. My sons are not having as much time to play with their children as I did.

Julie: We try not to talk about one child to the other. I did not like it when my grandmother came to visit, and she talked about one uncle to us, and then went and talked to another about us. If you do, later you can be quoted.

Leon: The kids like to include us in activities because they know we don't make comments, and they can be relaxed around us. I like all my sons- and daughters-in-law. They are all different, and each brings a new dimension to the family. If you don't like them, it comes through, and they don't like you. My sons-in-law are more comfortable around Julie because I am unpredictable, and they don't know what I might say.

Julie: We tried to teach the children to be happy for each other's successes. Sometimes kids are jealous, and they almost don't like to see the other succeed. We tried to say that your successes will come, too, so be happy for this one.

Leon: The kids appreciate each others' strengths and faults. If I ever detect little jealous criticisms in conversations, I put a stop to it right away.

I like to see all the cousins get along with each other. I was disappointed not to be closer to my nieces and nephews and not to have them close with my children, so I was determined that would not happen with my grandchildren. We have activities where all the cousins can be together and have fun.

It is so important that children know you love them. You don't just say it, but you are thoughtful about them and interested in them and ask them questions about what they are doing. Our granddaughter [eighteen] has called Julie a lifesaver. Julie has always been there for her when her divorced parents didn't get along. She came to live with us the last few months of high school and the summer after graduation because her father lived so far away from her friends, and she and her mother were not getting along. My parents were there for me. I could always call my father, get advice. He wrote me insightful letters, and I have continued that with my children. When I became an adult, I felt secure, knowing people cared for me and were cheering for me. We try to do that for our children and our grandchildren.

Promoting Positive Relationships between Parents and Adult Children

From working with adults and from experiences in his own family with his wife and nine children, Stephen Covey has developed the seven habits of highly effective families. These habits emphasize positive communication, understanding others' points of view, making plans to improve relationships and taking action to create the kinds of relationships one wants, and doing enjoyable activities with family members, including extended family members.[39]

Covey has always valued intergenerational relationships and activities and has emphasized them in his family life. He believes that such activities provide support to all members. To illustrate the point with his children, he showed them that they can easily break one Popsicle stick, but five Popsicle sticks stacked on top of each other are impossible to break. Similarly, family members together are stronger than anyone alone, and joint activities among family members provide energy and strength for all.

Covey's principles provide individuals ways to change themselves from the inside out. Over time, others will likely change in response, and change will be faster if all family members are following the same program. In parenting adult children, one person alone may want the changes but can promote change in others by taking the first step.

PARENTING DEPENDENT ADULTS

Some parents will always have parenting responsibilities in some form, because their children have significant disabilities that require active help. Adult children may suffer from mental retardation, congenital or birth injury, developmental problems such as autism, or serious psychological disorders that have limited their capacity for independence. Many forms of difficulty require ongoing parenting.

In the last three decades, many changes have increased the numbers of children with special needs living with parents—the closing of institutions that formerly provided residential care for many people, changes in medications that control behaviors, improved care and education of people so there is less need of institutionalization, increased number of community programs providing work and activities, and increased community and government services.[40] All these changes have created a larger role for parents as the ongoing caregiver and advocate for the child.

The new parental responsibilities for lifespan care of children create stress and the need for coping strategies to maintain parents' own well-being. Difficulties can be so different, and parents' resources in meeting them so varied, that one can only paint a very broad picture of parenting adult dependent children. The adult parent-child relationship is shaped by cultural context, type of family, nature of the problem, resources of the family, and services the family obtains from outside agencies.[41]

Studies of family caregiving of mentally retarded and mentally ill adults reveal that in many ways the nature of the difficulty affects caregiving. Mental retardation, for example, appears to involve less stress for caregivers than does mental illness. Diagnosed early in life, mental retardation proceeds in generally predictable fashion. It has less stigma attached to it than do psychological problems, as it is no one's "fault." Caregivers often receive sympathy and admiration for providing in-home care.

In contrast, mental illness often is diagnosed in late adolescence or early adulthood after decades of competent development.[42] Caregivers go through a period of mourning for the time of normal development. Mental illness takes an unpredictable course, and symptoms may appear suddenly. In the minds of many, mental illness is the "fault" of parents or family members, and so they feel some shame. As a result, caregivers of mentally ill children have a small support network that usually includes someone who also has a child with similar problems.

Siblings are affected differently by the two disorders. Adults who have siblings with mental illness are more affected, in part because they wonder if this could happen to them or their children.[43] Some decide not to have children for fear of the risk of psychological problems.

Providing care for dependent adult children places demands on parents and family but gives them satisfaction as well.

African American caregivers, and in some studies Latina/o caregivers, cope better with such stresses and consequently feel less burdened. The mutual-aid system that African Americans emphasize reduces stress even when they have fewer financial resources to help than do wealthier European Americans with a more extensive support system. Women of all ages are more likely to be caregivers than are men, who provide less help and experience less strain.[44]

Rachel Simon describes the satisfaction and insights she received from her relationship with her sister, Beth, who was mentally retarded and lived in a group home.[45] Rachel began to become a part of Beth's world when she took time to ride the buses with her. Laid off from her job, Beth spent her time riding the buses in Philadelphia from morning to night. She became friends with the drivers, the dispatcher, and the regular riders. On the other hand, Rachel was a hard-driving professional person who was devoted to work. She let friendships lapse and could not make a commitment to a long-term boyfriend when he asked her to marry him.

When Beth had to undergo eye surgery and became very nervous about the surgery and the recovery that would have to follow, Beth drew on her network of friends, who came to the hospital with her, took her into their homes following the surgery, and cared for her until she recovered. Witnessing the strong, caring bonds Beth had formed with other people changed Rachel, who said,

> I came to want a different life for myself than the one I'd had. And a few months after that, I phoned Sam [the boyfriend to whom she could not make a commitment]. We talked for a long time, and I was no longer scared. From there we began a surprising and wonderful courtship that resulted in our wedding in May 2001.[46]

So, Beth changed Rachel and helped her achieve a major life goal.

At some point in the course of caring for a dependent adult child, the question of placement occurs, such as in a group home. Parents may involve siblings in the plans and in the ongoing care that will have to continue when parents die. The move to some form of care may occur naturally as a part of general plans for the dependent adult, either because the parent cannot continue the caregiving or because the dependent adult is too difficult or erratic or even violent to maintain. Professionals and support group members can give guidelines and emotional support, but only parents can make the painful and saddening decisions required of them.

A PRACTICAL QUESTION: WHAT IF ADULT CHILDREN VACILLATE BETWEEN DEPENDENCE AND INDEPENDENCE?

As we saw in parenting adult dependent children, it is stressful when adult children have sporadically increasing needs parents must meet. This happens with children who have some form of serious psychological problems, such as bipolar disorder, criminal behavior, or some forms of substance abuse. How can parents manage?

Depending on the particular circumstance, professional consultations can give guidance and direction for the most helpful behaviors. George McGovern, a former U.S. senator from South Dakota and a presidential nominee in 1972, wrote a poignant book about parenting his daughter, who died of alcoholism at age forty-five. He and his wife had paid for many therapy programs and tried to help in various ways, but professionals advised that they keep a little more distance from her.[47]

> As I have . . . reflected on what I would do differently with the benefit of hindsight, several thoughts have emerged. I would make a greater effort to share in her life and development from the beginning. I would watch over her more carefully—especially in the adolescent high school years. I would, if I detected signs of alcoholism, inform myself thoroughly about this disease and do everything in my power to get her into a sound recovery program as quickly as possible. . . .
>
> Once the disease had fastened on to her, I would stay in close communication with her, expressing my love and concern for her at all times. I would call her every few days in a nonjudgmental manner, just to let her know I shared and understood her pain.
>
> I regret more than I can describe the decision Eleanor and I made under professional counsel to distance ourselves from Terry in what proved to be the last six months of her life. . . .
>
> But if I could recapture Terry's life, I would never again distance myself from her no matter how many times I had tried and failed to help her. Better to keep trying and failing than to back away and not know what is going on. If she had died despite my best efforts and my close involvement with her life up to the end, at least she would have died with my arms around her, and she would have heard me say one more time: "I love you, Terry."[48]

PARENTING ONE'S OWN PARENT

Parenting one's own parent is a gradual process that actually begins when one is young. The preschooler who points out the location of an item the parent is searching for, the older child who sympathizes with a parent's difficult workload, the college student who gives the parents valuable insight on a problem all involve supporting and caring for the parent.

Parents today not only have longer lifespans, but they are healthier and wealthier than previous generations as they age. As such, some adult children may only parent their parent by giving advice on certain topics such as investment strategies or giving care for a brief period when a parent has an acute illness. Nonetheless, many adult children will become their parent's parent during these years for a variety of reasons. Increasing divorce means many aging parents do not have care from a spouse and have reduced economic resources as well.[49] Young adult children, however, must often work full-time and answer their own children's needs; they are often not geographically available to give care. Further, today's smaller families mean there are fewer children to share the caregiving.

There are many similarities between parenting adult dependent children and parenting an aging parent. Wives and daughters do the primary caregiving, husbands do less, and sons the least.[50]

While they are healthy and well-functioning, parents tend to give rather than receive help. When needs arise, though, children do step in to meet parents' needs, especially when relationships are good.[51] Children are most likely to give advice and help with home chores, repairs, shopping, and errands. Financial help is rarer;

in one survey, only 3 percent of parents reported receiving $200 or more in five years. The more children one has, the more likely one is to receive help, so having many children continues to ensure help in older age. Those women who have been caregivers for so many years are more likely to receive aid than are men.

As noted earlier, divorce affects relationships through the generations. Parental divorce, which is becoming more frequent, reduces contact between parents and children and decreases the quality of their relationship, so that there is less mutual help between generations.[52] Interestingly, elderly widows receive more assistance than do married parents, perhaps because they have fewer resources.

Most cultures emphasize care of older parents. Both generations prefer parents to live independently when they are healthy and functioning well, but this does not always happen. A major transition occurs when a parent can no longer live alone. This decision is usually made by children, the parents, and the physician. A variety of alternatives exist. Parents may hire live-in help, but the most common arrangement is that the parent comes to live with the child; if needed, hired caregivers can come to the home or live in. Parents may also go to some form of residential living that involves levels of care—independent living, assisted living, and nursing care. There are also nursing homes and board-and-care homes. Even then, children will be involved in visiting, overseeing care, paying bills, and doing other necessary chores for parents. Making the decision for a parent to go into residential care is difficult for children. Parents sometimes spare children this task when they move into places with graded levels of care when healthy and simply move to the next level of care as needed.

Caregivers experience stress from many sources. They become depressed and isolated from others.[53] Conflict with noncaregiving brothers and sisters increases the stress, as does the decision to leave work to meet parents' needs. Caregiving can so take over caregivers' lives that they feel they have lost their personal identities. Social support from friends, siblings, and spouses reduces this stress. Married caregivers feel less strain than do single or divorced caregivers. Sibling support reduces strain as well. Caregivers who are active problem solvers manage the stress most effectively. Formal support, like day care programs, can reduce stress as well. Too many caregivers do not have access to them.

PARENTS' EXPERIENCES IN FACING TRANSITIONS

We have seen throughout this chapter the full span of parenting adults, which began when children first left home to be adults. "Empty nest" refers to the sad, empty feelings many parents have as children leave home and make their own lives. Even when children still live at home, parents' roles as caregiver and as primary authority decrease. Although parents welcome children's growing independence and competence, many long nostalgically for the days when everyone was together and all activities outside of work were family activities. Others, however, see these years as times of possibility for themselves.

Barbara Unell and Jerry Wyckoff describe this stage of parenthood as the *family remodeling stage*.[54] The home is no longer occupied as it once was. Children come

---

INTERVIEW
It's Never Too Late

Knowing my interest in parenting, Harry Sirota, a Chicago optometrist, shared these anecdotes from his own life.

Harry said to me, "It's never too late to learn and to change. And you can even be a parent to your parent. When my father was eighty-nine, he had a big birthday party, and I went home for it. There were lots of guests, but my father was sitting off to the side of the garden. He motioned me over to him and said, 'Sit down, I want to talk to you. I want to apologize for all the things I did when you were growing up. I wish I had been a different father.'"

"What did you do?" Harry asked his father.

"You know what I did. Why are you hurting me by making me tell you now?"

"I know that I know, but I want to know what you're apologizing for."

His father stopped, thought, then talked for half an hour about all the things he did. When he was through, he concluded, "I didn't mean to hurt you. I love you."

Harry replied, "I hated you for doing those things, but I want to thank you for apologizing to me. If I had to do it to my children, I would find it very difficult."

His father said, "I want you to know I loved you then, I love you now, and I always will love you."

"Why are you telling me these things now?" Harry asked.

His father explained, "I'm sitting here looking at all these children and how parents behave with them, and I realize I made some terrible mistakes with you."

Harry said to me, "There was a great release from the anger I carried all those years." His father died a year later.

Harry went on to tell me how he had changed his mother's behavior. "In all my childhood she never told me she loved me. So when she was about ninety, I thought I would give her what she couldn't give to me. I called every week, and it was usually a superficial conversation, "How are you? What are you doing?" At the end of one phone conversation, I took a deep breath, and said, 'I . . .' It was so hard to say, I almost gave up, but I gritted my teeth and blurted out, 'I love you, Mom.' And she replied she loved me. Each week it was a little easier.

"Then about the sixth week, no sooner had I got into the conversation, she said, 'You know, son, I really love you.'"

"Giving them what they could not give to me has been healing for them and healing for me."

---

and go during the college years or are out and working, so the home needs psychological "remodeling."

With more time and possibly more resources for their needs, parents often look at what they want to do with the rest of their lives. For example, Jane Pauley, an anchorwoman at NBC for about thirty years, decided to leave that job when her twins started college. She wanted time to figure out what she was going to do with the rest of her life. So, while children's leaving brings sadness, it can also spark excitement and renewed energy for the possibilities that greater freedom brings to adults.

The next stage of parenting is the plateau period. Children are grown and independent. Parents have created a satisfying lifestyle and are ready to enjoy grandparenting. Plateau parents have a sense of the circle of life and their role in it themselves. As their children become parents and they grandparents, they move on to mentor another generation. Plateau parents sometimes have to make choices about nurturing and giving, as they are part of the "sandwich generation" that nurtures aging parents as well as adult children.

Unell and Wyckoff describe the final years of parenthood as the *rebounding years,* when aging parents bounce back from the stresses of illness or other crises and also respond to the overtures of other family members for contact and help. They seek attention and are waiting for family members to interact with them and help as needed. Unell and Wyckoff identify three types of rebounders—the proud independents, the humble submissives, and the aged sages. Proud independents, as the name suggests, want to retain their autonomy as long as possible. They reject any offer of help and worry their children with their independent behaviors. Humble submissives feel apologetic at inconveniencing their children and rarely ask for help directly. As a result, they often do not get the help they want and do not recognize the help that is offered. They tend to feel rejected and complain about their life circumstances. Aged sages try to maintain independence but request help as they need it and express their appreciation for what others do for them. They enjoy others' company and do whatever they can to reciprocate the help they receive:

> When I stopped complaining that my daughter never called or my sons never came to see me, I suddenly became more popular. I had to learn not to push my grandchildren into taking care of me. Instead I asked them about their lives and didn't complain about mine. Like magic, they then started coming to family night at the retirement center where I live, showing off their children's report cards and pictures of their latest vacation. They even remembered to include me on the invitation list for my grandchildren's and great-grandchildren's birthday parties.[55]

Rebounders are in the stage of arriving at what Erik Erickson termed a "sense of integrity" (see Chapter 2), which involves feeling satisfied with one's life and accomplishments.

While parents usually have a greater emotional stake in children than children have in parents, still many adult children treasure their connection with their aging parent. They rely on being parented with advice and support even when they themselves are giving significant help to their parents.

Reviewing this chapter, we can see that acceptance, availability, nurturance, positive support, and problem solving are the basic strategies of parenting in the adult years, as in all the preceding years.

SUPPORT FOR PARENTS

Support groups provide services for parents across the lifespan. When children have developmental delays or special problems, parents' groups help parents cope with the diagnosis.[56] Support groups also help parents cope with marital and personal issues that arise from dealing with a child with special needs. As noted, such groups are especially important to help caregivers cope with mental illness, as caregivers often feel that only someone who has been in their shoes can understand their situation and feelings. Support groups are equally important for those parenting aging parents.

In addition to receiving emotional support, people who attend support groups get information on new treatments, resources in the community and how to access them, and coping strategies that work, as well as establishing a personal network they can rely upon for help.

Certainly, services need to be available for disabled adult children and their caregivers. Such programs need to be designed to counteract some families' tendencies to want to hide the disabled person and to counteract cultural beliefs that caring relatives should not rely on social programs to care for family members.[57]

Although we have focused on the demands of caregiving, benefits exist also. Many parents gain satisfaction from providing care for the adult child who lives with them. As parents age, the adult dependent child with mental illness can sometimes care for the parent. Living with one's own aging parent can bring the joys of intergenerational closeness discussed earlier.

MAIN POINTS

Criteria for adulthood include being

- over eighteen
- financially and psychologically self-sustaining
- taking on adult roles of parent and worker

Theoretical perspectives include

- Erikson's lifespan theory
- attachment theory, emphasizing communication, availability, and nurturance from attachment figure
- the theory of emerging adulthood

Families

- differ in closeness, agreement, proximity, contact, and amount of help exchanged
- fall into five typologies—tight-knit, sociable, intimate but distant, obligatory, and detached, with women more likely to be in tight-knit families and men in sociable and obligatory family relationships
- give several types of support—financial, emotional, instrumental, and informational
- are most likely to give help when members are close, see each other frequently, and grandchildren are involved

When adolescents take on adult roles of parent and worker, they

- look to parental support to live at home
- contribute their labor and earnings to help their families
- can gain responsibility and independence

College youth

- who emphasize self-governance as a definer of adulthood have high self-esteem and feel connected to others
- enter adulthood influenced by childhood events such as parents' divorce
- suffer an increasing number of psychological and substance abuse problems

Adolescents with chronic physical health problems

- attain levels of education, income, marriage, and self-esteem comparable to youth with no physical problems
- have added problems when they must depend on technology

Conflicts with adult children center on

- communication/interaction style
- lifestyle habits and personal choices
- child-rearing values and practices

Positive relationships are promoted

- when grandparents and grandchildren enjoy the grandchildren's childhood together
- when parents emphasize positive communications, win-win solutions, and doing enjoyable activities together to increase family solidarity

Parenting dependent adults and older parents

- involves caregiving and seeking support
- can be enriching psychologically and emotionally
- often involves looking for some form of placement outside the home

The stages parents experience as children go through adulthood include

- the family remodeling stage
- the plateau stage
- the rebounding stage

As in other phases of life, parenting in the adult years of life involves

- acceptance, availability, nurturance
- positive support and problem-solving help

EXERCISES

1. If you were a parent of two teenage children, what actions would you take so that your children would have a smooth transition to adulthood?
2. If you were an aging parent, what actions would you take to promote positive relationships with your children and grandchildren?
3. Have the class divide into small groups and discuss reasons for the growing number of psychological problems experienced by students in the college years. Also discuss what college administrations can do to reduce the problems students experience.

4. Imagine that you are the parent of a dependent adult child with mental retardation. Look in the community for the kinds of out-of-home living arrangements possible for such individuals. What is the cost of such arrangements? Would the average person be able to afford them?

5. Imagine that you are the child of an aging parent who could not live alone. What living arrangements are possible for such a parent in the community? What is the cost of such arrangements?

ADDITIONAL READINGS

Epstein, Joel. *Sex, Drugs, and Flunking Out*. Center City, MN: Hazelden, 2001.

Kastner, Laura S., and Wyatt, Jennifer. *The Launching Years*. New York: Three Rivers Press, 2002.

Koplewicz, Harold S. *More Than Moody*. New York: Putnam, 2002.

Levine, Mel. *Ready or Not, Here Life Comes*. New York: Simon & Schuster, 2005.

Peel, Kathy. *Family for Life*. New York: McGraw-Hill, 2003.

Unell, Barbara C., and Wyckoff, Jerry L. *The Eight Seasons of Parenthood*. New York: Times Books, 2000.

III

Parenting in Varying Life Circumstances

C H A P T E R

13

Parenting and Working

Test Your Knowledge: Fact or Fiction?

1. Children in dual-earner families report lack of time with parents as the source of greatest stress for them.
2. In a survey, children report employed mothers and fathers as equally good at controlling their tempers when children do something wrong.
3. Research shows that, in predicting children's competence, parenting matters much more than day care.
4. Early adolescents are old enough to engage in self-care without negative consequences.
5. The fees for good-quality day care are not very different from fees for mediocre care.

Combining working and parenting is a major challenge for today's men and women. The majority of mothers work from the time their children are infants, and more fathers than ever before are involved in child care. How do parents solve the problems that arise in integrating work and family lives? How do they find child care that promotes children's development? How do they adjust routines to enhance the quality of time they spend with children? How do they adapt to their many responsibilities yet maintain a sense of well-being?

This chapter examines the impact of working on parents, on their parenting, and on their children. In Chapter 2, Urie Bronfenbrenner described parents' work as part of the exosystem that exerts a major influence on children's development.[2] Our understanding of the relationship between parents' work and family life is limited for many reasons. First, parents' work varies in many ways from parent to parent— number of hours worked, level of job satisfaction, amount of stress. So, conclusions regarding parenting and work have to be generalized cautiously, because they may apply to only subgroups of parents. Second, families may experience several work and child-care patterns over even a short time in response to the family's economic and child-care needs, so it is difficult to identify one pattern that can be related to parents' and children's functioning. Third, research suggests that parents' work may have different effects on different children in the family, depending on birth order and personal characteristics.[3] Fourth, the relationship between parents' work and family life may change as the nature of work itself changes and society makes further adaptations to parents' work.

In our present society, most parents work. In 2001, both parents were employed in 68 percent of two-parent families with children under eighteen. In families maintained by women, 73 percent of women were employed.[4]

In this chapter, we look at how men and women integrate working and parenting, the day care options available when neither parent can care for the child, the impact of day care on children, and ways parents care for themselves as they rise to the challenges of working and parenting.

DIMENSIONS OF PARTICIPATION IN WORK AND FAMILY LIFE

Graeme Russell describes six domains of parental involvement in family life and two levels of activity—involvement and responsibility.[5] The six domains that apply to either mothers' or fathers' participation are

1. Employment and financial support
2. Day-to-day care and interaction with children (physical and psychological availability to the child)
3. Child management and socialization (looking after basic needs for health care, social experience, emotional connections, cognitive stimulation)
4. Household work (cleaning, shopping, preparing meals)
5. Maintaining relationships between caregivers (exchange of information about the child, raising and resolving areas of conflict)
6. Parental commitment and investment (amount of time spent with the child relative to paid work and leisure time and the degree to which the child's needs have priority over parents' needs)

The roles in each of these areas will differ for each parent, depending on whether the person is involved or takes primary responsibility for the area. Men may care for children for a specified number of hours, but this differs from taking responsibility for the child's well-being—arranging doctor visits, social activities. Similarly, women may work and provide income but not feel the responsibility of being the financial provider for the family.

In 1960, fathers were the primary financial providers and put in 1 hour of work at home for every 4 hours worked by mothers who cared for the children and the house. In 1996, women spent about 3.7 hours per day on household chores and child care, and men spent about 3 hours per day.[6] Men, however, worked an average of 48 hours per week at full-time jobs, and women worked 42. So, women did about 55 percent of the work at home, and men worked longer hours at a job. Although fathers in dual-earner families participate more than fathers in single-earner families, mothers in both families perform more child care.

Types of Families

There is no one way for parents to meet work and family needs. One study identified three family types in terms of work and parenting characteristics.[7] In *high-status families,* both parents had high levels of education and occupational status, were highly involved in their work, and earned more money than did the other two groups of families. In addition, the couples held less traditional ideologies on sex-role activities and shared tasks equally. They experienced a great deal of work overload and stress, however, and as a result had more marital conflict, less marital satisfaction, and less love between the spouses than did the other two groups. Parents confined tension to the marital relationship, and children in the families were not aware of the marital problems because the stress did not affect the ways parents treated the children.

In *low-stress families,* both parents reported low levels of work overload, high levels of marital satisfaction and love between the spouses, and low levels of conflict. Parents were available to take an active role in monitoring children, and such monitoring improved children's functioning.

In *main-secondary families,* fathers were the primary financial providers, and mothers provided a small supplementary income, frequently through employment in lower-status occupations. These families had the lowest incomes of the three types of families and the most traditional ways of organizing family activities. Girls in main-secondary families were more likely to engage in feminine tasks than were girls in other families. Marital satisfaction fell between that of the other two groups, as did their level of conflict.

After interviewing 150 families, Francine Deutsch identified four patterns of working and parenting, which she termed *equal sharers, 60–40 couples, 75–25 couples, and alternating shifters.*[8] She found that families sometimes moved among these patterns. When children were infants, some families were unequal sharers, becoming equal sharers after children were older. Even within the types of families, there were many variations. Equal sharers could be providing all the day care with flexible work hours, or they could have child care and work the same hours outside the home. Alternating shifters tended to have working-class occupations, as it is these types of occupations that offer daytime and evening shifts. Women's income in alternating-shift families was often very important, and women felt they had power and received appreciation for their contributions.

Deutsch found that these patterns of work influenced parents' ways of being with children but not the total amount of time they spent with children. Equal-sharing couples spent the same amount of time with children as did the other three groups of couples, but equal-sharing mothers were alone with children less frequently than were the other mothers. Equal-sharing fathers compensated for this, as they were alone with children more often than were fathers of the other groups. Further, equal-sharing parents were more often together with children than were parents of the other groups.

Deutsch found that the couples in the four groups did not differ markedly in politics, education, or class, but they did vary in how they negotiated the everyday issues of child care and household tasks. Couples who wanted equal sharing of parenting and working made every effort to distribute both kinds of tasks equally and to find friends who supported their decisions.

An interview study of middle-class men and women in dual-earner families looked at families at different points in the life cycle—some before or after having children but most in the child-rearing stages of life.[9] This study focused on middle managers and professionals, as these people not only determine their own fates but also tend to shape the work lives of people they supervise. Sampling couples from upstate New York rather than those from an urban area may have resulted in an overrepresentation of families who have scaled back working demands, however.

In this sample, few participants had dual-career families in which both parents were highly involved in work and both were single-mindedly pursuing work goals. Dual-career couples usually had no children at home, or they hired help to meet many of the family demands. The vast majority of couples relied on one of three strategies for scaling back work demands to carve out time for the family. Although most couples had an egalitarian gender ideology, choices in day-to-day behaviors often resulted in traditionally gendered roles for men and women.

The three work-family strategies were termed *placing limits, job-versus-career,* and *trading-off.* Couples who placed limits (about 30 percent) turned down jobs or promotions that required relocation or traveling, refused overtime hours, and limited the number of hours worked. Women often did this when a child was born, and men sometimes did this when careers became established and parenting involvement grew. Job-versus-career strategies (relied on by about 40 percent) involved one parent's having an absorbing career and the other parent's having a job that produced income but was subordinated to the needs of the family and the parent with the career. In about two-thirds of these families, men had the career and women had the job, but in one-third, the wife had the career and the man the job. Often, chance or early advancement or opportunity determined which parent had the career. In the trading-off group, parents shifted back and forth between jobs and careers, depending on family needs and career opportunities.

The researchers were concerned that couples' scaling-back strategies appeared to be private solutions to public workplace problems. They believe that private solutions do not challenge the underlying assumptions that work can make demands on parents—such as 60-hour weeks—while doing little to help them meet family and work needs. The couples appeared to make few demands for formal policies of flextime, job-sharing, or on-site day care and instead sought informal arrangements to meet family needs. Unfortunately, workers at lower levels in the employment hierarchy might not get such benefits without formal policies.

One can see that there are many ways to meet work and family needs and that families use more than one strategy to meet these needs over time. In a later section, we discuss ways parents can minimize stress in using these strategies.

Children's Ratings of Parents

Regardless of the strategies used by parents to meet their family and work responsibilities, children give their parents high marks. Ellen Galinsky, the president of the Families and Work Institute, has expressed concern that children's opinions have not been included in the discussions of the effects of parents' work on children and family life. In 1998, Galinsky interviewed a representative sample of 605 employed parents with children under eighteen and surveyed a representative sample of 1,023 third- to twelfth-grade children.[10] The sample of children varied with respect to the parents' work status—employed or nonemployed—and number of hours worked. Children's attitude toward their mother and their assessment of the parent-child relationship did not depend on the work status of the mother or the number of hours the mother worked. Nonemployed fathers were rated lower than were employed fathers in the areas of (1) making their children feel important and loved and (2) participating in important events in their children's lives. Children tended to give parents higher grades when the family was seen as financially secure. We discuss the influence of economic factors on parenting in greater detail in a later section.

Seventy-four percent of children felt mothers were very successful in managing work and family life, and 67 percent of children felt fathers were very successful. As shown in Table 13-1, parents received high marks for making children feel important and loved, being understanding, appreciating children, and being there for conversation. Although mothers were overwhelmingly seen as the parent who was there for children at times of sickness, more frequently involved than fathers in school matters, and someone children could go to when upset, the ratings for fathers on other qualities were similar to those given to mothers. Fathers were seen as being appreciative of who the child really was, as spending time in conversation, and as controlling their temper with the child as well as the mother.

Parents gave themselves equally high marks in these areas. Children's ratings of parents were higher when they spent more time with parents and when the time with parents was not rushed. About 40 percent of mothers and children and 32 percent of fathers, however, felt that their time together was somewhat or very rushed.

Divergent Realities

Mothers, fathers, and children do not always share the same views of experiences. We therefore need to understand these divergences in order to avoid false assumptions about the meanings of events.

Divergences in Men's and Women's Perceptions   Recall the study in Chapter 10 in which mothers, fathers, and early adolescents carried pagers for a week. When

■ **TABLE 13-1**
STUDENTS'* LETTER GRADES FOR PARENTS' BEHAVIORS

Letter Grade	A		B		C		D		E	
Parents' Behavior	**M†**	**F‡**	**M**	**F**	**M**	**F**	**M**	**F**	**M**	**F**
Being there for me when I'm sick	85	58	8	20	4	12	2	7	1	3
Appreciating me for who I am	72	69	15	16	6	8	4	5	3	2
Making me feel loved for who I am	72	66	16	18	8	9	4	4	1	2
Attending important events in my life	69	60	18	20	7	12	3	4	3	5
Being someone I can go to when I'm upset	57	48	18	19	11	14	6	8	8	10
Being involved in what's happening to me at school	55	45	22	24	11	15	7	10	5	6
Spending time talking to me	48	47	31	25	12	16	5	8	4	4
Controlling their temper when I do something wrong	28	31	31	28	19	18	11	11	11	12

*Students in third through twelfth grades
†M indicates percentage of students giving mother that grade
‡F indicates percentage of students giving father that grade
From Ellen Galinsky, *Ask the Children: What America's Children Really Think about Working Parents* (New York: Morrow, 1999).

beeped, family members wrote down their activities and their feelings. That study found that men and women experienced different levels of stress at work and at home.[11]

Though some were teachers and nurses, mothers who worked were usually low-paid office and service workers who worked longer hours than did husbands and had as much stress and conflict. Still, their average emotional rating at work was higher than that of men and of nonemployed women because of the social rewards with coworkers and feelings of having their work appreciated.

At home, however, they felt overwhelmed by household tasks and the responsibilities of caring for family members, and their emotional well-being was only slightly higher than that of nonemployed women. When work created extra stress, their emotional well-being fell below that of nonworking mothers. Nonworking mothers lacked the stimulation and the stress of work, and their overall mood ratings were only slightly lower than those of working women with minimal stress.

Regardless of the nature of their job, men were focused and absorbed at work. They felt alert, competent, and highly involved, as they felt primarily responsible for the family's financial well-being. They experienced frustration at work and saw the home as their place to unwind, rest, and relax. They did household chores, but at a relaxed, self-determined pace.

So, work appears more socially and emotionally rewarding for mothers than for fathers, though both are highly involved in it, and home appears more relaxing for fathers than for mothers. Thus, fathers and mothers feel more relaxed in the area traditionally assigned to the opposite sex.

Divergences in Parents' and Children's Perceptions   The survey responses Galinsky obtained from children revealed discrepancies between parents' and children's perceptions.[12] Children were more satisfied with the amount of time parents spent with them than were parents. About 44 percent of mothers and 56 percent of fathers felt they spent too little time with their children, whereas only 28 percent of children felt mothers spent too little time, and 35 percent of children felt fathers spent too little time. The survey asked children to name one wish that would change how parents' working affected the family. Parents expected children to say they wanted more time with parents. Children, however, had three more-important wishes. They wished that parents could earn more money, that they could return from work less stressed, and that they felt less tired. Also, when asked if they worried about their parents, approximately one-third of children aged eight to eighteen said that they often or very often worried about their parents, and another third said they sometimes worried. So, about two-thirds of children worry about parents at least some of the time. Children said they worried because they were part of a caring family, but they also worried because they felt their parents had a lot of stress from work. Thirty percent of children aged twelve to eighteen said the worst thing about having working parents was that they were stressed out from work. Given their concern about parents' stress level, one suspects that children wanted them to make more money so they would feel less stressed.

Further, children saw their parents as less emotionally available to them than parents believed they were, and children were more concerned about parents' anger than parents were. Ninety-six percent of mothers and 90 percent of fathers gave themselves As and Bs for being emotionally available when their children were upset, but only 75 percent of children gave mothers As and Bs, and 67 percent gave fathers As and Bs. Only 4 percent of mothers and 5.5 percent of fathers gave themselves Ds and Fs for controlling their tempers, whereas 22 percent of children gave mothers Ds and Fs, and 23 percent gave fathers Ds and Fs.

So, parents are sometimes not aware of children's wishes and priorities. Children want parents to be happier and less stressed and available for them emotionally without being angry.

THE FLOW OF WORK AND FAMILY LIFE

Galinsky believes that words such as *balancing, integrating, and combining* do not describe how parents deal with working and family life, as they imply that these two spheres of activity are separate. From her research and interviews, she believes work and family life flow together to form a stream of experience that adults navigate rather than balance or combine, as illustrated in Figure 13-1. Experiences at home carry over to work, and experiences at work spill over to feelings at home.

> Let's think of ourselves as navigating the stream. To steer through these waters, we need to understand the many outside forces affecting our passage—some of which are beyond our control; others of which are not. And we need to know ourselves: our life priorities and where we really want to go. We are at the helm, with at least some control over the course of our voyage.[13]

Parent-Child Interactions

Meeting children's basic psychological and physical needs absorbs parents' time at home. Galinsky describes eight basic needs children have that parents must meet—loving the child, responding to the child's cues, appreciating the child's individuality while also expecting success, providing values, providing constructive discipline, establishing structure and routine, helping with the child's education, and being emotionally available to the child. Parents meet children's needs in many ways.

■ **FIGURE 13-1**
A MODEL OF WORK AND FAMILY LIFE

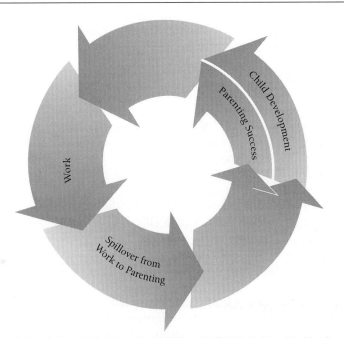

Ellen Galinsky, *Ask the Children: What America's Children Really Think about Working Parents* (New York: Morrow, 1999), 205. Copyright © 1999 by Ellen Galinsky. Reprinted by permission of HarperCollins Publishers, Inc., William Morrow.

Focusing on Children's Needs   A major strategy for employed parents is to focus their energy on meeting children's needs, especially their needs for relationships with parents. Fathers who engage in much child care when children are little maintain strong involvements in daily activities with children across the childhood years and into adolescence.[14] Such fathers play more games and share educational activities during the week, spending equal time with sons and daughters. The children of involved fathers are more socially mature at age six and more academically successful at age seven than are children of uninvolved fathers.

Employed mothers who work more than twenty hours a week spend less time with their infants and preschoolers than do nonemployed mothers. Mothers with a higher education compensate for time at work by spending more time with children in the evenings and on weekends. Children appear to become willing partners in this arrangement. They sleep more during the day care hours and remain awake and play for longer periods in the evening. In single-earner families, evening time is reserved for fathers, but in dual-earner families, mothers use this time to relate to children, giving them verbal stimulation. Although fathers are "crowded out" in these early family interactions, they have their own time alone with children and, in fact, spend more time with their children than do fathers in single-earner families.[15]

Although employed mothers spend less time with their infants, they are as sensitive and responsive as nonemployed mothers.[16] Mothers who are satisfied with their work and feel they get support are more responsive with their toddlers than are unemployed mothers; they give more guidance and use lower power-assertive techniques.[17]

Once children reach school age, mothers spend more time in single activities[18] with children than do fathers (90 minutes versus 60 minutes per week). Although no significant differences exist between single- and dual-earner fathers in the amount of time spent with children, they allot the time differently. (See the interview with Susan McHale.)

Time with children fluctuates seasonally for some mothers, with nonemployed and seasonally employed mothers spending more time in activities with children in the summer than in the winter.[19] Mothers who are employed the same number of hours throughout the year do not show this seasonal variation. Parenting of seasonally employed mothers becomes more traditional in the summer, as they have more involvement with children at that time than do fathers. Parenting becomes more egalitarian when mothers return to work.

Maintaining mother-child activities is important because such activities may buffer the child against possible negative effects from maternal absence.[20] When mothers with full-time employment or an increase in work hours maintain their time in shared activities with their children, the children show no decrease in social and cognitive functioning, as compared with children of nonemployed mothers. When mothers' hours of employment decrease and activities shared with the children increase, the children's functioning improves; if activities do not increase when work hours decrease, there is no improvement.

In the early adolescent years, the overall amount of time children spend with parents does not differ in single- and dual-earner families, but again, the difference

INTERVIEW
with Susan McHale

Susan McHale is an associate professor of human development at Pennsylvania State University and a codirector of the Pennsylvania State University Family Relations Project.

From your experience in studying dual-earner families, what kinds of things make it easiest for parents when both work?

We look at how the whole family system changes when mothers work, and we have found very interesting changes in how fathers relate to children between nine and twelve years old when their wives are employed. We collect a measure of "exclusive" or dyadic time—how much time the father spends alone with the child doing some fun activity like attending a concert or school activity. In single-earner families, fathers spend about 90 minutes a week with boys in "exclusive" (dyadic) activities and about 30 minutes with girls, so there is quite a sex distinction in these families. In dual-earner families, fathers spend equal amounts of "exclusive" time with boys and girls—about 60 minutes per week—so mother's working may enhance the relationship between *father* and daughter and decrease involvement between father and son.

We do not get any straightforward sex differences in the effects of mother's working—that is, boys do not necessarily do less well—unless these are mediated by some other process. For example, we have just finished a paper on parental monitoring of children's activities. To collect data on monitoring, we telephone both the parent and the child and ask specific questions about what has happened that day: Did the child do his homework? Did he have a special success at school that day? Our measure of monitoring is the discrepancy between the children's report and the parent's report. (We presume the children are right.) We thought that monitoring might be related to children's adjustment. We do find that in families where the child is less well monitored, boys are a little bit more at risk for problems in conduct and school achievement. This is independent of who does the monitoring; as long as you have at least one parent who is a good monitor, you do not get these effects.

When we look at what helps families function well when parents work, we find one factor is the agreement between *values* and *attitudes* on the one hand and the *actual roles* family members assume in daily life. This finding applies to adults and children. I am talking about sex-role attitudes. When parents have young children, we found the incongruencies between sex-role attitudes and behavior are related to problems in the marital relation. Specifically, when husbands and wives have traditional sex-role attitudes but the organization of daily life is egalitarian, couples were much more likely to fight, to have lower scores on a measure of love, and to find the relationship less satisfying.

When we looked at children's involvement in household chores, we found additional evidence of the importance of congruence between attitudes and family roles. For example, the more chores boys in dual-earner families perform, the better their adjustment; the reverse was true for boys in single-earner families, however. The mediating factor seems to be the father's sex-role attitudes. In single-earner families, fathers

(continued)

INTERVIEW with Susan McHale

(continued)

are more traditional and less involved in tasks themselves. Therefore, when sons do a lot of housework, their behavior is out of concordance with their fathers' values. In both kinds of families, dual and single earners, boys whose roles are incongruent with their fathers' values feel less competent and more stressed, and they report less positive relationships with their parents.

The congruence between values and beliefs and the kinds of family roles children and adults assume is what predicts better adjustment. Whether you can change people's attitudes and beliefs or whether it is easier to change family roles is hard to say. Part of the problem is that the work demands in dual-earner families require that family roles change before people feel really comfortable with that.

---

is in *how* the time is spent. Full-time employed mothers spend more time doing homework with children and less time in leisure activities.[21] Children of mothers employed part-time report more time spent playing sports with parents.

Monitoring A major task of parenting is monitoring and supervising children's activities. Although working parents are often not home after school, they can monitor what school-age children do and make certain children engage in approved activities. Studies have found that parents in dual-earner families monitor as carefully as parents in single-earner families.[22] This is important because less well monitored boys have lower school grades and less skill in school-related activities, regardless of whether mothers are employed. Studies have not found girls' behavior as clearly related as boys' behavior to monitoring.

In a recent study of after-school experiences and social adjustment of early adolescent boys and girls, Gregory Pettit found that parents' careful monitoring of their early adolescents was related to a lack of externalizing problems such as disobeying and fighting.[23] Careful monitoring counterbalanced the effects of living in an unsafe neighborhood and having a lot of unsupervised activities with peers, two other predictors of externalizing problems. As children progress through adolescence, parents' lack of monitoring is also associated with both boys' and girls' engaging in disapproved activities such as drinking.[24]

Intentional Parenting Galinsky uses the term *intentional parenting* to refer to the time, energy, and focus that working parents must bring to the process of meeting children's needs.[25] Parents feel good about their parenting when they spend time eating meals together and engaging in such activities as exercising, having fun together, or doing homework. They feel successful as parents and less stressed. Having supportive family and friends, having good day care, and having confidence that they are raising their child the way they want to also contribute to parents' feelings of success.

Despite the many demands these family activities make on parents, parents feel much less stress in caring for children than they do at work. Only 6 percent of parents say they feel a great deal of stress in caring for children, and an additional 36 percent say they feel a moderate amount of stress. By comparison, 24 percent experience a large amount of stress at work, and 45 percent experience a moderate amount.

To feel successful, though, parents have to maximize time with family members. Family time need not be considered only as time for leisure or relaxation but also as time for accomplishing tasks. When families work together, parents not only spend time with children, but they create more time for other activities as household work decreases for parents.

Encouraging Family Cooperation in Household Work   Although women usually retain primary responsibility for household management, men's participation in traditionally female household chores serves as a positive example for boys and girls, who do less stereotyping when fathers perform such chores.[26] Further, children who participate routinely in chores that benefit the family tend to show concern for others' welfare.[27]

Although women have traditionally borne the major responsibility for meeting the household needs, they are shifting the responsibility to the family as a whole. Jacqueline Goodnow and Jennifer Bowes's interviews with parents and children concerning the distribution of household work reveal that the meanings people attach to particular jobs (men's/women's work, Dad's/Mom's responsibility), the feelings they have about the jobs (like/dislike, feel competence/incompetence), and underlying principles of fairness shape how families distribute work.[28]

Several recommendations emerge from the discussion with families. First, a problem-solving approach that focuses on the specific question of "Who does this particular job?" is useful. Second, families must negotiate chores in an atmosphere of fairness, respect, and open-mindedness. When chores are assigned, people's preferences are respected and considered. Principles of fairness operate. Families naturally divide household chores into two categories: (1) self-care (making one's bed, picking up clothes or toys) and (2) family care (setting the table, taking out the garbage). Most families assign self-care responsibilities to children as the children become able to do them. Performing self-care chores gives children feelings of independence and competence, because they can care for themselves. As family chores are distributed among family members, children receive their share to promote feelings of being important participants in family life.

With a changing society expressing such varying opinions about family members' household responsibilities, families often feel dissatisfied with what they are doing and want to alter their patterns. Table 13-2 (page 446) contains suggestions for handling work responsibilities by maintaining respect and caring for each family member, staying flexible, and focusing on the positive benefits of all members' contributing to family life.

In brief, parents feel more satisfied with their family life and with their relationships with children when they have more time, do not feel rushed, and can focus on their children.[29] When they feel they have support from family and friends and can raise their children as they want, parents feel more successful. The same qualities related to parents' feelings of satisfaction and success are also associated with parents' reporting that their children have fewer problems with anxiety, depression, and inattention.

■ **T A B L E 13-2**
MOVING TO NEW PATTERNS OF HOUSEHOLD WORK

1. *Take a look at what bothers you*. Ask yourself why you are doing this chore. What specifically bothers you about the chore? What is the worst part of the chore for you?

2. *List the alternatives*. Jobs can be changed in many ways—eliminated, reassigned to someone else in the family, reduced (e.g., iron only some things but not everything), moved outside the family.

3. *Look carefully at the way you frame the problem and at the way you talk and negotiate*. Explain what you want, stick to the point in discussing the problem, and frame the issues in terms of practicality, logic, or benefits to all family members. Avoid name-calling.

4. *Be prepared for difficulties*. The greatest difficulty is dealing with family members' having different standards for completing chores. Children often do not want to do chores, because of criticism. Focus on the effort each person puts in and do not insist on perfect completion.

5. *Remember that there is more than one way to express caring and affection in a family*. Men and women have to give up old beliefs that caring must be shown by being a "good provider" or a "good homemaker." Caring for a family is more than doing housework.

6. *Keep in mind the gains as well as the costs*. Although all family members give up time to do household chores, everyone gains. All family members gain in doing chores and contributing to family functioning. They gain self-respect, skills, and the primary benefit of greater closeness to other family members.

Jacqueline J. Goodnow and Jennifer M. Bowes, *Men, Women and Household Work* (Melbourne, Australia: Oxford University Press, 1994), 197–201.

Spillover from Home to Work

About 70 percent of parents with children under eighteen say that their positive feelings about their children often or very often carry over to work, and about one-third say they often or very often have more energy on the job because of their children.[30] The parents who are more likely to have positive spillover from home to work are those who (1) are fathers, (2) put a higher priority on family life, (3) feel they have support for doing their work—they have day care they trust and parental support at times of difficulty, (4) work more days per week but feel fewer stresses and strains at work, (5) have better-quality jobs with more autonomy and learning opportunities, and (6) have more workplace support from coworkers. The fact that fathers more often experience positive feelings at home is similar to the finding of Larson and Richards that fathers have more positive moods at home than do mothers.

When mothers want to work, when they feel that their children do not suffer from their working, and when they have husbands' support, they feel increased satisfaction with themselves and with life.[31] Even if they work when they would prefer to be at home, they do not experience depression or decreased well-being, provided they think that what they are doing is important for the family. Women who want to work but who stay at home for fear of adverse effects on their children become depressed.[32] Further, their children do not function as well as those whose mothers are satisfied with their choice. One study found that academic and social performance of kindergartners was related to mothers' satisfaction with their work status.[33] Children of mothers who stayed at home when they wanted to work or thought they should work had lower levels of performance than did their peers whose mothers either worked and enjoyed it or stayed home and enjoyed that.

Men have high self-esteem and morale when their wives work, provided that these men have nontraditional attitudes about working. When men have traditional beliefs that wives' working reflects negatively on their ability as a provider, then they show decreased morale.[34] Like mothers, fathers also experience a drop in morale when they are concerned about child care and children's adjustment to mothers' working.[35]

Spillover from Work to Home

Whether one or two parents are employed, parents' work shapes family life in many ways. Parents' job classification—professional, business, skilled or unskilled labor—is the main determiner of the family's social status. The family's social status, in turn, influences its social attitudes and child-rearing practices. Middle-class parents value self-reliance and independence in children. To encourage these qualities, such parents tend to explain what they want to their children to motivate them to do what is necessary on their own. Working-class parents value obedience and conformity in children and tend to use power-assertive techniques to force compliance. They use physical punishment more than do middle-class parents; they refuse to give explanations, simply stating, "Because I said so." They are less interested in explanations, saying, "Do it now."[36]

Social status also determines the effects of mothers' employment. In a broad range of middle-class children, followed from age one through adolescence, mothers' work status per se had little effect on children's development. The children of employed and nonemployed mothers were equivalent on cognitive, academic, social-emotional, and behavioral development. The quality of the homes and parent-child relationships, regardless of mothers' work status, determined children's growth. In lower-status African American families, however, mothers' employment was related to children's language and achievement.[37]

In another study, children of single working mothers had higher self-esteem and greater academic achievement and academic self-esteem, and they reported greater family cohesiveness, than did children whose mothers received aid to dependent children. In families with fewer resources, added income may be the main factor, but the influence of an achieving parent may be what contributes to the difference.

In addition to providing income for basic support and forming a pattern of family life, work also brings many psychological benefits in terms of advancing parents' social, cognitive, and emotional development.[38] Work helps parents develop a sense of competence and self-esteem. Mothers who worked as volunteers in Head Start programs, for example, became more confident and motivated to go on in school. One of the benefits of this child-centered program has been to empower the parents who have worked there.[39]

Work often helps parents develop interpersonal skills that they then use at home. Workers in a manufacturing plant described how they used democratic work practices in solving problems at home. One man told how he started holding team meetings with his family: "After all, a family is kind of a team."[40] A mother commented to a psychologist, "Well, my daughter was having trouble going to sleep so I decided to handle the problem like we would at work. I asked her what she thought would solve the problem, and she said 'Reading two stories to me.' I did that, and she went to sleep. That cured the problem."[41]

Work also offers a range of friendships and supports. When asked to describe how she handled stress at home, a mother said, "I go to work. At work we are like a family. Friends listen to me, and we have fun even though there is a lot of work."[42] Supervisors also offer support and help at times of trouble. When one father was seriously ill, his supervisor organized coworkers to donate vacation hours so he could keep his benefits as long as possible.

About 77 percent of parents report that they often or very often feel successful at work.[43] Success is related to having time to get work done but more importantly to being able to focus on work without interruptions, being able to complete a task before getting another job to do. Having a say in how the work is done, positive relationships with coworkers, and feeling the job is meaningful also contribute to feeling successful.

Nevertheless, a sizable proportion of parents also report stress and frustration from work. Sixty-nine percent of parents report that they feel a moderate or large amount of stress, and 55 percent say they feel a moderate or large amount of frustration.[44] Stress appears to be related to job demands—working more hours per day and more days per week, having to take work home, having to travel more, feeling pressured to complete work in short periods of time with little control of how it is done, and feeling that the job is meaningless. Frustration has similar origins but is more related to the daily work schedule than to the total amount of time worked. Inability to focus, feeling unable to make decisions, feeling that the job entails no learning also increase frustration.

Galinsky's study revealed that the parents who were most likely to experience negative spillover from work to home were those who (1) put a higher priority on work than family, (2) were more likely to be managers or professionals with relatively large responsibilities at work, (3) had demanding jobs that were difficult to complete on time, (4) had jobs that were too stimulating or not stimulating enough, and (5) had less parenting support than did those who did not feel stress.[45]

Couples' diaries concerning work stress and home activities revealed that fathers with work overload were less active, less communicative, and more withdrawn.[46] Mothers compensated and did household chores, but fathers were not likely to reciprocate when mothers experienced overload. When parents had conflicts with supervisors or coworkers, they tended to argue more than before with spouses about home responsibilities. They confined arguments to spouses and did not include children.

A study of mothers and preschool children found that when mothers had stressful workdays, they were more withdrawn and less attentive, caring, and loving with their children.[47] Children tried to please mothers and engage them in activity but sometimes seemed less happy. Job stress was most upsetting to women who already had feelings of anxiety and depression.

Parents who felt positive spillover from work to home (about a third of the parents participating in Galinsky's study) were those who (1) were married, (2) had jobs that demanded more days per week, (3) experienced less stress and more autonomy at work, (4) had more supportive supervisors and coworkers, (5) had more parental support from family and friends, and (6) felt they were raising their children as they wanted.[48]

STRATEGIES FOR NAVIGATING WORK AND FAMILY LIFE

We have moved through the circular flow of work and family life and have seen common threads in feelings of success or stress in both places and in the process of making transitions between the two. Parents feel most successful and least stressed when they have time—time just to be with children and family without feeling rushed, time to engage in activities with them, and time to accomplish tasks at work. They feel successful when they have control of how they raise their children and how they do their work. They feel successful when they have support from family, friends, and coworkers and the work culture and when they can rely on trustworthy day care.[49]

Galinsky makes various specific suggestions for increasing positive feelings and reducing stress.[50] Navigating work consists of keeping job demands reasonable by seeking flextime, prioritizing work, and using problem-solving techniques. Parents improve their focus at work by finding ways to work without interruptions. They improve the quality of their jobs by learning new skills and gaining meaning from their work. They encourage positive relationships with supervisors and coworkers by appreciating support when given and making requests for reasonable modifications to the work environment to meet family needs.

Parents minimize difficulties in making transitions from work to home and from home to work in several ways. Parents do best in making the transition from work to home when they have some act or ritual that separates work from their home life—some do breathing exercises, some listen to music or books on tape or read on the way home. Parents also develop rituals that allow time with children to meet their needs when they first get home and then time to prepare dinner and do other household tasks. If parents have had a bad day at work, they are advised to tell their children and take extra time to reduce their stress. In making the transition from home to work, parents reduce stress by preparing for the next day (laying out clothes, making lunches) and allowing enough time in the morning to avoid rushing.

To navigate family life, Galinsky believes, parents need to reconsider the way they think about the time they spend with children. Children do not necessarily want more hours with parents. Children want stress-free, focused time with parents. They want parents to be calm and emotionally available to them. Galinsky recommends that parents spend time with children by hanging around and being available for conversation and supporting children's interests and activities. Because children are concerned about parents' control of anger, parents can improve relationships by communicating feelings in ways that encourage children to listen. Summarizing what she learned about promoting positive family life, Galinsky quotes a twelve-year-old:

> Listen. Listen to what your kids say, because you know, sometimes it's very important. And sometimes a kid can have a great idea and it could even affect you. Because, you know, kids are people. Kids have great ideas, as great as you, as great as ideas that adults have.[51]

Galinsky also recommends that parents talk about their work. Children hear little about work, especially from fathers. They often do not understand the positive aspects of their parents' work, and so they have a limited view of the meaning of work in people's lives. One of the reasons children are so concerned about parents' stress is that they hear mostly negative things about parents' work. Parents need to

Parents have to make stress-free, fun times with children a major priority of family life.

discuss what they do and the importance of their work. Children learn many indirect lessons about work from the way parents discuss coworkers and strategies for getting along.

On the basis of her interviews with parents, Francine Deutsch also recommends that parents be proactive in making daily choices that enable both parents to have careers and be parents.[52] Couples committed to equal careers and parenting make choices at home and at work that support equality. That means scaling back work—limiting work hours per day, workdays per week, travel, overtime—and "allowing family obligations to intrude on work as a significant part of identity."[53] When both parents make adjustments, neither one has the traditional career.

Mothers also have to be willing to relinquish their identity as primary caregivers and let fathers assume major responsibility for child care and decisions about children. They have to recognize that children benefit when fathers are equal parents, because children can develop closer relationships with them. Marriages benefit as well, because couples share the responsibilities of parenting and work and neither partner feels overburdened.

DAY CARE

Types of Day Care

Parents seek child care in many places. Recent data concerning child care for children under five with employed mothers reveal that 47 percent were cared for by parents or other relatives, 30 percent in center-based programs, 17 percent in family day care homes, and 5 percent by a sitter at home.[54]

The most important factor in selecting day care, particularly for a child in the first year, is the quality of the caregiver. For toddlers and preschoolers as well, having a secure attachment with a sensitive caregiver promotes social competence. Once parents have a reliable, sensitive caregiver, they can focus on the opportunities available for the child to socialize with others and to be involved in stimulating activities.[55] The child's needs will depend somewhat on his or her age and temperament.

Each form of care has certain advantages and possible drawbacks. Care by parents and relatives has the advantage that children know these people and have special ties to them. Although parental care is usually of high quality, a parent may need to sleep after working a shift or may provide child care to other children. Thus, the quality of parental care can vary.[56]

Substitute care at home is expensive but requires that the child adjust to only the new person; and it has the advantage of being available when the child is sick. As children get older, home care is often supplemented with nursery school attendance or other group activities so the child can be with peers.

Family day care—that is, care in the home of another family with other children—is cheaper than home care and has some advantages. A family day care setting provides an environment where children can engage in many of the same activities of home care with a mother or father figure.[57]

Because there are fewer children, family day care is sometimes more flexible than a center in meeting children's individual needs. Family day care homes are licensed;

some are part of a larger umbrella organization that supplies toys and training to home caregivers. Caregivers who are part of such a network can give higher-quality care than can untrained caregivers. Guidelines for making a choice of a family day care home are similar to those for choosing a day care program. Parents should make one visit with the child and one visit alone when gathering information.

Day care centers provide care for children from infancy and may provide after-school care for children in the elementary grades. In most states, such centers must meet specific standards intended to ensure the health and safety of the children. The parent whose child goes to a day care center is sure of having child care available every day—at some centers from 7 A.M. until 7 P.M. Many centers have credentialed personnel who have been trained to work with children, and many centers have play equipment and supplies not found in most home-care situations. All centers provide opportunities for contact with same-age children.

When children start elementary school, they receive care there for three to six hours per day and require special provision only before or after school and over holidays. Approximately two to ten million children aged six to eleven are unsupervised after school.[58] Diaries of 1,500 children indicate that about 12 to 14 percent of American children aged five to twelve are home alone for, on average, an hour after school.[59] The older the child, the larger the percentage in self-care— 1 percent of children five to seven, 8 percent of children eight to ten, and 23 percent of children eleven to twelve.

Older, better-educated mothers are more likely to have children in self-care, perhaps because they are more available by phone than are less-educated mothers, who may have jobs where phone access is limited. Quiet children who are not aggressive and children living in stable neighborhoods are likely to be in self-care. Children from higher-income families are more likely to be involved in sports and other activities after school than are children from lower-income families. Although problems can arise with self-care, some children describe benefits such as increased independence, responsibility, and time to think and to develop hobbies.

Availability, Affordability, and Quality of Day Care

We have described the kinds of care possible, but how available and affordable are they? The average cost of care can vary from $4,000 to $10,000 per year, with the cost higher for infants and preschoolers.[60] Child care takes about 10 percent of an average family's income but about 22 to 25 percent of a poor family's income.[61]

Families receive little governmental support in arranging child care. A tax credit depending on the amount spent for child care does not cover the full cost of the care and helps primarily middle-class and upper-middle-class families. Single parents and lower-income parents do not pay sufficient taxes to benefit much from the credit. Although federal subsidies provide some block support for child-care expenses of poorer families, only about 10 to 15 percent of those eligible receive such benefits.

Quality of Care during Infancy and Early Childhood   Quality of care is a major determiner of the effects of nonparental child care on children. There are two kinds of indexes of quality of care—process measures and structural measures.[62] *Process measures* examine appropriate caregiving for children—that is, sensitive, responsive interactions and appropriate activities in a safe, stimulating setting. *Structural measures* look at the amount of teacher or caregiver training/experience, staff turnover, and recommended staff ratios of 1:4 for infants and 1:7 for preschoolers. In both center care and family day care, the quality of the interactions with the caregiver—the positive, sensitive responsiveness of the caregiver—is the best measure of the quality of the care.[63] Caregivers' salaries are good measures of caregiver stability; when salaries are high, caregivers stay.

In high-quality day care settings, children build secure attachments to teachers and develop the many positive social qualities associated with early secure attachment to parents.[64] Secure attachment to an available, stable, sensitive, responsive caregiver who provides stimulating activities and monitors the child's behavior to increase self-regulation promotes competent development. The child uses this figure as a safe base for exploring the world, just as he or she uses the secure attachment with the mother or father. In the child's first thirty months, it is important for the teacher to remain the same; but after thirty months, the teacher can change and the child-teacher relationship will still remain stable.[65]

There are, of course, confounding factors. Highly motivated, stable parents seek out high-quality care for children.[66] Those infants who go into low-quality care often have parents who are less organized and use less appropriate socialization practices. A vicious cycle may develop for the infant in low-quality care. Highly stressed families give less attention to the child, and the child goes into a day care setting with few adults to interact with and little to do. These children have less contact with adults and receive less stimulation both at home and in day care than do children of motivated parents. Thus, they have cumulative risks for problems in development.

Availability of Good-Quality Care   Most experts agree that shortages exist in services for infants and school-age children. Recent studies have found that, even when available, day care is most often of mediocre quality.[67] Observations of care in centers and family day care found that in centers, 14 percent were of sufficiently high quality to promote development, 74 percent were of mediocre quality, and 12 percent were of such low quality as to be unstimulating and unable to fully meet children's health and safety needs. Forty percent of care for infants and toddlers was described as low quality. In family day care homes, 9 percent were found to be of good quality, 56 percent of adequate or custodial quality, and 35 percent of inadequate quality. The average family day care provider was described as "nonresponsive or inappropriate in interactions with children close to half the time."[68]

While good-quality care is expensive to provide because it requires recommended staffing ratios, as well as educated and trained staff members who stay, still the fees charged to parents for good-quality care are not that different from those for

INTERVIEW
with Jay Belsky

Jay Belsky is the initiator and director of the Pennsylvania Infant and Family Development Project, an ongoing study of 250 firstborn children whose parents were enrolled for study when the mothers were pregnant in 1981. He has done systematic research on the effects of day care.

What advice would you give to parents about day care in the first two years?

For working parents I say again and again that nothing matters as much as the person who cares for your baby. All too often parents don't look "under the hood" of the child care situation. They walk in, the walls are painted nicely, the toys are bright, the lunches are nutritious. Especially with a baby, once the minimal safety standards are met, what matters more than anything else psychologically is to find out about this person who'll care for the baby. So, who is this person, and what is his or her capacity to give individualized care? Because babies need individualized care, this issue matters above all else.

The second thing to consider is whether the caregiver and parent can talk together easily. Each person spends less than full time with the baby. The time factor is not necessarily handicapping them, but it can if information is not being communicated back and forth. So the trick then is, "If the caregiver gets to know my baby during the day, what can she tell me in the afternoon, and if I have the baby in the evening and the morning, what can I tell her when I drop the baby off?" There has to be an effective two-way flow of information.

The third thing to consider in selecting care is that the arrangement has to last a decent interval of time. That doesn't mean that you must take the child to the same center for a year's time; it means that the same *persons* take care of him or her for a year or so. If you find a great person who treats the child as an individual and communicates well with the parent but stays for only a few months, you are not buying yourself a lot. In a baby's life, changing caregivers more than once a year will be stressful. If a baby goes through three or four changes in a year, it may not matter what kind of caregiver he or she gets. Even though the caregivers may get to know the child, the child won't know them. Each has to know the other.

mediocre care. Parents need training and awareness to identify quality care. When they compared parents' ratings of quality to their own, researchers found that parents identified as good quality what researchers described as mediocre.[69] See the interview with Jay Belsky on this topic.

The Impact of Nonparental Care on Children

Reviewing studies on the effects of day care on children, the psychologist Michael Lamb writes,

> Exclusive maternal care through adulthood was seldom an option in any phase of human society; it emerged as a possibility for a small elite segment of society during one small portion of human history.[70]

Nonparental Care during Infancy and Early Childhood   In evaluating research, we must keep in mind first that a selection process related to mothers' education, personality, and interests determines who, in fact, chooses to return to work once children are born.[71] Second, the meaning of maternal employment in a child's life depends on (1) the child's characteristics (age, sex, temperament), (2) family characteristics (education and socioeconomic level, father's involvement in the home, mother's satisfaction with working), (3) work characteristics (the number of hours the mother works, the level of her stress at work), and, perhaps most important, (4) the nature of the child's substitute care. Because researchers cannot control all these factors, we have to interpret findings from several studies and draw our own conclusions. In discussing the research, we focus on children's social-emotional and cognitive functioning.

We know that early and continuing intervention programs that stimulate cognitive development, promote intellectual growth during the school years[72] and reduce grade retention and the need for special programs in the elementary school years. These programs stimulate intellectual growth in children from economically disadvantaged families. However, even controlling for effects of social class and family background, high-quality care in infancy is related to academic performance and verbal skills at age eleven.

Early research raised concerns that early and extensive day care could have negative effects on attachment and children's social-emotional and cognitive functioning. Longitudinal data from the National Longitudinal Survey of Youth revealed that maternal employment in the first year, especially early in the first year, was related to poorer cognitive and behavioral functioning in European American children at ages three and four and continuing on to age seven or eight. A sensitive, nurturing home environment appears to buffer children from the effects of mothers' early employment. African American children's functioning did not decrease when mothers worked in the first year.[73]

To respond to concerns about the effects of day care, the National Institute of Child Health and Human Development recruited a network of researchers and, in 1991, a sample of 1,261 newborns and their families to participate in extensive assessments and observations of children at home and at day care from the age of one month through childhood. The babies were first seen at one month, then at six, fifteen, twenty-four, thirty-six, and fifty-four months, with phone calls at scheduled intervals as well. The research has focused on the family and day care qualities that predict children's intellectual and social-emotional functioning, and their relationships with peers. Children were tested, then observed at home, at day care, and in the laboratory setting. Ratings were obtained from and about parents and day care workers. At present, the group of researchers has presented data about the children's functioning up to the age of fifty-four months. These are the basic findings at this point in the data analysis:[74]

1. Sensitive, responsive parenting consistently and strongly predicted children's competence in all areas at all ages.

2. High-quality day care was defined as day care that provided sensitive, responsive caregiving as well as language and intellectual stimulation.

High-quality care predicted intellectual skills and most social-emotional behaviors, as well as some peer ratings to a modest degree.

3. Quantity of child care, or the number of hours children spent in child care, related to children's behavior in different ways. At twenty-four and thirty-six months, a greater number of hours in day care was related to verbal and cognitive skills but to more problem behaviors at thirty-six and fifty-four months and more conflict with the caregiver at fifty-four months. Children were also observed to show more negative behavior with a peer at fifty-four months as well.

4. The only form of day care related to child outcomes was center care. In early childhood, more time in center care predicted greater language and cognitive skills, but it also predicted more behavior problems. At fifty-four months, more time in center care predicted positive peer relationships.

The researchers discussed the usefulness of these findings for parents of young children. "The primary conclusion is that parenting matters much more than does child care, so parents might make decisions that allow them to have quality time with their children."[75] Some mothers may decide to cut back the number of hours they work so they can spend more quality time with children, and others may decide that cutting back hours would create such financial stress for the family that parenting would be negatively affected.

The researchers highlighted that "exclusive maternal care was not related to better or worse outcomes for children. There is, thus, no reason for mothers to feel as though they are harming their children if they decide to work."[76] High-quality day care clearly contributes to children's competence.

Nonparental Care during Later Childhood and Adolescence   Extensive poor-quality care in the first year of life is related to hitting, kicking, and conflictful interactions in the first three years of elementary school.[77] Contemporaneous after-school day care that is not high quality is also related to children's being rated as noncompliant by teachers and less well liked by peers.[78] As in the early years, quality after-school care is related to effective functioning.[79]

Research suggests that low-income third-graders in formal after-school programs receive better grades in math, reading, and conduct than do children with other forms of care, including maternal care. From about the fifth grade on, children in self-care behave and perform similarly whether an adult is present or not.[80] Nevertheless, lack of supervision and monitoring of early adolescents is related to increased use of alcohol, cigarettes, and marijuana.[81] Eighth-graders in self-care for more than eleven hours a week—whether from dual- or single-earner families, from high- or low-income families, with good or poor grades, or active or nonactive in sports—were more likely than those not in self-care to use these substances. Self-care leads to feelings of greater autonomy and puts early teens at risk of being influenced by peers who are substance abusers.

In adolescence, however, maternal employment is also associated with self-confidence and independence. The benefits are more pronounced for girls who obtain good grades and think of careers for themselves, most likely because their mothers serve as role models of competence.[82]

Boys of employed mothers may not do as well in school, but that has not been a consistent finding in recent research.[83] Because fathers' involvement in the home is found to stimulate cognitive performance, it may be that fathers' increasing participation reduces that problem.

Gender Differences in Response to Nonparental Care   In several studies, boys were found to be more vulnerable than girls when their mothers worked during the boys' early childhood. It is not clear whether boys require more attention, nurturance, and supervision; whether they are more sensitive to deficiencies in child-care settings; or whether they make more demands on parents who are stressed from working, have less patience with them, and see them more negatively.

Lois Hoffman concludes that boys may have a more difficult time in dual-earner families, and girls more problems in single-earner families.[84] In single-earner families, girls are more at risk for insecure attachments, their behavior is viewed more negatively by mothers, they have less time with fathers, and they receive less encouragement for independence. So, girls profit from living in dual-earner families (that is, having more time with fathers), but boys may not. It is possible, however, to combine the best of both forms of family life so boys and girls get an optimal balance of nurturance, attention, supervision, and independence.

A PRACTICAL QUESTION: HOW DO WORKING PARENTS TAKE CARE OF THEMSELVES?

In the excitement and busyness of working, parents forget that the family started with the primacy of the couple. Further, the satisfaction that the couple has with each other and their ways of doing things make solutions effective. The continuance of a strong, loving bond between parents is a primary factor in the successful combining of work and parenting.

Further, more than anything else in the world, children want the family to stay together. To do this, parents need a strong relationship. Their relationship, however, usually gets put aside during child rearing, especially in the earliest years.

James Levine and Todd Pittinsky suggest that parents make a weekly date to do something without the children.[85] If money is a problem, they can set aside some special time at home—rent a video, have a special dinner. Baby-sitting, an expensive item, can be exchanged in baby-sitting cooperatives. The date should be exclusive time with the spouse to reconnect and share what is happening. Parents can organize daily rituals that give them special time together—reading the paper together, sitting close to each other while listening to music, talking after dinner, or just being physically close together watching TV. Telephone calls during the day also help parents stay connected.

Working parents who take care of themselves can take better care of their children and each other. Couples who exercise regularly, eat a balanced diet, and make sure they have private time for thinking and pursuing interests are less likely to be tense and tired and more likely to enjoy their job and family. Gloria Norris and JoAnn Miller suggest the following ways for parents to be good to themselves:[86]

1. Keep up friendships—exercising with a friend several times a week is ideal.
2. Develop ways of easing the transition from office to home—walk the last block or two, take a quick shower before dinner, rest for ten minutes after arriving home.
3. Learn personal signs of stress and do not ignore them; get rest and spend time relaxing.
4. Discover the most stressful times of the day and find ways of relieving tension; a different morning or evening routine can reduce stress.
5. Develop a quick tension reliever, like yoga exercises, deep breathing, or meditation.

The life of the working parent is challenging and demanding. Yet most working parents find the challenges worth the efforts required, as work makes life richer and more exciting for the whole family.

MAIN POINTS

Work

- influences social values in child rearing and the social life and status of families
- develops adults' skills and provides many supports
- creates stress that disrupts parenting skills

Among the many strategies they use to navigate the flow of work and family, parents

- place primary importance on spending time with children to meet their needs
- create time for children and family by sharing the workload at home
- maintain control of work demands through problem-solving methods
- build support systems at work and use high-quality child care

Nonparental care of children

- must meet established criteria to be considered high-quality care—specified child-staff ratios that vary according to the age of the child, staff training, safety, structure, organized activities programs

- is not as predictive of children's development as are parental qualities

- in early childhood promotes competence when children have secure attachments to sensitive teachers who provide stimulating activities and monitor them

- in the elementary school years and adolescence is associated with social and intellectual competence if children are supervised

- sometimes includes self-care by older children who enjoy independence but also require some form of monitoring

Effectively combining working and parenting

- requires that parents make daily decisions to share the workload at home

- involves parents' devoting time to sustaining their relationship

EXERCISES

1. Break into small groups and discuss the research finding that the effect of mothers' working seems to depend on the sex of the child. Discuss the finding that boys may experience more negative effects because they need more monitoring. How can parents take action to optimize effects for both boys and girls?

2. Imagine you had a child under age five—infant, toddler, or preschooler. Investigate day care options in the community for a child of that age. You might form groups to investigate care for a child of a particular age, with each student visiting at least one center to get information and summarize impressions. One group might investigate family day care in the area and compare the quality and the cost of care with that available in a center.

3. Design an ideal day care program for infants or toddlers, specifying the number of caregivers, their qualities, the physical facilities, and the daily routine.

4. Imagine what your family and work life will be like in ten years. Write diary entries for a day during the week and for a day on the weekend about your life at home and at work.

5. Write a short paper containing advice you could give to a parent of the same sex as you who feels frustrated and pressured trying to incorporate an infant and the care of the infant into his or her work life.

ADDITIONAL READINGS

Deutsch, Francine M. *Halving It All: How Equally Shared Parenting Works*. Cambridge, MA: Harvard University Press, 1999.

Galinsky, Ellen. *Ask the Children: What America's Children Really Think about Working Parents*. New York: Morrow, 1999.

Levine, James A., and Pittinsky, Todd L. *Working Fathers: New Strategies for Balancing Work and Family*. Reading, MA: Addison-Wesley, 1997.

Mason, Linda. *The Working Mother's Guide to Life*. New York: Three Rivers Press, 2002.

Steiner, Leslie Morgan, ed. *Mommy Wars*. New York: Random House, 2006.

14

Parenting in Diverse Family Structures

CHAPTER TOPICS

In this chapter, you will learn about:

- Experiences of unmarried mothers and their children

- The process of divorce and whether parents should stay together for their children's sake

- Fathers' roles in children's lives

- The challenges of stepfamilies and foster families

- How lesbian and gay families function

IN THE NEWS

New York Times, May 19[1]: Children leaving foster care at ages eighteen and nineteen face many hurdles. See pages 490–492.

Test Your Knowledge: Fact or Fiction?

1. When single mothers have stable living arrangements and use positive parenting principles, their children function competently.
2. As long as parents in conflict stay married, their children experience fewer problems than those children whose parents divorce.
3. Children in stepfamilies have fewer difficulties than children in single-parent families because they benefit from the resources in two-parent households.
4. In foster homes, children are able to deal with the difficulties that brought them there, and they have fewer difficulties when they leave.
5. Authoritative parenting has positive effects in intact families, but does not provide benefits in divorced families and stepfamilies because of the many transitions that occur.

Biologically speaking, it takes two parents to create a new life. In our society, family has traditionally meant a mother and a father and their biological children. But now, more children are born to single mothers, and a sizable number of children experience the divorce of their parents or the death of a parent with subsequent remarriage. How is life different for children in single-parent households? In households with gay or lesbian parents? How does life change when parents remarry or when children go into foster homes? How can parents help children cope with all the special circumstances of living in these types of families?

As we noted in Chapter 3, in 2004, 68 percent of children in the United States lived with two parents, 23 percent lived in households headed by single women, 5 percent with single fathers, and 4 percent with neither parent.[2] Single women raising children may be widowed, divorced, or separated from husbands, but a sizable number are never-married mothers. The rate of births to unmarried women has increased in recent years, and in 2002, 34 percent of babies were born to unmarried mothers.[3]

Both numbers and proportions of single-parent families have increased in all Western countries and in all ethnic groups in the United States. African American families have a somewhat higher rate of single-parent families than do other groups; this does not appear to be the result of increased sexual activity among young women but rather of the fact that birthrates have remained the same in this group while rates of marriage have dropped. Thus, more children are born to unmarried mothers.[4]

Because the child's experience depends on the specific conditions in his or her family, it is difficult to generalize about the effects of being reared in a single-parent family. Many studies suggest that children in single-parent families are at greater risk for developing emotional and academic problems.[5] This should not be surprising, as it is more difficult for one parent to provide as much nurturance, monitoring, and supervision as two parents, who have the additional benefits of greater resources and support from each other.

A major reason for the difficulties of single-parent families may be the increased rate of poverty. In 2003, the median income for female-headed households was $29,307; for male-headed households, $41,959; and for married-couple families, $62,405.[6] Half of all single parents are poor, and "no other major demographic group is so poor and stays poor for so long."[7] As noted in Chapter 3, economic hardship and poverty bring stress, which decreases parents' abilities to be nurturant and effective in setting limits.

Another factor is lack of support in dealing with increased stress. In studies of single mothers committed to raising their children alone, single mothers reported more stress than did mothers in two-parent families, even when families were matched on education, income, and area of residence.[8] The single mothers had to work longer hours and were more worried about finances than were their married counterparts. The greatest difference between these two groups of mothers, however, was that single mothers had fewer social and emotional supports when their children were young. It was precisely this kind of support that predicted optimal parent-child interactions in both single- and two-parent families. When single mothers had social-emotional support, their children's behavior was similar to that of children in two-parent families. Stressful life events such as poverty, which occurs more frequently in single-parent families, reduced overall parent effectiveness. Mobilizing both economic and social-emotional resources can help single-parent families function as effectively as two-parent families.

THE EXPERIENCES OF UNMARRIED MOTHERS AND THEIR CHILDREN

Recall the information in Chapter 6 on the characteristics of unmarried mothers prior to the birth. Approximately one-third of babies are born to never-married mothers living alone, with the child's father, or with a same-sex partner. Here we look at what happens to them and their children and focus on the unmarried mothers in the years following the birth and beyond.

Unmarried Mothers in the Years after the Birth

Those women who marry following their child's birth have family incomes that parallel those of children born to married parents. "This pattern suggests that the order of these two events—birth and marriage—[is] not as critical for demographic and economic outcomes as whether both events do occur."[9]

One study found that other actions mothers took after birth also had an impact on their economic self-sufficiency when the child was aged five to seven. Getting more education and postponing another child contributed to greater stability.[10]

Outcomes of Children Born to Unmarried Mothers

Children born to unmarried mothers take many paths to adulthood; no one outcome characterizes them all. One study found that living with two legal parents through adoption had a positive impact on children's high school completion, which in turn predicted their economic self-sufficiency in adulthood.[11] Living in a stepfamily with two parents did not produce such positive benefits and was associated with lower educational attainment and leaving home early. Living in a stable single-parent family, however, seemed to provide a secure base for children, who as adults did as well as or better than children living in other arrangements. They had more education and slower transitions to independence. The stability of legally adopted children and the consistency children experienced in a stable single-parent home may have reduced the stress experienced by children in stepfamilies, who had many transitions to make.

Living with grandparents without the mother was related to lower educational attainment and to a higher probability of leaving home by age eighteen. Children who lived with their grandparents and mother in a three-generation family, by contrast, appeared to experience greater stability and achieve higher education than did those who lived with their grandparents alone.

Protective factors in the child, the mother, the parent-child relationship, and the larger social context buttress children from stress and predict positive outcomes for them.[12] In one study, eight protective factors were divided into four categories: the child's characteristics (positive sociability and attentiveness), maternal qualities (efficacy and low risk of depression), parenting qualities (positive parent-child relationship and the father's involvement), and qualities of the larger social context (social support and few difficult life experiences). In a sample of disadvantaged mothers, 95 percent of whom were never married, families averaged three out of the eight protective factors, and 20 percent of families had five or more protective factors.

Protective factors assessed when children were eighteen and twenty-one months of age predicted measures of cognitive and social functioning at forty-two months of age. All protective factors except the father's involvement predicted competent psychological functioning, as measured by low scores on a behavior problem index covering aggressive, anxious, depressed, hyperactive, dependent, and withdrawn behaviors. Only the child's characteristics and positive parent-child relationship predicted cognitive competence, as measured by higher scores on a school-readiness test. The most important aspect of the parent-child relationship for later well-being was the absence of harsh discipline. Economic disadvantage may have its greatest impact on families by intensifying maternal distress that leads to harsh discipline. The more protective factors in the child's family, the better the child functioned. Nevertheless, even the children with the greatest number of protective factors scored below average, at the thirty-second percentile, on the measure of school readiness.

The evidence from many studies, then, suggests that there is not a single outcome for children of never-married mothers. When children (1) have stable living arrangements through legal adoption, living in a three-generation family, or living with a stable single mother and (2) experience positive parenting, they have greater social and cognitive competence. As we can see, the same qualities that predict effective functioning in children in two-parent households predict positive outcomes for children of never-married mothers.

MARITAL OR PARTNER CONFLICT

We have seen in earlier chapters that marital or partner satisfaction and intimacy contribute to parents' sense of well-being, their confidence, and their skills as parents. Nonetheless, even when parents are happily married, they argue. As noted in Chapter 4, parents' disagreements need not distress children. When parents argue in moderate emotional tones and resolve their conflicts in mutually agreeable ways, children respond in the same way they do to friendly interactions. In fact, children can learn valuable negotiating skills. Even when anger is unresolved, children feel no ill effects if parents encapsulate the anger and confine it to the marital or partner relationship and refuse to allow it to spill over to the parent-child relationship.[13]

Unresolved conflicts affect children in two ways. Observed anger that goes unresolved directly affects children's physiological and social functioning in negative ways, as noted in Chapter 4. Second, marital conflict affects children indirectly by impairing parents' skills and behavior with children.[14]

Other aspects of conflict determine its effects on children as well. When conflicts are intense, center on child-related issues, and imply that the child is to blame, the child feels more upset. If parents directly explain to the child that he or she is not at fault in the argument, the child feels less distress, even when the conflict is intense and is associated with child-rearing issues.[15]

In a negative atmosphere, children develop behavior problems. Children from high-conflict homes are at risk for developing (1) externalizing problems such as increased aggressiveness, noncompliance, and unacceptable conduct; (2) internalizing problems such as depression, anxiety, and social withdrawal; (3) problems in school such as poor grades; and (4) an angry, negative view of themselves and the world.[16] These problems persist, and in adolescence, both boys and girls who experienced parental disagreements in the preschool years are poorly controlled and interpersonally challenged.[17] Boys also show difficulties in intellectual functioning. So, boys whose parents later divorce are already impulsive and poorly controlled ten years before a divorce.[18]

Again, the keys to minimizing the impact of conflict on children are to resolve the conflicts in mutually agreeable ways and to remove any feelings of self-blame the child may have about the conflict.

THE PROCESS OF DIVORCE

When parents cannot resolve their conflicts, they often seek a divorce. Mavis Hetherington, who has carried out longitudinal studies of intact, divorced, and remarried families, describes four considerations that underlie all her research: (1) divorce is not a single event but an event that triggers many changes for children and parents over time; (2) changes associated with marital transitions have to be viewed as changes in the entire family system; (3) the entire social milieu—peer group, neighborhood, school, friendship network—influences an individual's response to the transition; and (4) there is great diversity in the ways children and parents respond to marital transitions.[19] Most studies of families in transition focus on European American middle-class families, and we do not know how widely we can generalize these findings.

Hetherington and Kathleen Camara emphasize that divorce is a parental solution to parental problems.[20] Children often view divorce as the cause of all their problems. For both parent and child, however, divorce brings many related stresses. Reduced income means many families must move, so the child has a new neighborhood, new school, and new friends. As resources grow more limited, parents may become more irritable, discouraged, and impatient with children.

As the divorce rate has risen, society has begun to accommodate the needs of divorcing families. The legal system has changed, making it easier for both parents to continue to be involved in the care of children. When parents have difficulty coming to agreement about custody issues, many states now provide court mediation services. Professional counselors help parents explore children's and parents' needs and reach agreement on reasonable living arrangements.

Further, laws have been passed to make it easier for single mothers to obtain child support payments decreed by the court. This is imperative because, as noted, mothers who are single heads of household have incomes far below those of other family units.

Telling Children about Divorce

When a couple decides to divorce, it is best if both parents together tell the children about the divorce before one parent leaves the home. Judith Wallerstein suggests wording like this: "We married fully hoping and expecting to love each other forever, but we have discovered that one (or both) of us is unhappy. One (or both) does not love the other anymore. We fight with each other. The divorce is going to stop the fighting and restore peace."[21] Parents present the decision as rational but sad:

> The goal is to present the child with models of parents who admit they made a serious mistake, tried to rectify the mistake, and are now embarking on a moral, socially acceptable remedy. The parents are responsible people who remain committed to the family and to the children even though they have decided to go their separate ways.[22]

When parents express their sadness at the solution, then children have permission to mourn without hiding their feelings from adults. It is also important to express reluctance at the solution, because children need to hear that parents know how upsetting this will be for them: "Put simply, parents should tell the children they are sorry for all the hurt they are causing."[23]

There are many things, however, divorcing parents should *not* say. First, they should not burden their children with their own negative views of each other. Second, they should not blame the other parent for all the problems. Third, they should not ask children to take sides—children usually need and want to be loyal to both parents.

Wallerstein comments on how little support most children get as they go through the initial turmoil of divorce. Often, no one talks to them, no one listens to them talk about their feelings or answers their questions, and few relatives give added help and support.

Children's Reactions to Divorce

Emotional reactions to divorce, common to children of all ages, include sadness, fear, depression, anger, confusion, and sometimes relief; the predominant emotions vary with the child's age and require somewhat different reactions from parents.[24] In the preschool years, children often feel abandoned and overwhelmed; they worry that they may have caused the divorce. Children may regress, begin wetting their bed, have temper tantrums, and develop fears. Parents can help most by providing emotional support. Outside interventions are not as useful as interventions by parents. Parents are urged to (1) communicate with the child about the divorce and the new adjustments, explaining in simple language the reasons for each change that occurs, and (2) reduce the child's suffering, where possible, by giving reassurance that the child's needs will be met and by taking actions such as arranging visits with the absent parent.

Preschool children are often protected initially by their ability to deny what is happening. Five- to seven-year-olds are vulnerable because they understand more but do not have the maturity to cope with what they see and hear. The most common reaction of a child this age is sadness and grief. One little girl, whose parents had just divorced, was asked what she would like if she could have just three

The increased conflict children witness during divorce, not the divorce itself, may be what leads to children's poorer adjustment after divorce.

wishes. Her reply: "First, that my daddy would come home. Second, that my parents would get back together. And third, that they would never, ever divorce again."[25]

Fear is another frequent response. Children worry that no one will love them or care for them. Their world has fallen apart and is no longer safe. Many children feel that only a father can maintain discipline in the family.

Children aged five and older may find outside intervention useful, and several weeks of counseling can help them sort out their feelings about the divorce, custody, and visitation. It is reassuring for them to hear a counselor or therapist say, "Yes, this is a very difficult time, and it is understandable that you feel upset and sad." Children can then accept their feelings more easily.

In helping older children handle divorce, parents need to keep in mind that these children may feel responsible—they may believe they have done something that has brought about the divorce or that they could have fixed the marital difficulties. Parents need to say clearly and often, when opportunities arise, that the divorce was *not* caused by the children but was caused by difficulties between the parents. In addition, parents need to remember that children worry about them and how they are doing. Parents cannot always confine their grief and distress to times when the children are not there, but parents can help children by trying to do so.

Thus far, we have seen the reactions of children who regret their parents' divorce, but about 10 percent of children feel relieved when their parents divorce.[26] Often, these are older children who have witnessed violence or severe psychological suffering on the part of a parent or other family member. These children feel that dissolution of the marriage is the best solution, and progressing from a conflict-ridden home to a more stable environment with one parent helps these children's overall level of adjustment and functioning.

From a follow-up of children fifteen years after divorce, Wallerstein and Sandra Blakeslee conclude that it is very difficult to determine the long-term adjustment of the child based on the child's reactions at the time of the divorce.[27]

Parents' Reactions to Divorce

Parents react to divorce in many and varied ways, almost all intense. They often suffer many symptoms—headaches, rapid heartbeat, fatigue, dizziness.[28] Their moods and behavior change at the time of the divorce, and these mood changes may be one of the most upsetting aspects of the divorce process for their children. Children are helpless in the face of their parents' extreme moods. Divorced men and women both start dating again, though men date in larger numbers and older women tend to remain isolated and alone, and children may have less time with each parent.

Long-term emotional reactions to the divorce are diverse. Seventy-five percent of divorced custodial mothers report that at the end of two years, they feel happier than they did in the last year of the marriage. Many of these women go on to develop independent lives and careers that increase their self-esteem. Some divorced women, however, report depression, loneliness, and health problems six to eleven years after the divorce. Still, they do not have as many problems as do nondivorced women in high-conflict marriages, who are more depressed and anxious and have more physical problems.[29]

Factors Affecting Adjustment to Divorce

Several factors influence how well a family adapts to divorce:[30] (1) the amount of conflict among family members, (2) the availability of both parents to their children, (3) the nature of the relationship changes in the family, (4) the responsibilities family members take, and (5) the defensibility of the divorce from the child's point of view.[31]

Moving from a household with two parents always in conflict to a stable household with one parent can lead to better adjustment for children.[32] Parents often continue the fighting when they live separately, however, and this is harmful to children; boys tend to react with undercontrolled behavior and girls with overcontrolled behavior.[33] The increased conflict children witness during divorce, not the divorce itself, may be what leads to their poorer adjustment. Increased conflicts can also occur between parents and children in a one-parent household in which the second parent is not available as a buffering agent. In addition, a parent may find the child a convenient target for feelings aroused by the other parent. In the midst

■ **TABLE 14-1**
OUT OF HARM'S WAY: PROTECTING CHILDREN FROM PARENTAL CONFLICT

Children can continue to grow and thrive even through a divorce if their parents insulate them from intense or prolonged hostilities. Parents who can accomplish this share some important qualities:

1. They make it clear that they value their child's relationship and time with them *and* with the other parent.

2. They work out a fair and practical time-sharing schedule, either temporary or long-term, as soon as possible.

3. Once that agreement is reached, they make every effort to live up to its terms.

4. They tell each other in advance about necessary changes in plans.

5. They are reasonably flexible in "trading off" to accommodate the other parent's needs.

6. They prepare the child, in a positive way, for each upcoming stay with the other parent.

7. They *do not* conduct adult business when they meet to transfer the child.

8. They refrain from using the child as a confidant, messenger, bill collector, or spy.

9. They listen caringly but encourage their child to work out problems with the other parent directly.

10. They work on their problems with each other in private.

Robert Adler, *Sharing the Children* (New York: Adler & Adler, 1988). Used with permission of the author.

of this raging conflict, the child feels quite alone. Minimizing the fighting in all arenas aids everyone's adjustment.

Parents can help insulate their children from the conflict that accompanies a divorce. Table 14-1 lists some behavior characteristics of parents who work to protect their children from the parents' own conflicts.

When children have continuing relationships with both parents, they are more likely to adjust well following the divorce process.[34] Fathers are more likely to maintain relationships with their sons than with their daughters. In fact, many mothers relinquish custody of older sons to fathers because they feel sons need a male role model.

Not only do children need relationships with both parents; they also need to be able to relate to each separately as a parent.[35] Recently divorced parents, however, often find it difficult to direct their energy to parenting. Thus, at this time of great need in the first year following divorce, when they actually need *more* attention, children receive less. As in the past, however, children function most effectively when both parents take time to monitor their behavior and enforce the usual rules.

In the family with two households and both parents working, the need for children to take on more responsibilities increases.[36] When demands are not excessive and are tailored to the abilities of children, then children may feel pleased by contributing to the family and developing greater competence. When the demands are too great, however—when they are given too much responsibility for caring for younger children or doing chores—then children become resentful, feeling they are being robbed of their childhood. Realistic demands for responsibility can help children grow in this situation.

Children seem better able to cope with divorce and its aftermath when the divorce is a carefully thought out, reasonable response to a specific problem.[37] When the problem improves after the divorce, children are better able to accept it.

Protective Factors for Children

Protective factors for children as they adjust to divorce include qualities of the child, supportive aspects of the family system, and external social supports.[38] The child's age, sex, and intelligence serve as protection. Younger children appear less affected than elementary school children or early adolescents at the time of the divorce or remarriage. Because they are becoming increasingly independent of the family, late adolescents seem less affected than younger children. Boys appear to suffer more difficulties at the time of the divorce, and girls appear to have more problems at the time of the mother's remarriage. Intelligence can help children cope with the stress.

The child's temperament also influences the process of divorce. An easy, adaptable temperament is a protective factor. In contrast, children with a difficult temperament are more sensitive and less adaptable to change; they can become a focal point for parental anger. In part, they elicit the anger with their reactive behavior; in part, they provide a convenient target for parental anger that may belong elsewhere.

We have already touched on some forms of family interaction that are protective—reduced conflict between the parents, structure and organization in daily life, and reasonable assignment of responsibilities within the family. Mothers must be especially firm and fair in establishing limits with boys, as their tendency is to develop a vicious repetitive cycle of complaining and fighting.

Researchers point to siblings and grandparents as potential supports.[39] When family life is harmonious after divorce, then sibling relationships resemble those in intact families.[40] When conflict between parents arises, siblings fight, with the greatest difficulty occurring between older brothers and younger sisters.

Grandparents can support grandchildren directly with time, attention, and special outings and privileges that help ease the pain of the divorce. As one girl said, "If it weren't for my grandparents, I don't think I could have made it past sixteen."[41] Grandparents provide support indirectly by helping one of the parents. In fact, returning to live in the home of one's parents is a solution many young parents choose when they do not have the resources to live on their own. Grandparents can be loving, stable baby-sitters who enrich children's lives in ways that no one else can. The mother can work and carry on a social life, knowing that her child is well cared for in her absence. This arrangement also usually reduces living expenses. When the mother and grandparents agree on child-rearing techniques and the mother is respected in the household as a mature adult, this solution may be attractive.

School is another major source of support for children. Authoritative, kind teachers and peer friendships give pleasure and a sense of esteem to children. Educational and athletic accomplishments contribute to feelings of competence that stimulate resilience.

Some protective factors lie beyond a parent's control, including the age, sex, and temperament of the child, but many lie within it, such as setting aside anger, establishing structure, monitoring behavior, and seeking out external supports for children.

Family Changes over Time

Right after a divorce, custodial mothers are under pressure because of all the changes occurring in their lives.[42] Many of these women become more negative with their children than they were earlier, particularly with boys, and less involved in monitoring their behavior; a small group of these mothers, however, become too lenient and permissive. In response, both boys and girls become more anxious, demanding, aggressive, and noncompliant with peers and adults. As time passes, however, custodial mothers adjust and become more nurturant and more consistent in behavior management. Girls' behavior improves, and mothers and daughters often grow very close. Relationships with boys improve somewhat, but many boys continue to have some behavior problems.

Custodial fathers initially complain of feeling overwhelmed, angry, confused, and isolated, but after two years, they report better adjustment.[43] After the divorce, noncustodial fathers tend to become either permissive and indulgent or disengaged. They are less likely to be disciplinarians and more likely to play the role of recreational companion than are custodial mothers.[44] Many times, however, noncustodial fathers do not stay involved. One study reported that two years after the divorce, 25 percent of children had not seen their fathers in the past year; eleven years after the divorce, the number rose to 50 percent.[45] More recent work indicates, however, that three and a half years after the divorce, two-thirds of adolescents still have contact with their fathers, even if only at holidays and over summer vacation.[46] Noncustodial fathers are most likely to stay involved when they feel they play an important role in their children's lives and their long-term development.

Noncustodial mothers of adolescents are more likely to stay involved than are noncustodial fathers. Noncustodial mothers are more active and involved with and supportive of children than are noncustodial fathers, who often continue their role of recreational companion.[47]

Children's Behavior over Time

Children's behavior problems do improve over the first two years, but boys continue to have some difficulties six to eleven years after the divorce. Beginning at age ten, girls, especially early-maturing girls, show behavior problems as well. Both boys and girls are less competent in school, more defiant and noncompliant with rules, and more negative in mood—anxious, depressed, sometimes suicidal—compared with children of nondivorced parents.[48]

Early adolescents' rule breaking and resistance to custodial parents' authority may result from the early autonomy and independence many experienced during the family adjustment period immediately after the divorce. They have been joint decision makers with their custodial parents, and parents have been less insistent and demanding that children meet family rules. Therefore, they feel entitled to pursue their own ends.[49]

In intact families, parents exert more constraint on early adolescents. They insist that teens do chores and follow the rules. These parents monitor carefully; there are more arguments and less harmony in intact families than in divorced families. Divorced custodial mothers, however, become careful monitors in mid-adolescence, especially with daughters. So, at a time when parents in intact families are disengaging and trusting children's judgment in mid-adolescence (age fifteen), divorced mothers are often becoming more authoritative.[50]

Children in divorced families resist custodial mothers' authority; these mothers are more successful and the children have fewer problems when another adult (such as a grandparent, *not* a stepparent) lives in the home and reinforces the mother's authority.[51]

Feeling caught between divorced parents who are in conflict intensifies adolescents' anxiety, depression, and poor adjustment.[52] Even when parents have high conflict with each other, adolescents can do well, provided parents do not put them in the middle. The feeling of being caught between parents contributes to these children's problems.

Again, we find great diversity in children's adjustment.[53] Although many children of divorce show aggressive and insecure behaviors in adolescence, others are caring, competent teenagers who cooperate with divorced parents and make significant contributions to family functioning. Still others are caring, responsible teenagers who worry that they will be unable to meet the demands placed on them. Those children who have the most difficulty with externalizing behaviors do not have a single caring adult in their lives. Their parents are neglectful, disengaged, and authoritarian, and the children cannot find support outside the family. Hetherington and her coworkers found in their studies of children in remarriages that one of the biggest stresses in the remarriage was children's experiences during the divorce.[54] Divorce, with all its changes and losses—changes in economic resources, schools, friends, neighborhoods, and the exposure to parental fighting—affects children in fundamental ways.

Paul Amato and Brian Keith reviewed ninety-two studies to determine the degree of difficulty children of divorce experience.[55] They concluded that divorce is associated with increased risk for problems in cognitive and social competence. However, recent, better-controlled studies reveal that the differences between children of divorce and children in intact families are small and that there is much overlap in the functioning of the two groups.

Amato and Keith examined three possible sources of increased difficulties for children: parental loss, economic deprivation, and family conflict. Parental loss—whether as a result of divorce or the death of a parent—is a significant contributor to problems, but it is not the only cause of difficulties in children of divorce.

Similar findings occur with economic disadvantage. When studies control for income, children of divorce still appear to have more problems than do children in intact families, and when parents remarry and income increases, children's behavior problems continue.

The third factor, family conflict, appears to be the main contributor to children's difficulties. Children in high-conflict, intact marriages have greater difficulties in self-esteem and adjustment than do children in divorced families in which such conflict is reduced. The level of family conflict and family conflict resolution styles are more powerful predictors of children's overall adjustment status than is family status (intact, divorced, or remarried).

We now find that the effects of divorce do not necessarily end with childhood.[56] Young adults whose parents divorced when they were children (1) have lower educational attainment than do adults from intact families, (2) earn less money, (3) are more likely to have a child out of wedlock, (4) are more likely to get divorced, and (5) are more likely to be alienated from one parent. Again, outcomes vary. Most adult children of divorce function well within the normal range on most measures of adjustment. The only exception is in having poor relations with the father. Later in the chapter, we examine general guidelines for parenting at times of marital transitions.

SHOULD PARENTS STAY TOGETHER FOR THE SAKE OF THE CHILDREN?

Hetherington has conducted studies on divorce and remarriage and seeks to provide an answer to the often-asked question, "Should parents stay together for the sake of the children?"[57] The answer depends on the nature of the conflict in the marriage, the various changes that follow the divorce, the quality of the postdivorce family relationships, and the degree to which the custodial parent relies on authoritative parenting.

Before the Divorce

Research comparing children in low-conflict nondivorced families with children in high-conflict nondivorced families and with children whose parents later divorce indicates that children are more disadvantaged in a highly conflictual family atmosphere than in one in which parents will later divorce. Hetherington concludes, "Before the divorce the family dynamics leading to divorce are less deleterious than those associated with extremely high levels of overt marital conflict."[58]

Wallerstein would add another criterion for parents to consider in their deciding whether to stay together.[59] She believes that if parents can live together and parent together, they should stay together, as children benefit enormously from having two adults help them through childhood. She does not believe in continuing abusive or violent marriages, but she says that sometimes parents divorce not because the marriage is bad but because they want more stimulating, satisfying lives. In these situations, she recommends staying together to rear the children. Two parents together, she says, place children's needs at the forefront of family life. Parents talk about how to help children change behaviors; they work together to provide stimulating activities and relaxing time together. Children feel increased security in this atmosphere of support. Wallerstein acknowledges that some single parents can maintain children-focused families, but it is not easy or frequent in her experience.

After the Divorce

In the first two years after a divorce, boys and girls in divorced families have more behavior problems, even if they are living in a low-conflict divorced family.

Two years after the divorce, children from high-conflict families—whether divorced or nondivorced—had the greatest number scoring in the range of clinical problems. Low-conflict families—whether divorced or nondivorced—had small numbers of girls scoring in the range of clinical problems. Although more boys in low-conflict divorced families than boys in low-conflict nondivorced families had clinical problems, the number was well below that of the number of boys from high-conflict families—whether divorced or nondivorced.

So, if conflict continues after the divorce, children might as well remain in a high-conflict nondivorced family and avoid all the trauma and changes of divorce. If, however, the divorce leads to a harmonious divorced family, then both boys and girls benefit, though girls appear to benefit more.

> The answer to our question about staying together for the sake of the children appears to be that if the stresses and disruptions in family processes, associated with an unhappy conflictual marriage and that erode the well being of children, are reduced by the move to a divorced single-parent family, divorce may be advantageous. If the diminished resources and increased risks associated with divorce also are accompanied by inept parenting and sustained or increased conflict, not only between the divorced couple but also between parents and children and siblings, it is better for children if parents remain in an unhappy marriage. Unfortunately, these "ifs" are difficult to determine when parents are considering divorce.[60]

FATHERS' ROLE IN CHILDREN'S LIVES

We saw in Chapter 13 that fathers' increased role in dual-earner families benefits children as well as mothers who are both working and rearing children. How, then, does the father's diminished role in the families of single mothers affect children?

Fathers' Absence

Using data from several longitudinal samples, Sara McLanahan and Julien Teitler report the consequences of father absence for children's development, along with the factors underlying those consequences.[61] They report that, in comparison with children growing up in two-parent families, children growing up apart from their biological fathers had lower grades, achieved less education, were more likely to drop out of school, and were less likely to get and keep a job. Adolescent girls in father-absent homes were far more likely to initiate sexual activity at an early age and to have a teen birth or a birth outside of marriage. In one study, 11 percent of adolescent girls in two-parent families had a teen birth, compared with 27 percent of girls in father-absent families. Father absence had a greater effect on the risk for teen births for European American and Latina teens than for African American teens.

The effects of father absence on educational attainment did not vary as a result of gender or racial or ethnic status of the family. Boys and girls of all ethnic groups had reduced educational attainment when fathers were absent. It did not seem to matter when father absence occurred or how long it lasted. Nor did it matter what family structure the child lived in, with one exception: Children in homes with widowed mothers did nearly as well as children in two-parent families. In general, father absence matters more than the circumstances causing it, except in the case of widowhood.

Fathers' Contributions to Children's Lives

McLanahan and Teitler looked at fathers' contributions in three ways but cautioned that these three features—financial, social, and community—may be the result of another, as-yet-unidentified factor. They point to fathers' financial contribution, which improves the resources available for child rearing. Without the additional resources, families may not have services such as health care and may live in poorer neighborhoods with poorer schools and fewer community services. They estimate that reduced income accounts for approximately 50 percent of the effects of father absence.

These researchers estimate that about half the disadvantage of father-absent homes results from poorer parent-child relationships, poorer relationships with adults, and a loss of resources in the community. As noted, it is extremely difficult for one parent to provide as much time, attention, and balance in parenting as two parents; nevertheless, some single-parent mothers do establish low-conflict homes in which children's functioning improves.

In contrast to McLanahan and Teitler, who have used large sociological surveys to support their views, Paul Amato has conducted new analyses of data to determine fathers' contributions to children's lives.[62] He looks at both mothers' and fathers' contributions in terms of human, financial, and social capital. *Human capital* refers to parents' skills, abilities, and knowledge that contribute to achievement in our culture. A useful measure of human capital is parent's education. *Financial capital* refers to the economic resources available to the family to purchase needed goods and services. *Social capital* refers to family and social relationships available to promote children's development.

Amato distinguishes between the benefits of the coparental relationship and those of the parent-child relationship. In a positive coparental relationship, the child views a model of how two people relate, cooperate, negotiate, and compromise. Children who learn these skills tend to get along better with peers and later partners. In providing a unified authority structure to children, two parents teach that authority is consistent and rational. Amato writes,

> Social closure between parents helps children to learn and internalize social norms and moral values. Also, a respect for hierarchical authority, first learned in the family, makes it easier for young people to adjust to social institutions that are hierarchically organized, such as schools and the workplace.[63]

Looking at many studies, Amato demonstrates that children's well-being is positively associated with (1) the father's education, (2) the father's income, (3) the quality of the coparental relationship, and (4) the quality of the parent-child relationship. These relationships hold in two-parent and one-parent families as well, even in studies where mothers' contributions are controlled for.

In his own longitudinal study, Amato interviewed individuals originally studied as children and followed up to early adulthood. He has found that fathers' education and income are related to children's education and that children's education has positive implications for such areas as friendships, self-esteem, and life satisfaction. Fathers' characteristics appear to account for more variance in children's education, self-esteem, and lack of psychological distress than do mothers' characteristics. Mothers' characteristics account for more variance in children's developing kin ties and close friends than do fathers' characteristics. Fathers' and mothers' characteristics account for equal amounts of variance in life satisfaction. Amato summarizes,

> Current research suggests that fathers continue to be important for their contributions of human and financial capital. Current research also suggests, however, that children benefit when fathers are involved in socioemotional aspects of family life . . . the current trend for fathers to be less involved in their children's lives (due to shifts in family structure) represents a net decline in the level of resources available for children.[64]

Studies show that nonresidential fathers who confine their activities with children to fun outings play a minimal role in children's development. Amato concludes that fathers matter "to the extent that they are able to provide appropriate support, guidance, and monitoring—especially if this occurs in the context of cooperation between the parents."[65]

Encouraging Fathers' Participation

James Levine, the founder of the Fatherhood Project in 1981, has written extensively on the advantages for children and fathers of fathers' increased involvement regardless of whether fathers are married to mothers.[66] He identifies three lessons he has learned over the years.

The first important ingredient in successfully involving fathers is the recognition that fathers want to be involved and can be effective parents with preparation and help. Second, single fathers need a support network that guides their behavior. Third, women play a key role in supporting men as fathers.

Fathers who confine their activities with children to fun outings play a minimal role in children's lives. Fathers matter when they provide appropriate support, guidance, and monitoring with children.

Figure 14-1 describes the "on-ramps" that facilitate men's connections with their children and families. Such on-ramps come from those in the community who interact with fathers—at the hospital, at doctors' visits, at schools. Levine writes,

> Our model does not absolve any man from primary responsibility; indeed, it holds that all fathers—whether unmarried, married, or divorced—are responsible for establishing and maintaining connection to their children. But it broadens that responsibility so it is also shared appropriately by all those in the community who, in their everyday work, have the opportunity and the capacity to build—or influence the building of—the on-ramps to connection.[67]

As Levine mentioned in his interview in Chapter 6, the context of interactions with fathers can help involve them. One example is the Hospital Paternity Establishment Program in West Virginia, which has increased the number of unwed fathers who establish paternity from 600 per year to 3,000 per year. Recall that changing expectations emphasize that new fathers need education about establishing paternity and that they need to be approached in terms of the benefits to the father and the child rather than to the state. Hospital staff were educated to involve fathers when they visited their newborns. Fathers then met with professionals, such as a child psychologist, who could explain the psychological importance of the father to the child; a doctor, who could explain the medical importance; and a

■ **F I G U R E   14-1**
CONNECTION: A SHARED RESPONSIBILITY

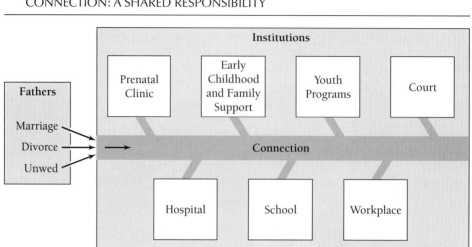

James A. Levine with Edward W. Pitt, *New Expectations: Community Strategies for Responsible Fatherhood* (New York: Families and Work Institute, 1995), 41. Reprinted with permission of the author.

lawyer, who could discuss the legal benefits to the child of having a father who is known. "Public education is the key," says Gary Kreps, who designed the program.[68]

REMARRIAGE

As many as 35 percent of children, 54 percent of women, and 60 percent of men live in second marriages.[69] Remarriage provides many benefits to parents. First, it provides emotional closeness, intimacy, and sexual satisfaction. In caring relationships, parents feel greater self-esteem, contentment, and happiness. Second, parents have someone with whom they can share both the financial and caregiving responsibilities. Wallerstein and Blakeslee find that many parents do not repeat the mistakes of the first marriage.[70] Although remarried parents report feelings of stress and depression related to the many demands they experience, the marriages still are as happy as those in nondivorced families, perhaps because the couples are more pragmatic in their expectations and in seeking solutions to problems.[71]

We know most about remarried families that consist of the custodial mother, her children, and the stepfather, who may or may not have children. There are fewer studies of stepmothers. Few studies focus on marriages of single mothers who have children, even though these may have many characteristics of stepfamilies.

Challenges of Stepfamilies

Stepparenting is more demanding than parenting in intact families for several reasons.[72] First, a stepparent does not have long-standing emotional bonds with the children to help all of them overcome the feelings of frustration and stress that occur as a result of remarriage.

Second, a stepfamily includes more people than does a nuclear family, so it has different needs and interests to consider. There are husbands and wives, their biological children, ex-spouses, stepbrothers and stepsisters, half-brothers and half-sisters, and stepgrandparents. Parents have the multiple tasks of solidifying and maintaining marital ties while sustaining relationships with their biological children and promoting positive sibling relationships.

Third, members of stepfamilies may have deep feelings of jealousy and ambivalence. Because so many more people are involved and the newly married parents want to devote time to their relationship, stepparents may have less time to give to individual children. Children may feel that the new marriage is depriving them of their parent. Parents must accept those feelings as realistic—there *is* less time for each child. Conversely, the parents may feel that the children are intruding on the marriage.

Fourth, both parents and children are haunted by the earlier marriage. Stepparents may feel insecure, as they live with children who are constant proof that the spouse loved another person. Further, the biological parent usually continues to have contact with the former spouse because of the children.

Fifth, former spouses may use the children and their needs to attack the biological parent and the stepparent. One father and stepmother reported that the mother never bought the children clothes, and when the father did this in addition to making the monthly child support payment, the mother would not launder them. Conversely, one mother reported that the father and stepmother, rather than providing money for clothes for the children, instead bought the children fancy clothes that were appropriate for the lifestyle of the father and stepmother but not for the children's needs at school and play.

Sixth, there are no clear guidelines for being a stepparent. There are few enough for biological parents, but the role of stepparent remains even more vague. The stepparent must create his or her role according to his or her individual personality, the ages and sexes of the children, and the family's living arrangements. Stepparents who are forewarned about the problems of stepparenting and who think and talk in advance about how to cope with these problems can find their new roles rewarding and exciting.

Family Changes over Time

Just as parents' behavior changes after a divorce, remarried custodial mothers' behavior changes as well at the time of the remarriage.[73] These mothers become more negative and less controlling, and there is much conflict between mother and children, particularly daughters. Regardless of the child's age at remarriage, conflicts increase in early adolescence, and relationships are more conflictual than in intact families. Even in mid-adolescence, children remain more distant from their custodial, remarried mothers.

When children live with remarried custodial fathers, girls again are the ones who have greater difficulty.[74] Frequent contact with their biological mothers seems to

INTERVIEW
with Emily Visher and John Visher

Emily Visher, a clinical psychologist, and John Visher, a psychiatrist, are founders of the Stepfamily Association and authors of such books as Stepfamilies: Myths and Realities *and* Old Loyalties, New Ties: Therapeutic Strategies with Stepfamilies.

You have worked with stepparents and stepfamilies for many years, so I want to talk to you about what you feel are the important things for parents to do in order to ease the difficulties that can arise in stepfamilies.

E. Visher: We talk about a parenting coalition that is the coalition between all the adults in the child's life. For example, you see, there could be three or four parenting adults— if both parents have remarried, there will be four. If those adults can somehow develop a working relationship around raising the children, the loyalty conflicts of the children will be much less. The adults will get a lot out of it, too, because there is less tension, and better relationships develop between stepparent and stepchild.

We chose the word *coalition* because it means a temporary alliance of separate entities for accomplishing a task. The households and couples are separate, and it is a temporary alliance among all the adults. The task they are working on together is raising the children.

Families can flounder on the basis of the stepparent's trying to be a parent and the children saying basically, "I've got a mother or a father." We have moderated panels of teenagers in stepfamilies, and we always ask them, "What do you want your stepparents to be? What is their role?" I don't think we have ever heard anyone say anything other than "a friend." The difficulty is that by "friend," they mean something very different. They don't mean a pal; it's closer than that.

They are able to talk to the stepparent in a meaningful way that is different from the way they would talk to a parent. They are freer to talk to a stepparent because they are not so involved. One teenager on a panel said she wanted her stepfather to be her friend, and then later she said, "I love my stepfather, and I've never told him." She's saying she wants a friend, but she has very deep feelings for him. He was in the back of the room and heard her.

It is important to take a role that is satisfying to the adult and to the child, and that may be different for children living in the same household and for children in different households. The relationship is different depending on the age of the child—a six-year-old needs something different from a sixteen-year-old. For the young child, the stepparent may well become a parent.

J. Visher: The only power the stepparent has as a parent is delegated from the remarried parent.

E. Visher: The adults need to be supportive of one another. Together they need to decide what the house rules are, and the parent of the children takes care of enforcing the rules until a relationship is set up.

J. Visher: Another major tip is to develop realistic expectations about what it is going to take to make everything work. So many people feel that they have failed after a few weeks or months, that the remarriage has faltered because things are chaotic. It takes four or five years for things to settle down and for people really to get satisfaction out of the whole family relationship.

One of the keys is for people to inform themselves by reading or talking to other people who also are in stepfamilies. They learn that making the stepfamily work takes time and that you shouldn't expect close family relationships quickly.

The most common pattern now is for children to move back and forth and feel part of two households. If all the adults form a parenting coalition, then children are most likely to feel they belong in both places.

Working out the parenting coalition so that it is at least civil makes an enormous difference to everybody. The children can go through the remarriage smoothly if there is not constant warfare. Sometimes parents who divorce or separate are tied together in bonds of anger. The anger can reflect an inadequate separation between the biological parents. They keep together by fighting.

E. Visher: Truman Capote said, "It's easy to lose a good friend, but it's hard to lose a good enemy." The anger ties you together. Hostility eats you up, and you are not free to go on.

J. Visher: Most people don't understand how much damage they are doing to themselves and to the children. Sometimes people say, "How can I work with that S.O.B. when I couldn't even stay married to him?" We say maybe you can split off the part that does not want to be married to him and share the parenting experience.

E. Visher: What the children need from that parent is different from what the spouse needed.

What can you do to decrease the hostility?
J. Visher: One thing is to trade assurances between the households that you are not trying to take the child away from them or trying to get the child to like you better. Often, in a single-parent household, the parent is afraid of further loss, afraid that the ex-spouse and his or her new spouse will encourage the child to stay there and the child will want to because it is a more attractive place or there is more money. This fear fuels the anger and makes the parent cling to the child more and try to influence the child to turn against the other parent.

E. Visher: So we think that sometimes the anger is not left over from the former marriage but has to do with the fear that builds up between the two households, the fear of more loss. The other household becomes a threat, and the ex-spouses become like enemies rather than like people trying to raise a child. The parents are afraid of each other, and they are not aware that the anger substitutes for fear. If they are more aware of it, they can deal with it.

Also important is the guilt the remarried parent feels. He or she feels guilty that the children have been unhappy through the death or divorce and then the remarriage. That parent has a real investment in its being a big, happy family right away. Yet they have difficulty setting limits for the children who live there or visit there. The stepparent goes up the wall.

Sometimes they feel that to form a good couple relationship and make that primary is a betrayal of their relationship with their child. The parent-child relationship is different from the relationship with the spouse.

(continued)

INTERVIEW with Emily Visher and John Visher

(continued)

J. Visher: There may be an unusually strong bond between parent and child; perhaps it has lasted for many years, and the new spouse is a rival. It becomes a power struggle between spouse and child for the loyalty of the biological parent. The child is sometimes suddenly out of a job as confidant.

E. Visher: I don't think people realize the change for the children, that now they have to share. One mother described that she and her daughter had lived together for five years. When she came home from work, she talked to her daughter. Now that she is remarried, she talks to her husband. That one little thing is not so little, as the daughter has to share her mother.

If people are aware of the losses for the children in the new structure, they can acknowledge those changes with the children and do things differently—sit down with the children alone and talk. When children sense their feelings are accepted, they will talk about them. One stepmother commented to her stepson that when the father talked to the son, she felt left out, and she wondered if he felt left out when the father talked to her. He agreed he did, and they talked about it. There was not a lot they could change, but after they had the talk, they got along better.

J. Visher: We hope that as people are more informed, they will be able to deal more effectively with the situation.

---

increase the difficulty, but this unusual finding may be the result of biological mothers' having special problems that argued against their having custody. However, the longer girls live in such families, the more positive the relationship grows between the daughter and the stepmother.

There are no differences in how biological parents parent their own children in nondivorced and remarried families. Regardless of family status, mothers and fathers are warmer, more supportive, and closer to their biological children than to their stepchildren, and their children are more often closer to them.[75]

No matter what the age of a child at a parent's remarriage, stepfathers initially feel less close to their stepchildren than to their biological children, and they do not monitor behavior as well as fathers do in intact families. When children are relatively young at the time of the remarriage, stepfathers may be able to build relationships with stepchildren by taking on the role of a warm and supportive figure and forgoing the role of disciplinarian until a relationship is established. Preadolescent boys may settle down in a relationship with a stepfather, but preadolescent girls usually resist stepfathers' overtures and direct angry, negative behavior to the custodial mother.[76]

When children are early adolescents at the time of the remarriage, there appears to be little adaptation to the new family over a two-year period.[77] Children are negative and resistant and, as a result, stepfathers remain disengaged, critical, and distanced from the day-to-day monitoring of children. When, however, stepparents can be authoritative parenting figures—warm, positive, appropriate in monitoring—then children's adjustment improves. With adolescents, stepparents fare better when they are authoritative from the start.

Adolescents at the time of the remarriage are often unwilling to become involved with stepparents, and they frequently retreat from the families and establish strong relationships with families of friends. At the same time, they become more argumentative with the biological parents, both custodial and noncustodial. As noted, adolescents feel closer to noncustodial mothers than to noncustodial fathers.[78]

In stepfamilies, marital happiness has a different relation to children's behavior than it has in intact families.[79] In nondivorced families, marital happiness is related to children's competent functioning and positive relationships with parents. In stepfamilies, marital happiness is related to children's negative and resistant behavior with parents. Girls may especially resent the loss of the close relationship with their custodial mother.

Relationships with siblings are less positive and more negative in remarried families than in nondivorced families.[80] Although girls tend to be warmer and more empathetic than boys, they are almost equally aggressive. As siblings become adolescents, they become more separated from each other. Interestingly, relationships with their stepsiblings appear less negative than relationships with their own siblings.

Children's Behavior over Time

Children's adjustment in stepfamilies varies. Often, initial declines in cognitive and social competence follow the remarriage, but when boys are young and stepparents are warm and authoritative, problem behaviors improve, and boys in these stepfamilies show levels of adjustment similar to those of boys in nondivorced families. Young girls continue to have more acting-out and defiant behavior problems than do girls in intact or divorced families.[81] Most gender differences in adjustment disappear at early adolescence, when both boys and girls have more problems.

At all ages, children in remarried families, like children in divorced families, have poorer school performance, more problems in social responsibility, and more rule-breaking behaviors than do children in intact families.[82] Still, the majority do well. Between two-thirds and three-quarters score within the average range on assessment instruments. Although this falls below the comparable figure of 90 percent for children of nondivorced parents, it indicates that most children in remarried families are doing well.[83]

As with children of divorced families, children of remarried families are at a disadvantage in early adulthood.[84] Compared with children of nondivorced parents, they are more likely to leave home at an early age, less likely to continue in school, and more likely to leave home as a result of conflict. As adults, they feel they can rely less on their families. Still, responses vary, and many of these children feel close to and supported in stepfamilies.

Many of the difficulties stepfamilies encounter can be avoided or lessened if they are anticipated and prepared for. Stepfamilies can strengthen their ties in many ways, such as nurturing relationships, finding personal space and time, and building family trust.[85]

Types of Stepfamilies

From his ten-year study of 100 stepfamilies made up of custodial mothers, stepfathers, and young children and a controlled sample of 100 nondivorcing families, James Bray has provided a basic understanding of developmental issues facing stepfamilies.[86] His major findings include the following:

1. A stepfamily has a natural cycle of changes and transition points.
2. A stepfamily takes many years to form a basic family unit.
3. The greatest risk to the stepfamily occurs in the first two years, when about 25 percent of remarriages fail.
4. In a stepfamily, there is no honeymoon period of high satisfaction followed by a gradual decrease, as there is in a first marriage; in a stepfamily, marital satisfaction starts at a moderate level and builds up from there or decreases to the point of divorce.
5. A stepfamily has four basic tasks to achieve cohesion:

   a. Integrating the stepfather into the family
   b. Creating a satisfying second marriage
   c. Separating from the ghosts of the past
   d. Managing all the changes

6. A stepfamily eventually takes one of three forms: *neotraditional, matriarchal, or romantic.* Neotraditionals almost always succeed, matriarchals succeed much of the time, and romantics face great risk of divorce.

The neotraditional family is described as a "contemporary version of the 1950s, white-picket fence; it is close-knit, loving, and works very well for a couple with compatible values."[87] The matriarchal family is one in which the wife-mother is a highly competent woman who directs and manages all the family activities. The romantic family seeks everything the neotraditional family does but wants it all immediately, as soon as the marriage occurs. The romantic family is at great risk for not surviving the conflicts and changes of the first two years. The three types of families do not differ in the crises and turning points they face, but they do differ in their expectations and their willingness to change their expectations and their behaviors to solve the problems they confront.

The first cycle of change that stepfamilies experience in the process of their formation occurs in the first two years of the remarriage. In this stressful period, all members of the family try to find ways to live together, deal with ex-spouses and noncustodial parents, and form a stable unit that brings everyone happiness. By the end of two years, the second cycle begins; family members find mutually satisfying ways of getting along, and a family unit is established. Tensions are reduced, and happy stepfamilies resemble nondivorced families. A third cycle of change occurs when children move into adolescence and become more insistent on independence and individuality.

Neotraditional families successfully navigate the changes because they give up unrealistic expectations and because they communicate feelings and solve problems.

Bray describes the neotraditional family as having the ability to (1) identify and express feelings clearly, (2) identify and understand other family members' thoughts, feelings, and values so differences are bridged, (3) resolve conflicts, (4) state a complaint so the other person feels empathy for the complaint, (5) establish new rituals that help define the family as a unit, and (6) accept other family members. Romantic families seek the same cohesiveness and close ties that neotraditional families do, but they find it very difficult to give up unrealistic expectations and solve the problems at hand.

Bray reports that despite the crises and difficulties of remarriage, many stepfamilies succeed and form stable, cohesive family units that give all members a sense of warmth and accomplishment. A significant number of stepfamilies do not succeed, however, and dissolve the marriages because the parents do not have the commitment to work through the problems to reach a joint resolution. A third group of families stay together and seem happy enough, but they lack a sense of vitality and seem to "just get by." These families do not want open communication or to really understand each other and instead choose habitual ways of relating to each other.

Bray asked successful families what got them through all the stressful periods. "The consistent answer was commitment. Commitment to a life together, not just getting by but living and loving fully, communicating about issues, building a stable family, and enjoying a good life together."[88]

LESBIAN AND GAY PARENTS

Lesbian and gay parents are a heterogeneous group.[89] The majority of lesbian and gay parents have children in the context of heterosexual marriages and later divorce, adopt a lesbian or gay identity, and rear children with partners of the same sex. These families face not only all the stresses of remarried families but also the pressure of prejudice against lesbian and gay parents. Much of the initial research done on lesbian and gay parents and their children has been conducted in order to prevent their being denied custody of and visitation with their children.

More and more lesbian and gay parents are choosing parenthood after proclaiming a lesbian or gay identity. They are usually living with partners and choose to have a child through assisted reproductive technology or surrogate parenthood. The child may have a biological relationship with one parent, with the other parent becoming a coparent through legal adoption of the child, or the child may have no biological relationship with either parent. A single lesbian or gay person may have a child in the same way.

Divorced Lesbian and Gay Parents

The largest group studied has been divorced lesbian mothers. Concerns have focused on their mental health and on their sex-role behavior and its effects on children. Most studies have compared lesbian and heterosexual mothers and find no differences between them on self-concept, overall psychological adjustment, psychiatric status, sex-role behavior, or interest in children and child rearing. Divorced lesbian mothers are more worried about custody issues than are divorced hetero-sexual mothers. They are more likely to be living with partners. Studies reveal no differences between the biological fathers of children of lesbian mothers and fathers divorced from heterosexual mothers in terms of paying child support, but fathers in the former group are more likely to have frequent visitation.

Research is just beginning on such topics as when and how lesbian mothers should reveal their sexual identity to children. Although there is no firm agreement, it is thought best to avoid doing this during the child's adolescence so that the child's own sexual identity and identity formation can occur without distraction.

Much less is known about divorced gay fathers. There is no research comparing the psychological stability of gay and heterosexual divorced fathers, perhaps be-cause men do not often seek physical custody. Research comparing their parenting behaviors suggests that gay fathers are more responsive, more careful about moni-toring, and more likely to rely on authoritative parenting strategies than are hetero-sexual divorced fathers. Studies of the family lives of gay fathers, teen sons, and fathers' partners indicate greater family happiness when the partner has a good re-lationship with the adolescent boy. Comparisons of divorced lesbian mothers and gay divorced fathers reveal that gay fathers report more income and more frequent sex-stereotypic toy play by their children.

Lesbian and Gay Couples' Transition to Parenthood

In the 1990s, many lesbian and gay individuals in committed partnerships chose to have children either through assisted reproductive technology or through adop-tion, but such couples often faced prejudice in a situation that is stressful enough. Little research has addressed the questions of how and when lesbian and gay cou-ples decide to have children. Research has focused instead on how lesbian and gay couples make the transition to parenthood and divide the responsibilities of child care and household work.

In lesbian partnerships, the biological mother takes primary care of the child in the earliest months, but nonbiological parents often report an immediate attach-ment to the child and take a larger role when the child is twelve months or older. There was more equal sharing of child care and household work in lesbian partner-ships than in heterosexual marriages. Lesbian partners also report a high level of rela-tionship satisfaction and greater satisfaction with the division of labor. Nonbiological mothers were seen as more knowledgeable about child care and more willing to as-sume equal care of the child than were heterosexual fathers.

A study comparing single and coupled lesbian mothers with single and coupled heterosexual mothers found that (1) single heterosexual and lesbian mothers were warmer and more positive with their children than were coupled heterosexual mothers, and all lesbian mothers were more interactive with their children than were single heterosexual mothers, and (2) single heterosexual and lesbian mothers reported more serious, though not more frequent, disputes with children than did coupled heterosexual mothers.

In a study of gay fathers choosing parenthood, gay fathers reported higher self-esteem and fewer negative attitudes about homosexuality than did gay men who elected not to become fathers.[90] There are few other differences between the two groups of men, and the author speculates that higher self-esteem may be a result of parenthood rather than a determiner of it.

Children of Lesbian and Gay Parents

A major question of research has been whether lesbian and gay parents influence the gender identity of their children in the direction of lesbian/gay gender identity and same-sex sexual orientation (choice of partner). There is no evidence that children of lesbian and gay parents have an increased likelihood of having a lesbian/gay gender identity or same-sex sexual orientation. Nor is there evidence that they are at increased risk of sexual abuse in lesbian or gay homes.

Children living with lesbian and gay parents are as well adjusted and socially competent as children living with heterosexual parents. Children of lesbian parents show no special problems with self-concept, gender identity, or sexual orientation. The results of research on lesbian and gay parents and their children indicate that the sexual adjustment of the parent does not predict the child's adjustment and that family process variables operate in much the same way in lesbian and gay families as in heterosexual families—that is, when parents are warm and involved, as many lesbian and gay parents are, their children do well.

FOSTER FAMILIES

Foster parents care for children whose parents cannot care for them, for a variety of reasons. Parents may have died and left no relatives or friends to care for the child. Parents may have been incarcerated or hospitalized for psychiatric or medical reasons, and no relatives or friends could step in to provide care. But most often, children live in foster families because parents' care has been found to be neglectful or abusive. The topic of child maltreatment is discussed at length in Chapter 15.

Approximately 300,000[91] children are taken into foster care each year, and approximately 500,000[92] children live in foster care, some with biological relatives but a half or more with nonrelatives. At present, the average length of stay in foster care is twenty-two months. About 20 to 25 percent of children will not return to their biological parents to live.

Because many parents who abuse children are from poor families, and because Native American, African American, and Latina/o families are overrepresented among the poor, as we saw in Chapter 3, children from these ethnic groups can be overrepresented among children going into foster care.[93] Racial bias may play a role, however, as one study found that substance-abusing, pregnant African American women were ten times more likely to be reported to authorities than European American women, despite the fact that the rates of pregnancy drug tests were the same for the two groups. Once infants were in foster care, agency caseworkers had less contact and made fewer case plans for African American families.

The major law governing foster care is the Adoption and Safe Family Act (AFSA), passed by Congress in 1997.[94] One main thrust of the law is to provide services for families at high risk of abuse, to enable children to remain with biological parents. These services include, for example, parenting programs, anger management programs, and therapy. If, however, children are removed from the home, the second main thrust of the program is to motivate parents to make changes in their behavior within about eighteen months. Agencies and parents set up plans for change, with periodic checks to note progress. If changes are not made, and if the child cannot be returned to biological parents within about eighteen months, then parental rights are terminated. This is to maximize the possibility that the child can be adopted and have a permanent home. Before the time frame was established, some children were in foster care for years, waiting for parents to change, and by the time parents' rights were terminated, children were considered hard to adopt because they were older.

Foster Parents

There is no national registry of foster parents, and our knowledge about them is based on small surveys. They are generally married (60 percent), with an average education of high school level; about half are of middle-class background, 15 percent are of upper-middle-class background, and 35 percent are of working-class background. Still, 40 percent are single parents, and many have limited financial resources.[95]

Adults who become foster parents give several reasons: (1) to have children, (2) to be altruistic, (3) to help deprived children. People who foster for these reasons receive higher ratings as parents than adults who become parents to nurture children. The latter group of parents may feel disappointed when children do not respond to their nurturance.[96]

Foster parents undertake a daunting challenge.[97] They have all the stresses and strains that any parent experiences, plus several others. The children who come into their homes arrive with a history of difficult life experiences—the death of a parent, physical or sexual abuse, neglect—and they are often dealing with strong emotional reactions to those experiences. In addition, they have the stress of being separated from their parents, brothers and sisters, and often friends as well. Finally, there is the stress of living with a new family, adjusting to new rules and expectations. Children may express their anger, disappointment, or sadness in their interactions with their foster parents, and resist efforts to follow the family routines. Foster parents, like stepparents, have had no previous attachment relationship with children, and it is such ties that often motivate children to cooperate. Building such relationships at times of crises is difficult. A further difficulty for foster parents is that they have to relinquish the ties when children leave their care.

Because of the numerous sources of difficulties, foster parents need to be trained to understand what children have been through, to be patient, sensitive, and warm yet firm and supportive in helping children meet age-appropriate demands at home and at school. One study found that, when foster parents learned ways to stimulate verbal and cognitive development of preschoolers, the children had fewer emotional and behavioral problems, perhaps because they felt more competent.

The Web of Foster-Care Relationships

In carrying out their caregiving responsibilities, foster parents are enmeshed in a web of what can be competing responsibilities.[98] First, they are to provide good care to the children, and they often feel strongly protective of them. Second, they are to work with the agency workers, helping to implement reunification programs with biological parents. Third, they work with biological parents, helping them and their children to establish effective patterns of interaction, sometimes arranging or supervising visits, sometimes helping parents' understand children's feelings. Looming over the system are the judge and court, which make final decisions about what will happen with children.

When there is clear communication and everyone is working together for the child's best interests, such a system can work well. But competing interests can easily surface. Foster parents may feel critical of parents and the protective agencies if they feel not enough is being done to safeguard the child or children. Birth parents may feel angry that children were taken, because parents had little help and support to do well, and frustrated that they are competing for their children with foster parents who have more resources. Agency workers may feel frustrated with many cases and many demands on them.

A California case illustrates how the system can fail the child and all who are caring for him.[99] Judge Marta Diaz went over thousands of pages of court records regarding a little boy who lived almost his entire life in foster care yet died after a two-day, unsupervised home visit that she authorized. Angelo was taken into foster care when he was twelve days old because he had unexplained broken ankles and cracked ribs. The person who abused him was never specifically identified. After about eight months, when parents had taken parenting classes and had had supervised and two unsupervised visits with him, the judge permitted him to go home with his parents for the two-day Christmas visit. He died at the end of the visit from shaken baby syndrome, and his father was arrested.

In reviewing the case, the judge learned that she had not had all the information she needed to make the recommendation for unsupervised visitation, and she had given social workers too much discretion in allowing the visits to go on after difficulties surfaced. The social worker assigned to the case for the first three months failed to report that there were problems with Angelo and his parents around the visits, and she never identified the initial abuser, although that was one of her tasks. The second social worker did not tell the judge that the foster parents, the child's doctor, and the parents' therapist had all recommended that the child not have unsupervised visits, because he had received injuries on two previous unsupervised visits. And the social worker did not cancel the Christmas visit in the light of this information.

The judge took full responsibility for having issued the order for unsupervised visitation but recommended several changes in the system to ensure greater training for social workers as well as better communication and more effective interactions among social workers, attorneys, agencies, judges, and foster parents involved in the cases of foster children.

Foster Children

There is less research than we would like on contemporary foster children. In the earlier days of foster care, older children typically came to these homes from stable families because of the death or absence of a parent. As child maltreatment cases have increased, children come to foster care with many emotional and behavioral problems. As drug abuse has increased among young women, infants have been sent to foster care from the hospital, and they make up a growing percentage of children in foster care.[100] Little is known about their attachment experiences and how foster care will affect their development over time, because there can be many moves within the foster-care system.

A small, well-controlled study provides information on children's experiences in foster care.[101] Following a sample of high-risk families (at risk because of young age of mothers, parents' low levels of education, poverty income, unstable environments) as children progressed through childhood to adulthood, University of Minnesota researchers were able to select three groups of children: (1) children who were maltreated and remained with the maltreating parent, (2) children who were removed from the home but lived with relatives or family friends, and (3) children who went into foster care with strangers. In 70 percent of the cases, removal from the home was for parental maltreatment or neglect, and in 30 percent, it was because of death of a parent, homelessness, or parent's being in jail. The remainder of the high-risk sample served as a control group of children who were not maltreated or placed in foster care.

There was detailed information on these children prior to the abuse and the removal from the family as well as after they left foster care. Prior to placement, maltreated children at home and those going into out-of-home placement showed more behavior problems than the control group, and those who stayed at home and those who were in out-of-home care did not differ from each other. Age at entry and length of time out of the home did not predict later functioning.

As soon as placement occurred, behavior problems of foster children sharply increased. Those who remained at home had no such spike. At the time of release from foster care, those leaving foster care had slightly higher levels of emotional and behavioral problems than those who had remained at home. Both groups of maltreated children continued to have more problems than those in the control group who did not experience maltreatment. Assessments of all groups of children in adolescence up to age seventeen and a half revealed that those who stayed at home with the maltreating parent had slightly fewer problems than those who went into foster care.

Going into foster care may well place an extra layer of stress on children and increase the behavior problems children have even after they leave foster care. Those who went into homes with familiar adults were less anxious, depressed, and withdrawn than those who went into foster care with strangers. Although this study is small, there were many controls for the social status of the groups and for the children's behavior ratings, as they were done by teachers, not by social workers or parents, who might have been less objective.

Support for the stressfulness of foster care with strangers comes from the fact that those children who go into foster homes of working-class and lower-social-status families, which are more like the families children lived in before foster care, have greater success, perhaps because the child feels more familiar with the routines and values expressed there.[102]

Sadly, children in foster care are at increased risk for abuse.[103] More reports of abuse are made about children in foster families than those in families in the general community, but the rate of substantiation is much lower for children in foster families. Existing studies indicate that, although the abuse rate may be higher in foster families than in community families, the rate is lower in foster families than is the rate of repeated abuse when children remain with biological parents. Further, foster parents may not always be the abusers; it may be the biological parent on a visit or someone else living in the foster home. Abuse is more likely to be reported in foster families with a younger mother, lower income, poorer health of the foster parents, and a crowded situation where foster children slept together.

The largest study of children leaving foster care provided some good news and some bad news about experiences in foster care.[104] The good news is that, at age seventeen, 90 percent of the group of 732 young people leaving foster care in Illinois, Wisconsin, and Iowa felt optimistic about the future. More than half felt "lucky" to have been placed in foster care, and an even larger percentage felt "mostly satisfied" with their foster-care experience.

The bad news is that this sample of youth experienced more difficulties in their growing-up years than a national sample of young people their age, and they faced the future with fewer skills. In comparison to the national group, the foster-care group was more likely to have been held back a year in school, twice as likely to have been suspended, four times as likely to have been expelled. Though most at age seventeen were in the last grades of high school, they were reading, on average, at the seventh-grade level.

The foster-care sample was much more likely to have received counseling and medication for psychological problems, and a large number had had conflict with the law—one-fifth reported conviction for a crime, and more than half had been arrested.

When followed up at age nineteen, the group still "wrestled" with worse problems than the national sample of nineteen-year-olds.[105] More than a third had no high school diploma—the comparable figure for the national sample was 10 percent—and they were more likely to be unemployed, pregnant, unable to pay the rent, and sometimes hungry and homeless. Those who remained in foster care beyond their eighteenth birthdays were more likely to be in school or a training program to prepare for a future.

It is important to point out that the appropriate comparison group may not be a broad national sample of same-aged youths but a sample of poorer youths who have known many difficulties as well, or a group of children who were maltreated and did not go to foster care as in the Minnesota study. The children exiting foster care have suffered many negative experiences, including poverty and traumatic events of abuse (see Chapter 15 for a discussion of child maltreatment and its legacy of problems). Studies of maltreated children suggest that they had many emotional problems when they entered foster care, and foster care, even with counseling, has not remedied them.

Richard Wexler, executive director of the National Coalition for Child Protection Reform, says, "What these results should tell us is that we've got to stop throwing so many children into foster care in the first place. What you can see is, regardless of what the problems were going in, foster care surely didn't fix them."[106]

Despite all the problems, it is important to recall that half the children felt that they were lucky to have been in foster care. Box 14-1 describes innovations in foster care that may make it more effective.

Kinship Foster Care and Nonrelative Foster Care

As suggested in the Minnesota study, kinship foster care has some advantages. Kinship foster care appears to provide more stability.[107] Children are less likely to be moved from it, and biological parents appear to keep in closer contact with children, with 56 percent visiting at least once a month and 19 percent visiting four or more times a month; the comparable figures in nonrelative foster care are 32 percent once a month and 3 percent four or more times a month. In addition, abuse is less likely to be reported in kinship foster families than in nonrelative foster families. Some foster-care professionals have expressed concern that, in kinship foster homes, children may receive fewer services and may be exposed to the influences that created difficulties for the parent, but kinship foster homes do appear to provide greater stability, and children seem to have fewer problems there.

Termination of Parental Rights

In our country, the tie between biological parent and child is considered so important that it is severed only because the parent cannot meet his or her responsibilities to provide adequate care for the child for an extended period of time. Even if a child has been placed for adoption and has lived happily for two or three years with adoptive parents as the only parents he or she has known, the courts will return the child to a competent biological father who did not know of the child's existence before adoption and who seeks the child out as soon as he learns he has a child.[108]

Parents' rights can be relinquished voluntarily, as when young parents give up a baby for adoption. Parents' rights are terminated when they have demonstrated to a court that they are unable to care for the child or children for an extended period of time. These decisions are not easy, for there can be mitigating circumstances that make it hard to meet the time limit—loss of a job or place to live, time in jail. Still, the court is concerned about the child's right to permanent placement with parents who can care for him or her. The child's interest will be considered only if the parent has proved unable or unwilling to make changes to become a competent parent.

A PRACTICAL QUESTION: WHAT SHOULD PARENTS DO AT TIMES OF TRANSITION?

Research suggests several things parents going through family breakups or transitions can do. First, these parents should maintain positive emotional relationships with children. Even if there is pronounced conflict between parents, parent-child relationships can be satisfying if parents make a special effort to keep children out of the conflict. Parents need to make time for the open communication of feelings,

Box 14-1
INNOVATIVE FOSTER-CARE PROGRAMS

Two innovative programs seek to build a more effective, supportive foster-care system for everyone involved.

In 1998, New York City established the family-to-family program* to create an open family system in which biological and foster parents meet with each other, plan the care of the children, and have ongoing contact as parents work toward having children live at home again. Meetings are initially held in agency offices where biological parents can meet the foster parents, give information about their child's routines and habits, and express their preferences for such things as church attendance, dress rules, and hairstyles.

When visiting starts, parents sometimes come to the foster homes a number of times before they start unsupervised visits. Parents frequently maintain relationships with each other, and children go back to visit after return to their biological parents. Foster parents become part of the extended family system. In many ways, foster parents and biological parents form the kind of relationship we referred to in Chapter 4 as coparenting, even though foster parents are more like mentors to parents in the beginning.

The program in New York is a voluntary one unless the court prohibits it, and about 60 percent of parents have had some contact with foster parents. The program requires special training for agency workers and for foster parents, who frequently feel critical of parents because of their child maltreatment. The program has resulted in children's returning to their biological families about three months sooner than under the older system. The rate at which parental rights are terminated remains the same, but the parent understands better that he or she cannot provide an effective level of care.

In the midwest, Brenda Eheart, an Illinois sociologist who was concerned that many foster children were not able to return to their biological parents, started a program she called "Generations of Hope," to recreate for foster children the kind of close and caring social ties she had had growing up in a small town.[†] She was able to negotiate the purchase of part of a decommissioned air force base and organized a community to live there. She advertised for adults who would become foster parents with the goal of adopting the children. She also advertised for older adults who would live there, volunteer their services to care for children, tutor them, and teach them skills in exchange for reduced rent of comfortable homes. And she contacted the Illinois Department of Children and Family Services for hard-to-place children that she could bring into her program.

Her program provides therapy, tutoring, and respite services for children and families. Eheart compares her program with state-run residential programs. In those programs, which are expensive, children must leave at eighteen. She summarizes her program: "We give children a childhood, a sense of permanence." Older adults as well as children have gained from the program because they have important, useful jobs, and they, too, have community connections.

*Leslie Kaufman, "Birth Parents Retaining a Voice in New York Foster Care Model," *New York Times*, 3 June 2004, p. A1.
[†]Lou Ann Walker, "A Place Called Hope," *Parade Magazine*, 7 July 2002, pp. 10–12.

for asking and answering questions, and for sharing enjoyable activities. These same rules apply to relationships with stepchildren.

Second, parents must learn effective ways of resolving conflicts, regardless of who is involved. (See Table 14-1, which lists suggestions for minimizing harm from conflict between parents, and Chapter 4 for a discussion on effective ways of dealing with anger between parents and children.) According to Amato, the most important thing society can do to promote safe and secure environments for children is to encourage parents to learn ways to resolve conflicts within marriages and to settle disputes if they get divorced so children are not put in the middle.[109] Children's feelings of self-blame, whether parents are married or divorced, are one of the contributors to children's poor adjustment to life.

Third, parents need to model and encourage positive relationships with all family members—siblings, grandparents, and all the relatives involved in stepfamilies.

Fourth, parents need to help children seek positive experiences in their own social milieu—with friends, relatives, schoolmates, and teachers. These supports help children cope in times of change.

Finally, parents need to recall that, at times of marital transition, they need to do all the things that are beneficial in nondivorced families, but they need to do more of them to buffer children from the stress of change. It is harder to do these things when parents themselves are under stress. Still, parents promote children's growth and competence in all times of change when they foster close, positive emotional relationships with children and monitor their behavior carefully to ensure that it falls within appropriate limits.

THE POWER OF AUTHORITATIVE PARENTING

Hetherington's work,[110] as well as that of other researchers,[111] reveals that regardless of family structure (one or two parents, biological parent or stepparent, lesbian or gay parents), regardless of ethnic background or age or gender, children do well with authoritative parenting. When parents can respond to children's needs and individuality and also monitor and control behavior, children function well. Similarly, regardless of family structure, children do poorly with authoritarian and harsh, demanding parenting. Authoritative parenting not only contributes to positive parent-child relationships but also builds positive sibling relationships, which increase children's competence.

MAIN POINTS

Single parents are

- a heterogeneous group made up of never-married, separated or divorced, and widowed adults with children
- more frequently women than men, with 22 percent of families with children headed by women and 4 percent headed by men
- most effective when they organize stable living environments and use authoritative parenting

The process of divorce

- is often preceded by marital conflict, which upsets children and arouses their feelings of self-blame
- is a major disruption for all family members
- involves many changes that can include fewer economic resources as well as a new neighborhood, a new school, and new friends
- places stress on children and parents, which can be reversed if parents establish low-conflict divorced homes

Protective factors for children at the time of divorce include

- a child's age, sex, intelligence, and temperament
- manageable amounts of stress and appropriate support from grandparents and other relatives
- educational and athletic accomplishments that contribute to children's feelings of competence and stimulate resilience

Children's behavior

- becomes more problematic at the time of divorce but improves as time passes
- is less carefully monitored in single-parent than in dual-parent homes in early adolescence
- improves when parents resolve their anger and use authoritative parenting

Men make positive contributions to children's development when

- they provide their human, financial, and social capital to the family
- the social context encourages their involvement

When parents remarry, they

- experience many emotional benefits, such as closeness, intimacy, and sexual satisfaction
- do not necessarily repeat the mistakes of the first marriage
- experience stress as they integrate everyone into a new family with few guidelines

When parents remarry, children

- differ in their reactions, with girls having more difficulty in adjusting to parents' remarriage than do boys
- show initial declines in social and cognitive competence
- show improvements in behavior, following an initial decline, when parenting figures are warm and authoritative

Stepfamilies

- often have unrealistic expectations about how quickly closeness and cohesiveness of family members will develop
- need empathy and communication skills to work through the crises and conflicts that occur in the first two years

Lesbian and gay parents

- are as effective as parents in heterosexual marriages
- have children who function as well as children of heterosexual parents
- share child care and household work more equally than heterosexual parents

Parenting tasks at times of partner and marital transition include

- maintaining positive emotional relationships with children
- learning effective conflict resolution skills
- relying on authoritative parenting strategies
- modeling positive relationships with the extended family
- encouraging children to have positive experiences in their own social world

Foster parenting

- involves the satisfactions and challenges of providing care for children who are dealing with difficult life experiences and require support and understanding
- involves many other people and agencies and the ongoing supervision of parents
- has not yet been able to help children overcome many problems they come with, but innovative programs suggest useful interventions

EXERCISES

1. Suppose your friend's parents divorced when he or she was a small child, and now your friend fears intimacy and commitment. What could you do to help him or her be less fearful? What advice could you offer your friend to lessen such fears? In a class discussion, share your ideas on how to advise your friend.

2. Imagine that your married brother, sister, or friend came to you and said that he or she was getting a divorce and wanted help in making arrangements so his or her eight-year-old daughter and six-year-old son would experience the fewest negative effects. What guidelines would you give your relative or friend?

3. Pair off with a classmate, preferably of the same sex. Imagine one of you is eight and the other is fifteen. One of your parents has just married your partner's parent; you are now stepbrothers or stepsisters. Discuss how you feel now that you are going to be living intimately with each other—perhaps sharing a room, having your time with your biological parent reduced so the parent can spend time with this stranger, having the amount of money available to you dependent on the needs of these new people. Would being older or younger make a difference in your reactions? Describe what your parents could do to ease the adjustment process.

4. Attend divorce court for a morning and summarize the cases presented there. What issues do parents argue about? What issues about children arise? Describe whether you agree with the judge's ruling, and state why.

5. What would you say to an older brother or sister who said that he or she was thinking about becoming a foster parent and wondered what you thought would be the satisfactions and challenges?

ADDITIONAL READINGS

Bray, James H., and Kelly, John. *Stepfamilies: Love, Marriage, and Parenting in the First Decade.* New York: Broadway Books, 1998.

Hetherington, E. Mavis, and Kelly, John. *For Better or Worse: Divorce Reconsidered.* New York: Norton, 2002.

Lamb, Michael E., ed. *Parenting and Child Development in Nontraditional Families.* Mahwah, NJ: Erlbaum, 1999.

Levine, James A., and Pitt, Edward W. *New Expectations: Community Strategies for Responsible Fatherhood.* New York: Families and Work Institute, 1995.

Martin, April. *The Lesbian and Gay Parenting Handbook.* New York: HarperCollins, 1993.

Wallerstein, Judith S., Lewis, Julia M., and Blakeslee, Sandra. *The Unexpected Legacy of Divorce.* New York: Hyperion, 2000.

15

Parenting at Times of Loss, Trauma, Disaster, and Violence

IN THE NEWS

New York Times, October 20[1]: In response to disasters, families organize emergency plans for all members. See pages 526–527.

Test Your Knowledge: Fact or Fiction?

1. Childhood is a time of health and energy, and physical problems in the family concern parents and grandparents.
2. Children have many grief reactions similar to those of parents when a close family member dies.
3. Children who experience one form of child maltreatment often experience several other forms.
4. Children quickly get parents' assistance when they have witnessed violence in the neighborhood.
5. Disasters and national violence are so overwhelming that families can do little to plan effective responses in advance.

When traumatic events occur, parents face difficult challenges. What reactions can parents expect from children? What can parents do to manage their own reactions and help children cope? Which children are most likely to suffer long-term effects from traumatic events? What can parents do to protect children from violence and enable them to feel secure in a world that is sometimes unsafe?

In previous chapters, we have talked about the moderately stressful events of life, such as school and peer problems. Life also includes major losses, traumas, and violence. In Chapter 8, we talked about the challenging difficulties of a child's having major developmental delays, and in Chapter 14, we discussed divorce, which for most children is a major loss in life. In this chapter, we talk about the other major traumatic events: illness; the death of a parent, child, or other close relative; abuse and neglect; and violence in the home, the community, and the nation. Sadly, some people experience several major losses and traumas, and—ironically and unfairly—these major traumas often bring with them all the moderately stressful life events as well. (See Box 15-1.)

Sometimes we experience stressful events in our personal lives, and sometimes, in an increasingly interconnected world, in the lives of others whom we learn about through the media. As we noted in Chapter 5, motor neurons in the brain enable us to be especially sensitive to what we witness. This chapter focuses on how parents help themselves and their children cope with the difficulties of illness, family death, neglect, abuse, community and national disaster, and violence.

THE SYSTEMS PERSPECTIVE

A systems perspective emphasizes that all family members are affected by the stressful life event of one family member. One person may have the physical illness with pains and treatments, but everyone in the family feels pain at that person's illness. If it is the child who is ill, parents rearrange their own lives and their other children's to provide physical care for the one who is ill. Others must care for brothers and sisters or drive them to their activities. Everyone worries and sympathizes with the one who is sick, and the one who is sick usually worries about all the extra demands he or she is making on the family. If it is the parent who is ill, the child worries and wants to help even if there is little he or she can do. The whole extended family is on alert, and grandparents may take leaves from jobs to come and help out.

A systems perspective also highlights that a difficulty in one area of development can trigger difficulties in other areas as well. For example, when asthmatic children have many flare-ups, they miss school and begin to fall behind academically, and so they often develop school problems. They may be unable to participate in certain sports or attend parties at homes with pets, and they feel left out of social activities. As a result of increased difficulties at school and feelings of loneliness, children become angry and irritable and resist parents' requests at home, alienating the support that they need from parents.

Box 15-1
THE MANY STRESSES THAT CAN COME YOUR WAY*

In the book *Conquering Your Child's Chronic Pain*, Dr. Lonnie Zeltzer describes the case of Damien, whom she treated for pain related to his sickle-cell disease. Up to the age of eleven or twelve, he rarely came to the hospital with complaints of pain. He was a happy boy, doing well at school and having fun with his brothers.

When he entered middle school, however, he began to have school difficulties, and his grades started to drop; in retrospect, he seemed to have a learning disability with math. At thirteen, he experienced a traumatic event but said nothing to the doctors who were overseeing his medical care.

When Dr. Zeltzer met him, he was a quiet, thirteen-year-old boy who said little about himself or his life when he came for medical visits to control the pain that was causing him increasing difficulties. Gradually, over a two-year period, he told Dr. Zeltzer details of the trauma. His older brother had joined a gang and was killed in a gang-related shooting. Damien had worshipped him and blamed himself for his brother's death. Damien had telephoned his brother and asked him to come home and help him repair his bicycle. They were walking to the store to get parts for the bike when a car came by, and someone shot his brother.

Damien blamed himself because, had he not called, his brother would not have been on the street that day. Following the death, Damien began to have symptoms of anxiety and flashbacks of the shooting. He felt on the alert, was easily startled, and could not sleep at night. Tired during the day, he had even greater difficulty with schoolwork, and his grades dropped further. To make matters worse, the adrenaline that was racing through his system was increasing the pain of the sickle-cell disease.

He was also having problems with peers. Sickle-cell disease stunted his growth, and bullies at school began to tease him for being short. To escape the teasing, he began to cut school with his friends. His parents, caught up in their own grief, tried to handle Damien's problems by yelling and predicting that Damien would meet the same fate as his brother.

At this time, Damien's pain became unmanageable; he stopped taking his medications regularly, refused help from his parents, skipped his regular doctors' appointments, and began to show up in the emergency room at irregular intervals for pain-killing medications. Medical staff became concerned that he was using street drugs and gave only minimal pain medications in the emergency room. As a result, Damien ended up screaming for pain medications.

One can see how a combination of physical illness, his particular age, and, most of all, the trauma of his brother's death put Damien on a downhill course. Had he and his parents been able to talk about his brother's death, and had Damien received psychological help for his symptoms of post-traumatic stress disorder when they began, he and his parents might have been spared much psychological pain.

*Lonnie K. Zeltzer and Christina Blackett Schlank, *Conquering Your Child's Chronic Pain* (New York: HarperCollins, 2005).

A system of social support for parents and children enables everyone to cope well in the face of loss or trauma. Feeling loved and cared for helps people deal with all the extra stresses. Usually, immediate and extended family members offer the most help with emotional support and extra caregiving of children as needed. Friends often serve the same role that family members do. Groups at the family's church and work often provide enormous help in times of trouble. One couple grieving for the loss of their infant son described how grateful they were to fellow church members, who brought them dinner every night for a month.[2]

Although special support is needed at times of trauma, the basic skills important in all parenting activities—effective communication of information and feelings, and problem-solving skills—are important in dealing with traumatic situations as well.

ILLNESS

We think of childhood as a time of health and energy. Yet, more than 10 percent of children have serious or chronic illnesses.[3] The most common chronic illnesses are asthma (which is the most common and affects from 4 to 9 percent of children), diabetes, cerebral palsy, human immunodeficiency virus (HIV), cystic fibrosis (a genetic disorder involving many symptoms and daily treatments), cancer, sickle-cell disorder, juvenile rheumatoid arthritis, and hemophilia. In addition, up to 20 percent of children between the ages of five and seventeen suffer from chronic headaches, and many others from bowel and stomach pains.[4]

Illnesses differ in their symptoms, treatments, degree of pain, and life-threatening potential, but all create stress and worry and require interventions. They interrupt families' daily schedules and activities. We discuss special sources of stress for children and parents and special strategies for maintaining family closeness and effectiveness.

Sources of Stress for Children

When illness strikes, children experience discomfort and often must undergo procedures and follow routines that restrict their activities and frequently cause great pain. Stress comes from lack of knowledge and misinformation about illnesses, from anxiety and fear of what may happen, from pain and fear of it, from guilt, and from irritability at restrictions and routines that must be followed.

Children's Understanding of Their Bodies and Their Illnesses   Children do not have clear conceptions of their bodies and illnesses, and so they may not understand what is happening, or they may have upsetting misconceptions of the illness and their role in causing it.

Young children get their ideas about their bodies from colloquial expressions, from their own bodily sensations, and from time devoted to that part of the body.[5] For example, they think that nerves give you courage. One little girl thought hair was the most important part of the body because her mother spent so much time

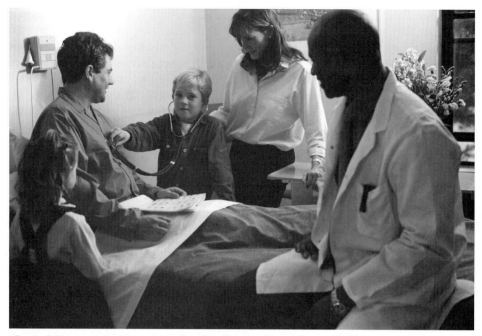

Physical illness and traumas are a family affair as all members are affected to one degree or another.

brushing it. It is wise to remember that children may hear parts of conversations about their illness and misinterpret what they hear. With increasing age, children's concepts of the body become more accurate, but their notions of how the body works remain rudimentary even in early adolescence. For example, one thirteen-year-old girl thought that lungs were in the throat and that one was for breathing and the other for eating.

Children's thoughts about illness also expand and become more detailed with age.[6] In the preschool years, children think of illness as a single symptom caused by a vague, distant thing or event, like the Sun. In these years, children sometimes think illness is caused by an immoral act—you are bad, and you get punished. As children move into the elementary school years, they see illness as several symptoms that are caused by germs, dirt, and—still—bad behavior. Direct contact with germs or dirt causes illness, and illness can be avoided if you stay away from direct contact with the cause.

Parents and health professionals must explore with children all their ideas about their physical functioning and what they think is the cause of their illness. When given accurate information in words they can understand, even children in pre-school years can develop scripts about what they must do and why in order to get over the illness or to control symptoms.

Anxiety and Fear of the Unknown   Children get anxious about shots and blood tests with which they have had experience, and about procedures they do not understand. Parents give accurate information about whether a shot will be given; they reassure the child that the pain will be brief, that it helps keep the child well, and that therefore, despite the pain, the shot or blood test serves a good purpose. When a child starts to cry, the parent can sympathetically comment that when things hurt, people cry, and it is okay to cry.

A parent can reduce a child's anxiety by encouraging the child to talk about feelings, clarifying any misconceptions, and giving the child strategies to reduce nervousness, such as slowing down breathing or focusing on other thoughts. If the child is very young, it is helpful for him or her to bring along a favorite toy or object. If a parent cannot reduce the child's anxiety, then consultation with a pediatric or clinical psychologist can be useful, for elevated anxiety can increase symptoms and obstruct healing.

Guilt   As noted, children often think that illness is a punishment for something they have or have not done, and so they feel guilty, making the illness experience even worse because they believe they have caused it themselves. Parents can be alert for any indication of such feelings and can even raise the topic in a casual way, saying, "Sometimes children believe they caused their illnesses. Do you ever feel this way?" Even if the child's behavior played a part in an accident or an injury, parents can reassure the child that everyone makes a mistake from time to time, and most often there is not such a heavy penalty. Or the parent can say that he or she knows the child did not intend to get injured. Sometimes parents are at a loss for words, as they never imagined that their child could feel responsible for the illness.

Pain   Pain is a common element of many illnesses and is stressful for children and parents. In the past, medical personnel minimized the pain that children felt, believing that it was different from adults' pain, and so they often failed to treat it effectively with medication. Since pain is a subjective experience, and very young children and some children with developmental disabilities do not have the language to express pain, it is difficult to determine how much pain a child has.

Dr. Lonnie Zeltzer, director of the Pediatric Pain Program at the University of California at Los Angeles, writes in her book for parents, "I believe that if a child complains of pain, the pain is real and the child is suffering. The job of parents and physicians is to figure out what might have started the pain and, more importantly, what is keeping the pain going. Typically the pain is continuing not because of one single thing such as torn cartilage but more commonly from an array of factors."[7] Parents work with medical personnel to plan a comprehensive pain relief program that includes medication, relaxation exercises, physical exercises, and a generally healthy lifestyle.

Anger and Irritability, Restrictions and Demands   Most illnesses limit the activities of children for varying amounts of time. Children may not be able to eat foods that all their friends eat, such as sugars, or play at certain games because grasses trigger asthma flare-ups. At the same time, they often have the frustrating demands of daily treatments or regimens. Asthmatic children must measure oxygen flow each day and take breathing treatments. Diabetic children must test their blood sugar and adjust insulin accordingly. Sometimes the procedures are painful, and all cut into time that children would rather spend elsewhere.

Parents must cope with children's resistance and also insist calmly that treatments be completed. It requires parents' organization to allow enough time for children to carry out the tasks and for monitoring to ensure completion. Parents must also keep their own emotions under control when children complain and direct their anger at the illness to parents who are there and can respond. It is difficult to listen to children's feelings and accept them while staying problem focused, but when parents do that, children usually comply once their feelings have been heard. Adolescents may have the most difficulties, even after years of compliance, because they want very much to do what their peers are doing, and because they want their independence and illness limits it.

Engaging the child in problem-solving to eliminate the most irritating aspects of the treatments helps, but parents must convey that, although they understand the child's reasons for anger, the restrictions must be followed and treatments must still be completed. When everyone in the family follows the restrictions of the ill child— if that is feasible and healthy—then the child feels less alone and less limited. For example, it is possible for everyone in the family to follow a diet very similar to the diabetic child's, with no refined sugars, limited carbohydrates (such as bread), many vegetables, and several smaller meals during the days at home. No candy is eaten at home. Brothers and sisters can have some sugary treats at school or with friends, but at home everyone eats a diet very similar to that of the person who is restricted. Further, the healthy lifestyles advised for all children with illnesses are followed by all family members. Everyone in the family joins with the ill child to the degree that is possible.

Sources of Stress for Parents and Strategies for Successful Coping

Parents' distress comes from many sources:[8]

1. Worries and uncertainties about what the illness and treatments involve and the possible lasting effects of the illness.
2. Feelings of guilt that they did not prevent and cannot cure the illness; such guilt may be intensified if the illness is a genetic one.
3. Feelings of helplessness at not having control over what is happening to their child and not being able to fix it.
4. Financial burdens from the cost of the illness and treatment.
5. Feelings of inadequacy to meet everyone's needs—the child's, their other children's, their spouse's, their own, their extended family members', the needs of the workplace.
6. Disruption of work life, the need for time off, diminished work performance.
7. Disruptions of social ties with extended family and friends.

Parents cope with all these stresses by clear and effective communication with everyone involved, expressing feelings and concerns and listening to others. They help sick children ask their questions and express their worries, and they find time to talk with other children in the family, their partners, and relatives. They try to keep pace with work demands if they can. Research indicates that it is the mother who is often the linchpin in this situation.[9] If she gets information and accepts the diagnosis, parenting stress is reduced. Fathers feel greater marital satisfaction and are more helpful and supportive. Children also feel more secure attachments to mothers when mothers accept the diagnosis.

Effective problem-solving and organization also help parents with the many extra activities involved with illness. Scheduling relatives and friends to help out with chores and provide support reduces stress. Parents must also take some time to unwind even if it is only a few minutes at the end of the day.

Other strategies to reduce the stress of illness include[10]

1. Forming a collaborative partnership with health-care providers, working as a team, sharing information and concerns, presenting the child's point of view

2. Balancing the needs of all family members, especially siblings, so that their needs are not ignored

3. Focusing on the positive aspects of the situation—the help and support given, the cooperation and caring of brothers and sisters, working together as a family

4. Emphasizing the commitment all family members feel toward the family, and helping everyone one in it do well

5. Maintaining ties to friends and extended family members

6. Being flexible with family roles and letting others take on new roles to get things done

7. Separating the illness from the child, and treating the sick child as nearly as possible like a healthy child even if the child is dying; seeing that they have chores within their capacities, go to school, and receive discipline like other children[11]

DEATH IN THE FAMILY

When a parent or child dies, nothing is the same. Although he was writing about the death of a parent, Earl Grollman's remarks apply to the death of a child as well. "Never again will the world be as secure a place as it was before. The familiar design of family life is completely disrupted."[12] Although there are differences in the ways that children and parents grieve, there are also many similarities. We touch on these first and then move on to what is unique for children and parents.

For both the child and the parent, the death of the other is "the worst loss."[13] The child has lost the figure he or she depended upon for security in life, and the parent has lost his or her central focus in life. Although the child may have been stillborn or may have lived for just a few minutes, the loss is devastating to parents, who feel they have lost their future with this child.

John Bowlby described four phases of the grief process: (1) a period of numbness, which lasts for hours or weeks, in which the person has taken in the fact of the death but has not registered it emotionally because the pain is so great; (2) a period of protest and yearning, in which the person refuses to accept the fact of the death and searches for the parent or child; (3) a period of sadness and despair, in which the reality of the death has sunk in emotionally and life without that person seems unbearable; and (4) a period of reorganization of life to go on without that person.[14]

Bowlby did not think of these as clear-cut stages but rather as a "succession of phases." It is possible to move back and forth between two phases while moving in the direction of adapting to and accepting the fact of the person's death.[15] Thus, a person can move from feeling sad to being engaged in reorganization and then back to feeling sad again. Bowlby believed it is not necessary to detach completely from the memory of the person; it is possible to reorganize your life in a meaningful way and still have a continuing sense of the dead person's presence in your life.

There is no specific length of time for grieving. Children may proceed through the phases of grief more rapidly than adults. It used to be thought that about a year was the usual length of mourning and that to be sad and grieving after a year indicated problems. Now, we realize it may take two or more years before people have reorganized their lives and are on an even emotional keel most of the time. Still, there will always be reminders and sudden experiences of intense grief. Psychological consultation is often recommended when the usual reactions to grief persist in intense ways that disrupt daily functioning. However, sometimes getting immediate professional advice eases the process of mourning and prevents the development of problems. For example, had Damien in Box 15-1 received psychological help when he first experienced fears and sleeplessness after his brother's death, he might have talked about his feelings of guilt right away and not experienced his downward spiral.

Children's Special Needs

A child's developmental level and temperament will guide what is said to the child. At the Dougy Center for Grieving Children, counselors have four guiding principles:

- Grief is a natural and expectable response to loss.
- Each individual carries within him an innate capacity to heal.
- The duration and intensity of grief is unique for each individual.
- Caring and acceptance are helpful to a person in resolving grief.[16]

Talking to Children   One must give as much accurate information as possible to children, in words they can understand.[17] Young children think of death as a reversible condition, and it is not until they are five to seven years old that they understand it is irreversible. Little children may ask when the parent or brother or sister will return. Regardless of their initial understanding, as they get older and their thinking becomes more mature, children may have new questions and new reactions they want to discuss. So, the initial explanation of the death is the beginning of conversations that will extend over the years.

Parents are sometimes told to wait for children to ask questions, but children may not know enough to ask questions at the time and only later may have the words or thoughts to which they need answers.[18] For example, for an extended period of time, a preschooler refused to go to bed after her infant sister died of SIDS because she thought she, too, would die in her sleep. She did not volunteer this information until her mother asked her what was upsetting her at bedtime.

As in dealing with illness, parents must be aware that children are prone to feel guilt and to blame themselves for the death of a loved one. One family was surprised to learn that their daughter blamed herself for her brother's death. She was not present when he died but blamed herself because she thought his death was God's punishment for not saying her prayers at night.

Ways Children's Reactions Differ from Adults'   The Dougy Center lists several ways in which children's grief differs from adults'.[19] First, children are more physical in their expressions of grief. They may want to ride a bike, shoot baskets, or run as a way to deal with grief. They also may have more physical complaints of stomachaches or headaches. Second, children are less verbal, and sometimes parents think they are not grieving because they are not talking about it. Children may use imaginative play or actions rather than words to express grief. Third, children express their anger about the death more directly and may do more quarreling or arguing or may simply express anger at everyone and life in general. Fourth, children may be more attuned to parents' needs and feelings than parents realize; as a result, they may behave in ways they think will please or help their parents. For example, if they see that their questions upset a parent, they may stop asking them even though they are still confused about the death. Fifth, children need breaks from grieving; parents may find it hard to understand that they can become immersed in an activity and not grieve. Parents misinterpret that as not caring for the dead person, but children do have the ability to live in the moment. They can grieve intensely and then happily be with friends.

Helping Children Grieve   Joan Huff, program director at the Dougy Center, believes that parents create a supportive emotional climate in which children feel it is safe to go through the process of grieving.[20] To create such a climate, she advises the following:

- In age-appropriate terms, give accurate, detailed information about the death, and answer all questions; be prepared to continue discussions in the future.

- Reassure children that the parent or parents will continue to nurture and care for them, and although the grief process may last an extended period of time, they will always be taken care of.

- "Keep your children with you, and include them in family and religious observances: viewings, funerals, burials, wakes, and the like. The question of at what age children should attend funerals comes up frequently. Talking with children, I hardly ever heard a child complain he was forced to attend a funeral against his will. Much more often, children complained that they had been sent away, excluded from this profoundly important event in their family's life."[21] If children are babies or toddlers, other relatives can hold them or supervise them. In the future, it will be valuable for them to know that they were there with the rest of the family even though they may not remember it.

- Talk to surviving children about what they want to do with their brother's or sister's or parent's possessions; parents make the final decision but get input from children.

- Express your grief in front of your children so they receive permission to grieve as well. Parents may worry that their grief will overwhelm children. Certainly in extreme form crying or sobbing can overwhelm them, so it is wise to try to strike a balance between expressing your feelings so children, too, feel free to grieve, and expressing them so intensely that children are overwhelmed and afraid.

- Structure observances of the death so that all close family members are included and have a role—lighting a candle on anniversaries, making a donation in the name of the child.

Parents' Special Needs

We all live with the assumption that we will grow up, marry, raise children, live for many years after children are grown, and then die when we have outlived our usefulness. The untimely death of a young parent or a child violates our sense of the order of life events and arouses fear that other frightening events or another untimely death can occur as well. Parents' expectations about life are dashed, and they have many of the same emotional reactions children have—anger, guilt, fear, insecurity. One father said, "When you lose a child, you lose a piece of yourself. You lose your illusions. You lose reason and predictability; all the order falls out of the universe. And you lose your future."[22] The same feelings exist when you lose your husband or wife or anyone close to you.

Parents need as much support and nurturance as their young children at this devastating time, and yet they also have the responsibility for providing and looking after other family members. So what helps them cope? Living in an emotionally safe environment with people who respect that they will grieve in their own individual way and who give them support as they find their way enables adults to get through the process of grieving.

Although there may be two parents grieving for a child, each parent is on his or her own timetable for grieving and may not be emotionally available to give support to the other when needed. In addition, they may have different temperaments and may grieve in different ways and so may not understand the other's needs. Each parent needs his or her own support network, and then both parents will have the energy to support each other.

Helpful strategies include these:[23]

- Talking to other people, sometimes in a group of people who have suffered a similar loss, such as Compassionate Friends; talking to other family members and staying connected. Expect to have to educate them about the grief process as you experience it.

- Knowing that life will not always be this painful, that you will get through this experience, that however painful it is and how many ups and downs you experience, you will survive.

- Striving for balance in your life with physical exercise, healthy eating, and little pleasures to offset the pain.

- Seeking a spiritual or broader connection to provide meaning in life; many people find help in a religious or spiritual understanding of the event; others seek meaning by becoming involved in groups to prevent the kind of tragedy that happened to them; still others find meaning and vitality to their lives by providing services to others, e.g., bringing pets or plants or services to people in nursing homes.

- Valuing what one has rather than focusing on what one has lost.

CHILD MALTREATMENT

Society has become more protective of children's well-being and in doing so has become more concerned that parents meet their responsibilities to care for children and protect their safety. Child maltreatment represents failure to protect children and to provide a healthy environment for their growth and development. Family violence and child maltreatment are traumatic to children, more traumatic than community and national disaster and violence, because the violence occurs at the hands of the very individuals who were expected to protect the child. So, in addition to the pain or damage of the abuse itself, the child experiences a great loss of trust in parents and authority in general, which cannot be easily restored. In this section, we look first at a bioecological view of abuse, then at the definitions, incidence, and prevalence of maltreatment, factors that place families at high risk for maltreatment, the problems children experience as a result of such experiences, and finally forms of intervention and prevention.

Dante Cicchetti and Michael Lynch propose an ecological/transactional model to describe how the child's environment interacts with the characteristics of the caregiver and the child to shape the child's level of risk and development subsequent to abuse.[24] They also refer to risk factors that increase the possibility of negative outcomes and protective factors that buffer children from the impact of negative events.

Risk factors and protective factors exist at the cultural, community, family, and individual levels of experience. Using Urie Bronfenbrenner's ecological model (presented in Chapter 2), the researchers describe the *macrosystemic* cultural beliefs that contribute to abuse—for example, that physical force is an acceptable way to settle differences, that children are property and one can spank them if one wishes, that sexual gratification is a sign of manliness.

At the *exosystemic level,* community factors such as the absence of supervised play areas and recreational activities for children, and the social isolation of poor neighborhoods, contribute to increased risk for abuse. Community factors interact with individual characteristics to increase risk.

Factors at the community level can interact with factors at the family level. For example, a neighborhood with high unemployment and drug addiction may have a higher rate of violent crime than a less stressed community; the prevalence of violent crime can in turn add to the distress of an unemployed father, who then becomes more physically punishing with his son. Unemployed parents lack the resources to move out of such neighborhoods and must deal with the ongoing frustrations that interfere with their parenting.

Children also experience violence at the *microsystemic level* in daily interactions with siblings, parents, peers, and teachers. Parents and children alike bring their individual characteristics to these interactions. Parents who maltreat children have their own difficult pasts, as we shall see. They tend to form unstable, conflicted adult-adult relationships,[25] and they interact with children in many negative ways besides the actual abuse. Children's individual characteristics also can influence the likelihood of abuse, as we shall see.

Finally, children experience violence at the *ontogenic level*—that is, in how they develop as individuals. Cicchetti and Lynch identify five areas that may be problematic for children's development following abuse: the attachment relationship with the parent, the regulation of emotion, the self-concept, peer relationships, and adaptation to school and learning.

The model developed by Cicchetti and Lynch also has implications for interventions that can help families and provide protective factors for them. First, there are interventions at the microsystemic level, with the individual and the family, that can provide positive protective factors: helping them deal with the situation, the feelings that arise from it, and the problems that ensue.

Then, there are interventions at the exosystemic level: helping parents and children reach out to social agencies and social structures, such as schools and community organizations, to get support to enable the family to cope. Community and state agencies offer a variety of programs to train parents in anger management, stress reduction, and effective disciplinary techniques. Such agencies seek to preserve the family by meeting its many needs for such services as financial and household management, help in finding employment, and treatment for alcohol abuse.

Community agencies also identify high-risk parents who, because of their own characteristics (for example, substance abuse) or characteristics of their children (physical conditions that make care difficult), need special services to prevent possible abuse.[26] These agencies provide, often in the home, training and modeling in appropriate caregiving and help parents adopt effective problem-solving skills.

Finally, there are interventions at the macrosystemic level: changing the societal views of violence and sexuality that permit victimization of children. Although this is a complicated process, giving all parents training in effective caregiving and child-rearing strategies makes abuse less likely.[27]

Definitions

Table 15-1 presents the number of cases of maltreatment reported to government agencies and substantiated through investigation in 2003, along with the forms of maltreatment and the ages and sexes of children who were maltreated. In 2000, 2,000 children died as a result of maltreatment.[28] It is estimated that 90 percent of abusers are parents.[29] This is not surprising, since 80 percent of the cases involve physical abuse and neglect, and parents are the primary providers of daily care.

Definitions of maltreatment are difficult because we do not have an agreed-upon code of acceptable parental care and discipline, so it is hard to define when a parent's behavior is unacceptable. In addition, cultural and ethnic differences exist within our country regarding "acceptable" discipline. Immigrants from other countries have cultural traditions that include hitting harder and hitting with objects; parents who cannot give up these traditions are more likely to be reported as abusive, although they would not be considered such in their countries of origin.

■ **TABLE 15-1**
VICTIMS OF CHILD MALTREATMENT IN 2003

Total number of reports: 1,576,000 involving 2,900,000 children	
Number of reports substantiated:	897,168
Neglect	61%
Physical abuse	19%
Sexual abuse	10%
Emotional abuse	5%
Medical neglect	2%
Sex of victims:	
Boys:	48%
Girls	52%
Age of victims:	
One and under	16%
2 to 5	25%
6 to 9	22%
10 to 13	21%
14 to 18	15%

U.S. Bureau of the Census, *Statistical Abstract of the United States: 2006*, 125th ed. (Washington, DC: United States Government Printing Office, 2005).

Definitions are difficult also because abusive behaviors have legal definitions and consequences, and the legal definitions are not the same as those used by health-care professionals and treatment providers.[30] Certainly, there is agreement about the extremes of behavior. We have clear ideas of sensitive, effective parenting, and we know that abuse has occurred when bones are broken, when children are sexually penetrated by adults, or when a young child plays unsupervised next to the railroad tracks. But as one moves toward the dividing line that separates abusive behavior from inappropriate behavior, the definitions are not so clear cut. Further, what is appropriate for a child of one age may be abusive at another age—e.g., it is neglect to leave a four-year-old at home alone, but not a fourteen-year-old.

Douglas Besharov, the first director of the National Center for Child Abuse and Neglect, has recommended reforms to achieve clearer, more specific definitions of the parenting behaviors that constitute abuse and therefore require reporting.[31] At present, laws are so vague, and so many reports are made, that endless hours go into investigating cases that turn out not to involve abuse or neglect. Once laws are clarified, professionals who make reports can be trained to make them more accurately. Reports should be screened carefully so that all are acted upon appropriately, and, finally, reporting individuals and agencies need feedback about their accuracy. Such clarity will not eliminate abuse and death from abuse, but without it, we will not make advances in eliminating abuse.

Dante Cicchetti and Sheree Toth[32] define four major areas of abuse:

Physical abuse: the infliction of bodily injury on a child by other than accidental means
Sexual abuse: sexual contact or attempted sexual contact between a caregiver or other responsible adult and a child for purposes of the caregiver's gratification
Neglect: the failure to provide minimum care and the lack of appropriate supervision
Emotional maltreatment: persistent and extreme thwarting of a child's basic emotional needs.

Other forms of abuse to the child are *moral-legal-educational maltreatment,* which involves failure to help the child develop appropriate moral and social values, e.g., involving the child in selling drugs,[33] and *domestic or family violence,* which is included as a form of abuse because, although the violence is directed to another party, children are traumatized by it, and exposure to it affects their behavior.[34] Further, a review of several studies reveals that 40 to 70 percent of children living in violent homes were physically abused, and 40 percent of physically abused children live in violent homes. The term *exposure* (to domestic or family violence) is used rather than *witness* to include children who hear the violence, see the effects of the violence, or are involved in interrupting the violence by calling the police. Although exposure to family violence refers to violence between adults, one suspects that children who are exposed to the parent-child abuse of a sibling suffer many of the same problems.

Prevalence

Incidence figures as reported in Table 15-1 report the number of new cases in a year. Prevalence figures report the total number of people who have had such experiences.

There are no statistics on the prevalence of family violence, but it is estimated that between 3 and 10 million children are exposed to it, beginning in utero.[35] Sixteen percent of women questioned in prenatal clinics reported abuse, by their spouses, and half of them reported several incidents.

Determining the incidence and prevalence of sexual abuse in childhood is extremely difficult, as the acts are taboo and most are not reported. In a sample of 1,800 college students, one-third of men *and* women reported experiencing sexual abuse in childhood. Only half of the women and a tenth of the men had reported the incident to an adult. Estimates are that one in four girls and one in six boys have experienced some form of sexual abuse by age eighteen.[36]

Diana Russell interviewed a random sample of San Francisco women concerning childhood sexual abuse.[37] Her definition of abuse included only actual sexual contact, not exhibitionism. She found that, by the age of eighteen, 16 percent of women had been abused by family members and 31 percent by a person outside the family, for a total of 38 percent of 930 women who reported at least one event. Only 2 percent of intrafamilial abuse and 6 percent of extrafamilial abuse were reported to police.

Although 3 million reports are made each year to agencies regarding all forms of abuse, self-reports of punishment and physical abuse by parents themselves are higher. In a 1985 national telephone survey, the caregivers for 60 percent of children reported that they used physical punishment and minor violence (pushing, grabbing, shoving, and slapping) with children. The caregivers for 10 percent of children reported one or more instances of physical abuse or severe violence, consisting of kicking, biting, hitting with a fist or object, or burning. Had the caregivers of 10 percent of children been reported, there would be 6 million children who are physically abused in this country.[38]

Although neglect is the most frequent form of abuse, accurate statistics on its prevalence are lacking. Similar figures are lacking for emotional and moral-legal-educational maltreatment. Emotional abuse is thought, however, to accompany most other forms of abuse.

Common Threads and Common Effects

When research was first carried out on families and children who were abused, the search was for single factors that led to each kind of abuse and for the specific problem that resulted from the abuse.[39] Although we distinguish the major forms of abuse listed above, they are not so much separate problems as several different ways children experience violence and trauma in a family setting. In fact, children often experience two or more different forms of abuse or two or more different episodes of the same form of abuse—recall from Chapter 6 that, in a sample of teen mothers, 60 percent of those sexually abused once were abused by several perpetrators in their growing-up years.[40] In a study of 160 adolescents who had been sexually abused, 20 percent experienced four other forms of abuse as well; 36 percent experienced three other kinds of abuse in addition to the sexual abuse, and only 6 percent of the sample had experienced only sexual abuse.[41] The search more recently has been for all the factors that put the family at risk for abuse.

In looking for common threads in maltreatment, it is important to recall that some abuse is experienced outside the home with strangers. The child's family may have done all the correct things to reduce the possibility of maltreatment, yet it occurred—perhaps at a reliable baby-sitter's or on the school grounds. To the extent that maltreatment comes through that route and neglect is not involved, then there are no family risk factors.

Children respond to trauma in many ways, and several different kinds of trauma lead to similar problems in children. For example, all forms of abuse are associated with difficulties in emotional control, in relationships with adults and with peers, in self-concept, and in school adjustment.[42] Further, the problems resemble those seen in children under stress, for example, when their parents divorce or lose their jobs. Sexualized behavior seems to be the one form of reaction that is most frequently linked to sexual abuse, but many sexually abused children do not show such behavior.

A common response in some children who experience either maltreatment or some form of disaster is post-traumatic stress disorder (PTSD).[43] The symptoms have been described in terms of adults' reactions to stress and their ability to verbalize their reactions, and have to be translated to fit children's level of development and their reactions. PTSD refers to a cluster of reactions that follow exposure to an unusual, threatening stress that arouses fear, helplessness, and horror in a person. The person suffers from repetitive recollections of the event, dreams about it, or relives it—in children, the repetitive themes can occur in play. There is also a cluster of symptoms around feeling numb, lack of interest in usual activities, avoidance of activities or thoughts that serve as reminders of the stress, feeling dissociated and detached from the events yet at the same time feeling a sense of a shortened future. The person also experiences heightened emotional arousal, along with difficulty sleeping, concentrating, being startled easily, irritability, and feeling on alert for another disaster. A diagnosis is not made until the person has had such symptoms for more than a month.

Research attention to individual responses to abuse continues, however, because even in a fairly narrowly defined form of abuse, children's responses can differ widely depending on the frequency of the event, the perpetrator, and the actions that followed disclosure.[44] For example, in a group of girls who, between ages six and sixteen, experienced within the family sexual abuse involving genital contact or penetration, responses differed, depending on the frequency of the abuse and whether the family member was the biological father or a nonbiological father-figure such as a stepfather or mother's boyfriend. So, parents must always pay attention to how their child experienced and reacted to the event.

Because maltreatment occurs more frequently in families of low socioeconomic status, a question arises as to whether abuse and violence contribute significant difficulties beyond those related to low income or negative life stress. A recent study statistically disentangled the contributions of physical abuse, low income, and life stress.[45] Indeed, physical abuse made a significant contribution to children's behavior problems beyond that related to economic disadvantage and stress as a result of negative life events.

Physical abuse was associated with additional problems in relationships with peers, and peer problems occurred after physical abuse, regardless of the sex, socioeconomic status, or stress level of the abused person. The abusive experience in the family appears to lead to distortions in how people relate to each other and what is required to get along. As noted earlier, this is especially sad because children then lose a major source of support in coping with their problems. Other stressors, such as low income and negative life events, produce few changes in self-perceptions or behavior problems unless they are unusually severe. Therefore, other difficulties in life appear to produce less marked changes in children's moods and behaviors. Abuse and violence damage children's trust in their parents and their peers and decrease their capacity for positive relationships, thus removing an important resource for such children.

Factors That Place Families at High Risk for Maltreatment

There are three general kinds of risk factors for child maltreatment.[46] First is the social context in which the family lives. Maltreatment is more likely to occur in poor families of low socioeconomic status, as just noted. As more Native American, African American, and Latina/o families are living below the poverty level, these groups have higher reports of child maltreatment. The majority of poor people do not abuse their children, but lack of resources for essential goods and services and living in neighborhoods with higher rates of crime and violence and fewer services increase parents' stress, which in turn can make parents more likely to act impulsively.

A second set of predisposing factors includes the stresses of everyday life—difficulties or layoffs at work, conflicts with spouse or neighbors—that increase parental stress and make it harder to be patient and calm in dealing with the demands that the average child makes. When you are worried about how you are going to buy groceries for dinner, it is hard to be patient and supportive when a child spills a quart of milk.

A third set of predisposing factors is the personal qualities parents bring to parenting. Recall the three basic qualities Christophe Heinicke described in Chapter 6 as making up the optimal parenting environment: parents' self-esteem and self-confidence, their positive relationships with partners and their extended family, and their problem-solving skills.[47] Parents in homes where maltreatment occurs have fewer of these qualities.

Between 25 and 40 percent of abusing parents were themselves abused, so their self-confidence, their networks of positive relationships, and their problem-solving skills are diminished.[48] They have many of the problems we describe as responses to abuse. They are often angry, depressed, and worried, and often form partnerships with people like themselves. Most parents who have been abused do not abuse their children (we look at what prevents this in the section on prevention), but a sizable portion continue the vicious cycle: the experience of maltreatment and violence, which leads to hostile, depressive reactions, which result in repetition of the maltreatment with their own children.

People who have been abused come to parenting with few models of positive parent-child interactions. They come to parenting with unrealistic expectations of children and what is required to meet their needs, and they often misinterpret the meanings of children's behavior.[49] For example, one mother of a toddler thought the child was clingy and dependent because he kept approaching her to show her his discoveries and see her reactions. She kept urging him to get away and play on his own. Contrast that with the responses of professional parents described in Chapter 2, who gave excited, positive verbal feedback to their toddlers every other minute, encouraging them to explore, to talk, to engage.

Because of their unrealistically high expectations, maltreating parents express less satisfaction with their children, and they use more disciplinary techniques than do nonmaltreating parents. Because such parents are often inconsistent, children learn to resist their directives, becoming involved in the coercive cycle Gerald Patterson and his coworkers describe in Chapter 2. When parents face problems with children, they have fewer problem-solving skills for dealing with them, perhaps because they are depressed and withdrawn, and perhaps because of substance abuse issues.

Substance abuse issues are a major contributor to all forms of abuse.[50] In a review of studies, substance and alcohol abuse figured in 80 to 90 percent of the cases of physical abuse and neglect. Substance abuse is considered a major risk factor for sexual abuse. And it is also a major reason for having children removed from the home.

The social networks of maltreating parents are smaller, and they feel more isolated. They often have marital problems or are single parents, and so they cannot turn to partners for support. They have fewer social supports. They are not connected to organizations or social groups, and so they have no friends who can help them or even offer a few encouraging words to get a parent through the day.

Specific risk factors for sexual abuse within a family are one or more of the following factors:

1. An alcoholic, domineering, and violent father
2. A mother who is away from home, physically ill, depressed, or passive
3. An older daughter who has had to act as a surrogate mother (doing most of the chores, caring for younger siblings or for her father)
4. Parents who have failed to establish a satisfying sexual relationship
5. Fathers and daughters who spend much time alone with each other
6. Any condition, such as psychosis or below-average intelligence, that reduces an individual's capacity for self-control
7. Previous incest in either parent's family
8. A romantic attachment, with an unusual amount of physical affection between adult and child[51]

A final set of risk factors for maltreatment concerns the child's qualities. Children who require highly skilled parenting because of prematurity, medical problems, disability, or difficult and overactive temperament put a highly stressed family at risk for neglect or abuse. The family does not have the resources, either financial or emotional, to deal with yet another source of stress and demand. In fact, even a colicky baby can tax the patience of highly educated parents with many resources, and many professionals report that one of the eye-opening experiences of parenthood has been how angry, frustrated, and helpless they can feel when confronted for hours with a crying baby.

It is important to emphasize, as we move to children's reactions and problems in response to abuse, that most poor people and most parents who have been abused do not maltreat their children. As we look at ways to intervene and prevent maltreatment, we describe how parents exit the vicious cycle of abuse and repetition of abuse.

Children's Responses to Maltreatment

Parents will better understand children's reactions when they are aware of the many changes associated with abuse in childhood.[52] First, there are biological changes; differences in the regulation of endocrine secretions and the startle response suggest disturbances in the biological arousal system that are present years after the abuse occurred. Other neurobiological changes suggest difficulties in memory and learning. These changes underlie and may help to explain children's chronic difficulties with nervousness, fear, and poor academic work.

Second, self-blame may play a role in continuing difficulties.[53] The more adolescents blame themselves, the more serious the behavior changes. Even though adolescents, and probably children as well, assign the perpetrator primary responsibility for the abuse, the majority of victims of all kinds of abuse consider that they, too, deserve blame because they did not prevent or avoid the abuse. Blaming oneself and feeling ashamed intensify feelings of depression and withdrawal that continue on into adulthood.

Changes in behavior are associated with the severity of the abuse and the age at which it occurred as well as the identity of the perpetrator. Some research suggests that the earlier the abuse occurred and the longer it lasted, the more behavioral effects are seen.[54] Those who experienced abuse in infancy and toddlerhood still showed differences in behavior from nonmaltreated children in the school years, and those abused in preschool were especially prone to developing aggressive and bullying behavior in the school years. The speculation is that ongoing stress is more disorganizing to the individual in periods in which the person is developing an understanding of the world and refining basic ways of relating to people. Still, abuse in childhood and adolescence is associated with many behavior changes as well.

Neglect   Less is known about the development of children who have been neglected. Physical and medical problems are often associated with neglect; half of the deaths in swimming pools are attributed to lack of appropriate supervision. Neglected children have a greater likelihood of attachment problems, low self-esteem, increased dependency, and anger, compared with physically abused and nonmaltreated children.[55] As they enter school, they have academic problems as well as emotional and social problems. They are passive and withdrawn, and with time are at risk for rule-breaking behavior.

Physical Maltreatment   Parental maltreatment very often results in a disoriented/disorganized form of attachment, in which the child happily approaches the parent on some occasions and at other times avoids the parent. Such attachments occur in as many as 80 percent of maltreated children and appear stable for at least a year. The attachment provides neither a secure base for exploration nor a positive inner working model of relationships in which the infant sees the self as lovable and worthy of care and protection and approaches others with the expectation of a loving response.[56]

When maltreatment occurs early in life and continues, children have great difficulty in understanding others' reactions and ways of thinking, and they find it hard to understand others' points of view.[57] As preschoolers, they have a more negative view of themselves and their relationships with their mothers, and they begin to be aggressive.[58] Children who are exposed to family violence are observed to be inattentive, less verbal, and more physically distant, and to have less positive affect in their interactions with mothers, even though many mothers are warm and try to be good parents.[59] Mothers do not seem to see these behaviors as difficulties, perhaps because they are not aware that other children respond in a more positive way with mothers.

As maltreated children enter school, they can have difficulties with emotional control, in part because their feelings are intense and in part because they do not have appropriate ways of expressing them verbally.[60] They may express their feelings in aggressive, demanding behaviors or in silent retreats from others. In either way, they are more likely to have peer problems because they do not have good control of their feelings. Because of their intense feelings, it will also be harder for them to focus and concentrate on schoolwork, so they may develop academic problems.

Sexual Abuse   The impact of sexual abuse depends very much on the child and the specific circumstances of the abuse—the nature, duration, and frequency of the physical contact and the identity of the perpetrator. Further, it is difficult to disentangle the effects of the family conflict prior to the abuse, the abuse itself, and the events around the disclosure of the abuse. A broad review of studies[61] suggests that sexual abuse that is likely to produce a greater number of symptoms involves (1) a close relationship with the perpetrator; (2) sexual acts of oral, anal, or vaginal penetration; (3) frequent occurrences; (4) a long duration; and (5) lack of maternal support at the time of disclosure. These separate aspects of abuse, however, are related to one another. A close family member often has greater opportunity for frequent contact with the victim over a long period of time.

Sexually abused children report many different symptoms following the abuse; no one symptom characterizes the majority of sexually abused children.[62] The most frequently reported symptoms are fears, nightmares, sexualized behaviors (sexualized play with dolls or toys, putting things in the vagina or anus, public or inappropriate masturbation) that suggest sexual stimulation from adults or peers, depression, aggression, withdrawal, school problems, poor self-esteem, acting out, regression of behavior, and symptoms of post-traumatic stress (reliving the experience, dread of dire consequences to the victim).

Preschoolers most often report fears, nightmares, sexualized behaviors, withdrawal, and aggressive and uncontrolled behaviors. School-age children report all these symptoms as well as school problems, hyperactivity, and regressive behaviors. Adolescents most often report depression, suicidal acting out, anger, running away, and antisocial behavior. Depression is the most commonly reported symptom in adults who have been sexually abused.

Between one-third and one-half of children who have been sexually abused report no symptoms initially.[63] These may be the children who experienced the least damaging abuse or received the most supportive response at the time of disclosure, and they may be the most resilient children. It is possible, however, that they have suppressed their feelings and may experience difficulties later. Evidence from longitudinal work suggests that between 10 and 24 percent of children report an increasing number of symptoms over a two-year period. In most cases, though, symptoms decrease over an eighteen-month period, with fears, nightmares, and anxiety disappearing first and anger and aggressiveness with peers and siblings tending to remain longer.

Children who experienced sexual abuse involving genital contact with family members are at risk for ongoing problems.[64] Children who had such experiences between the ages of six and sixteen years of age, who were assessed within six months of the abuse and followed up seven years later, had problems in several areas. Girls who were abused by their biological fathers over a long period of time had the greatest number of problems with aggressive, rule-breaking behavior and feelings of depression, anxiety, and low competence. Those girls who experienced abuse over a brief period of time by a single perpetrator who was not the biological father had fewer problems six months after the abuse than they did seven years later, when they, too, had feelings of depression and anxiety and were aggressive and noncompliant.

Many girls who have been sexually abused have been required to testify in court against the perpetrators, and their stress levels have increased.[65] To reduce such stress, children are now allowed in some courts to testify in another room, from which they cannot see the perpetrator, and their testimony is televised in court. The effects on the child in the short and long run depend very much on the circumstances of the abuse, the child's age and characteristics, and the legal proceedings and final disposition of the case.

Domestic and Family Violence   Children show a range of reactions to family violence, depending on their age and temperament, the specific nature of the violence, its severity and chronicity, and their involvement in it.[66] Children's emotional responses to the events include terror, fear of death, and fear of loss of the parent. As a result of the violence, children may experience the world as a hostile, unpredictable place where disaster may strike suddenly.

Children suffer other symptoms as well. Compared with children from nonviolent homes, children exposed to domestic violence are at higher risk for physical symptoms of insomnia, nightmares, tics, and bed-wetting.[67] They are more likely to have increased externalizing behavior problems (aggressiveness, temper tantrums, fighting with peers) and increased internalizing problems (anxiety, fear, depression, loss of self-esteem). The problems begin early; preschool children are observed to have distance and lack of positive relationships with mothers prior to reports of problem behaviors with others. Mothers appear warm, trying to compensate for family violence; they do not consider their children's behavior a problem, but trained observers find that the children pay less attention, stay physically distant from mothers, and are less positive in their interactions with her. In addition to peer problems, children from homes with family violence also score lower on measures of verbal, motor, and cognitive skills and have poorer concentration and attention for schoolwork.

Before leaving this topic, it is important to emphasize that, despite the abuse they experience, a sizable number of maltreated children develop competence and caring and are resilient and resourceful in surmounting problems. The most competent and best-functioning children are those who have developed ego control, ego resilience, and self-esteem.[68] The capacity for a more reserved, controlled, and rational way of interacting with others predicts overall competence in maltreated children. In a follow-up study of adults abused as children, 22 percent of the abused sample were doing well in major areas of life—education, work history, lack of psychiatric symptoms and criminal record.[69] Still, that figure was about half the number (40 percent) of the nonmaltreated adults who were doing well in these same areas.

Interventions and Prevention

The first step in intervention is to ensure the safety of the maltreated child. This can take several forms. In violent families at risk for imminent harm, it may mean getting the nonabusive parent and children to a shelter. In physically and sexually abusive families, it may mean removing the abusive family member from the family, or it may mean out-of-home placement for the child in the event that there is no other parent or relative to care for the child. Out-of-home placement can be with relatives or family friends known to the child, or it can be in foster care with strangers. The out-of-home care can last for weeks, months, or years and may be episodic throughout childhood for some children.

Although studies reveal that foster care has potential benefit for the children it serves (see more detailed discussion of foster care in Chapter 14), a small[70] but carefully controlled study suggests that out-of-home placement with strangers may place an extra layer of stress on children already under emotional siege.[71]

Once safety is established for family members, then home visitation programs, parenting programs, and psychotherapy can be instituted to prevent abuse or to help children and families cope with the many effects of maltreatment.[72] Home visitation programs can help young mothers who lack resources to provide adequate care for children. One program, which followed high-risk families from pregnancy to the child's fifteenth birthday, found that regular nurse visits during pregnancy and the first two years of life resulted in less maltreatment in these homes and, when maltreatment occurred, fewer problem behaviors in children. The nurse was able to form a relationship with the mother, give information on early child development and care, and connect the mother to other resources.

The relationship formed with the mothers seems critical. In two studies of treatment for abusing mothers—mothers of infants and mothers of preschool children—mothers received home visits and counseling that focused on either (1) the transmission of parenting information and skill building or (2) helping mothers build positive mother-child attachments by means of infant- or preschooler-mother psychotherapy. In the latter form of visit, the focus was on helping mothers to see connections between their past and present relationships with others and their way of relating to their children in the present. The therapists were supportive and respectful with mothers, hoping to give mothers new experiences in ways to relate to others. Therapists also focused on expanding mothers' sensitivity, responsiveness, and skills in granting autonomy to children.

Both kinds of visits, lasting about an hour and a half and occurring each week for a year, had significant impacts. In the study of infants, the percentage of infants with secure attachments in the infant-mother psychotherapy group rose from 3.6 to 61 at the end of the year; in the psychoeducational group, there was a similar increase, from 0 percent secure attachments to 54 percent secure attachments.[73] Secure attachments in the control maltreated group, who received community services, increased from 0 percent to 1.9 percent. The study indicated that attachment did not need to be the focus of the home visits in order for attachment classification to change. Further, the study showed that interventions could reverse the effects of maltreatment and perhaps interrupt the persistent course of problems that could be expected without intervention.

When mothers of preschoolers received the intensive parent psychotherapy sessions for a year, their preschoolers decreased their negative views of themselves and their parents and increased their positive views of themselves.[74] Although those preschoolers whose mothers received parenting information and skill-building and self-care strategies made similar kinds of changes, they were not so marked as those seen in the families who received the psychotherapy sessions. Families in the educational groups made changes that were not as marked as those in the psychotherapy group.

Positive relationships appear to be critical to breaking the cycle of maltreatment and ongoing social-emotional problems. In the Minnesota study (see Chapter 14), it was possible to follow the children into adulthood and look at those adults abused as children who did not continue this pattern, to determine what helped them avoid it.[75] Researchers looked at the 30 percent of the sample who provided good care to their infants, and compared them with the 40 percent who abused their children (30 percent of abused children provided borderline care). Three kinds of positive relationships helped young adults escape the cycle of abuse. Mothers who had emotionally supportive relationships with an adult outside the family or who received emotional support in psychotherapy did not abuse their infants. The third form of positive relationship was with a partner in adulthood. None of these factors were found in the lives of mothers who continued the abuse. Nonabusing mothers also tended to have come to terms with their childhood experiences of abuse and to have been able to form an integrated sense of self.

So, the main forms of helpful intervention are (1) providing increased emotional support for mothers and families to prevent abuse, (2) helping mothers establish more positive attachments with children, and (3) helping children find activities and relationships that give them more positive views of themselves. Psychotherapy can be supportive and helpful in directing children and families to form new patterns of relationships.

COMMUNITY AND NATIONAL DISASTERS

In this section, we discuss violence and disaster at both the community level and the national level. It is an unfortunate fact that many children have experienced, or are likely to experience, some form of severely traumatic event outside the home.

Community Violence

We have seen that, in any form, exposure to unresolved anger and aggression harms children, whether they witness it or experience it. Children do not face aggression only in their personal lives. Our society has become increasingly violent, and many children are exposed to traumatic events. Although a large proportion of violence occurs in areas of lower socioeconomic status, people are exposed to violence in restaurants, schools, and middle-class communities. No child is immune to the effects of community violence. Even if it does not touch a child personally, he or she may be acquainted with someone whose family member has died or experienced harm from violence.

Prevalence   Children are more likely to witness violence outside the home than to experience it. In a study in a low-income, moderately violent neighborhood in Washington, D.C., 19 percent of children in grades one and two had been physically threatened, chased, mugged, or shot, and 61 percent had witnessed such acts as muggings, stabbings, and illegal drug use not once but several times per year.[76] By grades five and six, 32 percent of children had been victims, and 72 percent had witnessed violence.

When questioned, older children reported that none of the victimizations took place at home. Nonetheless, 48 percent occurred near home, and 55 percent took place at or near school. Thus, the violence the children witnessed took place in their immediate environment. Although it occurred outside the home, children knew about two-thirds of the perpetrators; the rest were strangers to them.

Similar results are found in surveys conducted in Miami, Baltimore, and Detroit and in rural areas as well, so exposure to violence occurs in all parts of the country.[77] The effects of exposure are intensified if the child's family contains a great deal of conflict as well.

Parents report that their children experience or witness less violence than the children report. However, children may not tell parents all they see. Anecdotal reports suggest that parents may discourage children from talking about the violence they see.[78] This is unfortunate in that it prevents children from dealing with their feelings and parents from helping their children cope with the violence.

Effects on Children   Children exposed to community violence develop many of the symptoms of children who have been physically or sexually abused. They have difficulty sleeping, remembering, and concentrating, and they exhibit anxious attachment to parents (not wanting them to leave), aggressive play, severe limitation of activities and exploration, and regressive behavior.[79] Lenore Terr describes the denial and numbing children use to block out frightening reality.[80]

Children also experience feelings of grief and loss when a significant loved one dies as a result of violence.

All these reactions make it hard for children to develop intellectually and socially. They come to expect violence and develop a sense of fatalism about their lives, a feeling that they have no future. They believe that planning is unimportant because they could be crippled or killed before their plans are fulfilled.

Even in adverse circumstances, a significant number of children function well at school and appear to have few behavior problems. Such children are active individuals who seek to surmount obstacles. The main agent for helping them is their family and the stability it provides.[81] A second source of help is their own internal sense that life can improve, that they can influence what happens to them and make life better in the future.[82] Children who live in difficult circumstances but still maintain positive expectations of the future are more successful later on. But again, the immediate family members do the most to help children build positive expectations about the future. James Garbarino and his colleagues summarize the parents' role and its dangers:

> If parents, or other significant caregivers, can sustain a strong attachment to their children, can maintain a positive sense of self, and can have access to basic resources, children will manage, although it may be at great cost to the psychic and physical welfare of those parents, who may be "used up" caring for their children.[83]

Coping Resources   Several factors influence how children cope with violence.[84] Intelligence, self-confidence, self-esteem, sociability, an easygoing attitude, and an affectionate nature all increase children's coping ability. Such children demand little, yet they relate positively and happily to others and tend to receive support. Environmental factors include the presence of at least one stable emotional relationship with a caregiver who serves as a model of coping, as well as social relationships outside the family with relatives and family friends. The community can give support in many ways; friends, neighbors, teachers, and members of religious groups can provide support and encourage the competence of parents and children.

School is a major refuge for children who confront difficult experiences. After the family, school is the most important social institution in children's lives. Many resilient children find a source of self-esteem and competence in school activities. They make friends with and get support from schoolmates and from teachers who take an interest in them.

In *Children in Danger,* James Garbarino and his associates describe the schools as a major unit of intervention to counteract the community violence in children's lives.[85] He outlines a school-based intervention program in which teachers form close emotional attachments with students to promote their development. The researchers believe that these relationships serve as the basis for learning in all areas. Teachers and programs provide structure and control for these children, who adopt the values, behavior, and attitudes of a significant other person.

In Garbarino's plan, day-care centers can be included in programs to reach children below school age. An attachment teacher is assigned to every six or seven students, and a consistent substitute attachment and subgroup are assigned to each child. Children have an unvarying placement in small groups. Formal teaching programs stimulate the child's curiosity and level of development.

The organized school environment, with familiar teachers and programs, provides security and predictability in a changing world. By taking courses in child development and in understanding children's reactions to stress, violence, and loss, teachers are specially trained to work with these children. Teachers remain available to students who exhibit fluctuating or changing emotions and help the children deal with them.

Therapy can help children cope with their emotional reactions to trauma.[86] All major personality shifts resulting from trauma require treatment. Such personality changes occur in almost all physically and sexually abused children, as well as those who experience some form of trauma.

Parents should arrange for psychiatric treatment for a child as soon after a trauma as possible. If several children are involved, participants can be seen in a mini-marathon group session with a highly trained professional. When each member shares his or her experiences, the possibility of anyone's denying the situation (and thus prolonging traumatization) is lessened. Schools serve as familiar settings appropriate for such group sessions. If a family has been traumatized, then it can be treated as a unit. However, family therapy is not recommended when a parent has physically or sexually abused a child, because the child is not really free to express anger in the presence of the abuser.

Behavioral therapy is useful for children who have developed fears as a result of the trauma. Deconditioning can supplement individual treatment designed to deal with the emotional reactions, but behavioral therapy by itself is limited.

A person should begin treatment as soon as possible after the trauma. However, treatment is useful any time a person recognizes that he or she is suffering the effects of a trauma, even if therapy cannot reverse all the effects of the experience.

Parents want to know what to do to prevent violence and trauma in their children's lives. Working to create safe neighborhoods and to obtain support from community agencies can decrease violence. Although violence is difficult to eradicate, children who receive support are most likely to recover from the experience.

Natural Disasters Such as Hurricanes

In our country, we have seen the devastating effects of powerful hurricanes on the southern coast of the United States, and there is reason to think that we are in a phase of weather cycles or changes which will produce a continuation of such disasters.[87] In 2005, Hurricane Katrina damaged large sections of several Southern states, killed thousands of people, and upended the lives of hundreds of thousands of individuals and their families. Survivors are scattered around the country; although many will get their lives back together, it will take individuals, communities, and state agencies years to rebuild the structure of life as they knew it there.

Natural disasters vary in their predictability, and unpredictability increases stress. Hurricanes can be anticipated and sometimes escaped, but earthquakes and tornadoes are sudden and unpredictable. Even when predicted, the unprecedented damage of Hurricane Katrina was not planned for, and the country saw the anguished faces of families seeking safety or seeking loved ones whose whereabouts were unknown.

The effects of a natural disaster depend on its duration, which is usually short lived in comparison to abuse or community violence, which may be ongoing, and on the amount of damage it wreaks. In general, in the first year after the disaster, moderate to severe symptoms of post-traumatic stress disorder (PTSD) are found in 30 to 50 percent of children who experience the effects of the disaster. PTSD symptoms experienced after disasters more often include reexperiencing the event and having intrusive thoughts, and less often include numbing and avoidance of the topic. Long-term follow-ups of children are few, but generally symptoms decrease after the first year. Children who had problems prior to the disaster are more likely to have more serious problems after the disaster or to find their own difficulties intensified by the disaster.

The same kinds of interventions for community violence are useful for reactions following disasters: school programs that help children process events, help them normalize their reactions of immediate distress, and give creative outlets for expression of feelings. If schools are not in session, such programs can be carried out at community centers.

Massage therapy was found to be helpful in reducing elementary school children's feelings of anxiety and depression following Hurricane Andrew in Florida.[88] Children who reported many symptoms of PTSD were assigned either to receive back massages twice weekly for thirty minutes or to a control group who watched a video while sitting on the lap of a research assistant for the same amount of time. Children who received massages had lower levels of anxiety and depression and reduced levels of cortisol, indicating less stress after the massages. Parents were taught to give their children back massages.

As in all cases of trauma and disaster, returning to normal routines as soon as possible helps children and adults feel more secure. Even if people are not living at home, reviving daily routines and activities helps them feel less stressed.

Managing Fears of National Violence

On September 11, 2001, Americans across the country and people around the world witnessed via television the tragic and violent deaths of three thousand people killed in the terrorist attacks in New York, Washington, D.C., and Pennsylvania. All joined with their families and communities in mourning their deaths. Since September 11, 2001, Americans have lived with the fears of possible terrorist killings by bombs, biochemical agents released in the air or in the mail, and shootings. These fears have been heightened as the nation has engaged in war overseas. At the national level, we are now experiencing the ongoing fears people in inner cities have experienced for years, and the research on handling fear and stress in that situation can be applied to our present national tragedy.

Research after the Oklahoma City bombing revealed that symptoms following a terrorist attack can be long lived. School-aged children who lived a hundred miles away from Oklahoma City and suffered no physical or direct contact with the bombing were studied two years after the bombing. Almost a third of the children indicated knowing a friend who knew someone who had been injured or killed. Twenty percent of the children described bomb-related symptoms that decreased their level of functioning at home or in school.[89]

In studies of children's worries following the September 11 bombings, researchers found that children had fewer worries after the September bombings than they had in June of 2000.[90] Parents made a great effort to talk to children about their fears and concerns, and children felt reassured. Children who were members of panels that discussed these studies stated that they wanted parents to talk to them about such everyday concerns as bullying and television violence the same way they talked to them after September 11. They recommend that parents push to get information at times, even if children say they are not worried, because children will not talk spontaneously about their worries for fear of burdening their parents. One researcher commented, "When things are 'normal,' children seem to feel most alone and helpless in their fear, and unlike Code Orange times, parents can be clueless about kids' anxiety, and kids know that."

Parents want to know what to do to help their children in these scary times. Parents, as we have learned, are the most important figures in helping children cope with trauma and stress of all kinds, and their most important role is to talk to children. Here, as well as at the chapter's end, are suggestions parents can use.[91]

Parents should do the following:

1. Examine and manage their own fears, because children model their responses on their parents' behavior.

2. Turn off the television and radio when their children are awake, to reduce the stress of repeated exposure to visual images and discussion of the tragedies.

3. Listen and observe children to determine their level of stress as reflected in eating, sleeping, and level of energy. Parents should respond to children's questions and concerns in a supportive way.

4. Give honest statements of reassurance—saying they and the government are working to keep children safe, not promising that nothing bad will happen.

5. Respond in age-appropriate ways when talking to children. Preschoolers do not need the level of information and discussion useful for older children.

6. Maintain daily activities and routines, as familiar patterns of behavior provide reassurance and feelings of security.

7. Have the phone number handy of a friend outside the community whom all family members can call to report their safety and whereabouts in the event of a community disaster.

8. Appreciate and comment on the good things in life today—for example, the family's being together, the closeness with friends. Feelings of enjoyment provide a reserve of strength to deal with stress when it comes.

9. Read stories about the country's history that inspire and give confidence that we can survive and flourish in the face of sruggle and adversity—getting to the Pacific Coast from St. Louis, getting to the Moon, surviving the battles of the Revolution and of the War of 1812, when the White House burned.

10. Volunteer with children in some activity to make a part of the world a better place. We cannot directly influence those who might wish to hurt us now, but we can increase the pleasure and joy some people get out of life.

In all these difficult situations, the family remains the main source of support for children. Agencies and therapies can help, but it is individuals who are close and have a sense of the child's individuality who are truly helpful. If parents cannot do this, other relatives or family friends, teachers, or day care workers can step in.

The Commitment to Provide Safety

In New York, New Jersey, Florida, and California, the tragic deaths, disappearances, and injuries of children in the care of state agencies after they were removed from their families because of neglect or abuse have raised concerns about the ability of state agencies to step in and protect children, as is their mandate.

New York City Commissioner for the Administration for Children's Services, William C. Bell, described the changes the city made following the 1996 death of Elisa Izquierdo, who, despite many reports to agencies and the involvement of welfare personnel, was beaten and abused for most of her six years and was finally killed by her mother. The city reorganized services to improve its care of children, but he wrote that there is no quick fix to solve problems: "Lasting results came only with deliberate measures."[92]

Reform required the cooperation of city government leaders, child welfare agencies, court services, and union leaders. The number and education of caseworkers increased. Training programs and merit-based pay raises were established. Close collaboration with police and legal agencies enabled caseworkers to deal quickly with fatalities and severe trauma from abuse. Close collaboration with neighborhood agencies and the foster-care system made it possible for all individuals involved in a case to meet within seventy-two hours of the child's being taken into foster care. Parents received parenting training in their homes.

These changes have led to a reduction in cases from twenty-six per worker to eleven, and in the number of children in foster care from 41,000 in 1996 to about 26,000 in 2002.

William C. Bell, writing in the *New York Times*, stated:

Political will, competent leadership, level heads, and a clear plan of action were what were needed for sustained, lasting changes in children's services here in New York City. A commitment to engage in a long-term strategy—and not a knee-jerk response—is what can turn tragedies into the catalysts needed for successful change.[93]

THE PREVENTION OF VIOLENCE

In a chapter concerning the neurobiological effects of experiencing and witnessing trauma, Bruce Perry writes,

> The ultimate solution to the problems of violence, whether from the remorseless predator or the reactive, impulsive youth, is primary prevention. Our society is creating violent children and youth at a rate far faster than we could ever treat, rehabilitate, or even lock them away. No single intervention strategy will solve these heterogeneous problems. No set of intervention strategies will solve these transgenerational problems. In order to solve the problems of violence, we need to transform our culture.[94]

Where can we start? Katherine Christoffel describes the necessity of viewing violence in the form of firearm injuries and deaths as a public health problem rather than a criminal one.[95] Once we do that, the main goal becomes to decrease injuries, and we can search for a variety of strategies for doing this.

In describing how we reduced motor vehicle injury deaths, Christoffel illustrates how we might reduce violence. In the late 1960s, motor vehicle injury deaths were redefined as a public health problem, and a variety of actions were taken to decrease them. Car manufacturers improved the safety of cars, passenger restraints were developed, road construction was improved, and driving laws were amended to increase penalties for driving while intoxicated and failure to use seat belts. The number of deaths dropped from 55,000 in 1968 to 44,000 per year in 2003[96], although the number of cars and drivers increased.

Using a public health model, one can make the public aware of the risk we all face from firearms.[97] While deaths from motor vehicles are dropping, deaths from firearms are rising. By recognizing the lethality of guns and their risk to the general population, the public can shift the focus from crime, law enforcement, and civil liberties to a focus on preventing and reducing injuries and deaths from firearms. The emphasis is then placed on having handgun-free homes and neighborhoods, restricting handgun sales and ownership, and developing other self- and home-protection devices. For example, we can emphasize the safe storage of guns and ammunition in locked and separated areas, push for firearm manufacturers to install safety locks on guns, and urge state representatives to pass laws making owners responsible for others' use of their guns.

Although we have taken some action to regulate the purchase of guns, we have paid little attention to gun manufacturers and distributors. Licenses to distribute handguns are cheap and can be obtained through the mail. In 1990, there were more firearm licenses than gas stations in the United States. Many of these distributors, unknown to local officials, operate out of their homes. Thus, their compliance with existing laws may be minimal and could no doubt be improved if all distributors were known.

Another form of prevention is to encourage health professionals to advise and counsel all families on the danger of handguns and the need to have them locked away. They can track the number of injuries and deaths from handguns carefully and educate the public on the importance of reforms to control handgun use and storage.

We can also work to change the content of the media.[98] Research indicates that media violence contributes to violent behavior in three ways: (1) It increases aggressive behavior and the willingness to use violence; (2) it desensitizes viewers so that they accept violence as a normal part of life; and (3) it creates a "mean world syndrome" that makes people more fearful of the world because they see it as dangerous.

John Murray suggests that families need to act in three ways to counteract media violence.[99] First, they need to change their behavior at home. So that children can become informed consumers of television fare, parents need to watch television with children and talk about what they see. Parents and children can learn from each other in these discussions. Second, parents can lobby for the inclusion of media literacy courses, so that, again, children learn the habits of critical viewing. Third, parents can lobby the government and industries to make children's television less violent. For example, they might lobby the industry to reduce the amount of time allocated to violent programs during prime time. There are encouraging signs that the chairman of the Federal Communications Commission is ready to make changes. These are just a few of the actions that parents can pursue as they seek to make the world a safer place for children.

THE CHALLENGE MODEL

Therapy can help children deal with the effects of certain traumatic events and troubled family situations. Some therapists have become concerned, however, that certain forms of intervention so emphasize the pain and damaging effects of these difficulties that children and adults believe they are doomed to emotionally impoverished lives as a result of the trauma.

Steven Wolin and Sybil Wolin term this the *damage model* of human development, in that it focuses on the harmful effects produced by traumas; therapy in this model can only help individuals understand the damage and how it occurred. Drawing on clinical insights and on the research of such people as Ruth Smith and Emmy Werner (see the interview with Emmy Werner in Chapter 4), Wolin and Wolin have developed the *challenge model* of development.[100] Although adversity brings stress, harm, and vulnerability to the individual, Wolin and Wolin believe it also stimulates the person to branch out, to take measures to protect himself or herself, and to find other sources of strength that promote development. So, the individual experiences pain but develops resiliencies that can limit the pain and promote accomplishment and satisfaction.

In their book *The Resilient Self,* Wolin and Wolin identify seven resiliencies that help individuals rebound in the face of difficult circumstances:

1. *Insight*—[developing] the habit of asking tough questions and giving honest answers
2. *Independence*—drawing boundaries between yourself and your troubled parents; keeping emotional and physical distance while satisfying the demands of your conscience

Children cope best with community disasters when family members are supportive.

3. *Relationships*—[building] intimate and fulfilling ties to other people that balance a mature regard for your own needs with empathy and the capacity to give to someone else

4. *Initiative*—taking charge of problems; exerting control; [acquiring] a taste for stretching and testing yourself in demanding tasks

5. *Creativity*—imposing order, beauty, and purpose on the chaos of your troubling experiences and painful feelings

6. *Humor*—finding the comic in the tragic

7. *Morality*—[developing] an informed conscience that extends your wish for a good personal life to all of humankind[101]

Their book describes the many ways resiliencies grow in childhood, adolescence, and adulthood and offers an optimistic approach that encourages survivors of traumas and difficult childhood experiences to review their lives in terms of the strengths they have developed. As a result, people experience pride in their ability to overcome hardships—whether as a result of violence, abuse, or natural disasters such as floods and earthquakes—and confidence in their capacity to make further changes as needed. In focusing on pain and the sources of pain in the past, the damage model tends to discourage individuals, because the past cannot be changed nor the pain undone. In contrast, the challenge model asserts that life can be satisfying and productive despite the scars of the past.

A PRACTICAL QUESTION: HOW CAN WE KEEP CHILDREN SAFE IN EVERYDAY LIFE?

We have discussed interventions at times of disasters and trauma, but parents also have concerns about children's safety in everyday life. They want to help children be independent and safe in the world, yet they do not want to frighten them and make them afraid of strangers and new experiences. Grace Hechinger, an education consultant, has interviewed police officials, school safety officials, individuals involved in neighborhood safety programs, and victims of crime and assaults.[102] From this research, she has organized information to help parents prepare their children to be safe as they spend more time on their own.

Fostering children's awareness of danger, the sense of caution, and preparedness for unsafe situations does not mean making children live in fear. Children can learn that, even though most people in the world are good and helpful and most situations are safe, some people and experiences are not, and everyone must learn to protect himself or herself from dangers. Parents can help by putting this knowledge in perspective for children. Life has always involved danger of some sort, and many objects or experiences that are positive also have dangerous aspects. Cars are useful—they get us to work, to stores, to hospitals—but they can be dangerous if they hit us while we are crossing the street. The answer lies not in eliminating cars, because before we had cars, there were dangers from horses and horse-drawn vehicles. The solution is to take precautions to minimize the dangers and enjoy the benefits.

Families need to develop a set of instructions, to be discussed and revised as necessary, regarding certain dangerous situations. A one-time discussion is not enough; parents must periodically review instructions with children. Children can learn these safety rules gradually—for example, when and where they may go alone, or what they should do if bothered by someone on the street or in a store, even when parents are nearby. Learning safety rules can become as natural to children as learning to brush their teeth. Parents emphasize teaching children the skills to deal with the environment, to make them competent and independent.

Although parents worry that talk of possible fearful events will damage the child, the risks that come with ignorance are much greater. Parents can begin with simple discussions of traffic safety—where, when, and how to cross the street. They can move from that topic to others of importance for the child. Television may prompt some discussion. Hechinger recommends playing the game "What If?" Parents ask a variety of questions and give children chances to develop solutions to difficult situations. Parents should not be upset if their children's initial answers are impractical, because they can guide their children in learning more reasonable responses. Table 15-2 gives some sample "What If?" questions.

Parents should have clear safety rules about:

1. Behavior in the case of a fire at home
2. Traffic behavior, whether on foot or on a bicycle
3. Boundaries within which the child can come and go freely and outside of which an adult or parent must be present

■ **T A B L E 15-2**
SOME "WHAT IF?" QUESTIONS FOR YOUNG CHILDREN

Parents ask children what they would do if the following situations arose. If children give the impractical answers, parents can calmly tell them more practical alternative responses. What if:

1. We were separated in a shopping center, in the movies, at the beach?

2. You were lost in a department store, in the park, at a parade?

3. A stranger offered you candy or presents to leave the playground?

4. A stranger wanted you to get into his car?

5. A stranger started fussing with your clothing?

6. Your friends wanted to play with matches?

7. Someone you did not know asked [for] your name and phone number?

Grace Hechinger, *How to Raise a Street-Smart Child* (New York: Ballantine Books, 1984), 59.

4. Behavior in public with strangers

5. Behavior at home if strangers telephone or come to the house

6. Behavior when the child is a victim or witness of muggings by peers or adults

7. Behavior when sexual misconduct occurs

If a child is victimized—a bike is stolen, money is taken, a stranger approaches the child—parents' reactions can help speed the healing process. When parents listen to children's reactions and help children take constructive action, such as notifying the police, they help children cope. When parents' responses are exaggerated ("This is horrible!") or detached ("I cannot deal with this"), children get no help in coping with their feelings. If they cannot talk about how they feel, they will find it difficult to work out their feelings. Active listening and simple I-messages ("If that happened to me, I'd be really upset") give children a chance to say what the experience meant to them. Sometimes, children need to describe the event several times. Each time, more details emerge, as do more feelings. Gradually, after the incident, children regain their self-confidence. If a child's eating, sleeping, or play habits change, or if marked changes in schoolwork or personality continue for some time, professional help should be sought.

An important step in promoting children's safety is working with people in the community. Developing community awareness and programs gives everyone a positive feeling of working together, which does much to banish fear. Promoting public safety programs with school and police officials and organizing block-parent programs to help children in the neighborhood are useful steps. In block-parent programs, one house in the neighborhood is designated as a house where children can go if they need help or reassurance when no one is home at the child's own house.

Family members grow stronger when they face problems and work together to deal with them. The sense of community grows when families and agencies cooperate to make the environment safe for children.

MAIN POINTS

An ecological/transactional model of community violence and child maltreatment

- focuses on risk factors and protective factors
- describes characteristics of the child, parent, and environment that increase the risk of violence
- describes violence at several ecological levels: the macrosystemic, the exosystemic, the microsystemic, and the ontogenic, or personal, level
- emphasizes that factors at different levels interact to increase the likelihood of violence
- has implications for types of intervention at the various ecological levels

Exposure to family violence

- occurs in many different kinds of families
- affects a child's physical, psychological, and cognitive functioning
- requires interventions aimed at helping the nonabusing parent as well as the child
- requires organized community interventions to prevent family violence

Sexual abuse in childhood

- is experienced by one in four girls and one in six boys by the age of eighteen
- affects children in different ways, depending on the specific act, its duration, its frequency, and the identity of the perpetrator
- appears most traumatic when it involves someone close who frequently engages in forceful sexual acts of penetration over a long time period and when mothers provide little support
- results in behavior changes such as sexualized behavior and changes in emotional regulation, in attachment relations, in self-concept, in relations with peers, and in school adjustment
- does not always produce symptoms; about one-third to one-half of children show no symptoms at the time they are studied

Sexual child abuse victims

- require protection from the abuser
- can profit from individual, group, and family therapy

Physical child abuse

- is difficult to define precisely
- results from a variety of factors, including characteristics of the parents, the family, and the environment
- is learned in the context of the family
- results in a wide variety of symptoms relating to self-concept, emotional control, relations with peers and adults, and adjustment in school

- creates victims who can nevertheless be resourceful and surmount problems
- requires therapy for the victim, the perpetrator, and the family
- may be so severe on a single occasion that the child should not live with the abuser again

Neglect
- is a common but little-studied form of abuse
- occurs in families with other risk factors such as poverty and substance abuse
- can be prevented with increased services to children and families
- requires community-wide programs to prevent it and treat its victims

Community violence
- affects all children but mostly those in poor neighborhoods
- is more often witnessed than experienced
- has a negative impact when it erodes the safety and stability of family life
- results in many symptoms that hinder children's development
- requires interventions at the community level to decrease the violence and provide support for children who experience such violence
- creates effects that parents and individual, group, and family therapy can mitigate

Following national disasters and other trauma, parents should
- model realistic response to ongoing fear
- talk to children about fears and worries
- turn off television
- focus on the positive in life and carry out actions to make the world a better place

The challenge model
- focuses on strengths people develop to cope with negative family experiences or other traumas
- identifies seven resiliencies: insight, independence, relationships, initiative, creativity, humor, and morality
- presents an optimistic view of people's capacity to create satisfying lives despite the scars of painful experiences

Keeping children safe
- requires that parents teach children about potential dangers and ways to minimize them
- means that parents and society as a whole have to work to provide a safer community for everyone

EXERCISES

1. Imagine that a close friend told you that her four-year-old had just showed her how a twenty-five-year-old male relative had touched her genitals. The daughter said he told her it was a secret between them, but she decided to tell her mother because they do not keep secrets from each other. How would you advise your friend to help her daughter after she has reported the event to the authorities? What would you advise her to do to help herself?

2. Divide into groups of four and describe the general information you would choose to include in an eight-session parenting course for men and women who have physically abused their children. Share your group's results with the entire class. What elements were chosen by only one or two groups? Combine the best information from all groups and come up with one eight-session program. If possible, compare it with a program offered in your area, such as Parental Stress.

3. Divide into groups of four and describe a parenting program for adolescent mothers and fathers to prevent physical child abuse. Is it identical to the program designed for those who have already committed abuse? In what ways does it differ?

4. Imagine that you had unlimited money to go into a low-income housing project in a high-crime area. What kinds of programs would you devise to help children cope with the violence they witness around them?

5. Think about what you most feared as a young child. What would you tell a nine-year-old brother or sister who was afraid of being kidnapped on the street? Of experiencing an earthquake or hurricane or flood? Of being shot?

ADDITIONAL READINGS

Adams, Caren, and Fay, Jennifer. *Helping Your Child Recover from Sexual Abuse*. Seattle: University of Washington Press, 1992.

Kraizer, Sherryll. *The Safe Child Book*. New York: Fireside, 1996.

Osofsky, Joy D., ed. *Children in a Violent Society*. New York: Guilford, 1997.

Rosoff, Barbara D. *The Worst Loss*. New York: Henry Holt, 1994.

Zeltzer, Lonnie K., and Schlank, Christine Blackett. *Conquering Your Child's Chronic Pain*. New York: HarperCollins, 2005.

EPILOGUE

We have looked at parenting behaviors in many different circumstances. We have discussed parenting children of all ages living in families of diverse values and goals and in diverse family structures with one or two parents, who are sometimes of the same sex. We have looked at parenting in ordinary times and in times of special stress such as divorce or trauma. No matter what the age of the child; no matter whether the child is a biological or an adopted child, a child with special gifts or special needs, or a child with the usual gifts and needs; no matter whether parents are married, single, or remarried—four basic principles stand out.

The four basic principles are straightforward. First, parents give children positive attention. Positive attention does not mean accepting and approving all behaviors. It does mean that parents view children in terms of their special qualities and strengths, and that parents maintain their positive view of children while helping them make needed changes in behavior.

Second, parents provide support for the growth of children's competence by modeling positive behavior, guiding children's behavior, and teaching them problem-solving skills to deal with challenges. Third, parents talk about what is happening, listen to children's feelings, and answer children's questions so children have a clear understanding of situations and a chance to express their concerns. Fourth, parents deal with unresolved anger and hostility directed at the child or expressed to or about others in the child's presence. The persistence of such feelings destroys children's good feelings and their effectiveness in the world.

Relying on these four principles, parents can help children grow and realize their potential. No matter how strong the desire, parents cannot guarantee children a problem-free life, especially in these historical times, but they can guarantee children a lifetime attachment that provides the support and help necessary to grow and to meet life's challenges.

Throughout the book, we have seen that parents benefit from support as they go about rearing the next generation. In our individualistic society, this support usually comes from individuals and voluntary organizations. Government programs do not give much help to the vast array of parents, though such programs are effective in providing services—for example, home visiting programs for parents of infants or early childhood stimulation programs for children with special needs.

In most parents' lives, support comes primarily from marital partners, extended family members such as grandparents, friends, coworkers, and organizations like CHADD (Children and Adults with Attention Deficit Disorder) designed to help special groups of parents and children. More recently, organizations like the National Parenting Association have addressed the broader needs of all parents. Further, parents themselves have followed the Youth Charter plan of William Damon to organize the entire community to address the needs of all youth. This is vitally important for all of us, because children are the future of our society.

If you are not a parent or grandparent, you may wonder what you can do to help parents. First, every one of us can give parents the respect and acknowledgment for their hard work and sacrifice that our society generally withholds from parents.

Second, with whatever your special skills, you may be able to take actions in your everyday life to support parents and parenting. A single individual has tremendous power, as the actions of Barbara Barlow illustrate.[1] A pediatric surgeon at Harlem Hospital in New York, she became concerned at the growing number of preventable injuries she was treating. Children fell from open windows, were hit by automobiles while playing in the street, and were victims of violence.

In 1988, Barlow started Harlem Hospital's Injury Prevention Project (IPP) with a grant from the Robert Wood Johnson Foundation. With a staff of three, she worked to rebuild playgrounds and parks in the community, making them safe places to play. She photographed all the parks and playgrounds and took the information to the Parks Department and the Board of Education. The Parks Department has since made nearly all the parks in the area safe. Private funding was obtained, and with the suggestions of teachers and students, eight new parks were built.

The Injury Prevention Program has expanded to include activities that foster children's competence. For example, an in-hospital art program allows patients to express their feelings about illness and hospitalization. Children have exhibited and sold their work, with half of the profits going to the children and half to the art program. The IPP also sponsors baseball teams, a soccer team, a dance program serving 200 children, and a greening program in which children can grow vegetables and flowers.

Since the implementation of this program, major injuries to children in Harlem have decreased by 37 percent. Motor vehicle accidents have decreased by 50 percent, and fewer children fall from windows. In addition, dancers, athletes, artists, and gardeners have developed skills they would not have been able to develop without the programs.

An increase in violent injuries led Barlow to start the Anti-Violence Project, which contains several specific programs for (1) teaching children how to stay safe, (2) helping children deal with violence after they experience it, and (3) teaching the children, their parents, and educators, conflict resolution techniques and other ways to avoid violence.

Funding for all these programs comes from individuals, corporations, foundations, and fees from Barlow's speaking engagements. Barlow concludes,

> You have to give to get in this world, and we give a lot. We put in lots of hard work, but it's immensely satisfying. There is no such thing as not being able to make things better. In any community, every individual can make a tremendous difference if they truly care, if they look around to see what needs to be done.[2]

NOTES

PREFACE

1. David Gutmann, "Parenthood: A Key to the Comparative Study of the Life Cycle," in *Life Span Developmental Psychology: Normative Life Crises,* ed. Nancy Daton and Leon H. Ginsberg (New York: Academic Press, 1975), 175.
2. Arthur T. Jersild et al., *Joys and Problems of Child Rearing* (New York: Bureau of Publications, Teachers College, Columbia University, 1949), p. 1.

CHAPTER 1

1. Amy Harmon, "That Wild Streak? Maybe It Runs in the Family," *New York Times,* 15 June 2006, p. A1.
2. U.S. Bureau of the Census, *Statistical Abstract of the United States: 2006,* 125th ed. (Washington, DC: U.S. Government Printing Office, 2005).
3. William Morris, ed., *The American Heritage Dictionary of the English Language* (Boston: American Heritage Publishing and Houghton Mifflin, 1969).
4. Lois Wladis Hoffman and Martin L. Hoffman, "The Value of Children to Parents," in *Psychological Perspectives on Population,* ed. James T. Fawcett (New York: Basic Books, 1973), 19–76; Sarah Blaffer Hrdy, *Mother Nature* (New York: Ballantine Books, 1999).
5. Lois Wladis Hoffman and Jean Denby Manis, "The Value of Children in the United States: A New Approach to the Study of Fertility," *Journal of Marriage and the Family* 41 (1979): 583–596.
6. Donald G. McNeil, Jr., "Demographic 'Bomb' May Only Go Pop!," *New York Times,* 29 August 2004, Section 4, p. 1.
7. *People* 10 November 1997, Cover.
8. Personal communication.
9. Hoffman and Manis, "The Value of Children."
10. Arthur T. Jersild et al., *The Joys and Problems of Child Rearing* (New York: Bureau of Publications, Teachers College, Columbia University, 1949).
11. Gerald Y. Michaels, "Motivational Factors in the Decision and Timing of Pregnancy," in *The Transition to Parenthood,* ed. Gerald Y. Michaels and Wendy Goldberg (New York: Cambridge University Press, 1988), 23–61.
12. Jersild et al., *The Joys and Problems of Child Rearing.*
13. Jay Belsky, "The Determinants of Parenting: A Process Model," *Child Development* 55 (1984): 83–96.
14. David F. Bjorklund, Jennifer L. Yunger, and Anthony D. Pellegrini, "The Evolution of Parenting and Evolutionary Approaches to Childrearing," in *Handbook of Parenting,* 2nd ed., ed. Marc H. Bornstein, vol. 2: *Biology and Ecology of Parenting* (Mahwah, NJ: Erlbaum, 2002), 3–30.
15. Urie Bronfenbrenner and Pamela A. Morris, "The Ecology of Developmental Processes," in *Handbook of Child Psychology,* 5th ed., ed. William Damon, vol. 1: *Theoretical Models of Human Development,* ed. Richard Lerner (New York: Wiley, 1998), 996, 1015.
16. Belsky, "Determinants of Parenting."
17. Catherine E. Ross and Maurieke Van Willigen, "Gender, Parenthood, and Anger," *Journal of Marriage and Family* 58 (1996): 572–584.
18. Richard M. Lerner, Elizabeth F. Sparks, and Laurie D. McCubbin, "Family Diversity and Family Policy," in *Handbook of Family Diversity,* ed. David H. Demo, Katherine R. Allen, and Mark A. Fine (New York: Oxford University Press, 2000), p. 391.
19. Diana Baumrind and Ross A. Thompson, "The Ethics of Parenting," in *Handbook of Parenting,* 2nd ed., ed. Marc H. Bornstein, vol. 5. *Practical Issues in Parenting* (Mahwah, NJ: Erlbaum, 2002), 3–34.
20. Belsky, "Determinants of Parenting."
21. Jay Belsky et al., "Intergenerational Transmission of Warm-Sensitive-Stimulating Parenting: A Prospective Study of Mothers and Fathers of 3-Year-Olds," *Child Development* 76 (2005): 384–396.
22. Joan Vondra, Helen Bittman Sysko, and Jay Belsky, "Developmental Origins of Parenting," in *Parenting: An Ecological Perspective,* 2nd ed., ed. Tom Luster and

Lynn Okagaki (Mahwah, NJ: Erlbaum, 2005), 35–71.

23. Paul R. Amato, "More than Money? Men's Contributions to Their Children's Lives," in *Men in Families: When Do They Get Involved? What Difference Does It Make?* ed. Alan Booth and Ann C. Crouter (Mahwah, NJ: Erlbaum, 1998), 241–278.

24. Ronald L. Simons et al., "Social Network and Marital Support As Mediators and Moderators of the Impact of Stress and Depression on Parental Behavior," *Developmental Psychology* 29 (1993): 368–381.

25. Baumrind and Thompson, "Ethics of Parenting."

26. Pauline M. Pagliocca et al., "Parenting and the Law," in *Handbook of Parenting*, ed. Bornstein, vol. 5, p. 464.

27. Ibid.

28. Ibid.

29. Laura Landro, "Parents Barred From Teen Health Files," *Wall Street Journal*, 8 August 2005, p. D1.

30. Pagliocca et al., "Parenting and the Law."

31. Greg Lucas and Carla Marinucci, "Rock Toss Case To Be Mediated," *San Francisco Chronicle*, 4 August 2005, p. B1.

32. Jeffrey Marx, *Season of Life* (New York: Simon & Schuster, 2003).

33. Judith Warner, *Perfect Madness: Motherhood in the Age of Anxiety* (New York: Penguin, 2005).

34. Peter N. Stearns, *Anxious Parents* (New York: New York University Press, 2003).

35. Jacob Needleham, *The American Soul* (New York: Penguin, 2002), p. 19.

36. Jim Taylor, *Your Children Are Under Attack* (Naperville, IL: Sourcebooks, 2005).

37. U.S. Bureau of the Census, *Statistical Abstract of the United States, 2006.*

38. Gerald Nadler, "Not Much Change in Children's Death Rate," *San Francisco Chronicle*, 8 October 2004, p. A13.

39. Victoria Colliver, "Uninsured Ranks Hit Record High," *San Francisco Chronicle*, 27 August 2004, p. A1.

40. Elizabeth Olson, "U.N. Surveys Paid Leave for Mothers," *New York Times*, 16 February 1998, p. A5.

41. Warner, *Perfect Madness.*

42. Stearns, *Anxious Parents.*

43. James Garbarino, "Supporting Parents in a Socially Toxic Environment," in *Parenthood in America*, ed. Jack C. Westman (Madison:

University of Wisconsin Press, 2001), 220–231.

44. Michael Rutter, "Nature, Nurture, and Development: From Evangelism through Science toward Policy and Practice," *Child Development* 73 (2002): 15.

45. Vern Bengston, "Beyond the Nuclear Family: The Increasing Importance of Multigenerational Bonds," *Journal of Marriage and Family* 63 (2001): 1–16.

46. Ibid., p. 5.

47. Steven H. Zarit and David J. Eggebeen, "Parent-Child Relationships in Adulthood and Later Years," in *Handbook of Parenting*, 2nd ed., ed. Marc H. Bornstein, vol. 1: *Children and Parenting* (Mahwah, NJ: Erlbaum, 2002), 135–161.

48. Bengston, "Beyond the Nuclear Family," p. 7.

49. Ibid.

50. Carol C. Gohm et al., "Culture, Parental Conflict, Parental Marital Status, and the Subjective Well-Being of Young Adults," *Journal of Marriage and the Family* 60 (1998): 319–334.

51. Jay Belsky, Elliot Robins, and Wendy Gamble, "The Determinants of Parental Competence: Toward a Contextual Theory," in *Beyond the Dyad*, ed. Michael Lewis (New York: Plenum, 1984), 251–280.

52. Judith Rich Harris, *The Nurture Assumption: Why Children Turn Out the Way They Do* (New York: Free Press, 1998), p 351.

53. Belsky, Robins, and Gamble, "The Determinants of Parental Competence."

54. W. Andrew Collins et al., "Contemporary Research on Parenting: The Case for Nature and Nurture," *American Psychologist* 55 (2000): 218–232.

55. Lynn Singer et al., "Relationship of Prenatal Cocaine Exposure and Maternal Postpartum Psychological Distress to Child Development Outcome," *Development and Psychopathology* 9 (1997): 473–489.

56. Gurney Williams III, "Toxic Dads," *Parenting*, October 1998, p. 94.

57. Arnold Sameroff et al., "Family and Social Influences on the Development of Child Competence," in *Families, Risk, and Competence*, ed. Michael Lewis and Candice Feiring (Mahwah, NJ: Erlbaum, 1998), 161–185.

58. Ronald Seifer et al., "Child and Family Factors That Ameliorate Risk between 4 and 13 Years of Age," *Journal of the American*

Academy of Child and Adolescent Psychiatry 31 (1992): 893–903.

59. Sameroff et al., "Family and Social Influences."

60. Ibid., pp. 178–179.

61. Arnold Sameroff, "Democratic and Republican Models of Development; Paradigms or Perspectives," *APA Division 7 Newsletter* (Fall 1996): 8.

62. Collins et al., "Contemporary Research on Parenting."

63. Stephen J. Suomi, "Attachment in Rhesus Monkeys," in *Handbook of Attachment: Theory, Research, and Clinical Applications,* ed. Jude Cassidy and Phillip R. Shaver (New York: Guilford, 1999), 181–197.

64. Jerome Kagan, Doreen Arcus, and Nancy Snidman, "The Idea of Temperament: Where Do We Go From Here?' in *Nature and Nature in Psychology*, ed. Robert Plomin and Gerald E. McClearn (Washington, DC: American Psychological Association, 1993), 197–210.

65. Eleanor E. Maccoby, "Parenting and Its Effects on Children: On Reading and Misreading Behavior Genetics," *Annual Review of Psychology* 51 (2000): 1–27.

66. C. Robert Cloninger et al., "Predispositions to Petty Criminality in Swedish Adoptees. II. Cross-Fostering Analysis of Gene-Environment Interaction, *Archives of General Psychiatry* 39 (1982): 1242–1247.

67. Laraine Masters Glidden, "Parenting Children with Developmental Disabilities: A Ladder of Influence," in *Parenting and the Child's World: Influences in Academic, Intellectual, and Socio-Emotional Development*, ed. John G. Borkowski, Sharon Landesman Ramey, and Marie Bristol-Power (Mahwah, NJ: Erlbaum, 2002), 329–344.

68. Ibid., p. 336.

69. Benjamin S. Bloom, ed., *Developing Talent in Young People* (New York: Ballantine, 1985).

70. Matthew Purdy, Andrew Jacobs, and Richard Lezin Jones, "Life Behind Basement Doors: Family and System Fail Boys," *New York Times*, 12 January 2003, p. A1.

71. David Kocieniewski, "State Admits Losing Track of Children," *New York Times*, 11 January 2003, p. A15.

72. Richard Lezin Jones and Leslie Kaufman, "Gaps in Children's Safety Net Are Seen in New Jersey Case," *New York Times*, 14 March 2003, p. A25.

73. Robert Pear, "US Finds Fault in All 50 States' Child Welfare Programs and Penalties May Follow," *New York Times*, 26 April 2004, p. A17.

74. Ibid.

75. Katherine Ellison, *The Mommy Brain: How Motherhood Makes Us Smarter* (New York: Basic Books, 2005).

76. Ibid., p. 7.

77. Michael Numan and Thomas R. Insel, *The Neurobiology of Parental Behavior* (New York: Springer, 2003).

78. Ibid.

79. Ellison, *The Mommy Brain*.

80. Numan and Insel, *The Neurobiology of Parental Behavior*.

81. James J. Dillon, "The Role of the Child in Adult Development," *Journal of Adult Development* 9 (2002): 267–275.

82. Ibid., p. 271.

83. Ibid., p. 272.

84. Jersild et al., *The Joys and Problems of Child Rearing*, p. 122.

85. Sandra T. Azar, "Parenting and Child Maltreatment," in *Handbook of Parenting*, 2nd ed., ed. Marc H. Bornstein, vol. 4: *Social Conditions and Applied Parenting* (Mahwah, NJ: Erlbaum, 2002), 361–388.

86. Interview with Steven Wolin in Jane B. Brooks, *The Process of Parenting*, 5th ed. (Mountain View, CA: Mayfield, 1999), 458–459.

87. Ibid.

88. Ibid.

89. June Lichtenstein Phelps, Jay Belsky, and Keith Crnic, "Earned Security, Daily Stress, and Parenting: A Comparison of Five Alternative Models," *Development and Psychopathology* 10 (1998): 21–38.

90. Daniel J. Siegel and Mary Hartzell, *Parenting from the Inside Out: How a Deeper Self-Understanding Can Help You Raise Children Who Thrive* (New York: Penguin, 2003), p. 4.

91. Ibid., p. 248.

92. Dorothy H. Eichorn, Jane V. Hunt, and Marjorie P. Honzik, "Experience, Personality and IQ: Adolescence to Middle Age," in *Present and Past in Middle Life*, ed. Dorothy H. Eichorn et al. (New York: Academic Press, 1981), 89–116.

93. Carolyn Pape Cowan and Philip A. Cowan, *When Partners Become Parents* (New York: Basic Books, 1992).

CHAPTER 2

1. Judith Warner, "Kids Gone Wild," *New York Times*, 27 November 2005, sect. 4, p. 1.
2. Valerie French, "History of Parenting: The Ancient Mediterranean World," in *Handbook of Parenting*, 2nd ed., ed Marc H. Bornstein, vol 2: *Biology and Ecology of Parenting* (Mahwah, NJ: Erlbaum, 2002), 345–376.
3. Ibid., p. 447.
4. Ibid., p. 350.
5. Ibid.
6. Ibid.
7. Ibid.
8. Linda A. Pollock, *Forgotten Childhood: Parent-Child Relations from 1500 to 1900* (New York: Cambridge University Press, 1983).
9. Ibid., p. 268.
10. Ibid., p. 123.
11. Ibid., p. 270.
12. Judith A. Schickedanz et al., *Understanding Children*, 2nd ed. (Mountain View, CA: Mayfield, 1993).
13. Ross A. Thompson, "Early Sociopersonality Development," in *Handbook of Child Psychology*, 5th ed., ed William Damon, vol. 3: *Social, Emotional, and Personality Development*, ed. Nancy Eisenberg (New York: Wiley, 1998), 25–104.
14. John M. Belmont, "Cognitive Strategies and Strategies of Learning," *American Psychologist* 44 (1989): 142–148; Laboratory of Human Cognition, "Culture and Cognitive Development," in *Handbook of Child Psychology*, 4th ed., ed. William Kessen, vol. 1: *History, Theory, and Methods* (New York: Wiley, 1982), pp. 295–356; James V. Wertsch and Peter Tulviste, "L. S. Vygotsky and Contemporary Developmental Psychology," *Developmental Psychology* 28 (1992): 548–557.
15. E. Mark Cummings and Jennifer S. Cummings, "Parenting and Attachment," in *Handbook of Parenting*, 2nd ed., ed Marc H. Bornstein, vol. 5: *Practical Issues in Parenting* (Mahwah, NJ: Erlbaum, 2002), 35–58.
16. Herbert Ginsburg and Sylvia Opper, *Piaget's Theory of Intellectual Development* (Englewood Cliffs, NJ: Prentice-Hall, 1969); Jean Piaget and Barbel Inhelder, *The Psychology of the Child* (New York: Basic Books, 1969).
17. Jean Piaget, *The Child's Conception of the World* (Paterson, NJ: Littlefield, Adams & Co., 1963).
18. Robert B. Cairns, "The Making of Developmental Psychology," in *Handbook of Child Psychology*, 5th ed., ed. William Damon, vol. 1: *Theoretical Models of Human Development*, ed. Richard M. Lerner (New York: Wiley, 1998), 25–105.
19. Arnold Gesell, *Infancy and Human Growth* (New York: Macmillan, 1928), p. 375.
20. Arnold Gesell, "Foreword," in Frances L. Ilg and Louise Bates Ames, *Child Behavior* (New York: Harper & Row, 1955), p. vii.
21. Cairns, "The Making of Developmental Psychology," p. 70.
22. Erik H. Erikson, *Childhood and Society*, 2nd ed. (New York: Norton, 1963).
23. Erik H. Erikson, "Human Strength and the Cycle of Generations," in *Insight and Responsibility* (New York: Norton, 1964), 109–157.
24. Thompson, "Early Sociopersonality Development," p. 35.
25. Cummings and Cummings, "Parenting and Attachment."
26. Thompson, "Early Sociopersonality Development."
27. Ibid.
28. Karlen Lyons-Ruth et al., "Infants at Social Risk: Maternal Depression and Family Support Services as Moderators of Infant Development and Security of Attachment," *Child Development* 61 (1990): 85–98.
29. Thompson, "Early Sociopersonality Development."
30. L. Alan Sroufe et al., *The Development of the Person: The Minnesota Study of Risk and Adaptation from Birth to Adulthood* (New York: Guilford, 2005).
31. Jay Belsky et al., "Instability of Infant-Parent Attachment Security," *Developmental Psychology* 32 (1996): 921–924.
32. Claire E. Hamilton, "Continuity and Discontinuity of Attachment from Infancy through Adolescence," *Child Development* 71 (2000): 690–694; Everett Waters et al., "Attachment Security in Infancy and Early Adulthood: A Twenty-Year Longitudinal Study," *Child Development* 71 (2000): 684–689.
33. Michael Lewis, Candace Feiring, and Saul Rosenthal, "Attachment over Time, *Child Development* 71 (2000): 707–727; L. Alan Sroufe and Byron Egeland, "Attachment

from Infancy to Early Adulthood in a High-Risk Sample: Continuity, Discontinuity, and Their Correlates," *Child Development* 71 (2000): 695–702.

34. Sroufe et al., *The Development of the Person*.

35. Gilbert Gottlieb, Douglas Wahlsten, and Robert Lickliter, "The Significance of Biology for Human Development: A Developmental Psychobiological Systems View," in *Handbook of Child Psychology*, 5th ed., ed. Damon and Lerner, vol. 1, 233–273.

36. Lynn Singer et al., "Relationship of Prenatal Cocaine Exposure and Maternal Postpartum Psychological Distress to Child Development Outcome," *Development and Psychopathology* 9 (1997): 473–489; Gurney Williams III, "Toxic Dads," *Parenting*, October 1998, p. 94.

37. Urie Bronfenbrenner and Pamela A. Morris, "The Ecology of Developmental Processes," in *Handbook of Child Psychology*, 5th ed., ed. Damon and Lerner, vol. 1, pp. 993–1028.

38. Rima Shore, *Rethinking the Brain* (New York: Families and Work Institute, 1997), p. 15.

39. Arnold J. Sameroff et al., "Family and Social Influences on the Development of Child Competence," in *Families, Risk, and Competence*, ed. Michael Lewis and Candace Feiring (Mahwah, NJ: Erlbaum, 1998), 161–185.

40. David T. Lykken, "Parental Licensure," *American Psychologist* 56 (2001): 883–894.

41. David F. Bjorklund and Anthony D. Pellegrini, "Child Development and Evolutionary Psychology," *Child Development* 71 (2000): 1687–1708; David F. Bjorklund, Jennifer L. Yunger, and Anthony D. Pellegrini, "The Evolution of Parenting and Evolutionary Approaches to Child Rearing," in *Handbook of Parenting*, 2nd ed., ed. Bornstein, vol. 2, 3–30.

42. Bjorklund and Pellegrini, "Child Development and Evolutionary Psychology."

43. Bronfenbrenner and Morris, "The Ecology of Developmental Processes."

44. Urie Bronfenbrenner, "Growing Chaos in the Lives of Children: How Can We Turn It Around?" in *Parenthood in America*, ed. Jack C. Westman (Madison: University of Wisconsin Press, 2001), 197–210.

45. Bronfenbrenner and Morris, "The Ecology of Developmental Processes."

46. Ibid.

47. Bronfenbrenner, "Growing Chaos in the Lives of Children."

48. John B. Watson, *Psychological Care of Infant and Child* (New York: Norton, 1928).

49. Cairns, "The Making of Developmental Psychology," p. 70.

50. Watson, *Psychological Care of Infant and Child*, pp. 81–82.

51. Benjamin Spock, *Baby and Child Care* (New York: Pocket Books, 1946).

52. Ann Hulbert, *Raising America: Experts, Parents, and a Century of Advice about Children* (New York: Alfred A. Knopf, 2003), p. 264.

53. Haim G. Ginott, *Between Parent and Child* (New York: Avon, 1969).

54. Thomas Gordon, *P.E.T.: Parent Effectiveness Training* (New York: New American Library, 1975).

55. Rudolf Dreikurs with Vicki Soltz, *Children: The Challenge* (New York: Hawthorn, 1964).

56. James Dobson, *Dare to Discipline* (Wheaton, Il: Tyndale House, 1970); James Dobson and Gary L. Bauer, *Children at Risk* (Dallas, TX: Word, 1990).

57. Dobson and Bauer, *Children at Risk*.

58. William Sears, Introduction to *Attachment Parenting*, by Katie Allison Granju with Betsy Kennedy (New York: Pocket Books, 1999).

59. Hulbert, *Raising America*.

60. T. Berry Brazelton and Stanley I. Greenspan, *The Irreducible Needs of Children* (Cambridge, MA: Perseus, 2000).

61. Dr. Phil McGraw, *Family First: Your Step by Step Plan for Creating a Phenomenal Family* (New York: Free Press, 2004).

62. Deborah Carroll and Stella Reid, *Nanny 911: Expert Advice for All Your Emergencies* (New York: HarperCollins, 2005).

63. Ibid., p. xvii.

64. Ibid., p. xviii.

65. McGraw, *Family First*, p. xiv.

66. Ibid.

67. Dobson and Bauer, *Children at Risk*.

68. McGraw, *Family First*.

69. Myla Kabat-Zinn and Jon Kabat-Zinn, *Everyday Blessings: The Inner Work of Mindful Parenting* (New York: Hyperion, 1997).

70. Ibid., p. 378.

71. Diana Baumrind, "The Development of Instrumental Competence through Socialization," in *Minnesota Symposium on Child Psychology*, ed. Ann D. Pick, vol. 7

(Minneapolis: University of Minnesota Press, 1973), pp. 3–46.

72. Ibid., pp. 42–43.

73. Ibid., p. 3.

74. Gerald R. Patterson et al., *A Social Learning Approach to Family Intervention*, vol. 1: *Families with Aggressive Children* (Eugene, OR: Castalia, 1975).

75. Gerald R. Patterson and Philip A. Fisher, "Recent Developments in Our Understanding of Parenting: Bidirectional Effects, Causal Models, and the Search for Parsimony," in *Handbook of Parenting*, 2nd ed., ed. Bornstein, vol. 5, pp. 59–88.

76. Gerald R. Patterson, "The Early Development of the Coercive Family Process," in *Antisocial Behavior in Children and Adolescents*, ed. John B. Reid, Gerald R. Patterson, and James Snyder (Washington, DC: American Psychological Association, 2002), pp. 25–44.

CHAPTER 3

1. David L. Kirp, "Life Way After Head Start," *New York Times Magazine*, 21 November 2004, p. 32.

2. Joseph E. Illick, *American Childhoods* (Philadelphia: University of Pennsylvania Press, 2002).

3. Stephen Moore, "More Immigrants, More Jobs," *Wall Street Journal*, 11 July 2005, p. A13.

4. William Morris, ed., *The American Heritage Dictionary of the English Language* (Boston: American Heritage Publishing Co., 1969).

5. Sara Harkness and Charles Super, "Culture and Parenting," in *Handbook of Parenting*, 2nd ed., ed. Marc H. Bornstein, vol. 2: *Biology and Ecology* (Mahwah, NJ: Erlbaum, 2002), 253–280.

6. Rebecca I. New and Amy L. Richman, "Maternal Beliefs and Infant Care Practices in Italy and the United States," in *Parents' Cultural Belief Systems: Their Origins, Expressions, and Consequences*, ed. Sara Harkness and Charles M. Super (New York: Guilford, 1996), 385–404.

7. Velma McBride Murry, Emilie Phillips Smith, and Nancy E. Hill, "Race, Ethnicity, and Culture in Studies of Families in Context," *Journal of Marriage and Family* 63 (2001): 912.

8. Daphne Blunt Bugental and Jacqueline J. Goodnow, "Socialization Processes," in *Handbook of Child Psychology*, 5th ed., ed.

William Damon, vol. 3: *Social, Emotional, and Personality Development*, ed. Nancy Eisenberg (New York: Wiley, 1998), 389–462.

9. Rogers Brubaker, *Ethnicity without Groups* (Cambridge, MA: Harvard University Press, 2004).

10. Jean L. Briggs, "Mazes of Meaning: How a Child and a Culture Create Each Other," in *Interpretive Approaches to Socialization*, ed. William A. Corsaro and Peggy J. Miller, *New Directions for Child Development*, no. 66 (San Francisco: Jossey Bass, 1992), p. 25.

11. William A. Corsaro and Katherine Brown Rosier, "Documenting Productive-Reproductive Processes in Children's Lives: Transition Narratives of a Black Family Living in Poverty," in *Interpretive Approaches to Children's Socialization*, ed. Corsaro and Miller, pp. 67–91.

12. Bugental and Goodnow, "Socialization Processes."

13. James Youniss, "Rearing Children for Society," in *Beliefs about Parenting: Origins and Developmental Implications*, ed. Judith G. Smetana, *New Directions for Child Development*, no. 66 (San Francisco: Jossey Bass, 1994), 37–50.

14. Cynthia Garcia Coll et al., "Parental Involvement in Children's Education: Lessons from Three Immigrant Groups," *Parenting: Science and Practice* 2 (2002): 303–324.

15. Ross D. Parke and Raymond Buriel, "Socialization in the Family: Ethnic and Ecological Perspectives," in *Handbook of Child Psychology*, 5th ed., ed. Damon, vol. 3, 463–552.

16. "California Seeks to Stop the Use of Child Medical Interpreters," *New York Times*, 30 October 2005, p. A17.

17. Murry, Smith, and Hill, "Race, Ethnicity, and Culture."

18. Nicholas Wade, "Race Is Seen As Real Guide to Track the Roots of Disease," *New York Times*, 30 July 2002, p. D1.

19. Parke and Buriel, "Socialization in the Family."

20. Cynthia Garcia Coll et al., "An Integration Model for the Study of Developmental Competencies in Minority Children," *Child Development* 67 (1996): 1891–1914.

21. Cynthia Garcia Coll and Lee M. Pachter, "Ethnic and Minority Parenting," in

Handbook of Parenting, 2nd ed., ed. Marc H. Bornstein, vol. 4: *Social Conditions and Applied Parenting* (Mahwah, NJ: Erlbaum, 2002), 1–20.

22. Ibid.
23. Robert H. Bradley et al., "The Home Environments of Children in the United States: Part II: Relations with Behavioral Development through Age Thirteen," *Child Development* 72 (2001): 1868–1886.
24. Annette Lareau, *Unequal Childhoods: Class, Race, and Family Life* (Berkeley: University of California Press, 2003), p. 274.
25. Patricia M. Greenfield and Lalita K. Suzuki, "Culture and Human Development: Implications for Parenting, Education, Pediatrics, and Mental Health," in *Handbook of Child Psychology*, 5th ed., ed. William Damon, vol. 4: *Child Psychology in Practice*, ed. Irving E. Sigel and K. Ann Renninger (New York: Wiley, 1998), 1059–1109.
26. Ibid.
27. U.S. Bureau of the Census, *Statistical Abstract of the United States: 2006*, 125th ed. (Washington, DC: Government Printing Office, 2005).
28. Parke and Buriel, "Socialization in the Family."
29. Samuel Eliot Morison, *Oxford History of the American People* (New York: Oxford University Press, 1965), p. 3.
30. Ibid., p. 15.
31. Ben A. Franklin, "American Indians Open a Massive New Museum in Washington," *Washington Spectator*, 15 October 2004, p. 2.
32. Illick, *American Childhoods.*
33. Walter T. Kawamoto and Tamara C. Cheshire, "American Indian Families," in *Families in Cultural Context*, ed. De Genova, pp. 15–34; Morison, *Oxford History of the American People*; Parke and Buriel, "Socialization in the Family."
34. Ibid.
35. U.S. Bureau of the Census, *Statistical Abstract of the United States: 2006.*
36. Parke and Buriel, "Socialization in the Family."
37. Kawamoto and Cheshire, "American Indian Families," p. 21.
38. Ibid., p. 20.
39. Parke and Buriel, "Socialization in the Family."
40. U.S. Bureau of the Census, *Statistical Abstract of the United States: 2006.*
41. Garcia Coll and Pachter, "Ethnic and Minority Parenting."
42. Niara Sudarkasa, "Interpreting the Afro-American Family Organization," in *Black Families*, 2nd ed., ed. Harriette Pipes McAdoo (Newbury Park, CA: Sage, 1988), 27–43.
43. Ibid.
44. John Hope Franklin, "A Historical Note on Black Families," in *Black Families*, 2nd ed., ed. McAdoo, pp. 23–26.
45. Ibid.
46. Morison, *Oxford History of the American People.*
47. Robert E. Martin, "Lynching," in *The Encyclopedia Americana*, vol. 17 (Danbury, CT: Grolier, 2000), 884–885.
48. Morison, *Oxford History of the American People.*
49. Andrew Billingsley, *Climbing Jacob's Ladder: The Enduring Legacy of African-American Families* (New York: Simon & Schuster, 1992); Franklin, "Historical Note on Black Families."
50. Billingsley, *Climbing Jacob's Ladder.*
51. Parke and Buriel, "Socialization in the Family."
52. Vonnie C. McLoyd, "The Impact of Economic Hardship on Black Families and Children: Psychological Distress, Parenting, and Socioemotional Development," *Child Development* 61 (1990): 311–346.
53. Ibid., p. 326.
54. Jacquelynne Faye Jackson, "Issues in Need of Initial Visitation: Race and Nation Specificity in the Study of Externalizing Behavior Problems and Discipline," *Psychological Inquiry* 8 (1997): 204–211.
55. Tom Luster and Harriette Pipes McAdoo, "Family and Child Influences on Educational Attainment," in *Black Children*, 2nd ed., ed. Harriette Pipes McAdoo (Thousand Oaks, CA: Sage, 2002), 141–174.
56. Peter Irons, *Jim Crow's Children* (New York: Viking, 2002).
57. Billingsley, *Climbing Jacob's Ladder.*
58. David M. Halbfinger and Steven A. Holmes, "Military Mirrors a Working-Class America," *New York Times*, 30 March 2003, pp. A1, B12, B13.
59. Ibid., p. B12.
60. Billingsley, *Climbing Jacob's Ladder.*

61. Jim Herron Zamora, "Black Men Bring Hope to Bloody Streets," *San Francisco Chronicle*, 29 September 2002, p. A23.

62. Billingsley, *Climbing Jacob's Ladder*, p. 354.

63. U.S. Bureau of the Census, *Statistical Abstract of the United States*: 2006.

64. Parke and Buriel, "Socialization in the Family."

65. Morison, *Oxford History of the American People*.

66. Robin Harwood et al., "Parenting among Latino Families in the United States," in *Handbook of Parenting*, 2nd ed., ed. Bornstein, vol. 4, pp. 21–46.

67. Parke and Buriel, "Socialization in the Family."

68. Ibid., p. 509.

69. Harwood et al., "Parenting among Latino Families."

70. Robin L. Harwood et al., "Cultural Differences in Maternal Beliefs and Behaviors: A Study of Middle-Class Anglo and Puerto Rican Mother-Infant Pairs in Four Everyday Situations," *Child Development* 70 (1999): 1005–1016.

71. Andrew J. Fuligni, Vivian Tseng, and May Lam, "Attitudes toward Family Obligations among American Adolescents with Asian, Latin American, and European Backgrounds," *Child Development* 70 (1999): 1030–1044.

72. Harwood et al., "Parenting among Latino Families."

73. Diana Jean Schemo, "Education Study Finds Hispanics Both Gaining and Lagging," *New York Times*, 8 September 2002, p. A23.

74. Ibid.

75. Ruth Chao and Vivian Tseng, "Parenting of Asians," in *Handbook of Parenting*, 2nd ed., ed. Bornstein, vol. 4, pp. 59–93.

76. Ibid.

77. Parke and Buriel, "Socialization in the Family."

78. Ibid.

79. U.S. Bureau of the Census, 2006.

80. Chao and Tseng, "Parenting of Asians."

81. Parke and Buriel, "Socialization in the Family."

82. Chao and Tseng, "Parenting of Asians."

83. Fred Rothbaum et al., "Immigrant Chinese and Euro-American Parents' Physical Closeness with Young Children: Themes of Family Relatedness," *Journal of Family Psychology* 14 (2000): 334–348.

84. Chao and Tseng, "Parenting of Asians."

85. Ibid.

86. Mary Martini, "How Mothers in Four American Cultural Groups Shape Infant Learning During Mealtimes," *Zero to Three* 22 (February–March, 2002): 14–20.

87. Ibid., p. 20.

88. Arab American Institute Foundation, online at www.aaiusa.org/demographics.htm.

89. Barbara C. Aswad, "Arab American Families," in *Families in Cultural Context*, ed. DeGenova, pp. 213–237.

90. Helen Hatab Samhan, "Who Are Arab-Americans?" Arab American Institute Foundation, online at www.aaiusa.org.

91. Aswad, "Arab American Families," p. 231.

92. Ibid.

93. Ibid.

94. Ibid.

95. Arab American Demographics, www.aaiusa/census/Demographics.htm

96. Ibid.

97. Samhan, "Who Are Arab-Americans?"

98. Aswad, "Arab American Families."

99. Ibid., p. 225.

100. Jean M. Twenge and Jennifer Crocker, "Race and Self-Esteem: Meta-Analyses Comparing Whites, Blacks, Hispanics, Asians, and American Indians, and Comment on Gray-Little and Hafdahl (2000)," *Psychological Bulletin* 128 (2002): 371–408.

101. Paul R. Amato and Frieda Fowler, "Parenting Practices, Child Adjustment, and Family Diversity," *Journal of Marriage and Family* 64 (2002): 703–716.

102. Marjory R. Gray and Laurence Steinberg, "Unpacking Authoritative Parenting: Reassessing a Multidimensional Construct," *Journal of Marriage and the Family* 61 (1999): 574–587.

103. Vonnie C. McLoyd and Julia Smith, "Physical Discipline and Behavior Problems in African American, European American, and Hispanic Children: Emotional Support As a Moderator," *Journal of Marriage and Family* 64 (2002): 40–53.

104. Mary Kay DeGenova, "Introduction," in *Families in Cultural Context*, ed. DeGenova, p. 6.

105. Erika Hoff, Brett Laursen, and Twila Tardif, "Socioeconomic Status and Parenting," in *Handbook of Parenting*, 2nd ed., ed. Bornstein, vol. 2, pp. 231–252.

106. Betty Hart and Todd R. Risley, *Meaningful Differences in the Everyday Experiences of Young American Children* (Baltimore: Brookes, 1995).
107. Lareau, *Unequal Childhoods.*
108. Rand D. Conger et al., "Family Economic Stress and Adjustment of Early Adolescent Girls," *Developmental Psychology* 29 (1993): 206–219; Rand D. Conger et al., "A Family Process Model of Economic Hardship and Adjustment of Early Adolescent Boys," *Child Development* 63 (1992): 526–541; Constance A. Flanagan, "Change in Family Work Status: Effects on Parent-Adolescent Decision-Making," *Child Development* 61 (1990): 163–177; Constance A. Flanagan and Jacquelynne S. Eccles, "Changes in Parents' Work Status and Adolescents' Adjustment at School," *Child Development* 64 (1993): 246–257.
109. Leslie Morrison Gutman and Jacquelynne S. Eccles, "Financial Strain, Parenting Behaviors, and Adolescent Achievement: Testing Model Equivalence between African American and European American Single- and Two-Parent Families," *Child Development* 70 (1999): 1464–1476.
110. Nancy E. Hill, Kevin R. Bush, and Mark W. Roosa, "Parenting and Family Socialization Strategies and Children's Mental Health: Low-Income African American and Euro-American Mothers and Children," *Child Development* 74 (2003): 189–204.
111. Ronald L. Simons et al., "Support from Spouse as Mediator and Moderator of the Disruptive Influence of Economic Strain on Parenting," *Child Development* 63 (1992): 1282–1301.
112. Ronald L. Simons et al., "Social Network and Marital Support as Mediators and Moderators of the Impact of Stress and Depression on Parental Behavior," *Developmental Psychology* 29 (1993): 368–381.
113. Vonnie C. McLoyd, "Children in Poverty: Development, Public Policy, and Practice," in *Handbook of Child Psychology*, 5th ed., ed. Damon, vol. 4, pp. 135–208.
114. Robert Pear, "Number of People Living in Poverty Increases in U.S.," *New York Times*, 25 September 2002, p. A1.
115. McLoyd, "Children in Poverty."
116. U.S. Bureau of the Census (online): www.census.gov.
116. U.S. Bureau of the Census, *Statistical Abstract of the United States: 2006.*

117. Mary E. Corcoran and Ajay Chaudry, "The Dynamics of Childhood Poverty," *Future of Children* 7, no. 2 (1997): 40–54.
118. McLoyd, "Children in Poverty."
119. Jeanne Brooks-Gunn and Greg J. Duncan, "The Effects of Poverty on Children," *Future of Children* 7, no. 2 (1997): 55–71.
120. Ibid.
121. Richard Rothstein, "Rx for Good Health and Good Grades," *New York Times*, 11 September 2002, p. A30.
122. Greg J. Duncan and Jeanne Brooks-Gunn, "Family Poverty, Welfare Reform, and Child Development," *Child Development* 71 (2000): 188–196.
123. John M. Love et al., "The Effectiveness of Early Head Start for Three-Year-Old Children and Their Parents: Lessons for Policy and Programs," *Developmental Psychology* 41 (2005): 885–901.
124. Aletha C. Huston et al., "Impacts on Children of a Policy to Promote Employment and Reduce Poverty for Low-Income Parents: New Hope after 5 Years," *Developmental Psychology* 41 (2005): 902–908.
125. David L. Kirp, "Life Way After Head Start," *New York Times Magazine*, 21 November 2004, 32–38.
126. Tammy L. Mann, "Findings from the Parent-Child Project and the Impact of Values on Parenting: Reflections in a 'Scientific' Age," *Zero to Three* 20 (December 1999–January 2000): 3–8.
127. Ibid., p. 8.
128. Ibid.
129. Vivian J. Carlson and Robin L. Harwood, "Understanding and Negotiating Cultural Differences Concerning Early Developmental Competence: The Six-Raisin Solution," *Zero to Three* 20 (December 1999–January 2000): 19–24.
130. Ibid., p. 24.

CHAPTER 4
1. Benedict Carey, "Holding Loved One's Hand Can Calm Jittery Nerves," *New York Times*, 31 January 2006, p. D7.
2. Lois Wladis Hoffman and Jean Denby Manis, "The Values of Children in the United States: A New Approach to the Study of Fertility," *Journal of Marriage and the Family* 41 (1979): 583–596.
3. Steven Farkas et al., *A Lot Easier Said Than Done: Parents Talk About Raising Children* (New York: Public Agenda, 2002).

4. John H. Grych, "Marital Relationships and Parenting," in *Handbook of Parenting*, 2nd ed., ed. Marc H. Bornstein, vol. 4: *Social Conditions and Applied Parenting* (Mahwah, NJ: Erlbaum, 2002), 203–225.

5. Ibid.

6. Patrick T. Davies, E. Mark Cummings, and Marcia A. Winter, "Pathways between Profiles of Family Functioning, Child Security in the Interpersonal System and Child Psychological Problems," *Development and Psychopathology* 16 (2004): 525–550.

7. Jay Belsky and R. M. Pasco Fearon, "Exploring Marriage-Parenting Typologies and Their Contextual Antecedents and Developmental Antecedents," *Development and Psychopathology* 16 (2004): 501–523.

8. Jelani Mandara and Carolyn B. Murray, "Development of an Empirical Typology of African American Family Functioning," *Journal of Family Psychology* 16 (2002): 318–337.

9. Belsky and Fearon, "Exploring Marriage-Parenting Typologies."

10. James McHale et al., "Coparenting in Diverse Family Systems," in *Handbook of Parenting*, 2nd ed., ed. Marc H. Bornstein, vol. 3: *Being and Becoming a Parent* (Mahwah, NJ: Erlbaum, 2002), 75–107.

11. Ibid., p. 76.

12. Ibid.

13. Jennifer M. Jenkins et al., "Change in Maternal Perception of Sibling Negativity: Within- and Between-Family Influence," *Journal of Family Psychology* 19 (2005): 533–541.

14. Jim Snyder, Lew Bank, and Bert Burraston, "The Consequences of Antisocial Behavior in Older Male Siblings for Younger Brothers and Sisters," *Journal of Family Psychology* 19 (2005): 643–653.

15. Barbara Shebloski, Katherine J. Conger, and Keith F. Widaman, "Reciprocal Links Among Differential Parenting, Perceived Partiality and Self-Worth: A Three-Wave Longitudinal Study," *Journal of Family Psychology* 19 (2005): 633–641.

16. Laurie Kramer and Amanda K. Kowal, "Sibling Relationships Quality from Birth to Adolescence: The Enduring Contributions of Friends," *Journal of Family Psychology* 19 (2005): 503–511.

17. Barbara L. Fredrickson, "The Role of Positive Emotions in Positive Psychology: The Broaden-and-Build Theory of Positive Emotions," *American Psychologist* 56 (2001): 218–226.

18. Ann S. Masten, "Ordinary Magic: Resilience Processes in Development," *American Psychologist* 56 (2001): 227–238.

19. Charles C. Carlson and John C. Masters, "Inoculation by Emotion: Effects of Positive Emotional States on Children's Reactions to Social Comparison," *Developmental Psychology* 22 (1986): 760–765.

20. Jane B. Brooks and Doris M. Elliott, "Prediction of Psychological Adjustment at Age Thirty from Leisure Time Activities and Satisfactions in Childhood," *Human Development* 14 (1971): 61–71.

21. Ashley Montague, *Touching*, 2nd ed. (New York: Harper & Row, 1978).

22. Tiffany Field, "Infant Masssage Therapy," in *Handbook of Infant Mental Health*, 2nd ed., ed. Charles H. Zeanah (New York: Guilford, 2000), 494–500.

23. Urs A. Hunziker and Ronald G. Barr, "Increased Carrying Reduces Crying: A Randomized Controlled Trial," *Pediatrics* 77 (1986): 641–647.

24. Tiffany Field, "The Effects of Mother's Physical and Emotional Availability on Emotion Regulation," in *Development of Emotion Regulation: Biological and Behavioral Considerations*, ed. Nathan A. Fox, *Monographs of the Society for Research in Child Development* 59, serial no. 240 (1994): 208–227.

25. Field, "Infant Massage Therapy."

26. Carey, "Holding Loved One's Hand Can Calm Jittery Nerves."

27. Field, "The Effects of Mother's Physical and Emotional Availability on Emotion Regulation."

28. Dorothy C. Briggs, *Your Child's Self-Esteem* (Garden City, NY: Doubleday, 1970), 61–62.

29. John M. Gottman, Lynn Fainsilber Katz, and Carole Hooven, "Parental Meta-Emotion Philosophy and the Emotional Life of Families: Theoretical Models and Preliminary Data," *Journal of Family Psychology* 10 (1996): 243–268.

30. John Gottman with Joan DeClaire, *The Heart of Parenting: Raising an Emotionally Intelligent Child* (New York: Simon & Schuster, 1997).

31. Ibid.

32. Nancy Eisenberg et al., "Parental Reactions to Children's Negative Emotions: Longitudinal

Relations to Quality of Children's Social Functioning," *Child Development* 70 (1999): 513–534.

33. Beverly J. Wilson and John M. Gottman, "Marital Conflict, Repair, and Parenting," in *Handbook of Parenting*, 2nd ed., ed. Bornstein, vol. 4: 227–258.

34. Thomas Gordon, *P.E.T.: Parent Effectiveness Training* (New York: New American Library, 1975); Thomas Gordon with Judith G. Sands, *P.E.T. in Action* (New York: Bantam Books, 1978); Thomas Gordon, *Teaching Children Self-Discipline* (New York: Random House, 1989).

35. Gordon with Sands, *P.E.T. in Action*, p. 47.

36. Judy Dunn, Jane Brown, and Lynn Beardsall, "Family Talk about Feeling States and Children's Later Understanding of Others' Emotions," *Developmental Psychology* 27 (1991): 448–455.

37. Adele Faber and Elaine Mazlish, *Liberated Parents/Liberated Children* (New York: Avon Books, 1975).

38. John A. Clausen, Paul H. Mussen, and Joseph Kuypers, "Involvement, Warmth, and Parent-Child Resemblance in Three Generations," in *Present and Past in Middle Life*, ed. Dorothy H. Eichorn et al. (New York: Academic Press, 1981), 299–319.

39. Steven J. Wolin and Linda A. Bennett, "Family Rituals," *Family Process* 23 (1984): 401–420.

40. Linda A. Bennett et al., "Couples at Risk for Transmission of Alcoholism: Protective Influences," *Family Process* 26 (1987): 111–129.

41. Barbara Fiese et al., "A Review of 50 Years of Research on Naturally Occurring Family Routines and Rituals: Cause for Celebration?" *Journal of Family Psychology* 16 (2002): 381–390.

42. Ibid.

43. Robert Serpell et al., "Intimate Culture of Families in the Early Socialization of Literacy," *Journal of Family Psychology* 16 (2002): 391–405.

44. Fiese et al., "A Review of 50 Years of History."

45. William J. Doherty, *The Intentional Family* (New York: Avon, 1997).

46. Susan Engel, *The Stories Children Tell* (New York: Freeman, 1999).

47. Ibid., p. 4.

48. Ibid.

49. Ibid.

50. Ibid.

51. Don P. McAdams, *The Redemptive Self* (New York: Oxford University Press, 2006).

52. Barbara H. Fiese and Kathleen A. T. Marjinsky, "Dinnertime Stories: Connecting Family Practices with Relationship Beliefs and Child Adjustment," in *The Stories That Families Tell: Narrative Coherence, Narrative Interaction and Relationship Beliefs*, ed. Barbara H. Fiese et al., *Monographs of the Society for Research in Child Development* 64 (2, serial no. 257) (19199): 52–68.

53. Arnold J. Sameroff and Barbara H. Fiese, "Narrative Connections in the Family Context: Summary and Conclusions," in *The Stories That Families Tell*," ed. Fiese et al., p. 122.

54. Brooks and Elliott, "Prediction of Psychological Adjustment."

55. Farkas et al., *A Lot Easier Said Than Done.*

56. John P. Robinson and Geoffrey Godbey, *Time for Life* (University Park: Pennsylvania State University Press, 1997).

57. Ibid., pp. 48–49.

58. Sandra L. Hofferth, "Changes in American Children's Time, 1981–1997," *Brown University Child and Adolescent Behavior Letter*, March, 1999, p. 1.

59. Robinson and Godbey, *Time for Life.*

60. Ibid., p. 149.

61. Ibid., p. 316.

62. Keith Crnic and Christine Low, "Everyday Stresses and Parenting," in *Handbook of Parenting*, 2nd ed., ed. Marc H. Bornstein, vol. 5: *Practical Issues in Parenting* (Mahwah, NJ: Erlbaum, 2002), 243–267; Theodore Dix, "The Affective Organization of Parenting: Adaptive and Maladaptive Processes," *Psychological Bulletin* 110 (1991): 3–25.

63. Ernest N. Jouriles, Christopher M. Murphy, and K. Daniel O'Leary, "Effects of Maternal Mood on Mother-Son Interaction Patterns," *Journal of Abnormal Child Psychology* 17 (1989): 513–525.

64. John U. Zussman, "Situational Determinants of Parenting Behavior: Effects of Competing Cognitive Activity," *Child Development* 51 (1980): 772–780.

65. Crnic and Low, "Everyday Stresses and Parenting."

66. Crnic and Low, "Everyday Stresses and Parenting"; Jay Belsky, Keith Crnic, and Sharon Woodworth, "Personality and Parenting:

Exploring the Mediating Role of Transient Mood and Daily Hassles," *Journal of Personality* 63 (1995): 905–929.

67. Mona El-Sheikh, E. Mark Cummings, and Virginia Goetsch, "Coping with Adults' Angry Behavior: Behavioral, Physiological, and Verbal Responses in Preschoolers," *Developmental Psychology* 25 (1989): 490–498.

68. John M. Gottman and Lynn F. Katz, "Effects of Marital Discord on Young Children's Peer Interaction and Health," *Developmental Psychology* 25 (1989): 373–381.

69. E. Mark Cummings, "Coping with Background Anger in Early Childhood," *Child Development* 58 (1987): 976–984.

70. Jennifer S. Cummings et al., "Children's Responses to Adult Behavior As a Function of Marital Distress and History of Interparent Hostility," *Child Development* 60 (1989): 1035–1043.

71. John H. Grych and Frank D. Fincham, "Children's Appraisals of Marital Conflict: Initial Investigation of the Cognitive-Contextual Framework," *Child Development* 64 (1993): 215–230.

72. Katherine Covell and Brenda Miles, "Children's Beliefs about Strategies to Reduce Parental Anger," *Child Development* 63 (1992): 381–390.

73. E. Mark Cummings et al., "Resolution and Children's Responses to Interadult Anger," *Developmental Psychology* 27 (1991): 462–470.

74. Katherine Covell and Rona Abramovitch, "Understanding Emotion in the Family: Children's and Parents' Attributions of Happiness, Sadness, and Anger," *Child Development* 57 (1987): 985–991.

75. Nancy Samalin with Catherine Whitney, *Love and Anger: The Parental Dilemma* (New York: Penguin Books, 1992).

76. Jane Nelson, *Positive Discipline* (New York: Ballantine Books, 1981).

77. Rudolf Dreikurs with Vicki Soltz, *Children: The Challenge* (New York: Hawthorne, 1964), pp. 55–56.

78. Timothy F. J. Tolson and Melvin N. Wilson, "The Impact of Two- and Three-Generational Family Structure on Perceived Family Style," *Child Development* 61 (1990): 416–428.

79. Jane L. Pearson et al., "Black Grandmothers in Multigenerational Households: Diversity in Family Structures on Parenting in the Woodlawn Community," *Child Development* 61 (1990): 434–442.

80. Peter K. Smith and Linda M. Drew, "Grandparenthood," in *Handbook of Parenting*, 2nd ed., ed Marc H. Bornstein, vol. 3: *Being and Becoming a Parent* (Mahwah, NJ: Erlbaum, 2002), 141–172.

81. Ibid., p. 147.

82. Ibid.

83. Ibid.

84. Natalie Angier, "Weighing the Grandma Factor," *New York Times*, 5 November 2002, p. D1.

85. Ibid.

86. Smith and Drew, "Grandparenthood."

87. Peter C. Scales, Peter L. Benson, and Eugene C. Roehlkepartain, *Grading Grownups: American Adults Report on Their Real Relationships with Kids* (Minneapolis: Lutheran Brotherhood and Search Institute, 2001).

88. Anita Weiner, Haggai Kuppermintz, and David Guttmann, "Video Home Training (The Orion Project): A Short-Term Preventive and Treatment Intervention for Families of Young Children," *Family Process* 33 (1994): 441–453.

89. Jay D. Schvaneveldt, Marguerite Fryer, and Renee Ostler, "Concepts of 'Badness' and 'Goodness' of Parents As Perceived by Nursery School Children," *The Family Coordinator* 19 (1970): 98–103.

90. John R. Weisz, "Autonomy, Control and Other Reasons Why 'Mom Is the Greatest': A Content Analysis of Children's Mother's Day Letters," *Child Development* 51 (1980): 801–807.

91. Personal communication.

CHAPTER 5

1. Sandra Blakeslee, "Cells That Read Minds," *New York Times*, 10 January 2006, p. D1.

2. Steve Farkas et al., *A Lot Easier Said Than Done: Parents Talk about Raising Children in Today's America* (New York: Public Agenda, 2002).

3. Lynn Okagaki and Diana Johnson Divecha, "Development of Parental Beliefs," in *Parenting: An Ecological Perspective*, ed. Tom Luster and Lynn Okagaki (Hillsdale, NJ: Erlbaum, 1993), 35–67.

4. E. Mark Cummings, Patrick T. Davies, and Susan B. Campbell, *Developmental Pathology and Family Process: Theory, Research, and Clinical Implications* (New York: Guilford, 2000).

5. Lea Winerman, "The Mind's Mirror," *Monitor on Psychology*, October, 2005: 49–50.

6. Blakeslee, "Cells That Read Minds."

7. Beth Azar, "How Mimicry Begat Culture," *Monitor on Psychology*, October, 2005: 54–56.

8. Sadie F. Dingfelder, "Autism's Smoking Gun?" *Monitor on Psychology*, October, 2005: 52–53.

9. Bruce D. Perry, "Incubated in Terror: Neurodevelopmental Factors in the Cycle of Violence," in *Children in a Violent Society*, ed. Joy D. Osofsky (New York: Guilford, 1997), 124–149.

10. Tiffany Field, "Psychologically Depressed Parents," in *Handbook of Parenting,* ed. Mark H. Bornstein, vol. 4: *Applied and Practical Parenting* (Mahwah, NJ: Erlbaum, 1995), 85–99.

11. Blakeslee, "Cells That Read Minds."

12. Carol Zander Malatesta and Jeanette M. Haviland, "Learning Display Rules: The Socialization of Emotion Expression in Infancy," *Child Development* 53 (1982): 991–1003.

13. Marion Radke-Yarrow et al. "Learning Concern for Others," *Developmental Psychology* 8 (1973): 240–260.

14. Elizabeth L. Pollard and Mark L. Rosenberg, "The Strength-Based Approach to Child Well-Being: Let's Begin with the End in Mind," in *Well-Being: Positive Development Across the Life Course*, ed. Marc H. Bornstein et al. (Mahwah, NJ: Erlbaum, 2003), 13–21.

15. Farkas et al., "Easier Said Than Done."

16. Tara Parker-Pope, "How to Give Your Child a Longer Life," *The Wall Street Journal*, 9 December 2003, p. R1.

17. David A. Sleet and James A. Mercy, "Promotion of Safety, Security, and Well-Being," in *Well-Being*, ed. Bornstein, 81–97.

18. Wanda M. Hunter et al., "Injury Prevention Advice in Top-Selling Parenting Books," *Pediatrics* 116 (2005): 1080–1088.

19. Linda C. Mayes and Sean D. Truman, "Substance Abuse and Parenting," in *Handbook of Parenting*, 2nd ed., ed Marc H. Bornstein, vol. 4: *Special Conditions and Applied Parenting* (Mahwah, NJ: Erlbaum, 2002), 329–359.

20. Caroline H. Leavitt, Thomas F. Tonniges, and Martha F. Rogers, "Good Nutrition—The Imperative for Positive Development," in *Well-Being*, ed. Bornstein, 35–49.

21. Gina Kolata, "Thinning the Milk Does Not Mean Thinning the Child," *New York Times*, 12 February 2006, section 4, p. 3.

22. Leavitt, Tonniges, and Rogers, "Good Nutrition."

23. Kaiser Family Foundation Report, "Role of Media in Childhood Obesity," February, 2004. www.kff.org.

24. Parker-Pope, "How to Give Your Child a Longer Life."

25. Kolata, "Thinning the Milk Does Not Mean Thinning the Child."

26. Jeanette M. Connor, "Physical Activity and Well-Being," in *Well-Being*, ed. Bornstein, 65–79.

27. Kim Severson, "Politicians Prodded on Child Obesity," *San Francisco Chronicle*, 12 December 2002, p. A1.

28. Jane E. Brody, "Time to Get Out, for the Body and the Mind," *New York Times*, 14 February 2006, p. D7.

29. Connor, "Physical Acitivity and Well-Being."

30. Beth Azar, "Wild Findings in Animal Sleep," *Monitor on Psychology*, January, 2006: 54–55.

31. David Tuller, "Poll Finds Even Babies Don't Get Enough Rest," *New York Times*, 30 March 2004, p. D5.

32. James C. Sillbury et al., "Sleep Behavior in an Urban U.S. Sample of School-Aged Children," *Archives of Pediatric and Adolescent Medicine* 158 (2004): 988–994.

33. Lea Winerman, "Brain Heal Thyself," *Monitor on Psychology*, January, 2006: 56–57.

34. Lea Winerman, "Let's Sleep On It," *Monitor on Psychology*, January, 2006: 58–60.

35. Marc Weissbluth, *Healthy Sleep Habits, Healthy Child* (New York: Fawcett, 1999).

36. Avi Sadeh, Reut Gruber, and Amiram Raviv, "The Effects of Sleep Restriction and Extension on School-Aged Children: What a Difference an Hour Makes," *Child Development* 74 (2003): 444–455.

37. Weissbluth, *Healthy Sleep Habits, Happy Child*.

38. Alice M. Gregory and Thomas G. O'Connor, "Sleep Problems in Childhood: A Longitudinal Study of Developmental Change and Association I Behavioral Problems, "*Journal of the American Academy of Child and Adolescent Psychiatry* 41 (2000): 964–971.

39. Robert M. Bradley and Robert F. Corwyn, "Productive Activity and the Prevention of Behavior Problems," *Developmental Psychology* 41 (2005): 89–98.

40. Victoria Rideout, Donald F. Roberts, and Ulla G. Foehr, "Generation M: Media in the Lives of 8–18-Year-Olds," Kaiser Family Foundation Report No. 7250, March, 2005. www.kff.org.

41. Victoria Rideout and Elizabeth Hamel, "The Media Family: Electronic Media in the Lives of Infants, Toddlers, Preschoolers, and Their Parents," Kaiser Family Foundation, Report No. 7500, May 2006. www.kff.org.

42. Ibid.

43. Rideout, Roberts, and Foehr, "Generation M."

44. Ibid.

45. Aimee Dorr, Beth E. Rabin, and Sandra Irlen, "Parenting in a Multimedia Society," in *Handbook of Parenting*, 2nd ed., ed. Marc H. Bornstein, vol. 5: *Practical Issues in Parenting* (Mahwah, NJ: Erlbaum, 2002), 349–373.

46. Rideout and Hamel, "The Media Family."

47. Ibid.

48. Ibid.

49. Dorr, Rabin, and Irlen, "Parenting in a Multimedia Society."

50. Donna L. Mumme and Anne Fernald, "The Infant as Onlooker: Learning from Emotional Reactions Observed in a Television Scenario," *Child Development* 74 (2003): 221–237.

51. Daniel R. Andersoon et al., "Early Childhood Television Viewing and Adolescent Behavior," *Monographs of the Society for Research in Child Development* 66 (2001): 1, Serial No. 264.

52. Darcy A. Thompson and Dimitri A. Christakis, "The Association between Television Viewing and Irregular Sleep Schedules among Children Less Than Three Years of Age," *Pediatrics* 116 (2005): 851–856.

53. Dimitri A. Christakis et al., "Early Television Exposure and Subsequent Attentional Problems in Children," *Pediatrics* 113 (2004): 708–713.

54. Frederick J. Zimmerman and Dimitri A. Christakis, "Children's Television Viewing and Cognitive Outcomes: A Longitudinal Analysis of National Data," *Archives of Pediatric and Adolescent Medicine* 159 (2005): 619–625.

55. Dina L. G. Borzekowski and Thomas N. Robinson, "The Remote, the Mouse, and the No. 2 Pencil," *Archives of Pediatric and Adolescent Medicine* 159 (2005): 607–613.

56. Thomas N. Robinson, "Reducing Children's Television to Prevent Obesity: A Randomized Controlled Trial," *Journal of the American Medical Association* 282 (1999): 1561–567.

57. John D. Coie and Kenneth A. Dodge, "Aggression and Antisocial Behavior," in *Handbook of Child Psychology*, 5th ed., ed. Damon, vol. 3, 799.

58. L. Rowell Huesmann et al., "Longitudinal Relations between Children's Exposure to TV Violence and Their Aggressive and Violent Behavior in Young Adulthood: 1977–1992," *Developmental Psychology* 39 (2003): 201–221.

59. Brian H. Bornstein and Monica K. Miller, "Just a Game? Psychologists Play a Critical Role in Video Game Controversy," *Monitor on Psychology*, May 2006: 99.

60. Liliana Escobar-Chaves, "Impact of the Media on Adolescent Sexual Behavior," *Pediatrics* 116 (2005): 297–331.

61. Rebecca L. Collins et al., "Watching Sex on Television Predicts Adolescent Initiation of Sexual Behavior," *Pediatrics* 114 (2004): 280–289.

62. Jane D. Brown et al., "Sexy Media: Exposure to Sexual Content in Music, Movies, Television, and Magazines Predicts Black and White Adolescents' Sexual Behavior," *Pediatrics* 117 (2006): 1018–1027.

63. Escobar-Chaves, "Impact of Media on Adolescent Sexual Behavior."

64. Rideout and Hamel, "The Media Family."

65. Rideout, Roberts, and Foehr, "Generation M."

66. Ibid.

67. Dorr, Rabin, and Irlen, "Parenting in a Multimedia Society."

68. Robinson, "Reducing Children's Television Viewing to Prevent Obesity"; Thomas N. Robinson et al., "Effects of Reducing Children's Television and Video Game Use on Aggressive Behavior: A Randomized Controlled Trial," *Archives of Pediatric and Adolescent Medicine* 155 (2001): 17–23.

69. American Academy of Pediatrics Committee on Public Education. "Media Education." *Pediatrics* 104 (1999): 341–343.

70. Ross A. Thompson, Sara Meyer, and Meredith McGinley, "Understanding Values in Relationships: The Development of Conscience," in *Handbook of Moral Development,* ed. Melanie Killen and Judith Smetana (Mahwah, NJ: Erlbaum, 2006), 267–297.

71. Grazyna Kochanska et al., "Maternal Parenting and Children's Conscience: Early Security as Moderator," *Child Development* 75 (2004): 1229–1242.

72. Gerald R. Patterson and Philip A. Fisher, "Recent Developments in Our Understanding of Parenting: Bidirectional Effects, Causal Models, and the Search for Parsimony," in *Handbook of Parenting,* 2nd ed., ed. Marc H. Bornstein, vol. 5: *Practical Issues in Parenting* (Mahwah, NJ: Erlbaum, 2002), 59–88.

73. Barbara Rogoff, "Cognition as Collaborative Process," in *Handbook of Child Psychology,* 5th ed., ed. William Damon, vol. 2: *Cognition, Perception, and Language,* ed. Deanna Kuhn and Robert S. Siegler (New York: Wiley, 1998), 679–744.

74. Ibid.

75. Ibid.

76. Watty Piper, *The Little Engine That Could* (New York: Platt & Monk, 1930).

77. Rudolf Dreikurs with Vicki Soltz, *Children: The Challenge* (New York: Hawthorn, 1964).

77. Rudolf Dreikurs with Vicki Soltz, *Children: The Challenge* (New York: Hawthorn, 1964).

78. Ibid., p. 39.

79. Ibid., p. 108.

80. Farkas et al., "Easier Said Than Done."

81. Haim Ginott, *Between Parent and Child* (New York: Avon, 1969), p. 39.

82. Carolyn Saarni, Donna L. Mumme, and Joseph J. Campos, "Emotional Development Action, Communication and Culture," in *Handbook of Child Psychology,* 5th ed., ed. William Damon, vol. 3: *Social, Emotional, and Personality Development,* ed. Nancy Eisenberg (New York: Wiley, 1998), 237–309.

83. Inge Bretherton et al., "Learning to Talk about Emotions: A Functionalist Perspective," *Child Development* 57 (1986): 534.

84. Dymphna van den Boom, " Do First-Year Interventions Effects Endure?" Follow-Up during Toddlerhood of a Sample of Dutch Irritable Infants," *Child Development* 66 (1995): 1798–1816.

85. Thompson, Meyer, and McGinley, "Understanding Values in Relationships."

86. Ibid.

87. Florence L. Goodenough, *Anger in Young Children* (Minneapolis: University of Minnesota Press, 1931).

88. Judy S. DeLoache, Kevin F. Miller, and Sophia L. Pierroutsakos, "Reasoning and Problem Solving," in *Handbook of Child Psychology,* 5th ed., ed. Damon, vol. 2: *Cognition, Perception, and Language,* ed. Kuhn and Siegler, 801–850.

89. Farkas et al., "Easier Said Than Done," p. 18.

90. De Loache, Miller, and Pierroutsakos, "Reasoning and Problem Solving."

91. Ross D. Parke and Raymond Buriel, "Socialization in the Family: Ethnic and Ecological Perspectives," in *Handbook of Child Psychology,* 5th ed., ed Damon and Eisenberg, vol. 3, 463–552.

92. Maurice J. Elias, and Roger P. Weissberg, "School-Based Social Competence Promotion as a Primary Prevention Strategy: A Tale of Two Projects," *Prevention in Human Services* 7 (1990): 177–200.

93. Daniel Goleman, *Emotional Intelligence* (New York: Bantam, 1995).

94. Mary Gauvain and Ruth Duran-Huard, "Family Interaction, Parenting Style, and the Development of Planning: A Longitudinal Analysis Using Archival Data," *Journal of Family Psychology* 13 (1999): 75–92.

95. Albert Bandura, *Self-Efficacy: The Exercise of Control* (New York: W.H. Freeman, 1997).

96. George A. Bonanno, "Loss, Trauma, and Human Resilience: Have We Underestimated the Human Capacity to Thrive after Extremely Aversive Events?" *American Psychologist* 59 (2004): 20–28.

97. John Hope Franklin, *Mirror to America* (New York: Farrar, Straus and Giroux, 2005), p. 374.

98. Nancy Eisenberg and Bridget Murphy, "Parenting and Children's Moral Development," in *Handbook of Parenting,* ed. Marc H. Bornstein, vol. 4: *Applied and Practical Parenting* (Mahwah, NJ: Erlbaum, 1995), 227–257.

99. William Damon, *The Moral Child* (New York: Free Press, 1988), p. 2.

100. Robert Coles, *The Moral Intelligence of Children* (New York: Random House, 1997), p. 5.

101. Dreikurs with Soltz, *Children: The Challenge.*

102. Thomas Gordon, *P.E.T.: Parent Effectiveness Training* (New York: New American Library, 1975).

103. Chamberlain and Patterson, "Discipline and Child Compliance in Parenting."

104. Lawrence S. Wissow, "What Clinicians Want to Know about Teaching Families New Disciplinary Tools," *Pediatrics* 98 (1996): 815–817.

105. Thomas F Caltron and John C. Masters, "Mothers' and Children's Conceptualizations of Corporal Punishment," *Child Development* 64 (1993): 1815–1828.

106. Murray A. Straus, "Spanking and the Making of a Violent Society," *Pediatrics* 98 (1996): 837–844.

107. Farkas et al, "Easier Said Than Done."

108. Diana Baumrind, "Necessary Distinctions," *Psychological Inquiry* 8 (1997): 176–182.

109. Vonnie C. McLoyd and Julia Smith, "Physical Discipline and Behavior Problems in African American, European American, and Hispanic Children: Emotional Support As Moderator," *Journal of Marriage and Family* 64 (2002): 40–53.

110. Elizabeth Thompson Gershoff, "Corporal Punishment by Parents and Associated Child Behaviors and Experiences: A Meta-Analysis and Theoretical Review," *Psychological Bulletin* 128 (2002): 539–579; Ray Guarendi with David Eich, *Back to the Family* (New York: Simon & Schuster, 1991).

111. Anthony M. Graziano, Jessica L. Hamblen, and Wendy A. Plante, "Subabusive Violence in Child-Rearing in Middle-Class Families," *Pediatrics* 98 (1996): 845–848.

112. Randal D. Day, Gary W. Peterson, and Coleen McCracken, "Predicting Spanking of Younger and Older Children by Mothers and Fathers," *Journal of Marriage and the Family* 60 (1998): 79–94; Jean Giles-Sims, Murray A. Straus, and David B. Sugarman, "Child, Maternal, and Family Characteristics Associated with Spanking," *Family Relations* 44 (1995): 170–176.

113. Glenn D. Wolfner and Richard J. Gelles, "A Profile of Violence toward Children: A National Study," *Child Abuse and Neglect* 17 (1993): 199–214.

114. Graziano, Hamblen, and Plante, "Subabusive Violence."

115. Day, Peterson, and McCracken, "Predicting Spanking."

116. Giles-Sims, Straus, and Sugarman, "Child, Maternal, and Family Characteristics."

117. Day, Peterson, and McCracken, "Predicting Spanking"; Gershoff, "Corporal Punishment"; Giles-Sims, Straus, and

Sugarman, "Child, Maternal, and Family Characteristics."

118. Diana Baumrind, "The Development of Instrumental Competence through Socialization," in *Minnesota Symposium on Child Psychology,* vol. 7, ed. Ann D. Pick (Minneapolis: University of Minnesota Press, 1973), 3–46.

119. Day, Peterson, and McCracken, "Predicting Spanking."

120. McLoyd and Smith, "Physical Discipline and Behavior Problems."

121. Giles-Sims, Straus, and Sugarman, "Child, Maternal, and Family Characteristics."

122. Day, Peterson, and McCracken, "Predicting Spanking."

123. Giles-Sims, Straus, and Sugarman, "Child, Maternal, and Family Characteristics."

124. Ibid.

125. Day, Peterson, and McCracken, "Predicting Spanking."

126. Guarendi with Eich, *Back to the Family.*

127. Wissow, "What Clinicians Want to Know about Teaching Families New Disciplinary Tools."

128. Baumrind, "Discipline Controversy Revisited."

129. McLoyd and Smith, "Physical Discipline and Behavior Problems."

130. Ibid., p. 50.

131. Robert E. Larzelere, "A Review of Outcomes of Parental Use of Nonabusive or Customary Physical Punishment," *Pediatrics* 98 (1996): 824–828.

132. Gershoff, "Corporal Punishment."

133. Diana Baumrind, Robert E. Larzelere, and Philip A. Cowan, "Ordinary Physical Punishment: Is It Harmful? Comment on Gershoff (2002)," *Psychological Bulletin* 128 (2002): 580–589.

134. Straus, "Spanking and the Making of a Violent Society."

135. Baumrind, "The Disciplinary Controversy Revisited," p. 413.

136. Patterson and Fisher, "Recent Developments."

137. Robert W. Chamberlin, "'It Takes a Whole Village': Working with Community Coalitions to Promote Positive Parenting and Strengthen Families," *Pediatrics* 98 (1996): 805.

138. Baumrind, "The Discipline Controversy Revisited," p. 413.

139. Bruce Cedar and Ronald F. Levant, "A Meta-Analysis of the Effects of Parent

Effectiveness Training," *American Journal of Family Therapy* 18 (1990): 373–384; Paul C. Burnett, "Evaluation of Adlerian Parenting Programs," *Individual Psychology* 44 (1988): 63–76.

140. Anthony M. Graziano and David M. Diament, "Parent Behavior Training: An Examination of the Paradigm," *Behavior Modification* 16 (1992): 3–39.

141. Gerald R. Patterson and Carla M. Narrett, "The Development of a Reliable and Valid Treatment Program for Aggressive Young Children," *International Journal of Mental Health* 19 (1990): 19–26.

142. Amy Wolfson, Patricia Lacks, and Andrew Futterman, "Effects of Parent Training on Infant Sleeping Patterns, Parents' Stress, and Perceived Parental Competence," *Journal of Consulting and Clinical Psychology* 60 (1992): 41–48.

143. Carolyn Pape Cowan and Philip A. Cowan, *When Partners Become Parents* (New York: Basic Books, 1992).

144. Carolyn Pape Cowan, Philip A. Cowan, and Gertrude Heming, "Two Variations of a Preventive Intervention for Couples: Effects on Parents and Children during the Transition to School," in *The Family Context of Parenting in Children's Adaptation to Elementary School,* ed. Philip A. Cowan et al. (Mahwah, NJ: Erlbaum, 2005), 277–312.

145. Gene H. Brody, "The Strong African-American Families Program: Translating Research into Prevention Programming," *Child Development* 75 (2004): 900–917.

146. Camille Smith, Ruth Perou, and Catherine Lesesne, "Parent Education," in *Handbook of Parenting,* ed. Marc H. Bornstein, vol. 4: *Social Conditions and Applied Parenting,* 405.

147. Arnold Gesell and Frances L. Ilg, *The Child from Five to Ten* (New York: Harper & Row, 1946), p. 308.

CHAPTER 6

1. Jane Brody, "Easing the Trauma for the Tiniest in Intensive Care," *New York Times,* 27 June 2006, p. D7.

2. U.S. Census Bureau, *Statistical Abstract of the United States*: 2006, 125th ed. (Washington, DC: Government Printing Office, 2005).

3. Philip A. Cowan, Douglas Powell, and Carolyn Pape Cowan, "Parenting Interventions: A Family Systems Perspective," in *Handbook of Child Psychology,* 5th ed., ed. William Damon, vol. 4: *Child Psychology in Practice,* ed. Nancy Eisenberg (New York, Wiley, 1998), 3–72.

4. David Lykken, "Parental Licensure," *American Psychologist* 56 (2001): 883–894.

5. Christoph Heinicke, "The Transition to Parenting," in *Handbook of Parenting,* 2nd ed., ed. Marc H. Bornstein, vol. 3: *Being and Becoming a Parent* (Mahwah, NJ: Erlbaum, 2002), 363–388.

6. Jeanette M. Connor and James E. Dewey, "Reproductive Health," in *Well-Being: A Positive Development Across the Life Course,* ed. Marc H. Bornstein et al. (Mahwah, NJ: Erlbaum, 2003), 99–107.

7. Kelly Musick, "Planned and Unplanned Childbearing Among Unmarried Women," *Journal of Marriage and Family* 64 (2002): 915–929.

8. Ibid.

9. Carolyn Pape Cowan and Philip A. Cowan, *When Partners Become Parents* (New York: Basic Books, 1992).

10. Robert Schoen and Paula Tufis, "Precursors of Nonmarital Fertility in the United States," *Journal of Marriage and Family* 65 (2003): 1030–1040.

11. U.S. Bureau of the Census, *Statistical Abstract of the United States*: 2006.

12. E. Michael Foster, Damon Jones, and Saul D. Hoffman, "The Economic Impact of Nonmarital Childbearing: How Are Older, Single Mothers Faring?" *Journal of Marriage and Family* 60 (1998): 163–174.

13. Schoen and Tufis, "Precursors of Nonmarital Fertility in the United States."

14. Musick, "Planned and Unplanned Childbearing."

15. Gerald Y. Michaels, "Motivational Factors in the Decision and Timing of Pregnancy," in *The Transition to Parenthood,* ed. Gerald Y. Michaels and Wendy A. Goldberg (New York: Cambridge University Press, 1988), 23–61.

16. Nancy J. Cobb, *Adolescence* (Mountain View, CA: Mayfield, 1992).

17. Brenda W. Donnelly and Patricia Voydanoff, "Factors Associated with Releasing for Adoption among Adolescent Mothers," *Family Relations* 40 (1990): 404–410.

18. Marsha Weinraub, Danille L. Horvath, and Marcy B. Gringlas, "Single Parenthood," in *Handbook of Parenting,* 2nd ed., ed. Marc H. Bornstein, vol. 3, 109–140.

19. Melisa Ludtke, *On Our Own: Unmarried Motherhood in America* (New York: Random House, 1997).

20. Jane Mattes, *Single Mothers by Choice,* 2nd ed. (New York: Times Books, 1997).

21. Musick, "Planned and Unplanned Childbearing."

22. Wendy D. Manning, "The Implications of Cohabitation for Children's Well-Being," in *Just Living Together,* ed. Alan Booth and Ann C. Crouter (Mahwah, NJ: Erlbaum, 2002), 121–152.

23. Judith A. Seltzer, "Families Formed Outside of Marriage," *Journal of Marriage and Family* 62 (2000): 1247–1268.

24. Stacy Rosenkrantz Aronson and Aletha C. Huston, "The Mother-Infant Relationship in Single, Cohabiting, and Married Families: A Case for Marriage?" *Journal of Family Psychology* 18 (2004): 5–18.

25. Charlotte J. Patterson, "Lesbian and Gay Parenthood," in *Handbook of Parenting,* 2nd ed., ed. Bornstein, vol. 3, 317–338.

26. Ibid.

27. Conner and Dewey, "Reproductive Health."

28. Jennifer S. Barber, William G. Axinn, and Arland Thornton, "Unwanted Childbearing, Health, and Mother-Child Relationships," *Journal of Health and Social Behavior* 40 (1999): 231–257.

29. Henry P. David, Zdenek Dytrych, and Zdenek Matejcek, "Born Unwanted," *American Psychologist* 58 (2003): 224–229.

30. Adam Pertman, *Adoption Nation* (New York: Perseus, 2000), pp. 47–48.

31. Edward Zigler et al., *The First Three Years and Beyond* (New Haven: Yale University Press, 2002).

32. Ibid.

33. Janet A. Di Pietro et al., "Maternal Stress and Affect Influence Fetal Neurobehavioral Development," *Developmental Psychology* 38 (2002): 659–668.

34. Aronson and Huston, "The Mother-Infant Relationship."

35. Ellen Galinsky, *Between Generations: The Six Stages of Parenthood* (New York: Times, 1981).

36. Frank F. Furstenberg, J. Brooks-Gunn, and S. Philip Morgan, *Adolescent Mothers in Later Life* (Cambridge: Cambridge University Press, 1990), pp. 145–146.

37. Lianne Woodward, David M. Fergusson, and L. John Horwood, "Risk Factors and Life Processes Associated with Teenage Pregnancy: Results of a Prospective Study from Birth to Twenty Years," *Journal of Marriage and Family* 63 (2001): 1170–1184.

38. Laura V. Scaramella et al., "Predicting Risk for Pregnancy by Late Adolescence: A Social Contextual Perspective, *Developmental Psychology* 34 (1998): 1233–1245.

39. Judith Musick, "The Special Role of Parenting in the Context of Poverty: The Case of Adolescent Motherhood," in *Threats to Optimal Developmental: Integrating Biological Psychological and Social Risk Factors,* ed. Charles A. Nelson (Hillsdale, NJ: Erlbaum, 1994), 179–216.

40. Lisa A. Serbin et al., "Intergenerational Transfer of Psychosocial Risk in Women with Childhood Histories of Aggression, Withdrawal, or Aggression and Withdrawal," *Developmental Psychology* 34 (1998): 1242–1262.

41. Woodward, Fergusson, and Horwood, "Risk Factors and Life Processes."

42. Joy D. Osofsky, Della M. Hann, and Claire Peebles, "Adolescent Parenthood: Risks and Opportunities for Mothers and Infants," in *Handbook of Infant Mental Health,* ed. Charles H. Zeanah, Jr. (New York: Guilford, 1993), 106–119.

43. Osofsky, Hann, and Peebles, "Adolescent Parenthood."

44. Ibid.

45. Terrence P. Thornberry, Carolyn A. Smith, and Gregory J. Howard, "Risk Factors for Teenage Fatherhood," *Journal of Marriage and the Family* 59 (1997): 505–522.

46. James McCarthy and Janet Hardy, "Age at First Birth and Birth Outcomes," *Journal of Research on Adolescence* 3 (1993): 373–392.

47. Osofsky, Hann, and Peebles, "Adolescent Parenthood."

48. Nan Marie Astone, "Are Adolescent Mothers Just Single Mothers?" *Journal of Research on Adolescence* 3 (1993): 353–371.

49. Ibid.

50. Mignon R. Moore and Jeanne Brooks-Gunn, "Adolescent Parenthood," in *Handbook of Parenting,* 2nd ed., ed. Bornstein, vol. 3, 173–214.

51. Lisa A. Serbin, Patricia L. Peters, and Alexander E. Schwartzman, "Longitudinal Study of Early Childhood Injuries and Acute Illnesses in the Offspring of Adolescent Mothers Who Were Aggressive, Withdrawn,

or Aggressive-Withdrawn in Childhood," *Journal of Abnormal Psychology* 105 (1996): 500–507.

52. Moore and Brooks-Gunn, "Adolescent Parenthood."

53. Janet B. Hardy et al., "Like Mother, Like Child: Intergenerational Patterns of Age at First Birth and Associations with Childhood and Adolescent Characteristics and Adult Outcomes in the Second Generation," *Developmental Psychology* 34 (1998): 1220–1232.

54. Sara Jaffee et al., "Why are Children Born to Teen Mothers at Risk for Adverse Outcomes in Young Adulthood? Results from a 20-year Longitudinal Study," *Development and Psychopathology* 13 (2001): 377–397.

55. Ariel Kalil and James Kunz, "Teenage Childbearing, Marital Status, and Depressive Symptoms in Later Life," *Child Development* 73 (2002): 1748–1760.

56. U.S. Bureau of the Census, *Statistical Abstract of the United States: 2002.*

57. Carol Harkness, *The Infertility Book*, 2nd ed. (Berkeley, CA: Celestial Arts, 1992).

58. Andrew Yarrow, *Latecomers: Children of Parents over 35* (New York: Free Press, 1991).

59. Tamar Lewin, "Unwed Fathers Fight for Babies Placed for Adoption by Mothers," *New York Times*, 19 March 2006, p. A1.

60. Jason B. Johnson, "Father Grows Up," *San Francisco Chronicle*, 3 September 2002, p. A15.

61. Ronald Mincy, Irwin Garfinkel, and Lena Nepomnyaschy, "In-Hospital Paternity Establishment and Father Involvement in Fragile Families," *Journal of Marriage and Family* 67 (2005): 611–626.

62. Ibid.

63. Sara R. Jaffe et al., "Life With (or Without) Father: The Benefits of Living with Two Biological Parents Depend on the Father's Antisocial Behavior," *Child Development* 74 (2003): 109–126.

64. Emma Ross, "Patience for Parenthood," *San Francisco Chronicle*, 4 July 2002, p. A6.

65. Susan Golombok, "Parenting and Contemporary Reproductive Technologies," in *Handbook of Parenting*, 2nd ed., ed. Bornstein, vol. 3, 339–360.

66. Sylvia Pagan Westphal, "At Fertility Clinics, A New Emphasis on Gentle Methods," *Wall Street Journal*, 23 March 2006, p. A1.

67. Pam Belluck, "From Stem Cell Opponents, an Embryo Crusade," *New York Times*, 2 June 2005, p. A1.

68. Pam Belluck, "It's Not So Easy to Adopt an Embryo," *New York Times*, 12 June 2005, section 4, p. 5.

69. Belluck, "From Stem Cell Opponents."

70. Debora Spar, *The Baby Business: How Money, Science, and Politics Drive the Commerce of Conception* (Boston: Harvard University Press, 2006).

71. Lori B. Andrews, "Designer Babies," *Reader's Digest*, July 2001, p. 72.

72. Golombok, "Parenting and Contemporary Reproductive Technologies."

73. Susan Golombok et al., "Parenting Infants Conceived by Gamete Donations," *Journal of Family Psychology* 18 (2004): 443–452.

74. Susan Golombok et al., "Families Created Through Surrogacy Arrangements: Parent-Child Relationships in the 1st Year of Life," *Developmental Psychology* 40 (2004): 400–411.

75. Golombok, "Parenting and Contemporary Reproductive Technologies."

76. David Plotz, "Who's Your Daddy?" *New York Times*, 19 May 2005, p. A35.

77. Peggy Orenstein, "Looking for a Donor to Call Dad," *The New York Times Magazine*, 18 June 1995, p. 28.

78. David M. Brodzinsky and Ellen Pinderhughes, "Parenting and Child Development in Adoptive Families," in *Handbook of Parenting*, 2nd ed., ed. Marc H. Bornstein, vol. 1: *Children and Parenting* (Mahwah, NJ: Erlbaum, 2002), 279–311.

79. Spar, *Baby Business.*

80. Ibid.

81. Brodzinsky and Pinderhughes, "Parenting and Child Development in Adoptive Families."

82. Leslie Granston, "A World of Possibilities: International Adoption," *Vassar*, Summer, 2002, pp. 14–19.

83. Brodzinsky and Pinderhughes, "Parenting and Child Development in Adoptive Families."

84. Ibid.

85. Ibid.

86. Ibid.

87. Ibid.

88. Ibid

89. Ibid.

90. Golombok, "Parenting and Contemporary Reproductive Technologies."

91. Brodzinsky and Pinderhughes, "Parenting and Child Development in Adoptive Families."

92. Gail S. Goodman, Robert E. Emery, and Jeffrey J. Haugaard, "Developmental Psychology and Law: Divorce, Child Maltreatment,

Foster Care, and Adoption," in *Handbook of Child Psychology*, 5th ed., ed. William Damon, vol. 4: *Child Psychology in Practice*, ed. Irving E. Sigel and K. Ann Renninger (New York: Wiley, 1998), 775–874.

93. DiAnne Borders, Judith M. Penny, and Francine Portnoy, "Adult Adoptees and Their Friends: Current Functioning and Psychosocial Well Being," *Family Relations* 49 (2000): 407–418.

94. Brodzinsky and Pinderhughes, "Parenting and Child Development in Adoptive Families."

95. C. Robert Cloninger et al., "Predisposition to Petty Criminality in Swedish Adoptees: Cross-Fostering Analysis of Gene-Environment Interaction," *Archives of General Psychiatry* 39 (1982): 1242–1247.

96. Brodzinsky and Pinderhughes, "Parenting and Child Development in Adoptive Families."

97. Heinicke, "The Transition to Parenting."

98. Melissa Curran et al., "Representations of Early Family Relationships Predict Marital Maintenance During Transition to Parenthood," *Journal of Family Psychology* 19 (2005): 189–197.

99. Ross D. Parke and Barbara J. Tinsley, "Family Interaction in Infancy," in *Handbook of Infant Development*, 2nd ed., ed. Joy Doniger Osofsky (New York: Wiley, 1987), 579–641.

100. Jay Belsky and John Kelly, *The Transition to Parenthood* (New York: Delacorte Press, 1994).

101. Galinsky, *Between Generations*.

102. Myra Leifer, "Psychological Changes Accompanying Pregnancy and Motherhood, *Genetic Psychology Monographs* 95 (1977): 55–96.

103. Cowan and Cowan, *When Partners Become Parents*.

104. Belsky and Kelly, *Transition to Parenthood*.

105. Susan Goldberg and Barbara DiVitto, "Parenting Children Born Preterm," in *Handbook of Parenting*, 2nd ed., ed. Bornstein, vol. 1, 329–354.

106. Ibid.

107. Ruth Feldman et al., "Testing a Family Intervention Hypothesis: The Contribution of Mother-Infant Skin-to-Skin Contact (Kangaroo Care) to Family Interaction Proximity and Touch," *Journal of Family Psychology* 17 (2003): 94–107.

108. Sara Goldstein Ferber and Imad R. Makhoul, "The Effect of Skin-to-Skin Contact (Kangaroo Care) Shortly after Birth on the Neurobehavioral Responses of the Term Newborn: A Randomized, Controlled Trial," *Pediatrics* 113 (2004): 858–865.

109. Ibid., pp. 863–864.

110. Galinsky, *Between Generations*.

111. Ibid., p. 317.

112. Kathryn E. Barnard, Colleen E. Morisett, and Susan Spieker, "Preventive Interventions: Enhancing Parent-Infant Relationships," in *Handbook of Infant Mental Health*, ed. Zeanah, 386–401.

113. Amy Wolfson, Patricia Lacaks, and Andrew Futterman, "Effects of Parent Training on Infant Sleeping Patterns, Parents' Stress, and Perceived Parental Competence," *Journal of Consulting and Clinical Psychology* 60 (1992): 41–48.

114. Cowan and Cowan, *When Partners Become Parents*.

CHAPTER 7

1. Amy Harmon, "And Baby Makes Three in One Bed," *New York Times*, 29 December 2005, p. E1.

2. Thomas Anders, Beth Goodlin-Jones, and Avi Sadeh, "Sleep Disorders," in *Handbook of Infant Mental Health*, 2nd ed., ed. Charles H. Zeanah, Jr. (New York: Guilford, 2000), 326–328.

3. Marc Weissbluth, *Crybabies* (New York: Arbor House, 1984).

4. Ibid.

5. Daphne Blunt Bugental and Jacqueline J. Goodnow, "Socialization Processes," in *Handbook of Child Psychology*, 5th ed., ed. William Damon: vol. 3: *Social, Emotional, and Personality Development*, ed. Nancy Eisenberg (New York: Wiley, 1998), 1256–1297.

6. Andrew Meltzoff and M. Keith Moore, "Imitation of Facial and Manual Gestures by Human Neonates," *Science* 198 (1977): 75–78.

7. Tiffany Field, "The Effects of Mother's Physical and Emotional Availability on Emotion Regulation," in *Development of Emotional Regulation: Biological and Behavioral Considerations*, ed. Nathan A. Fox, Monographs of the Society for Research in Child Development 59, serial no. 240 (1994): 208–227.

8. Jayne Standley, "Music Therapy in the NICU: Promoting Growth and Development of Premature Infants," *Zero to Three* 23, no. 1 (2002): 23–30.

9. Colwyn Trevarthen and Stephen Malloch, "Musicality and Music before Three: Human Vitality and Invention Shared with Pride," *Zero to Three* 23, no.1 (2002): 10–18.

10. Carol Zander Malatesta and Jeannette M. Haviland, "Learning Display Rules: The Socialization of Emotion Expression in Infancy," *Child Development* 53 (1982): 991–1003.

11. Jeannette M. Haviland and Mary Lelwica, "The Induced-Affect Response: 10-Week-Old Infants' Responses to Three Emotion Expressions," *Developmental Psychology* 23 (1987): 97–104.

12. Carol Z. Malatesta et al., "Emotion Socialization and Expression Development in Preterm and Full Term Infants," *Child Development* 57 (1986): 316–330.

13. Ross A. Thompson, "Early Sociopersonality Development," in *Handbook of Child Psychology*, 5th ed., ed. Damon, vol. 3, pp. 25–104.

14. Ibid.

15. Ibid.

16. Robin Hornick, Nancy Risenhoover, and Megan Gunnar, "The Effects of Maternal Positive, Neutral, and Negative Affect Communication on Infant Responses to New Toys," *Child Development* 58 (1987): 936–944.

17. Susan Crockenberg and Esther Leerkes, "Infant Social and Emotional Development in Family Context," in *Handbook of Infant Mental Health*, 2nd ed., ed. Zeanah, pp. 60–90.

18. Gwen E. Gustafson, "Effects of the Ability to Locomote on Infants' Social and Exploratory Behaviors: An Experimental Study," *Developmental Psychology* 20 (1984): 397–405.

19. Herbert Ginsburg and Sylvia Opper, *Piaget's Theory of Intellectual Development* (Englewood Cliffs, NJ: Prentice-Hall, 1969); Jean Piaget and Barbel Inhelder, *The Psychology of the Child* (New York: Basic Books, 1969).

20. James V. Wertsch and Peeter Tulviste, "L. S. Vygotsky and Contemporary Developmental Psychology," *Developmental Psychology* 28 (1992): 548–557.

21. Lois Bloom, "Language Acquisition in Its Developmental Context," in *Handbook of Child Psychology*, 5th ed., ed. William Damon, vol. 2: *Cognition, Perception, and Language*, ed. Deanna Kuhn and Robert S. Siegler (New York: Wiley, 1998), 309–370.

22. Ibid.

23. Inge Bretherton et al., "Learning to Talk about Emotions: A Functionalist Perspective," *Child Development* 57 (1986): 529–548.

24. Ibid., p. 534.

25. Bloom, "Language Acquisition."

26. Malatesta and Haviland, "Learning Display Rules."

27. Ibid.

28. Eleanor J. Gibson and Richard D. Walk, "The Visual Cliff," *Scientific American* 202 (April 1960): 64–71.

29. Robin Hornick, Nancy Risenhoover, and Megan Gunnar, "The Effects of Maternal Positive, Neutral, and Negative Affect Communication on Infant Responses to New Toys," *Child Development* 58 (1987): 936–944.

30. Michael Lewis, "The Emergence of Emotions," in *Handbook of Emotions*, ed. Michael Lewis and Jeanette M. Haviland (New York: Guilford Press, 1993), 223–235.

31. Deborah Stipek, Susan Recchia, and Susan McClintic, *Self-Evaluation in Young Children*, Monographs of the Society for Research in Child Development 57, serial no. 226 (1992).

32. Pamela M. Cole, Karen Caplovitz-Barrett, and Carolyn Zahn-Waxler, "Emotion Displays in Two-Year-Olds during Mishaps," *Child Development* 63 (1992): 314–324; Deborah J. Stipek, J. Heidi Gralinski, and Claire B. Kopp, "Self-Concept Development in the Toddler Years," *Developmental Psychology* 26 (1990): 972–977.

33. Marion Radke-Yarrow et al., "Learning Concern for Others," *Developmental Psychology* 8 (1973): 240–260; Herbert Wray, *Emotions in the Lives of Young Children*, Department of Health, Education, and Welfare Publication no. 78-644 (Rockville, MD: 1978); Carolyn Zahn-Waxler et al., "Development of Concern for Others," *Developmental Psychology* 28 (1992): 126–136.

34. Florence L. Goodenough, *Anger in Young Children* (Minneapolis: University of Minnesota Press, 1931)..

35. Ibid.

36. Claire B. Kopp, "Regulation of Distress and Negative Emotions: A Developmental View," *Developmental Psychology* 25 (1989): 343–354.

37. Ibid.

38. Harriet L. Rheingold, Kay V. Cook, and Vicki Kolowitz, "Commands Cultivate the Behavioral Pleasure of Two-Year-Old Children," *Developmental Psychology* 23 (1987): 146–151.

39. Susan Harter, "The Development of Self-Representations," in *Handbook of Child Psychology*, 5th ed., ed. Damon, vol. 3, pp. 553–617.

40. Claire B. Kopp, "Antecedents of Self-Regulation: A Developmental Perspective," *Developmental Psychology* 18 (1982): 199–214.

41. Donelda J. Stayton, Robert Hogan, and Mary D. Salter Ainsworth, "Infant Obedience and Maternal Behavior: The Origins of Socialization Reconsidered," *Child Development* 42 (1971): 1057–1069.

42. Kopp, "Antecedents of Self-Regulation."

43. Brian E. Vaughn et al., "Process Analysis of the Behavior of Very Young Children in Daily Tasks," *Developmental Psychology* 22 (1986): 752–759.

44. Marianne S. De Wolff and Marinus van IJzendoorn, "Sensitivity and Attachment: A Meta-Analysis on Parental Antecedents of Infant Attachment," *Child Development* 68 (1997): 571–591.

45. Mary Jane Gandour, "Activity Level As a Dimension of Temperament in Toddlers: Its Relevance for the Organismic Specificity Hypotheses," *Child Development* 60 (1989): 1092–1098.

46. Ross D. Parke, "Fathers and Families," in *Handbook of Parenting*, 2nd ed., ed. Marc H. Bornstein, vol. 3: *Being and Becoming a Parent* (Mahwah, NJ: Erlbaum, 2002), 27–73.

47. W. Jean Yeung et al., "Children's Time with Fathers in Intact Families," *Journal of Marriage and Family* 63 (2001): 136–154.

48. Ibid.

49. Parke, "Fathers and Families."

50. Kathryn E. Barnard and JoAnn E. Solchany, "Mothering," in *Handbook of Parenting*, 2nd ed., ed. Bornstein, vol. 3, pp. 3–25.

51. Parke, "Fathers and Families."

52. Jay Belsky, Bonnie Gilstrap, and Michael Rovine, "The Pennsylvania Infant and Family Development Project I: Stability and Change in Mother-Infant and Father-Infant Interaction in a Family Setting at One, Three, and Nine Months," *Child Development* 55 (1984): 692–705.

53. Marc H. Bornstein, "Parenting Infants," in *Handbook of Parenting*, 2nd ed., ed. Marc H. Bornstein, vol. 1: *Children and Parenting* (Mahwah, NJ: Erlbaum, 2002), 3–43.

54. T. Berry Brazelton and Stanley I. Greenspan, *The Irreducible Needs of Children* (Cambridge, MA: Perseus, 2000).

55. Patricia M. Greenfield and Lalita K. Suzuki, "Culture and Human Development: Implications for Parenting, Education, Pediatrics, and Mental Health," in *Handbook of Child Psychology*, 5th ed., ed. William Damon, vol. 4: *Child Psychology in Practice*, ed. Irving E. Sigel and K. Ann Renninger (New York: Wiley, 1998), 1059–1109.

56. Sylvia M. Bell and Mary D. Salter Ainsworth, "Infant Crying and Maternal Responsiveness," *Child Development* 43 (1972): 1171–1190.

57. Judy Dunn, *Distress and Comfort* (Cambridge, MA: Harvard University Press, 1977), 23.

58. Urs A. Hunziker and Ronald G. Barr, "Increased Carrying Reduces Crying: A Randomized Controlled Trial," *Pediatrics* 77 (1986): 641–647.

59. William A. H. Sammons, *The Self-Calmed Baby* (Boston: Little, Brown, 1989).

60. Gilda A. Morelli et al., "Cultural Variations in Infants' Sleeping Arrangements: Questions of Independence," *Developmental Psychology* 28 (1992): 604–613.

61. Klaus Minde, "The Sleep of Infants and Why Parents Matter," *Zero to Three* 19 (October–November 1998): 9–14.

62. Richard Ferber, *Solve Your Child's Sleep Problems* (New York: Simon & Schuster, 1985).

63. Athleen B. Godfrey and Anne Kilgore, "An Approach to Help Very Young Infants Sleep through the Night," *Zero to Three* 19 (October–November 1998): 15–18.

64. Morelli et al., "Cultural Variations in Infants' Sleeping Arrangements."

65. Suad Nakamura, *"Adult Beds Are Unsafe Places for Children under Age Two to Sleep,"* American Medical Association media briefing on children's health, New York, 29 September 1999.

66. James J. McKenna, Sarah S. Mosko, and Christopher A. Richard, "Bedsharing Promotes Breastfeeding," *Pediatrics* 100 (1997): 214–219

67. Nakamura, "Adult Beds Are Unsafe."

68. John Seabrook, "Sleeping with the Baby," *New Yorker*, 8 November 1999.

69. James J. McKenna, "Cultural Influences on Infant and Childhood Sleep Biology, and the Science That Studies It: Toward a More Inclusive Paradigm," *Zero to Three* 20 (December 1999–January 2000): 17.

70. William Sears, introduction to *Attachment Parenting*, by Katie Allison Granju with Betsy Kennedy (New York: Pocket Books, 1999).

71. Katie Allison Granju with Betsy Kennedy, *Attachment Parenting* (New York: Pocket Books, 1999).

72. Ibid., p. 9.

73. Ibid., p. 10.

74. Kopp, "Antecedents of Self-Regulation."

75. Eleanor E. Maccoby and John A. Martin, "Socialization in the Context of the Family: Parent-Child Interaction," in *Handbook of Child Psychology*, 4th ed., ed. Paul H. Mussen and E. Mavis Hetherington, vol. 4: *Socialization, Personality, and Social Development* (New York: Wiley, 1983), 1–101.

76. Susan Crockenberg and Cindy Litman, "Autonomy As Competence in Two-Year-Olds: Maternal Correlates of Child Defiance, Compliance, and Self-Assertion," *Developmental Psychology* 26 (1990): 961–971.

77. George Holden, "Avoiding Conflicts: Mothers As Tacticians in the Supermarket," *Child Development* 54 (1983): 233–240; George W. Holden and Meredith J. West, "Proximate Regulation by Mothers: A Demonstration of How Differing Styles Affect Young Children's Behavior," *Child Development* 60 (1989): 64–69; Thomas G. Power and M. Lynne Chapieski, "Childrearing and Impulsive Control in Toddlers: A Naturalistic Investigation," *Developmental Psychology* 22 (1986): 271–275.

78. J. Heidi Gralinski and Claire B. Kopp, "Everyday Rules for Behavior: Mothers' Requests to Young Children," *Developmental Psychology* 29 (1993): 573–584.

79. Ibid.

80. Cheryl Minton, Jerome Kagan, and Janet A. Levine, "Maternal Control and Obedience in the Two-Year-Old," *Child Development* 42 (1971): 1873–1894.

81. Jeanne Brooks-Gunn and P. Lindsay Chase-Lansdale, "Adolescent Parenthood," in *Handbook of Parenting*, ed. Marc H. Bornstein, vol. 3: *Status and Social Conditions of Parenting* (Mahwah, NJ: Erlbaum, 1995), 113–149.

82. Joy D. Osofsky, Della M. Hann, and Claire Peebles, "Adolescent Parenthood: Risks and Opportunities for Mothers and Infants," in *Handbook of Infant Mental Health*, 2nd ed., ed. Zeanah, pp. 106–119.

83. Brooks-Gunn and Chase-Lansdale, "Adolescent Parenthood."

84. Ibid.

85. Sara Jaffee et al., "Why Are Children Born to Teen Mothers at Risk for Adverse Outcomes in Young Adulthood? Results from a 20-Year Study," *Development and Psychopathology* 13 (2001): 377–397; Judith Musick, "The Special Role of Parenting in the Context of Poverty: The Case of Adolescent Motherhood," in *Threats to Optimal Development: Integrating Biological, Psychological and Social Risk Factors*, ed. Charles A. Nelson (Hillsdale, NJ: Erlbaum, 1994), 179–216.

86. Musick, "The Special Role of Parenting."

87. Brooks-Gunn and Chase-Lansdale, "Adolescent Parenthood."

88. Frank F. Furstenberg, J. Brooks-Gunn, and S. Philip Morgan, *Adolescent Mothers in Later Life* (Cambridge, England: Cambridge University Press, 1990), 145–146.

89. Ross D. Parke and Raymond Buriel, "Socialization in the Family: Ethnic and Ecological Perspectives," in *Handbook of Child Psychology*, 5th ed., ed. Damon, vol. 3, pp. 463–552.

90. Ibid.

91. Beverly I. Fagot et al., "Becoming an Adolescent Father: Precursors and Parenting," *Developmental Psychology* 34 (1998): 1217.

92. Furstenberg, Brooks-Gunn, and Morgan, *Adolescent Mothers in Later Life*.

93. Tiffany Field, "Psychologically Depressed Parents," in *Handbook of Parenting*, ed. Marc H. Bornstein, vol. 4: *Applied and Practical Parenting* (Mahwah, NJ: Erlbaum, 1995), 85–99.

94. Ibid.

95. Linda C. Mayes and Sean D. Truman, "Substance Abuse and Parenting," in *Handbook of Parenting*, 2nd ed., ed. Marc H. Bornstein, vol 4: *Social Conditions and Applied Parenting* (Mahwah, NJ: Erlbaum, 2002), 329–359.

96. Ibid.

97. Ibid.

98. Rina Das Eiden, Felipa Chavez, and Kenneth E. Leonard, "Parent-Infant Interactions among Families with Alcoholic Fathers," *Development and Psychopathology* 11 (1999): 745–762.

99. Mayes and Truman, "Substance Abuse and Parenting."

100. Linda C. Mayes, "Developing Brain and In Utero Cocaine Exposure: Effects on Neural Ontogeny," *Development and Psychopathology* 11 (1999): 685–714.

101. Ibid., p. 706.

102. Carolyn Pape Cowan and Philip A. Cowan, *When Partners Become Parents* (New York: Basic Books, 1992), 142.

103. Ibid.

104. "Surge in Multiple Births Drives Premature Babies to Record," *New York Times*, 19 December 2002, p. A24.

105. Klaus Minde, "Prematurity and Serious Medical Conditions in Infancy: Implications for Development, Behavior, and Intervention," in *Handbook of Infant Mental Health*, 2nd ed., ed. Zeanah, pp. 176–194.

106. Susan Goldberg and Barbara DiVitto, "Parenting Children Born Preterm," in *Handbook of Parenting*, 2nd ed., ed. Bornstein, vol. 1, pp. 329–354.

107. Ibid.

108. Ibid., p. 339.

109. Ibid.

110. Mark T. Greenberg and Keith Crnic, "Longitudinal Predictors of Developmental Status and Social Interaction in Premature and Full-Term Infants at Age Two," *Child Development* 59 (1988): 544–553.

111. Goldberg and DiVitto, "Parenting Children Born Preterm."

112. Marilyn Stern and Katherine A. Hildebrandt, "Prematurity and Stereotyping: Effects on Mother-Infant Interaction," *Child Development* 57 (1986): 308–315.

113. Cynthia I. Zarling, Barton J. Hirsch, and Susan Landry, "Maternal Social Networks and Mother-Infant Interactions in Full-Term and Very Low Birthweight, Preterm Infants," *Child Development* 59 (1988): 178–185.

114. Glenn Affleck et al., "Effects of Formal Support on Mothers' Adaptation to the Hospital-to-Home Transition of High Risk Infants: The Benefits and Costs of Helping," *Child Development* 60 (1989): 488–501.

115. Leila Beckwith, "Prevention Science and Prevention Programs," in *Handbook of Infant Mental Health*, 2nd ed., ed. Zeanah, pp. 439–456.

116. Ellen Galinsky, *Between Generations: The Six Stages of Parenthood* (New York: Times Books, 1981).

117. Linda Mayes, "Harris Programs in Perinatal Mental Health at the Yale Child Study Center," *Zero to Three* 22, no. 6 (2002): 24–30.

118. Mayes, "Harris Programs."

119. Patricia K. Coleman and Katherine H. Karraker, "Self-Efficacy and Parenting Quality: Findings and Future Applications," *Developmental Review* 18 (1997): 47–85.

CHAPTER 8

1. Gretchen Cook, "Siblings of Disabled Have Their Own Troubles," *New York Times*, 4 April 2006, p. D5.

2. Allison Gopnick, Andrew N. Meltzoff, and Patricia K. Kuhl, *The Scientist in the Crib* (New York: Morrow, 1999).

3. Jean Piaget and Barbel Inhelder, *The Psychology of the Child* (New York: Basic Books, 1969).

4. Ross A. Thompson, "Early Sociopersonality Development," in *Handbook of Child Psychology*, 5th ed., ed. William Damon, vol. 3: *Social, Emotional, and Personality Development*, ed. Nancy Eisenberg (New York: Wiley, 1998), 25–104.

5. Lois Bloom, "Language Acquisition in Its Developmental Context," in *Handbook of Child Psychology*, 5th ed., ed. William Damon, vol. 2: *Cognition, Perception, and Language*, ed. Deanna Kuhn and Robert S. Siegler (New York: Wiley, 1998), 309–370.

6. Ibid.

7. Sally K. Donaldson and Michael A. Westerman, "Development of Children's Understanding of Ambivalent and Causal Theories of Emotions," *Developmental Psychology* 22 (1986): 655–662.

8. Richard A. Fabes et al., "Preschoolers' Attributions of the Situational Determinants of Others' Naturally Occurring Emotions," *Developmental Psychology* 24 (1988): 376–385.

9. Gertrude Nunner-Winkler and Beate Sodian, "Children's Understanding of Moral Emotions," *Child Development* 59 (1988): 1323–1338.

10. Frank A. Zelko et al., "Adult Expectancies about Children's Emotional Responsiveness: Implications for the Development of Implicit Theories of Affect," *Developmental Psychology* 22 (1986): 109–114.

11. William Roberts and Janet Strayer, "Parents' Responses to the Emotional Distress of Their Children: Relations with Children's Competence," *Developmental Psychology* 23 (1987): 415–422.

12. Michael Lewis, Catherine Stanger, and Margaret Sullivan, "Deception in Three-Year Olds," *Developmental Psychology* 25 (1989): 439–443.

13. Pamela M. Cole, "Children's Spontaneous Control of Facial Expressions," *Child Development* 57 (1986): 1309–1321.

14. Kurt W. Fischer and Daniel Bullock, "Cognitive Development in School Age Children: Conclusions and New Directions," in *Development during Middle Childhood: The Years from Six to Twelve*, ed. W. Andrew Collins (Washington, DC: National Academy Press, 1984).

15. Nancy Eisenberg et al., "The Relations of Emotionality and Regulation to Children's Anger-Related Reactions," *Child Development* 65 (1994): 109–128.

16. E. Mark Cummings, "Coping with Background Anger in Early Childhood," *Child Development* 58 (1987): 976–984.

17. Jerome Kagan and Nancy Snidman, "Temperamental Factors in Human Development," *American Psychologist* 46 (1991): 856–862.

18. Anders Broberg, Michael E. Lamb, and Philip Hwang, "Inhibition: Its Stability and Correlates in Sixteen- to Forty-Month-Old Children," *Child Development* 61 (1990): 1153–1163.

19. Jerome Kagan and Howard A. Moss, *From Birth to Maturity* (New York: Wiley, 1962).

20. Fabes et al., "Preschoolers' Attributions."

21. David Matsumoto et al., "Preschoolers' Moral Actions and Emotions in Prisoner's Dilemma," *Developmental Psychology* 22 (1986): 663–670.

22. Marion Radke-Yarrow et al., "Learning Concern for Others," *Developmental Psychology* 8 (1973): 240–260; Herbert Wray, *Emotions in the Lives of Young Children* (Rockville, MD: U.S. Department of Health, Education, and Welfare, 1978), publication no. 78–644.

23. Susan Harter, "The Development of Self-Representations," in *Handbook of Child Psychology*, 5th ed., ed. Damon, vol. 3, pp. 553–617.

24. Deborah J. Stipek, Theresa A. Roberts, and Mary E. Sanborn, "Preschool-Age Children's Performance Expectations of Themselves and Another Child As a Function of the Incentive Value of Success and the Salience of Past Performance," *Child Development* 55 (1984): 1983–1989.

25. Beverly I. Fagot, "Parenting Boys and Girls," in *Handbook of Parenting*, ed. Marc H. Bornstein, vol. 1: *Children and Parenting* (Mahwah, NJ: Erlbaum, 1995), 163–183.

26. Diane N. Ruble and Carol Lynn Martin, "Gender Development," in *Handbook of Child Psychology*, 5th ed., ed. Damon, vol. 3, pp. 933–1016.

27. Susan Golombok and Robyn Fivush, *Gender Development* (New York: Cambridge University Press, 1994).

28. Carolyn Pope Edwards and Wen-Li Liu, "Parenting Toddlers," in *Handbook of Parenting*, 2nd ed., ed. Marc H. Bornstein, vol. 1: *Children and Parenting* (Mahwah, NJ: Erlbaum, 2002), 45–71.

29. Golombok and Fivush, *Gender Development*, p. 111.

30. Ruble and Martin, "Gender Development."

31. Beverly I. Fagot and Mary D. Leinbach, "The Young Child's Gender Schema: Environmental Input, Internal Organization," *Child Development* 60 (1989): 663–672.

32. Patricia J. Bauer, "Memory for Gender-Consistent and Gender-Inconsistent Event Sequences by Twenty-five-Month-Old Children," *Child Development* 64 (1993): 285–297.

33. Ruble and Martin, "Gender Development."

34. Deanna Kuhn, Sharon Churnin Nash, and Laura Brucken, "Sex Role Concepts of Two-and Three-Year-Olds," *Child Development* 49 (1978): 445–451.

35. Campbell Leaper, "Parenting Boys and Girls," in *Handbook of Parenting*, 2nd ed., ed. Bornstein, vol. 1, pp. 189–225; Ruble and Martin, "Gender Development."

36. Carolyn Zahn-Waxler, "Warriors and Worriers: Gender and Psychopathology," *Development and Psychopathology* 5 (1993): 79–89.

37. Margaret Beale Spencer and Carol Markstrom-Adams, "Identity Processes among Racial and Ethnic Minority Children in America," *Child Development* 61 (1990): 290–310.

38. Frances E. Aboud, "The Development of Ethnic Identification and Attitudes," in *Children's Ethnic Socialization*, ed. Jean S. Phinney and Mary Jane Rotheram (Beverly Hills, CA: Sage, 1987).

39. Claire B. Kopp, "Antecedents of Self-Regulation: A Developmental Perspective," *Developmental Psychology* 18 (1982): 199–214.

40. J. Heidi Gralinski and Claire B. Kopp, "Everyday Rules for Behavior: Mothers' Requests to Young Children," *Developmental Psychology* 29 (1993): 573–584.

41. Leon Kucynski and Grazyna Kochanska, "Development of Children's Noncompliance Strategies from Toddlerhood to Age 5," *Developmental Psychology* 26 (1990): 398–408.

42. Susan Crockenberg and Cindy Litman, "Autonomy As Competence in Two-Year-Olds: Maternal Correlates of Child Defiance, Compliance, and Self-Assertion," *Developmental Psychology* 26 (1990): 961–971; Eleanor E. Maccoby and John A. Martin, "Socialization in the Context of the Family: Parent-Child Interaction," in *Handbook of Child Psychology*, 4th ed., ed. Paul H. Mussen and E. Mavis Hetherington, vol. 4: *Socialization, Personality, and Social Development* (New York: Wiley, 1983), 1–101.

43. Sandra R. Kaler and Claire B. Kopp, "Compliance and Comprehension in Very Young Toddlers," *Child Development* 61 (1990): 1997–2003.

44. Keng-Ling Lay, Everett Waters, and Kathryn A. Park, "Maternal Responsiveness and Child Compliance: The Role of Mood As Mediator," *Child Development* 60 (1989): 1405–1411.

45. Ross D. Parke and Raymond Buriel, "Socialization in the Family: Ethnic and Ecological Perspectives," in *Handbook of Child Psychology*, 5th ed., ed. Damon, vol. 3, pp. 463–552.

46. Thompson, "Early Sociopersonality Development."

47. Leaper, "Parenting Boys and Girls"; Ruble and Martin, "Gender Development."

48. Campbell Leaper, "Gender Affiliation, Assertion, and the Interactive Context of Parent-Child Play," *Developmental Psychology* 36 (2000): 381–393.

49. Fagot, "Parenting Boys and Girls."

50. Leaper, "Parenting Boys and Girls."

51. Kay Bussey and Albert Bandura, "Self-Regulatory Mechanisms Governing Gender Development," *Child Development* 63 (1992): 1247.

52. Leaper, "Parenting Boys and Girls"; Ruble and Martin, "Gender Development."

53. Robert H. Bradley et al., "Home Environments of Children in the United States Part I: Variations by Age, Ethnicity, and Poverty Status," *Child Development* 72 (2001): 1844–1867.

54. Robert H. Bradley et al., "The Home Environments of Children in the United States Part II: Relations with Behavioral Development through Age Thirteen," *Child Development* 72 (2001): 1868–1886.

55. Catherine S. Tamis-LeMonda, Ina C. Uzgiris, and Marc H. Bornstein, "Play in Parent-Child Interaction" in *Handbook of Parenting*, 2nd ed., ed. Marc H. Bornstein, vol. 5, *Practical Issues in Parenting* (Mahwah, NJ: Erlbaum, 2002), 221–241.

56. Grazyna Kochanska, "Mutually Responsive Orientation between Mothers and Their Young Children: Implications for Early Socialization," *Child Development* 68 (1997): 94–112.

57. Jane B. Brooks, *The Process of Parenting*, 5th ed. (Mountain View, CA: Mayfield, 1999), 193.

58. Gerald R. Patterson, "The Early Development of the Coercive Family Process," in *Antisocial Behavior in Children and Adolescents*, ed. John B. Reid, Gerald R. Patterson, and James Snyder (Washington, DC: American Psychological Association, 2002), 25–44.

59. Jay Belsky, Sharon Woodworth, and Keith Crnic, "Troubled Family Interaction during Toddlerhood," *Development and Psychopathology* 8 (1996): 477–495.

60. Patricia M. Greenfield and Lalita K. Suzuki, "Culture and Human Development: Implications for Parenting, Education, Pediatrics, and Mental Health," in *Handbook of Child Psychology*, 5th ed., ed. William Damon, vol. 4: *Child Psychology in Practice*, ed. Irving E. Sigel and K. Ann Renninger (New York: Wiley, 1998), 1059–1109.

61. Ibid.

62. Ibid.

63. Robert B. Stewart et al., "The Firstborn's Adjustment to the Birth of a Sibling: A Longitudinal Assessment," *Child Development* 58 (1987): 341–355.

64. Wyndal Furman and Richard Lanthier, "Parenting Siblings," in *Handbook of Parenting*, 2nd ed., ed. Bornstein, vol. 1, pp. 165–188.

65. Radke-Yarrow et al., "Learning Concern for Others."

66. Gene H. Brody, Zolinda Stoneman, and Michelle Burke, "Child Temperaments, Maternal Differential Behavior, and Sibling

Relationships," *Developmental Psychology* 23 (1987): 354–362; Robert B. Stewart et al., "The Firstborn's Adjustment to the Birth of a Sibling: A Longitudinal Assessment," *Child Development* 58 (1987), 341–355; Clare Stocker, Judy Dunn, and Robert Plomin, "Sibling Relationships: Links with Child Temperament, Maternal Behavior, and Family Structure," *Child Development* 60 (1989): 715–727.

67. Judith F. Dunn, Robert Plomin, and Denise Daniels, "Consistency and Change in Mothers' Behavior toward Young Siblings," *Child Development* 57 (1986): 348–356; Judith F. Dunn, Robert Plomin, and Margaret Nettles, "Consistency of Mothers' Behavior toward Infant Siblings," *Developmental Psychology* 21 (1985): 1188–1195.

68. Carollee Howes, *Peer Interaction of Young Children*, Monographs of the Society for Research in Child Development 53, serial no. 217 (1987).

69. Tiffany Field, Louis De Stefano, and John H. Koewler, III, "Fantasy Play of Toddlers and Preschoolers," *Developmental Psychology* 18 (1982): 503–508.

70. Donald S. Hayes, "Cognitive Bases for Liking and Disliking among Preschool Children," *Child Development* 49 (1978): 906–909.

71. Willard W. Hartup et al., "Conflict and the Friendship Relations of Young Children," *Child Development* 59 (1988): 1590–1600.

72. Michael P. Leiter, "A Study of Reciprocity in Preschool Play Groups," *Child Development* 48 (1977): 1288–1295.

73. Kenneth H. Rubin, William Bukowski, and Jeffrey G. Parker, "Peer Interactions, Relationships, and Groups," in *Handbook of Child Psychology*, 5th ed., ed. Damon, vol. 3, pp. 619–700.

74. Ibid.

75. Patty Rhule, "Sleep Trouble in School-Age Kids," *USA Weekend*, 15–17 November 2002, p. 16.

76. Alice M. Gregory and Thomas G. O'Connor, "Sleep Problems in Childhood: A Longitudinal Study of Developmental Change and Association with Behavioral Problems," *Journal of the American Academy of Child and Adolescent Psychiatry* 41 (2002): 964–971.

77. Rhule, "Sleep Trouble."

78. Richard Ferber, *Solve Your Child's Sleep Problems*, rev. ed. (New York: Simon & Schuster, 2006).

79. Ibid., p. 163.

80. Adele Faber and Elaine Mazlish, *Liberated Parents/Liberated Children* (New York: Avon, 1975).

81. Thomas Gordon with Judith Gordon Sands, *P.E.T. in Action* (New York: Bantam Books, 1978).

82. Rudolf Dreikurs with Vicki Soltz, *Children: The Challenge* (New York: Hawthorn, 1964).

83. John D. Krumboltz and Helen B. Krumboltz, *Changing Children's Behavior* (Englewood Cliffs, NJ: Prentice-Hall, 1972).

84. Stanley Turecki and Leslie Tonner, *The Difficult Child* (New York: Bantam Books, 1985).

85. Faber and Mazlish, *Liberated Parents/Liberated Children*.

86. David M. Buss, Jeanne H. Block, and Jack Block, "Preschool Activity Level: Personality Correlates and Developmental Implications," *Child Development* 51 (1980): 401–408.

87. David M. Buss, "Predicting Parent-Child Interactions from Children's Activity Level," *Developmental Psychology* 17 (1981): 59–65.

88. Donald H. Meichenbaum and Joseph Goodman, "Training Impulsive Children to Talk to Themselves: A Means of Developing Self-Control," *Journal of Abnormal Psychology* 77 (1971): 115–126.

89. Robert Eimers and Robert Aitchison, *Effective Parents/Responsible Children* (New York: McGraw-Hill, 1977).

90. Kenneth H. Rubin and Kim B. Burgess, "Parents of Aggressive and Withdrawn Children," in *Handbook of Parenting*, 2nd ed., ed. Bornstein, vol. 1, pp. 383–418.

91. Patterson, "Early Development of the Coercive Family Process"; Gerald R. Patterson, "Future Extensions of the Model," in *Antisocial Behavior in Children and Adolescents*, ed. Reid, Patterson, and Snyder, pp. 273–283.

92. Paul D. Hastings et al., "The Development of Concern for Others in Children with Behavior Problems," *Developmental Psychology* 36 (2000): 531–546.

93. Rubin and Burgess, "Parents of Aggressive and Withdrawn Children."

94. Linda Gilkerson and Frances Stott, "Parent-Child Relationships in Early Intervention with Infants and Toddlers with Disabilities and Their Families," in *Handbook of Infant Mental Health*, 2nd ed., ed. Charles H.

Zeanah, Jr. (New York: Guilford, 2000), 457–471.

95. Ibid., p. 460.

96. Penny Hauser-Cram et al., *Children with Disabilities*, Monographs of the Society for Research in Child Development 66, serial no. 266 (2001).

97. Ellen Galinsky, *Between Generations: The Six Stages of Parenthood* (New York: Times Books, 1981).

98. Ibid., pp. 136–137.

99. Philip A. Cowan and Carolyn Pape Cowan, "What an Intervention Design Reveals about How Parents Affect Their Children's Academic Achievement and Behavior Problems," in *Parenting and the Child's World: Differences in Academic, Intellectual and Socio-Emotional Development*, ed. John G. Borkowski, Sharon Landesman Ramey, and Marie Bristol-Power (Mahwah, NJ: Erlbaum, 2002), 75–97.

CHAPTER 9

1. Jay Matthews, "Importance of Parents' Role in Academics Downplayed," *San Francisco Chronicle*, 26 November 2005, p. A2.

2. J. David Hawkins, "Academic Performance and School Success: Sources and Consequences," in *Enhancing Children's Wellness*, ed. Roger P. Weissberg et al. (Thousand Oaks, CA: Sage, 1997), 278–305.

3. Robert Serpell et al., "Intimate Culture of Families in the Early Socialization of Literacy," *Journal of Family Psychology* 16 (2002), 391–405.

4. Arthur J. Reynolds, Suh-Ruu Ou, and James W. Topitzes, "Paths of Effects of Early Childhood Intervention on Educational Attainment and Delinquency: A Confirmatory Analysis of the Chicago Child-Parent Centers," *Child Development* 75 (2004): 1299–1328; Leon Feinstein and John Bynner, "The Importance of Cognitive Development in Middle Childhood for Adult Socioeconomic Status, Mental Health, and Problem Behavior," *Child Development* 75 (2004): 1329–1339.

5. Clancy Blair, "School Readiness: Integrating Cognition and Emotion in a Neurobiological Conceptualization of Children's Functioning at School Entry," *American Psychologist* 57 (2002): 111–127.

6. W. Andrew Collins, Stephanie D. Madsen, and Amy Susman-Stillman, "Parenting during Middle Childhood," in *Handbook of Parenting*, 2nd ed., ed. Marc H. Bornstein, vol. 1: *Children and Parenting* (Mahwah, NJ: Erlbaum, 2002), 73–101.

7. Jacquelynne S. Eccles, Allan Wigfield, and Ulrich Schiefele, "Motivation to Succeed," in *Handbook of Child Psychology*, 5th ed., ed. William Damon, vol. 3: *Social, Emotional, and Personality Development*, ed. Nancy Eisenberg (New York: Wiley, 1998), pp. 1017–1095.

8. Ben Carson with Gregg Lewis, *The Big Picture* (Grand Rapids, MI: Zondervan, 1999).

9. Ibid., p. 50.

10. Deborah A. Phillips, "Socialization of Perceived Academic Competence among Highly Competent Children," *Child Development* 58 (1987): 1308–1320.

11. Peter Ernest Haiman, "How Children Manage Frustration Affects Ability to Focus and Learn," *Brown University Child and Adolescent Newsletter* 16 (February 2000): 1.

12. Sheppard G. Kellam et al., "The Effect of the Level of Aggression in the First Grade Classroom on the Course and Malleability of Aggressive Behavior in Middle School," *Development and Psychopathology* 10 (1998): 165–185.

13. Hawkins, "Academic Performance and School Success."

14. Karl L. Alexander and Doris R. Entwisle, *Achievement in the First Two Years of School: Patterns and Processes*, Monographs of the Society for Research in Child Development 53, serial no. 218 (1988).

15. Gary W. Ladd and Joseph M. Price, "Predicting Children's Social and School Adjustment Following the Transition from Preschool to Kindergarten," *Child Development* 58 (1987): 1168–1189.

16. Karin S. Frey and Diane Ruble, "What Children Say about Classroom Performance: Sex and Grade Differences in Perceived Competence," *Child Development* 58 (1987): 1066–1078.

17. Karen Klein Burhans and Carol S. Dweck, "Helplessness in Early Childhood: The Role of Contingent Worth," *Child Development* 66 (1995): 1719–1738.

18. Eccles, Wigfield, and Schiefele, "Motivation to Succeed."

19. Patricia M. Greenfield and Lalita K. Suzuki, "Culture and Human Development: Implications for Parenting, Education, Pediatrics, and Mental Health," in *Handbook of Child Psychology*, 5th ed., ed. William Damon,

vol. 4: Child *Psychology in Practice*, ed. Irving E. Sigel and K. Anne Renninger (New York: Wiley, 1998), 1059–1109.

20. Harold W. Stevenson, Chuansheng Chen, and David H. Uttal, "Beliefs and Achievements: A Study of Black, White, and Hispanic Children," *Child Development* 61 (1990): 508–523.

21. Deborah J. Stipek and Karen M. DeCotis, "Children's Understanding of the Implications of Causal Attributions for Emotional Experiences," *Child Development* 59 (1988): 1601–1616.

22. Dayna Fuchs and Mark H. Thelen, "Children's Expected Interpersonal Consequences of Communicating Their Affective State and Reported Likelihood of Expression," *Child Development* 59 (1988): 1314–1322.

23. Nancy Eisenberg et al., "The Relations of Children's Dispositional Prosocial Behavior to Emotionality, Regulation, and Social Functioning," *Child Development* 67 (1996): 974–992.

24. Charles L. McCoy and John C. Masters, "The Development of Children's Strategies for the Social Control of Emotion," *Child Development* 56 (1985): 1214–1222.

25. Nancy Eisenberg and Paul H. Mussen, *The Roots of Prosocial Behavior in Children* (Cambridge, England: Cambridge University Press, 1989).

26. Steven R. Asher et al., "Peer Rejection and Loneliness in Childhood," in *Peer Rejection in Childhood*, ed. Steven R. Asher and John D. Coie (Cambridge, England: Cambridge University Press, 1990), 253–273.

27. Michael Rutter, Jack Tizard, and Kingsley Whitmore, eds., *Education, Health and Behavior* (Huntington, NY: Kruger, 1981).

28. Kaoru Yamamoto et al., "Voices in Unison: Stressful Events in the Lives of Children in Six Countries," *Journal of Child Psychology and Psychiatry* 28 (1987): 855–864.

29. Elaine Shaw Sorensen, *Children's Stress and Coping* (New York: Guilford, 1993).

30. Jennifer L. Altshuler and Diane N. Ruble, "Developmental Changes in Children's Awareness of Strategies for Coping with Uncontrollable Stress," *Child Development* 60 (1989): 1337–1349.

31. Sorensen, *Children's Stress and Coping*.

32. Molly Reid et al., "My Family and Friends: Six- to Twelve-Year-Old Children's Perceptions of Social Support," *Child Development* 60 (1989): 907.

33. Mary J. Levitt, Nathalie Guacci-Franco, and Jerome L. Levitt, "Convoys of Social Support in Childhood and Early Adolescence," *Developmental Psychology* 29 (1993): 811–818.

34. Susan Harter, "The Development of Self-Representations," in *Handbook of Child Psychology*, 5th ed., ed. Damon, vol. 3, pp. 553–617.

35. David M. Brodzinsky and Ellen Pinderhughes, "Parenting and Child Development in Adoptive Families," in *Handbook of Parenting*, 2nd ed., ed. Bornstein, vol. 1, pp. 279–311.

36. Ibid., p. 290.

37. Phyllis A. Katz and Keith R. Ksansnak, "Developmental Aspects of Gender Role Flexibility and Traditionality in Middle Childhood and Adolescence," *Developmental Psychology* 30 (1994): 272–282.

38. Joel Szkrybalo and Diane N. Ruble, "God Made Me a Girl: Sex-Category Constancy Judgments and Explanations Revisited," *Developmental Psychology* 35 (1999): 392–402.

39. Lynn S. Liben and Rebecca S. Bigler, *The Developmental Course of Gender Differentiation*, Monographs of the Society for Research in Child Development 67, serial no. 269 (2002); Diane N. Ruble and Carol Lynn Martin, *Commentary: The Developmental Course of Gender Differentiation*, Monographs of the Society for Research in Child Development 67, serial no. 269 (2002).

40. Frances E. Aboud, "The Development of Ethnic Self-Identification and Attitudes," in *Children's Ethnic Socialization*, ed. Jean S. Phinney and Mary Jane Rotheram (Beverly Hills, CA: Sage, 1987), 32–55.

41. Sandra L. Hofferth and John F. Sandberg, "How American Children Spend Their Time," *Journal of Marriage and Family* 63 (2001): 295–308.

42. Frances E. Aboud, "The Formation of In-Group Favoritism and Out-Group Prejudice in Young Children: Are They Distinct Attitudes?" *Developmental Psychology* 39 (2003): 48–60.

43. Susan Harter, "Causes, Correlates, and the Functional Role of Global Self-Worth: A Life-Span Perspective," in *Competence Considered*, ed. J. Kolligian and Robert

Sternberg (New Haven, CT: Yale University Press, 1990), 67–97.

44. Jean M. Twenge and Jennifer Crocker, "Race and Self-Esteem: Meta-Analysis Comparing Whites, Blacks, Hispanics, Asians, and American Indians and Comment on Gray-Little and Hofdahl (2000)," *Psychological Bulletin* 128 (2002): 371–408.

45. Tamara J. Ferguson, Hedy Stegge, and Ilse Damhuis, "Children's Understanding of Guilt and Shame," *Child Development* 62 (1991): 827–839.

46. Hazel J. Markus and Paula S. Nurius, "Self-Understanding and Self-Regulation in Middle Childhood," in *Development during Middle Childhood*, ed. W. Andrew Collins (Washington, DC: National Academy Press, 1984), pp. 147–183.

47. Eliot Turiel, "The Development of Morality," in *Handbook of Child Psychology*, 5th ed., ed. Damon, vol. 3, pp. 863–932.

48. Melanie Killen et al., *How Children and Adolescents Evaluate Gender and Racial Exclusions*, Monographs of the Society for Research in Child Development 67, serial no. 271 (2002).

49. Turiel, "Development of Morality."

50. Collins, Madsen, and Susman-Stillman, "Parenting during Middle Childhood."

51. Kenneth H. Rubin, William Bukowski, and Jeffrey G. Parker, "Peer Interactions, Relationships, and Groups," in *Handbook of Child Psychology*, 5th ed., ed. Damon, vol. 3, pp. 619–700.

52. Ronald Seifer et al., "Child and Family Factors That Ameliorate Risk between 4 and 13 Years of Age," *Journal of the American Academy of Child and Adolescent Psychiatry* 31 (1992): 893–903.

53. Robert L. Nix et al., "The Relation between Mothers' Hostile Attribution Tendencies and Children's Externalizing Problems: The Mediating Role of Mothers' Harsh Discipline Practices," *Child Development* 70 (1999): 896–909.

54. Thomas G. O'Connor et al., "Genotype-Environment Correlations in Late Childhood and Early Adolescence: Asocial Behavioral Problems and Coercive Parenting," *Developmental Psychology* 34 (1998): 970–981.

55. Collins, Madsen, and Susman-Stillman, "Parenting during Middle Childhood."

56. Judith G. Smetana, "Adolescents' and Parents' Reasoning about Actual Family Conflict," *Child Development* 60 (1989): 1052–1067.

57. Graeme Russell and Alan Russell, "Mother-Child and Father-Child in Middle Childhood," *Child Development* 58 (1987): 1573–1585.

58. Frances K. Grossman, William S. Pollack, and Ellen Golding, "Fathers and Children: Predicting the Quality and Quantity of Fathering," *Developmental Psychology* 24 (1988): 822–891.

59. Russell and Russell, "Mother-Child and Father-Child."

60. Molly Reid, Sharon Landesman Ramey, and Margaret Burchinal, "Dialogues with Children about Their Families," in *Children's Perspectives on the Family*, ed. Inge Bretherton and Malcolm W. Watson, New Directions for Child Development, no. 48 (San Francisco: Jossey-Bass, 1990), 5–28.

61. Eleanor E. Maccoby, "Middle Childhood in the Context of the Family," in *Development during Middle Childhood*, ed. Collins, pp. 184–239.

62. Michael C. Thornton et al., "Sociodemographic and Environmental Correlates of Racial Socialization by Black Parents," *Child Development* 61 (1990): 401–409.

63. Ibid.

64. Algea O. Harrison et al., "Family Ecologies of Ethnic Minority Children," *Child Development* 61 (1990): 347–362; Carolyn Bennett Murray and Jelani Mandara, "Racial Identity Development in African American Children: Cognitive and Experiential Antecedents," in *Black Children*, 2nd ed., ed. Harriette Pipes McAdoo (Thousand Oaks, CA: Sage, 2002), 73–96; Margaret Beale Spencer and Carol Markstrom-Adams, "Identity Processes among Racial and Ethnic Minority Children in America," *Child Development* 61 (1990): 290–310.

65. Collins, Madsen, and Susman-Stillman, "Parenting during Middle Childhood;" Wyndol Furman and Richard Lanthier, "Parenting Siblings," in *Handbook of Parenting*, 2nd ed., ed. Bornstein, vol. 1, pp. 165–188.

66. Ibid.

67. Clare M. Stocker and Lise Youngblade, "Marital Conflict and Hostility Links with Children's Sibling and Peer Relationships," *Journal of Family Psychology* 13 (1999): 598–609.

68. Clare M. Stocker, Rebecca A. Burwell, and Megan L. Briggs, "Sibling Conflict in Middle Childhood Predicts Children's Adjustment in Early Adolescence," *Journal of Family Psychology* 16 (2002): 50–57.

69. Gene H. Brody et al., "Sibling Relationships in Rural African American Families," *Journal of Marriage and the Family* 61 (1999): 1046–1057.

70. Rubin, Bukowski, and Parker, "Peer Interactions, Relationships, and Groups."

71. Ibid.

72. Nicki R. Crick and Jennifer K. Grotpeter, "Relational Aggression, Gender, and Social-Psychological Adjustment," *Child Development* 66 (1995): 710–722.

73. Ibid.

74. John D. Coie and Gina Krehbiel Koeppl, "Adapting Intervention to the Problems of Aggressive and Disruptive Children," in *Peer Rejection in Childhood*, ed. Asher and Coie, pp. 309–337.

75. Dan Olweus, "Annotation: Bullying at School: Basic Facts and Effects of a School Based Intervention Program," *Journal of Child Psychology and Psychiatry* 35 (1994): 1171–1190.

76. Nicki R. Crick and Jennifer K. Grotpeter, "Children's Treatment of Peers: Victims of Relational and Overt Aggression," *Development and Psychopathology* 8 (1996): 367–380.

77. David Schwartz et al., "Peer Group Victimization As a Predictor of Children's Behavior Problems at Home and at School," *Development and Psychopathology* 10 (1998): 87–99.

78. Susan K. Egan and David G. Perry, "Does Low Self-Regard Invite Victimization?" *Developmental Psychology* 34 (1998): 299–309.

79. Avi Sadeh, Reut Gruber, and Amiram Raviv, "The Effects of Sleep Restriction and Extension in School-Age Children: What a Difference an Hour Makes," *Child Development* 74 (2003): 444–455.

80. Barbara H. Fiese et al., "A Review of 50 Years of Research on Naturally Occurring Family Routines and Rituals: Cause for Celebration?" *Journal of Family Psychology* 16 (2002): 381–390.

81. Kelly J. Kelleher, "Increasing Identification of Psychosocial Problems: 1979–1996," *Pediatrics* 105 (2000): 1313–1321.

82. Tim Murphy and Loriann Hoff Oberlin, *The Angry Child* (New York: Three Rivers Press, 2001).

83. Gerald R. Patterson, "The Early Development of the Coercive Family Process," in *Antisocial Behavior in Children and Adolescents*, ed. John B. Reid, Gerald R. Patterson, and James Snyder (Washington, DC: American Psychological Association, 2002), 25–44.

84. Martin E. P. Seligman, *The Optimistic Child* (Boston: Houghton Mifflin, 1995)..

85. Philip G. Zimbardo and Shirley Radl, *The Shy Child* (Garden City, NY: Doubleday, 1982).

86. Sherri Oden and Steven R. Asher, "Coaching Children in Social Skills for Friendship Making," *Child Development* 48 (1977): 495–506.

87. Marlene Jacobs Sandstrom and John D. Coie, "A Developmental Perspective on Peer Rejection: Mechanisms of Stability and Change," *Child Development* 70 (1999): 955–966.

88. Olweus, "Annotation: Bullying at School."

89. Joyce L. Epstein and Mavis G. Sanders, "Family, School, and Community Partnerships," in *Handbook of Parenting*, ed. Marc H. Bornstein, vol. 5: *Practical Issues in Parenting* (Mahwah, NJ: Erlbaum, 2002), 407–437.

90. Ellen Galinsky, *Between Generations: The Six Stages of Parenthood* (New York: Times Books, 1981).

91. Joan Beck, *Effective Parenting* (New York: Simon & Schuster, 1976).

92. Emmy E. Werner and Ruth S. Smith, *Overcoming the Odds* (Ithaca, NY: Cornell University Press, 1992), p. 177.

93. Robert Coles, *The Spiritual Life of Children* (Boston: Houghton Mifflin, 1990), 127.

CHAPTER 10

1. Curtis Sittenfeld, "Parental Supervision Required," *New York Times*, 7 September 2005, p. A29.

2. Jeanne Brooks-Gunn and Edward O. Reiter, "The Role of Pubertal Processes," in *At the Threshold: The Developing Adolescent*, ed. S. Shirley Feldman and Glen R. Elliott (Cambridge, MA: Harvard University Press, 1990), 16–53.

3. Ibid.

4. Ibid.

5. Eric Stice, Katherine Presnell, and Sarah Kate Bearman, "Relation of Early Menarche to Depression, Eating Disorders, Substance Abuse, and Comorbid Psychopathology among Adolescent Girls," *Developmental Psychology* 37 (2001): 608–619.

6. Brooks-Gunn and Reiter, "The Role of Pubertal Processes."

7. L. LaBerge et al., "Development of Sleep Patterns in Early Adolescence," *Journal of Sleep Research* 10 (2001): 59–67.

8. Peter Huttenlocher, *Neural Plasticity* (Cambridge, MA: Harvard University Press, 2002).

9. Susan Harter, "Self and Self-Identity," in *At the Threshold*, ed. Feldman and Elliott, pp. 352–387.

10. Stice, Presnell, and Bearman, "Relation of Early Menarche to Depression."

11. Mary C. Jones and Nancy Bayley, "Physical Maturing among Boys Related to Behavior," *Journal of Educational Psychology* 41 (1950): 129–148.

12. Jane Norman and Myron Harris, *The Private Life of the American Teenager* (New York: Rawson Wade, 1981).

13. Herbert Ginsburg and Sylvia Opper, *Piaget's Theory of Intellectual Development* (Englewood Cliffs, NJ: Prentice-Hall, 1969); Jean Piaget and Barbel Inhelder, *The Psychology of the Child* (New York: Basic Books, 1969).

14. Jacquelynne Eccles et al., "Development during Adolescence: The Impact of Stage-Environment Fit on Young Adolescents' Experiences in Schools and in Families," *American Psychologist* 48 (1993): 90–101.

15. Ibid.

16. Edward Seidman et al., "The Impact of School Transition in Early Adolescence on the Self System and Perceived Social Context of Poor Urban Youth," *Child Development* 65 (1994): 507–522.

17. James Patrick Connell, Margaret Beale Spencer, and J. Lawrence Aber, "Educational Risk and Resilience in African American Youth: Context, Self, Action, and Outcomes in School," *Child Development* 65 (1994): 493–506.

18. Seidman et al., "Impact of School Transition."

19. Gene H. Brody et al., "Financial Resources, Parent Psychological Functioning, Parent Co-Caregiving and Early Adolescent Competence in Rural Two-Parent African American Families," *Child Development* 65 (1994): 590–605.

20. Robert W. Roeser, Jacquelynne S. Eccles, and Arnold J. Sameroff, "Academic and Emotional Functioning in Early Adolescence: Longitudinal Relations, Patterns, and Prediction by Experience in Middle School," *Development and Psychopathology* 10 (1998): 321–352.

21. Reed Larson and Maryse H. Richards, *Divergent Realities: The Emotional Lives of Mothers, Fathers, and Adolescents* (New York: Basic Books, 1994).

22. Reed Larson and Mark Ham, "Stress and 'Storm Stress' in Early Adolescence: The Relationship of Negative Events and Dysphoric Affect," *Developmental Psychology* 29 (1993): 130–140.

23. Larson and Richards, *Divergent Realities*.

24. Christy Miller Buchanan, Jacquelynne S. Eccles, and Jill B. Becker, "Are Adolescents the Victims of Raging Hormones? Evidence for Activational Effects of Hormones on Mood and Behavior at Adolescence," *Psychological Bulletin* 111 (1992): 62–107.

25. David Elkind, *Children and Adolescents*, 2nd ed. (New York: Oxford University Press, 1974).

26. Larson and Ham, "Stress and 'Storm Stress' in Early Adolescence."

27. Reed W. Larson, "Toward a Psychology of Positive Youth Development," *American Psychologist* 55 (2000): 170–183.

28. Ibid., p. 170.

29. Anne C. Petersen et al., "Depression in Adolescence," *American Psychologist* 48 (1993): 155–168.

30. Roberta G. Simmons et al., "The Impact of Cumulative Changes in Early Adolescence," *Child Development* 58 (1987): 1220–1234.

31. Mary J. Levitt, Nathalie Guacci-Franco, and Jerome L. Levitt, "Convoys of Social Support in Childhood and Early Adolescence: Structure and Function," *Developmental Psychology* 29 (1993): 811–818.

32. Susan Harter, "The Development of Self-Representations," in *Handbook of Child Psychology*, 5th ed., ed. Damon, vol. 3, pp. 553–617.

33. Erik H. Erikson, *Childhood and Society*, 2nd ed. (New York: Norton, 1963).

34. James E. Marcia, "Identity in Adolescence," in *Handbook of Adolescent Psychology*, ed. Joseph Adelson (New York: Wiley, 1980), 159–187.

35. Harold D. Grotevant, "Adolescent Development in Family Contexts," in *Handbook of Child Psychology*, 5th ed., ed. Damon, vol. 3, pp. 1097–1149.

36. William E. Cross, Jr., "A Two-Factor Theory of Black Identity: Implications for the Study of Identity Development in Minority Children," in *Children's Ethnic Socialization: Pluralism and Development*, ed. Jean S. Phinney and Mary Jane Rotheram (Beverly Hills, CA: Sage, 1987), 117–133.

37. Nancy L. Galambos, David M. Almeida, and Anne C. Petersen, "Masculinity, Femininity, and Sex Role Attitudes in Early Adolescence: Exploring Gender Intensification," *Child Development* 61 (1990): 1905–1914.

38. Phyllis A. Katz and Keith R. Ksansnak, "Developmental Aspects of Gender Role Flexibility and Traditionality in Middle Childhood and Adolescence," *Developmental Psychology* 30 (1994): 272–282; Thalma E. Lobel et al., "The Role of Gender-Related Information and Self-Endorsement of Traits in Preadolescents' Inferences and Judgments," *Child Development* 64 (1993): 1285–1294.

39. Jean S. Phinney, "Stages of Ethnic Identity Development in Minority Group Adolescents," *Journal of Early Adolescence* 9 (1989): 34–49.

40. Margaret Beale Spencer and Carol Markstrom-Adams, "Identity Processes among Racial and Ethnic Minority Children in America," *Child Development* 61 (1990): 290–310; Michael C. Thornton et al., "Sociodemographic and Environmental Correlates of Racial Socialization by Black Parents," *Child Development* 61 (1990): 401–409.

41. Phinney, "Stages of Ethnic Identity Development."

42. Jane B. Brooks, "Social Maturity in Middle Age and Its Developmental Antecedents," in *Present and Past in Middle Life*, ed. Dorothy H. Eichorn et al. (New York: Academic Press, 1981), 243–265.

43. Jack Block with Norma Haan, *Lives through Time* (Berkeley, CA: Bancroft Books, 1971).

44. Reed Larson and Maryse H. Richards, "Daily Companionship in Late Childhood and Early Adolescence: Changing Developmental Contexts," *Child Development* 62 (1991): 284–300.

45. Larson and Richards, *Divergent Realities*, p. 189.

46. Judith G. Smetana, "Adolescents' and Parents' Reasoning about Actual Family Conflict," *Child Development* 60 (1989): 1052–1067; Judith G. Smetana, "Concepts of Self and Social Convention: Adolescents' and Parents' Reasoning about Hypothetical and Actual Family Conflicts," in *Development during the Transition to Adolescence: Minnesota Symposia on Child Psychology*, vol. 21, ed. Megan R. Gunnar and W. Andrew Collins (Hillsdale, NJ: Erlbaum, 1988), 79–122.

47. Smetana, "Concepts of Self and Social Convention."

48. Laurence Steinberg, "Impact of Puberty on Family Relations: Effects of Pubertal Status and Pubertal Timing," *Developmental Psychology* 23 (1987): 451–460.

49. Per F. Gjerde, "The Interpersonal Structure of Family Interaction Settings: Parent-Adolescent Relations in Dyads and Triads," *Developmental Psychology* 22 (1986): 297–304.

50. Andrew J. Fuligni and Jacquelynne S. Eccles, "Perceived Parent-Child Relationships and Early Adolescents' Orientation toward Peers," *Developmental Psychology* 29 (1993): 622–632.

51. Holmbeck, Paikoff, and Brooks-Gunn, "Parenting Adolescents."

52. Ibid.

53. Hakan Stattin and Margaret Kerr, "Parental Monitoring: A Reinterpretation," *Child Development* 71 (2000): 1072–1085; Margaret Kerr and Hakan Stattin, "What Parents Know, How They Know It, and Several Forms of Adolescent Adjustment: Further Support for a Reinterpretation of Monitoring," *Developmental Psychology* 36 (2000): 366–380.

54. Eva S. Lefkowitz, Marian Sigman, and Terry Kit-fong Au, "Helping Mothers Discuss Sexuality and AIDS with Adolescents," *Child Development* 71 (2000): 1383–1394.

55. Martha A. Rueter and Rand D. Conger, "Reciprocal Influences between Parenting and Adolescent Problem-Solving Behavior," *Developmental Psychology* 34 (1998): 1470–1482.

56. Cynthia Garcia Coll and Lee M. Pachter, "Ethnic and Minority Parenting," in *Handbook of Parenting*, 2nd ed., ed. Marc H. Bornstein, vol. 4: *Social Conditions and*

Applied Parenting (Mahwah, NJ: Erlbaum, 2002), 1–20.

57. Carolyn Bennett Murray and Jelani Mandara, "Racial Identity Development in African American Children: Cognitive and Experiential Antecedents," in *Black Children*, 2nd ed., ed. Harriette Pipes McAdoo (Thousand Oaks, CA: Sage, 2002), 73–96.

58. David Elkind, *The Hurried Child*, 3rd ed. (Cambridge, MA: Perseus Books, 2001).

59. Bruce E. Compas et al., "Parents and Child Stress Symptoms: An Integrative Analysis," *Developmental Psychology* 25 (1989): 550–559.

60. Norman and Harris, *Private Life of the American Teenager*.

61. Ibid.

62. Kenneth H. Rubin, William Bukowski, and Jeffrey G. Parker, "Peer Interactions, Relationships, and Groups," in *Handbook of Child Psychology*, 5th ed., ed. Damon, vol. 3, pp. 619–700.

63. Lynne Zarbatany, Donald P. Hartmann, and D. Bruce Rankin, "The Psychological Functions of Preadolescent Peer Activities," *Child Development* 61 (1990): 1067–1080.

64. Maryse H. Richards et al., "Developmental Patterns and Gender Differences in the Experience of Peer Companionship during Adolescence," *Child Development* 69 (1998): 154–163.

65. Holmbeck, Paikoff, and Brooks-Gunn, "Parenting Adolescents," p. 95.

66. Don Dinkmeyer and Gary D. McKay, *STEP/TEEN Systematic Training for Effective Parenting of Teens* (Circle Pines, MN: American Guidance Service, 1983).

67. Adele Faber and Elaine Mazlish, *How to Talk So Kids Will Listen and Listen So Kids Will Talk* (New York: Rawson Wade, 1980), 165.

68. Myrna B. Shure with Roberta Israeloff, *Raising a Thinking Preteen* (New York: Henry Holt, 2000).

69. Larson, "Toward a Psychology of Positive Youth Development," p. 170.

70. Ibid., p. 177.

71. Ibid., p. 179.

72. Ibid.

73. Kathryn R. Wentzel and Cynthia A. Erdley, "Strategies for Making Friends: Relations to Social Behavior and Peer Acceptance in Early Adolescence," *Developmental Psychology* 29 (1993): 819–826.

74. Sandra Graham and Cynthia Hudley, "Attributions of Aggressive and Nonaggressive African-American Male Early Adolescents: A Study of Construct Accessibility," *Developmental Psychology* 30 (1994): 365–373; Sandra Graham, Cynthia Hudley, and Estella Williams, "Attributional and Emotional Determinants of Aggression among African-American and Latino Young Adolescents," *Developmental Psychology* 28 (1992): 731–740.

75. Wentzel and Erdley, "Strategies for Making Friends."

76. Philip Zimbardo and Shirley Radl, *The Shy Child* (Garden City, NY: Doubleday, 1982).

77. Haim G. Ginott, *Between Parent and Teenager* (New York: Avon, 1969).

78. Robert Eimers and Robert Aitchison, *Effective Parents/Responsible Children* (New York: McGraw-Hill, 1977).

79. Mary Pipher, *Reviving Ophelia* (New York: Ballantine Books, 1994), 283.

80. Ibid., p. 257.

81. William Pollack, *Real Boys* (New York: Henry Holt, 1998).

82. Ibid., p. xxiv.

83. Ibid., p. 391.

84. Ibid., p. 398.

85. Ellen Galinsky, *Between Generations: The Six Stages of Parenthood* (New York: Times Books, 1981).

86. William Damon, *The Youth Charter: How Communities Can Work Together to Raise Standards for All Our Children* (New York: Free Press, 1997).

87. Ibid., p. ix.

CHAPTER 11

1. Benedict Carey, "Study Pursues a Genetics Link to Depression," *New York Times*, 10 December 2004, p. A27

2. Susan G. Millstein and Iris F. Litt, "Adolescent Health" in *At the Threshold: The Developing Adolescent*, ed. S. Shirley Feldman and Glen R. Elliott (Cambridge, MA: Harvard University Press, 1990), 431–456.

3. Cathy Schoen et al., *The Commonwealth Fund Survey of the Health of Adolescent Girls* (New York: Commonwealth Fund, 1997).

4. Millstein and Litt, "Adolescent Health."

5. Schoen et al., *Commonwealth Fund Survey.*

6. Jerald G. Bachman et al., "Transition in Drug Use during Late Adolescence and Young Adulthood," in *Transitions through Adolescence: Interpersonal Domains and Context*, ed. Julie A. Graber, Jeanne Brooks-Gunn, and Anne C. Petersen (Mahwah, NJ: Erlbaum, 1996), 111–140.

7. Schoen et al., *Commonwealth Fund Survey*.
8. Herant Katchadourian, "Sexuality," in *At the Threshold*, ed. Feldman and Elliott, pp. 330–351.
9. Joseph Lee Rodgers, "Sexual Transitions in Adolescence," in *Transitions through Adolescence*, ed. Graber, Brooks-Gunn, and Petersen, pp. 85–110.
10. Roger P. Weissberg and Mark T. Greenfield, "School and Community Competence-Enhancement and Prevention Programs," in *Handbook of Child Psychology*, 5th ed., ed. William Damon, vol. 4: *Child Psychology in Practice*, ed. Irving E. Sigel and K. Ann Renninger (New York: Wiley, 1998), 877–954.
11. Nancy J. Cobb, *Adolescence: Continuity, Change, and Diversity* (Mountain View, CA: Mayfield, 1992).
12. Rodgers, "Sexual Transitions in Adolescence."
13. James Jaccard, Patricia J. Dittus, and Vivian V. Gordon, "Parent-Adolescent Congruency in Reports of Adolescent Sexual Behavior and in Communications about Sexual Behavior," *Child Development* 69 (1998): 247–261.
14. Katchadourian, "Sexuality."
15. Patricia Barthalow Koch, "Promoting Healthy Sexual Development during Early Adolescence," in *Early Adolescence: Perspectives on Research, Policy, and Intervention*, ed. Richard M. Lerner (Hillsdale, NJ: Erlbaum, 1993), 293–307.
16. Lisa J. Crockett, "Early Adolescent Family Formation," in *Early Adolescence*, ed. Lerner, pp. 93–110.
17. Ibid.
18. Katherine Fennelly, "Sexual Activity and Childbearing among Hispanic Adolescents in the United States," in *Early Adolescence*, ed. Lerner, pp. 335–352.
19. Jeanne Brooks-Gunn and Frank F. Furstenberg, "Adolescent Sexual Behavior," *American Psychologist* 44 (1989): 249–257.
20. Melvin Zelnick and John F. Kantner, "Sexual Activity, Contraceptive Use, and Pregnancy among Metropolitan-Area Teenagers 1971–1979," *Family Planning Perspectives* 12 (1980): 230–237.
21. Daniel P. Keating, "Adolescent Thinking," in *At the Threshold*, ed. Feldman and Elliott, pp. 54–89.
22. Karen Bartsch, "Adolescents' Theoretical Thinking," in *Early Adolescence*, ed. Lerner, pp. 143–157.

23. Jacquelynne S. Eccles, Allan Wigfield, and Ulrich Schiefele, "Motivation to Succeed," in *Handbook of Child Psychology*, 5th ed., ed. William Damon, vol. 3: *Social, Emotional, and Personality Development*, ed. Nancy Eisenberg (New York: Wiley, 1998), 1017–1095.
24. Ibid.
25. Sanford M. Dornbusch et al., "The Relation of Parenting Style to Adolescent School Performance," *Child Development* 58 (1987): 1244–1257.
26. Robert B. McCall, Cynthia Evahn, and Lynn Kratzer, *High School Underachievers* (Newbury Park, CA: Sage, 1992).
27. U.S. Bureau of the Census, *Statistical Abstract of the United States: 2002*, 122nd ed. (Washington, DC: U.S. Government Printing Office, 2001).
28. Frank F. Furstenberg, "The Sociology of Adolescence and Youth in the 1990s: A Critical Commentary," *Journal of Marriage and the Family* 62 (2000): 896–910.
29. Ellen Greenberger and Laurence D. Steinberg, "The Workplace As a Contest for the Socialization of Youth," *Journal of Youth and Adolescence* 10 (1981): 185–210; Laurence Steinberg and Ellen Greenberger, "The Part-Time Employment of High School Students: A Research Agenda," *Children and Youth Services Review* 2 (1980): 161–185.
30. Mihaly Csikszentmihalyi and Reed Larson, *Being Adolescent* (New York: Basic Books, 1984), 234.
31. Michael Windle, "A Longitudinal Study of Stress Buffering for Adolescent Problem Behaviors," *Developmental Psychology* 28 (1992): 522–530.
32. Suniya S. Luthar, "Vulnerability and Resilience: A Study of High Risk Adolescents," *Child Development* 62 (1991): 600–616.
33. Jeanne Brooks-Gunn and Michelle P. Warren, "Biological and Social Contributions to Negative Affect in Young Adolescent Girls," *Child Development* 60 (1989): 40–55.
34. Albert Bandura, *Self-Efficacy: The Exercise of Control* (New York: Freeman, 1997).
35. Susan Harter et al., "The Development of Multiple Role-Related Selves," in *Development and Psychopathology* 9 (1977): 835–853.
36. Jack Block and Richard W. Robins, "A Longitudinal Study of Consistency and Change in Self-Esteem from Early Adolescence to

Early Adulthood," *Child Development* 64 (1993): 909–923.

37. Jack Block, "Some Relationships Regarding the Self from the Block and Block Longitudinal Study," paper presented at the Social Science Research Council Conference on Selfhood, Stanford, CA, October 1985.

38. Patricia Barthalow Koch, "Promoting Healthy Sexual Development during Early Adolescence," in *Early Adolescence*, ed. Lerner, pp. 293–307.

39. Katchadourian, "Sexuality."

40. Koch, "Promoting Healthy Sexual Development during Early Adolescence."

41. Jean S. Phinney and Victoria Chavira, "Ethnic Identity and Self-Esteem," *Journal of Adolescence* 15 (1992): 271–281.

42. Jean S. Phinney and Mona Devich-Navarro, "Variations in Bicultural Identification among African-American and Mexican-American Adolescents," *Journal of Research on Adolescence* 7 (1997): 3–32.

43. Nancy Eisenberg et al., "Prosocial Development in Adolescence: A Longitudinal Study," *Developmental Psychology* 27 (1991): 849–857.

44. Harold D. Grotevant, "Adolescent Development in Family Contexts," in *Handbook of Child Psychology*, 5th ed., ed. Damon, vol. 3, pp. 1097–1149.

45. Richard Jessor et al., "Protective Factors in Adolescent Problem Behavior: Moderator Effects and Developmental Change," *Developmental Psychology* 31 (1995): 923–933.

46. Bachman et al., "Transitions in Drug Use."

47. Diana Baumrind, "The Influence of Parenting Style on Adolescent Competence and Problem Behavior," paper presented at the American Psychological Association Meetings, New Orleans, LA, August 1989.

48. Ibid., p. 16.

49. Laurence Steinberg et al., "Authoritative Parenting and Adolescent Adjustment: An Ecological Perspective," in *Examining Lives in Context*, ed. Phyllis Moen, Glen H. Elder, Jr., and Kurt Lusher (Washington, DC: American Psychological Association, 1995), 423–466.

50. Ibid., p. 443.

51. Anne C. Fletcher, Laurence Steinberg, and Elizabeth B. Sellers, "Adolescents' Well Being As a Function of Interparental Consistency," *Journal of Marriage and the Family* 61 (1999): 599–610.

52. Brooks-Gunn and Furstenberg, "Adolescent Sexual Behavior."

53. Ibid.

54. Ellen Greenberger and Laurence Steinberg, *When Teenagers Work* (New York: Basic Books, 1986).

55. Judith G. Smetana, "Adolescents' and Parents' Reasoning about Actual Family Conflict," *Child Development* 60 (1989): 1052–1067; Judith G. Smetana, "Concepts of Self and Social Convention: Adolescents' and Parents' Reasoning about Hypothetical and Actual Family Conflicts," in *Development during the Transition to Adolescence*, Minnesota Symposia on Child Psychology, vol. 21, ed. Megan R. Gunnar and W. Andrew Collins (Hillsdale, NJ: Erlbaum, 1988), 79–122.

56. Joseph P. Allen et al., "Longitudinal Assessment of Autonomy and Relatedness in Adolescent-Family Interactions As Predictors of Adolescent Ego Development and Self-Esteem," *Child Development* 65 (1994): 1179–1194.

57. R. Rogers Kobak et al., "Attachment and Emotion Regulation during Mother-Teen Problem Solving: A Control Theory Analysis," *Child Development* 64 (1993): 231–245.

58. Duane Buhrmester and Wyndol Furman, "Perceptions of Sibling Relationships during Middle Childhood and Adolescence," *Child Development* 61 (1990): 1387–1398.

59. B. Bradford Brown, "Peer Groups and Peer Culture," in *At the Threshold*, ed. Feldman and Elliott, pp. 171–196.

60. Wyndol Furman, "Friends and Lovers: The Role of Peer Relationships in Adolescent Romantic Relationships," in *Relationships As Developmental Contexts: The 30th Minnesota Symposium on Child Development*, ed. W. Andrew Collins and Brett Laursen (Hillsdale, NJ: Erlbaum, 1999), 133–154.

61. Brown, "Peer Groups and Peer Culture."

62. Duane Buhrmester, "Intimacy and Friendship, Interpersonal Competence, and Adjustment during Preadolescence and Adolescence," *Child Development* 61 (1990): 1101–1111.

63. Jane Norman and Myron Harris, *The Private Life of the American Teenager* (New York: Rawson Wade, 1981).

64. Brown, "Peer Groups and Peer Culture."

65. Brown, "Peer Groups and Peer Culture."

66. Ritch Savin-Williams and Thomas Berndt, "Friendships and Peer Relations," in *At the*

Threshhold, ed. Feldman and Elliott, pp. 277–307.

67. Furman, "Friends and Lovers."
68. Candice Feiring, "Concepts of Romance in Fifteen-Year-Old Adolescents," *Journal of Research on Adolescence* 6 (1996): 181–200.
69. Ibid.
70. Furman, "Friends and Lovers."
71. Michael D. Resnick et al., "Protecting Adolescents from Harm," *Journal of the American Medical Association* 278 (1997): 823–832.
72. Barbara J. Tinsley and Nancy B. Lees, "Health Promotion for Parents," in *Handbook of Parenting*, ed. Marc H. Bornstein, vol. 4, *Applied and Practical Parenting* (Mahwah, NJ: Erlbaum, 1995), 187–204.
73. Judy A. Andrews, Hyman Hops, and Susan C. Duncan, "Adolescent Modeling of Parent Substance Use: The Moderating Effect of the Relationship with the Parent," *Journal of Family Psychology* 11 (1997): 259–270.
74. Baumrind, "Influence of Parenting Style"; Jonathan Shedler and Jack Block, "Adolescent Drug Use and Psychological Health: A Longitudinal Inquiry," *American Psychologist* 45 (1990): 612–630.
75. Resnick et al., "Protecting Adolescents from Harm."
76. Melissa R. Herman et al., "The Influence of Family Regulation, Connection, and Psychological Autonomy on Six Measures of Adolescent Functioning," *Journal of Adolescent Research* 12 (1997): 34–67.
77. Grace M. Barnes and Michael P. Farrell, "Parental Support and Control As Predictors of Adolescent Drinking, Delinquency, and Related Problem Behaviors," *Journal of Marriage and the Family* 54 (1992): 763–776; Grace M. Barnes et al., "The Effects of Parenting on the Development of Adolescent Alcohol Misuse: A Six-Wave Latent Growth Model," *Journal of Marriage and the Family* 62 (2000): 175–186.
78. Resnick et al., "Protecting Adolescents from Harm."
79. Richard Jessor et al., "Protective Factors in Adolescent Problem Behavior: Moderation Effects and Developmental Change," *Developmental Psychology* 31 (1995): 923–933.
80. Resnick et al., "Protecting Adolescents from Harm."
81. Marcia Herrin and Nancy Matsumoto, *The Parent's Guide to Childhood Eating Disorders* (New York: Holt, 2002).
82. Ibid.
83. Ibid.
84. Resnick et al., "Protecting Adolescents from Harm."
85. Ibid.
86. Ibid.
87. Karen Bogenschneider et al., "'Other Teens Drink, but Not My Kid': Does Parental Awareness of Adolescent Alcohol Use Protect Adolescents from Risky Consequences?" *Journal of Marriage and the Family* 60 (1998): 356–373.
88. Ibid.
89. Resnick et al., "Protecting Adolescents from Harm."
90. Beth Polson and Miller Newton, *Not My Kid: A Parent's Guide to Kids and Drugs* (New York: Avon, 1985).
91. Baumrind, "Influence of Parenting Style"; Shedler and Block, "Adolescent Drug Use."
92. Nikki Babbit, *Adolescent Drug and Alcohol Abuse: How to Spot It, Stop It, and Get Help for Your Family* (Sebastopol, CA: O'Reilly, 2000).
93. James Garbarino, *Lost Boys: Why Our Sons Turn Violent and How We Can Save Them* (New York: Free Press, 1999).
94. Ibid., p. 74.
95. Ibid., p. 75.
96. Ibid., p. 149.
97. Deborah M. Capaldi and Mike Stoolmiller, "Co-occurrence of Conduct Problems and Depressive Symptoms in Early Adolescent Boys: III. Prediction to Young-Adult Adjustment," *Development and Psychopathology* 11 (1999): 59–84.
98. Ibid., p. 78.
99. Alice W. Pope and Karen L. Bierman, "Predicting Adolescent Peer Problems and Antisocial Activities: The Relative Roles of Aggression and Dysregulation," *Developmental Psychology* 35 (1999): 335–346.
100. Capaldi and Stoolmiller, "Co-occurrence of Conduct Problems."
101. Dante Cicchetti and Sheree L. Toth, "The Development of Depression in Children and Adolescents," *American Psychologist* 53 (1998): 221–241.
102. Ibid.
103. Donald H. McKnew, Leon Cytryn, and Herbert Yahraes, *Why Isn't Johnny Crying?* (New York: Norton, 1983).
104. Cicchetti and Toth, "Development of Depression."
105. Harold S. Koplewicz, *More Than Moody: Recognizing and Treating Adolescent Depression* (New York: Putnam, 2002).

106. Ibid.
107. Anne C. Petersen et al., "Depression in Adolescence," *American Psychologist* 48 (1993): 155–168.
108. Petersen et al., "Depression in Adolescence."
109. Ibid.
110. Koplewicz, *More Than Moody*.
111. Ibid.
112. Petersen et al., "Depression in Adolescence."
113. Koplewicz, *More Than Moody*.
114. Martin E. P. Seligman, *The Optimistic Child* (New York: Houghton Mifflin, 1995).
115. Susan Harter, "Visions of Self beyond the Me in the Mirror," university lecture, University of Denver, 1990, 16.
116. Andrew J. Fuligni and Jacquelynne S. Eccles, "Perceived Parent-Child Relationships and Early Adolescents' Orientation toward Peers," *Developmental Psychology* 29 (1993): 622–632.
117. W. Andrew Collins et al., "Conflict Processes and Transitions in Parent and Peer Relationships," *Journal of Adolescent Research* 12 (1997): 178–198.
118. McCall, Evahn, and Kratzer, *High School Underachievers*.
119. Fitzhugh Dodson, *How to Discipline with Love* (New York: Rawson, 1977), 410.
120. Ibid, pp. 410–411.
121. Herrin and Matsumoto, *Parent's Guide to Childhood Eating Disorders*.
122. Koplewicz, *More Than Moody*.
123. Harold S. Koplewicz, "More Than Moody: Recognizing and Treating Adolescent Depression," *Brown University Child and Adolescent Newsletter* 18 (December 2002): 7.
124. Jane E. Brody, "Adolescent Angst or a Deeper Disorder? Tips for Spotting Serious Symptoms," *New York Times*, 24 December 2002, p. D5.
125. Babbit, *Adolescent Drug and Alcohol Abuse*.
126. Laurence Steinberg with Wendy Steinberg, *Crossing Paths: How Your Child's Adolescence Triggers Your Own Crisis* (New York: Simon & Schuster, 1994).
127. Phyllis York, David York, and Ted Wachtel, *ToughLove* (Garden City, NY: Doubleday, 1982).

CHAPTER 12

1. Jeffrey Zaslow, "The Coddling Crisis: Why Americans Think Adulthood Begins at Age 26," *Wall Street Journal*, 6 January 2004, p. D1.
2. Karen Bogenschneider, "Has Family Policy Come of Age? A Decade Review of the State of U.S. Family Policy in the 1990s," *Journal of Marriage and the Family* 62 (2000): 1136–1159.
3. Gail S. Goodman, Robert E. Emery, and Jeffrey J. Haugaard, "Developmental Psychology and Law: Divorce, Child Maltreatment, Foster Care, and Adoption," in *Handbook of Child Psychology*, 5th ed., ed. William Damon, vol. 4: *Child Psychology in Practice*, ed. Irving E. Sigel and Ann Renninger (New York: Wiley, 1998), 775–874.
4. Jeffrey Jensen Arnett, "Conceptions of the Transition to Adulthood: Perspectives from Adolescence through Midlife," *Journal of Adult Development* 8 (2001): 133–143.
5. DeWayne Moore, "Parent-Adolescent Separation: The Construction of Adulthood by Late Adolescents," *Developmental Psychology* 23 (1987): 298–307.
6. Erik H. Erikson, *Childhood and Society*, 2nd ed. (New York: Norton, 1963).
7. John Bowlby, *The Making and Breaking of Affectional Bonds* (London: Tavistock, 1979), 129.
8. Mary D. Salter Ainsworth, "Some Considerations Regarding Theory and Assessment Relevant to Attachments beyond Infancy," in *Attachment in the Preschool Years: Theory, Research, and Intervention*, ed. Mark T. Greenberg, Dante Cicchetti, and E. Mark Cummings (Chicago: University of Chicago Press, 1990), 474.
9. Ibid., pp. 463–488.
10. Glen H. Elder, Jr., "The Life Course in Human Development," in *Handbook of Child Psychology*, 5th ed., ed. William Damon, vol. 1: *Theoretical Models of Human Development*, ed. Richard M. Lerner (New York: Wiley, 1998), 961.
11. Jeffrey Jensen Arnett, "Emerging Adulthood: A Theory of Development From the Late Teens Through the Twenties," *American Psychologist* 55 (2000): 469–480.
12. Ibid., p. 469.
13. Ann S. Masten et al., "Resources and Resilience in the Transition to Adulthood: Continuity and Change," *Development and Psychopathology* 16 (2004): 1071–1094.
14. Vern L. Bengtson, "Beyond the Nuclear Family: The Increasing Importance of Multigenerational Bonds," *Journal of Marriage and Family* 63 (2001): 1–16.
15. Moncrieff Cochran, "Parenting and Personal Social Networks," in *Parenting: An Ecological Perspective*, ed. Tom Luster and Lynn Okagaki (Hillsdale, NJ: Erlbaum, 1993), 149–178.

16. Frances K. Goldscheider, Arland Thornton, and Li-Shou Yang, "Helping out Kids: Expectations about Parental Support in Young Adulthood," *Journal of Marriage and Family* 63 (2001): 727–742.

17. Cochran, "Parenting and Personal Social Networks."

18. Bertram J. Cohler and Judith S. Musick, "Adolescent Parenthood and the Transition to Adulthood," in *Transitions through Adolescence*, ed. Julia A. Graber, Jeanne Brooks-Gunn, and Anne C. Petersen (Mahwah, NJ: Erlbaum, 1996), 214.

19. Katherine S. Newman, "Working Poor: Low-Wage Employment in the Lives of Harlem Youth," in *Transitions through Adolescence*, ed. Graber, Brooks-Gunn, and Petersen, pp. 323–343.

20. Ibid., p. 338.

21. Ibid., p. 341.

22. Moore, "Parent-Adolescent Separation."

23. Kathy Bell et al., "Family Factors and Young Adult Transitions: Educational Attainment and Occupational Prestige," in *Transitions through Adolescence*, ed. Graber, Brooks-Gunn, and Petersen, pp. 345–366.

24. Carol L. Gohm et al., "Culture, Parental Conflict, Parental Marital Status, and the Subjective Well Being of Young Adults," *Journal of Marriage and the Family* 60 (1998): 319–334.

25. Erica Goode, "Students' Emotional Health Worsens," *San Francisco Chronicle*, 3 February 2003, p. A9.

26. Ray Delgado, "Report on College Drinking's Toll Shows Health Crisis, Experts Say," *San Francisco Chronicle*, 10 April 2002, p. A7.

27. Suniya Luthar and Bronwyn Becker, "Privileged but Pressured? A Study of Affluent Youth," *Child Development* 73 (2002): 1593–1610.

28. Leslie Morrison Gutman and Arnold J. Sameroff, "Continuities in Depression from Adolescence to Young Adulthood: Contrasting Ecological Influences," *Development and Psychopathology* 16 (2004): 967–984.

29. Andrea M. Hussong and Laurie Chassin, "Stress and Coping among Children of Alcoholic Parents through the Young Adult Transition," *Development and Psychopathology* 16 (2004): 985–1007.

30. David Gortmaker et al., "An Unexpected Success Story: Transition to Adulthood in Youth with Chronic Physical Health Conditions," *Journal of Research on Adolescence* 3 (1993): 317–336.

31. Ibid., p. 333.

32. Harold D. Grotevant, "Adolescent Development in Family Contexts," in *Handbook of Child Psychology*, 5th ed., ed. William Damon, vol. 3: *Social, Emotional, and Personality Development*, ed. Nancy Eisenberg (New York: Wiley, 1998), 1097–1149.

33. Steven H. Zarit and David J. Eggebeen, "Parent-Child Relationships in Adulthood and Later Years," in *Handbook of Parenting*, 2nd ed., ed. Marc H. Bornstein, vol. 1: *Children and Parenting* (Mahwah, NJ: Erlbaum, 2002), 135–161.

34. Gail Sheehy, "It's about Pure Love," *Parade Magazine*, 12 May 2002, pp. 6–8.

35. Ibid., p. 8.

36. Ibid., p. 7.

37. Valerie King, "The Legacy of Grandparents' Divorce: Consequences for Ties between Grandparents and Grandchildren," *Journal of Marriage and Family* 65 (2003): 170–183.

38. Edward J. Clarke et al., "Types of Conflicts and Tensions between Older Parents and Adult Children," *Gerontologist* 39 (1999): 261–270.

39. Stephen R. Covey, *The Seven Habits of Highly Effective Families* (New York: Golden Books, 1997).

40. Marsha Mailick Seltzer and Tamar Heller, "Families and Caregiving across the Life Course: Research Advances on the Influence of Context," *Family Relations* 46 (1997): 321–323.

41. Ibid.

42. Jan S. Greenberg et al., "The Differential Effects of Social Support on the Psychological Well Being of Aging Mothers of Adults with Mental Illness or Mental Retardation," *Family Relations* 46 (1997): 383–394.

43. Marsha Mailick Seltzer et al., "Siblings of Adults with Mental Retardation or Mental Illness: Effects on Lifestyle and Psychological Well Being," *Family Relations* 46 (1997): 395–405.

44. Harriet P. Lefley, "Synthesizing the Family Caregiving Studies: Implications for Service Planning, Social Policy, and Further Research," *Family Relations* 46 (1997), 445–450.

45. Rachel Simon, "Riding the Bus with Beth," *Reader's Digest*, September 2002, pp. 140–145.

46. Ibid., p. 145.
47. George McGovern, *Terry: My Daughter's Life and Death Struggle with Alcoholism* (New York: Villard, 1996).
48. Ibid., pp. 189–190.
49. Zarit and Eggebeen, "Parent-Child Relationships."
50. Ibid.
51. Ibid.
52. Ibid.
53. Ibid.
54. Barbara G. Unell and Jerry L. Wyckoff, *The Eight Seasons of Parenthood* (New York: Times, 2000).
55. Ibid., p. 270.
56. Lefley, "Synthesizing."
57. Ibid.

CHAPTER 13

1. Sue Shellenbarger, "Fairer Flextime: Employers Try New Policies for Alternative Schedules," *Wall Street Journal*, 17 November 2005, p. D1.
2. Urie Bronfenbrenner, "Ecology of the Family As a Context for Human Development," *Developmental Psychology* 22 (1986): 723–742.
3. Ann C. Crouter et al., "Conditions Underlying Parents' Knowledge about Children's Daily Lives in Middle Childhood: Between- and Within-Family Comparisons," *Child Development* 70 (1999): 246–259.
4. U.S. Bureau of the Census, *Statistical Abstract of the United States: 2006*, 125th ed. (Washington, DC: U.S. Government Printing Office, 2005).
5. Graeme Russell, "Primary Caregiving Fathers," in *Parenting and Child Development in Nontraditional Families*, ed. Michael E. Lamb (Mahwah, NJ: Erlbaum, 1999), 57–81.
6. James A. Levine and Todd L. Pittinsky, *Working Fathers: New Strategies for Balancing Work and Family* (Reading, MA: Addison-Wesley, 1997).
7. Ann C. Crouter and Beth Manke, "Development of a Typology of Dual-Earner Families: A Window into Differences between and within Families in Relationships, Roles, and Activities," *Journal of Family Psychology* 11 (1997): 62–75.
8. Francine M. Deutsch, *Halving It All: How Equally Shared Parenting Works* (Cambridge, MA: Harvard University Press, 1999).
9. Penny Edgell Becker and Phyllis Moen, "Scaling Back: Dual-Earner Couples' Working Family Strategies," *Journal of Marriage and the Family* 61 (1999): 995–1007.
10. Ellen Galinsky, *Ask the Children: What America's Children Really Think about Working Parents* (New York: Morrow, 1999).
11. Reed Larson and Maryse H. Richards, *Divergent Realities: The Emotional Lives of Mothers, Fathers, and Adolescents* (New York: Basic Books, 1994).
12. Galinsky, *Ask the Children.*
13. Ibid., p. 205.
14. Adele Eskeles Gottfried, Allen W. Gottfried, and Kay Bathurst, "Maternal and Dual-Earner Employment Status and Parenting," in *Handbook of Parenting*, ed. Marc H. Bornstein, vol. 2: *Biology and Ecology of Parenting* (Mahwah, NJ: Erlbaum, 1995), 139–160.
15. Ann C. Crouter and Susan M. McHale, "The Long Arm of the Job: Influences of Parental Work on Child Rearing," in *Parenting: An Ecological Perspective*, ed. Tom Luster and Lynn Okagaki (Hillsdale, NJ: Erlbaum, 1993), 179–202.
16. Cynthia A. Stifter, Colleen M. Coulehan, and Margaret Fish, "Linking Employment to Attachment: The Mediating Effects of Maternal Separation Anxiety and Interactive Behavior," *Child Development* 64 (1993): 1451–1460.
17. Cheryl D. Hayes, John L. Palmer, and Martha J. Zaslow, eds., *Who Cares for America's Children?* (Washington, DC: National Academy Press, 1990).
18. Crouter and McHale, "The Long Arm of the Job."
19. Ann C. Crouter and Susan M. McHale, "Temporal Rhythms in Family Life: Seasonal Variation in the Relation between Parental Work and Family Processes," *Developmental Psychology* 29 (1993): 198–205.
20. Martha J. Moorehouse, "Linking Maternal Employment Patterns to Mother-Child Activities and Children's School Competence," *Developmental Psychology* 27 (1991): 295–303.
21. Maryse H. Richards and Elena Duckett, "The Relationship of Maternal Employment to Early Adolescent Daily Experience with and without Parents," *Child Development* 65 (1994): 225–236.
22. Ann C. Crouter, "Processes Linking Families and Work: Implications for Behavior and

Development in Both Settings," in *Exploring Family Relationships with Other Contexts*, ed. Ross D. Parke and Sheppard G. Kellam (Hillsdale, NJ: Erlbaum, 1994), 9–28.

23. Gregory Pettit, "After-School Experience and Social Adjustment in Early Adolescence: Individual, Family, and Neighborhood Risk Factors," paper presented at the Meetings of the Society for Research in Child Development, Washington, DC, April 11, 1997.

24. Jean L. Richardson et al., "Substance Use among Eighth-Grade Students Who Take Care of Themselves after School," *Pediatrics* 84 (1989): 556–566.

25. Galinsky, *Ask the Children*.

26. Grace G. Baruch and Rosalind C. Barnett, "Fathers' Participation in Family Work and Children's Sex Role Attitudes," *Child Development* 57 (1986): 1210–1223.

27. Joan E. Grusec, Jacqueline J. Goodnow, and Lorenzo Cohen, "Household Work and the Development of Concern for Others," *Developmental Psychology* 32 (1996): 999–1007.

28. Jacqueline J. Goodnow and Jennifer M. Bowes, *Men, Women and Household Work* (Melbourne, Australia: Oxford University Press, 1994).

29. Galinsky, *Ask the Children*.

30. Ibid.

31. Ellen Greenberger and Robin O'Neil, "Parents' Concerns about Their Child's Development: Implications for Fathers' and Mothers' Well Being and Attitudes toward Work," *Journal of Marriage and the Family* 52 (1990): 621–635; Ellen Greenberger and Robin O'Neil, "Spouse, Parent, Worker: Role Commitments and Role-Related Experiences in the Construction of Adults' Well Being," *Developmental Psychology* 29 (1993): 181–197.

32. Ellen Hock and Debra K. DeMeis, "Depression in Mothers of Infants: The Role of Maternal Employment," *Developmental Psychology* 26 (1990): 285–291.

33. Anita M. Farel, "Effects of Preferred Maternal Roles, Maternal Employment and Sociodemographic Status on School Adjustment and Competence," *Child Development* 50 (1980): 1179–1186.

34. Lois Wladis Hoffman, "Effects of Maternal Employment in the Two-Parent Family," *American Psychologist* 44 (1989): 283–292.

35. Greenberger and O'Neil, "Parents' Concerns about Their Child's Development"; Greenberger and O'Neil, "Spouse, Parent, Worker."

36. Melvin L. Kohn, *Class and Conformity: A Study in Values* (Homewood, IL: Dorsey Press, 1969).

37. Crouter, "Processes Linking Families and Work."

38. Elizabeth Menaghan and Toby Parcel, "Parental Employment and Family Life: Research in the 1980s," *Journal of Marriage and the Family* 52 (1990): 1079–1098.

39. Crouter, "Processes Linking Families and Work."

40. Ibid., p. 21.

41. Personal communication to author.

42. Ibid.

43. Galinsky, *Ask the Children*.

44. Ibid.

45. Ibid.

46. Niall Bolger et al., "The Contagion of Stress across Multiple Roles," *Journal of Marriage and the Family* 51 (1989): 175–183.

47. Rena L. Repetti and Jennifer Wood, "Effects of Daily Stress at Work on Mothers' Interactions with Preschoolers," *Journal of Family Psychology* 11 (1997): 90–108.

48. Galinsky, *Ask the Children*.

49. Ibid.

50. Ibid.

51. Ibid., p. 330

52. Deutsch, *Halving It All*.

53. Ibid., p. 232.

54. Sandra L. Hofferth, "Child Care in the United States Today," *The Future of Children*, no. 2 (1996): 41–61.

55. Carollee Howes, Deborah A. Phillips, and Marcy Whitebook, "Thresholds of Quality: Implications for the Social Development of Children in Center-Based Child Care," *Child Development* 63 (1992): 449–460.

56. Harriet B. Presser, "Child Care Supply and Demand: What Do We Really Know?" in *Child Care in the 1990s: Trends and Consequences*, ed. Alan Booth (Hillsdale, NJ: Erlbaum, 1992), 26–32.

57. Sally Provence, Audrey Naylor, and June Patterson, *The Challenge of Daycare* (New Haven, CT: Yale University Press, 1977).

58. Edward F. Zigler and Mary E. Lang, *Child Care Choices* (New York: Free Press, 1991).

59. Leslie Berger, "What Children Do When Home and Alone," *New York Times*, 11 April 2000, p. D8.

60. Alice Sterling Honig, "Choosing Child Care for Young Children," in *Handbook of Parenting*, 2nd ed., ed. Marc H. Bornstein, vol. 5, *Practical Issues in Parenting* (Mahwah, NJ: Erlbaum, 2002), 375–405.

61. Hofferth, "Child Care in the United States."

62. Michael E. Lamb, "Nonparental Child Care: Context, Quality, Correlates," in *Handbook of Child Psychology*, 5th ed., ed. William Damon, vol. 4: *Child Psychology in Practice*, ed. Irving E. Sigel and K. Ann Renninger (New York: Wiley, 1998), 73–133.

63. NICHD Early Child Care Research Network, "Early Child Care and Self-Control, Compliance, and Problem Behavior at Twenty-Four and Thirty-Six Months," *Child Development* 69 (1998): 1145–1170.

64. Hayes, Palmer, and Zaslow, *Who Cares for America's Children?*

65. Carollee Howes, Claire E. Hamilton, and Catherine C. Matheson, "Children's Relationships with Peers: Differential Associations with Aspects of the Teacher-Child Relationship," *Child Development* 65 (1994): 253–263.

66. Carollee Howes, Catherine C. Matheson, and Claire E. Hamilton, "Maternal, Teacher, and Child Care History Correlates of Children's Relationships with Peers," *Child Development* 65 (1994): 264–273.

67. Suzanne W. Helburn and Carollee Howes, "Child Care Cost and Quality," *The Future of Children* 6, no. 2 (1996): 62–82.

68. Ibid., p. 69.

69. Ibid.

70. Michael E. Lamb, "Nonparental Child Care," in *Parenting and Child Development in Nontraditional Families*, ed. Lamb, p. 39.

71. Crouter, "Processes Linking Families and Work."

72. Lamb, "Nonparental Child Care," in *Handbook of Child Psychology*, 5th ed., ed. Damon, vol. 4.

73. Wen-Jui Han, Jane Waldfogel, and Jeanne Brooks-Gunn, "The Effects of Early Maternal Employment on Later Cognitive and Behavioral Outcomes," *Journal of Marriage and Family* 63 (2001): 336–354.

74. NICHD Early Child Care Research Network, "Child Care Effect Sizes for the NICHD Study of Early Child Care and Youth Development," *American Psychologist* 61 (2006): 99–116.

75. Ibid., p. 111.

76. Ibid., p. 111.

77. Ron Haskins, "Public School Aggression among Children with Varying Day-Care Experience," *Child Development* 56 (1985): 689–703.

78. Deborah Lowe Vandell and Mary Ann Corasaniti, "The Relation between Third-Graders' After-School Care and Social, Academic, and Emotional Functioning," *Child Development* 59 (1988): 868–875.

79. Hayes, Palmer, and Zaslow, *Who Cares for America's Children?*

80. Lamb, "Nonparental Child Care," in *Parenting and Child Development in Nontraditional Families*, ed. Lamb.

81. Richardson et al., "Substance Use among Eighth-Grade Students."

82. Hoffman, "Effects of Maternal Employment."

83. Ibid.

84. Ibid.

85. Levine and Pittinsky, *Working Fathers*.

86. Gloria Norris and JoAnn Miller, *The Working Mother's Complete Handbook* (New York: Dutton, 1979).

CHAPTER 14

1. Monica Davey, "Those Who Outgrow Foster Care Still Struggle, Study Finds," *New York Times*, 19 May 2005, p. A14.

2. U.S. Bureau of the Census, *Statistical Abstract of the United States: 2006*, 125th ed. (Washington, DC: U.S. Government Printing Office, 2005).

3. "Women in Their 20s Create a Baby Boomlet," *San Francisco Chronicle*, 27 March 2000, p. A8.

4. Marsha Weinraub, Danielle L. Horvath, and Marcy B. Gringlas, "Single Parenthood," in *Handbook of Parenting*, 2nd ed., ed. Marc H. Bornstein, vol. 3: *Being and Becoming a Parent* (Mahwah, NJ: Erlbaum, 2002), 109–140.

5. Ibid.

6. U.S. Bureau of the Census, *Statistical Abstract: 2006*.

7. Marsha Weinraub and Marcy B. Gringlas, "Single Parenting," in *Handbook of Parenting*, ed. Marc H. Bornstein, vol. 3: *Status and Social Conditions of Parenting* (Mahwah, NJ: Erlbaum, 1995), 66.

8. Weinraub and Gringlas, "Single Parenthood," p. 66.

9. Anne K. Driscoll et al., "Nonmarital Childbearing among Adult Women," *Journal of Marriage and the Family* 61 (1999): 186.

10. Jodi R. Sandfort and Martha S. Hill, "Assisting Young, Unmarried Mothers to Become Self-Sufficient: The Effects of Different Types of Early Economic Support," *Journal of Marriage and the Family* 58 (1996): 311–326.

11. William S. Aquilino, "The Life Course of Children Born to Unmarried Mothers: Child Living Arrangements and Young Adult Outcomes," *Journal of Marriage and the Family* 58 (1996): 293–310.

12. Martha J. Zaslow et al., "Protective Factors in the Development of Preschool-Age Children of Young Mothers Receiving Welfare," in *Coping with Divorce, Single Parenting, and Remarriage*, ed. E. Mavis Hetherington (Mahwah, NJ: Erlbaum, 1999), 193–223.

13. E. Mavis Hetherington, "Should We Stay Together for the Sake of the Children?" in *Coping with Divorce, Single Parenting, and Remarriage*, ed. Hetherington, pp. 93–116.

14. Robert Fauber et al., "A Mediational Model of the Impact of Marital Conflict on Adolescent Adjustment in Intact and Divorced Families: The Role of Disrupted Parenting," *Child Development* 61 (1990): 1112–1123.

15. John H. Grych and Frank D. Fincham, "Children's Appraisals of Marital Conflict: Initial Investigation of the Cognitive-Contextual Framework," *Child Development* 64 (1993): 215–230; John H. Grych, Michael Seid, and Frank D. Fincham, "Assessing Marital Conflict from the Child's Perspective," *Child Development* 63 (1992): 558–572.

16. E. Mark Cummings and Patrick Davies, *Children and Marital Conflict: The Impact of Family Disputes and Resolution* (New York: Guilford Press, 1994).

17. Brian E. Vaughn, Jeanne H. Block, and Jack Block, "Parenting Agreement on Child Rearing during Early Childhood and the Psychological Characteristics of Adolescents," *Child Development* 59 (1988): 1020–1033.

18. Jeanne H. Block, Jack Block, and Per F. Gjerde, "The Personality of Children prior to Divorce: A Prospective Study," *Child Development* 57 (1986): 827–840.

19. E. Mavis Hetherington, "An Overview of the Virginia Longitudinal Study of Divorce and Remarriage with a Focus on Early Adolescence," *Journal of Family Psychology* 1 (1993): 39–56.

20. E. Mavis Hetherington and Kathleen A. Camara, "Families in Transition: The Process of Dissolution and Reconstruction," in *A Review of Child Development Research*, vol. 7, ed. Ross D. Parke (Chicago: University of Chicago Press, 1984), pp. 398–439.

21. Judith S. Wallerstein and Sandra Blakeslee, *Second Chances* (New York: Ticknor & Fields, 1989), 286.

22. Ibid.

23. Ibid., p. 287.

24. Judith S. Wallerstein and Joan B. Kelly, *Surviving the Breakup* (New York: Basic Books, 1980).

25. Ibid., p. 66.

26. Ibid.

27. Wallerstein and Blakeslee, *Second Chances*.

28. M. Janice Hogan, Cheryl Buehler, and Beatrice Robinson, "Single Parenting: Transitioning Alone," in *Stress and the Family*, vol. 1: *Coping with Normative Transitions*, ed. Hamilton I. McCubbin and Charles R. Figley (New York: Brunner/Mazel, 1983), 116–132.

29. Hetherington, "Overview of the Virginia Longitudinal Study."

30. Hetherington and Camara, "Families in Transition."

31. Wallerstein and Kelly, *Surviving the Breakup*.

32. Ibid.

33. Hetherington and Camara, "Families in Transition."

34. Hetherington and Camara, "Families in Transition"; Wallerstein and Kelly, *Surviving the Breakup*.

35. Ibid.

36. Ibid.

37. Wallerstein and Kelly, *Surviving the Breakup*.

38. E. Mavis Hetherington, "Coping with Family Transitions: Winners, Losers, and Survivors," *Child Development* 60 (1989): 1–14.

39. Wallerstein and Blakeslee, *Second Chances*.

40. Carol E. MacKinnon, "An Observational Investigation of Sibling Interactions in Married and Divorced Families," *Developmental Psychology* 25 (1989): 36–44.

41. Wallerstein and Blakeslee, *Second Chances*, p. 110.

42. Hetherington, "Overview of the Virginia Longitudinal Study."

43. James H. Bray and E. Mavis Hetherington, "Families in Transition: Introduction and Overview," *Journal of Family Psychology* 7 (1993): 3–8.

44. Sanford L. Braver et al., "A Longitudinal Study of Noncustodial Parents: Parents

without Children," *Journal of Family Psychology* 7 (1993): 9–23.

45. Hetherington, "Overview of the Virginia Longitudinal Study."

46. Eleanor E. Maccoby et al., "Postdivorce Roles of Mothers and Fathers in the Lives of Their Children," *Journal of Family Psychology* 7 (1993): 24–38.

47. E. Mavis Hetherington and Kathleen M. Jodl, "Stepfamilies As Settings for Child Development," in *Stepfamilies: Who Benefits? Who Does Not?* ed. Alan Booth and Judy Dunn (Hillsdale, NJ: Erlbaum, 1994), pp. 55–79.

48. Hetherington, "An Overview of the Virginia Longitudinal Study."

49. Sanford M. Dornbusch et al., "Single Parents, Extended Households and the Control of Adolescents," *Child Development* 56 (1985): 326–341; Judith G. Smetana et al., "Adolescent-Parent Conflict in Married and Divorced Families," *Developmental Psychology* 27 (1991): 1000–1010.

50. E. Mavis Hetherington and W. Glenn Clingempeel, *Coping with Marital Transitions: A Family Systems Perspective*, Monographs of the Society for Research in Child Development 57, serial no. 227 (1992): 2–3.

51. Dornbusch et al., "Single Parents."

52. Christy M. Buchanan, Eleanor E. Maccoby, and Sanford M. Dornbusch, "Caught between Parents: Adolescents' Experience in Divorced Homes," *Child Development* 62 (1991): 1008–1029.

53. Hetherington, "Overview of the Virginia Longitudinal Study."

54. Edward R. Anderson et al., "The Dynamics of Parental Remarriage: Adolescent, Parent, and Sibling Influences," in *Coping with Divorce, Single Parenting, and Remarriage*, ed. Hetherington, pp. 295–319.

55. Paul R. Amato and Brian Keith, "Parental Divorce and the Well Being of Children: A Meta-Analysis," *Psychological Bulletin* 110 (1991): 26–46; Dornbusch et al., "Single Parents."

56. Nicholas Zill, Donna Ruane Morrison, and Mary Jo Coiro, "Long-Term Effects of Parental Divorce on Parent-Child Relationships, Adjustment, and Achievement in Young Adulthood," *Journal of Family Psychology* 7 (1993): 91–103.

57. Hetherington, "Should We Stay Together?"

58. Ibid., p. 101.

59. Judith S. Wallerstein, Julia M. Lewis, and Sandra Blakeslee, *The Unexpected Legacy of Divorce* (New York: Hyperion, 2000).

60. Hetherington, "Should We Stay Together?" p. 115.

61. Sara McLanahan and Julien Teitler, "The Consequence of Father Absence," in *Parenting and Child Development in Nontraditional Families*, ed. Michael E. Lamb (Mahwah, NJ: Erlbaum, 1999), 83–102.

62. Paul R. Amato, "More Than Money? Men's Contributions to Their Children's Lives," in *Men in Families: When Do They Get Involved? What Difference Does It Make?* ed. Alan Booth and Ann C. Crouter (Mahwah, NJ: Erlbaum, 1998), 241–278.

63. Ibid., p. 244.

64. Ibid., pp. 271–272.

65. Ibid., p. 257.

66. James A. Levine with Edward W. Pitt, *New Expectations: Community Strategies for Responsible Fatherhood* (New York: Families and Work Institute, 1995).

67. Ibid., p. 41.

68. Ibid., p. 108.

69. Monica McGoldrick and Betty Carter, "Forming a Remarried Family," in *The Changing Family Life Cycle*, 2nd ed., ed. Betty Carter and Monica McGoldrick (New York: Gardner Press, 1988), 399–429.

70. Wallerstein and Blakeslee, *Second Chances*.

71. Hetherington and Clingempeel, "Coping with Marital Transitions."

72. Fitzhugh Dodson, *How to Discipline with Love* (New York: Rawson Associates, 1977).

73. Hetherington and Jodl, "Stepfamilies As Settings for Child Development."

74. W. Glenn Clingempeel and Sion Segal, "Stepparent-Stepchild Relationships and the Psychological Adjustment of Children in Stepmother and Stepfather Families," *Child Development* 57 (1986): 474–484.

75. Hetherington and Jodl, "Stepfamilies As Settings for Child Development."

76. Ibid.

77. Hetherington, "Overview of the Virginia Longitudinal Study."

78. Hetherington and Clingempeel, "Coping with Marital Transitions."

79. Hetherington and Jodl, "Stepfamilies As Settings for Child Development."

80. Hetherington and Clingempeel, "Coping with Marital Transitions."

81. Hetherington and Jodl, "Stepfamilies As Settings for Child Development."

82. Ibid.
83. Ibid.
84. Lynn White, "Stepfamilies over the Life Course: Social Support," in *Stepfamilies*, ed. Booth and Dunn, pp. 109–137.
85. Emily Visher, "The Stepping Ahead Program," in *Stepfamilies Stepping Ahead*, ed. Mala Burt (Baltimore: Stepfamilies Press, 1989), 57–89.
86. James H. Bray and John Kelly, *Stepfamilies: Love, Marriage, and Parenting in the First Decade* (New York: Broadway Books, 1998).
87. Ibid., p. 16.
88. Ibid., p. 265.
89. Charlotte J. Patterson and Raymond W. Chan, "Families Headed by Lesbian and Gay Parents," in *Parenting and Child Development in Nontraditional Families*, ed. Lamb, pp. 191–219.
90. Ibid.
91. Gregory K. Fritz, "The Foster Care System: Can't Live With It and Can't Live Without It," *The Brown University Child and Adolescent Behavior Letter*, March, 2004, p. 7.
92. Jeffrey Haugaard and Cindy Hazan, "Foster Parenting," in *Handbook of Parenting*, 2nd ed., ed. Marc H. Bornstein, vol. 1: *Children and Parenting* (Mahwah, NJ: Erlbaum, 2002), 313–327.
93. Fritz, "The Foster Care System."
94. Haugaard and Hazan, "Foster Parenting."
95. Ibid.
96. Ibid.
97. Ibid.
98. Ibid.
99. Matthew B. Stannard, "Judge Takes Responsibility in Death of Foster Child," *San Francisco Chronicle*, 4 April 2003, A19.
100. Haugaard and Hazan, "Foster Parenting."
101. Catherine R. Lawrence, Elizabeth A. Carlson, and Byron Egeland, "The Impact of Foster Care on Development," *Development and Psychopathology* 18 (2006): 57–76.
102. Haugaard and Hazan, "Foster Parenting."
103. Gail S. Goodman, Robert E. Emery, and Jeffrey J. Haugaard, "Developmental Psychology and Law: Divorce, Child Maltreatment, Foster Care, and Adoption," in *Handbook of Child Psychology*, 5th ed., ed. William Damon, vol. 4: *Child Psychology in Practice*, ed. Irving E. Sigel and K. Ann Renninger (New York: Wiley, 1998), 775–874.
104. Monica Davey, "Youths Leaving Foster Care Are Found Facing Obstacles," *New York Times*, 24 February 2004, A10.
105. Monica Davey, "Those Who Outgrow Foster Care Struggle, Study Finds," *New York Times*, 19 May 2005, A14.
106. Ibid.
107. Goodman, Emery, and Haugaard, "Developmental Psychology and Law."
108. Ibid.

CHAPTER 15

1. Ruth LaFerla, "Families Confront a Perilous World," *New York Times*, 20 October 2005, p. E7.
2. Barbara D. Rosoff, *The Worst Loss* (New York: Henry Holt, 1994).
3. Barbara G. Melamed, "Parenting the Ill Child," in *Handbook of Parenting*, 2nd ed., ed. Marc H. Bornstein, vol. 5: *Practical Issues of Parenting* (Mahwah, NJ: Erlbaum, 2002), 329–348.
4. Lonnie K. Zeltzer and Christine Blackett Schlank, *Conquering Your Child's Chronic Pain* (New York: HarperCollins, 2005).
5. Elizabeth Gellert, "Children's Conceptions of the Content and Functions of the Human Body," *Genetic Psychology Monographs* 65 (1962): 293–405.
6. Roger Bibace and Mary E. Walsh, "Developmental States of Children's Conceptions of Illness," in *Health Psychology*, ed. George C. Stone, Frances Cohen, and Nancy E. Adler (San Francisco: Jossey-Bass, 1979), 285–301.
7. Zeltzer and Schlank, *Conquering Your Child's Chronic Pain*, p. 32.
8. Melamed, "Parenting the Ill Child."
9. Ibid.
10. Ibid.
11. Fred A. Rogosch et al., "Parenting Dysfunction in Child Maltreatment," in *Handbook of Parenting*, ed. Marc H. Bornstein, vol. 4: *Applied and Practical Parenting* (Mahwah, NJ: Erlbaum, 1995), 127–159.
12. Earl Grollman, "Prologue," in *Explaining Death to Children*, ed. Earl Grollman (Boston: Beacon, 1967), p. 15.
13. Rosoff, *The Worst Loss*.
14. John Bowlby, *Attachment and Loss*, vol. 3: *Loss: Sadness and Depression* (New York: Basic Books, 1980).
15. Ibid., p. 85.
16. Rosoff, *The Worst Loss*, p. 108.
17. Ibid.
18. Ibid.
19. Ibid.

20. Ibid.

21. Ibid., p. 128.

22. Ibid., p. 14.

23. Ibid.

24. Dante Cicchetti and Michael Lynch, "Toward an Ecological/Transactional Model of Community Violence and Child Maltreatment: Consequences for Child Development," *Psychiatry* 56 (1993): 96–118.

25. Rogosch et al., "Parenting Dysfunction in Child Maltreatment."

26. David A. Wolfe, "The Role of Intervention and Treatment Services in the Prevention of Child Abuse and Neglect," in *Protecting Children from Abuse and Neglect*, ed. Gary B. Melton and Frank D. Barry (New York: Guilford, 1994), 224–303.

27. Ibid.

28. Sandra T. Azar, "Parenting and Maltreatment," in *Handbook of Parenting*, 2nd ed., ed. Marc H. Bornstein, vol. 4: *Social Conditions and Applied Parenting* (Mahwah, NJ: Erlbaum, 2002), 361–388.

29. Edward F. Zigler, Matia Finn-Stevenson, and Nancy W. Hall, *The First Three Years and Beyond* (New Haven: Yale University Press, 2002).

30. Azar, "Parenting and Maltreatment."

31. Douglas J. Besharov et al., "Four Commentaries: How We Can Better Protect Children from Abuses and Neglect," in *The Future of Children* 8, no. 1 (1998): 120–132.

32. Dante Cicchetti and Sheree L. Toth, "Developmental Psychopathology and Preventive Intervention," in *Handbook of Child Psychology*, 6th ed., ed. William Damon and Richard M. Lerner, vol. 4: *Child Psychology in Practice*, ed. K. Ann Renninger and Irving E. Sigel (New York: Wiley, 2006), 497–547.

33. Gail S. Goodman, Robert E. Emery, and Jeffrey J. Haugaard, "Developmental Psychology and Law, Divorce, Child Maltreatment, Foster Care, and Adoption," in *Handbook of Child Psychology*, 5th ed., ed. William Damon, vol. 4: *Child Psychology in Practice*, Irving E. Sigel and K. Ann Renninger (New York: Wiley, 1998), 775–874.

34. John W. Fantuzzo and Wanda K. Mohr, "Prevalence and Effects of Child Exposure to Domestic Violence," *The Future of Children* 9, no. 3 (1999): 21–32.

35. Lucy Salcido Custer, Lois A. Weithorn, and Richard E. Berman, " Domestic Violence and Children: Analysis and Recommendations," *The Future of Children* 9, no. 3 (1999): 4–20.

36. Sally Zierler, "Studies Confirm Long-Term Consequences of Childhood Sexual Abuse," *Brown University Child and Adolescent Newsletter* 8 (1992): 3.

37. Diana E. H. Russell, "The Incidence and Prevalence of Intrafamilial and Extrafamilial Sexual Abuse of Female Children," in *Handbook on Sexual Abuse of Children*, ed. Lenore A. Auerbach Walker (New York: Springer, 1988), 19–36.

38. Glenn D. Wollfner and Richard J. Gelles, "A Profile of Violence toward Children: A National Study," *Child Abuse and Neglect* 17 (1993): 199–214.

39. Dante Cicchetti, "An Odyssey of Discovery: Lessons Learned through Three Decades of Research on Child Maltreatment," *American Psychologist* 59 (2004): 731–741.

40. Judith Musick, "The Special Role of Parenting in the Context of Poverty: The Case of Adolescent Motherhood," in *Threats to Optimal Development: Integrating Biological, Psychological, and Social Risk Factors*, ed. Charles A. Nelson (Hillsdale, NJ: Erlbaum, 1994), 179–216.

41. Robin McGee, David Wolfe, and James Olson, "Multiple Maltreatment, Attribution of Blame, and Adjustment among Adolescents," *Development and Psychopathology* 13 (2001): 827–846.

42. Cicchetti and Lynch, "Toward an Ecological/Transactional Model of Community Violence and Child Development."

43. American Psychiatric Association, *Diagnostic and Statistical Manual of Mental Disorders,* 4th ed. (Washington, DC: American Psychiatric Association, 1994).

44. Penelope K. Trickett et al., "Variants of Intrafamilial Sexual Abuse Experience: Implications for Short- and Long-Term Development," *Development and Psychopathology* 13 (2001): 1001–1019.

45. Alexandra Okun, Jeffrey G. Parker, and Alytia A. Levendosky, "Distinct and Interactive Contributions of Physical Abuse, Socioeconomic Disadvantage and Negative Life Events to Children's Social, Cognitive, and Affective Adjustment," *Development and Psychopathology* 6 (1994): 77–98.

46. Azar, "Parenting and Maltreatment."

47. Christoph Heinicke, "The Transition to Parenthood," in *Handbook of Parenting,*

2nd ed., ed. Marc H. Bornstein, vol. 3: *Being and Becoming a Parent* (Mahwah, NJ: Erlbaum, 2002), 363–388.

48. Azar, "Parenting and Maltreatment," L. Alan Sroufe, *The Development of the Person* (New York: Guilford, 2005).

49. Azar, "Parenting and Maltreatment."

50. Ibid.

51. Karen C. Meiselman, *Resolving the Trauma of Incest* (San Francisco: Jossey-Bass, 1990).

52. Cicchetti, "Odyssey of Discovery."

53. McGee, Wolfe, and Olson, "Multiple Maltreatment, Attribution of Blame, and Adjustment among Adolescents."

54. Jody Todd Manly et al, "Dimensions of Child Maltreatment and Children's Adjustment: Contributions of Developmental Timing and Subtype," *Development and Psychopathology* 13 (2001): 759–782.

55. Howard J. Dubowitz, "The Families of Neglected Children," in *Parenting and Child Development in Nontraditional Families,* ed. Michael E. Lamb (Mahwah, NJ: Erlbaum, 1999), 327–345.

56. Robert E. Emery and Lisa Laumann-Billings, "An Overview of the Nature, Causes, and Consequences of Abusive Family Relationships: Toward Differentiating Maltreatment and Violence, *American Psychologist* 53 (1998): 121–135.

57. Dante Cicchetti et al, "False Belief Understanding in Maltreated Children," *Development and Psychopathology* 15 (2003): 1067–1091.

58. Sheree L. Toth et al., "The Relative Efficacy of Two Interventions in Altering Maltreated Preschool Children's Representational Models: Implications for Attachment Theory," *Development and Psychopathology* 14 (2002): 877–908.

59. Alytia A. Levendosky et al., "The Impact of Domestic Violence on the Mother-Child Relationship and Preschool-Age Children's Functioning," *Journal of Family Psychology* 17 (2003): 275–287.

60. Manly et al, "Dimensions of Child Maltreatment."

61. Kathleen A. Kendall-Tackett, Linda Meyer Williams, and David Finkelhor, "Impact of Sex Abuse on Children: A Review and Synthesis of Recent Empirical Studies," *Psychological Bulletin* 113 (1993): 164–180.

62. Ibid.

63. Ibid.

64. Trickett et al., "Variants of Intrafamilial Sexual Abuse Experience."

65. Jodi A. Quas et al., "Childhood Sexual Assault Victims: Long-Term Outcomes after Testifying in Criminal Court," *Monographs of the Society for Research in Child Development* 70 (2005): (2 Serial No. 280).

66. Betsy McAlister Groves, "Mental Health Services for Children Who Witness Domestic Violence," *The Future of Children* 9, no. 3 (1999): 122–133.

67. Bruce D. Perry, "Incubated in Terror: Neurodevelopmental Factors in the 'Cycle of Violence,'" in *Children in a Violent Society,* ed. Joy D. Osofsky (New York Guilford, 1997).

68. Dante Cicchetti et al., "Resilience in Maltreated Children: Processes Leading to Adaptive Outcome," *Development and Psychopathology* 5 (1993): 629–647.

69. Jean Marie McGloin and Cathy Spatz Widom, "Resilience among Abused and Neglected Children Grown Up, " *Development and Psychopathology* 13 (2001):1021–1038.

70. Goodman, Emery, and Haugaard, "Development, Psychology, and Law."

71. Catherine R. Lawrence, Elizabeth A. Carlson, and Byron Egeland, "The Impact of Foster Care on Development," *Development and Psychopathology* 18 (2006): 57–76.

72. John Eckenrode et al., "Child Maltreatment and the Early Onset of Problem Behaviors: Can a Home Visitation Break the Link?" *Development and Psychopathology* 13 (2001): 873–890.

73. Cicchetti and Toth, "Developmental Psychopathology and Preventive Intervention."

74. Toth et al., "The Relative Efficacy of Two Interventions."

75. Sroufe et al., *The Development of the Person.*

76. John E. Richters and Pedro Martinez, "The NIMH Community Violence Project: I. Children as Victims of and Witnesses to Violence," *Psychiatry* 56 (1993): 7–21.

77. Janis B. Kupersmidt, Ariana Shahinfar, and Mary Ellen Voegler-Lee, "Children's Exposure to Community Violence," in *Helping Children Cope with Disasters and Terrorism,* ed. Annette M. LaGreca et al. (Washington, DC: American Psychological Association, 2002), 381–401.

78. Pedro Martinez and John E. Richters, "The NIMH Community Violence Project: II. Children's Distress Symptoms Associated with Violence Exposure," *Psychiatry* 56 (1993): 22–35.

79. John E. Richters and Pedro Martinez, "Violent Communities, Family Choices, and Children's Choices: An Algorithm for Improving the Odds," *Development and Psychopathology* 5 (1993): 609–627.
80. Lenore Terr, *Too Scared to Cry* (New York: Harper & Row, 1990).
81. James Garbarino et al., *Children in Danger* (San Francisco: Jossey-Bass, 1992).
82. Peter A. Wyman et al., "The Role of Children's Future Expectations in Self-System Functioning and Adjustment to Life Stress: A Prospective Study of Urban At-Risk Children," *Development and Psychopathology* 5 (1993): 649–661.
83. Garbarino, *Children in Danger,* p. 10.
84. Ibid.
85. Ibid.
86. Terr, *Too Scared to Cry.*
87. Annette M. LaGreca and Mitchell J. Prinstein, "Hurricanes and Earthquakes," in *Helping Children Cope with Disasters and Terrorism,* ed. LaGreca et al., 107–138.
88. Ibid.
89. Robin H. Gurwitch et al., "The Aftermath of Terrorism," in *Helping Children Cope with Disasters and Terrorism,* ed. LaGreca et al., 327–357.
90. Deborah Smith, "Everyday Fears Trump Worries about Terrorism," *Monitor on Psychology,* May 2003, pp. 22–23.
91. Joshunda Sanders, "What to Tell Kids about War," *San Francisco Chronicle,* 19 March 2003, p. A21.
92. William C. Bell, "Tough Lessons in Child Welfare Reform," *New York Times,* 21 January 2003, p. A23.
93. Ibid.
94. Perry, "Incubated in Terror," p. 144.
95. Katherine Kaufer Christoffel, "Firearm Injuries Affecting United States Children and Adolescents," in *Children in a Violent Society,* ed. Osofsky, 42–71.
96. U.S. Bureau of the Census, *Statistical Abstract of the United States: 2006,* 125th ed. (Washington, DC: U.S. Government Printing Office, 2005).
97. Christoffel, "Firearm Injuries Affecting United States Children."
98. John P. Murray, "Media Violence and Youth," in *Children in a Violent Society,* ed. Osofsky, 72–106.
99. Ibid.
100. Steven J. Wolin and Sybil Wolin, *The Resilient Self* (New York: Villard Books, 1993).
101. Ibid., pp. 5–6.
102. Grace Hechinger, *How to Raise a Street-Smart Child* (New York: Ballantine Books, 1984).

EPILOGUE
1. Amy Arner Sgarro, "A Surgeon and Community," *Vassar Quarterly,* Spring 1993, pp. 10–13.
2. Ibid, p. 13.

CREDITS

Text Credits

Figure 1.1, from "Beyond the Nuclear Family: The Increasing Importance of Multi-generational Bonds," by Vern L. Bengston, *Journal of Marriage and Family,* 63. Copyright © 2001 by the National Council on Family Relations, 3989 Central Ave. NE, Suite 550, Minneapolis, MN 55421. **Table 1.2**, from Jay Belsky, Elliot Robins, and Wendy Gamble, "The Determinants of Parental Competence: Toward a Contextual Theory," in *Beyond the Dyad,* ed. Michael Lewis (New York: Plenum, 1984), p 253. Reprinted with kind permission from Springer Science and Business Media. **Table 3.1**, from Patricia Greenfield and Lalita K. Sazuki, "Culture and Human Development: Implications for Parenting, Education, Pediatrics and Mental Health," *Handbook for Child Psychology,* 5th ed., vol. 4, p. 1085. Reprinted with permission of John Wiley and Sons, Inc. **Table 3.6**, "Typology of Differences in Children Rearing," from Annette Lareau, *Unequal Childhoods: Class, Race, and Family Life* (Berkeley: University of California Press, 2003), p. 31. Reprinted by permission from the University of California Press. **Table 3.7**, from Jeanne Brooks-Gunn and Greg J. Duncan, "The Effects of Poverty," *The Future of Children* 7 (2), pp. 58-59. Reprinted with permission of the David and Lucile Packard Foundation. **Table 5.1**, "Developmental Challenges Faced by Children and Caregivers from Infancy through Adolescence," from E. Mark Cummings, Patrick T. Davies, and Susan B. Campbell, *Developmental Psychopathology and Family Process* (New York: Guildford, 2000), p. 207. Reprinted with permission from Guilford. **Table 5.4**, "Time Spent Using Media and in Other Activities, by Age" from *The Media Family: Electronic Media in the Lives of Infants, Toddlers, Preschoolers, and Their Parents* (#7500), The Henry J. Kaiser Family Foundations, May 2006. This information was reprinted with permission from the Henry J. Kaiser Family Foundation. The Kaiser Family Foundation, based in Menlo Park California, is a non-profit, private operating foundation focusing on the major health care issues facing the nation and is not associated with Kaiser Permanente or Kaiser Industries. **Table 5.2 and Table 5.3**, "Time Spent with the Media" and "Time Spent in Non-Media Activities" from *Generation M: Media in the Lives of 8–18 Year Olds* (#7251), The Henry J. Kaiser Family Foundation, March 2005. The Kaiser Family Foundation, based in Menlo Park California, is a non-profit, private operating foundation focusing on the major health care issues facing the nation and is not associated with Kaiser Permanente or Kaiser Industries. **Box 5.1**, Excerpted from the book *Children Learn What They Live.* Copyright © 1998 by Dorothy Law Nolte and Rachel Harris. The poem "Children Learn What They Live." Copyright © 1972 by Dorothy Law Nolte. Used by permission of Workman Publishing Co., Inc., New York. All rights reserved. **Table 7.1**, from J. Heidi Gralinski and Claire B. Kopp, "Everyday Rules for Behavior: Mothers' Request to Young Children," *Developmental Psychology* 29 (1993): 576. Reprinted with permission of the American Psychological Association. **Figure 9.1**, Mary J. Levitt, Nathalie Guacci

Franco, and Jerome L. Levitt, "Convoys of Social Support in Childhood and Early Adolescence: Structure and Function," *Developmental Psychology* 29 (1993): p. 815. Reprinted with permission from the American Psychological Association. **Figure 10.1**, from William J. Cross, Jr., "A Two-Factor Theory of Black Identity," in *Children's Ethnic Socialization*, ed. Jean S. Phinney and Mary Jane Rotheram (Newbury Park, CA: Sage, 1987), p. 122. Reprinted by permission of Sage Publications. **Figure 11.1**, from Cathy Schoen et al., *The Commonwealth Fund Survey of the Health of Adolescent Girls* (New York: The Commonwealth Fund, 1997), p. 25. **Figure 12.1**, table adapted from Jeffrey Jensen Arnett, "Conceptions of the Transition to Adulthood: Perspectives from Adolescence to Midlife," *Journal of Adult Development* 8 (2001): p. 127. Reprinted with kind permission from Springer Science and Business Media. **Table 12.2**, Vern L. Bengston, "Beyond the Nuclear Family: The Increasing Importance of Multigenerational Bonds. Copyright © 2001 by the National Council on Family Relations. Reprinted by permission. **Table 13.1**, from Ellen Galinsky, *Ask the Children*. Copyright © 1999 by Ellen Galinsky. Reprinted by permission of HarperCollins Publishers, Inc. **Figure 14.2**, from *New Expectations: Community Strategies for Responsible Fatherhood* by James Levine and Edward W. Pitt, (New York: Families and Work Institute, 1995), p. 41. Reprinted with permission of the Families and Work Institute.

Photo Credits

Page 5, © Brand X Pictures/PunchStock. **Page 18**, © Getty Images. **Page 62**, © Corbis/PunchStock. **Page 89**, © Andrew Fox/Corbis. **Page 109**, © Digital Vision/Getty Images. **Page 132**, © Brand X. **Page 150**, © Photos.com. **Page 176**, © Ryan McVay/Getty Images. **Page 187**, © Royalty-Free/Corbis. **Page 222**, © Getty Images. **Page 264**, © Brand X Pictures/PunchStock. **Page 282**, © Robert Brenner/PhotoEdit. **Page 311**, © Brand X Pictures/PunchStock. **Page 349**, © BananaStock/PunchStock. **Page 368**, © Digital Vision. **Page 383**, © McGraw-Hill Companies, Inc./Gary He, photographer. **Page 410**, © Ryan McVay/Getty Images. **Page 417**, © Richard Hutchings/PhotoEdit. **Page 444**, © Myrleen Ferguson Cate/PhotoEdit. **Page 461**, © BananaStock/PunchStock. **Page 471**, © Buccina Studios/Getty Images. Page 496, © Getty Images/Mark Thornton. **Page 524**, © Michael Okoniewski/The Image Works.